Reform Judaism
in America

Also Available in Jewish Denominations in America

Conservative Judaism in America: A Biographical Dictionary and Sourcebook
Pamela S. Nadell

Reform Judaism in America

A BIOGRAPHICAL DICTIONARY AND SOURCEBOOK

Edited by
Kerry M. Olitzky,
Lance J. Sussman,
and Malcolm H. Stern

Jewish Denominations in America

Marc Lee Raphael, *Advisory Editor*

Greenwood Press
Westport, Connecticut • London

Library of Congress Cataloging-in-Publication Data

Reform Judaism in America : a biographical dictionary and sourcebook /
  edited by Kerry M. Olitzky, Lance J. Sussman, and Malcolm H. Stern.
      p.   cm.—(Jewish denominations in America)
    Includes bibliographical references and index.
    ISBN 0–313–24628–9
    1. Reform Judaism—United States. 2. Jews—United States—
  Biography—Dictionaries. 3. Union of American Hebrew
  Congregations. 4. Hebrew Union College-Jewish Institute of
  Religion. 5. Central Conference of American Rabbis. I. Olitzky,
  Kerry M. II. Sussman, Lance Jonathan. III. Stern, Malcolm H.
  IV. Series.
  BM750.R39   1993
  296.8′346′0973—dc20   92–25794

British Library Cataloguing in Publication Data is available.

Library of Congress Catalog Card Number: 92–25794
ISBN: 0–313–24628–9

First published in 1993

Greenwood Press, 88 Post Road West, Westport, CT 06881
An imprint of Greenwood Publishing Group, Inc.

Printed in the United States of America

The paper used in this book complies with the
Permanent Paper Standard issued by the National
Information Standards Organization (Z39.48–1984).

10 9 8 7 6 5 4 3 2 1

CONTENTS

PREFACE

Reform Judaism in America: A Biographical Dictionary and Sourcebook is the second in a series of three volumes on American Judaism. Conceived by Professor Marc Lee Raphael, the series will provide "the first extensive documentation of the lives and careers of the most important leaders" in the history of American Judaism, short histories of each movement, and essays on the central institutions, as well as comprehensive lists of the presidents of all denominational organizations. *Reform Judaism in America* is designed to serve as a basic reference tool for a wide range of users and libraries. Hopefully, it will stimulate both research and general interest in the history of Judaism and its leadership in the United States and Canada.

In the first book of the series, *Conservative Judaism in America* (1988), Professor Pamela S. Nadell established the style, format and structure for the entire collection. In two respects, however, the current volume differs from its predecessor. First, because of inherent religious differences between the Reform and Conservative movements, different criteria for determining the entries in the biographical dictionary were developed. Second, producing this reference work was a cooperative rather than a solo enterprise. Whereas Nadell both researched and wrote all the entries in her biographical dictionary, three editors worked on this volume and invited a large number of contributors from both the scholarly community and the Reform movement to participate.

Perhaps the most difficult task the editors faced was to create a relatively short list—numbering approximately 170—of the most important leaders in the history of American Reform Judaism. This work was complicated by both ideological and historiographical factors. First, religious authority in the Reform movement is essentially located in the individual Jew, who is free to combine elements of contemporary culture with select beliefs and practices from Jewish tradition in his or her search for meaningful religious self-expression. Consequently, the spirit of the age and the laity often take priority over the theophany at Sinai and the rabbinate as the historical and social bases of Torah in the Reform tradition. As the volume editors, we made a special effort to identify and research the contributions of a wide range of leaders, especially women, in the Reform movement.

It is also important to note that while Reform's twin commitments to progressive revelation and individualism enfranchise a broader spectrum of religious leaders than do most of the other branches of modern Judaism, rabbis have continued to play the most prominent role in shaping and articulating American Reform Judaism by virtue of their personal commitment, collective ability to influence the movement and superior Jewish education. Thus, most entries detail the lives and careers of the leading rabbis in the American Reform movement, reflecting the enduring but modified role of the rabbinate in modern Judaism's most liberal branch.

With respect to periodization, we begin with Isaac Harby and the first attempt at organizing a Reform movement in the United States in 1824. Our terminus ad quem is the 1976 Centenary Perspective. Also known as the San Francisco Platform, this is Reform's most recent statement of principles and reflects over 40 years of theological discussion and changes in the movement's ritual life. Individuals who have emerged as national leaders since 1976 have not been included in this book even though they might already have been active to some degree before the U.S. bicentennial. Except for Uri Herscher, Executive Vice President of Hebrew Union College–Jewish Institute of Religion, and Sally Priesand, the first woman ordained as a Reform rabbi, everyone in our biographical dictionary was born before 1940.

A basic criterion applied to all potential entries for our biographical dictionary was that the impact of an individual's work had to be deemed of national significance in the development of the American Reform movement. In each case, the broader implications of a leader's work were carefully and comparatively evaluated. Numerous categories, including originality of thought, sphere of operation and peer recognition, were considered. Regrettably, highly talented and successful leaders who primarily functioned at the local or regional level were thus eliminated from this study of Reform leadership.

Using the standard of national significance and the other initial parameters of our study, we created a preliminary list of over 400 names, more than triple the size projected for each volume in the series on American Jewish denominations. Obviously, further criteria were needed to help us identify the core group of leaders in American Reform Judaism, 1824–1976. At this point, we returned to our original concept of diversity in Reform's leadership and created a number of categories that needed to be represented in the biographical dictionary. These include architects of the central Reform institutions, national organizational leaders, distinguished pulpit rabbis, leading academicians and intellectuals, outstanding cantors and musical directors, volunteer lay activists and women. When leaders met the criteria for several categories, they were evaluated in terms of their most-important or best-known contribution.

   Another problem we encountered in defining standards of eligibility involved leaders whose geographical or ideological positions changed significantly over time. Immigrant leaders who were distinguished for their earlier work outside of North America but who were less influential or active in the United States or Canada have been omitted, as have American Reform leaders who primarily served abroad or in other religious movements. The exception is Richard Hirsch, who has served as the Executive Director of the World Union for Progressive Judaism since 1973. Individuals who only temporarily functioned within the Reform fold but did not view it as their spiritual home or seek to define themselves vis-à-vis Reform, like Abraham Joshua Heschel, are not included here. Felix Adler, on the other hand, who began in Reform but left and founded the Ethical Culture movement, is included because of his continued dialogue and impact on Reform Judaism.

   Before the reorganization of the Reform movement as an American-style denomination during the last 30 years of the nineteenth century, a number of leaders helped shape both the ideology and the ritual practice of North America's most liberal branch. In addition to Isaac Harby, the principal leaders of early American Reform Judaism included Samuel Adler, David Einhorn, Bernhard Felsenthal, James Gutheim, Samuel Hirsch, Max Lilienthal, Leo Merzbacher and Gustavus Poznanski. Emil Hirsch, Benjamin Szold and Jacob Voorsanger were the most important leaders of a transitional generation of congregational rabbis who, although trained in Europe, served in American Reform pulpits at the end of the last century.

   The architects of Reform's denominational institutions and organizations include two of the most distinguished names in the history of American Judaism. Isaac M. Wise was directly responsible for founding both Hebrew Union College (1875) and the Central Conference of American Rabbis (1889). He also influenced the creation of the Union of American Hebrew Congregations (1873). Stephen S. Wise (no relation to Isaac) opened the Jewish Institute of Religion in New York City in 1922. It merged with Hebrew Union College in 1950.

   The intellectual fountainhead of Reform Judaism, Hebrew Union College–Jewish Institute of Religion (HUC-JIR) currently operates on four campuses: Cincinnati, New York, Los Angeles and Jerusalem. It has been led by a handful of presidents who played major roles in shaping generations of Reform Jewish leadership. After Isaac M. Wise, Kaufmann Kohler and Julian Morgenstern served as presidents of HUC. Nelson Glueck was president during and after the merger with JIR. He was succeeded by Alfred Gottschalk, the current president. The college's presidents were aided by a number of capable and influential administrators, including Henry Englander, Uri Herscher, Eugene Mihaly and Paul Steinberg.

   A number of HUC-JIR faculty and staff have also had a profound influence on the development of Reform Judaism by virtue of their research, personal commitment to the movement and influence on its rabbis and other leaders. Leading HUC-JIR teachers include Israel Bettan, Sheldon H. Blank, Eugene B.

Borowitz, Samuel Cohon, Abraham Cronbach, Gotthard Deutsch, Abraham Franzblau, Robert Katz, Jacob Z. Lauterbach, Jacob R. Marcus, Michael A. Meyer, Moses Mielziner, David Neumark, Jakob Petuchowski, Alvin Reines, Ellis Rivkin, Samuel Sandmel, Sylvan Schwartzman, Henry Slonimsky and Max Wiener. Two college librarians, Edward Kiev and Adolph Oko, also made significant contributions to the Reform movement. A professor who did not teach at the college but nevertheless profoundly influenced American Reform Judaism was Bernard Martin.

HUC-JIR has also been shaped by an impressive array of lay leaders and philanthropists. In the area of lay leadership, Jules Backman, Bernhard Bettmann, Herbert Bloch, Sr., Alfred M. Cohen, Simon Scheuer, Ted Tannenwald and Frank Weil have served with distinction. Among the many financial supporters of HUC-JIR, the Klau and Dalsheimer families were outstanding, especially in their contributions to the school's library system. Rabbi Jack Skirball was also a major benefactor of HUC-JIR.

The Union of American Hebrew Congregations (UAHC), the umbrella organization of Reform Judaism in North America, was founded and profoundly influenced by lay Jewish leaders, including Jacob Aronson, Emil Baar, Julius Freiberg, J. Walter Freiberg, Robert Goldman, S. S. Hollender, Moritz Loth, Ralph Mack, Horace Stern, and Ludwig Vogelstein. Other UAHC lay activists, particularly in the area of social justice, include Marcus Aaron and Kivie Kaplan. Ironically, perhaps the two most important lay leaders within the Reform movement, Louis Marshall and Lessing Rosenwald, were not active with the UAHC.

The staff of the UAHC has also been rich with impressive leaders. Lipman Levy and George Zepin served as early national administrators. Since 1946, two well-known rabbis, Maurice Eisendrath and Alexander Schindler, have served as president of the UAHC and have functioned as major spokesmen for American Jewry in general. Other significant UAHC administrators include Louis Egelson, Myron Schoen and Al Vorspan. In the area of Jewish education, two UAHC leaders, Emanuel Gamoran and Jack Spiro, have been outstanding. The North American Federation of Temple Youth was founded by Samuel Cook.

The third of Reform's central organizations, the Central Conference of American Rabbis (CCAR), has been another major source of collective and individual leadership in the movement. The conference was guided by 39 presidents between its founding, in 1889, and 1976. Previously unmentioned leaders include Bernard J. Bamberger, Philip S. Bernstein, Barnett R. Brickner, Edward N. Calisch, Max C. Currick, Hyman Enelow, Abraham J. Feldman, Leon I. Feuer, Joseph L. Fink, Leo M. Franklin, Solomon B. Freehof, Roland B. Gittelsohn, Samuel H. Goldenson, Moses J. Gries, Louis Grossman, James Heller, Maximilian Heller, Robert I. Kahn, Joseph Krauskopf, David Lefkowitz, Emil W. Leipziger, Arthur J. Lelyveld, Felix A. Levy, Albert Minda, Morris Newfield, Levi A. Olan, David Philipson, David Polish, William Rosenau, Jacob Philip Rudin, Samuel Schulman, Abba Hillel Silver, Joseph Silverman, Abram Simon, Joseph Stolz, Jacob J. Weinstein and Louis Wolsey.

For many years, the conference's extensive *Yearbook* was edited by its volunteer recording secretary, Isaac Marcuson. However, after World War II the administrative work of the CCAR became increasingly professionalized. Sidney Regner and Joseph Glaser have both served as executive vice president. Malcolm H. Stern, an accomplished genealogist, served as the CCAR's first placement director.

A number of congregational rabbis have also distinguished themselves and played a major role in the history of American Reform Judaism. Earl Grollman, Bertram W. Korn, Joshua Loth Liebman, Daniel Jeremy Silver and Arnold J. Wolf are important writers and intellectuals. Gustavus Gottheil and Judah L. Magnes were leading Zionists. Elmer Berger, Isaac Landman and Morris Lazaron, on the other hand, were important anti-Zionists. Henry Berkowitz, who graduated in HUC's first class in 1883, was a leading interfaith activist. Leonard Beerman, Balfour Brickner, Sidney Goldstein, Edward Israel, Ferdinand Isserman, Jacob Rothschild and Horace J. Wolf exemplified the Reform movement's quest for social justice. William G. Braude and W. Gunther Plaut have urged a return to tradition, whereas David Max Eichhorn, Abraham Klausner, Clifton Harby Levy, Morris and Tehilla Lichtenstein, Solomon Schindler, Harry Stern, Sherwin Wine and Ray Zwerin have advocated innovation and change.

One of the most distinctive features of the Reform synagogue is, of course, its music. Born in controversy over the use of the organ on the Sabbath and festivals, the Reform musical tradition has been shaped by a number of cantors, composers and music directors. The basic contours of the musical heritage of the Reform movement were shaped by Abraham W. Binder, Gershon Ephros, Benjamin Grobani, Abraham Z. Idelsohn, Max Janowski, Alois Kaiser, Will Sharlin, Ben Steinberg, Lazar Weiner and Eric Werner. Contributions were also made by Hugo Adler, Isador Freed, Herbert Fromm, Max Helfman, Heinrich Schalit and Edward Start.

Women have only begun to make progress in gaining national leadership positions in the Reform movement in recent years. The National Federation of Temple Sisterhoods, founded in 1913, offered Reform women their first public forum in the movement at the denominational level but generally did not seek to redefine the role of women in Reform Judaism. The most significant breakthrough for Reform women occurred in 1972 when Sally Priesand was ordained as the first female Rabbi by HUC-JIR. Other significant women in the history of American Reform Judaism include Paula Ackerman, Sadie American, Fannie Brinn, Rae Cook, Jane Evans, Norma Levitt, Ray Frank Litman, Audrey Friedman Marcus, Carrie Simon, Hannah Greenebaum Solomon and Rosa F. Sonneschein.

While each entry in the biographical dictionary tells part of the larger story of American Reform Judaism, the introductory essay on the history of the movement attempts to place the rise and development of Reform Judaism in a broad historical context. In addition, the essays on HUC-JIR, the CCAR and the UAHC help to place all of these leaders in context. At the same time, the constituent organizations of the Reform movement served as a model for other Jewish religious movements in North America. These essays provide the reader with an overview of the milieu in which these leaders have labored. Finally, all of this material is followed by a series of lists and a bibliography that will aid the reader and researcher in a further exploration of Reform Judaism from a historical perspective.

ACKNOWLEDGMENTS

Since this volume, by design, speaks of the lives of so many people, it is impossible to thank all of them—even those among the living. In no small way have they contributed to our growth as rabbis, scholars and human beings. Their stories have become our stories. And so thank them we must.

We also want to thank the many contributors whose essays are included in this volume, as well as those who contributed essays that, in the end, had to be excised from such a modest volume. Their work has not been forgotten and will one day find a place in a larger volume on the Reform movement.

In particular, there are those who require a special note of thanks. The American Jewish Archives continues to be a source of our strength. Our beloved teacher Jacob Rader Marcus is unrelenting in his mastery of the material we sought and unending in his unique ability to give of self. Abraham Peck, friend and colleague, saw us through the many difficult hours of assembling the material. Archivists Fannie Zelcer and Kevin Profitt always found the time and energy to fulfill our requests—no matter how busy they were.

We owe a great deal to Alfred Gottschalk, our president; Paul Steinberg and Uri Herscher, vice presidents; and Norman J. Cohen, dean of HUC-JIR, without whom none of our work would be possible. Their presence is felt in this book alongside our own.

Students of HUC-JIR, New York—many of whom are now rabbis and will assuredly be listed in future volumes of this kind—helped in the tedious task of rechecking dates and references and tracking down the elusive data of history. These include Carole Balin, Karen Bookman, Paula Feinstein, Ellen Lippman and Michelle Paskow. Ida Walker of Binghamton, New York, also devoted a great deal of time to our project.

The series editor deserves special thanks. He stood by this project throughout the process of completion. While the words are our own, without Marc Lee Raphael none of the words in this book would have been written.

This book is also a tribute to a personal, rabbinic friendship among three people who have a love for American Jewish history. Over a period of several years we brought our individual perspectives to this project and brought it to completion.

We also thank our families. They stand by us wherever our lives take us, and we are eternally grateful for their love and support.

Kerry M. Olitzky
Lance J. Sussman
Malcolm H. Stern

INTRODUCTION

Reform Judaism is one of the principal branches of Judaism in the United States and Canada and the largest movement in liberal or modern religion in the world. Developing first in West European Jewish communities, most importantly in Germany during the early decades of the nineteenth century, Reform's greater institutional success in North America was predicated on the appeal of both its general belief in Jewish cultural accommodation and its highly adaptive religious program, especially its reduction of ritualism.

For most of its first century, with the exception of the original Reformed Society of Israelites (1825–1833), which was led by a small coterie of Sephardic Jews, American Reform Judaism almost exclusively attracted Jews of Central European origin or descent. Beginning in the 1920s, East European Jews and their descendants began to join Reform temples in steadily increasing numbers. By the 1940s, they constituted a majority in the movement. After World War II, subethnic differences diminished in general among American Jews and played virtually no role in the shaping of postwar Reform Judaism. The social structure of the Reform movement began to change again during the 1970s as the rate of mixed and conversionary marriages soared. From its inception, the American Reform movement has largely maintained a middle-class social base. It has also been successful in appealing to a significant portion of the socioeconomic elite of the American Jewish community.

Reform Judaism was the first religious movement among American Jews to organize itself on a denominational basis. Pioneering a tripartite polity in American Judaism that was subsequently adopted by all the major branches of modern Judaism in North America, Reform's primary national institutional superstructure consists of (1) an umbrella organization of independent synagogues, the Union of American Hebrew Congregations (UAHC); (2) a seminary system, Hebrew Union College–Jewish Institute of Religion (HUC-JIR); and (3) a professional association of rabbis, the Central Conference of American Rabbis (CCAR).

By the beginning of the 1980s, over 750 American synagogues with more than a million individual members were affiliated with the Reform movement. Outside of North America, Reform congregations are represented by the World Union for Progressive Judaism.

The basic mode of governance in the American Reform movement is congregationalist. Power is principally vested in the board and officers of the individual synagogue. Since World War II, the national institutions of the movement have dramatically widened the scope of their operations. The UAHC presidency, a professional position held by a rabbi since 1943, is now the most visible and, perhaps, most influential leadership role in the movement. The authority of the congregational rabbinate, on the other hand, is inherently weak because of the Reform movement's liberal theology and its tradition of trusteeism, which is based, in part, on the constitutional separation of the institutions of state and religion in the United States. Nevertheless, professionalism and traditional respect for the rabbinic office [kavod ha-rav] function as mitigating factors. Jewish scholarship, the traditional basis of rabbinic power, has largely given way to the individual rabbi's powers of persuasion, personal warmth and pastoral skills as the basis for his or her authority at the local level.

THEOLOGY

Unlike their counterparts in Europe, early American Reformers did not initially see Halachic justifications as part of their effort to adapt Judaism to the American cultural milieu. Influenced by the American belief in the sovereign self, they began with their own religious present and then drew eclectically both from contemporary culture and from the cumulative Jewish tradition to express and validate their understanding of Judaism. Subsequently, the American Reform movement generally remained more radical than its counterpart in Germany. Although currently more favorably inclined toward a number of traditional practices than in the past, the overall religious ideology of the movement remains as liberal as ever. For example, the CCAR's 1983 endorsement of patrilineal descent can be seen as one of the most radical policies ever adopted by an official body of the Reform movement.

The initial theology of the American Reform movement was Deistic. Although popular religious thought in Reform largely remains in line with that of general American civil religion, an elitist theology, first articulated in Germany and subsequently brought to the United States and Canada by immigrant "rabbi-doctors" during the middle decades of the nineteenth century, is usually presented as the official "religion" of the movement. In addition to "ethical monotheism," two doctrines—"progressive revelation" and the "mission of Israel," derived from classical Jewish sources and Romantic German (Hegelian) philosophy— shaped much of the ideological character of American Reform during its formative years. In the Reform tradition, revelation is not usually understood in terms of a historical theophany at Sinai nor as a philosophically determined truth.

Rather, it is redefined as an ongoing process of individual and collective inspiration in Jewish history. Not only did progressive revelation account for the development of the Written (Bible) and, to a lesser extent, the Oral (Talmud) Law, but it also sanctioned the work of the reformers themselves. In short, progressive revelation held that religious change was divinely sanctioned and that the Reform movement and the Jewish people were God's vanguard on earth.

The second concept, the Mission of Israel, proved more problematic and has gradually waned within the Reform movement. Basically, it suggested that the Hebrew prophets served as the apostles of ethical monotheism, with the goal of creating a just society on earth. Mission theology thus helped justify and define the continued existence of the Jewish people in the postemancipatory era. However, the mission concept was more than a mere universalistic reinterpretation of Judaism's ancient theological view of history. It was also a radical reformulation of the idea of the chosen people. It committed Reform Judaism to the maintenance of Jewish endogamy and provided the movement with an effective buttress against Christian missionary activity. In its heyday, the mission idea not only complemented the more enduring notion of progressive revelation but actually gave the American Reform movement a triumphalist edge.

Closely allied to the nineteenth-century belief in infinite human progress, Reform's "classical" theology was shaken by the terrible carnage of World War I. Subsequently, the mission concept was gradually abandoned as Reform reconciled itself with Zionism and embraced Jewish particularism during the 1930s and 1940s. An echo of the doctrine remains in the movement's commitment to social justice and political action. For the most part, however, contemporary Reform Judaism is no longer characterized by "immediatism," and its religious program increasingly serves as a handmaiden to American Jewry's commitment to Jewish survival and American modalities of domesticity. In limited circles, especially among rabbis, attempts to redefine Reform theology in terms of religious existentialism with an emphasis on personal spirituality have been highly successful.

RELIGIOUS PRACTICES

While Reform Judaism remains ideologically committed to a program of open-ended religious innovation and theological reevaluation, fundamental changes in its liturgical life tend to be carefully controlled at both the congregational and the national levels. The potential for religious anarchy within Reform is also checked by the widespread respect that Reform Jews hold for the normative religious principles and practices sanctioned by their movement. Reform's early and frequently cited antinomianism relaxed during the course of the twentieth century, and especially within rabbinic circles, an openness toward Jewish legal traditions has developed. Currently, the CCAR issues a number of religious guides for Reform Jews as well as several collections of Reform responsa.

Current Reform practice is characterized by the slow, eclectic restoration of numerous traditional customs, along with the presentation of more radical Reform practices and a continual commitment to ritual innovations and experimentation. Although only a tiny percentage of Reform Jews regularly attend services on a weekly basis, the vast majority worship annually at Temple during the High Holy Days. Reform Jews generally do not celebrate the "second day" of Jewish festivals.

The main Sabbath service in Reform is held on Friday nights after dinner, an innovation that can be traced back to the late 1860s but that was not widely adopted by Reform congregations until the 1930s. Men and women sit together during worship, and except for some congregations during the High Holy Days, seating is universally unassigned. The reading of the liturgy is usually supplemented with organ music and choral singing. The Reform choir is generally made up of non-Jewish semiprofessional singers, although many congregations also employ a cantor. Since World War II, the music of the American Reform synagogue has evolved away from nineteenth-century German Jewish liturgical traditions and has come to include Israeli, Hasidic, and folk-style American tunes, especially in youth services and at the movement's summer camps. Influenced by Israeli practice, most Reform synagogues have switched from Ashkenazic pronunciation to the Sephardic style of Hebrew. The amount of Hebrew read in the Reform service has also increased steadily since World War II. However, extensive use of the vernacular continues to distinguish the American Reform service, as does its decorum and relative congregational passivity.

Outside the synagogue, many Reform Jews tend to maintain a number of ritual practices. Passover and Hannukah are widely observed, and in a large percentage of households, Sabbath candles are lit. Observance of the dietary laws, not required by the Reform tradition, is rarely maintained in full, although some restrictions are respected. Reform Jews tend to maintain strong ethnic identities as American Jews and consider general education and ethics to be of paramount importance. In recent years, a large number of Reform males have returned to wearing the ritual head covering (*kippah* or *yarmulke*) during worship at home and in Temple. Many reform synagogues provide *kippot* for those who want to wear them. *Tallitot* (prayer shawls), on the other hand, are generally worn only by the rabbis, cantors and other regular participants in morning services. Some women are also adopting these practices.

Most Reform Jews send their school-age children to supplementary Jewish education programs on the weekends and after regular school during the week. However, a Reform day school movement has emerged in several large cities and, after considerable debate, has received UAHC sanction. Most Reform children remain in religious school through the tenth grade and confirmation. Since World War II, Bar and Bat Mitzvah have also been widely observed by American Reform Jews. Adult-education programs are increasingly popular. Distinguished-speaker series and seminar-style study groups, in particular, have both proven to be successful formats.

In response to the soaring rate of exogamy and pressure from congregants whose children have chosen to marry non-Jews, nearly half of all Reform rabbis now officiate at the weddings of religiously mixed couples, in contravention of CCAR guidelines. The vast majority of these rabbis, however, insist that the children of such unions be raised as Jews and that the couple receive either premarital counseling or some instruction in Judaism. Few Reform rabbis will co-officiate at a wedding with either a minister or a priest. Reform policy on conversion has been a source of increasing controversy in the larger Jewish community in recent years, and the "Outreach Program" represents a significant softening of traditional Judaism's attitude toward prospective converts. In general, Reform rabbis continue to be involved in both Jewish and general communal affairs and are often active in interfaith circles, civic organizations and social-welfare activities.

HISTORY

Constantly seeking to create a mode of Judaism compatible with contemporary culture, American Reform Judaism can be divided into six distinct periods: (1) Beginnings, 1824–1865; (2) The Golden Age of Liberal Judaism, 1865–1900; (3) Reform Judaism and Uptown Progressivism, 1900–1920; (4) Reorientation, 1920–1945; (5) Reform on the Suburban Frontier, 1945–1965; and (6) Reform since 1965. During the interwar years, the Reform movement experienced an official shift in its basic ideology from a primary emphasis on theological universalism to a greater appreciation of Jewish particularism. The "reorientation," however, did not result in either a permanent institutional schism or an abandonment of the movement's essential religious modernism.

Beginnings, 1824–1865

During its initial period of development, the American Reform movement, although small and internally divided, generated a considerable amount of religious controversy among American Jews. By the time the Civil War began, no more than eight of the 200-plus synagogues in the United States and Canada were either openly Reform or had evidenced some Reformistic tendencies. On the other hand, the Reform movement had several outstanding rabbinic champions, including the indefatigable Isaac M. Wise (1819–1900) and the brilliant radical reformer David Einhorn (1809–1879).

The first attempt to organize a Reform movement in American Judaism occurred in Charleston, South Carolina, one of the great cultural centers of the Old South and a site of continuous Jewish settlement since the 1670s. The leaders were young, highly Americanized Jews, many of Sephardic descent, who had only a faint knowledge of the European Reform movement. The group of nearly 50 members of Charleston's *Kehillah*, Congregation Beth Elohim, petitioned the synagogue-community's Board and requested the reading of select prayers in the English language, a weekly "discourse" in the vernacular, and greater decorum and dignity in a variety of congregational activities, including worship and fund raising. When Beth Elohim's trustees refused to discuss the group's proposals, the dissidents decided to organize an independent Reformed Society of Israelites (1825–1833). The society flourished for only a few years; it held annual dinners for its male members and produced its low liturgy. The untimely death of its principal leader, Isaac Harby (1788–1828), and sustained communal and family pressures resulted in the society's decline. Subsequently, however, the Charleston Reform movement experienced a resurgence at the end of the 1830s. Led by a young attorney, Abraham Moise (1799–1869), who received the unforeseen support of Beth Elohim's hazzan, Gustavus Poznanski (1805?–1879), the Reformers not only succeeded in having an organ installed in the community's new synagogue building but also won custody of the building in a protracted and bitter legal action against the Orthodox members of the congregation. The latter subsequently withdrew from Beth Elohim and formed a synagogue of their own, Shearith Israel.

A second line of development in the American Reform movement began in the early 1840s with the arrival of Central European immigrants, who quickly became the new majority of American Jews. The Jewish population of the United States grew geometrically, from 2,700–3,000 in 1820 to approximately 15,000 in 1840. By 1860, the total U.S. Jewish population approached 150,000. Included in their midst were a small number of Reform Jews and rabbis who laid the foundation for the development of an indigenous American Reform movement. Typical of all immigrant faiths, Reform Jews debated the merits of cultural and linguistic accommodation. By the 1870s, however, the Americanizers had clearly gained the upper hand.

The first immigrant Reform groups were organized in Baltimore, the Har Sinai Verein, in 1842, and in New York, Congregation Emanu-El, three years later. Both groups' activities were essentially informed by the contemporary Reform movement in Germany. Emanu-El, in particular, quickly prospered and attracted many of New York's most successful immigrants to its pews. It engaged Leo Merzbacher (1809–1856), who had studied with the renowned Orthodox scholar the Hatam Sofer Moses Schreiber, and at several German universities, to serve as its spiritual leader. Although he preached exclusively in German, Merzbacher published his own prayerbook, *Seder Tefillah*, in English and Hebrew in 1855.

Isaac M. Wise, a native of Bohemia and the leading organizer of nineteenth-century American Reform Judaism, arrived in the United States in 1846. Committed to Americanizing Judaism, Wise, whose personal education was considerably more modest than he publicly claimed, was a highly industrious, pragmatic leader, a prodigious reader, a writer and, above all, a practical Reformer. At the age of 27, he was sent to Albany by his friend Max Lilienthal (1815–1882), who was then serving as the "Chief Rabbi" of New York's three traditional German congregations. There Wise immediately began introducing reforms, including a mixed choir. Tensions mounted when Wise insisted on leading services on the Jewish New Year in 1850. After a melee in the synagogue on

Rosh Hashanah, Wise and his followers withdrew and organized Congregation Anshe Emeth. Established as a Reform congregation, Anshe Emeth was the first synagogue in the United States to permit men and women to sit together during services.

In 1854, Wise was called to the pulpit of Bene Jeshurun in Cincinnati, where he remained for the rest of his life. The following year, Lilienthal, who also was moving in the direction of moderate Reform, also relocated to Cincinnati when he accepted the rabbinic position at Bene Israel Congregation, the oldest in the city. Of the two, Wise quickly emerged as the superior leader. He founded a monthly newspaper, the *Israelite*, which enabled him to circulate his views on a national basis. Hoping to unite American Jewry under one banner, Wise, along with his archrival, Isaac Leeser (1806–1868), the leading Orthodox religious leader in antebellum America, unsuccessfully attempted to convene a conference of American "rabbis" in 1848. Seven years later, the relentless Wise organized a rabbinic conference in Cleveland, which Leeser reluctantly attended.

Wise hoped to use the Cleveland Conference to establish a single mode of American Judaism, a common prayerbook (*Minhag America*), and a rabbinic college in Cincinnati. In conceding the authority of the Talmud to his Orthodox colleagues, however, Wise offended the religious sensibilities of numerous radical reformers, especially Rabbi David Einhorn, who vigorously and publicly attacked Wise. Einhorn's protests not only dashed Wise's hopes for a common American Judaism but also indicated the serious religious divisions growing within the American Reform movement.

Einhorn differed from Wise on a number of issues. A Bavarian rabbi who had studied at several German universities, Einhorn was a rigorous and systematic thinker, an uncompromising reformer and a political liberal. Arriving in the United States in 1855 to serve Baltimore's Har Sinai congregation, he published a monthly German-language journal, the *Sinai*, and his own prayer book, *Olath Tamid*, an original German work that later became the basis for the CCAR's *Union Prayer Book*. Despite his support of abolitionism, Einhorn emerged as a leading theologian of the Reform movement in the years before and immediately after the Civil War. In the postwar period, his ideology and liturgy dominated the Reform movement while Wise's national institutions and organizations reshaped the character of the Reform polity.

The Golden Age of Liberal Judaism, 1865–1900

The complex period between the end of the Civil War and the death of Isaac M. Wise in 1900 witnessed the transformation of the Reform movement in America into an American-style denomination. It also witnessed the growth of the radical and "classical" branches within the Reform movement and the expansion of Reform, in general, in American Judaism. Several factors contributed to these developments. First, the process of Americanization among German Jews accelerated rapidly during their "second generation," a process that was greatly fortified by their general economic success. Second, "liberal religion" flourished in the United States in general during much of the latter half of the nineteenth century and helped pave the way for reinterpreting Judaism in the light of contemporary philosophy and science.

After 1880, however, the established German Jewish community experienced a double displacement. As the nineteenth century drew to a close, indigenous anti-Semitism rose significantly and resulted in widespread discrimination against American Jews, including elite German Jews. Moreover, within the American Jewish community, the Reformers were being displaced by East European Jews who began arriving in North America in increasing numbers after 1880. Membership in a Reform Temple symbolically helped to define the "elite" character and subethnic status of the German Jew in America.

In the years immediately following the Civil War, Einhorn took the first step to define the character of American Reform Judaism in the postwar period. In November 1869, at the Philadelphia home of a distinguished colleague, Samuel Hirsch (1815–1889), he convened a small rabbinic conference. Among other things, the Philadelphia Conference, animated by the doctrines of progressive revelation and the mission of Israel, rejected the idea of Jewish restoration to Palestine and the Orthodox belief in physical resurrection and also attempted to strengthen the role of women in various Jewish life-cycle occasions. Ten years later, in his last sermon, Einhorn, who was never fully at home in America, cautioned his followers, "If you sever Reform from . . . the German language, you will have torn it from its native soil and the lovely flower must wilt." Although his theology prevailed, Einhorn's struggle to preserve the German character of American Reform Judaism proved to be a lost cause.

Wise, who attended the Philadelphia Conference but contributed little to it, had plans of his own to rally moderate Reform rabbis under one banner. Instead, a series of meetings inspired or organized by Wise early in the 1870s proved highly divisive and pitted the East Coast radicals against Wise's group. To support their rabbi, a lay group, led by Moritz Loth (1832–1913), then president of Wise's congregation, organized the Union of American Hebrew Congregations in July 1873. Thirty-four congregations joined, mainly from the Midwest and South. By the following year, the number of affiliated synagogues had increased to 55, and another 17 congregations joined in 1875. By the end of the decade, 118 congregations, more than half of all the identified synagogues in the United States, were affiliated with the UAHC. The Reform movement had taken the decisive step toward becoming an American-style denomination.

One of the principal purposes of the UAHC was to serve as the patron of a rabbinic school. In 1875, Hebrew Union College was established in Cincinnati, and Wise was named its president, thus fulfilling one of his lifelong dreams. Hoping that HUC could serve all sectors of American Jewish religious life, Wise carefully controlled the curriculum so that ideas and methods repugnant to traditionalists were not offered. However, his initial nondenominational approach to rabbinic education proved to be a pipe dream. In 1883, at a dinner honoring

HUC's first four ordinees and attended by representatives of over 100 UAHC congregations, shellfish (prohibited by Jewish law) was inadvertently served by the hosts. This "Trefa Banquet" quickly became a symbol of the differences between the Reform movement and the more traditional branches of Judaism in America. HUC survived the incident, but Wise's dream of a common American Judaism had been dealt a fatal setback.

Two years later, a controversy between two scholarly pulpit rabbis in New York set the stage for the promulgation of a platform for "classical" Reform Judaism in America. Alexander Kohut (1842–1894), a Hungarian rabbi recently arrived in the United States, initiated the debate by giving a series of lectures attacking Reform's rejection of Jewish law. Kohut's charge—"Reform is a Deformity"—was answered by the German-born Kaufmann Kohler (1843–1926), a son-in-law of David Einhorn's as well as his successor at Beth El congregation. The debate attracted wide attention, filled the two rabbis' synagogues with partisan crowds and clarified many of the differences between Reform and traditional Judaism.

At the same time the Kohler-Kohut debate was raging, Reform Judaism was also being attacked by Felix Adler (1851–1933), a founder of the Society for Ethical Culture (est. 1876) and son of Samuel Adler, a distinguished Reform rabbi. The young Adler, who had rejected both monotheism and Jewish ethnicity, charged that Reform, even at its most radical, had failed to liberate itself completely from religious orthodoxy and embrace a universal code of ethics. Adler's views appealed to many Reform Jews and elicited strong replies from a number of leading Reform rabbis, including the intellectually adroit Kohler.

Seeking a middle ground between Kohut's positive-historical approach to Judaism and Adler's ethical atheism, Kohler convened a conference of Reform rabbis in Pittsburgh in 1885. Labeled a "Declaration of Independence" by Wise, the eight planks of Kohler's "Pittsburgh Platform" were unequivocally modern in spirit. However, in its subtext, the platform also preserved Reform's emotional connection to historical Judaism. It described the Bible as "reflecting the primitive ideas of its own age," rejected all Jewish customs "not adapted to the views and habits of modern civilization" and announced that the Jews were "no longer a nation but a religious community." On the other hand, it also affirmed that "Judaism presents the highest conception of the God-idea" and that Jews continue to exist as a "religious community" with a messianic mission.

While the Pittsburgh Platform again stirred Reform's critics, on both the left and the right, it was also defended by a number of leading Reform Jews. Most important, a Conference of Southern Rabbis, organized in New Orleans later in 1885, strongly endorsed Kohler's work. A quasi-professional organization, it planned to meet on an annual basis. Wise responded by organizing a parallel Central Conference at a UAHC convention in Detroit four years later and successfully recruited rabbis from midwestern states as well as his former students.

An organizational success, the CCAR emerged as the third national branch of Reform's denominational superstructure. It quickly sought to strengthen the religious authority and improve the professional standing of the average Reform rabbi. It also set out to standardize religious policy and practice in the Reform movement. In 1892, the CCAR issued its first *Union Prayer Book*, which was followed two years later with a liturgy for the High Holy Days. Both works were essentially Einhornian in theology and literary style but were published principally in English, with some Hebrew but no German. In 1897, the CCAR also published its first *Union Hymnal*, modeling it after an Episcopalian work, in an effort to standardize the music as well as the texts used in the Reform liturgy. That same year, led by their aging president and in anticipation of the first Zionist Congress in Basle, Switzerland, the rabbis of the CCAR declared, "We totally disapprove of any attempt for the establishment of a Jewish state." "Classical" Reform had reached its high-water mark.

Reform Judaism and Uptown Progressivism, 1900–1920

The changes that occurred in the American Reform movement during the first two decades of the twentieth century were deeper than the emergence of new leaders in the wake of Isaac M. Wise's death in 1900. Immigration had already radically altered the profile of American Jewry, which had quadrupled in size from 250,000 in 1880 to approximately one million people at the end of the nineteenth century, increasing to nearly 3.5 million by 1920. The Reform movement, by contrast, could claim only 99 congregations with 9,800 members in 1900 and 200 congregations with 23,000 members twenty years later. Even more important than the demographic marginalization of the Reform movement was the diminution of its leadership role, lay and rabbinic, in the American Jewish community. In 1906, an elite group of German Jews formed the oligarchical American Jewish Committee and thereby signaled a major structural change in American Jewish life. Hereafter, defense and philanthropic agencies—and, still later, Zionist organizations—would represent the broadest consensuses in American Jewish life, replacing the older religious and fraternal groups like the UAHC and B'nai B'rith. Similarly, the independent National Council of Jewish Women, founded in 1892, won an increasingly widespread following among German-Jewish women, as did Hadassah in Zionist circles after its formal organization in 1914.

The demographic and political challenges faced by Reform did not shake the movement's confidence. A new synthesis, however, was needed, and various new positions were adopted and old, religiously radical ideas modified. Beginning in 1902, when the CCAR voted to maintain the Seventh-Day Sabbath, Reform's ties to many aspects of traditional Judaism were reestablished as a response to the development of an East European majority in American Jewish life and, perhaps, the reorganization of the Conservative movement's rabbinic seminary under the guidance of the scholarly and vigorous Solomon Schechter. In 1906, the CCAR rejected a proposal to establish, under its auspices, a general Synod for American Jews and instead established a Reponsa Committee the following year. In 1909 it declared, "Mixed marriages are contrary to the Jewish religion." Although the majority of Reform Jews remained "classical" in their orientation, the movement as a whole was slowly abandoning its goal of recasting Judaism in terms of mainstream American Protestantism.

Challenged during the nineteenth century by both David Einhorn and his Chicago-based son-in-law, Emil G. Hirsch (1851–1923), to incorporate "social justice" into the core body of Reform doctrines, the American Reform movement nevertheless remained largely unconcerned about the massive social problems caused by industrialization and urbanization in the United States, until the early 1900s. Following the lead of the Social Gospel movement, which culminated in the organization of the Federal Council of Churches in 1908, the CCAR finally spoke out against child labor that same year. However, it did not formulate a "Declaration of Principles" on the rights of workers in general for another decade. By contrast, in 1904, at the urging of its president, Joseph Krauskopf (1858–1923), the CCAR actively campaigned to strengthen the "wall of separation" between the institutions of government and religion.

Reform's ambivalence regarding organized labor was paralleled by its qualified support of the suffrage movement. After 1900, women were increasingly accepted as members of Reform synagogues but were generally not allowed to serve on Temple boards and thus remained outside the power structure in the Reform movement. Similarly, the National Federation of Temple Sisterhoods (NFTS), founded in 1913, stressed the role of Jewish women in the home and the virtues of feminine piety. At its inception, NFTS was administered by Rabbi George Zepin (1878–1963), secretary of the UAHC. The CCAR rejected two resolutions in favor of women's suffrage before passing a motion in 1917. Finally, in the years following World War I, both the faculty of the Hebrew Union College and members of the CCAR voted in favor of ordaining women as rabbis but were overruled by HUC's powerful board of governors in 1923.

Reorientation, 1920–1945

During the interwar years, the American Reform movement reevaluated and largely rejected its earlier, equivocal views of Jewish particularism. Spurred by the increase in domestic anti-Semitism, the rise of Hitler in Germany and the success of the *Yishuv* in building a modern Jewish society in British Palestine, the American Reform movement not only embraced the concept of "Jewish peoplehood" but ultimately endorsed the idea of Jewish statehood as well. In a step widely viewed as the great turning point in the history of the American Reform movement, the CCAR adopted a Zionist platform in 1937 and thereby paved the way for a fundamental shift in the ideology of the movement in North America. By contrast, Reform's liturgical practices did not change as dramatically during this period.

Reform's ideological reorientation clearly had a social basis. American isolationism and xenophobia in the wake of World War I led to a severe tightening of American immigration laws during the course of the 1920s and also accelerated the pace of the Americanization of the East European Jews already in the United States, many of whom began to join Reform temples. These new Reform Jews, especially in rabbinic circles, often maintained a warm feeling for old-world Jewish traditions as well as Zionist ideology. In 1930, before the Depression temporarily disrupted further growth, the movement peaked at 285 congregations with more than 60,000 members at a time when less than one-third of all American Jewish families were affiliated with a synagogue. However, Reform, like liberal religion in general, did not flourish during the 1920s and 1930s. One American church historian even referred to the period beginning in the latter half of the 1920s as the beginning of a "religious depression." Weakened by numerous changes in popular American culture including the expansion of the automobile market and the development of new entertainment industries, Reform temples often found themselves serving as little more than "ornaments" of middle-class Jewish culture, and in fact, numerous costly synagogues were built by Reform congregations during the 1920s. Symptomatic of the general religious decline of the period, the Reform movement helped foster and participated in a number of inter- and intrafaith organizations during this period.

The most significant change in the Reform movement during the interwar years, however, was in its attitude toward Zionism. The CCAR's original hard-line opposition to political Zionism was never unanimous and began to soften after the Balfour Declaration of 1917. In 1922, Rabbi Stephen S. Wise (1874–1949, no relation to Isaac M. Wise), an outstanding orator, social activist and Zionist leader, founded the Jewish Institute of Religion (merged with HUC in 1950) in New York, which largely produced pro-Zionist rabbis, many of whom served in Reform congregations. One year later, in 1923, the UAHC hired a pro-Zionist director, Emanuel Gamoran (1895–1962), to head its education commission, a position he held until shortly before his death. Finally, the CCAR, after some debate, agreed to include "Hatikvah" in the 1932 *Union Hymnal*.

The great debate over Zionism in the American Reform movement, however, was yet to come. Sparked by the empowerment of Nazism in Germany in 1933, by a parallel surge in domestic anti-Semitism and by the publication of Mordecai Kaplan's *Judaism as a Civilization* in 1934, which advocated both Jewish peoplehood and theological naturalism, the CCAR agreed, in 1935, to reevaluate the theology and antinationalism of the 50-year-old Pittsburgh Platform. The Zionist faction in the conference was led by the militant Abba Hillel Silver (1893–1963), but it was Samuel S. Cohon (1888–1959), a professor of Jewish theology at HUC, who drafted the "Guiding Principles of Reform Judaism," which were overwhelmingly adopted by the CCAR at its annual convention in Columbus, Ohio, in 1937. Expanding on Reform's traditional theism and re-affirming its commitment to social justice, Cohon's "Columbus Platform" also spoke of "the obligation of all Jewry to aid in [the] upbuilding [of Palestine] as a Jewish homeland" and the positive role of ceremonialism and Hebrew in

Jewish worship. That same year, the UAHC also adopted a resolution calling for "the establishment of a Jewish [home] and in Palestine."

Reform opposition to Zionism, however, did not end in 1937. As late as 1942, the movement split over the twin issues of raising a Jewish army in Palestine and demanding immediate statehood. An anti-Zionist splinter group, the American Council for Judaism, composed mainly of Reform rabbis and their lay followers, formed and brought American Reform Judaism to the brink of schism. News of the destruction of European Jewry and the establishment of the State of Israel rapidly sapped the council of its strength. Reform's anti-Zionism was now largely a thing of the past, and the movement, theologically redefined and institutionally reinvigorated, refocused its attention on the rapidly changing religious and social realities of postwar America.

Reform on the Suburban Frontier, 1945–1965

The massive expansion of organized religious life in America in the years immediately following World War II transformed the Reform movement into a major American denomination. In 1940, the UAHC could claim 265 affiliate congregations with a total of 59,000 members. Just 15 years later, in 1955, it could boast of 520 congregations with 255,000 members representing perhaps as many as a million people. Although Reform's growth curve began to slow thereafter, the UAHC continued to expand and reported a total of 660 member-temples in 1964.

The reasons for the movement's immense growth can basically be explained in terms of the general sociology of religion in postwar America. Suburbanization, the vast social process that resulted in the development of huge rings of single-family house tracts around established urban centers, as well as the creation of entirely new suburban cities, especially in the Southwest, had an enervating effect on both extended-family networks and ethnic neighborhoods, which had supported much of prewar Jewish life. To retain a modicum of ethnic Jewish culture in their lives, maintain social contacts with other Jews and, above all, instill a Jewish identity in their children, hundreds of thousands of otherwise secular and highly Americanized Jews joined synagogues for the first time. Thus, while the clergy, academics and the press debated the depth and religious quality of the postwar revival, new synagogue construction soared, and temples became remarkably busy social centers for suburban Jewry.

If the underlying causes for the Reform movement's rapid institutional growth were typical of the American religious scene, the movement's postwar leadership was remarkable. Two rabbis in particular, Maurice Eisendrath (1902–1973) and Nelson Glueck (1900–1971), were responsible for reshaping the American Reform movement. Eisendrath was named the executive director of the UAHC in 1943 and became its president in 1946. Determined to revitalize the UAHC and invigorate the Reform movement, Eisendrath successfully campaigned to move

UAHC's headquarters from Cincinnati to New York and built an impressive "House of Living Judaism" on Fifth Avenue across the street from Temple Emanu-El. Glueck, a world-renowned archaeologist, succeeded Julian Morgenstern as president of HUC in 1947 and, shortly thereafter, oversaw HUC's merger with Stephen Wise's Jewish Institute of Religion. An energetic president of the two-campus HUC-JIR, he established a third branch in Los Angeles in 1954 and dedicated a fourth campus in Jerusalem in 1963. The CCAR was also transformed by the dramatic growth of the Reform movement. Run entirely on a volunteer basis since its inception, the CCAR opened a national office in New York in 1954 and engaged its first executive vice president, Rabbi Sidney Regner (1903–   ). Ten years later, the CCAR began regulating rabbinic placement—heretofore a process largely controlled by select faculty members and the president of HUC-JIR—and thereby preserved the CCAR's position in the overall polity of the Reform movement. The professionalization of the CCAR, as well as the Reform rabbinate, was also reflected in the CCAR's decision to begin publishing a quarterly journal of opinion, currently called the *CCAR Journal: A Reform Jewish Quarterly*, early in the 1950s.

The Reform movement of the 1950s and early 1960s focused much of its energies on social justice issues, including civil liberties, civil rights and the American peace movement. After a bitter debate, the UAHC resolved to develop a lobby in Washington, D.C., and, with the financial help of Kivie Kaplan (1904–1975), a Reform Jew and prominent civil rights activist, opened a Religious Action Center in 1961 in the former Ecuadorian Embassy on Connecticut Avenue. Although many southern rabbis and congregations publicly urged caution on civil rights issues (often while privately supporting the civil rights movement) and although numerous other voices challenged Eisendrath's and others' increasingly vocal opposition to American military involvement in Vietnam after 1964, Reform Jews broadly favored their movement's liberal political agenda. Reform rabbis, mostly from the North, marched with other civil rights leaders in the Deep South and, a few years later, in mass antiwar demonstrations. By mid-decade, the movement had gained much of its earlier messianic zeal. However, the enthusiasm was shortlived, and by the end of the 1960s, the Reform movement, like many liberal and mainstream religious groups, found itself wallowing in a deep malaise.

Reform since 1965

A combination of at least three different factors accounted for the sudden dramatic change in the mood of the Reform movement. By 1965, the direction of the civil rights movement had begun to change, away from integration and toward "black power." Two years later, in the wake of Israel's stunning six-day victory, many Reform Jews found themselves torn between their opposition to the war in Vietnam, opposition that was in many cases undistinguished from antimilitarism in general, and their elation over Israel's success on the battlefield. Furthermore, they felt betrayed by the failure of the Christian clergy to rally behind Israel in its most perilous hour and were angry at much of the American political Left, which quickly adopted an anti-Zionist position after June 1967. Finally, a specifically religious crisis also developed, especially within the Reform rabbinate, leading, as in American religion in general, to greater personal spirituality and a broad rethinking of the place of tradition in worship and practice.

Tensions in the movement during this period focused on several key issues. First, the congregational rabbis successfully campaigned for curricular changes at HUC-JIR, with a new emphasis on ''social and practical relevance.'' Second, a debate over Diaspora-Israeli relations was opened but to a large extent was muted after the 1973 Yom Kippur War and the expansion of local Jewish Federations and the United Jewish Appeal (UJA). The bitterest fight in the Reform movement during this period, however, was over the question of rabbinic officiation at mixed marriages. A deeply divided Central Conference of American Rabbis debated the issue at its 1973 meeting in Atlanta and, by a three-to-two margin, reaffirmed its ''opposition to participation by its members in any ceremony which solemnizes a mixed marriage.'' An additional clause recognizing ''divergent interpretations of Jewish tradition'' helped control a potentially schismatic movement within the CCAR and the larger Reform movement. Ironically, the number of Reform rabbis who did solemnize such marriages continued to rise; according to information gathered by the Rabbinic Center for Research and Counseling, founded by Rabbi Irwin H. Fishbein in 1970, over 500 Reform rabbis officiated at the marriages of religiously mixed couples ''under specified conditions'' just ten years after the Atlanta vote.

Neither the fight over rabbinic officiation at mixed marriages nor the movement's religious crisis resulted in a schism. Remarkably, by the mid-1970s, the Reform movement had largely regained its equilibrium. The sources of renewal were diverse. Women played an exceptionally important role in raising the movement out of its malaise. First, by the 1970s, they had gained access to the board rooms of most Reform synagogues, and in 1972, HUC-JIR conferred rabbinic ordination on Sally Priesand (1946–   ). Second, women made up the vast majority of the wave of converts to Reform Judaism during the 1970s, many of whom became highly involved in the affairs of their congregations. Finally, a group of national leaders, all male and many German-born, emerged as the new stewards of the movement.

In 1971, both the CCAR and HUC-JIR engaged new chief executives. American-born Rabbi Joseph Glaser (1925–   ) was named executive vice president of the CCAR and launched a massive campaign to revise the entire liturgy of the Reform movement to reflect its growing religious diversity. Four years later, the CCAR published the *Gates of Prayer*, a prayerbook anthology of services and readings ranging from ''traditional'' to nontheistic, and, in 1978, a parallel volume for the High Holy Days. The CCAR also issued numerous guides to Reform practice as well as a few inspirational works. Also, to help ''heal the wounds'' in the movement, the CCAR sponsored the writing of ''A Centenary Perspective'' in 1976. Authored by Rabbi Eugene Borowitz (1924–   ), a professor at the New York campus of HUC-JIR and a noted covenant theologian, this San Francisco platform (as it is also called) labels ''diversity . . . the hallmark of Reform.'' Nondirective and nondogmatic, it warmly discusses traditional theological themes and talks of the religious ''obligations'' of the individual Reform Jew. Its core teaching, however, remains closely linked to the theologian Abraham Geiger's notion of progressive revelation.

A second national leader to emerge during the early 1970s was Rabbi Alfred Gottschalk (1930–   ). Gottschalk fled Nazi Germany as a child and resettled in the United States. Rising quickly in HUC-JIR's ranks after his ordination, he became president of HUC-JIR in 1971. An exceptional fund raiser, he greatly expanded his predecessor's program to enlarge the college-institute, physically and programmatically. The two largest projects involve the expansion of the Jerusalem campus and the building of a Cultural Center for American Jewish Life in Los Angeles.

The third major national leader to emerge in the Reform movement during the 1970s was Rabbi Alexander Schindler (1925–   ), a European-born Jew and the first Reform religious leader to head the prestigious Conference of Presidents of Major American Jewish Organizations. A dramatic speaker, Schindler helped launch the Reform movement's Outreach Program, which has greatly softened much of modern Judaism's approach to proselytism and which subsequently challenged the CCAR to adopt a resolution on patrilineal descent. Passed in 1983, the CCAR vote played a significant role in escalating the highly divisive ''Who is a Jew?'' debate throughout the Jewish world, especially in the weeks following the 1988 Israeli general election. Eleven years earlier, in 1977, the American Reform movement had created the Association of Reform Zionists of America (ARZA) to promote Jewish religious pluralism in Israel and give American Reform Jews a voice in the World Zionist Organization.

Assessments of the Reform movement's future well-being vary widely. The most optimistic position is held by the movement's premier historian, Michael A. Meyer (1937–   ), a professor of Jewish history at HUC-JIR in Cincinnati. In a 1978 essay, Meyer wrote, ''With all its diversity, [Reform Judaism] alone offered [its adherents] a religious expression of Judaism both intellectually attractive and emotionally satisfying.'' The Rabbi Jakob J. Petuchowski (1925–1991), on the other hand, a former colleague of Meyer's at HUC-JIR (Cincinnati), wrote in the *Journal of Reform Judaism* in 1986 of ''the process of Reform Judaism's self-dissolution, which is already well under way, seeing that Reform Judaism keeps changing not only its outward forms, as might indeed be expected, but even its theological contents and its demographic make-up.''

The reality of Reform's current religious and institutional situation probably lies somewhere between its official triumphalism and the warnings of its

Jeremiah-like critics. However, at the present time, the American Reform movement is growing in terms of its total membership and number of affiliated synagogues. In fact, it is not unreasonable to suggest that Reform will be the largest
sector in organized American Judaism in the early decades of the twenty-first
century.

NOTE

This chapter is a revised version of an essay written by Lance J. Sussman which originally
appeared in *Jewish-American History and Culture: An Encyclopedia*, edited by Jack Fischel
and Sanford Pinsker, and published by Garland Publishing, Inc.

Reform Judaism
in America

A

AARON, MARCUS (1869–1954). Businessman. Aaron was born on December 14, 1869, in Pittsburgh, Pennsylvania, the son of Louis I. and Mina Lippman Aaron. He attended the University of Western Pennsylvania but left after six months due to typhoid fever. Much later, in 1924, he received the honorary LL.D. from the University of Pittsburgh. (The University of Pittsburgh was chartered as the University of Western Pennsylvania.) Aaron was president of the Homer Laughlin China Co. in Newell, West Virginia, having been associated with it since 1897 when the company was located in East Liverpool, Ohio. After a long and successful career, he retired to devote his full energies to community and civic concerns, primarily in Pittsburgh.

He was a member of the Board of Public Education in Pittsburgh (1911–1947), serving as its president (1922–1928), as well as the State Board of Education of Pennsylvania (1916–1923) and the State Council of Education (1921–1923). Aaron served as a trustee of the Carnegie Institute, the Carnegie Library and the Carnegie Institute of Technology and was a member of the Board of Governors of Hebrew Union College. He was also a member of the Board of the Union of American Hebrew Congregations (1940–1941), as well as a trustee of the Jewish Publication Society. Aaron served on the board of Rodef Shalom Congregation in Pittsburgh from 1898 to 1943 and was its president from 1930 to 1941.

In 1893, Aaron married Stella Hamburger. They had one son: Marcus Lester Aaron. Aaron died June 21, 1954.

References: *Universal Jewish Encyclopedia* (New York, 1943), 1:8; *Who's Who in American Jewry* (New York, 1939), p. 1.

ACKERMAN, PAULA (1893–1989). Spiritual leader, lecturer, teacher. Born in Pensacola, Florida, on December 7, 1893, Paula was the daughter of Joseph and Dora Herskovitz Ackerman. She was passionately interested in Judaism and active in Pensacola's Reform temple, Beth-El, first as a student and later as a teacher. She also received private Hebrew lessons from a local Orthodox rabbi, apparently becoming the first Jewish girl in Pensacola to formally study Hebrew.

Ackerman graduated from high school in 1911 as valedictorian of her class and was awarded a full scholarship to Sophie Newcomb College in New Orleans. However, financial difficulties at home, coupled with her father's refusal to allow her to prepare for the study of medicine, led her to decline the scholarship. She taught in the Pensacola public schools until 1919, when she married William Ackerman, Temple Beth-El's rabbi.

The Ackermans lived in Natchez, Mississippi, from 1920 to 1922, when William was appointed rabbi of Temple Beth Israel, a congregation of approximately 150 families in Meridian, Mississippi. During her husband's 28-year tenure as rabbi, Paula taught preconfirmation class and was active on a local and national level in the National Federation of Temple Sisterhoods.

In November 1950, after her husband's death, Ackerman was asked by the congregation to become their spiritual leader. Accepting their offer, she served from January 1951 through September 1952, leading services, preaching, teaching, performing marriages, funerals and even conversions. In so doing, she became the first woman to serve as the religious leader of a mainstream American Jewish congregation.

Ackerman's appointment was publicized in newspapers throughout the world. Although questions arose within the American Jewish community as to her qualifications for leadership, the congregation staunchly defended the appointment, even after Maurice Eisendrath, president of the Union of American Hebrew Congregations, issued a press release denying that he had previously given his approval. On retirement, Ackerman remained in Meridian, serving on city, state and national religious boards. She also traveled throughout the country, lecturing on religious themes. In 1962 she agreed to serve as spiritual leader of Temple Beth-El in Pensacola until a new rabbi could be found. Six months later she returned to Meridian, later moving to Pensacola (1970), Atlanta (1981) and Thomaston, Georgia (1985).

In 1986, at a special ceremony at the temple in Atlanta, the Union of American Hebrew Congregations formally honored Paula Ackerman's pioneering contribution to Jewish communal life, but since she had not received the requisite training, no retroactive ordination was conferred. She died in Thomaston on January 12, 1989.

Writings: Unfortunately, there seem to be no extant sermons by Paula Ackerman. However, letters by and to her, as well as newspaper clippings and transcribed interviews, can be found in the American Jewish Archives in Cincinnati.

References: "Correspondence pertaining to the election of Paula Ackerman as 'rabbi,' " Meridian, Mississippi, and New York, New York, 1951, American Jewish Archives; "Reform's Lost Woman Rabbi: An Interview with Paula Ackerman," *Genesis 2* 17 (June/July 1986): 18–20.

                                                                                    E.M.U.

ADLER, FELIX (1851–1933). Founder of the Ethical Culture movement, social reformer, professor of social and political ethics at Columbia University. The son of Henrietta and Rabbi Samuel Adler, Felix Adler was born in Alzey, Germany, in 1851. In 1857 he was brought to New York with his family when his father was called to serve as rabbi at Temple Emanu-El. While he received a secular education at Columbia Grammar School and Columbia College, his religious training took place at the temple's Jewish School and from the instruction of his father. From 1870 to 1873, Adler pursued rabbinical studies at the Hochschule für Wissenschaft des Judentums in Berlin. While completing a Ph.D., summa cum laude, in Semitics at Berlin University, he did additional work at the University of Heidelberg. The three years spent abroad put Adler in touch with several of the most illustrious scholars in the German Reform movement as well as with noted scholars in the fields of philosophy, science, biblical criticism and comparative religion. At the Hochschule, Adler studied under Hymann Steinthal and Abraham Geiger. The latter was the major theoretician of German Reform, whose concepts of the historical evolution of Jewish spirituality greatly affected Adler's changing religious outlook. Adler's work with Hermann Cohen and the historian Friedrich Lange at Berlin University exposed him to a neo-Kantian framework as a basis for morality.

On his return to New York in 1873 Adler was invited to give a sermon before his father's congregation. In his sermon, "The Judaism of the Future," which reflected the progressive spirit of the age, Adler praised the work of reformers, underscored Judaism's ethical dimension and identified Judaism as a religion "not of creed but of the deed." At the same time he implied that religion was not sufficiently addressing the social evils of the day and suggested that Judaism must rise to embrace the entire human family.

Adler's developing universalism, as well as his critique of the biblical sanction for morality, made him unsuited for a career in the rabbinate. Instead, he took a teaching position in the field of Hebrew and Oriental literature at Cornell University. But in 1876, with the help of several prominent members of Temple Emanu-El, Adler returned to New York City to found the Society for Ethical Culture, which proved to be the spearhead of a new religious movement. Committed to freedom of conscience in matters of belief, Adler made clear that the movement would be dedicated to promoting ethical ideals, particularly the dignity of the person, independent of explicit doctrine and without the support of ritual.

The Ethical Culture movement became a significant force for progressive social change, especially in its efforts to redress the inequities brought about by the industrial revolution. Adler contended that ethics is the essential element of religion but that monotheism is inadequate as its foundation. In its stead he developed his own idealistic formulation of the Godhead, which he termed "the infinite ethical manifold." It was a metaphysical notion of human interrelatedness in which individual identity would, nevertheless, be preserved.

Adler and his movement came under considerable attack from Reform Jewish leaders in the late 1870s, not only because of his radical views but also, ironically, because of his popularity among Jewish audiences, often heavily composed of Reform Jews. In part, the Pittsburgh Platform (1885) can be seen as a reaction of Reform rabbinic leaders to some of the challenges Adler posed to their movement.

Although Adler drew from many sources, one can, in part, interpret his work as an effort to transpose some of the major categories of American Reform Judaism to a universal context. His emphasis on the centrality of ethics, his search for a universal religious essence, his appropriation of Kantian idealism and his critique of Zionism all bear the stamp of the Reform ideology of his time.

In his early years Adler divided his time between leading the Ethical Culture movement, promoting social reform and teaching at Columbia University. At Columbia he continued to defend his neo-Kantian idealism against proponents of philosophical naturalism, including John Dewey.

Adler died on April 24, 1933, in New York City.

Writings: *Creed and Deed* (New York, 1877); *An Ethical Philosophy of Life* (New York, 1918); *The Reconstruction of the Spiritual Ideal* (New York, 1924).

References: "Autobiography of Samuel Adler" and "Biography File," American Jewish Archives; Horace Friess, *Felix Adler and Ethical Culture* (New York, 1981); Benny Kraut, *From Reform Judaism to Ethical Culture: The Religious Evolution of Felix Adler* (Cincinnati, 1979); Howard B. Radest, *Toward Common Ground* (New York, 1969).

                                                                                                                                                        J.C.

ADLER, SAMUEL (1809–1891). Rabbi, religious thinker. The son of Rabbi Isak Adler of Worms, Germany, Adler received traditional training at Frankfurt Yeshiva and privately from Rabbi Jacob Bamberger. He studied at the University of Bonn from 1831 to 1833 and at Giessen from 1833 to 1835, where he came under the influence of Joseph Hillebrand, a Hegelian. He played a major role in transplanting the intellectual tradition of the German Reform movement to the United States.

Adler's first rabbinical position was in Worms. There he initiated various changes in ritual, including removing the partition between men and women, translating the liturgy into German and eliminating prayers of vengeance. In 1842 he went to Alzey, where he remained for 14 years. At the Frankfurt Reform rabbinical conference in 1845 and at the Breslau conference in 1846, Adler advocated the role of the Jewish masses in changing rituals to fit contemporary conditions and the need to advance the status of women in education and worship. He posited that the Sabbath principle of sanctification would be preserved if nonstrenuous work affecting the welfare of the state, itself a moral institution, was permitted. In 1856 Adler accepted an invitation to succeed Leo Merzbacher of Temple Emanu-El in New York and emigrated the following year. In the United States he continued to advocate and develop his philosophy of religion. He openly rejected supernatural revelation and the eternal validity of Mosaic law. He omitted phrases from the liturgy referring to the return to Zion and advocated the removal of head coverings during those parts of the service that did not deal directly with devotion to God, such as sermons.

In his various published essays, Adler speaks of an ontological morality, an ethical *Weltall* (cosmos) created and maintained by God. Humanity, he proposes, is never outside its borders yet is not totally identified with the cosmos lest the individual and collective identity of being human be lost. Human history unfolds the content of the eternal *Weltall* in time. The process is inevitable, for morality is ultimately all reality, and history becomes an even better mediator between humanity and the *Weltall*. God, according to Adler, intervenes in history to reinforce the development of this mediation. Until Adler left Germany, he believed that it was fertile soil for redemption, relying on Germany for absolute value and truth. On emigrating to America, he quickly changed his ideological loyalties.

The nation of Israel, according to Adler's conception, has special intimacy with the moral ideal and provides access to it for other nations. The Hebrew prophets reveal morality from eternity to time, awakening humanity's moral consciousness and enlivening human moral potential. Hebrew Scripture preserves the work of the prophets in tangible form, while the synagogue provides a living vehicle, a perennial depository for moral awareness and a source for ever-intensified moral awakening.

With regard to the intellectual issues of the day, Adler took positions in line with his moral theology. He saw the scientific study of Judaism as a God-given method to draw moral insight from literature and history. He saw cultic activity, on the other hand, as a religious garment, secondary to moral concerns, which must be evaluated in the contemporary context according to scientific study. For Adler, a ceremony devoid of moral content becomes an "abominable corpse" before God. He regarded the Talmud as an expression of moral consciousness and, following Isaac Reggio's *Torah and Philosophy* of 1827, as a record of various branches of scientific study. But the Talmud is also a manifestation of postexilic life under oppression. Its contribution in the medieval period, for Adler, lay in preserving Jewish identity through ceremonies until Judaism could express its moral core in the larger world. Since modern society does provide for scientific ethics and study, the Talmudic vehicle should be replaced by nonregressive instruments. Adler regarded Orthodoxy as an anachronism obsessed with postexilic oppression and with preserving dead material as holy inheritance. He believed that history had reached a point where it served as an open channel between humanity and God's morality, a point in which Reform Judaism is at home.

Adler died in New York City on June 9, 1891.

Writings: *Guide to Instruction in the Israelite Religion* (New York, 2d ed., 1864); *Kovetz al Yad: Collection of Scientific Articles Dispersed in Periodicals* (New York, 1886).

References: "Autobiography," "Biography," "Religious Essay and Caricature Pertaining to S. Adler and D. Einhorn," American Jewish Archives; Gershon Greenberg,

"The Dimension of Samuel Adler's Religious View of the World," *Hebrew Union College Annual* 46 (1975): 377–412; L. Mayer, in Central Conference of American Rabbis *Yearbook* 2 (1892): 27–32.

G.G.

AMERICAN, SADIE (1862–1944). Social welfare worker, clubwoman, suffragist. Born to Oscar and Amelia Smith American in Chicago, on May 3, 1862, Sadie was educated in that city's public schools. In 1893 American was asked to organize the National Council of Jewish Women (NCJW) at the 1893 World's Parliament of Religions, an event she helped organize. She served as executive secretary of the NCJW until 1914, when she resigned in the midst of controversy. In 1901 American moved to New York City and became president of her local NCJW section. She also founded the NCJW's Ellis Island programs, its Department of Immigrant Aid and the Lakeview Home, on whose board she served even after severing ties with NCJW.

Sadie American was active in more than 100 philanthropic organizations in addition to the NCJW, including the General Federation of Women's Clubs, the International Council of Women and the Consumer's League. She earned recognition as a pioneer in combating the white slave trade and in establishing vocational schools and public playgrounds in immigrant neighborhoods. Widely acclaimed for her frequent conference papers, she acted as consultant to several governments. American also helped found Jewish women's organizations in England (1899) and Germany (1904) as well as the International Council of Jewish Women (1923).

American was a follower of Rabbis Isaac S. Moses and Emil G. Hirsch. She taught Sunday School at Chicago Sinai Congregation, supported the Sunday Sabbath and was invited to speak from the pulpit of several Reform congregations. She favored the ordination of women and was among the first to apply domestic feminist theory to the Jewish community. She argued that the home and motherhood were sacred but that domestic duties extended to society at large, requiring women to participate in social reform work outside the home. In NCJW recruiting speeches, she exhorted women to return to Judaism, claiming that because women stayed at home to raise children, only mothers could save Judaism from the perils of assimilation.

Sadie American died at the Aurora Sanitarium in Morristown, New York, on May 3, 1944.

Writings: *Journal of Sociology* (November 1898, January 1899); *Papers of the Jewish Women's Congress* (Philadelphia, 1894), pp. 218–62; "Reports of the Executive Secretary," in *National Council of Jewish Women Triennial Proceedings*, 1896–1914 (7 volumes).

References: *American Jewish Year Book* 7 (1905): 44–46; Charlotte Baum, Paula Hyman and Sonya Michel, *The Jewish Woman in America* (New York, 1976), pp. 49, 51, 165–68, 171–73, 176, 177; "Biography," American Jewish Archives; *Jewish Encyclopedia* (New York, 1972), 1:520; Anita Libman Lebeson, *Recall to Life* (New York, 1970), p. 203; Library of Congress Manuscript Division, National Council of Jewish

Women Collection, Boxes 1, 34, 103; Mary Simmerson Logan, *The Part Taken by Women in American History* (Wilmington, Del., 1912), pp. 642–46; for coverage of the controversy with the National Council of Jewish Women, selected issues of *Reform Advocate* (Chicago, 1900–1914) and *American Hebrew* (New York, 1900–1916); *New York Times*, obituary, and *New York Herald Tribune*, obituary, May 4, 1944.

F.R.

ARONSON, JACOB (1887–1951). Lawyer. Born in Brooklyn, New York, on January 2, 1887, the son of William B. and Hannah Kalins Aronson, Jacob was also educated there. After graduation from high school, he was employed as a stenographer and studied law in the evening at Brooklyn Law School, St. Lawrence University. He graduated with an LL.B. in 1906. In 1934, an honorary Doctor of Laws degree was conferred on him by the same institution. Soon after his graduation he entered the law department of the New York Central Railroad Company, serving in various positions until he was named general counsel in 1929 and vice president in 1933. He remained in that post until his retirement, one week before his death.

Serving the railroad industry, Aronson argued before the U.S. Supreme Court on several occasions. He served as chief counsel for the eastern railroads in the railway wage cases of 1921 and 1922 and as chief counsel for all the railroads in the United States in the railway wage cases of 1943 and 1944. He also led the court fight in the celebrated railway pension case of 1934.

Aronson served as chairman of the executive board of the UAHC from 1946 to 1951 and was honorary chairman at the time of his death. It was under Aronson's initiative that the headquarters of the UAHC were moved from Cincinnati to New York, where its own religious center was built. The Jacob Aronson Memorial was established in the boardroom of the newly built House of Living Judaism, UAHC's headquarters in New York City.

In 1914, he married Sadie Michaels. They had two children: Ruth Meyer and Hubert. Aronson died on January 13, 1951, in New York.

References: "Biography," American Jewish Archives; *New York Times*, obituary, January 14, 1951; *Who's Who in American Jewry* (New York, 1938), p. 39; *Who Was Who in America* (Chicago, 1960), 3:33.

B

BAAR, EMIL N. (1891–1985). Lawyer. Emil Baar was born on September 9, 1891, in Vienna, Austria, and emigrated to the United States in 1893 at the age of two, settling with his parents, Jacob and Fannie Sonnenschein Baar, in the Williamsburg section of Brooklyn. After attending public schools in Brooklyn and graduating from Boys High School, Baar worked his way through college and law school, earning an A.B. from Columbia College (1913) and an LL.B. and J.D. from Columbia University Law School (1915). Immediately beginning the practice of law, Baar was admitted to the bar the following year.

Between 1915 and 1920, Baar was associated with the firm of Johnson and Galston, before developing his practice (1921–1926). In 1926 he formed the firm in which he remained active throughout his career. Beginning as Baar, Palmer and Seales, the firm went through several evolutions, finally emerging as Baar and Bennett, in which he was an active senior partner until shortly before his death. Active in politics as well, he ran an unsuccessful campaign for Brooklyn borough president in 1940. Eleven years later, in 1951, he was named a justice of the Supreme Court of New York State. In 1955 Baar was retained by the attorney general of New York State as special assistant to defend (successfully) the constitutionality of emergency commercial and business rent-control laws.

Baar was active in a wide range of community organizations, serving as president of Union Temple of Brooklyn (1941–1949), then honorary president; as president of Jewish Hospital of Brooklyn (1948–1954), then honorary chairman of the board; and as chairman of the board, Union of American Hebrew Congregations (1959–1963), then honorary lifetime chairman (in 1964). Baar served in various capacities in the following bodies: Federation of Jewish Philanthropies of New York (trustee), Brooklyn Jewish Community Council (trustee), Brooklyn Institute of Arts and Sciences (trustee), Brooklyn Museum (governing committee), Children's Museum Governing Committee (chairman),

United Hospital Fund of New York (trustee), Brooklyn Advisory Committee (chairman), Brooklyn Society for the Prevention of Cruelty to Children (trustee), Boys Welcome Hall of Brooklyn (trustee), Men's League of Brooklyn (trustee), Board of Governors, HUC-JIR (1958–1975, elected honorary member in 1975), Jewish Braille Institute of America (director, president, 1962–1969), Corporal Sidney Rosenberg Post No. 670, American Legion, and County Commander of Kings County American Legion (1925), Fresh Meadow Country Club (president and chairman of the board), National Republican Club (NYC), Bankers Club (NYC), Unity Club (Brooklyn), Columbia University Club (NYC), National Conference of Christians and Jews (officer), World Union for Progressive Judaism (vice-president) and Leo Baeck School in Haifa (trustee).

In 1951 Baar became the founding Israel Bond chairman for the Borough of Brooklyn, a post he held for three years; he was active in Israel Bonds throughout his life. Baar was also a trustee of Brevoort (later Metropolitan) Savings Bank and on the advisory board of Manufacturers Trust Company in Brooklyn. He was a member of the Brooklyn Bar Association, the Association of the Bar of the City of New York, the New York State Bar Association (executive committee, 1952–1953), American Bar Association, Federation Lawyer's Club of Brooklyn (honorary president), National Sojourners Chapter 13, B.P.O. Elks Lodge No. 22, Anthon #769F and A.M. Lodge, New York University and Kismet Temple A.N.O.M.N.S. (32nd degree), the Brooklyn Lodge of B'nai B'rith and the Society of Old Brooklynites.

In 1951 he was given a citation by the Men's League of Brooklyn for distinguished service to Jewry; in 1952 he was cited by the American Legion, Kings County, for outstanding citizenship; in 1956 UAHC/HUC-JIR gave him their Man of the Year award; in 1958 he was cited by the Commission on Synagogue Activities, Federation of Jewish Philanthropies, for distinguished service to Jewry; in 1963 he was named Man of the Year by the National Federation of Temple Brotherhoods; in 1964 he was awarded the Downtown Brooklyn Association's Gold Medal for Most Distinguished Service for Brooklyn; in 1965, he received an honorary D.Hum.L. (Doctor of Humane Letters) from HUC-JIR; and in 1981 he was given the Maurice Eisendrath Bearer of Light Award by the UAHC.

In 1919 Baar married Amelia Augusta Wasch. After his wife's death in 1966, he married Grace George Arenson in 1974. Baar died in New York on November 11, 1985.

References: "Biography," *American Jewish Archives*; May Okon, "Brooklyn's Good Samaritan," *New York Sunday News*, May 9, 1971, pp. 8–9; *Who's Who in American Jewry* (Los Angeles, 1980), p. 19.

BACKMAN, JULES (1910–1982). Economist, educator. Jules Backman was born on May 3, 1910, in New York City, the son of Nathan and Gertrude Schell Backman. Growing up in New York, he attended high school in Brooklyn and studied at New York University, where he received a B.C.S. (1931), A.M.

(1932), M.B.A. (1933) and D.C.S. (1935). An authority on prices, labor and antitrust problems, Backman was appointed to the Securities and Exchange Commission after receiving his doctorate. Three years later he began teaching at NYU as an instructor in its School of Commerce. In the 1940s he worked in the Office of Price Administration and was an advisor to the president's Cost of Living Committee. Later, he was a member of the New York State Committee on Milk Prices. He was an advisor to the steel industry in many of its national wage cases, to the railroad industry in several rate cases and to New York City banks in several mergers. For many years he was also an editorial writer for the *New York Times*. He remained at NYU, teaching courses throughout his career. Even after his retirement as a professor of economics, he continued to teach as research professor emeritus. Backman was an honorary fellow of the American Statistical Association.

Backman received the New York University Alumni Medal for distinguished service (1943) and the School of Commerce Madden Award for distinguished achievement (1960). In 1961 he was elected Man of the Year by the alumni of the Graduate School of Business Administration, and in 1964 he received a Presidential Citation from NYU for distinguished service to the community. In 1976 Backman was given the Great Teacher Award by NYU, and in 1979 the university established the Jules Backman Faculty Fellowship in Business Economics in his honor. Backman was also a founder and first chairman of the board of trustees of the NYU Club.

Long active in Reform Jewish affairs, Backman served as national chairman of the Reform Jewish Appeal from 1965 to 1969 and was a member of the executive committee of the Union of American Hebrew Congregations. Backman was elected to the Board of Governors at Hebrew Union College–Jewish Institute of Religion in 1963 and served as its chairman from 1976 until his death.

Backman was instrumental in relocating the New York school of HUC-JIR to a site adjacent to the NYU campus. HUC-JIR awarded him the American Judaism Award in 1970 and the Founders Medal in 1979.

In 1935 Backman married Grace Straim. They had two children: John and Susan Frank. He died in New York on March 25, 1982.

Writings (selected): *Advertising and Competition* (New York, 1967); *Price Practices and Price Policies* (New York, 1953); *Regulation or Deregulation* (Indianapolis, 1980); *Social Responsibility and Accountability* (New York, 1975).

References: ''Biography'' and ''Scrapbooks, New York, New York, 1955–1967,'' American Jewish Archives; *Who's Who in American Jewry* (Los Angeles, 1980), p. 19; *Who's Who in World Jewry* (New York, 1981), p. 36.

BAMBERGER, BERNARD J. (1904–1980). Rabbi, scholar, author. Born in Baltimore, Maryland, on May 30, 1904, to William and Gussie (Erlanger) Bamberger, he received his B.A. from Johns Hopkins University in 1923, where he was elected to Phi Beta Kappa, and his rabbinical training from Hebrew Union College, where he was ordained in 1926. He continued his studies with a fellowship at Hebrew Union College while serving his first congregation, Temple Israel in Lafayette, Indiana (1926–1929). In 1929, he earned a D.D. at HUC, which, in 1950, awarded him an honorary Doctor of Hebrew Letters.

In 1929 he left Lafayette to become rabbi of Temple Beth Emeth in Albany, New York, where he served until 1944, when he accepted a call to (the West End Synagogue) Temple Shaaray Tefila in New York. He remained there for the rest of his career and, on his retirement in 1970, he was elected rabbi emeritus.

Bamberger was one of the few rabbis who successfully combined devotion to their congregational duties with the leadership of national and international organizations and, in addition, with the pursuit of scholarship on the highest level.

He served as president of the Synagogue Council of America (1950–1951), the Central Conference of American Rabbis (1959–1961) and the World Union for Progressive Judaism (1970–1972). He was a liberal of the classical type and was convinced that Reform Judaism held the key to a meaningful continuation of Jewish existence. At the same time, his great scholarship prevented him from indulging in narrow, sectarian attitudes, and his intellectual openness made him an ideal participant in a collaborative enterprise he prized highly: working on the new English translation of the *Tanakh*, sponsored by the Jewish Publication Society of America, on whose board of editors he served for many years and whose work he helped to its completion.

He was also vice president of the Jewish Book Council (1950), served on the Board of Governors of HUC-JIR, was a member of the Commission on Jewish Education and was president of the Liberal Ministers Club of New York City.

A number of important books established him as a respected scholar, beginning with his pathbreaking study *Proselytism in the Talmudic Era*. He was also a contributing editor of the *Universal Jewish Encyclopedia*. Beginning in the late 1960s, he helped plan the creation of a modern commentary on the Torah, a large-scale enterprise sponsored by the Union of American Hebrew Congregations. Bamberger wrote the commentary on Leviticus, which was published as a separate volume (1979), but he died a year before the publication of the entire pentateuchal commentary, which incorporated his interpretation of Leviticus and also contained his essay "The Torah and the Jewish People."

Bamberger married Ethel ("Pat") Kraus in 1932. They had two children: Henry and David S. He died on June 14, 1980, in New York City.

Writings (partial listing): *The Bible—A Modern Jewish Approach* (New York, 1956); *Fallen Angels* (Philadelphia, 1952); "President's Message," Central Conference of American Rabbis *Yearbook* 52 (1960): 3–10 and 71 (1961): 3–12; *Proselytism in the Talmudic Era* (Cincinnati, 1939; New York, 1968); *Reform Judaism* (Cincinnati, 1949); *The Search for Jewish Theology* (1978); *The Story of Judaism* (New York, 1957, 1964); *Studies in Jewish Law, Custom and Folklore* (New York, 1970).

References: "Biography Nearprint Box" and "Biography Nearprint File," American Jewish Archives; Central Conference of American Rabbis *Yearbook* 90 (1980): 224–25; *Encyclopaedia Judaica* 4:150–51 (with picture). For a critique of his commentary on Leviticus, see Robert Alter, "Reform Judaism and the Bible," *Commentary* 73 (February 1982): 31–35; *Who's Who in American Jewry* (Los Angeles, 1980), p. 374.

W.G.P.

BEERMAN, LEONARD (1921–   ). Rabbi, social activist. Born on April 9, 1921, in Altoona, Pennsylvania, Leonard Beerman is the son of Tillie (Grossman) and Paul Beerman. After moving to Blue Island, Illinois (1928–1929), and Owosso, Michigan (1929–1937), his family returned to Altoona the year before he graduated high school. He attended Pennsylvania State College (now University), where he received a B.A. in 1942 with Phi Beta Kappa and Phi Kappa Phi honors. Beerman dropped out of college briefly in 1941 to work in a machine gun factory as an unskilled laborer, encountering a great deal of anti-Semitism. The experience marked a turning point in his life. After graduation, he entered the U.S. Marine Corps as a private first class (1942–1943). He entered Hebrew Union College in 1943, where he received an M.H.L. and rabbinic ordination in 1949. Before ordination, he studied at Hebrew University and served in the Haganah (1947–1948). Hebrew Union College–Jewish Institute of Religion awarded him a D.D. (honorary) in 1974.

Immediately after graduation, Beerman accepted an invitation to become rabbi of the newly formed Leo Baeck Temple in Los Angeles, where he remained until his retirement in 1986.

Beerman's special field of interest is the ethical implications of religion in areas of social concern. For many years, he has been involved in the fields of civil and human rights and in the movement for world peace. The emphasis of his rabbinate is reflected in his involvement over the years as a board member, Los Angeles Community Relations Conference, Committee for Sane Nuclear Policy; Committee to Abolish Capital Punishment, Religion and Labor Council; United National Association of Los Angeles; member, Commission on Justice and Peace; member, Human Subjects Committee of Cedars-Sinai Medical Center; executive board member, Breira; executive board member, Jewish Peace Fellowship; member, National Advisory Council, Emergency Civil Liberties Committee; member, Committee of One-Hundred of Committee for National Health Insurance; and Committee of Psychiatry and Religion of the CCAR. Beerman has also been president of the Pacific Association of Reform Rabbis and vice president of the Southern California Board of Rabbis.

Beerman married Martha Fechheimer (d. 1986) on December 20, 1945. They had three daughters: Judith O'Hanlon, Eve and Elizabeth. After his wife's death, Beerman married Joan Willen in 1988.

References: "Biography Nearprint Box," American Jewish Archives; Mark Davidson, "The Rabbi: His Career Reflects an Inspiration That Has Shaped the World," *Herald-Examiner*, November 6, 1977; Freda Kerner Furman, *Beyond Yiddishkeit* (Albany, 1987).

BERGER, ELMER (1908–   ). Rabbi, organization executive. The son of Samuel and Selma (Turk) Berger, he was born in Cleveland, Ohio, on May 27, 1908. He received his B.A. at the University of Cincinnati (Phi Beta Kappa) in 1931 and was ordained at Hebrew Union College in 1932. From 1932 to 1936, he served Temple Beth Jacob of Pontiac, Michigan, and then was invited to serve Temple Beth El of nearby Flint, where he was rabbi from 1935 to 1943.

Berger was well known to Rabbi Louis Wolsey, the founder of the American Council for Judaism, and it was Wolsey who selected Berger to become the council's executive director (named executive vice president in 1956) at the moment the organization received sufficient lay support to become financially viable as the voice of anti-Zionism. Berger accepted with enthusiasm and fulfilled his responsibilities with considerable ingenuity. He developed a newsletter that was widely read, despite the growing unpopularity of its viewpoint. He engaged like-minded colleagues to produce a series of religious-school textbooks presenting the "Pittsburgh Platform approach" to Reform Judaism. At every opportunity, he secured media attention, offering counterviews to the steps that led to the birth of the State of Israel. He published two works conveying his viewpoint. After 1948, he developed a political outlook that sought empathy for the Arabs, and he created a philanthropy that enabled council members to aid human, rather than nationalist, causes. He continued to write books on the same theme.

The Six-Day War of 1967, with its astounding victories for Israel, proved Berger's undoing; he wrote a major article in the *New York Times* on July 16, 1967, in which he pointed to the council's opposition to Israel's belligerence and named a number of council leaders without securing their permission to do so. Within a year, his relationship with the council was terminated. With support from a few admirers, he proceeded to create American Jewish Alternatives to Zionism, with himself as president, but its influence has been minimal. He retired to Longboat Key, Florida.

Berger married Ruth Rosenthal on August 27, 1946.

Writings (partial listing): *The Jewish Dilemma* (New York, 1945); *Judaism or Jewish Nationalism* (New York, 1957); *Memoirs of an Anti-Zionist Jew* (Beirut, 1978); *A Partisan History of Judaism* (New York, 1951); *United States Politics and Arab Oil* (New York, 1974); *Who Knows Better Must Say So* (New York, 1956).

References: "Biography Nearprint Box" and "Biography Nearprint File," American Jewish Archives; *Who's Who in American Jewry* (Los Angeles, 1980), p. 34; *Who's Who in World Jewry* (New York, 1981), p. 67.

BERKOWITZ, HENRY (1857–1924). Rabbi, interfaith activist. Henry Berkowitz was born in Pittsburgh, Pennsylvania, on March 15, 1857, the fourth of seven children of Louis and Henrietta (Jarolawski) Berkowitz. At age 15 he enrolled at Cornell University intending to prepare for law, but the Panic of 1873 impoverished his father, and Berkowitz was forced to return home. A lecture by Isaac M. Wise at Pittsburgh's Rodef Shalom, announcing his plan to open a rabbinical college in Cincinnati, inspired Berkowitz to study with his local rabbi and cantor to prepare to enter Hebrew Union College's first class. Berkowitz graduated from H.U.C. in 1883.

Berkowitz's first pulpit was at Congregation Shaarai Shomayim in Mobile, Alabama, where he remained for nearly five years. His pastoral and social concerns became evident when he organized the Humane Movement for the

Protection of Children and Animals from Cruelty and, in 1888, wrote *Judaism on the Social Question*, a book on labor-capital relations. Mobile proved an unhealthy spot for his family: a son died of yellow fever, his wife and daughter were frequently ill and the powerful president of the congregation objected to religious innovation. Flora Berkowitz described their mutual plight in an article she signed "Auntie Apathy," published in Wise's *The Israelite*. It resulted in several job offers in 1887, including the pulpit of B'nai Jehudah of Kansas City, which Berkowitz promptly accepted. In 1893, officials of Philadelphia's Congregation Rodeph Shalom heard him speak and invited him to become the successor to the aging Marcus Jastrow. Berkowitz accepted, only to discover that Jastrow deeply resented his presence and frequently obstructed his work. Eventually, he succeeded in winning the affection of his older colleague. Under Berkowitz's ministry, Rodeph Shalom identified with the Reform movement and reorganized its religious instruction for children, creating a children's choir and a junior congregation.

Berkowitz is best remembered for founding the Jewish Chautauqua Society. Impressed by what the Methodists achieved at Lake Chautauqua with summer programs to train teachers and educate adults, Berkowitz in 1893 persuaded a mass meeting of Philadelphia's Jews to inaugurate a parallel movement. He gained additional adherents to Chicago's Columbian Exposition, where a Parliament of Religions was held later that same year. Reading circles were created around the country to engage in Judaic study. By 1894, an adult assembly had been arranged at the vacation homes of Rodeph Shalom members at Lake Placid, New York, later moving to Atlantic City, New Jersey, for a decade and then to a series of regional assemblies.

In 1910, Berkowitz was asked by the University of Tennessee at Knoxville to provide a seminar on the Bible. Julian Morgenstern, a young professor (later president) of Hebrew Union College, was sent, despite heated opposition from Christian fundamentalists. The program was so successful that Berkowitz changed the primary focus of the Jewish Chautauqua Society from education of Jews to educating Christian College students about Judaism.

Known to his colleagues and congregants as "the beloved rabbi," Berkowitz was the first secretary of the Central Conference of American Rabbis and directed its first major project: a survey of contemporary rabbis' attitudes toward the circumcision of proselytes. He also served on various CCAR committees and was the first president of the Hebrew Union College Alumni Association.

Berkowitz's interest in social reform found a fertile field in Philadelphia, where, in 1901, he united the proliferating Jewish social agencies into the Federation of Jewish Charities. Concern about the rise of prostitution among immigrant Russian Jewish girls led to his appointment to the mayor's vice commission. He also helped develop playgrounds and became an honorary vice president of the municipal Playgrounds Association.

During World War I, Berkowitz toured army camps and ministered to soldiers. Worn by exertions during the influenza epidemic of 1919, he developed a heart condition that compelled him to retire. His last years were spent in Atlantic City, where he died on February 27, 1924. He was survived by his wife and their daughter, Etta Reefer, and son, Max.

Writings: with Joseph Krauskopf, *Bible Ethics* (Cincinnati, 1895); *The Fire Eater* (Philadelphia, 1941); *How to Organize a Sabbath School* (Cincinnati, n.d.); *Intimate Glimpses of the Rabbi's Career* (Cincinnati, 1921); *Judaism on the Social Question* (New York, 1888); *Kiddush: Sabbath Sentiment in the Home* (Philadelphia, 1921); *The New Education in Religion with a Curriculum of Jewish Studies* (Philadelphia, 1913); *The Open Bible* (Philadelphia, 1896); *Symbol of Lights* (Philadelphia, 1893).

References: "Henry Berkowitz Manuscript Collection," American Jewish Archives; Max E. Berkowitz, *The Beloved Rabbi* (New York, 1932).

BERNSTEIN, PHILIP SIDNEY (1901–1985). Rabbi, political activist, Zionist. The son of immigrant parents, Abraham M. and Sarah (Steinberg) Bernstein, Bernstein was born in Rochester, New York, on June 29, 1901, into an Orthodox home. He was deeply influenced during his youth by Rabbi Paul Chertoff and, as a result, embraced Zionism. Bernstein graduated from Syracuse University (A.B., 1921) and began teaching at Temple Society of Concord in Syracuse, New York. During this time he served as personal secretary to Rabbi Benjamin Friedman, who introduced him to Reform Judaism. He completed his rabbinic studies at the Jewish Institute of Religion and was ordained in 1926, when he also received an M.H.L. He did graduate study at Columbia University, Cambridge University and the Hebrew University. A graduate of the Jewish Institute of Religion's first class, Bernstein began his rabbinic career at Temple B'rith Kodesh, Rochester, New York, as assistant to Rabbi Horace Wolf. On Wolf's death, some six months later, Bernstein became the spiritual leader of the congregation he was to serve for over half a century.

Bernstein was a committed pacifist until Hitler's invasion of Poland in 1939, when he became convinced there were evils worse than war. Thus, in 1942 Bernstein accepted the position of executive director of the Committee on the Army and Navy Religious Activities of the National Jewish Welfare Board, responsible for the supervision of the 300 American rabbis serving as chaplains in the U.S. Armed Forces, a post he held until 1946. During this time he published a series of articles in the *Nation* under the title "The Jews of Europe," in which he expressed his intense Zionist commitment. As director of the Jewish Chaplaincy program in World War II, Bernstein was deeply involved in national and international Jewish life. He became a member of the Zionist Emergency Council and helped form the American Christian Palestine Committee, dedicated to organizing groups of sympathetic Christians for the purpose of channeling non-Jewish opinion toward Zionist objectives.

In February 1946, Bernstein returned to his congregation in Rochester. That same year, he received an invitation to serve as the second advisor on Jewish affairs to the U.S. Army. He accepted and served from May 1946 to August 1947, specifically responsible for aiding in the tragic and complicated problems presented by the surviving Jews of Europe in Displaced Persons Camps. After completing his service as Jewish advisor, Bernstein returned to his Rochester congregation once again but remained active in national Jewish affairs. His series of articles on Judaism, printed in *Life* magazine, was expanded into a book, *What the Jews Believe*, published in 1950. Also in 1950, Bernstein was elected president of the Central Conference of American Rabbis, which he led for two years, the first graduate of JIR to do so. From 1954 to 1968 he was president of the American Israel Public Affairs Committee and advised congressional representatives, senators and presidents on the Middle East. He was a vice president of the American Jewish Congress and a member of the Western Hemisphere Executive of the World Jewish Congress. He published *Rabbis at War*, an account of his years as director of the spiritual program for the 600,000 Jews in the U.S. Armed Forces stationed all over the world. In 1966, Bernstein received the coveted Herbert Lehman Israel Award in recognition of his four decades of leadership in the American Jewish community. When he retired, Bernstein's many friends and admirers in both the Jewish and non-Jewish communities of Rochester established the Philip S. Bernstein Chair of Jewish Studies at the University of Rochester.

In 1925, he married Sophie Rubin. They had three children: Jeremy, Stephen and Alice. Bernstein died in Rochester on December 3, 1985.

Writings: "The New Israel and American Jewry," Central Conference of American Rabbis *Yearbook* 58 (1948): 285–86; *Rabbis at War* (Walther, MA, 1971); *To Dwell in Unity* (Philadelphia, 1983); *What the Jews Believe* (New York, 1950).

References: Yehuda Bauer, *Flight and Rescue: Brichah the Organized Escape of the Jewish Survivors of Eastern Europe* (New York, 1970); "Interview" and "Biography Nearprint Box," American Jewish Archives; Thomas P. Liebschutz, "Rabbi Philip S. Bernstein and the Jewish Displaced Person" (Rabbinic thesis, Hebrew Union College–Jewish Institute of Religion, 1965); Leo Schwarz, *The Redeemers* (New York, 1953).

T.P.L.

BETTAN, ISRAEL (1889–1957). Rabbi, professor. The son of Moses Isaac and Anna Itta (Fishman) Bettan, he was born in Kovno, Lithuania, on January 16, 1889. After an early education in the *hadarim* (Jewish grade schools) and *yeshivot* of Kovno, he came to the United States in 1907 where he enrolled in the Rabbi Isaac Elchanan Yeshiva. Shortly thereafter he transferred to the Hebrew Union College in Cincinnati, enrolling simultaneously at the University of Cincinnati. He received his B.A. degree from U.C. in 1910, his rabbinic ordination in 1912, and the D.D. degree in 1915 from Hebrew Union College.

Bettan served Congregation B'nai Israel of Charleston, West Virginia, for the first decade of his rabbinate. He took a leave of absence during World War I to become a chaplain in the American Expeditionary Force in France (1918–1919). He then returned to Charleston, where he served until the fall of 1922. Active in civic and philanthropic affairs in Charleston, he also honed his considerable preaching skills and deepened his scholarship.

In 1922, Dr. Julian Morgenstern, president of HUC, invited Bettan to return to his alma mater to assume the chairmanship of the Department of Homiletics. For 35 years Bettan taught homiletics, including the rubrics of the textual and nontextual sermon, wedding addresses, eulogies, benedictions and talks for life-cycle occasions. He also supervised the program of required student preaching in the college chapel. The students knew him as a demanding but fair critic.

As a logical extension of his teaching in homiletics, Bettan was assigned to also teach Midrash. He offered many diverse courses in this area and compiled several literary anthologies for classroom use. Bettan's love of the rabbinic commentary on the biblical text ultimately led, in 1950, to his book *The Five Scrolls, a Commentary*.

Bettan did not view the disciplines he taught, whether Midrash or homiletics, as ends in themselves. For Bettan, the Bible and its exegesis were the font of the Jewish soul; homiletics, which educates, edifies and inspires, was the vessel whereby the Jewish soul might be informed. Central to his concept of the rabbinate was a pulpit that had the power and the influence to move Jews toward greater spiritual commitment and knowledge. He labored in the classroom to impart this view to a generation of Reform rabbis and sought to provide them with the tools with which they might stir the hearts of their congregants.

Bettan played an active and influential role in the Central Conference of American Rabbis. He had strong feelings about the nature of prayer and the purpose of liturgy, and he applied his great creative talents and writing skills as a member of committees that twice revised the *Union Prayer Book*. His interest in responsa, already reflected in the topic of his doctoral dissertation, "Early Reform in Contemporaneous Responsa," ultimately brought him to the chairmanship of the CCAR Committee on Responsa. He represented the CCAR on the Joint Committee (with the Union of American Hebrew Congregations) on Ceremonies. His rabbinic colleagues recognized his contribution to the Reform Movement, his vision and his leadership by electing him vice president of the conference in 1954 and president in 1956. In 1957 he retired from his faculty position at HUC and was reelected to the CCAR presidency.

Bettan married Ida Goldstein on April 7, 1927. They had one daughter: Anita Ester. He died on August 5, 1957, in Cincinnati, Ohio.

Writings (partial listing): *The Five Scrolls, a Commentary* (Cincinnati, 1950); *Studies in Jewish Preaching: Middle Ages* (Cincinnati, 1939). A complete bibliography of articles, reviews and published sermons was compiled by Theodore Wiener for the *Israel Bettan Memorial Volume* (New York, 1961), pp. 52–62. This book also contains articles on Bettan by Samuel S. Cohon, Solomon B. Freehof and Albert S. Goldstein.

References: "Biography Nearprint File," American Jewish Archives; *Encyclopaedia Judaica* (Jerusalem, 1973), 14:775; Samuel Karff, Hebrew Union College-Jewish Institute of Religion, *At One Hundred Years* (Cincinnati, 1976), pp. 91–92, 93, 328, 332; Michael A. Meyer, *Response to Modernity* (New York, 1988), p. 302.

E.A.G.

BETTMANN, BERNHARD (1834–1915). Businessman, public official, communal leader. Born in Weidnitz, Bavaria, Germany, on August 2, 1834, the son of Jacob and Jeannette Kann Bettmann, he was educated there before coming to Cincinnati in 1850. As soon as he arrived, he became active in community life, appointed to serve the Zion Collegiate Association by Isaac M. Wise in 1855. Later, in 1875, he was the first chairman of the Board of Governors of Hebrew Union College, holding that position until 1910, when he was named honorary president. (Actually, Henry Mack was the first chairman, but he resigned before HUC opened.) Not one to give up after the failure of Zion College, he was one of the leaders in the movement toward, and the establishment of, the Union of American Hebrew Congregations; he joined its executive board on its founding in 1873. Later, when Moses Mielziner retired as president of HUC, Bettmann was asked to succeed him, but he dismissed the offer, contending that the president should be a scholar, not a layperson. Bettmann was also treasurer of Congregation Bene Jeshurun (1884–1910), where Isaac Mayer Wise served as rabbi. A pioneer in the development of community-wide social services, Bettmann was the first president of the United Jewish Charities of Cincinnati (1896–1903). Bettmann was also a member of the board of the Talmud Yelodim Institute, a parochial school affiliated with Congregation Bene Jeshurun, for 22 years. In 1899, as part of the German Day Association, Bettmann served as president of the Golden Jubilee Saengerfest.

Active in politics within the ranks of the Republican Party, Bettmann often presided over city and county conventions. From 1884 to 1898 he served as an elected member of the School Board for the Seventeenth Ward in Cincinnati. And in 1897, President William McKinley named him Collector of Internal Revenue for the First District of Ohio, a position he left in 1905 in order to travel abroad. Two years later, after his return to the United States, President Theodore Roosevelt reappointed him. This appointment was reconfirmed under the administration of William Howard Taft. And so Bettmann served until 1913, when he resigned to go abroad once again.

A clothier by trade, Bettmann was a director of the First National Bank and was a delegate of the United States to the International Convention of the Chambers of Conference held in Belgium in 1906.

Like many of his contemporaries, Bettmann was a non-Zionist who contended that Israel's mission was to preach the word of God and the brotherhood of man. He argued that there was no need for a return to Palestine, but he did concede that it might be a haven for the oppressed and persecuted Russian Jews.

A man of many interests, Bettmann wrote *German Ritual for Masonic Lodges*; he was a member as Master Mason. And many of his poems appeared in various periodicals, including *Die Gartenlaube* (Leipzig). He also prepared a new version of the "Memorial Service" for his own congregation, Bene Jeshurun, based on Isaac M. Wise's original German.

On October 6, 1859, he married Matilda Ward. He died in Cincinnati on June 18, 1915.

Writings: *Some Addresses and Poems of Bernhard Bettmann* (Cincinnati, 1904).

References: *Hebrew Union College Monthly* 2 (November 1915): 76–88; *Jewish Tribune*, July 2, 1915; *Universal Jewish Encyclopedia* (New York, 1943), 2:272–73.

BINDER, ABRAHAM WOLFE (1895–1966). Composer, conductor, educator, musicologist. A. W. Binder, as he was known in his adult years, was born on May 5, 1895, in New York City to Cantor Sholem Binder and Leah (Wittes) Binder. As a child, he sang in synagogue choirs, especially in the choir of Cantor Abraham Frachtenberg, composing pieces for his father's choir by age seven. His musical education was first acquired at the Settlement Music School and later the Neighborhood Musical School (now the Manhattan School of Music). For his general education, he graduated from Townsend Harris High School. By age 14, he was already leading a choir, and Shirmer and Co., music publishers, had issued a number of his compositions. In 1911, he was organist and choir director at Temple Beth El in Brooklyn. In 1913, he had a musical position at Temple Adath Israel in the Bronx. In 1916, he formed the Hadassah Choral Union and subsequently was choir director of the Kamenetzer Shul in New York. In 1918, he supplemented his busy schedule by being the music director at Mordecai Kaplan's newly formed Jewish Center Congregation and soon after at Temple Emanu-El (New York City) Religious School as well. Binder attended Columbia University (1917–1920), where he was awarded the Mosenthal Fellowship in musical composition. In 1964, Hebrew Union College–Jewish Institute of Religion awarded him a D.H.L. (honorary).

After graduation, he was named musical director of the Stephen S. Wise Free Synagogue in New York from 1924, as well as the 92nd St. YM/YWHA in the same city (1918–1965). Binder also served as professor of liturgical music at the Jewish Institute of Religion (later, HUC-JIR) since its founding in 1923 and was one of the founders of the HUC-JIR School of Sacred Music (1948) and the Jewish Music Forum (1939), serving as chairman from 1939 to 1943.

As a composer, Binder created works for orchestra, chamber orchestra, chorus, chamber music, operetta, dramatic musical narrative, solo voice, violin, cello and piano. He also composed eight sacred services for the Sabbath and holidays. As one of the few early choirmasters in a Reform synagogue in America, Binder's work attempted to revitalize synagogue music by bringing it closer to its sources. He was music editor of the third edition of the *Union Hymnal* (1920) issued by the Central Conference of American Rabbis. During World War II, Binder served as one of the music editors for *Army and Navy Hymnal*. His score for "City of the Ages" was produced to celebrate the 300th anniversary of the founding of Jerusalem. And in 1954, he was commissioned by the American Tercentary Committee to compose "The Heart of America," a choral poem. He also actively introduced Palestinian (later Israeli) music to America.

Throughout his career he lectured at universities across North America, including Yale, Barnard, Cornell, Illinois, Ohio State, Michigan and Maryland. He was also visiting professor at Hebrew University in 1951, where he conducted the Kol Israel Orchestra, and was visiting lecturer at the Union Theological Seminary School of Sacred Music from 1954 until his death. Binder was a member of the board of the American Guild of Organists and vice president of the National Jewish Music Council. In 1956, the same Jewish Music Council awarded him a citation of merit for his work.

Binder was associated with numerous other organizations, including the American Society of Composers and Conductors, Hymn Society of America, American Academy for Jewish Research, American Musicology Society and Bohemian.

In 1921, he married Anne Friedman (d. 1936). They had two daughters: Leah (Silverman) and Hadassah (Markson). In 1938, he married Priscilla Dreyer (d. 1953). In 1953 Binder married Helen F. Danton (div. 1961). He died in New York on October 10, 1966.

Writings, Compositions and Recordings (partial listing): *Amos on Times Square* (New York, 1943); *Biblical Chant* (New York, 1959); *Hibbath Shabbath* (New York, 1928); *Jewish Year in Song* (New York, n.d.); *New Songs of Palestine* (New York, 1926); *Prayers and Songs for the Sabbath* (New York, 1948).

References: L. Appleton, ed., *The Music of A. W. Binder* (mimeographed) (New York, 1964); *Canadian Jewish Chronicle*, April 7, 1950; Herbert Fromm, *A. W. Binder: Jewish Liturgical Composer* (New York, 1972); I. Heskes, *A. W. Binder: His Life and Work* (New York, 1965); Irene Heskes, *Studies in Jewish Music* (New York, 1971); "Nearprint Biography Box," American Jewish Archives; *New York Times*, obituary, October 11, 1966; *Universal Jewish Encyclopedia* (New York, 1940), 2:354–55; *Who's Who in American Jewry* (New York, 1939), p. 96.

BLANK, SHELDON HAAS (1896–1989). Rabbi, academic. Born in Mt. Carmel, Illinois, on September 17, 1896, Blank was the son of Solomon H. and Byrde Haas Blank. In 1914, Blank left to attend the University of Cincinnati and Hebrew Union College. His studies were interrupted in 1918, when he served in the Infantry Officers Training Corps, and he was commissioned a second lieutenant just as Armistice was reached in November 1918. Blank received a B.A. from the University of Cincinnati in 1918 and an M.A. in 1920 and was ordained at HUC in 1923.

In mid-1923, Blank joined a group of fellow newly ordained HUC alumni—Nelson Glueck, Walter Rothman and Jacob Marcus—and the four enrolled that fall in the University of Berlin. While Marcus adapted well to Berlin, Blank and the two others transferred to Jena in Thurigen in the spring of 1924. His program focused on the German philosophy of Idealism—Kant, Hegel and their descendants. Blank wrote a dissertation on "Das Wort *Torah*" and earned his Ph.D. in 1925.

After finishing at Jena, Blank went to London, England, to assist with High Holy Day services at a local temple. There he met Amy Kirchberger, his future wife. While in England, Blank received an invitation to join the faculty of HUC and a suggestion that he spend time in British Palestine to improve his Hebrew. Blank briefly studied at the American School of Oriental Research in Jerusalem and visited numerous archaeological sites with other Biblical scholars. Returning to London in the summer of 1926, Blank participated in a July meeting of world Jewish leaders, which resulted in the founding of the World Union for Progressive Judaism.

Later that year, Blank joined the HUC faculty as an instructor of Bible. His method involved more than exercises in text and translation; he maintained that the discipline can and should promote a social consciousness. Blank found inspiration for this conviction in his own mentor and instructor in Bible at HUC, Moses Buttenwieser, and in the interpretation of the prophets that Buttenwieser put forth in his *The Prophets of Israel from the Eighth to the Fifth Century* (1914). Blank inherited his teacher's courses and their focus on the prophetic literature and eventually became a full professor of Bible at the college-institute. In 1977 he was named Nelson Glueck Professor of Bible Emeritus. Blank was editor of the *Hebrew Union College Annual* for more than six decades.

Blank served as president of the Middle West branch of the American Oriental Society and of the Mid-West Section of the Society of Biblical Literature and Exegesis. He was national president of the Society of Biblical Literature in 1952. Blank also served a number of years as chairman of the faculty at HUC.

Blank married Amy Kirchberger on July 21, 1926. They had two daughters: Elizabeth and Miriam. Blank died on February 14, 1989, in Cincinnati.

Writings: *Jeremiah: Man and Prophet* (Cincinnati, 1961); "Men against God: The Promethian Element in Biblical Prayer," *Journal of Biblical Literature* 72 (March 1953): 1–14; *Prophetic Faith in Isaiah* (New York, 1958); *Understanding the Prophets* (New York, 1969). See "Bibliography of the Writings of Sheldon H. Blank," covering the years 1920–1976, in *Prophetic Thought, Essays and Addresses* (Cincinnati, 1977), pp. 159–67.

References: "Biography Nearprint File," American Jewish Archives; Central Conference of American Rabbis *Yearbook* 96 (1986): 7; Festschrift in *Hebrew Annual Review* 8:2–3; *Who's Who in World Jewry* (New York, 1981), p. 87.

BLOCH, HERBERT R. (1889–1957). Investment broker, community activist, chairman of the board of HUC-JIR. Born on February 3, 1889, in Cincinnati, Ohio, to Abraham and Rebecca (Friedenwald) Bloch, Herbert Bloch attended lower school in Cincinnati, entering the University of Michigan at the age of 15. Bloch was a senior partner with the securities firm of Benjamin D. Bartlett and Co., a member of the New York and Cincinnati stock exchanges, and director of many business corporations. Bloch's public career was marked by his active leadership of institutions devoted to the perpetuation of modern Judaism.

He was a founder, in 1946, of the Federation of Jewish Agencies and was also its president. He was president of the Isaac M. Wise Temple and served as a member of its board of trustees for many years. He played a major part in the establishment of the Child Guidance Home and In-Patient Clinic for the Treatment of Mentally and Emotionally Disturbed Children, a joint activity of the Jewish Hospital Association, the Community Chest and the Department of Psychiatry of the College of Medicine of the University of Cincinnati. He was active in the American Red Cross, the United Jewish Social Agencies, the Jewish Welfare Fund of Cincinnati and many other organizations. He was a member of the board of trustees of the University of Cincinnati and served as president of the board from 1935 to 1943.

He was a national chairman of the Combined Campaign of the Hebrew Union College–Jewish Institute of Religion and the Union of American Hebrew Congregations. Bloch was elected chairman of the board of HUC-JIR in 1952, a post he held at the time of his death on March 17, 1957.

On June 1, 1914, Bloch married Jean Kaufman. They had three children: Herbert Jr., John and Sue B. Strauss.

References: ''Biography Nearprint File,'' American Jewish Archives.

BOROWITZ, EUGENE G. (1924–   ). Rabbi, theologian. The son of Benjamin and Molly (Schafronik) Borowitz, Borowitz was born in New York City on February 20, 1924. Both his parents had arrived in the United States about 15 years earlier, his father from what is now Poland, his mother from Hungary. Borowitz received a B.A. from Ohio State University in 1943, a B.H.L. from Hebrew Union College in 1945, an M.H.L. and ordination in 1948. From 1948 to 1950, he served as assistant rabbi of Shaare Emeth Congregation in St. Louis, Missouri. Deciding to return to the academy, Borowitz left St. Louis and in 1952 received a D.H.L. from the newly consolidated Hebrew Union College–Jewish Institute of Religion.

From 1951 to 1953, the years of the Korean War, he served as a chaplain in the U.S. Navy. Back in civilian life, Borowitz took a pulpit in the community in which he resides to this day, serving as rabbi at Community Synagogue in Port Washington, New York, from 1953 to 1957. Deeply involved in Jewish education, Borowitz was named national director of education of the Union of American Hebrew Congregations in 1957, serving for five years. In 1958 he received an Ed.D. from Teachers College, Columbia University. In 1962, Borowitz joined the faculty of Hebrew Union College–Jewish Institute of Religion, New York campus, as professor of education and Jewish religious thought, a post he still holds.

Borowitz is widely regarded as the leading theologian of liberal Judaism in the United States. In his ''postmodern, systematic theology of Judaism'' (*Judaism as Covenant*, 1991), Borowitz describes Judaism by analogy to personal relationships rather than in terms of law, peoplehood or universal ethics. He identifies the root Jewish religious experiences of our time as the absoluteness of value and Jewish particularity, with God as their ground. He then creates a theory of non-Orthodox Jewish duty based on the Jewish self's intimate involvement with God, with the Jewish people today, its tradition and its messianic hope, and thus with a self fully individual, yet primarily shaped by its Jewish relationships, Covenant.

A prolific author and editor, Borowitz's 1974 work, *The Mask Jews Wear*, received the National Jewish Book Award in the field of Jewish thought. He is perhaps most widely known as the editor of *Sh'ma: A Journal of Jewish Responsibility*, a magazine of social ethics he founded in 1970. Concurrently with his teaching at the college-institute, Borowitz has served as visiting professor at a number of institutions, including Columbia University, Princeton University, Temple University, Woodstock College (the Jesuit graduate school of theology) and Jewish Theological Seminary. In 1982–83, Harvard University Divinity School invited him to inaugurate its newly established Albert A. List Professorship of Jewish Studies.

Borowitz was the first Jew to serve as president of the American Theological Society. He also served as chair of the Central Conference of American Rabbis committee that drafted the statement of principle "Reform Judaism: A Centenary Perspective," in 1976, and as chair of the HUC-JIR faculty from 1976 to 1980. Borowitz has also been a vice president of the Religious Association of America and a trustee of the Fund for Jewish Education, New York.

Borowitz married Estelle Covel on September 7, 1947. They have three daughters: Lisa, Drucy and Nan (Langowitz). Borowitz serves on the HUC-JIR faculty as Sigmund L. Falk Distinguished Service Professor of Education and Jewish Religious Thought.

Writings (partial listing, not including numerous articles, earlier works or edited publications, especially *Sh'ma*, 1970–present): *Choices in Modern Jewish Thought* (New York, 1983); with Naomi Patz, *Explaining Reform Judaism* (New York, 1985); *Exploring Jewish Ethics* (Detroit, 1989); *Liberal Judaism* (New York, 1984); *The Mask Jews Wear* (New York, 1974).

References: *American Jewish Biographies* (New York, 1982), pp. 44–45; *Who's Who in American Jewry* (Los Angeles, 1980), p. 59; *Who's Who in World Jewry* (New York, 1981), p. 100.

BRAUDE, WILLIAM GORDON (1907–1988). Rabbi, scholar. Braude was born Gershon Z'ev Braude in 1907, the son of Yitzhak Aisik and Chiene Rachel (Halperin) Braude, in the town of Telz in the Russian province of Kovno, Lithuania. His father was a rabbi, as were his maternal grandfather and two uncles, who were scholars of the Telz Yeshiva.

In 1920 the family left Europe for New York, where Braude was enrolled in the Rabbi Isaac Elchanan Yeshiva. Shortly thereafter, the family moved to Denver, Colorado, and at the age of 13, Braude entered public school for the first time. In 1922 his father moved the family to Dayton, Ohio, where William Braude developed an interest in the Reform rabbinate. He entered the University of Cincinnati in 1925, receiving a junior Phi Beta Kappa key and a B.A., summa cum laude, in 1929. Concurrently enrolled at Hebrew Union College, he was ordained in 1931.

Braude's first full-time rabbinic position was at Temple Beth-El in Rockford, Illinois. He combined his congregational duties with scholarship, a pattern maintained throughout his rabbinate. In 1932, he became rabbi of Congregation Sons of Israel and David, Temple Beth-El, in Providence, Rhode Island, and continued in this position until his retirement in 1974, when he became rabbi emeritus.

While serving Temple Beth-El, Braude enrolled at Brown University and studied for both the M.A. (1934) and the Ph.D. (1937). Later, in 1955, he received an honorary D.D. from Hebrew Union College–Jewish Institute of Religion and an honorary D.H.L. in 1959.

In 1937–38, Braude was appointed assistant lecturer in Hebrew at Brown University and two years later was promoted to lecturer in Biblical literature. He served in this capacity until the summer of 1942.

Besides teaching at Brown and Providence College, he also taught courses at Yale, the Hebrew University in Jerusalem and Leo Baeck College in London. In 1980 he retired from university teaching.

As a congregational rabbi, William Braude was known as a forceful and articulate advocate for Reform Judaism, reclaiming traditional Jewish practices and observances such as kashruth and yarmulkes, as well as promoting the importance of Jewish study. He was an early proponent of day schools, and the Temple Beth-El library, which bears his name, contains more than 25,000 volumes. In 1965, he participated in the civil rights demonstration led by the Reverend Dr. Martin Luther King in Montgomery, Alabama.

Braude was president of the World Affairs Council of Rhode Island and vice president of the Urban League. He was on the board of governors of HUC-JIR and on the executive board of the Central Conference of American Rabbis. He was a member of the Jewish Family Welfare Society, Phi Beta Kappa, the Providence Anthenaeum, American Academy for Jewish Research and the Commission on Jewish Education of the Union of American Hebrew Congregations.

On June 19, 1938, he married one of his students, Pearl Finkelstein. They were the parents of Joel Isaac, Benjamin Meir and Daniel. William G. Braude died on February 25, 1988.

Writings (partial listing); *Jewish Proselytising in the First Five Centuries of the Common Era, the Age of the Tannaim and Amoraim* (Providence, 1940); *Midrash on Psalms* (New Haven, 1959); trans., *Pesikta de Rav Kahana* (Philadelphia, 1975); *Pesikta Rabbati* (Cambridge, MA, 1968); trans., *Tanna debe Eliyyahu* (Philadelphia, 1980).

References: "Biography Nearprint File," American Jewish Archives; *Encyclopaedia Judaica* (Jerusalem, 1973), 4:1315; *Who's Who in American Jewry* (Los Angeles, 1980), p. 61; *Who's Who in World Jewry* (New York, 1981), pp. 103–4.

L.Y.G.

BRICKNER, BALFOUR (1926–   ). Rabbi, social activist, author. The son of Rabbi Barnett R. and Rebecca Aaronson Brickner, Brickner was born in Cleveland, Ohio, on November 18, 1926. Initially educated in Cleveland schools, Brickner served in the U.S. Navy from 1943 to 1946. After discharge, he received his B.A. in philosophy from the University of Cincinnati in 1948 and his M.H.L. and ordination from Hebrew Union College–Jewish Institute of Religion in 1952.

After ordination, Brickner accepted a pulpit at Temple Sinai in Washington,

D.C. In that same year, 1952, he toured Israel, Western Europe and North Africa, lecturing on behalf of the United Jewish Appeal. Between 1957 and 1961, Brickner was the Jewish Chautauqua Society's resident lecturer at American University.

A leader among Reform rabbis in political activism, Brickner has maintained that right-wing secular and political trends are historically threatening to Jews. His social activism led him to become codirector, in 1961, of the National Commission on Social Action of the Union of American Hebrew Congregations, a post he held until 1978. He also coupled his political work with interreligious efforts; for example, he led a mission of rabbis to West Germany in 1966 to teach Judaism to hundreds of young, non-Jewish students and teachers-in-training. In 1961, Brickner became director of the UAHC Department of Interreligious Affairs.

Between 1961 and 1964, Brickner was actively involved in the civil rights movement, traveling extensively through the South under a Merrill Foundation grant, where his attempt to provide Jewish support for civil rights often landed him in local jails. Brickner also took the lead in religious opposition to the Vietnam War. He was a founder and active member of the Clergy and Laity Concerned about Vietnam (CALC) between 1966 and 1973 and served on its executive committee. In 1970, he visited Saigon on a fact-finding mission at the request of the Fellowship of Reconciliation. Later, Brickner agitated for women's rights as an executive board member of the National Association for the Repeal of Abortion Laws (NARAL) and as a founder of Religious Leaders for Free Choice.

During this period, Brickner hosted a popular weekly radio program, "Adventures in Judaism," which won the State of Ohio Award for outstanding religious broadcasts in 1965, 1966, 1967 and again in 1968, when it also won the Religious Heritage Foundation award. Brickner initiated, and codirected, a summer seminar program in Israel for Christian scholars. He has written on cross-faith understanding, as in *An Interreligious Guide to Passover and Easter* (1968) and a study guide to *Jesus Christ Superstar* (1978). Brickner was also a founder of UPACA (Upper Park Avenue Community Association) in New York, an interracial, interreligious nonprofit housing corporation, rehabilitating and constructing housing in a six-block-square area of East Harlem.

In 1980, Brickner returned to the congregational rabbinate, accepting a post at the Stephen Wise Free Synagogue in New York City. From the pulpit, he continued his work in the larger arenas of American Jewish life. During the 1980s, he chaired or cochaired a variety of organizations, including the National Religious Cabinet, State of Israel Bonds; the Mass Media Committee; Religion in American Life; the Interreligious Coalition for Health Care; and the Martin Steinberg Center of the American Jewish Congress. He also serves on the steering committee of the International Jewish Committee for Interreligious Consultations, a group that meets periodically with representatives of the World Council of Churches and the Vatican for the purpose of joint consultation and action.

Brickner married Barbara Michaels on January 20, 1954. They had three children: Adam, Barnett and Alisa (deceased). After a divorce, he married Doris Gottlieb on February 20, 1975.

Writings (partial listing, does not include numerous other articles and pamphlets): *As Driven Sands: The Arab Refugees*, UAHC pamphlet (New York, 1960); "No Ease in Zion for Us: Christian-Jewish Relations after the Arab-Israeli War," *Christianity and Crisis* 27, no. 15 (September 18, 1967): 200–204; with Albert Vorspan, *Searching the Prophets for Values* (New York, 1981); "The Synagogue: Reality or Relic?" *Jewish Spectator* 36, no. 8 (October 1971): 7–11.

References: *American Jewish Biographies* (New York, 1982), pp. 47–48; "Nearprint Biography File," American Jewish Archives; *Who's Who in American Jewry* (Los Angeles, 1980), p. 64; *Who's Who in World Jewry* (New York, 1981), p. 109.

BRICKNER, BARNETT ROBERT (1892–1958). Rabbi, Zionist leader. Brickner was born on September 14, 1892, in New York City, the son of Joseph and Bessie (Furman) Brickner. Schooled in New York City, Brickner attended Columbia University (B.S., 1913; M.A., 1914), where he did postgraduate work as well. Concurrently, he attended the Teachers Institute of the Jewish Theological Seminary of America (1910–1915) before entering Hebrew Union College in Cincinnati. He was ordained at HUC in 1919 and received a Ph.D. in social sciences from the University of Cincinnati the following year. Later (in 1945), he received a D.D. (hon.) from HUC. An outspoken Zionist even in his youth, Brickner was one of the founders of the Young Judea movement (1910). He also served as director of extension education at the Bureau of Jewish Education in New York (1910–1915) and then as executive director of United Jewish Social Agencies in Cincinnati (1918–1920).

After earning his doctorate, Brickner became rabbi of Holy Blossom Temple in Toronto, where he introduced the practice and ideology of Reform Judaism (1920–1925). In 1925, he was elected rabbi of Cleveland's Euclid Avenue Temple (later called Fairmont Temple), where he remained until his death. There he had introduced Sunday services, which were later discontinued.

One of the foremost orators in the Zionist movement in the United States, Brickner was a pivotal figure in the United Palestine Appeal. He argued forcefully for the primary position of Israel in the life of American Jews. Suggesting that Reform rabbis be partially trained in Israel long before it was fashionable to do so, he also believed that the only way the liberal religious position in Israel could be fostered was through the creation of a political movement by American Reform Jews. A leading advocate in the fields of Jewish education, refugee relief and social service, Brickner was responsible for the Training School for Jewish Welfare Workers in military camps in the United States and abroad during World War I. He was cofounder (921) and contributing editor (1921–1925) of the *Canadian Jewish Review*. While organizing the Jewish Farm School in Canada, he was among a small group of people to persuade the Canadian government to allow 5,000 Russian Jewish refugees, stranded in Rumania, to settle in Canada in 1923. Later, a scholarship in social service was established in his honor at the University of Toronto. Brickner was an arbitrator for the dry-cleaning industry in Cleveland (1928–1929), the leader of a movement to oppose ousting the Cleveland city manager in 1930, an arbitrator between Cleveland Railway Co. and Street Car Men's Union (1934, 1935), and an arbitrator for Employed Bakers of Cleveland (1935–1936).

As the administrative chairman for army and navy religious activities of the National Jewish Welfare Board and later the chairman of the chaplains committee of the Central Conference of American Rabbis in World War II, Brickner was designated by President Roosevelt to tour all the theaters of war in connection with religious missions to chaplains and troops in the U.S. Army and Navy. He received a naval citation for meritorious personal service, as well as a Medal of Merit (1947), the highest award the government confers on a civilian and the first time it had ever been awarded to a rabbi.

Brickner was also active in numerous organizations: Jewish Welfare Fund Committee in Cleveland (chairman); CCAR (chairman of the Social Justice Committee; CCAR president, 1955–1956); National Conference of Jewish Social Work; Religious Education Association of America; American Academy of Political and Social Science; Foreign Policy Association of Jewish Academicians; Zionist Organization of America (executive committee); Actions Committee of the World Zionist Organization; National Council for Jewish Education (executive board); UAHC (board member); Jewish Welfare Federation of Cleveland (vice chairman); and Bureau of Jewish Education in Cleveland (vice president).

On August 10, 1919, Brickner married Rebecca Ena Aaronson. They had two children: Joy Marion (Rabinowitz) and Arthur James Balfour Brickner (known as Balfour). Brickner died on May 14, 1958, of causes indirectly related to an auto accident, in Spain, on return from a tour to Israel under the auspices of the UAHC.

Writings: *The God Idea in Light of Modern Thought* (New York, 1930); *History of the Jews in Canada* (Toronto, 1925).

References: "Nearprint Biographies Box and File," American Jewish Archives; *New York Herald Tribune*, obituary, May 15, 1958; Samuel Silver, *Portrait of a Rabbi: An Affectionate Memoir on the Life of Barnett R. Brickner* (Cleveland, 1959); *Who's Who in American Jewry* (New York, 1939), p. 137; *Who Was Who in America* (Chicago, 1960), 3: 102.

C

COHEN, ALFRED MORTON (1859–1949). Politician, lawyer, lay leader. The son of Morton S. and Phebe Phillips Cohen, Alfred Cohen was born in Cincinnati, Ohio, on October 19, 1859. Although his parents were Orthodox, as a young man Cohen was drawn to the Reform movement. He attended public school in Cincinnati as well as a school Isaac M. Wise established as a precursor to Hebrew Union College. From the pool of available students, Wise chose five, including 12-year-old Cohen, for HUC's first class. However, Cohen's interest turned to law, and he subsequently enrolled in the University of Cincinnati Law School. He received an LL.B. in 1880 in the same class as the future president and chief justice William H. Taft, a lifelong friend and political foe of Cohen's.

Early in his career Cohen immersed himself in Cincinnati and Ohio politics. He served several terms in Cincinnati's city council, the first when he was only 24 years old. At age 27 he was nominated to the corporation council of Cincinnati. At various times Cohen served in the Ohio Senate (two terms), as presidential elector (three times), and as president of the Ohio Electoral College (two times). He also was nominated for the governorship and in 1900 ran for mayor of Cincinnati as a Democratic candidate.

Early in life Cohen became involved in Jewish organizations. At age 17 he helped organize the Cincinnati YMHA. Later he served as president of both the local and the national YMHA.

Politically and civically, Cohen was a committed advocate for equal rights for blacks and was active in the Urban League. Cohen also served as head of the Negro Division of the local Community Chest. At age 85 Cohen fought to suppress Jim Crow barriers in Cincinnati hotels and restaurants and often used his prestige to gain guarantees of unbiased service from other local businesses.

Much of Cohen's Jewish communal work revolved around B'nai B'rith. Cohen joined Cincinnati's Jerusalem Lodge of B'nai B'rith in 1890 and served it in various offices. When Cincinnati's seven lodges united, Cohen was chosen president of the organization. In 1925 he was elected national president of the organization, a post he held until 1938. During Cohen's tenure—which spanned the onset of the Depression and the Nazi rise to power in Germany—B'nai B'rith expanded its operations into many new areas. Beginning in 1925, the organization initiated the B'nai B'rith Hillel Foundation, designed to promote religious and cultural consciousness among Jewish university and college students. In addition to his support for Hillel, Aleph Zedik Aleph, the junior B'nai B'rith, emerged during Cohen's leadership. This organization was established to initiate young Jewish men into the fraternity and cultural activity of B'nai B'rith. Also during his presidency, the Anti-Defamation League emerged as perhaps B'nai B'rith's best-known branch.

In 1933, after Hitler's election as chancellor of Germany, Cohen, along with representatives of the American Jewish Congress and American Jewish Committee, helped found the Joint Consultative Council. The purpose of the council was to achieve a unified Jewish response to the struggle against Nazism. The little the council or Cohen may have accomplished in trying to influence U.S. governmental response to developments on the Continent cannot be attributed to a lack of effort. Cohen lobbied, petitioned and exerted himself in every way possible to effect a change in the progress of events in Europe.

Cohen was chairman of the board of governors of Hebrew Union College from 1918 to 1937; after that he held the post of honorary chairman. In 1929 HUC recognized his service to the Jewish community by granting him an honorary Doctor of Hebrew Law degree. Cohen was a senior member of the law firm Cohen, Hurtig and Cohen and chairman of the board of People's Bank and Savings Company.

Cohen married Millie Phillips on June 19, 1889; they had three children: Ruth, Hannah and Phillip. Alfred Cohen died on March 9, 1949 in Cincinnati.

References: *B'nai B'rith National Jewish Monthly* (October 1934), pp. 4–15; *Encyclopaedia Judaica* (Jerusalem, 1971) 5:605; "Nearprint Biography Box" and "Scrapbooks," American Jewish Archives; *New York Times*, March 10, 1949; *Who Was Who in America* (1960), 3:169.

COHEN, HENRY (1863–1952). Rabbi, social activist. The son of David and Josephine Cohen, Henry Cohen was born in London on April 7, 1863. At age nine Cohen was sent to N'veh Tzedek, a boarding school established for the children of needy Jews. He studied traditional Judaism and secular subjects. At age 15 he worked for the Board of Guardians, a Jewish welfare agency, distributing bread tickets to the poor. At night he studied at Jews College. Cohen spent two years in South Africa, where he became an interpreter for the British Army during the Zulu War. In 1884, after his return to England, he completed his studies at Jews College and received the title of minister. This entitled him to perform all Jewish clerical duties except rendering decisions on Jewish law.

Cohen was sent by Chief Rabbi Herman Adler to Kingston, Jamaica, where he served as assistant reader in the Synagogue of Amalgamated Israelites. After one year he was forced to leave Jamaica because of his liberal views. Cohen became the rabbi of the House of Israel Reform congregation in Woodville, Mississippi.

In 1888 Cohen accepted the pulpit of B'nai Israel in Galveston, Texas. He remained the spiritual leader of B'nai Israel for 62 years. In 1900, after a catastrophic storm took the lives of 3,500 Galvestonians, Cohen was among the leaders who helped rebuild the shattered community. In 1907 he gave leadership and inspiration to the Galveston Movement, which enabled 10,000 Russian Jews to enter the United States through Galveston, the second largest port in the South at the time. The Galveston Movement helped the immigrants find economic opportunity in the South and Midwest. The movement ended in 1914 because of discriminatory restrictions by anti-Semitic Galveston port authorities and the preferences of most Jewish immigrants to settle on the East Coast, where there were large Jewish communities already established.

Hostilities between the United States and Mexico caused hundreds of U.S. citizens to return to this country through Galveston in 1914. Cohen supervised this relief effort as well. During the 1920s Cohen was an ardent and effective advocate for prison reform. For years he had been acting as a one-man parole board, finding jobs for released prisoners who reported to him weekly. He initiated a political campaign to revamp the state prison system and was appointed to the state prison board, where he advocated separation of first offenders from hardened criminals, as well as vocational rehabilitation and adequate health care. Most of the board's recommendations became law in 1930. During this time Cohen was working closely with Monsignor James Kirwin, vicar general of the Galveston/Houston diocese, to prevent the Ku Klux Klan from gaining influence in Galveston.

In 1921 Cohen was asked by the board of Hebrew Union College to become a candidate for the presidency of the college. He declined the honor, writing, "Among other reasons, I have not the adequate scholarship to be the successor of Dr. [Kaufmann] Kohler." President Woodrow Wilson called him "the first citizen of Texas" after signing, at Cohen's urging, a bill authorizing the first Jewish chaplains in the navy. In 1930 Rabbi Stephen Wise, on being asked by the *New York Times* to list ten outstanding religious leaders in the nation, gave the names of nine Christian clergy and Rabbi Cohen of Galveston.

Cohen retired from the active rabbinate in 1950. In 1889 he had married Mollie Levy; they had two children: Ruth and Harry. Henry Cohen died on June 12, 1952.

Writings: "A Brave Frontiersman," *ALHS*, no.· 8 (1900); "Henry Castro, Pioneer and Colonist," *AJHS*, no. 5 (1896); "The Hygiene and Medicine of the Talmud," *University of Texas Record*, December 1901; "Settlement of the Jews in Texas," *American Jewish Historical Society*, no. 2 (1894); *Talmudic Sayings* (New York, 1894); Henry Cohen's papers (correspondence, articles, documents, etc.) are at the Baker Historical Library, University of Texas at Austin. Some papers are held at the American Jewish Archives in Cincinnati.

References: Anne Cohen and Harry I Cohen, *The Man Who Stayed in Texas* (New York, 1941); Stanley Dreyfus, ed., *Henry Cohen: Messenger of the Lord* (New York, 1963); "Nearprint Biographies Box" and "Correspondence File," American Jewish Archives; Webb Waldron, "Rabbi Cohen, First Citizen of Texas," *Reader's Digest*, February 1939.

H.C.C.

COHON, SAMUEL S. (1888–1959). Rabbi. Born on March 22, 1888, in Lohi, Ninsk, Belorussia, the son of Solomon and Rachel Starobenitz Cohon, Samuel Cohon emigrated to the United States in 1904 and was naturalized in 1912. Cohon had attended *yeshivot* in Russia and summer school at the University of Chicago before matriculating at the University of Cincinnati (A.B., 1911). A year later he was ordained by Hebrew Union College, which he had been attending concurrently. Cohon continued his studies in the postgraduate department of the University of Chicago. In 1943, he was awarded the honorary D.D. from Hebrew Union College.

After ordination, Cohon served Oheb Zedakah Congregation in Springfield, Ohio (1912–1913). He moved to Chicago to become rabbi of Zion Congregation (1913–1919). In 1919 Cohon directed the merger of Zion Congregation with Congregation B'nai Abraham to form Congregation B'nai Abraham-Zion. That same year he assisted in the founding of Temple Beth Israel and organized Temple Mizpah, serving as its rabbi from 1919 to 1923. He then was named professor of Jewish theology at Hebrew Union College in Cincinnati.

While in Chicago, Cohon established the first modern study *kallah* and a Jewish training institution, which served as a precursor to the Spertus College of Judaica. He played a role in the creation of the Chicago Federation of Synagogues and the Chicago Jewish Normal School, which he directed from 1920 to 1923. Cohon also was responsible for encouraging Chicago's Jewish community to establish America's first post of Jewish chaplain for the city's institutions.

Unlike many of his contemporaries in the Reform rabbinate, Cohon took a positive approach toward traditional Jewish observance, Hebrew language and the idea of Jewish peoplehood. Cohon was chiefly responsible for the 1937 "Guiding Principles of Reform Judaism," or Columbus Platform, which reflected his warm approach to Jewish tradition. Cohon was active and articulate in defending Jewry against aggressive missionary campaign and stood as spokesman against the growing anti-Semitism of the 1930s and 1940s.

According to the historian Michael Meyer, Cohon was the central theological figure in the Reform movement in the United States between 1930 and 1960. Cohon's genius lay in his ability to adapt what was established by Abraham Geiger and Kaufmann Kohler to twentieth-century challenges. He supported much of the work of the earlier Reformers but parted from them when he felt they had strayed from the historical development of Judaism based on Jewish sources. However, his theology was not always systematic, as he preferred to focus on the religious experience of the individual.

Cohon helped the movement's *Union Haggadah* in 1923 and its *Rabbis Manual* in 1928. Between 1940 and 1945, Cohon was influential in the revision of the two volumes of the *Union Prayer Book*. In 1951 he served on the committee for the revision of the *Union Home Prayer Book*. He was also the editor of theology for the *Universal Jewish Encyclopedia*.

In 1956 Cohon was named professor emeritus and became a research fellow at HUC-JIR in Los Angeles. He later organized and became chairman of its graduate department, remaining there until his death. He donated his books, now named the Samuel S. Cohon Library Collection, to the institution. The books compose one of the West Coast's finest collections in Jewish theology and philosophy.

In 1912 Cohon married A. Irma Reinhart; they had one son: Baruch. Samuel Cohon died in Los Angeles on August 22, 1959.

Writings (partial listing): *B'nai B'rith Manual* (Cincinnati, 1926); coauthor, *Christianity and Judaism Compare Notes* (New York, 1927); *Essays on Jewish Theology* (Cincinnati, 1957); *Every Mother* (Cincinnati, 1936); *Jewish Theology* (Assen, 1971); *Judaism—A Way of Life* (Cincinnati, 1948); *Religious Affirmations* (Los Angeles, 1983); *What We Jews Believe* (Cincinnati, 1931).

References: Michael Meyer, "Samuel S. Cohon: Reformer of Reform Judaism," *Judaism* 15, no. 3 (Summer 1966): 319–28; *National Cyclopaedia of American Biography*, vol. 47; "Nearprint Biographies Box," American Jewish Archives; Theodore Weiner, "The Writings of Samuel S. Cohon," *Studies in Bibliography and Booklore* 2, no. 4 (December 1956): 160–78.

COOK, SAMUEL (1907–   ). Rabbi. Samuel Cook was born on January 8, 1907, in Philadelphia to Morris and Else Sophi Cook. He received his B.A. (Phi Beta Kappa) from Haverford College in 1927 and attended graduate school there. He was ordained at Hebrew Union College in 1934. In 1959 Cook received an honorary D.D. from HUC-JIR.

From 1934 to 1936 Cook was director of the B'nai B'rith Hillel Foundation at the University of Alabama, teaching on its faculty in 1935 and 1936. In 1937 he was named director of religious education and assistant rabbi at Reform Congregation Keneseth Israel in Philadelphia, a position he held until 1940, when he was called to Temple Beth Israel in Altoona, Pennsylvania. While in Philadelphia he also served as Jewish chaplain of the National Farm School in nearby Doylestown, Pennsylvania. Although he stayed in Altoona until 1946, he took a leave of absence to serve in the Pacific with the U.S. Army Chaplain Corps from 1943 to 1946.

Cook is credited with the development of a national organization of Reform Jewish youth groups. Beginning in 1941, as rabbi in Altoona, he combined his youth group with the one in nearby Johnstown. Subsequently he was instrumental in establishing the Middle Atlantic Federation of Temple Youth, the beginning of a regional structure system for the National Federation of Temple Youth (NFTY). Cook also took a leading role in the Reform movement's camping program. In 1946 he became director of the youth department at UAHC and finally founded NFTY (later called the North American Federation of Temple Youth). In 1967 he was named executive director of the UAHC Department of College Education. These positions he held until his retirement in 1973.

In 1938 he married Ray Clara Marcus; they have two sons: Joel, and Michael, a Reform rabbi and professor at HUC-JIR, Cincinnati.

References: *Who's Who in World Jewry* (New York, 1981), p. 150.

CRONBACH, ABRAHAM (1882–1965). Rabbi, professor. Born in Indianapolis, Indiana, on February 16, 1882, Cronbach was the son of Marcus and Hannah Itzig Cronbach. He attended the University of Cincinnati, graduating Phi Beta Kappa (B.A., 1902), and Hebrew Union College (B.H., 1902), where he was ordained in 1906. Later he received a D.D. (1915) and an honorary D.H.L. in 1950 from HUC-JIR. Cronbach pursued graduate study at Cambridge University in England (1911–1912) and at the Lehrenstalt des Judenthums in Germany (1912).

After ordination, Cronbach served as rabbi of Temple Beth El in South Bend, Indiana (1906–1915), Free Synagogue of New York City (1915–1917) and Temple Israel in Akron, Ohio (1917–1919). He was an institutional chaplain serving hospitals and prisons for the Chicago Federation of Synagogues (1919–1922) and professor of social studies at Hebrew Union College in Cincinnati (1922–1950).

Cronbach was an early proponent of the modern concept that a relationship exists between religious thought and social action. The courses he taught as a faculty member at HUC were among the first in America to integrate studies of social science with practical community social-welfare experience. A dedicated pacifist and opponent of capital punishment, he unsuccessfully sought clemency for the convicted spies Ethel and Julius Rosenberg and officiated at their funeral in 1953.

Cronbach was a member of the Fellowship of Reconciliation and the Jewish Peace Fellowship. He founded the Peace Heroes Memorial Society to pay Memorial Day tribute to nonmilitary heroes such as firemen and policemen.

Cronbach earned many honors during his lifetime. A chapel at the Leo Baeck School in Haifa was named in his honor. He was made an honorary life member of the CCAR (1950) and received the Social Justice Award of the Religion and Labor Foundation (1960). Other honors include honorary life member, National Federation of Temple Youth (1960); official "godfather," Temple Micah, Denver, Colorado (1962); and honorary rabbi emeritus, Valley Temple, Cincinnati, Ohio (1963).

Cronbach married Rose Hentel on October 7, 1917; they had one daughter: Marion Hentel Davis. Abraham Cronbach died in Cincinnati on April 2, 1965.

Writings (partial listing): "Autobiography," *American Jewish Archives* (April 1959); *Jewish Peace Book* (Cincinnati, 1932); *Prayers of the Jewish Advance* (New York, 1924);

The Quest for Peace (Cincinnati, 1937); *The Realities of Religion* (New York, 1957); *Religion in Its Social Setting* (Cincinnati, 1933).

References: "Abraham Cronbach Manuscript Collection," "Autobiographies File," "Nearprint Biographies Box," "Interview with Cronbach, Robert Alan Siegel, July 8, 1964," American Jewish Archives; Robert Alan Siegel, "A Biography of Abraham Cronbach" (Rabbinical thesis, Hebrew Union College–Jewish Institute of Religion, 1965); *Who Was Who in America* (Chicago, 1968), 4:215–16.

CURRICK, MAX COHEN (1877–1947). Rabbi. Currick was born on September 1, 1877, the son of Fishel Currick and Hannah Ganut Currick. Like his classmates at Hebrew Union College at the time, he studied at the University of Cincinnati, where he received an A.B. in 1898, the same year he was ordained at HUC. Later, he received an honorary D.D. from HUC. After ordination, he served United Hebrew Congregation in Fort Smith, Arkansas (1898–1901). In 1901, he was elected rabbi of Congregation Anshe Hesed in Erie, Pennsylvania, a position he held until his death in 1947.

Beginning in 1910, Currick was editor (1910–1912) of the *Erie Dispatch* and contributing editor from 1919. Currick was chairman of the board of editors of *Liberal Judaism*, the house organ of the Union of American Hebrew Congregations. He was active in assisting the victims of Nazism and was chairman of the Central Conference of American Rabbis Committee on International Peace (1927–1935), which drafted a resolution in 1935 that asserted, "War is an unmitigated evil . . . and we should all refrain from it."

He served the CCAR in various other capacities as well, including vice president (1935–1937) and president (1937–1939). He was also a member of the Board of Governors of Hebrew Union College and the B'nai B'rith Home for Children (where he was chairman of its committee on religion, education and library). Currick was a trustee of the Erie Hebrew Institute and a director of the Jewish Welfare Society, as well as vice president of the Erie Public Library and the Community Chest of Erie County. He was a member of the Erie County Peace Council (president 1929–1936) and the Academy for Jewish Research, as well as a board member of the following organizations: Erie section, American Red Cross; Erie Boys Club; Anti-Tuberculosis Society; The Playhouse (chairman, 1915–1930); Erie County Relief Board; and Child-Parent Bureau. During World War I, he was chairman of the Council of National Defense and Four-Minute Men. In 1945, he was presented with the Award of Merit, Isadore Sobel Lodge of B'nai B'rith.

In 1910, Currick married Florence Baker. He died on May 29, 1947, in New York.

Writings: "The Rabbis Talk," Central Conference of American Rabbis *Yearbook* 37 (1927): 242–49; "The Synagogues and Philanthropies," CCAR *Yearbook* 26 (1916): 313–34.

References: *New York Times*, obituary, May 224, 1947; *Universal Jewish Encyclopedia* (New York, 1943), 3:435.

D

DALSHEIMER, HELEN (1900–1974). Lay leader, philanthropist. Helen Miller Dalsheimer was born in Baltimore on April 16, 1900, the daughter of Solomon F. and Millie K. Miller. A graduate of Goucher College, Dalsheimer made national headlines in 1956 when she was elected president of the Baltimore Hebrew Congregation, the first woman to serve a large congregation in that capacity. She served as president of the National Federation of Temple Sisterhoods and on the boards of the Union of American Hebrew Congregations and HUC-JIR.

Committed to Reform Judaism, Helen Dalsheimer's scope of leadership reached into the Jewish community at large. She was the first woman to be elected president of the World Federation of YMHAs and Jewish Community Centers. She served on the boards of the National Conference of Christians and Jews and the national Council of Jewish Federations and Welfare Funds. In 1960 the national Jewish Welfare Board awarded Dalsheimer the Frank L. Weil Award for outstanding service.

Helen Dalsheimer was a talented and articulate speaker who addressed forums across the United States about issues of concern to the American Jewish community. She manifested both a rigorous attachment to religious tradition and an eager willingness to embrace change and innovation.

Helen and her husband both possessed an unshakable trust in the power of education. In the early 1960s their generous gift to HUC-JIR made possible the Dalsheimer Rare Book Room located on the Cincinnati campus. Also named in their honor are the Dalsheimer Auditorium of the Baltimore Hebrew Congregation and the Dalsheimer Youth Center of the Baltimore Jewish Community Center.

Helen and Hugo Dalsheimer were married on October 31, 1921, and had two sons: Roger and George. Helen Dalsheimer died in Baltimore on December 25, 1974.

References: "Nearprint Biographies Box," American Jewish Archives.

J.R.K.

DALSHEIMER, HUGO (1891–1978). Lay leader, philanthropist. The son of Bertha and Simon Dalsheimer, Hugo Dalsheimer was born in Baltimore on May 10, 1891. He received a B.S. from the University of Pennsylvania in 1912. During World War I he earned the rank of major in the Army Coast Artillery Corps. A business executive who headed a prominent Baltimore publishing firm, the Lord Baltimore Press, Hugo Dalsheimer served as vice chairman of the board of governors of HUC-JIR, which awarded him an honorary doctorate in 1973. He also served as president of the Jewish Historical Society of Maryland and as a board member of the Associated Jewish Charities in Baltimore.

The Dalsheimers both possessed an unshakable trust in the power of education. In the early 1960s their generous gift to HUC-JIR made possible the Dalsheimer Rare Book Room located on the Cincinnati campus. Also named in their honor are the Dalsheimer Auditorium of the Baltimore Hebrew Congregation and the Dalsheimer Youth Center of the Baltimore Jewish Community Center.

Helen and Hugo Dalsheimer were married on October 31, 1921, and had two sons: Roger and George. Hugo Dalsheimer died in Baltimore, on September 27, 1978.

References: "Nearprint Biographies Box," American Jewish Archives.

J.R.K.

DEUTSCH, GOTTHARD (1859–1921). Rabbi, historian. Born in Moravia to Rabbi Bernhard L. and Elise Wiener Deutsch, Gotthard Deutsch attended the Breslau Rabbinical Seminary, where he studied with the historian Heinrich Graetz. Deutsch was ordained by another great scholar, Isaac Hirsch Weiss, and later earned his Ph.D. in history at the University of Vienna. In 1891 Deutsch came to the United States to become professor of Jewish history and philosophy at Hebrew Union College, a position he retained until his death. He was given the honorary D.D. degree by HUC in 1916.

Deutsch was a prolific writer and regularly wrote articles for Jewish and other periodicals on a variety of topics; he published books, lectures and essays on Jewish history. He served on the editorial board of the *Jewish Encyclopedia* (1901–1906), responsible for its department of modern Jewish history. Deutsch was committed to the philosophy of Reform and was critical of many Orthodox customs, yet he remained emotionally attached to tradition and prayed in the Orthodox synagogues of Cincinnati.

Deutsch admired German culture and served as editor of the German-Jewish monthly *Die Deborah* from 1901 to 1903. He coupled this love for German with an appreciation of Yiddish culture, eventually becoming sufficiently well versed in the language to enjoy its poetry and contribute to its press. Deutsch opposed political Zionism but nevertheless demanded that the movement be given a fair hearing and sympathized with many of its efforts.

Deutsch was active in the larger Cincinnati German immigrant community. These loyalties proved problematic with the outbreak of World War I. Deutsch was accused of disloyalty to the United States as anti-German sentiment spread across the country. Great pressure was brought to bear on HUC's board of governors by the Cincinnati Jewish community to dismiss Deutsch, a move that was narrowly averted by the intervention of board members who lived elsewhere in the country and who were thus removed from the intensity of local feeling on this issue.

Deutsch's strength as a historian lay less in synthesis than in his ardent love of facts and determination to collect and impart them. While Deutsch devoted his attention to meticulous historical detail, he never wrote a full-scale account of Jewish history but was satisfied with a relatively small number of essays and papers. In his words, "History is more a scientific method than a science." Deutsch believed that Jewish history could be understood only in the context of world history. "We will understand every single Jewish fact of Jewish history in connection with the whole, and the whole of Jewish history in its drift toward the goal of humanity" (*Philosophy of Jewish History*). His impulse to collect and preserve information is epitomized by the Deutsch Card Catalogue of about 70,000 items of interest in Jewish history, now housed at the American Jewish Archives.

Deutsch married Hermine Bacher on May 10, 1888; they had one son: Hermann Bacher Deutsch. Gotthard Deutsch died in Cincinnati on October 12, 1921.

Writings: *Andere Zeiten* (Berlin, 1898); *The Epochs of Jewish History* (New York, 1894); *History of the Jews* (New York, 1921); *Israel Bruna: An Historical Tragedy in Five Acts* (Boston, 1908); *Jew and Gentile* (Boston, 1920); *Memorable Dates of Jewish History* (Cincinnati, 1904); *Philosophy of Jewish History* (Cincinnati, 1897); *Scrolls: Essays on Jewish History and Literature, and Kindred Subjects*, 2 vols. (Cincinnati, 1917); *Theory of Oral Tradition* (Cincinnati, 1896); *Unloshare Fesseln* (Berlin, 1903).

References: Stanley R. Brav, ed., *Telling Tales out of School* (Cincinnati, 1965), pp. 78–86; Martin A. Cohen, "History," in *Hebrew Union College–Jewish Institute of Religion at One Hundred Years*, ed. Samuel E. Karff (Cincinnati, 1976), pp. 433–35; G. A. Dobbert, "The Original of Gotthard Deutsch," *American Jewish Archives* 20 (November 1968): 129–55; Samuel Markowitz, "Gotthard Deutsch," *Hebrew Union College Monthly* 9 (February 1923): 3–6; "Nearprint Biographies Box and File," "Diaries," American Jewish Archives; Max Raisin, *Great Jews I Have Known: A Gallery of Portraits* (New York, 1952), pp. 143–52.

S.R.S.

E

EGELSON, LOUIS ISAAC (1885–1957). Rabbi, administrator. Louis Egelson was born on August 29, 1885, in Rochester, New York, the son of Samuel and Anna F. Seresky Egelson. He attended the College of the City of New York (B.A., 1904), Columbia University (M.A., 1907) and the Jewish Theological Seminary of America, where he was ordained in 1908. Later he received an honorary D.D. from HUC-JIR (1954).

After his ordination he served Congregation Adath Israel in Washington, D.C. (1908–1911) and Temple Emanuel in Greensboro, North Carolina (1911–1914). He also served as a chaplain in World War I (1918–1919). Although ordained as a Conservative rabbi, Egelson spent most of his career as an administrator for the national organization within the Reform movement.

Filling numerous positions at the UAHC after 1914, Egelson served as assistant director, Department of Synagogue and School Extension of Union of American Hebrew Congregations, Cincinnati, Ohio; director, San Francisco office (1917–1918); secretary, beginning in 1927, Tract Commission of Central Conference of American Rabbis and Union of American Hebrew Congregations; assistant executive secretary, National Federation of Temple Sisterhoods (1915–1917) and National Federation of Temple Brotherhoods (1923–1933); secretary of the Committee on Chaplain Procurement (1942–1947); Committee on Emergency Placement of Chaplains (1943–1947); member of the executive board, CCAR (1946–1949); secretary of the Commission on Information about Judaism; and editor of *Liberal Judaism*, the UAHC house publication of the time. In 1942 he was named administrative secretary of the UAHC, a position he held until his death.

In 1920 Egelson married Augusta Cronheim; they had one son: Louis Irving Egelson, Jr. Louis Egelson died on August 10, 1957, in New York City.

Writings: coauthor, *A Layman's Jewish Library* (Cincinnati, 1931); "The Part Played by Laymen in the Promotion of Reform Judaism," Central Conference of American Rabbis *Yearbook* 38 (1928): 521–60; *Reform Judaism—A Movement of the People* (Cincinnati, 1949).

References: "Nearprint Biographies Box," American Jewish Archives; *Who's Who in American Jewry* (New York, 1939), p. 224.

EICHHORN, DAVID MAX (1906–   ). Rabbi, chaplain, educator. David Eichhorn was born on January 6, 1906, in Columbia, Pennsylvania, the son of Joseph and Anna Zevi Eichhorn. After graduating from high school in Columbia in 1923, Eichhorn attended the University of Cincinnati, receiving a B.A. in 1928. He was ordained at Hebrew Union College in 1931 and received a D.D. from the same institution in 1938. In 1956 he received an honorary D.H.L. from HUC-JIR.

After ordination, Eichhorn remained at HUC for a year to pursue postgraduate studies. He served Sinai Temple in Springfield, Massachusetts (1932–1934), as its first rabbi but was forced to leave that pulpit when the Depression prohibited the congregation from paying his annual salary. His next pulpit was at Mt. Sinai Temple, Texarkana, Arkansas (1935–1938). While there, Eichhorn organized and served as secretary of the Texarkana School of Adult Education in conjunction with Texarkana Junior College. He left Arkansas to become the first rabbi at Temple Israel, Tallahassee, Florida. He also was the first state director of Florida Hillel Foundations (1939–1942), serving both the University of Florida in Gainesville and Florida State College for Women (later Florida State University) in Tallahassee. While in these positions, he organized and was the first president of the Leon County Interracial Council (1940–1942).

Eichhorn served in the U.S. Army from 1942 to 1945, enlisting as a chaplain. He was active in rescue work connected with the liberation of a number of concentration camps. He was the first Jewish chaplain to enter Dachau. As a result, he was awarded a Bronze Star. On discharge, Eichhorn was named director of field operations, Commission on Jewish Chaplaincy (then known as the Committee on Army and Navy Religious Activities) and director of religious activities at the National Jewish Welfare Board, a position he held until he retired in 1968. He served in the U.S. Army Reserve until 1960. During retirement, he has served Temple Israel of Merritt Island, Florida, and as chaplain at the Kennedy Space Center, Patrick Air Force Base. Eichhorn was also the founder and president of the Brevard County J.C.C. (1973–1975).

At the request of the Department of Defense, Eichhorn conducted spiritual retreats for chaplains and preaching missions for servicemen in Panama and Puerto Rico (1950), England, France, Germany and Austria (1952) and Japan and Korea (1954).

Eichhorn was chairman of the Committee on the Unaffiliated of the CCAR. He was also president of the Association of Jewish Chaplains of the Armed Forces and president of the Hebrew Union College–Jewish Institute of Religion Alumni Association. He was vice president of the Jewish Information Society of America.

An active Zionist, he was a frequent contributor to periodicals. David Eichhorn is best known for his expertise on the history of conversion to Judaism, as well as Christian attempts to convert American Jews, and as an advocate of rabbinic officiation at mixed marriages.

On June 23, 1935, Eichhorn married Zelda Socol; they have four children: Jonathan, Michael, Jeremiah and Judith.

Writings: *Cain: Son of the Serpent* (New York, 1957); *Conversion to Judaism* (New York, 1965); *Evangelizing the American Jew* (New York, 1978); *Jewish Intermarriages: Fact and Fiction* (Satellite Beach, FL, 1974); *Joys of Jewish Folklore* (New York, 1980); *Musings of the Old Professor* (New York, 1963).

References: "Nearprint Biographies File" and "Biographies File," American Jewish Archives; *Who's Who in American Jewry* (Los Angeles, 1980), p. 106.

EINHORN, DAVID (1809–1879). Rabbi, theologian. Born in Diespeck, Germany, on November 10, 1809, David Einhorn attended the *yeshivah* in Fuerth, where he studied under Rabbi Wolf Hamburger. He studied at the Universities of Würzburg and Munich. Einhorn's rabbinical career began at Birkenfeld, where he officiated from 1842 through 1847 as *Landsrabbiner*. He went on to Mecklenburg-Schwerin to succeed Samuel Holdheim and remained through 1851. Einhorn next briefly held a post in Pesth, Hungary. In 1855 he moved to Har Sinai Congregation in Baltimore and in 1859 to Keneseth Israel in Philadelphia; during this period he also founded and edited the journal *Sinai*. From Philadelphia, Einhorn went to Adath Jeshurun in New York in 1866 and remained there, through its merger with Anshe Chesed into Beth El, until his death. In 1869, Einhorn organized a rabbinic conference in Philadelphia to promote his radical views of Reform Judaism in America.

Einhorn's professional career was marked by repeated difficulties and disappointments. He was denied governmental approval for his initial rabbinical appointment in Wellhausen in 1838. When he left Mecklenburg-Schwerin, he was accused of betraying his congregants and subsequently was forced out of Pesth by local Orthodox forces. He left Baltimore with feelings of contempt for Baltimore Jewry and also was suspended from his post in Philadelphia.

In part, Einhorn's professional difficulties evolved from both his rigid personality and deeply held ideology. While in Europe, he was distressed that Emancipation still left Jews in Germany "crawling like worms among men." In America, he felt Jews demeaned their religion by enslaving blacks and by displaying unbridled materialism.

Nevertheless, Einhorn developed a concept of Judaism filled with optimism. For Einhorn, the religion of Israel began with a mystical bond between the people led by Moses and God. In the life of Israel, the bond manifests itself through rational mastery over the polarities of existence in a process that connects a transcendent and immanent God with spiritual and physical man. Ultimately, the religion of Israel will be fulfilled in the messianic age when the light shared with Israel is made universal. At this point, Israel's separate identity will disappear.

To reach this messianic goal, Einhorn struggled to make Reform Judaism a radical ideological movement. In place of Moses Mendelssohn's composite of revealed legislation and rational truth, Einhorn believed the divine absolute freedom shared with man is implicitly rational and that nothing in Judaism should remain outside reason. Like Mendelssohn, he proposed that rational explication of revelation brings man nearer to the messianic age. However, instead of Mendelssohn's concept of an ancient ideal Mosaic state from which organized society has declined, Einhorn looked on history as inherently positive. To Einhorn, history was the *Torah shebeal-Peh* (oral law) that activates reason. This was Einhorn's way of reconciling his "radical" reform with the historical sanctity of oral law. The beginning of exile, the breaking down of the ghetto walls and the liberty of America are all high points in history's inevitable progress. In contrast to Mendelssohn's emphasis on religious ceremonies, Einhorn generally considered ritual an obstacle to rational access to revelation. Ceremonies, he taught, are forms that must be disposed of as history and reason demand.

Einhorn's thought was crystallized and implemented in his highly innovative German-Hebrew prayerbook *Olat Tamid*, composed in Germany in 1848 and published in Baltimore in 1856. He omitted prayers for Zion, for bodily resurrection and for the personal messiah. Einhorn portrayed Israel as a light to the nations but not as inherently superior to them. The text proceeds from left to right, and little of the Hebrew of the traditional Ashkenazic prayerbook remains. *Olat Tamid* served as a basic liturgical model for the Central Conference of American Rabbis' original Hebrew-English *Union Prayer Book*.

Einhorn married Julia Henrietta Ochs; they had five daughters and four sons. The third daughter, Johanna, married Rabbi Kaufmann Kohler; the fourth, Mathilda, married Rabbi Emil Hirsch. These two sons-in-law were leading Reform rabbis at the turn of the century. Einhorn died in 1879 in New York City.

Writings: *David Einhorn Memorial Volume* (collected sermons), ed. Kaufmann Kohler (New York, 1911); *Ner Tamid (Eternal Light): The Doctrine of Judaism* (Leipzig, 1854) [German]; *The Principle of Mosaism and Its Relation to Paganism and Rabbinic Judaism* (Leipzig, 1854) [German]; "Principle Points of Difference between Old and New Judaism," *Sinai* 1–7 (July 1856–January 1863): passim [German].

References: Eric L. Friedland, "*Olat Tamid* by David Einhorn," *Hebrew Union College Annual* 45 (1974): 307–32; Gershon Greenberg, "The Significance of America in David Einhorn's Conception of History," *American Jewish Historical Quarterly* 63, no. 2 (December 1973): 160–84; idem, "Mendelssohn in America: David Einhorn's Radical Reform Judaism," *Leo Baeck Institute Yearbook* 27 (1982): 281–94.

G.G.

EISENDRATH, MAURICE NATHAN (1902–1973). Rabbi, organizational leader. The second child of Nathan Eisendrath and Clara Oesterreicher Eisendrath, Maurice Eisendrath was born in Chicago, Illinois, on July 10, 1902. At age 16, Eisendrath began his rabbinical studies at Hebrew Union College in Cincinnati. He earned a B.A. from the University of Cincinnati in 1925 and was ordained by Hebrew Union College in 1926.

After ordination, Eisendrath served as rabbi of the Virginia Street Temple in Charleston, West Virginia, for three years. In 1929, he accepted a rabbinic position at Holy Blossom Temple in Toronto, Ontario. An impassioned preacher and public orator, he quickly attracted public attention. A national weekly radio program, "Forum on the Air," gave him widespread exposure across Canada. Imbued with a sense of prophetic justice, Eisendrath felt compelled to speak out on many social and political issues. He advocated better housing and the clearing of urban slums and, during the 1930s, spoke out against the growing threat of Nazism. Eisendrath also was noted for his efforts on behalf of Jewish-Christian understanding and cochaired the Canadian Conference of Christians and Jews.

Though strong-willed and highly opinionated, Eisendrath did question and revise some of his beliefs as circumstances challenged them. A self-described "absolute and dogmatic pacifist," he later qualified this position in response to Nazism. Eisendrath also moved from an anti-Zionist position to one of strong advocacy of the importance of the Jewish state for Jewish people. Eisendrath was a scholar of modest dimensions and served as president of the Canadian Society for Biblical Studies. He published a small number of monographs and articles on religion.

In January 1943 Eisendrath became interim director of the Union of American Hebrew Congregations while the director, Nelson Glueck, was on assignment in the Middle East. In October of the same year, Eisendrath, who had quickly discovered his suitability for the post, was named the permanent director. During his subsequent 30-year tenure as director, and still later as president, of the UAHC (granted life tenure in 1952), the organization doubled in size. By 1960, the UAHC claimed the affiliation of approximately 600 congregations and more than one million members. Concurrently, the programs, staff and budget of the organization all significantly increased.

In 1946, before the declaration of independence of Israel, Eisendrath persuaded the UAHC to adopt an officially neutral stance. Later, he became a staunch supporter of Israel, calling Israel "the sole hope of democracy and the harbinger of progress in the politically and spiritually parched Near East." During his tenure, Eisendrath fought for religious reforms, including the ordination and placement of women as rabbis, and for the central role of the synagogue in the area of social action. One of Eisendrath's most notable achievements was the transfer of the UAHC's main offices from Cincinnati to New York City. He believed it was imperative that the organization come into greater contact with the mainstream of American Jewish life. This was reflected also in his orchestration of a shift in balance of the movement's power from the South and Midwest, where Isaac Mayer Wise had planted its roots, to the East. Eisendrath also oversaw the evolutionary swing from a classical Reform Judaism to one with a more inviting approach to Jewish tradition.

At the heart of Eisendrath's concerns was social justice. He was a forceful speaker on behalf of the black civil rights movement, though some Reform Jews in the South resented his proclamations on the subject. In the 1960s he was an early opponent of American involvement in Vietnam. As an ardent critic of the escalating war in Southeast Asia, especially during the Johnson administration, Eisendrath touched off a controversy that resulted in New York's Temple Emanu-

El, the Reform movement's largest congregation, seceding from the UAHC. Along with his many other opponents, leaders at Temple Emanu-El had long opposed the idea of having any one spokesman for Reform Judaism in America, and during this time of great controversy, their dissent became even more focused. Eisendrath also called for a halt to the proliferation of nuclear weapons, winning the Gandhi Peace Award in 1961. A leader in interfaith work throughout his career, Eisendrath worked to promote better understanding and cooperation between Christians and Jews. The interfaith program of the UAHC expanded widely during his years as president. He also organized special institutes for Christian clergy and Sunday school teachers. One of Eisendrath's crowning achievements was the establishment of a center for social action in Washington, D.C. Despite vehement opposition from Washington Hebrew Congregation and Temple Emanu-El of New York City, Eisendrath succeeded in convincing the majority of delegates at the 1961 UAHC Biennial Convention that Reform Judaism's views on public policy should be heard in the nation's capital. As a result, the Emily and Kivie Kaplan Religious Action Center was dedicated in November 1962.

An outstanding spokesman for Reform Judaism, he was active in many spheres of American and Jewish life. Among other offices held, Eisendrath served as national chairman of the Commission on Religious Organizations of the National Conference of Christians and Jews. He was one of the official American Jewish representatives to the Paris Peace Conference after World War II and served as a consultant to the San Francisco conference at which the charter for the United Nations was written.

Toward the end of his life, Eisendrath helped create the first International Conference on Religion and Peace, which convened in Kyoto, Japan, in 1970. Two years later, he was elected president of the World Union for Progressive Judaism.

Eisendrath married Rosa Brown on November 25, 1926. They had no children. Rosa Brown Eisendrath died on July 2, 1963. He married Rita Hands Greene on June 8, 1964. Eisendrath died in New York on November 9, 1973, at the biennial convention of the UAHC, just before his intended retirement.

Writings: *The Never Failing Stream* (Toronto, 1939); *Can Faith Survive: The Thoughts and Afterthoughts of an American Rabbi* (New York, 1964).

References: Michael A. Meyer, *Response to Modernity: A History of the Reform Movement in Judaism* (New York, 1988); *New York Times*, November 10, 1973; Avi M. Schulman, "Visionary and Activist: A Biography of Maurice N. Eisendrath" (Rabbinical thesis, Hebrew Union College–Jewish Institute of Religion, Cincinnati, 1984); Daniel B. Syme, "Interview with Maurice Eisendrath," May 10, 1972, American Jewish Archives.

Av.M.S.

ENELOW, HYMAN (1877–1934). Rabbi. Enelow was born in Kovno, Lithuania, on October 26, 1877, the son of Leopold Enelow and Matilda Marver Enelow. While he was still an infant, the family moved to Libau, before emigrating to Chicago in 1893. Hyman intended to go to the University of Heidelberg but, en route, changed his mind and followed his father to the United States. Under the influence of Emil G. Hirsch and Joseph Stolz, he entered the University of Chicago before going to Hebrew Union College, entering its collegiate department (because of his advanced knowledge of Hebrew) in 1895. He received his B.A. from the University of Cincinnati in 1897 and was a fellow in English there from 1897 to 1898. In 1898, he was ordained at Hebrew Union College. In 1900, he was awarded the D.D. degree by Hebrew Union College; his thesis was entitled "The Jewish Synod: A Study in the History of an Institution." He received an honorary D.H.L. from HUC in 1925.

After ordination, he served Temple Israel, Paducah, Kentucky (1898–1901); Temple Adath Israel, Louisville, Kentucky (1901–1912); and Temple Emanu-El, New York, New York (1912–1934).

While in Louisville, in addition to establishing the Adath Israel Sisterhood in 1903 and the Geiger Society (for the study of problems in liberal Judaism) in 1904, Enelow was a founder and member of the Executive Committee of the Federation of Jewish Charities (1908–1911) and president of the Kentucky State Conference of Charities and Corrections and of the Conference of Social Workers in 1910–1911. He also founded the *Temple*, a local Anglo-Jewish weekly newspaper, serving as editor during 1909–1910.

While at Temple Emanu-El in New York, his chief interest initially centered on religious education, of both children and adults, and he organized the Junior Society there. Likewise, he served as a member of the Commission on Jewish Education of the Union of American Hebrew Congregations for many years and served as chairman of its Committee on Adult Education.

During World War I, Enelow was a member of the Overseas Commission of the Jewish Welfare Board and went to France on its behalf in 1918–1919 as commander and general field secretary. While in France, he was appointed to the College of Letters at the A.E.F. University of Beaune.

A member of the Central Conference of American Rabbis (vice president 1925–1927; president 1927–1929), Enelow was active as chairman of its committee on Synod and advocated the establishment of an American Synod, which never materialized. He was also a member of the American Historical Association and the American Jewish Historical Society. He was a pivotal figure in the establishment of the Littauer Chair in Jewish Literature and Philosophy at Harvard University and the Nathan J. Miller Chair in Jewish History, Literature and Institutions at Columbia University, using his influence on donors.

Enelow wrote widely, contributing articles and essays to various volumes, including the *Jewish Encyclopedia* and yearbooks of the CCAR. His greatest scholarly contributions were probably *Menorat Ha-maor by R. Israel ibn Al-Nakawa, from a Unique Manuscript in the Bodleian Library, Oxford,* which he edited with a scholarly introduction, and *Mishnah of Rabbi Eliezer, or the Midrash of Thirty-Two Hermeneutic Rules.*

A collection of manuscripts in his memory, as well as his own personal library, was given to the Jewish Theological Seminary of America.

He died on February 6, 1934, at sea on his way to Europe.

Writings (partial listing): *The Faith of Israel* (Cincinnati, 1917); *A Jewish View of Jesus* (New York, 1920); *Selected Works,* 4 vols., ed. Felix Levy (Kingsport, TN, 1935); *The Synagogue in Modern Life* (New York, 1916); ed., *Menorat Ha-maor by R. Israel ibn Al-Nakawa, from a Unique Manuscript in the Bodleian Library, Oxford,* 4 vols. (New York, 1929–1932); ed., *Mishnah of Rabbi Eliezer, or the Midrash of Thirty-Two Hermeneutic Rules* (New York, 1933); ed., *Yahvism and Other Discourses by Adolph Moses* (Louisville, 1908).

References: *American Hebrew and Jewish Tribune,* February 9, 1934, pp. 256, 262–63; *American Jewish Year Book* 36 (1934): 25–53; "Hyman Enelow Manuscript Collection," American Jewish Archives.

ENGLANDER, HENRY (1877–1951). Rabbi, professor. The son of Max and Regina Goldstein Englander, Henry Englander was born in Hungary on February 17, 1877, and was brought to the United States as a young child. In 1901 he received his B.A. from the University of Cincinnati and was ordained at the Hebrew Union College. He received an M.A. (1906) and a Ph.D. (1909) from Brown University.

After rabbinical services in Ligonier, Indiana (1901–1905), Englander became rabbi of Temple Beth El in Providence, Rhode Island, serving from 1905 to 1910. In 1910 he was called back to HUC to serve as associate professor. Eventually he became both professor of medieval exegetical literature and registrar, serving in the latter capacity until his retirement in 1942. For many years he was one of the most beloved members of the faculty, significantly influencing the lives of three generations of rabbinical candidates as well as his colleagues in the Reform rabbinate.

A number of Englander's studies in Hebrew grammar were published in the *Hebrew Union College Annual* during the years 1920 to 1941. In 1920 he was elected president of the HUC Alumni Association. In 1940 he was honored with a D.D. degree from HUC.

Englander married Esther Straus in 1912. He died on April 9, 1951, in Cincinnati.

Writings: "The Exodus in the Bible," in *Studies in Jewish Literature* (Berlin, 1913), pp. 108–16; "Grammatical Elements and Terminology in Rashi's Biblical Commentaries, Part I," *HUCA* 11 (1936): 367–90; "Grammatical Elements . . . Part II," *HUCA* 12–13 (1937–938): 505–22; "Grammatical Elements . . . Part III," *HUCA* 14 (1939): 387–429; "Joseph Karas' Commentary on Micah in Relation to Rashi's Commentary," *HUCA* 16 (1941): 157–62; "Rabbener Jacob Ben Meir Teum as Grammarian," *HUCA* 15 (1940): 485–96.

References: "Biography Nearprint File," American Jewish Archives.

S.R.B.

EPHROS, GERSHON (1890–1978). Cantor, composer-arranger, teacher, an-
thologist. The son of Avraham Abba and Feiga Kronzak Ephros, Gershon Ephros
was born in Serotzk, Poland, on January 15, 1890. His father, a Hebrew teacher
and *baal koreh*, died when the younger Ephros was only ten years old. Ephros
received his initial musical training in the home of his stepfather, Cantor Moses
Fromberg, a *hazzan-shohet* from Yendzeve. As a child, Ephros sang in Fromberg's choir. After his bar mitzvah, he studied in the *yeshivot* of Brest, Litovsk
and Bialystok, where he continued his musical studies, sang in various choirs
and learned the art of conducting. At age 17 Ephros began to lead his own choir
in the synagogue in Sgersch. In 1909 he emigrated to Palestine, where he studied
cantorial music and harmony with Abraham Zvi Idelson, for whom he also
served as choir director and assistant hazzan in the Synagogue of the Lemel
Shule. In addition, he served as music instructor in the newly organized Machon
L'shirat Yisrael, the Institute of Jewish Music.

In 1911 Ephros came to the United States and continued his music studies
with Hermann Spielter (1918–1920), Joseph Achron (1930–1933) and Henry
Cowell (1952–1954). He was appointed music director at the newly formed
(New York) Bureau of Jewish Education. He also taught music at the Rabbi
Jacob Joseph Yeshivah, the H. A. Friedland School for Girls and the Herzliyah
Teachers Institute. As a cantor, he served three congregations: Congregation
Beth-El, Norfolk, Virginia, in 1918; Congregation Beth Elohim in the Bronx,
New York; and Congregation Beth Mordecai in Perth Amboy, New Jersey, from
1927 until his retirement in 1957 (when he was named emeritus). He was a
faculty member of the HUC-JIR School of Sacred Music almost from its incep-
tion, in 1948, through 1959. Ephros was also president of the Jewish Music
Forum and a member of the executive board of the National Jewish Music
Council, which he helped found.

The author of numerous articles and the composer of dozens of published and
unpublished musical compositions, Ephros is most widely known for compiling
the *Cantorial Anthology* for the entire year in six volumes (1929 to 1969). He
also helped prepare the *U.S. Army and Navy Hymnal*, including several of his
own compositions for the Jewish section. In addition, his music can be found
in various collections, including the CCAR *Hymnal*, the *Union Hymnal and
Songster* and the *Union Songster*.

Ephros was a member of Mailamm, the Jewish Liturgical Society, the American Society for Jewish Music, American Musicological Society, ASCAP, Composers Committee for Israel and American Jewish Music, National Association
of American Composers and Conductors and the American Music Center. He
was an honorary member of the American Conference of Cantors, the Cantors
Assembly and the Jewish Ministers and Cantors Association of America and
Canada.

In 1953 he was named Hazzan Mechubad B'yisrael by the HUC-JIR School
of Sacred Music, and in 1954 he was named a Fellow of the Cantors Institute
at the Jewish Theological Seminary of America.

1

Ephros received numerous awards, notably from the National Jewish Music Council (1957), the Jewish Education Committee of New York (1967) and the Board of Cantors of Greater Philadelphia (1967).

Ephros married Rose Hurwitz in 1912; they had two children: Helen Cooperman and Abraham. Gershon Ephros died in New York City on June 28, 1978.

Writings (partial listing): *Cantorial Anthology*, 6 vols. (New York, 1929–1969); *Children's Suite* (New York, 1944); *Services for Weekday Eve and Morning* (New York, 1952); *S'lichos for Cantor, Mixed Choir and Organ* (New York, 1962); *Toward a New Day* (New York, 1970).

References (partial listing): Irene Heskes, *The Resource Book of Jewish Music* (Westport, CT, 1985); Arthur Holde, *Jews in Music* (New York, 1959); Alfred Sendrey, *Bibliography of Jewish Music* (New York, 1951); Israel Shalita, *Encyclopedia of Music* [Hebrew] (Tel Aviv, n.d.); Nathan Stolnitz, *On Wings of Song* (Toronto, 1968); Albert Weisser, *The Modern Renaissance of Jewish Music* (New York, 1983).

                                                                                    I.A.G.

EVANS, JANE (1907–   ). Communal leader, lecturer. The only child of James and Maybelle Holden Evans, Jane Evans was born in New York City on October 31, 1907. Raised as a Reform Jew, she was confirmed at Congregation Beth Emeth in Brooklyn. Educated in public schools and by private tutors, Evans received a Bachelor of Philosophy degree from Xavier University in Cincinnati, Ohio, and an honorary D.H.L. from HUC-JIR in 1975.

Evans moved to St. Louis, Missouri, in 1928 to begin work as an interior designer. She also taught a number of art courses at the local YM/YWHA. In 1933 one of her students, Martha Steinfeld, president of the National Federation of Temple Sisterhoods, was impressed by Evans's speaking ability and Jewish education and invited Evans to become executive director of NFTS. Convinced by her close friend and rabbi, Julius Gordon, that she had been given a unique and important opportunity to enter into Jewish communal life, Evans accepted the invitation. In 1951, with the move of UAHC headquarters to New York, she relocated again and functioned as executive director of NFTS until 1976.

Under Evans's leadership, the work of NFTS took on new directions. It developed a more intense emphasis on Jewish education, actively addressed major issues of peace and world relations, became more involved in the work of the World Union for Progressive Judaism (on whose governing body Evans continues to sit) and expanded its work into other countries. At Evans's instigation, NFTS helped develop the Jewish Braille Institute (JBI), founded in 1931, and helped it evolve into a separate organization. Evans remained actively involved in the work of the JBI and saw it become the major institution in over 40 countries for meeting the religious and cultural needs of the Jewish blind. Serving for many years as its treasurer, she became its president in 1979, an office she still holds.

In the late 1940s Evans began advocating the idea that the Union of American Hebrew Congregations should construct a building of its own. She subsequently served as secretary of the UAHC's Site and Building Committee and, through NFTS, helped raise over half a million dollars for the building's completion.

Deeply interested in world affairs, Evans served as chairman of the Commission on Displaced Persons of the American Jewish Conference after World War II and was a consultant to the U.S. delegation during the early years of the United Nations (whose sessions she still attends as a nongovernmental observer). In the 1950s she taught courses in U.S. foreign policy at the New School for Social Research in New York City, specializing in U.S.-Asian and U.S.-South American affairs. Throughout her life, Evans has been a religious pacifist, active in many peace organizations, including the Jewish Peace Fellowship, of which she was a founder, president and current member of the executive board; the National Peace Conference, which she served as president during the beginning of World War II; and the World Conference on Religion and Peace, on whose U.S. Steering Committee she is still a member.

Having gained prominence as an outstanding lecturer, Evans has addressed Jewish audiences all over the world. Today she continues to lecture widely, focusing on such topics as the work of the United Nations, human rights, international relations and Reform Judaism. She is an honorary life member of Reform Judaism's Commission on Social Action and remains involved in labor negotiations and arbitration for the UAHC.

Evans has lived in New Rochelle, New York, since 1956. An active member of Temple Israel of New Rochelle, she sits on its board of directors and is chairman of its By-Laws Committee.

References: "Biography Nearprint Box," American Jewish Archives; "Jane Evans: A Builder of Reform Judaism," *Reform Judaism* 12, no. 1 (Fall 1983): 30; *Who's Who in American Jewry 1938–1939*, pp. 248–49.

                                                                                   E.M.U.

F

***

FELDMAN, ABRAHAM J. (1893–1977). Rabbi, Zionist, communal leader. The son of Jehiel and Elka Rubin Feldman, Abraham Feldman was born on June 28, 1893, in Kiev, Ukraine, U.S.S.R. He came to the United States in 1906 and settled on New York's Lower East Side. After attending the Baron de Hirsch School of the Educational Alliance, where he assisted in the publication of a Yiddish-English dictionary, Feldman was educated at the University of Cincinnati (B.A., 1917). He was ordained at Hebrew Union College in 1918, where he had previously received his B.H.L. Although he was a Zionist amid a largely anti-Zionist faculty, he received an honorary D.D. from HUC in 1944.

After ordination, he served as fellowship assistant at the Free Synagogue of Flushing, New York (1918–1919), a branch of Stephen S. Wise's Free Synagogue in New York City; the Congregation Children of Israel in Athens, Georgia (1919–1920); and Reform Congregation Keneseth Israel in Philadelphia (1920–1925). While Feldman had come to Philadelphia as Joseph Krauskopf's assistant, he took on most of the rabbinic duties when Krauskopf became ill in 1920. It was in Philadelphia that Feldman began his extensive community involvement. In 1925 he was elected rabbi of the Congregation Beth Israel in West Hartford, Connecticut, a position he held until his retirement in 1968.

Feldman was a leading ecumenist and an articulate defender of human rights and racial brotherhood. A foe of secularism, he believed his mission as a rabbi was "to speak the word of God and the message of religion in the hope of influencing human behavior in every sphere." A first-rate orator, Feldman believed sermons needed to "appeal to the ear as well as to the mind and heart." According to Feldman: "Reform is not a frozen idea. The concept of Reform is really the most authentic concept in Judaism. As the human mind expands, we change." He advocated the active observance of Judaism in all facets of life and the adherences to specific standards for Reform practice. Feldman resisted the trend to adopt traditional practices that Reform Judaism had already declared "nonessential."

Active in communal affairs in Hartford and the state of Connecticut, Feldman was director of education in the Hartford area for the National Recovery Administration (1933); state chairman of the National Recovery Administration Adjustment Board (1934–1935); president of the Hartford Council for Adult Education; president of the W. Hartford Public Library; chaplain of the U.S. Veterans Hospital in Newington, Connecticut; and member of the board of directors of the Jewish Federation, the United Jewish Social Service Agency and Mount Sinai Hospital of Hartford. He served on the United War Community Fund of Connecticut, was a member of the advisory board of the Salvation Army of Hartford and a commissioner of the Hartford Fellowship Commission. In 1929 he founded the *Connecticut Jewish Ledger* with Samuel Neusner and remained editor of the paper until 1977.

Feldman also saw himself as a Jewish ambassador to the non-Jewish community. For 37 years he delivered an annual Thanksgiving message to the Hartford Rotary Club. He maintained extensive contact with Christian clergy in the Hartford area and annually taught a course in Judaism at the Hartford Theological Seminary.

Nationally, Feldman served as a member of the Board of Governors of Hebrew Union College, a member of the executive council of the Union of American Hebrew Congregations, president of the Central Conference of American Rabbis (1947–1949) and chairman of its Committee on Ritual for Children's Holy Day Services and the Rabbinical Pension Board. He was president of the Alumni Association of Hebrew Union College and a member of the publications committee of the Jewish Publication Society, the National Committee of the Jewish Book Council of America and the administrative board of the (short-lived) School of Religious Education of Hebrew Union College and the Union of American Hebrew Congregations in New York City. Feldman also served the Synagogue Council of America and was elected to its presidency in 1955 (to 1957). As a member of the Union of American Hebrew Congregations' committee on ceremonies, Feldman designed the *atarah*, which many Reform rabbis still wear in place of a *tallit*. He also participated on the committee that revised the *Union Prayer Book* in 1940.

Feldman was a prolific writer, authoring more than 26 books, pamphlets and articles and contributing to the *Universal Jewish Encyclopedia* and the *Encyclopedia of Jewish Knowledge*. In 1955 he was designated Citizen of the Year in Hartford, Connecticut, where he also was chaplain colonel in the Connecticut State Guard. The same year he received the Connecticut Valley Council B'nai B'rith Americanism and Civic Award. In 1956 he received a George Washington Honor Medal for the Freedoms Foundation. In 1959 he received an Achievement Award in Religion from Phi Epsilon Pi National Fraternity. In 1961 he received the Silver Beaver decoration from the Boy Scouts. In 1962 he was recipient of the first appointment as Distinguished Alumni Professor at HUC-JIR, Cincinnati, and was named honorary rabbi by Temple Sinai in Newington, Connecticut (which he had helped found). He received honorary degrees from Trinity College (S.T.D.), Hillyer College (LL.D.) and Hartt College of Music (D.Hum.). In 1964 he was awarded the Charter Oak Leadership Medal by the Greater Hartford Chamber of Commerce.

Feldman married Helen Bloch in 1918; they had three children: Ella Norwood, Joan Helen Mecklenburger and Daniel. Abraham Feldman died in West Hartford on July 21, 1977.

Writings (partial listing): *The American Jew* (New York, 1964); *The American Reform Rabbi* (New York, 1965); *A Companion to the Bible* (New York, 1964); *Confirmation* (New York, 1948); *Why I Am a Zionist* (New York, 1948); *Words of My Mouth* (New York, 1969).

References: *Encyclopaedia Judaica* (Jerusalem, 1971); Lawrence Karol, "Rabbinic Leadership in the Reform Movement as Reflected in the Life and Writings of Rabbi Abraham Jehiel Feldman (1893–1977)" (Rabbinical thesis, Hebrew Union College–Jewish Institute of Religion, 1981); "Nearprint Biography Box and File," American Jewish Archives; *New York Times*, obituary, July 23, 1977; Ella Feldman Norwood, *Not Bad for an Immigrant Boy* (New Haven, 1979); *Universal Jewish Encyclopedia* (New York, 1943), 4:270; *Who's Who in American Jewry* (New York, 1939), pp. 261–62.

L.P.K.

FELSENTHAL, BERNHARD (1822–1908). Rabbi, mathematician. Bernhard Felsenthal was born in Münchweiler, Rhenish Bavaria, Germany, on January 2, 1822. He received his early education in Münchweiler, at Kreisgewerbschule in Kaiserslautern, Polytechnic High School in Munich (where he graduated as a civil engineer), and Teacher's Seminary at Kaiserslautern (graduated 1843). However, he was primarily self-taught and was privately ordained by David Einhorn and Samuel Adler. He originally wanted to enter the Bavarian civil service but recognized there would be no prospect for a Jew there. Thus, he entered the field of teaching and taught at a small congregational school in Steinbach for ten years. In the 1840s, when the Russian government had begun to entertain the notion of developing a system of schools, he was prepared to leave Germany. Since the system never materialized, he remained until 1854, when he immigrated to the United States with his father and sister. His mother had died in 1852, and two brothers had preceded them to the United States. After a few months in Louisville, Kentucky, Felsenthal went to Lawrenceburg, Indiana, as a tutor for a Jewish family. In 1856 he served as rabbi to an Orthodox congregation in Madison, Indiana. He left the pulpit to enter the banking house of Greenbaum Brothers in Chicago in 1858. At the same time, as secretary, Felsenthal became the guiding spirit behind Chicago's Jüdischer Reformeverein (which later became Sinai Congregation), and in 1861, he became its first rabbi. It was at this time (1859) that he wrote *Kol Kore Bamidbar: Über Jüdische Reform*, which pleaded for maintaining divergent views in Judaism and the right for religious autonomy. Felsenthal was particularly vocal in his advocacy of radical change in the Sabbath service and was adamantly opposed to slavery.

Declining a later invitation to serve a congregation in Mobile, Alabama, he could not understand how a Reform congregation could support slavery. In 1864, he declined reelection at Sinai Congregation to become rabbi at the neighboring and newly formed Zion Congregation, where he served until 1887, becoming rabbi emeritus in 1886.

Influenced by David Einhorn, Felsenthal was one of the first protagonists of Reform Judaism in the Midwest. He opposed Isaac Mayer Wise and the establishment of a rabbinical seminary. Felsenthal did not feel American Jewry was ready for it. As a result, he declined an invitation by Wise in 1878 to teach at Hebrew Union College. He was an advocate of Jewish day schools. Later in his career, feeling that Reform Judaism was preparing a "beautiful death" for Judaism, he became an ardent Zionist.

He took part in the Philadelphia Rabbinical Conference in 1869 but was generally opposed to establishing an American Synod. As a vocal community spokesperson, he headed a petition for systematic ethical instruction in public schools in 1881. And he strongly opposed the attempt by citizens to introduce Bible readings in public school. Felsenthal generally did not express himself politically; yet, in 1882, he wrote an article for the *Chicago Tribune* in which he opposed Sunday laws, prohibition and blind party loyalty in local affairs, declaring himself a candidate for the Senate.

In 1879, Felsenthal was named honorary vice president of the Free Religious Association. Felsenthal was active in the Jewish Publication Society since its founding in 1888 and helped found the American Jewish Historical Society in 1892. He also served as a member of the executive committee and as vice president of the Federation of American Zionists and was active in Chicago's B'nai B'rith and the Zion Literary Association.

He received an honorary Ph.D. from the University of Chicago (1866) and an honorary D.D. from Hebrew Union College (1902) and the Jewish Theological Seminary of America (1905).

In 1862, Felsenthal married Caroline Levi. They had one child: Ida. After Caroline's death (a result of childbirth complications), he married Henriette Blumenfield in 1865. They had five children. Felsenthal died in Chicago on January 12, 1908.

Writings (partial listing, excluding 250 miscellaneous essays): *Beginnings of Chicago Sinai Congregation* (Chicago, 1898); *An Instruction in the Post-Biblical History* (Cincinnati, n.d.); *Jüdische Frazen* (Chicago, 1896); *Jüdisches Schulweisen in Amerika* (Chicago, 1866); *Kritik des Christlichen Missionswesens* (Chicago, 1869); *A Practical Hebrew Grammar* (New York, 1868); *Zur Proselyten frage* (Chicago, 1878). A full bibliography is included in Emma Felsenthal's *Bernard Felsenthal: A Teacher in Israel* (New York, 1924).

References: "Biography File," American Jewish Archives; *Encyclopaedia Judaica* (Jerusalem, 1921), 6:1221–22; Central Conference of American Rabbis *Yearbook* 18 (1908): 161–68; Emma Felsenthal, *Bernard Felsenthal: A Teacher in Israel* (New York, 1924); *Jewish Encyclopedia* (New York, 1964), 5:361–62; *Publications of the American Jewish Historical Society* 17 (1909): 218; *Reform Advocate*, "Felsenthal Century

Number,'' December 21, 1921; Aaron Soviv, ''Bernhard Felsenthal: A Great American Jewish Educator,'' *Jewish Education* 25 (Summer 1954): 35–41, 64; *Universal Jewish Encyclopedia* (New York, 1941), 4:273–74.

FEUER, LEON ISRAEL (1903–1984). Rabbi, Zionist leader, educator, orator. The son of Isaac and Rose Gluckman Feuer, Leon Feuer was born into a traditional, observant family in Hazleton, Pennsylvania, on May 23, 1903, and was brought to Wilkes-Barre while still an infant. Seeking to improve their economic status, his parents moved to Cleveland, where Feuer graduated from Glenville High School at age 16. In 1920, at the age of 17, he entered Hebrew Union College. He received his B.A. from the University of Cincinnati in 1925, where he was a member of Tau Kappa Alpha, and was ordained at HUC in 1927, receiving a prize in homiletics. In 1955 Feuer received an honorary D.D. from HUC-JIR. After ordination, he returned to Cleveland as Assistant Rabbi and Minister of Religious Education at the Temple-Tifereth Israel. He served in that position until 1934.

Leaving Cleveland in 1934, he became rabbi of the Collingwood Avenue Temple, Congregation Shomer Emunim of Toledo, Ohio, where he served until his retirement in 1974. In Toledo he improved the religious school program and positively influenced the Zionist orientation of the members of the Temple and of the Toledo Jewish community. He also taught at the University of Toledo.

Feuer believed in the efficacy of the sermon as a means of teaching and persuasion. He utilized the pulpit as a means of communicating his ideals and convictions. At a time of grave economic crisis and the beginning of the era that culminated in World War II and the Holocaust, he turned to what he considered the critical requirements of the Reform Jewish community. He addressed the need for stronger Jewish education requirements with particular reference to customs, ceremonies and Hebrew. He called for liberal social legislation protecting the rights of workers, the unemployed, women and children. He was also an early advocate of transforming laws and institutions in search of racial equality.

During the 1930s the Reverend Walter Cole, a Unitarian minister, convinced Feuer that Father Charles Coughlin's anti-Semitic radio addresses represented a real danger to American democracy and American Jews. Feuer secured secret financing for Cole to purchase air time to broadcast rebuttals and helped ghost-write some of Cole's speeches.

It was, however, Feuer's impassioned oratory and relentless labors on behalf of Zionism and a Jewish state that gave him national prominence. In 1942, his book *Why a Jewish State?* was the first work in the United States openly advocating an independent Jewish commonwealth in Palestine. In 1943 he was appointed a panel hearing officer for the Regional War Labor Board. That same year he was given a year's leave of absence by his congregation to be director of the Washington bureau of the American Zionist Emergency Council (1943 to 1944). It was his responsibility to modify the American political position in favor of a Jewish state. He successfully lobbied members of Congress to oppose the British White Paper and to pass resolutions calling for the establishment of an independent Jewish country in Palestine following the successful end of World War II.

In 1945 Feuer was elected vice president of the Zionist Organization of America and in 1946 was a delegate to the World Zionist Congress in Basle, Switzerland, serving as floor whip of the Z.O.A. delegation. There Feuer adamantly strove for communal self-discipline and unity of purpose in achieving Zionist goals.

Following the establishment of the State of Israel, Feuer returned to active communal and congregational duties. He was organizing chairman of the Jewish Welfare Federation of Toledo and served the Central Conference of American Rabbis in many positions of leadership, notably as chairman of the Committee on Social Action; from 1963 to 1965 he served as its president. In 1967 he was appointed to the executive of the American section of the Jewish Agency. He was also president of the Toledo Zionist District; Toledo Lodge, B'nai B'rith; Jewish Community Council; United Jewish Fund; and the Toledo United Nations Association.

Feuer was a talented artist and exhibited his work at the Toledo Museum. After his retirement he served as a visiting professor at Emory University and received an honorary doctorate from Bowling Green University in 1975.

Feuer married Hortense Morgenstern in 1929; they had one child: Leon I. Feuer, Jr. After his wife's death he married Carmen Greenberg Smith in 1972. Leon Feuer died in 1984.

Writings: coauthor, *The Jew and His Religion* (New York, 1935); coauthor, *Jewish Literature since the Bible*, 2 vols. (Cincinnati, 1937, 1941); *Why a Jewish State?* (New York, 1942).

References: "Autobiography," "Biography File and Box," American Jewish Archives; *Who's Who in American Jewry* (Los Angeles, 1980), p. 126.

                                                                                          A.M.S.

FINK, JOSEPH LIONEL (1895–1964). Rabbi. The fifth of seven children and the only son of Rabbi Mendel and Tillie Kagen Finkelstein, Joseph Fink was born on May 12, 1895, in Springfield, Ohio, into a family from a long rabbinical line. He was raised in Dayton, Ohio, and received his B.A. from the University of Cincinnati in 1915, his M.A. from the University of Chicago in 1918 and his Ph.D. summa cum laude in philosophy from Niagara University in 1919. His dissertation was a study of the conflict between scholastic philosophy and pragmatism over the nature of truth. Fink was ordained at Hebrew Union College in 1919 and was awarded an honorary D.D. by Hebrew Union College in 1949.

Fink's first congregation was United Hebrew Congregation in Terre Haute, Indiana (1919–1924). There he became deeply involved in community work. As chairman of the Community Chest he incurred the wrath of the Ku Klux Klan, who abducted Fink and took him to a Klan rally. He called the Klansmen cowards and accused them of betraying their community. They released him, and a week later he received a check from the Klan in the amount of $1,800 for the Community Chest.

While en route to Germany for graduate studies in 1924, Fink stayed overnight in Buffalo, New York, where the ailing Rabbi Louis Kopald of Temple Beth Zion asked him to remain. Fink never left and succeeded Kopald as rabbi of Beth Zion in 1924. He served until 1958 and as emeritus rabbi until his death.

In Buffalo, Joseph Fink was widely known as the leading spokesman of the Jewish community and as a community affairs activist. From 1930 to 1956, his radio program, "The Humanitarian Hour," was a weekly broadcast on station WBEN. He presented messages concerning significant issues of the day and responded to the letters of listeners. Fink was sought as a speaker throughout the community and succeeded in creating interfaith dialogues with Buffalo's Catholic and Protestant leaders. In the 1930s he was among the first to identify the threat of Nazi Germany and spoke out loudly and forcefully in congregational and community forums for a firm American response to the danger.

Among his other activities, Fink served as chaplain to the Buffalo police and fire departments and was called in as mediator on a number of civil disputes. He was president of the Buffalo B'nai B'rith Lodge, founder of the local Board of Jewish Education and a 33rd Degree Mason and was adopted into the Bear tribe of the Tuscarora Indian Nation. He served on the boards of the local Old Folks Home, Community Chest, Board of Community Relations and the University of Buffalo. Fink was appointed to several commissions by the governor of the State of New York. He engaged several times in public debate with Eugene V. Debs and Clarence Darrow.

Fink's sermons demonstrated his belief in the indomitability of the human spirit in the face of difficulty. He addressed Jewish historical themes and related them to contemporary issues, seeking to foster an educated community that would address issues with civility and rationality. A Reform rabbi, he was committed to the entire Jewish community and sought to unify it, as he sought also to unify the entire Buffalo interfaith community.

Nationally, Joseph Fink was recognized as a leader and moderating force within the Central Conference of American Rabbis. For many years he chaired its Committee on Church and State and authored numerous positions papers. He advocated a strong wall of separation between church and state. From 1952 to 1954 he served as president of the CCAR. During his tenure he succeeded in strengthening the ties between the recently merged Hebrew Union College–Jewish Institute of Religion and initiated publication of the *CCAR Journal*, now subtitled *A Reform Jewish Quarterly*. A Zionist, he sought to bring together Jew and Arab for common benefit in the new state.

Fink married Janice Florence Gutfreund on June 14, 1932; they had two children: Arnold G. and R. Toby. Joseph Fink died in Buffalo on November 26, 1964.

References: Selig Adler and Thomas E. Connolly, *From Ararat to Suburbia* (Philadelphia, 1960); "Nearprint Biography File and Box," American Jewish Archives; *New*

York Times, November 28, 1964; Temple Beth Zion, 25th Anniversary publication, *In Honor of Dr. Joseph L. Fink* (Buffalo, 1949).

A.G.F.

FRANKLIN, LEO M. (1870–1948). Rabbi. The son of Michael and Rachel Levy Franklin, Leo Franklin was born in Cambridge City, Indiana, on March 5, 1870, but spent his boyhood and youth in Cincinnati. As a teenager he enrolled in Hebrew Union College and was ordained in 1892. In 1923 he was awarded an honorary Doctor of Law degree by the University of Detroit and by Wayne (State) University in 1940. Hebrew Union College also awarded him an honorary D.D. in 1940.

Franklin's first pulpit was Temple Israel in Omaha (1892–1898). He served Detroit's Temple Beth El from 1899 to 1941 and then as rabbi emeritus until his death in 1948. During his tenure, membership in the temple increased tenfold. As a result, he led the move to build two new temples, one in 1902, known as the Woodward Avenue Temple, and another in 1922.

Franklin was a talented organizational leader. Within months after his arrival in Detroit he reorganized the synagogue's Sabbath services, reinstituted late Friday-night services and in 1899 founded the United Jewish Charities of Detroit. In 1926 he helped found the Jewish Welfare Federation of Detroit. For many years he was editor of the *Detroit Jewish American*. At Beth El he organized a Sisterhood, a Brotherhood, and a youth group. He also led the first fight in America to abolish assigned seating and insisted that the congregation permit the education of children regardless of the parents' ability to pay. He established a College of Jewish Studies at the synagogue, again one of the first congregational rabbis to do so.

After World War I, Franklin was deeply involved in the many efforts to expose the anti-Semitism of Father Charles Coughlin. Franklin obtained a statement from Henry Ford denying that he endorsed anti-Semitism. Soon after, the *Dearborn Independent* suspended publication, and Ford issued a public apology to American Jews.

Throughout his ministry, Franklin was a strong ambassador of goodwill to the non-Jewish community. He was a founder of the Interdenominational Thanksgiving Service and of the Round Table of Catholics, Jews and Protestants and was presented with a Citation for Distinguished Living by the organization in 1941. He was one of the first pulpit rabbis to reach out to Jewish university students and organized a Jewish Student Organization at the University of Michigan in 1916, which became the forerunner of B'nai B'rith Hillel Foundations. He also helped to found many congregations in smaller cities throughout Michigan. He fought for the dignity and rights of the individual. Franklin believed the basic premises of American democracy grew from and were reinforced by the insights and teachings of the prophets of Israel. Thus, he proclaimed, one could become a better American by becoming a better Jew.

Despite the official position of the CCAR, Franklin was one of those who frequently officiated at intermarriages, but he always stipulated that the couple raise their children in the Jewish faith. He was considered a pastoral rabbi, tending to the needs of his congregation.

A proponent of classical Reform, Franklin was also a non-Zionist; he was a member of the American Council for Judaism until he resigned in 1948 and endorsed the State of Israel. Franklin was a consistent supporter of efforts to settle Jews on farms in Michigan. Franklin was president of the Hebrew Union College Alumni Association (1907–1908) and president of the Central Conference of American Rabbis (1919–1921).

Leo Franklin married Hattie Oberfelder in 1896; they had three children: Ruth Einstein, Leo I. and Margaret Fleishaker. Leo Franklin died on August 8, 1948. After his death, Temple Beth El established the Leo M. Franklin Memorial Chair in Human Relations at Wayne (State) University.

Writings: *Christ and Christianity from the Standpoint of the Modern Jew* (Omaha, 1897); *Order of Worship for Sunday Services* (Detroit, 1904); *An Outline History of Congregation Beth El* (Detroit, 1940); *The Rabbi, the Man and his Message* (New York, 1938); *A Ritual for Children's Sabbath Services and Sabbath School Devotions* (Detroit, 1903); *A Ritual for Children's Sabbath Services in Schools and Camps* (New York, 1927).

References: *The Bulletin of Temple Beth El* 23, no. 1 (September 10, 1948); Leo M. Franklin Section, Michigan Historical Collection, University of Michigan, Ann Arbor; "Nearprint Biography File and Box," American Jewish Archives; *Who Was Who in America* (Chicago, 1950), 2:197.

R.C.H.

FRANZBLAU, ABRAHAM NORMAL (1901–1982). Jewish educator, psychiatrist. The son of Manes and Esther Franzblau, Abraham Franzblau was born in New York City on July 1, 1901.

Educated in New York City schools, Franzblau received his B.S. from the College of the City of New York and his Ph.D. from Columbia University in 1935. He was also a graduate of the Teacher's Institute of the Jewish Theological Seminary of America. He went on to the University of Cincinnati, where he received his M.D. in 1937. Franzblau began his career as a psychologist in the Bureau of Reference, Research and Statistics of the Board of Education of New York City, and worked simultaneously at the Educational Clinic of C.C.N.Y. Franzblau also served as a psychologist for the Veteran's Administration. From 1923 to 1931 he served as the principal of the Hebrew Union College School for Teachers in New York City. At that time Julian Morgenstern appointed him professor of religious education and pastoral psychiatry at Hebrew Union College in Cincinnati, where he served from 1931 until 1946. Franzblau also served as director of the Commission on Research of the UAHC from 1927 to 1930. In 1946 he returned to New York to help found and serve as dean of the Jewish Institute of Religion's School of Education and Sacred Music. He also served as professor of psychiatry, a position he held until his retirement in 1959, at which time he was named emeritus. Franzblau then practiced psychiatry full time in New York City.

Franzblau was a pioneer in the application of psychiatry to the ministry, lecturing widely on the subject at Jewish and Christian theological seminars. As a physician he served as associate attending psychiatrist and chief of the Medicine-Psychiatry Liaison Service at Mt. Sinai Hospital in New York. He was a fellow of various medical societies, including the American Psychiatric Association and the New York Academy of Medicine. During World War II, Franzblau was attached to the office of the Surgeon General, responsible for disseminating information, through movies, magazines, and radio, relating to health and medical matters vital to civilian participation in the war effort.

As a Jewish educator, he introduced practical experience into the rabbinic program, requiring senior rabbinic students to direct local religious schools, and he introduced the concept of cantor-educator to the Reform movement.

Franzblau married Rose Nadler on December 21, 1923; they had two children: Michael and Jane Isay. Abraham Franzblau died in New York City on October 27, 1982.

Writings: *The Curriculum of Jewish Religious Education* (Cincinnati, 1935); *The Little Hebrew Schoolhouse* (Cincinnati, 1948); *A Primer of Statistics for Non-Statisticians* (New York, 1958); *A Quarter-Century of Training Rabbis* (New York, 1931); *Reform Judaism in the Large Cities* (Cincinnati, 1933); *Religious Belief and Character among Jewish Adolescents* (New York, 1934); *The Road to Sexual Maturity* (New York, 1954).

References: *The El Paso Jewish Historical Review* 5, no. 1 (January 1988): entire issue; "Nearprint Biographies Box," American Jewish Archives.

                                                                                            F.S.F.

FREEHOF, SOLOMON BENNETT (1892–1990). Rabbi, scholar, author, liturgist. The son of Isaac and Golda Blonstein Freehof, Solomon Freehof was born in London on August 8, 1892. He was brought to the United States in 1903 and reunited with his father and older brother Morris, who had immigrated a year and a half earlier. Freehof traces his ancestry to the "Alter Rebbe," Rabbi Shneur Zalman of Lyady (1745–1813), the founder of Lubavitch-Chabad Hasidism. The family line runs through Shneur Zalman's daughter Freda, from whom the name Freehof is derived. Shortly after settling in Baltimore, Freehof began studying with Rabbi William Rosenau (1865–1943) of Congregation Oheb Shalom. He then attended the University of Cincinnati, graduating in 1914, and was ordained at Hebrew Union College in 1915. With the exception of a short period of military service as a chaplain during World War I, Freehof remained on the HUC faculty until 1924. While at HUC he earned a D.D. degree in 1922.

Freehof's first pulpit was the K.A.M. (Kehillath Anshe Maarav) Temple in Chicago (1924–1934). Beginning in 1934 he led Pittsburgh's Rodef Shalom Congregation. After he was named emeritus in 1966, he returned to preach at the High Holy Days and on other occasions throughout his life.

During his pulpit rabbinate, Freehof was actively involved in a number of umbrella organizations of Reform Judaism. In 1939 he was appointed chairman of the CCAR Committee on Liturgy. In that capacity he oversaw the writing and editing of the *Union Prayer Book*, volumes 1 (*Siddur*) and 2 (*Machzor*). He served as president of the CCAR (1943–1945) and was appointed head of the Responsa Committee of the Conference in 1955. He also served the movement as chairman of its Commission on Jewish Education. On the international front, Freehof became the first American to hold the office of president of the World Union for Progressive Judaism, a post he held from 1959 until 1964. He also served on the Jewish Welfare Board.

Freehof's most passionate interest was Jewish law, halakah, particularly its development through the literature of the responsa. Through his work with the CCAR Responsa Committee, Freehof was instrumental in the evolution of Reform responsa, a major purpose of which was to reattach modern Reform Jews to their Jewish tradition. In 1944 he authored *Reform Jewish Practice and Its Rabbinic Background*, the first of many volumes that today compose a vital and growing Reform responsa literature. In 1960 *Reform Responsa* was published, the first volume of responsa to questions addressed directly to Freehof by Reform rabbis, congregations and lay people. Over the years, additional questions prompted additional responsa. The last published volume of Freehof's responsa— his seventh—appeared in 1980, titled *New Reform Responsa*. Hundreds of unpublished responsa continued to be collected by Freehof for eventual publication, which he called his halakic correspondence. Through his studies and published writings, Freehof was the acknowledged contemporary expert on the relationship between halakah and Reform Judaism. It is important to note that Freehof first started writing responsa while serving as chair of the Jewish Law Committee of the Commission on Jewish Chaplaincy during World War II. He answered questions for Jewish soldiers who wanted to know when Shabbat in Iceland should be observed, given that night lasted for six months. With the concurrence and support of the Orthodox and Conservative members, Freehof authored the permissive responsa that war made necessary, an unusual feat of cooperation seldom duplicated. Freehof saw his role as freeing Reform Judaism from the strictures of rabbinic law but at the same time helping individual Reform Jews remain faithful to the historical teachings of Judaism.

Freehof wrote general commentaries on Scripture as well as on several individual biblical books. No modern Reform Jew, he believed, could legitimately ignore the prophetic spirit embodied in the Bible, which Freehof perceived as the foundation on which halakah was established. Freehof took on himself the task of bringing the Bible once again into the everyday life of Jews who had lost touch with it.

In Freehof's hundreds of published works, he addressed diverse areas of concern in Reform Jewish life, including ceremonies and rituals, the institution of the synagogue, the role of the rabbi and the institution of public worship and prayer. His own library contained thousands of volumes, including one of the world's greatest collections of Jewish law; he also did his own bookbinding.

Freehof married Lillian Simon on October 29, 1934. Solomon Freehof died on June 12, 1990, in Pittsburgh, Pennsylvania.

Writings (partial listing): *Book of Isaiah: A Commentary* (New York, 1972); *New Reform Responsa* (Cincinnati, 1980); *Preface to Scripture* (Cincinnati, 1950); *Reform Jewish Practice and Its Rabbinic Background* (Cincinnati, 1944, 1960); *The Responsa Literature* and *A Treasure of Responsa*, 2 vols. (Philadelphia, 1955, 1963).

References: "Nearprint Biography Box and File," American Jewish Archives; *New York Times*, obituary, June 13, 1990; Rodef Shalom Congregation, *Essays in Honor of Solomon B. Freehof* (Pittsburgh, 1964); Kenneth Weiss, "Solomon B. Freehof—Reforging the Links: An Approach to the Authenticity of the Reform Rabbi in the Modern World" (D.H.L. dissertation, Hebrew Union College–Jewish Institute of Religion, 1980).
                                                                                      K.J.W.

FREIBERG, JULIUS (1823–1905). Communal leader. Born in Neu Leiningen, Rheinpfalz, Bavaria, on May 1, 1823, the son of Sigmund Freiberg. After a basic Jewish and secular education in Germany, he received a vocational education as well. He immigrated to the United States to Cincinnati, Ohio, in 1847 (after a short time in Kentucky). He engaged in vinegar trade, which he expanded to a general merchandise business. A cooper and wine maker by training, he was the founder (in 1855) of the distilling firm of Freiberg and Workum and the first to introduce bourbon whiskey to the world.

He was an honorary member of the Cincinnati Chamber of Commerce and a "potent in counsel" in B'nai B'rith. He was the president of Congregation Bene Israel (1860–1862; 1867–1884; 1887–1890) and the Union of American Hebrew Congregations (vice president, 1873–1889; president, 1889–1903), which he helped to found, as well as a member and vice president of the Board of Governors of Hebrew Union College (1875–1905), where he was active in its founding and served most of the time as vice chairman. Freiberg had served as chairman of the first meeting of the Union of American Hebrew Congregations held in Cincinnati, Ohio, on March 30, 1873, and was among the signers of a call to form a confederation of congregations, which brought the Union of American Hebrew Congregations into existence. Freiberg was a founder and director of the Jewish Hospital in Cincinnati and endowed its surgical pavilion. He served as an officer of the (Cincinnati) Jewish Charities. He also helped to found the Home for the Jewish Aged and Infirm, as well as the Jewish Foster Home in Cincinnati. In 1873, he was a delegate to the Ohio Constitutional Convention, nominated by both political parties of Hamilton County. Freiberg was also a member of the Board of Trustees of the Sinking Fund of Cincinnati. In 1894, Freiberg was elected an honorary member of the Cincinnati Chamber of Commerce.

In 1856, he married Duffie Workum. They had six children: J. Walter, Maurice, Mrs. Joseph Ransohoff, Mrs. E. L. Heinsheimer, Mrs. J. B. Frenkel and Mrs. Albert Freiberg. He died in Cincinnati on December 7, 1905.

References: *American Jewish Year Book* 7 (1905): 59; *Encyclopaedia Judaica* (Jerusalem, 1971), 7:131–32; David Philipson, "Julius Freiberg," *Publications of the Amer-*

ican Jewish Historical Society 19 (1910): 202–5; *Universal Jewish Encyclopedia* (New York, 1943), 4:434–35.

FREIBERG, J.(ULIUS) WALTER (1858–1921). Born in Cincinnati on December 20, 1858, J. Walter Freiberg was the son of Julius Freiberg and Duffie Workum Freiberg. He attended public schools in Cincinnati, graduating from high school in 1875. Immediately after graduation, he entered his father's distilling firm, Freiberg and Workum, later to head it. He was successful in business and later became the director of several banks and other business enterprises. He was a member of the board of directors of the First National Bank (1905–1921) and of the Market National Bank.

He served as president of the Union of American Hebrew Congregations (elected in 1911); he became a member of its executive board in 1903. Then a subsidiary organization, the Union of American Hebrew Congregations Department of School and Synagogue Extension invited him to become a member of its board of managers beginning in 1907. Freiberg was also active in the launching of the National Federation of Temple Sisterhoods in 1913. Active in the Cincinnati Chamber of Commerce, becoming a member of its Board of Directors in 1894, he served four terms. He was also a member of the American Jewish Relief Committee of New York.

From 1913 to 1914, Freiberg served as an elected member of the (Cincinnati) Charter Commission, until the charter was defeated at a special election. He also served as vice president of the National Denver Hospital for Consumptives (now called the National Jewish Hospital) from 1911 to 1921. A member of the Board of Trustees of K. K. Bene Israel (Rockdale Temple), he served as its president from 1908 to 1910.

He married Stella Heinsheimer. They had one son: Julius W. Freiberg. J. Walter Freiberg died in Cincinnati on June 9, 1921.

References: *Encyclopaedia Judaica* (Jerusalem, 1971), 7:131–32; *Publications of the American Jewish Historical Society* 29 (1925): 161–63; *Universal Jewish Encyclopedia* (New York, 1943), 4:434–35.

G

GAMORAN, EMANUEL (1895–1962). Educator. The son of Abraham Dov and Fanny Simchovitz Gamoran (originally spelled Gemoraman in Europe), Emanuel Gamoran was born in Betz, Bessarabia, Russia, on November 23, 1895. He and his family emigrated to the United States in 1907. Educated in New York City public schools and the Rabbi Jacob Joseph School, Gamoran planned to enter the rabbinical school of the Jewish Theological Seminary of America. On the advice of admissions officers, he entered its Teachers Institute instead, graduating in 1912. While attending the Teachers Institute, Gamoran advanced in his secular studies, completing his course at Townsend Harris High School in three years. In 1917 he was awarded an M.A. in education from Teachers College, Columbia University, and received a Ph.D. in 1922 from the same institution.

Gamoran taught in various New York City schools from 1914 to 1917. He was educational director of the Circle of Jewish Children in America from 1917 to 1920. While at Columbia he was one of Samson Benderly's "boys." Under Benderly's tutelage, Gamoran served as supervisor of Extension Schools in New York for the Bureau of Jewish Education in 1920 and 1921. Gamoran was principal of the Washington Heights Hebrew School and a member of the faculty of the Teachers Institute of the Jewish Theological Seminary of America from 1921 to 1923. In 1923 he became director of education for the board of editors, Department of Synagog [sic] and School Extension of the UAHC, which eventually evolved into the Commission on Jewish Education, serving the entire Reform movement. He kept this position until his retirement in 1958.

As a traditionalist, a graduate of the Conservative movement's educational program and a Zionist, Gamoran was an unusual choice for the first person to hold the central position in Reform Jewish education at the time. In that role, he influenced Jewish education in three major ways. First, he created a textbook-centered, grade-leveled curriculum for supplementary schools that could be adapted and adjusted for one-, two- or three-day-a-week schools. Second, he built a textbook literature to support this curriculum, publishing textbooks through the UAHC, guiding it to become the largest publisher of Jewish educational textbooks of its day. Third, to place trained teachers in the classrooms, he professionalized the field by training teachers, helping create the National Association of Temple Educators. This set into motion what eventually developed into the Schools of Education at HUC-JIR. Before Gamoran's appointment, Reform Jewish education was patterned on the catachetical model of the Christian Protestant Sunday School. Gamoran engineered the transition from that model to one that attempted to imitate the public school. His curriculum was a reflection of this new ideology, one that featured the cultural pluralism of John Dewey and Samson Benderly rather than the melting-pot theory of the early 1900s. In a sense, Gamoran's struggle was to move Jewish education from religious to ethnic education.

Although Gamoran's long relationship with the UAHC was occasionally strained, most of the progress made in Reform Jewish education from 1923 to 1958 was a result of his stewardship. The world of Reform education had been chaotic. He gave it order, purpose and new direction.

Gamoran was active in Jewish community life. He served as vice president of the Religious Education Association, member of the board of directors of the Hebrew Federation of America and president of the (national) Council for Jewish Education.

Gamoran wrote numerous articles, books and monographs, lectured widely in North America and Europe and trained teachers throughout the world. He was invited to become a member of the Jewish Academy of Arts and Sciences and in 1945 was given a citation by the Jewish Theological Seminary of America for his outstanding achievements in American Jewish education. At the invitation of Hebrew University, he addressed the first World Conference on Hebrew Education in Jerusalem. In 1953 he was awarded a special citation by the UAHC. From 1953 to 1954 Gamoran was a visiting lecturer at Hebrew University, and in 1956 he was awarded an honorary D.H.L. by HUC-JIR.

Gamoran married Mamie Goldsmith in 1922; they had three children: Abraham Carmi, Nathaniel Hillel and Judith Reenah.

Writings (partial listing): *Changing Conceptions in Jewish Education* (New York, 1924); coauthor, *Gilenu: The Fun Way to Hebrew* (Cincinnati, 1933–1935); *Methods of Teaching Jewish History* (New York, 1950); *Methods of Teaching the Bible* (New York, 1948); *A Survey of 125 Religious Schools* (Cincinnati, 1925); *Teacher Training for Jewish Schools* (Cincinnati, 1924).

References: "Biography File," "Emanuel Gamoran Manuscript Collection," "Nearprint Biographies Box," American Jewish Archives; Samuel Grand and Mamie Gamoran, eds., *Emanuel Gamoran: His Life and His Work* (New York, 1979); Kerry M. Olitzky, "A History of Reform Jewish Education During Emanuel Gamoran's Tenure as Educational Director of the Commission on Jewish Education of the Union of American Hebrew Congregations, 1923–1958" (D.H.L. dissertation, Hebrew Union College–Jewish Institute of Religion, Cincinnati, 1984); Robert J. Wechman, "Emanuel Gamoran: Pioneer in Jewish Religious Education" (Ph.D. dissertation, Syracuse University, 1970).

GITTELSOHN, ROLAND B. (1910–   ). Rabbi, theologian. The son of Reuben and Anna Manheim Gittelsohn (two Russian immigrants), Roland Gittelsohn was born in Cleveland, Ohio, on May 13, 1990. After attending Cleveland schools, Gittelsohn enrolled at Western Reserve University (now Case Western Reserve), receiving a B.A. in English in 1931. He enrolled at Hebrew Union College in Cincinnati, receiving a B.H. in 1934, and was ordained in 1936. In 1961 Gittelsohn received an honorary Sc.D. from Lowell Technological Institute.

In 1936 Gittelsohn took the rabbinical position at Central Synagogue of Nassau County, Rockville Centre, New York. He held this post until 1953. During World War II, Gittelsohn served as chaplain in the U.S. Navy (1943–1946) and had the distinction of being the first Jewish chaplain in U.S. history assigned to Marine Corps duty. He received three ribbons for his role in the Iwo Jima campaign and delivered the dedicatory sermon at Fifth Marine Division Cemetery on Iwo Jima. In 1953 Gittelsohn moved to Temple Israel in Boston, where he would remain as rabbi until his retirement in 1977 and rabbi emeritus until the present. He assumed the presidency of the Association of Reform Zionists of America in 1977, a post he held for seven years. In 1978 he became a member of the General Zionist Council of the World Zionist Organization.

Gittelsohn was always active as a scholar and writer, focusing his attention on adapting Jewish theology to the naturalistic, scientifically oriented Anglo-American philosophy of the latter twentieth century. His efforts to contemporize his beliefs extended to social issues as well. As an author and religious leader, he sought to apply the prophetic ethic to the consuming moral issues of contemporary society. Gittelsohn also produced revisions of liturgy and pedagogic materials in accordance with his theological and ethical work.

Gittelsohn has been very involved in the national administration of the Reform movement. From 1967 to 1969, he served as vice president of the Central Conference of American Rabbis; from 1969 to 1971, he served as president. Gittelsohn has worked with the Union of American Hebrew Congregations in a variety of capacities: as a member of the executive committee and the board of trustees, including a period as vice chairman of the board (1973–1977); on the Commission on Social Action; and as chairman of the Commission on Jewish Education (1959–1968).

Gittelsohn has also been a prominent civic leader with a special concern for social action, both in Massachusetts and nationally. In 1947 he served on President Harry S. Truman's Committee on Civil Rights. In the 1950s and 1960s, Gittelsohn focused his energies on the protection of the disenfranchised in Massachusetts, serving on the Commission on Abolition of the Death Penalty (1957–1958), the Governor's Committee on Migratory Labor (1960–1962) and the Governor's Committee to Survey Operation of Massachusetts Prisons (1961–1962).

Gittelsohn married Ruth Freyer on September 25, 1932; they had two children: David and Judith Sue. Roland Gittelsohn married Hulda Tishler on August 19, 1979.

Writings (partial listing, not including numerous articles, experimental liturgies and chapters contributed to anthologies): *Consecrated Unto Me* (New York, 1965); *Here I Am—Harnessed to Hope* (New York, 1988); *Little Lower Than the Angels* (New York, 1951); *Modern Jewish Problems* (New York, 1951); *Wings of the Morning* (New York, 1969).

References: "Nearprint Biography Box," American Jewish Archives; *Who's Who in American Jewry* (Los Angeles, 1980), p. 161; *Who's Who in World Jewry* (Jerusalem, 1981), p. 269.

GLASER, JOSEPH B. (1925–   ). Rabbi. The son of Louis and Dena Harris Glaser, Joseph Glaser was born in Boston, Massachusetts, on May 1, 1925. During World War II he served in the combat infantry (1943–1946) and was awarded a Purple Heart with oak leaf cluster. In 1948 he received an A.B. from UCLA. After graduation, he attended law school at the University of San Francisco, where he received a J.D. (1951). In 1954 he received his B.H.L. from HUC-JIR. Glaser was ordained at HUC-JIR in 1956 and received an M.H.L. He also studied at Johns Hopkins and Stanford universities and did postgraduate work as a Merrill Trust grantee at the Hebrew University Law School in Jerusalem (1969–1970) and at Oxford University in England. In 1981 he was awarded an honorary D.D. from HUC-JIR.

After ordination, Glaser served Temple Beth Torah of Ventura, California (1956–1959). Concurrently he served as registrar of and instructor at the newly opened Hebrew Union College–Jewish Institute of Religion in Los Angeles. From 1959 to 1971, Glaser was regional director, Union of American Hebrew Congregations, for the Northern California/Pacific Northwest Region. In 1971 he was appointed executive vice president of the Central Conference of American Rabbis, a position he still holds.

Glaser served as vice chairman of the San Francisco Interfaith Conference on Religion and Peace (1969–1971) and Religion and Race (1963–1968). He was also chairman of the Clergy Committee Farm Labor Negotiations, which helped arbitrate an agreement among the Teamsters' Union, the United Farm Workers' Organizing Committee (AFL-CIO) and Grape Growers (1967–1968). While in San Francisco, Glaser was administrative secretary of the Pacific Association of Reform Rabbis and directed Camp Swig. He was also chairman of the youth commission of the Western Association of Reform Rabbis.

Glaser was chairman of the Board of Religion in American Life (1977–1982), the first Jew to head the organization; chairman, Committee on Scope, Conference of Presidents of Major American Jewish Organizations; chairman, administrative committee of the Synagogue Council of America; vice president, American Friends of the Oxford Centre for Post Graduate Hebrew Studies;

chairman, Americans United to Save Uganda; and member of the board of American Jewish World Service.

In 1951 Glaser married Agatha Maier; they have four children: Simon, Meyer, Sara and John.

Writings: "The Fifth Amendment—Some Help from the Past," in *Jewish Law Association Studies I* (Chico, CA, 1985); ed., Central Conference of American Rabbis *Yearbook*, 1971–1975.

References: Central Conference of American Rabbis *Yearbook* 91 (1981): 154–60; "Nearprint Biographies," American Jewish Archives; *Who's Who in America* (Chicago, 1990–1991), p. 1211; *Who's Who in American Jewry* (Los Angeles, 1980), p. 162.

GLUECK, NELSON (1900–1971). Rabbi, archaeologist, academician. Born into an Orthodox family on June 4, 1900, in Cincinnati, Ohio, Nelson Glueck was the son of Anne Rubin Glueck and Morris Glueck (born Morris/Moshe Revel). While still in high school, he studied at Hebrew Union College in the afternoon and received his B.H.L. (1918). As an ROTC private, he entered the University of Cincinnati (A.B., 1922) and continued his studies concurrently at Hebrew Union College, where he was ordained (1923). After ordination, as the first Morgenthau Traveling Fellow, he studied in Europe. Like many students of his generation, he took classes at the Universities of Berlin and Heidelberg, before settling at the University of Jena, where he graduated (Ph.D., 1927).

After graduation, he went directly to Palestine and studied under William Foxwell Albright at the American School of Oriental Research (Jerusalem, 1928–1929) and dug at Tel Bet Mirsim near Hebron. When he returned to the United States, he joined the faculty of Hebrew Union College (instructor 1928; assistant professor, 1931; associate professor, 1934; professor, 1942–1971). In 1941 Glueck was named director of the Union of American Hebrew Congregations, but he never really fulfilled that responsibility. With Glueck still in Israel, Maurice Eisendrath eventually took the position. But in 1947 Glueck was elected president of Hebrew Union College. He held this position until his retirement in 1971.

A world-renowned archaeologist, Glueck executed a systematic survey of Transjordan and identified over 1,000 sites. In 1937 he uncovered a Nabatean Temple at Jebel el-Tannor and helped us understand the Nebatean contribution to civilization. Glueck excavated Tel el Kheleifeh (Etzion-Geber) in 1938. And beginning in 1952, at the request of David Ben Gurion, he surveyed ancient sites in the Negev in order to assist the incipient state of Israel in planning communities in the desert by identifying water sources.

During World War II, using his cover as an archaeologist, Glueck worked with the U.S. Office of Strategic Services in Transjordan to provide vital information should the Allies need an escape route from Rommel's Afrika Corps.

As president of Hebrew Union College, Glueck succeeded in securing its independence from the patronage of the Union of American Hebrew Congregations. In 1948 he succeeded Stephen S. Wise as president of the Jewish Institute of Religion as part of the merger plan of the two institutions (which took place in 1950). Under Glueck's presidency, Hebrew Union College expanded by establishing campuses in Los Angeles and Jerusalem. In Jerusalem he led a successful fight, amid right-wing opposition, for the inclusion of a chapel on the Hebrew Union College campus. He built the American Jewish Archives (with Jacob Rader Marcus), established the Hebrew Union College Museum and developed the interfaith fellows program, where non-Jews study toward the Ph.D. in Biblical and Cognate Studies. Under his stewardship, plans for all first-year students to study in Jerusalem were made. In addition, he helped pave the way for the admission of women as rabbinical students.

In his role as president of Hebrew Union College, Glueck was involved in many organizations and received numerous honors. He offered the prayer at the presidential inauguration of John F. Kennedy in 1961. He was named an honorary citizen of Beersheva and Eilat. Glueck was a Fellow of the Royal Geographical Society and the American Academy of Arts and Sciences and a trustee of the American School of Oriental Research and the JFK Memorial Library. He was a member of the American Philosophical Society, the Central Conference of American Rabbis, the Israel Exploration Society and Phi Beta Kappa.

Glueck received honorary degrees from the Jewish Theological Seminary (D.H.L., 1947), Jewish Institute of Religion (D.H.L., 1947), Dropsie College (Litt.D., 1955), Kenyon College (D.S.L., 1955), Drake University (D.D., 1956), University of Pennsylvania (L.H.D., 1961), Miami University (L.L.D., 1962), Wayne State University (L.H.D., 1962), New York University (L.H.D., 1963), University of Southern California (S.T.D., 1964), College of Holy Cross (D.D., 1965), Thomas Moore College (Litt.D., 1979), Instituti Divi Thome (D.D., 1968), Ripon College (S.T.D., 1969) and Xavier University (L.L.D., 1969).

He was a recipient of the Cincinnati Fine Arts Award (1939), Ohioana Medal (1956) and the Ohioana nonfiction book award (1960) for his *Rivers in the Desert).*

Nelson Glueck married Helen Iglauer in 1931. They had one son: Charles. Glueck died on February 12, 1971, in Cincinnati.

Writings (partial listing): *Dateline: Jerusalem* (Cincinnati, 1968); *Deities and Dolphins* (New York, 1965); *The Other Side of the Jordan* (New Haven, 1940); *The River Jordan* (Philadelphia, 1946); *Rivers in the Desert* (Philadelphia, 1949).

References: *Current Biography* (July 1969), pp. 28–30; *Encyclopaedia Judaica* (Jerusalem, 1971), 7:627–28; "Nelson Glueck Manuscript Collection," American Jewish Archives; *New York Times*, obituary, February 15, 1971, p. 25; James A. Sanders, *New Eastern Archaeology in the Twentieth Century: Essays in Honor of Nelson Glueck* (Garden City, 1980), includes biographical essays and bibliography; Ellen Norman Stern, *Dreamer in the Desert: A Profile of Nelson Glueck* (New York, 1980); *Time*, December 13, 1963; *Universal Jewish Encyclopedia* (New York, 1941), 4:627; *Who Was Who in America* (Chicago, 1964), 5:273.

GOLDENSON, SAMUEL H. (1878–1962). Rabbi, advocate of classical Reform. The son of Hyman and Fanny Leah Frankel Goldenson, Samuel Goldenson was born in Kalvaria, Poland, on March 26, 1878. His family came to the United

States in 1890 and settled in Rochester, New York. He received his B.A. from the University of Cincinnati and his rabbinic training at Hebrew Union College, Cincinnati, receiving ordination in 1904. Goldenson received a doctorate from Columbia University in 1917, where he studied under John Dewey. In 1925 he was awarded an honorary D.H.L. from HUC.

Goldenson's rabbinate began in Lexington, Kentucky, at the Adath Israel Congregation (1904–1907). In 1907 he moved to Temple Beth Emeth in Albany, New York, and in 1918 went to Rodef Shalom Congregation in Pittsburgh. In 1934 he went to Temple Emanu-El in New York and remained there until his retirement in 1937.

Samuel Goldenson was influenced deeply by prophetic Judaism, which formed the core of his rabbinate. He campaigned for civic reform and for social justice. His early series of sermons in Pittsburgh, titled "Reconstruction," encouraged a universalistic and idealistic spirit at the victorious conclusion of World War I. Seeking to influence his own congregation and the liberal Christian community in Pittsburgh, he often spoke about the rights of workers in their struggle for a better life. For Goldenson, his successful campaign to abolish private pews at Rodef Shalom reflected this struggle. A more radical note was struck by "Am I My Brother's Keeper?" which dealt with the great coal strike of 1928. He refrained, however, from direct involvement in union efforts.

Goldenson approached the problems of Judaism and the contemporary world through philosophical analysis. His sermons emphasized logic. He frequently combined the noblest thoughts of the biblical prophetic message with the pragmatic approach of John Dewey, though usually allowing biblical ideals to hold sway.

As president of the Central Conference of American Rabbis (1933–1935), Goldenson was confronted with the rise of Nazi Germany and the hopelessness felt by many American Jews during the Depression. He criticized and attacked Mordecai Kaplan's emphasis on Judaism as a civilization. Goldenson saw this as an outgrowth of secular Zionism and dangerous to his own view of prophetic religion. Although not opposed to Palestine as a place of refuge for persecuted Jews, he feared it would not live up to the high ethical expectations of a Jewish state. When the Zionist Felix Levy was elected as his successor to the CCAR presidency, Goldenson refused to serve on its executive board. Subsequently he joined the American Council for Judaism. Goldenson also served as the vice president of the World Union for Progressive Judaism. In 1927, as a member of the committee on Sacred Justice, he boldly influenced the UAHC adoption of six principles, including acknowledgment that "human rights take precedence over rights of property."

After his retirement at age 70, Goldenson made himself available to small, isolated congregations and sought to strengthen liberal prophetic Judaism in those settings.

In 1905 he married Claudia Myar of Camden, Arkansas (d. 1938); they had three children: Evelyn Glick, Robert and William. Samuel Goldenson died on August 31, 1962, in Stamford, Connecticut.

Writings: *World Problems and Personal Religion: Sermons, Addresses and Selected Writings*, ed. M. L. Aaron (Pittsburgh, 1975).

References: Central Conference of American Rabbis *Yearbook* 73 (1964): 125–26; Solomon B. Freehof, *Samuel Goldenson: A Tribute* (Pittsburgh, 1962); "Nearprint Biographies," American Jewish Archives; *New York Times*, obituary, September 1, 1962, p. 19; *Universal Jewish Encyclopedia* (New York, 1941), 5:19.

W.J.

GOLDMAN, ROBERT PHILIP (1890–1976). Attorney, communal and civic leader. Born in Cincinnati on May 17, 1890, the son of Louis and Rose Frohman Goldman, Robert Goldman attended Cincinnati public schools, the Ohio Military Institute and Franklin School before entering Yale College, from which he earned an A.B., Phi Beta Kappa (1911). Goldman studied law at Harvard University (LL.B., 1914) and the University of Paris (1919). He was admitted to the bar in Cincinnati in 1914 and was president of the Cincinnati Bar Association (1954–1955). In 1963 he was awarded an honorary D.H.L. from HUC-JIR.

During World War I, Goldman served as a private with the 309th Supply Train, 84th Division, and with the Sorbonne Detachment, U.S. Army A.E.F., 1918 to 1919.

Goldman was associated with the law firm of Paxton and Seasongood from 1919 until his death. He was a director of the Merry Manufacturing Co., the Wolf Machine Co., United States Shoe Corporation, Famous Surplus Stores, Inc., and the Hi-Code Trading Corporation.

Goldman was president (chairman of the board) of the Union of American Hebrew Congregations (1937–1943) and a member of the Board of Governors of HUC-JIR. Elected to the Board of Governors in 1953, he served as chairman from 1958 to 1962. Goldman was the only person to hold both offices, unique because he was a Zionist. He often was the force for rapprochement between HUC and the UAHC as they struggled for hegemony in the Reform movement, for example, over control of the College of Jewish Studies in Los Angeles and the Combined Campaign of Reform Judaism. Goldman played an active role in keeping the American Jewish Assembly (later known as the American Jewish Conference) an effective organization in American Jewish life. He headed the Jewish Community Council in Cincinnati from 1944 to 1947 and served for several years as vice president of the Foreign Policy Association of Cincinnati. Goldman was active as the cochairman of the local chapter of the National Conference of Christians and Jews. He was also president of Isaac M. Wise Temple (1926–1928) and trustee of Bellfaire, a Cleveland orphanage (1932–1953).

Goldman was a member of the Cincinnati Council on World Affairs. He was one of the leaders of the Charter movement there, which ousted Cincinnati's machine government in 1925. Goldman remained active in the Charter movement until his death, serving as chairman of the Board of Revision for the City Charter of Cincinnati in 1949 as well as trustee of the City Charter Commission and chairman of its board (1955–1958). A leading authority on representative voting, he was president of the (national) Proportional Representation League. He served as trustee of the Ohio State Archaeological and Historical Society (1932–1938) and trustee of the University School of Cincinnati. He was one of the founders of and a legal architect and advisor for the Greater Cincinnati Foundation. Goldman was secretary and trustee of the Legal Aid Society of Cincinnati and the National Alliance of Legal Aid Societies.

Goldman was chairman of the Committee on Banking and Commercial Law of the Ohio State Bar Association (1949–1961) and a member of the Association of the Bar of New York City. Active in efforts to bring about uniform corporation laws to avoid impediments in legal representation, he was a member of the American Law Institute and served on the editorial board of its Uniform Commercial Code (he was responsible for the adoption of the code in Ohio) as well as its Committee on Continuing Legal Education. Goldman served as president of the Cincinnati Bar Association (1954–1955) and was a founder of the Lawyers Club of Cincinnati.

Goldman wrote various articles on Cincinnati's political history, proportional representation elections and legal subjects. He was an expert not only in the field of corporate and commercial law but also in the fields of trusts, taxation, estate planning and laws affecting charitable institutions. In 1966 he received the Distinguished Service Medal of the Ohio State Bar Association and in 1969 the City of Peace Award from the State of Israel Bond Organization. In 1969 he received the Isaac M. Wise Temple's Good Neighbor Award.

On October 16, 1921, Goldman married Therese Wolfstein; they had three children: David, Agnes and Barbara Cohen. Robert Goldman died in Cincinnati on April 10, 1976.

Writings (partial listing): coauthor, *Anderson's Ohio Corporation Desk Book* (Cincinnati, 1951); coauthor, "Land Trust Certificates with Relation to Ohio Law," *Cincinnati Law Review* 2, no. 3 (May 1928); "Legal Aid Societies in the United States," *Legal Aid Review* 13, no. 1; "When Is a Trust Not a Trust?" *Cincinnati Law Review* 16, no. 3 (May 1942).

References: *Cincinnati Index*, May 17, 1960; Edward Treister, "Robert P. Goldman: A Leader in Reform Judaism, 1943–1963" (Term paper, Hebrew Union College–Jewish Institute of Religion, Cincinnati, 1969; *Who Was Who in America* (Chicago, 1981, 7:126.

GOLDSTEIN, SIDNEY EMANUEL (1879–1955). Rabbi, professor. Sidney Goldstein was born on March 7, 1879, in Marshall, Texas, to Jacob and Golda Mesritz Goldstein. He attended the University of Cincinnati (B.A., 1904) and Hebrew Union College (B.H.L., ordination 1905) simultaneously. Goldstein also did graduate work in social services at the University of Cincinnati, University of Chicago and Columbia University. In 1945 the Jewish Institute of Religion awarded him an honorary D.D.

From 1905 to 1907, Goldstein was assistant superintendent at Mt. Sinai Hospital in New York City. He left Mt. Sinai to become assistant rabbi at the Free

Synagogue of New York (1907), where he remained for the rest of his career. When the Free Synagogue's senior rabbi, Stephen S. Wise, began the Jewish Institute of Religion in 1922, Goldstein assisted in its founding and was named professor of social service.

This dual role of congregational rabbi and social service advocate shaped his entire career. At the Free Synagogue, Goldstein established its social service division, which stood as a model for other congregations. Especially innovative were his programs for children who had been mental-health patients and who were placed in half-way programs to help them readjust to daily life. These programs also helped tubercular patients become self-sufficient. Goldstein was well regarded as an early authority on marriage counseling and was an indefatigable supporter of the labor, women's suffrage and civil rights movements.

Like other rabbis, Goldstein was active in many community activities and organizations, serving as chairman, Commission on Social Justice of the CCAR, and member of its executive committee; chairman, Jewish Institute on Marriage and the Family; chairman, New York State Conference on Marriage and the Family (1936–1940); president, National Conference on Family Relations (1944–1946); member, Planning Committee of White House Conference on Children in a Democracy (1939–1940); member, White House Conference on Aging; member, board of directors, Planned Parenthood Federation of America; chairman, executive committee, Joint Committee on Unemployment (1930–1934); and chairman, executive committee, War Resisters League of America (1930–1942).

In 1906 Goldstein married Susan Sugarman (d. 1937); they had two daughters: Eleanore Mattye Nichthauser and Beatrice Sidbeth Konheim.

Writings: *Marriage and Family Counseling* (New York, 1945); *The Meaning of Marriage and the Foundation of the Family* (New York, 1942); *The Synagogue and Social Welfare* (New York, 1955).

References: *Encyclopaedia Judaica* (Jerusalem, 1971), 7:749–50; "Nearprint Biographies Box," American Jewish Archives; *New York Times*, obituary, March 21, 1955, p. 25; *Who Was Who in America* (Chicago, 1951–1960), 3:332.

GOTTHEIL, GUSTAV (1827–1903). Rabbi. Son of Bernard Gottheil, Gustav Gottheil was born on May 28, 1827, in Pinne-Posen, Prussian Poland. His mother's maiden name was Adersbach, but her first name is unknown. After graduation from his religious high school in 1847, he secured a position as teacher in a common school in a neighboring community. While continuing his education, he was a teacher in Gach, on the Belgian frontier, from 1851 to 1854 and served as preacher in this small Jewish community.

Gottheil studied at the University of Berlin and the Berlin Rabbinical College. While studying in Berlin, he became the assistant of Samuel Holdheim at the Berlin Reformgemeinde (1855). There he received his rabbinical ordination. Gottheil received his Ph.D. from the University of Jena. He moved to Manchester, England, in 1860. For 13 years he served the Manchester Congregation of British Jews at the Park Place Synagogue. There he also taught at Owens College, later renamed the University of Manchester (1867–1873). Unusual for his generation, Gottheil preached in English as well as German. Well known for his liberal views, he preached against slavery, attacking those who argued that slavery was in accord with Mosaic law. In Manchester he introduced moderate reforms and instituted a seven-year cycle for the reading of the Torah. In 1869, as a representative of Reform Judaism, he participated in the Leipsig Synod. Gottheil argued for the reinstitution of the Palestinian triennial cycle for the reading of the Torah.

In 1873 Gottheil moved to New York City as the assistant to Samuel Adler (whom he succeeded) at Temple Emanu-El. He held this position until his retirement in 1899. At Emanu-El he introduced more radical reforms, instituting an annual cycle for reading the Torah, with shortened weekly readings and English or German translations. The haftarah was read in German or English only, and the prayer book was completely revised. Through the years he was engaged in the controversy over Sunday services, which were not introduced at Emanu-El. At Emanu-El he challenged the ethical culture theories of Felix Adler. Gottheil spoke of a more traditional theistic Judaism than that espoused by the congregation. At Emanu-El he founded a preparatory school (1875–1885) and a short-lived rabbinical school (1881–1885), but there were few students. He also founded the Emanu-El Sisterhood of Personal Service, the first such organization in New York, which emphasized both creed and deed. He was active as well in the women's suffrage movement. It is especially noteworthy that Gottheil was vice president of the Federation of American Zionists at a time when Temple Emanu-El was utterly opposed to Zionism and forbade its rabbis to speak about it in the pulpit. Gottheil was involved in translating Jewish hymns, but he seems also to have collected hymns of Christian origin to create a hymnal on which the *Union Hymnal* was partly based. Gottheil's hymnal was one of the first Jewish hymnbooks published in the United States. Gottheil founded the Jewish Ministers Association in 1888, serving as president. He founded the Association of Eastern Rabbis, which in 1890 became part of the Central Conference of American Rabbis, where Gottheil took an active role. He was also one of the founders of the Jewish Publication Society and was chairman of the CCAR committee that revised the *Union Prayer Book*.

He was affiliated with the Society for Biblical Literature, the Oriental Club, and the advisory council of the American Common League School, which settled questions of religion in the New York City public schools. Gottheil was involved in a commission that busied itself with work in Palestine. He was founder and vice president of the Nineteenth Century Club, established as a response to the Christian bias in the Society for the Prevention of Cruelty to Children. He also founded the Society for the Aid of Jewish Prisoners (1893).

Gottheil was active beyond the Jewish community as one of the founders of the New York State Conference of Religions, where he assisted in editing its *Book of Common Prayers*. In 1892 he was a representative at the Parliament of

Religions held at the Chicago World's Fair. In commemoration of Gottheil's seventieth birthday, a Gustav Gottheil lectureship in Semitic languages was established at Columbia University.

In 1856 Gottheil married Sara (called Rosalie) Wollmann; they had five children: Richard, William, Ernest, Gertrude Rich and Theodora Levy. Gustav Gottheil died on April 15, 1903, in New York City.

Writings: *Sarah* (New York, 1896); *Sun and Shield* (New York, 1886).

References: "Biographies Nearprint File," American Jewish Archives; *Encyclopaedia Judaica* (Jerusalem, 1973), 7:821; Richard Gottheil, *The Life of Gustav Gottheil: Memoir of a Priest in Israel* (Williamsport, PA, 1936); "Gustav Gottheil," in J. Alexander Patten, *Lives of the Clergy of New York and Brooklyn* (New York, 1874); *Jewish Encyclopedia* (New York, 1964), 6:51–52; *New York Times*, obituary, April 16, 1903; *Universal Jewish Encyclopedia; Who Was Who in America* (Chicago, 1912), 1:473.

                                                                              S.M.G.

GOTTSCHALK, ALFRED (1930–   ). Rabbi, academician. Alfred Gottschalk was born in Oberwesel, Germany, the son of Max and Erna Trum-Gerson (later Nussbaum, after her husband's death) Gottschalk. In 1939 his family fled Nazi Germany and settled in New York, where Gottschalk attended Boys High School in Brooklyn. He studied at Brooklyn College, receiving his B.A. in 1952. After graduation he entered HUC-JIR, receiving a B.H.L. from HUC-JIR, New York (1954) and an M.A.H.L. from HUC-JIR, Cincinnati (1956). He was ordained in Cincinnati in 1957.

Immediately after ordination, Gottschalk helped to direct the newly formed Los Angeles campus of HUC-JIR as acting dean (1958–1959) and then as dean (1959–1971). Concurrently he completed his Ph.D. at the University of California (1965), after which he was named Professor of Bible and Religious Thought at HUC-JIR. Gottschalk taught courses in the extension division and summer school at UCLA periodically between 1965 and 1971.

While in Los Angeles, Gottschalk was active in the Southern California Historical Society and other civic groups, including the Mayor's Community Development Advisors Committee, the Governor's Poverty Support Corps Program, and the Joint Committee on the Master Plan for Higher Education. He also was president of the Southern California Association of Liberal Rabbis.

In 1971 Gottschalk was named president of HUC-JIR and returned to Cincinnati. In honor of his work in community outreach, HUC-JIR established the Alfred Gottschalk chair in Jewish Communal Service in 1979.

While Gottschalk is known for his work on Ahad Ha-am, the principal figure in the early development of Cultural Zionism, his greatest contributions can be seen in the pioneering direction he has moved HUC-JIR both in the United States and in Israel since his inauguration as president. He ordained the first woman rabbi and opened up cantorial and rabbinical programs to women. He instituted a program at the Jerusalem campus to train and ordain Israeli students for careers as Reform rabbis. This made possible the first ordination of trained leaders for the Reform movement in Israel in 1980. Under Gottschalk's leadership, the modest beginnings of each campus of HUC-JIR have been expanded into impressive academic, cultural and educational centers. Gottschalk has introduced and encouraged a broad range of new development at HUC-JIR. He pioneered the creation of a School of Jewish Communal Service, which became the model for others throughout the country.

As a refugee from Nazi Germany, Gottschalk has been active in various Holocaust-related memorial committees and commissions. He was involved in the interdenominational Holocaust Council, which evolved into the U.S. Holocaust Memorial Council.

Among the numerous fellowships, degrees and awards he has won is a Smithsonian Research Grant in 1963. The University of Southern California awarded him an honorary doctorate in 1968 and an LL.D. in 1976. In 1971 the University of Judaism awarded him the honorary degree of D.Hu.L. He has received an honorary L.H.D. from Dropsie University (1974); an honorary L.L.D. from the University of Cincinnati (1976); and an honorary D.Rel.Ed. from Loyola Marymount University (1977). In 1977 Gottschalk was elected an Honorary Fellow of Hebrew University in Jerusalem. When he inaugurated Xavier University's first chair of interreligious ecumenical studies, the university awarded him an honorary L.S.D. degree. St. Thomas Institute bestowed an honorary Litt.D. on Gottschalk in 1982; New York University followed with an honorary D.D. in 1985.

Gottschalk was awarded a State Department Research Grant in 1963 and a Smithsonian Institute Grant in 1967. In 1967 and 1969 he was a Bertha Guggenheim Fellow, and in 1971 the American Jewish Committee bestowed on him its Human Relations Award. Twice he has received the Los Angeles City Council Award for Contributions to Education (1965 and 1971) and was named Alumnus of the Year by Brooklyn College in 1971. Among Gottschalk's other honors are the Tower of David Award for Cultural Contributions to Israel and America by the Israeli Government (1972); the Gold Medallion Award of the Jewish National Fund (1972); Man of the Year Award, West Coast Chapter, Boys High School Alumni Association (1976); Myrtle Wreath Award, Southern Pacific Coast Region of Hadassah (1977); Louis Dembitz Brandeis Award of the Zionist Organization of American (1977); and the National Brotherhood Award, National Conference of Christians and Jews, New York (1979). The Dr. Alfred Gottschalk Department of Judaica was established in his honor in 1979 at the Kfar Silver Youth and Education Center in Israel.

Gottschalk serves on the executive committee of the CCAR, the American Jewish Committee, the National Association of Temple Educators and the board of trustees of the UAHC. He is a vice president of the World Union for Progressive Judaism, honorary president of the board of the Southern California Historical Society and an honorary vice president of the New York Board of Rabbis.

Among Gottschalk's academic affiliations are memberships in the Interreligious Institute of Loyola University in California, the American Philosophical Society, the Israel Exploration Society, the World Union of Jewish Studies, and the board of trustees of the Albright Institute of Archaeological Research.

Gottschalk has published over 65 essays, articles, translations, addresses and books. The themes of these publications are primarily problems of education, ethics, values and aspects of Jewish and general intellectual history.

In 1952 Gottschalk married Jeannie Schrag; they had two children: Marc and Rachel. In 1977 he married Deanna Zeff Frank. She has two children: Andrew and Charles.

Writings (partial listing): "Israel and Reform Judaism: A Zionist Perspective," *Forum* 36 (Fall/winter 1979): 143–60; "Maimonides, Spinoza and Ahad Ha-am," *Judaism* 21, no. 3 (Summer 1972): 303–10; *On Jewish Learning* (Cincinnati, 1962); "A Passion for Social Justice," in *Kivie Kaplan: A Legend in His Own Time*, ed. Norman Feingold and William B. Silverman (New York, 1976); *Your Future as a Rabbi: A Calling That Counts* (New York, 1967; rev., 1989).

References: *American Jewish Biographies* (New York, 1982), pp. 144–45; "Man in the News," *New York Times*, June 14, 1971; "Scrapbook," "Nearprint Biography File and Box," American Jewish Archives.

GROLLMAN, EARL A. (1925–   ). Rabbi, lecturer. Born in Baltimore, Maryland, on July 4, 1925, the son of Gerson Simon and Dorah Edith Steinbach Grollman, Earl Grollman attended the University of Maryland and the University of Cincinnati, where he received a B.A. in 1945. He was ordained with an M.H.L. at HUC-JIR (1950). He has done graduate work at the Boston University School of Theology and its School of Legal Medicine. On ordination he became assistant rabbi of Temple Israel in Boston. He served for a year, leaving in 1951 to assume the pulpit of Beth El Temple Center in Belmont, Massachusetts. He served there until his retirement in 1987.

A pioneer in the field of Jewish pastoral counseling, crisis intervention and thanatology, Grollman has been active in many organizations: president, Massachusetts Board of Rabbis; chairman, United Rabbinic Chaplaincy Commission; member, Governor's Council on Action for Mental Health; member, Massachusetts Committee on Services for the Aged; chairman, Massachusetts Ecumenical Council on Health and Morality; member, Bereavement Team, Harvard University, Community School of Psychiatry; member, Governors' Commission on Pornography; member, Massachusetts Advisory Council on Home and Family; member, editorial board, *Omega*, a "magazine devoted to death, dying and bereavement"; member, professional advisory board, Foundation of Thanatology, Columbia-Presbyterian Medical Center, New York; chairman, Committee on Judaism and Health, Central Conference of American Rabbis.

Grollman is the author of many books, including *Talking about Death*, which received the Trends Citation by UNESCO at the International Children's and Youth Book Exhibition in Munich, Germany. He has contributed to many publications and speaks about his work at universities and seminaries throughout the country. He also has appeared on television and radio.

In 1979 *Boston Magazine* voted him one of the 79 most exciting people in New England. He was awarded an honorary D.D. from Portia Law School (1964) in recognition of his outstanding spiritual leadership and an honorary D.D. from HUC-JIR in 1975.

In 1949 he married Netta D. Levinson; they have three children: David, Sharon and Jonathan.

Writings (partial listing): *Concerning Death*, ed. Earl A. Grollman (Boston, 1974); *Explaining Death to Children* (Boston, 1967); *Judaism in Sigmund Freud's World* (New York, 1966); *Rabbinical Counseling* (New York, 1967); *Talking about Death* (Boston, 1976); *Talking about Divorce* (Boston, 1975).

References: "Nearprint Biographies File," American Jewish Archives; *Who's Who in American Jewry* (Los Angeles, 1980), p. 197.

GUTHEIM, JAMES KOPPEL (1817–1886). Rabbi. James Gutheim was born in Westphalia, Germany, in 1817. While chiefly self-educated, he was trained at the Teacher's Institute in Münster. Gutheim immigrated to the United States in 1843 and engaged in business until he succeeded Isaac Mayer Wise as rabbi of K.K. Bene Jeshurun in Cincinnati, Ohio, in 1846. He went on to serve Shaare Chesed Congregation in New Orleans (1850–1853) and then Nefutzoth Yehudah, also in New Orleans (1853–1863). From 1863 to 1865, he served Kahl Congregation in Montgomery, Alabama, and B'nai Israel Congregation in Columbus, Georgia, having closed the doors to his synagogue in New Orleans once New Orleans was captured by the Union. He was a Confederate patriot who would not take the oath of allegiance to the United States and was forced to leave New Orleans. He did return to New Orleans in 1865, but he left in 1868 to serve Temple Emanu-El of New York City. He returned to New Orleans once again in 1872 to head the newly formed Temple Sinai. He remained there until his death.

Gutheim insisted that women should not be denied a Jewish education. Since he was one of the few rabbis who preached in English, he quickly became a popular southern orator. A firm believer that politics did not belong in the pulpit, he avoided such issues even when Lincoln was elected president and the southern states seceded from the Union.

Gutheim was first vice president of the Touro Infirmary, president of the Hebrew Benevolent Association and president of the New Orleans Board of Education. Gutheim was close to Isaac Mayer Wise and worked with him in the establishment of the Union of American Hebrew Congregations and Hebrew Union College.

Many of Gutheim's sermons were published in the *Jewish Times*. He also wrote most of the hymns included in Leo Merzbacher's prayer book.

James Gutheim married Emilie Jones on December 15, 1858. Gutheim died in New Orleans on June 11, 1886.

Writings: trans., *History of the Jews*, by Heinrich Graetz, vol. 4 (New York, 1873); *Temple Pulpit* (New York, 1872).

References: *Encyclopaedia Judaica* (Jerusalem, 1974), 7:568; Saul Teplitz, "The Rabbi for Whom Louisiana Sat Shivah," *Jewish Digest* (June 1961), pp. 49–50; *Universal Jewish Encyclopedia* (New York, 1941), 5:134.

H

HARBY, ISAAC (1788–1828). Journalist, drama critic, playwright, educator, religious reformer. The son of Solomon and Rebecca Moses Harby, Isaac Harby was born in Charleston, South Carolina, on November 9, 1788. He received his education at a private academy, where he excelled in the study of Greek, Latin and French literatures. He entered Charleston College in 1805 but soon left to apprentice in the law office of Langdon Cheves. Legal work did not sustain his interest, and he left the practice of law to open a private academy. This school, known as Harby's Academy, was a secular institution with a large Jewish enrollment. It would ultimately become his most reliable source of income; although Harby made many attempts to support himself and his family of six children through more literary occupations, he always relied on his academy to make a living.

Harby was one of the 47 Israelites of Charleston who petitioned the board of Congregation Beth Elohim in 1824 to institute some liturgical change. When this petition was rejected, Harby and others established the Reformed Society of Israelites in 1825—the first organized expression of Jewish religious reform in North America. Harby soon became the society's most prominent intellectual, and his widely circulated discourse, delivered before the society on November 21, 1825, remains a compelling statement of the group's goals and aspirations. Along with David N. Carvalho and Abraham Moise, Harby compiled the society's prayer book. He served as the group's president in 1827.

Hoping to advance his literary fortune, Harby moved to New York City in mid-1828, where he regularly contributed to the *New York Evening Post* and the *New York Mirror*, a leading literary journal.

Harby married Rachael Mordecai in 1810; they had six children: Solomon, Julian, Samuel, Horace, Armida and Octavia. Isaac Harby died in New York on December 14, 1828.

Writings: *The Sabbath Service and Miscellaneous Prayers of the Reformed Society of Israelites* (1825; Columbia, SC, 1974); *A Selection from the Miscellaneous Writings of the Late Isaac Harby*, ed. Abraham Moise and Henry L. Pinckney (Charleston, SC, 1829); correspondence in *The Jews of the United States*, ed. Joseph Blau and Salo W. Baron (New York, 1964), and in *AJA* 8 (1955): 68–72.

References: James L. Apple, *A Criticism and Critique of Isaac Harby's Plays and Essays* (Rabbinic thesis, Hebrew Union College–Jewish Institute of Religion, Cincinnati, 1965); Barnett A. Elzas, *The Jews of South Carolina* (Philadelphia, 1905); N. Bryllion Fagin, "Isaac Harby and the Early American Theatre," *American Jewish Archives* 8 (1956): 3–13; Max J. Kohler, "Isaac Harby: Jewish Religious Leader and Man of Letters," *Publications of the American Jewish Historical Society* 23 (1931): 35–53; L. C. Moise, *Biography of Isaac Harby* (Macon, GA, 1931); "Nearprint Biography File," American Jewish Archives; Lance J. Sussman, "Isaac Harby, Leadership, and the Liturgy of the Reformed Society of Israelites" (Term paper, Hebrew Union College–Jewish Institute of Religion, Cincinnati, 1979).

G.P.Z.

HARRIS, MAURICE HENRY (1859–1930). Rabbi. Son of Rachel Lewis and Rev. Henry Lionell Harris, Maurice Harris was born in London on November 9, 1859, and received his early education there.

After immigrating to the United States at the age of 19, Harris entered the business world, first as stenographer, then as secretary to the head of an early pioneer in telegraph promotion. Harris studied at Columbia University (A.B., 1887; A.M., 1888; Ph.D. 1889) and Temple Emanu-El Theological Seminary in New York (ordained, 1884). In 1883, he was a student preacher at Hand-in-Hand Congregation (later called Temple Israel) of Harlem, New York, and became its rabbi in 1887.

Harris was a pioneer in social service. Well-known among his peers as an eloquent preacher and author of popular books for children, Harris, as founder and president of the Federation Settlement and the Jewish Protectory, was involved in the settling and absorption of Russian immigrants. He was also active as a founder of the Jewish Board of Guardians and the New York Society for the Prevention of Crime. Harris served as president of the Association of Reform Rabbis of New York.

Harris married Kitty Green in London on August 14, 1888. They had three children: Adriel, Naomi Wolfson and Ruth. He died in New York on June 23, 1930.

Writings: *Judaism for the Jew* (New York, 1925); *Modern Jewish History* (New York, 1922); *The People of the Book*, 3 vols. (New York, 1895–1897); *Selected Addresses*, 3 vols. (New York, 1895).

References: "Box No. 1444," "Nearprint Box," American Jewish Archives; *Jewish Encyclopedia* (New York, 1964), 6:239; *New York Times*, obituary, June 24, 1930, p. 25; *Who's Who in American Jewry* (New York, 1928), p. 280; *Who Was Who in America* (New York, 1943), 1:525.

HARRISON, LEON (1866–1928). Rabbi. Harrison was born on August 13, 1866, the son of Gustave and Louisa (Nelson), in Liverpool, England. He came to the United States as a child and attended public schools where (he later claimed) he ranked first at high school graduation of all of New York City in 1880. He entered College of the City of New York, then studied at Columbia University, where he received his A.B. (in the first Honors Class) in 1886. He also attended Emanu-El Theological Seminary (a short-lived seminary established by Congregation Emanu-El in New York City), where he was ordained in 1886 by Kaufmann Kohler and Gustav Gottheil; after ordination, he studied philosophy at Columbia University for several years while serving Temple Israel in Brooklyn (1886–1891). Then he went to St. Louis to serve Temple Israel, from 1891 until his death.

In St. Louis, he introduced Sunday services, which were well attended by Jews and Gentiles alike. He eventually abandoned these services in favor of late Friday services. Harrison was often invited to represent the Jewish people at large gatherings. He offered the eulogy at the funeral of Henry Ward Beecher in Brooklyn in 1887 and delivered a memorial address on behalf of President McKinley in the St. Louis Coliseum, as well as offering the Thanksgiving oratory at Festival Hall for the St. Louis Exposition in 1904.

As manifestations of his social concerns in St. Louis, he was vice president, Anti-Tuberculosis Society, and director, Tenement-house Improvement Association. Harrison founded the Sisterhood of Personal Service in St. Louis, as well as the Social Settlement League and Fresh Air Society there. Throughout the years he was also a Lyceum of Jewish Chautauqua Society Lecturer.

Harrison was coeditor, for the Department of Semitics, of the *Editor's Encyclopedia.*

Harrison died in New York City in 1928.

Writings: *The Religion of a Modern Liberal* (New York, 1931).

References: *American Jewish Year Book* 5 (1903): 62; *Universal Jewish Encyclopedia* (New York, 1943), 5:222–23; *Who's Who in American Jewry* (New York, 1928), p. 281.

HELLER, JAMES G. (1892–1971). Rabbi, Zionist leader, musician-composer. Born in New Orleans, Louisiana, the son of Rabbi Maximilian and Ida Marks Heller, James Heller received his A.B. from Tulane University in 1912. He continued his studies at the University of Cincinnati (M.A., 1914) and at Hebrew Union College, where he was ordained in 1916. His rabbinic career included service to Congregation Keneseth Israel, Philadelphia (assistant rabbi, 1916–1919), Bene Israel Temple, Little Rock, Arkansas (1919–1920) and the Isaac M. Wise Temple, Cincinnati (1920–1952).

Heller was a forceful national voice for Zionism, specifically within the Reform movement, throughout his lifetime. He urged change in the anti-Zionist position of most Reform Jews of the day. Like his father, Heller demonstrated that American Jewish support of Zionism was not incompatible with American loyalty and patriotism. By the latter years of his career, Heller's perspective on Zionism came to be the guiding principles of Reform Judaism. Heller's commitment to his ideas earned the respect of many, and he became a Jewish leader of national stature. As such, he was chosen by President Truman to serve with a select group of clergy touring Europe to report on the status of post–World War II refugees. Other national positions of leadership included his service as president of the Labor Zionist Organization of America, as chairman (1945) of the national United Jewish Appeal and as a leader in the establishment of Bonds for Israel. In the Reform movement he served as president of the Central Conference of American Rabbis (1941–1943), as a member of the executive committee of the Union of American Hebrew Congregations and as a member of the board of governors of Hebrew Union College. After retiring as rabbi of Wise Temple in 1952, Heller became the executive director of the Development Corporation for Israel.

Heller wrote a history of the Wise Temple and a biography of Wise himself. In addition, many of his sermons and addresses were printed in pamphlet form. Heller was an outstanding orator who spoke throughout the country, particularly on behalf of Zionism.

Besides his energetic Zionist and rabbinic leadership activities, Heller was a talented musician and composer. Until his death he maintained a passionate involvement in music. In 1935 Heller was appointed professor of musicology at the Cincinnati Conservatory of Music, from which he held the degree of Mus.D. He composed numerous works for many different instrumental and vocal ensembles, including four solo services for Shabbat worship. In 1929 he received a prize from the Society for Publication of American Music for his string quartet "Aquatints."

Heller married Jean H. Bettmann on August 15, 1917; they had three daughters: Cecile, Claire and Joan. After Jean's death, Heller married Helen R. Bettman on December 5, 1952. James Heller died in Cincinnati on December 17, 1971.

Writings: *As Yesterday When It Is Past: A History of the Isaac M. Wise Temple K.K. B'nai Yeshurun, 1842–1942* (Cincinnati, 1942); *Isaac M. Wise: His Life, Work and Thought* (Cincinnati, 1965).

Compositions: Among many compositions, including the four solo services for Shabbat worship and "Aquatints," Heller composed an elegy and pastorale for voice and string quartet and an oratorio, based on Psalms, titled "Watchman, What of the Night."

References: "Nearprint Biography File," "Nearprint Biography Box," American Jewish Archives.

                                                                        L.H.K.

HELLER, MAXIMILIAN (1860–1929). Rabbi, Zionist leader. The third child and only son among Simon and Mathilde Kassowitz Heller's five children, Maximilian Heller was born in Prague, Bohemia, on January 31, 1860. He resided in the heart of that city's Jewish ghetto until he was 19, although he was afforded the opportunity to study at the Prague Gymnasium. Heller came to the United States in 1879 to join his parents, who had immigrated two years earlier.

In 1884 he received rabbinical ordination from Hebrew Union College in Cincinnati, a member of that institution's second ordination class.

From 1884 to 1886, Heller served as assistant rabbi for Rabbi Bernhard Felsenthal at Chicago's Zion Congregation. Felsenthal, a reformer and later a Zionist, probably influenced the evolution of Heller's own ideology. After leaving Chicago, Heller spent a year at the Reform Jewish Congregation of Houston, Texas. Having established a reputation as a powerful orator and a sharp intellect, Heller was elected rabbi of Temple Sinai in New Orleans, where he remained for the rest of his life.

Heller was a devoted disciple of Isaac Mayer Wise, the founder of Hebrew Union College. Perhaps it was out of respect for Wise, who had publicly denounced Zionism in 1897, that Heller openly declared himself a Zionist only after Wise's death in 1900. In 1907 Heller became vice president of both the Federation of American Zionists and the Central Conference of American Rabbis. Heller's Zionist sympathies nearly cost him the presidency of the conference, a position customarily assumed by the vice president on retirement of the president. In becoming president in 1910, Heller personified the possible reconciliation of two seemingly divergent ideologies: Reform Judaism and Zionism.

Heller believed that the essence of the conflict between Reform and Zionism was the issue of what each side called the "true" mission of Judaism. Classical Reform ideology advanced the notion that Israel's highest mission was to cooperate with the best forces of human civilization to bring about a world of peace and justice. Building on Felsenthal's philosophy, Heller concluded that Zionism was "almost the literal fulfillment of prophetic vision." He argued that Zionism and the mission of Israel as Reform conceived it were "one and inseparable." The promulgation of the Balfour Declaration in 1917 proved to be a turning point in this controversy, and in the last years of his life Heller witnessed an increasing affirmation of his ideology within the ranks of the Reform rabbinate.

In addition to his organizational activities in the Reform and Zionist movements, Heller published many articles, sermons and addresses. He edited the *Jewish Ledger* from 1896 to 1897 and wrote regularly for the *American Israelite* and the *Maccabaean*.

Heller married Ida Annie Marks on March 6, 1889; they had four children: James (who also became a Reform rabbi), Cecile, Isaac and Ruth. Maximilian Heller died in New Orleans on March 30, 1929.

Writings: Heller published extensively in the Anglo-Jewish press, including the *Jewish Ledger*, *American Israelite*, the *Maccabaean*, the *Times-Picayune* and *Times-Democrat* of New Orleans and in the Central Conference of American Rabbis *Yearbooks*. He also wrote *My Month in Palestine* (New York, 1929).

References: Central Conference of American Rabbis *Yearbook* 39 (1929): 223; *Dictionary of American Biography*; David Philipson, *My Life as an American Jew* (Cincinnati, 1941); Gary P. Zola, "Reform Judaism's Pioneer Zionist: Maximilian Heller," *American Jewish History* 73, no. 4 (June 1984): 375–97.

G.P.Z.

HERSCHER, URI D. (1941-   ). Rabbi, academician, administrator. Born to German immigrants, Joseph and Lucy Strauss Herscher, in Tel Aviv, British Mandatory Palestine, Uri Herscher was seven when the State of Israel was proclaimed. In 1954 the wish to be reunited with surviving relatives forced his parents to leave Tel Aviv for San Jose, California. Ten years later Herscher earned a B.A. in sociology at the University of California at Berkeley. While a Berkeley undergraduate, he helped establish and then directed a camp for underprivileged children from the San Francisco Bay area. Herscher was ordained at HUC-JIR, Cincinnati, in 1970. While at HUC-JIR he received the Samuel Kaminker Memorial Award in Youth Work for his efforts on behalf of Jewish students in the Los Angeles area. After ordination, Herscher served a two-year term as national director of admissions for HUC-JIR and for three years was assistant to its president. In 1973 he earned a D.H.L. from HUC-JIR. His dissertation research laid the foundation for his later publications in immigration history.

Herscher was named professor of American Jewish history on the Cincinnati campus. In 1975 he was named executive vice president and moved his office to Los Angeles in 1979. In Los Angeles he has been active in Jewish community life and on the boards of agencies such as the Los Angeles Jewish Federation Council and the American Jewish Committee. His ongoing identification with Zionism has expressed itself in support for the Association of Reform Zionists of America from the date of its founding.

Herscher spearheaded HUC-JIR's effort to create in Los Angeles a new institution of nationwide scope, the HUC Skirball Cultural Center, whose purpose is to reinforce Jewish consciousness and serve the interests of American and American-Jewish pluralism. The cultural center, to be completed in the 1990s, will highlight the American-Jewish experience for a larger Jewish and general public.

Herscher married Eleanor Grant in 1969; they have two sons: Joshua and Gideon. In 1990, he married Myna Meshul Coleite, mother of Adam and Aron Coleite.

Writings (partial listing): *A Century of Memories, 1882–1982: The East European Jewish Experience in America* (Cincinnati, 1983); *Jewish Agricultural Utopias in America* (Detroit, 1981); coeditor and cotranslator, *On Jews, America and Immigration* (Cincinnati, 1980); coauthor, *Queen City Refuge: An Oral History of Cincinnati by Jewish Refugees from Nazi Germany* (Cincinnati, 1989).

References: "Nearprint Biography Box," American Jewish Archives; *Who's Who in American Jewry* (Los Angeles, 1980), p. 215; *Who's Who in World Jewry* (New York, 1981), p. 346.

                                                                                 S.F.C.

HIRSCH, EMIL G. (1851–1923). Born in Luxembourg on May 22, 1851, Emil G. Hirsch was the son of Louise Mickolls Hirsch and Rabbi Samuel Hirsch (who was chief rabbi of the Grand Duchess of Luxembourg). When his father left Luxembourg in 1866 to serve Keneseth Israel in Philadelphia, Emil Hirsch immigrated with his parents to the United States. Initially taught by his father, Hirsch continued his education at the Episcopal Academy of Philadelphia. After his graduation from the University of Pennsylvania in 1872, where he played on the football team, he studied at the Universities of Berlin (1872–1876) and Leipzig (Ph.D., 1876) as well as the Hochschule für die Wissenschaft des Judenthums in Berlin, where he was influenced by Abraham Geiger, Hermann Steinthal and Moritz Lazarus.

On his return to the United States, he preached a short time at Keneseth Israel. Then Hirsch served Har Sinai Congregation in Baltimore (1877) and Adath Israel (1878–1880) in Louisville before coming to Chicago Sinai Congregation, where he began serving in 1880. After a speaking engagement in New York, he was invited to lead Congregation Emanu-El in New York City, a position he accepted. However, after protest from his synagogue in Chicago, he asked to be released from his contract with Emanu-El and remained at Chicago Sinai until his death.

Hirsch was a spokesperson for the radical wing of Reform Judaism in the United States. Nevertheless, he was critical of ideologues like Felix Adler and his philosophy of Ethical Culture. Through eloquent prose and satirical wit, he expressed his belief in an evolutionary concept of Judaism, one that was nurtured by German idealist philosophy. Hirsch contended that halakah must yield to ethical ideas. The primary mission of the emancipated Jew, said Hirsch, was a commitment to social justice. Throughout his rabbinate and particularly in Chicago, he challenged organized labor and supported welfare reforms. In an age of industrial unrest, Hirsch was particularly successful in lightening the load of the working class by pressure for the passage of laws protecting women and in the area of worker's compensation. He also worked for prison reform and improvements in public education. In 1874, Hirsch introduced Sunday services at Chicago Sinai.

While in Chicago, he helped to found the University of Chicago and served as a professor of rabbinic literature and philosophy. He was the editor of the Bible section of the *Jewish Encyclopedia* (1905) and contributed numerous articles to the Hastings *Encyclopedia of Religion and Ethics*. From 1888 to 1893, he coedited *Zeitgeist*; he was coeditor and writer for the *Jewish Reformer* (1886–1892); and he founded the *Reform Advocate* (1891–1923), a weekly Anglo-Jewish newspaper that served as a vehicle for the public articulation of his ideas.

Hirsch was instrumental in the founding of the Manual Training School in Chicago (1888), Associated Jewish Charities of Chicago, (with Hannah G. Solomon) National Council of Jewish Women (1853), and Chicago Sinai Temple Sisterhood (1935). Hirsch also served as a member of the Hebrew Union College Board of Governors and the Illinois State Board of Charities in 1901 and was acting president of the Congress of Liberal Religions. He served as president of the Chicago Public Library (1888–1897). In 1896, he was presidential elector at large for the State of Illinois. In 1902, Hirsch was the Percy Trumbull Lecturer at Johns Hopkins University.

In honor of his seventieth birthday, Stephen S. Wise invited him to serve as honorary president of the Jewish Institute of Religion. This afforded him the opportunity to address rabbinical students in New York on numerous occasions. Hirsch received honorary degrees from Austin College (L.L.D., 1898), Western University of Pennsylvania (L.H.D., 1908), Hebrew Union College (D.D., 1901) and Temple University (D.L.L., 1908).

In 1878, Hirsch married Mathilda Einhorn, Rabbi David Einhorn's daughter. They had five children: David Einhorn, Dora, Beatrice Kirchheimer, Elsa Levi and Samuel. Hirsch died in Chicago on January 7, 1923.

Writings (partial listing): *The Crucifixion from a Jewish Standpoint* (New York, 1908); *Discourses* (Chicago, n.d.); *My Religion* (New York, 1925); ed., *David Einhorn Memorial Volume* (New York, 1911).

References (partial listing): *American Jewish Year Book* 27 (1930): 230–37; Central Conference of American Rabbis *Yearbook* 33 (1923): 145–54; *Encyclopaedia Judaica* (Jerusalem, 1971), 8:503–4; David Einhorn Hirsch, *Rabbi Emil G. Hirsch: The Reform Advocate* (Chicago, 1968); *Jewish Encyclopedia* (New York, 1905), 6:410–11; Bernard Martin, "The Religious Philosophy of Emil G. Hirsch," *American Jewish Archives* 4 (1952): 66–82; *Universal Jewish Encyclopedia* (New York, 1947), 5:373–75; *Who Was Who in America* (New York, 1942), 1: 569.

HIRSCH, RICHARD G. (1926–   ). Rabbi, civil rights activist. Richard Hirsch was born on September 13, 1926, in Cleveland, Ohio, the son of Abe and Bertha Gusman Hirsch. After his ordination from HUC-JIR in 1951, Hirsch assumed the pulpit at Temple Emanuel in Chicago. While at Temple Emanuel (1951–1953) Hirsch was among the founders of the Young People's Division of the Jewish Federation of Chicago and the rabbinic advisor to the Chicago Federation of Temple Youth. In 1953 Hirsch became corabbi of Temple Emanuel in Denver, Colorado, serving also as director of Camp Schwayder (1953–1956).

In 1956 Hirsch moved back to Chicago to become director of the Chicago Federation and Great Lakes Council of the UAHC. While there, he initiated many pioneering activities, particularly in the area of interfaith relations, establishing and appearing as the Jewish representative on the first interreligious prime-time television program in the United States, "The Understanding Heart." He helped found the Metropolitan Conference on Religion and Race, the first interreligious social-action organization in the country.

Hirsch moved to Washington, D.C., in 1962 to become the founding director of the Religious Action Center of the UAHC. It was here that his outstanding organizational and oratorical skills first came to national attention. While in Washington, he coordinated and led the Reform movement's response to the civil rights challenges of the 1960s, testifying on numerous occasions before Senate and congressional committees on such issues as church-state, civil liberties, civil rights, migrant workers, poverty and foreign policy. He organized the first joint interreligious testimony (Protestant, Catholic and Jewish) before congressional committees.

The Religious Action Center became the national nerve center for black-Jewish cooperation in the fight for civil rights. Hirsch worked closely with Dr. Martin Luther King, Jr., being the first Jew to respond to Dr. King's call to demonstrate in Selma, Alabama, and organizing Jewish participation in the march on Washington in August 1963.

During his 11 years in Washington, Hirsch was involved in a wide range of Jewish social-action concerns. He was elected secretary of the Citizen's Crusade Against Poverty, was a member of the executive committee of the Leadership Conference on Civil Rights and of the Religion and Labor Council, sat on the organizing committee of the National Conference on Soviet Jewry and was its representative in Washington, represented the Synagogue Council of America and served on the boards of the Jewish Community Council and the Jewish Community Center of Greater Washington.

In 1973 Hirsch initiated and implemented the transfer of the international headquarters of the World Union for Progressive Judaism (WUPJ) from New York to Jerusalem, becoming its executive director. A committed Zionist throughout his life, Hirsch now devoted himself to improving conditions for Reform Judaism in Israel. Under his dynamic leadership and through the force of his personality, the Reform movement took great strides toward becoming a full participant in Israeli society.

In 1974 Hirsch initiated the affiliation of the WUPJ with the World Zionist Organization (formal affiliation, 1976). He helped establish Kubbutz Yahel, the first Reform kibbutz, in 1976 and later Kibbutz Lotan. At the invitation of the prime minister, he served on the Horev Commission, which investigated immigration and absorption in Israel. He initiated and planned the establishment of the World Education Center for Progressive Judaism in Jerusalem, including Beit Shmuel, and founded Hemdat, the Council for Freedom of Science, Religion and Culture in Israel. Hirsch was actively involved in the leadership of movements on behalf of Soviet Jewry, including the establishment of the International Committee on Soviet Jewry and Progressive Judaism.

Since 1972 Hirsch has sat on the executive board of the World Zionist Organization and has been a member of the Board of Governors of the Jewish Agency for Israel. He has been active in numerous Jewish Agency projects, including serving as cochairman of the Jewish Agency Board of Governors Committee on Immigration and Absorption and cochairman of the Committee on the Israel Experience. In 1988 Hirsch was elected chairman of the Zionist General Council (Hava'ad Hapoel Hazioni).

Richard Hirsch married Bella Rosencweig on September 5, 1954; they have four children: Ora Pescovitz and Raphael, Ammiel and Emmet Hirsch.

Writings: *Judaism and Cities in Crisis* (New York, 1961); *There Shall Be No Poor* . . . (New York, 1965); *Thy Most Precious Gift* (New York, 1974); *The Way of the Upright* (New York, 1973).

References: "Nearprint Biography File," American Jewish Archives.

A.H.

HIRSCH, SAMUEL (1815–1889). Rabbi, religious philosopher. The son of Shlomo ben Shmuel and Tzorreleh bat Ya'ackov Hirsch, Samuel Hirsch was born in Thalfang near Trier, Germany, on June 8, 1815. He went to heder from the time he was three and after bar mitzvah studied at the yeshiva in Metz and the Mainz Gymnasium. Hirsch received university training in Bonn from 1835 to 1837, where he was influenced by the Protestant theologian and historian of religion Karl Immanuel Nitzsche. In Berlin he studied from 1837 to 1838 under the Hegelian scholar Karl Ludwig Michelet. Hirsch received a doctorate from the University of Leipzig in 1842. Samuel Holdheim ordained him in 1840, by which time he was already officiating as a rabbi in Dessau.

In Dessau, Hirsch published various sermons, including the confirmation address he gave in 1838. He worked actively to strengthen the Duke Leopold Friedrich Franz School for Jewish Children and published *The Messianic Doctrine of the Jews* as the ideological basis for instruction. His public opposition to *Schutzjude* status (protected Jew), however, led to his dismissal. In 1843 he moved to Luxembourg to assume the post of chief rabbi. During Hirsch's 22 years in this post, he attacked Bruno Bauer's arguments against Judaism in modern times, campaigned against the *more judaico* required of Jewish army recruits and published *Humanity as Religion*, lectures about religious principles common to Judaism and Christianity. Hirsch also expressed opposition to Zionist ideas and, along with Samuel Holdheim, proposed a Sunday Sabbath.

In 1866 he moved to the United States, where he succeeded David Einhorn at Philadelphia's Keneseth Israel. He remained there through 1888. He was an outspoken participant at Reform rabbinical conferences and a frequent contributor to German and French liberal Jewish periodicals.

The underlying motif of Hirsch's religious philosophy, especially as revealed in *The Religious Philosophy of the Jews* (1841), was his belief in Judaism's "absolute" status in the history of religion. He thereby hoped to mitigate any effort that sought to justify discrimination against Jews in modern society based on a hostile intellectual evaluation of Jewish religious ideology. Toward this end he probed the history of religion according to Hegel. Hirsch demonstrated how the biblical and rabbinic literature of Judaism was compatible with the German Idealist values of spirituality, freedom and morality. According to Hirsch, Abraham was the paradigm of these ideals, and ultimately all humankind would emulate him. Within its own history, Israel developed from a "child" leaving Egypt instilled with spirituality into an "adult" strengthened by Torah to withstand the sufferings consequent to its mission to spiritualize humanity. Christianity extended the essence of Israel's inner life with God to the rest of humankind. Ultimately all religions, including Christianity, would contribute positively to the expanding moral spirituality of Judaism and thereby share in the "absolute" religiosity of the messianic kingdom.

Hirsch's efforts to conceptualize Judaism's absolute role in human history became a process of redefining Judaism in terms of contemporary thought and experience by continually readdressing the central themes of Jewish philosophy:

the experience of the divine, the nature of history, the relation of God to human social and political entities, the status of Scripture and the role of cultic regulations and rituals. The stages of this process parallel Hirsch's movements from Dessau to Luxembourg to America.

Hirsch's views in Dessau highlighted absolute, ahistorical perspectives on Judaism, emphasizing, for example, the revealed and transcendental dimension of knowing God. Hirsch viewed this present and transcendent God as immanent in history, defining history itself as a joint product of divine-ontological and human-psychological processes. As an example of this notion of God's role in the world, Hirsch conceived of a possible state in which God would be present in the monarch. This in turn would compel unconditional human trust in the state. Scripture and rabbinical writings were viewed as having a superhuman, heteronomous nature, qualitatively different from human products; by implication, Hirsch embraced cultic regulations on the grounds that Scripture commanded them and the sages developed them.

Hirsch's thought in Luxembourg began to blend emphases on the historical and the transcendent, viewing, for instance, human reason and divine revelation as having a common root. Hirsch now conceived of history not as a coproduct of the divine and human but as having a measure of its own independent power. He began to see Scripture as a drama played out between God and humanity on the stage of history. Likewise, the state was conceived of as a focus of the unfolding of the divine human drama through time. At this time his concern with cultic rituals lay in their historical role in Israel's survival.

Hirsch extended the gradual emphasis on the historical and human-psychological aspects of Jewish philosophy when he moved to America. He dwelt more on human comprehension than divine revelation and insisted that Scripture was a product of the human mind. Hirsch felt the view of history should be revised from the pragmatic perspective of the experience of the contemporary Jew. From this perspective he saw the state as an instrument in which God is present for the purpose of developing morality. Similarly, he saw it as the individual's responsibility to decide in the context of contemporary experience whether cultic symbols and actions evoked consciousness of God and adequately expressed religious thoughts.

Hirsch married Louise Mickolls; they had one son, Emil, who became a prominent Reform rabbi. Samuel Hirsch died in Chicago on May 14, 1889.

Writings: *Humanity as Religion* (Trier, 1854); *Judaism, the Christian State and the Modern Critics: Letters to Shed Light on Bruno Bauer's Jewish Question* (Leipzig, 1843); *The Messianic Doctrine of the Jews* (Leipzig, 1843); *Peace, Freedom and Unity* (Dessau, 1839); *The Reform in Judaism and Its Calling in the Contemporary World* (Leipzig, 1844); *The Religious Philosophy of the Jews, or the Principle of the Jewish Religious Perception and its Relation to Paganism, Christianity and to Absolute Philosophy* (Leipzig, 1841).

References: Gershon Greenberg, "The Historical Origins of God and Man: Samuel Hirsch's Luxembourg Writings," *Leo Baeck Institute Yearbook* 20 (1975); idem, "Religion and History According to Samuel Hirsch," *Hebrew Union College Annual* 43 (1972): 103–4; idem, "Samuel Hirsch's American Judaism," *American Jewish Historical Quarterly* 42, no. 4 (June 1973): 363–82; Maurice Lefkowitz, "Samuel Hirsch," Central Conference of American Rabbis *Yearbook* 25 (1915), includes a list of books and articles by Hirsch and an article on Hirsch; "Nearprint Biographies," American Jewish Archives.

G.G.

HOLLENDER, SAMUEL S. (1900–1984). Optometrist, businessman. Hollender was born on December 8, 1900, the son of Joseph and Mary Koss Hollender. After growing up in Chicago, he attended Lewis Institute (Illinois Institute of Technology); Northwestern University of Accounting; John Marshall Law School, Chicago; and Northern Illinois College of Ophthalmology and Otology (D.D., 1923). He received an honorary D.H.L. from Hebrew Union College–Jewish Institute of Religion in 1956.

As a lay person, he served his local community, as well as the national community, and provided resources for program development and implementation. As chairman of the Union of American Hebrew Congregations, he oversaw growth from 300 to 500 congregations, representing more than one million people.

Hollender was chairman of the board of Almer Coe Optical Co. (from 1955) and general merchandise manager at The Fair, Chicago (1930–1932). He was also organizer and president of S.S. Hollender, Inc., since 1933, and general manager and partner of Merryweather Optical Co. with offices in Chicago and New York. Active in community life, he was a member of the Board of Directors, Mt. Sinai Hospital (1934–1939); Board of Governors, Opera Co., since 1935; Board of Directors, Jewish Charities (now Jewish Federation) since 1941, treasurer (1947–1950), vice president (1950), president (1955, 1958), all of Chicago; member, Board of Directors, Jewish Vocational Service and Employment Center (1938–1940); Executive Board, UAHC, since 1944, vice chairman (1946–1950), chairman (1951–1953), honorary chairman (since 1953), president, 42nd biennial assembly (1953); Board of Governors, Hebrew Union College, Cincinnati (1941); chairman, War Records Committee, JWB, Chicago, and National Armed Forces Committee (both 1944–1946); board, United Services Organizations Council of Chicago (1945–1946); American Jewish Committee; Board of Directors, United Jewish Building Fund (since 1946); Board of Directors, JDC (since 1947); Board of Trustees, Hebrew Union School of Education and Sacred Music (1950); National Board of Directors, Chicago Medical School (1950); board, World Union for Progressive Judaism (1951); president, Community Council: Jewish Charities (1939); Emanuel Congregation (1930–1945), life member, board of directors; Federation of Reform Synagogues, now Federation of UAHC (1944, 1945, all of Chicago); national chairman, combined campaign, UAHC-HUC-JIR (1948–1953); general chairman, Chicago Combined Jewish Appeal (1951), president (1952); Jewish Braille Institute, executive board member; member, Masons; member, B'nai B'rith; honorary member, Zeta Beta Tau; life member, Art Institute of Chicago.

In 1948, he received an award of merit from the Chicago Federation of Reform Synagogues. In 1955, he received the Man of the Year Award by the UAHC. In 1964, he was the recipient of the Julius Rosenwald Memorial Award presented by the Jewish Federation in Chicago. In 1967, he was named to the Golden Age of Fame Jewish Community Center of Chicago. In 1980, he was the honoree of 1,000 trees planted in the Leo Baeck Forest, Lahav, Israel.

In 1922, Hollender married Sylvia V. Jacobson. They had two children: Elaine Kaplan and Caryl Susman. He died in Chicago on October 16, 1984.

References: *Who Was Who in America* (Chicago, 1985), 8: 192–203.

I

IDELSOHN, ABRAHAM ZEVI (1882–1938). Ethnomusicologist, cantor, linguist, liturgist. Born in Felixberg, Russia, on July 1, 1882, the son of the local *shochet* and *baal tefilah* Azriel and Deborah Hirschfeld Idelsohn, Abraham Idelsohn received a traditional *yeshiva* education. He studied *chazanut* with Abraham Mordecai Rabinowitz in Libau, Latvia, and briefly with Eduard Birnbaum in Koenigsberg. In early 1901 he attended the Stern Conservatory in Berlin, transferring to the Leipzig Conservatory later in the year, where he also served as cantor. Idelsohn worked as hazzan in Regensburg from 1903 to 1905 and then in Johannesburg until 1907.

From 1907 to 1921, Idelsohn lived in Jerusalem, where he was a teacher, hazzan, choir director, composer and private music instructor. Among his pupils were Moshe Nathanson, Shlomo Zalman Rivlin and Yehoshua L. Ne'eman. In 1910 he and Rivlin founded the short-lived Institute of Jewish Music. However, Idelsohn's driving passion was the study of the unique musical traditions of the many Jewish and non-Jewish ethnic communities in the city.

Idelsohn's work came to the attention of the Academies of Science of Berlin and Vienna. They assisted him financially in making over 1,000 recordings on cylinders and disks. Subsequently he was invited to Vienna in the winter of 1913–1914 to present his preliminary findings, gaining recognition from such musicologists as Guido Adler and E. M. von Hornbostel. In 1914 Idelsohn published the first volume of his monumental ten-volume *Thesaurus of Hebrew-Oriental Melodies*. Subsequent volumes on other Oriental and Sephardic communities were also products of recordings, transcriptions and analyses made during his Jerusalem period.

Financial difficulties, poor health, and the lack of academic opportunities prompted Idelsohn to leave the *yishuv* in 1921. After a year in Berlin, he traveled to the United States in 1922, where he gave a year-long lecture tour. He was asked by the Hebrew Union College in Cincinnati to catalog the Eduard Birnbaum collection of Jewish Music. In 1924 he was appointed Professor of Liturgy and Jewish Music. The Birnbaum archives facilitated research for the later volumes of the *Thesaurus* (on German, Eastern European and Hasidic Jewish music). Idelsohn's *Jewish Music in Its Historical Development* (1929) became and has remained a classic in the field.

In the view of many Jewish music scholars, Idelsohn was the most significant figure in Jewish musicology and a leading pioneer in ethnomusicology. He treated oral tradition, especially that of Oriental Jewish communities, with the same respect as written musical sources. This enabled him to find musical elements common to all Jewish communities. Idelsohn's demonstration of similarities between Yemenite Jewish chant and Gregorian chant provided new perspectives on the development of music in the Christian church. Idelsohn's range of interests and achievements was impressive. He was involved not only in musicology and ethnomusicology but also in liturgy, folklore and linguistics and composed Jewish music, including several synagogue services, an opera and popular songs.

Idelsohn married Zilda Schneider on October 2, 1902. Abraham Idelsohn died in Johannesburg in 1938.

Writings: *Jewish Liturgy and Development* (New York, 1932); *Jewish Music in Its Historical Development* (New York, 1929); "Die Maqaman der arabischen Musik," *Sammelbände der Internationale Musikgesellschaft* 15 (1913): 1–63; "Parallelen zwischen gregorianischen and hebräisch-orientalischen Gesangweisen," *Zeitschrift für Musikwissenschaft* 4 (1922): 515–24; "Song and Singers of the Synagogue in the Eighteenth Century, with Special Reference to the Birnbaum Collection of the Hebrew Union College," *HUC Jubilee Volume* (1925), pp. 397–424; ed. *Thesaurus of Hebrew Oriental Melodies*, 10 vols. (Leipzig and Berlin, 1925–1932).

Compositions: *Jeptha* (Jerusalem, 1922); *The Jewish Song Book* (Cincinnati, 1928); *Shirei Tefilah L'shats U'makheilah* (Jerusalem-Berlin, n.d.).

References: Baruch J. Cohon and Israel J. Katz, "Idelsohn," *Encyclopaedia Judaica* (Jerusalem, 1971), 8:1125–26; Edith Gerson-Kiwi, "A. Z. Idelsohn: A Pioneer in Jewish Ethnomusicology," *Yuval* 5 (1986): 46–52; idem, "Idelsohn," *Die Musik in Geschichte und Gegenwart* 6 (1957), cols. 1038–40; idem, "Idelsohn," *New Grove Dictionary of Music and Musicians* 9 (1980): 18–19; Shlomo Hofman, "A. Z. Idelsohn's Music: A Bibliography," *Yuval* 5 (1986): 31–50 (Hebrew section); Eliyahu Schleifer, "Idelsohn's Scholarly Publications: An Annotated Bibliography," *Yuval* 5 (1986): 53–180; Moses C. Weiler and Theodore S. Ross, "Abraham Zevi Idelsohn," *Hebrew Union College Monthly* 20, no. 2 (December 1932): 9–10; Moses C. Weiler, "Remembering Abraham Zevi Idelsohn," *Jewish Affairs* 37, no. 8 (August 1982): 28–30.

                                                                                    G.C.G.

ISRAEL, EDWARD LEOPOLD (1896–1941). Rabbi, social activist, labor Zionist. The son of Charles and Emma Linz Israel, Edward Israel was born in Cincinnati, Ohio, on August 30, 1896. Educated at Harvard and the University of Cincinnati (A.B., 1917), Israel was ordained in 1919 at Hebrew Union College. In 1938 he was awarded an honorary LL.D. at Washington College (now University). From 1919 to 1920, he was rabbi at Temple B'rith Sholom in

Springfield, Illinois. He served as rabbi of Washington Avenue Temple (Adath B'nai Israel) Congregation in Evansville, Indiana, from 1920 to 1923. In 1923 he became senior rabbi of Har Sinai, Baltimore. He remained in that post until a few months before his death in 1941. He had been called to serve as executive director of the Union of American Hebrew Congregations, a position he was never able to fill.

Although reared in a classical Reform congregation, Israel was committed to the message of the prophets of Israel, social justice in America and the developing Jewish community of British Palestine. A confirmed Zionist, Israel was one of the leaders of the Histadrut movement. He served as an impartial arbitrator for the men's clothing industry and as chairman of the CCAR Social Action Commission. He was outspoken in denouncing the "yellow dog" contracts in American industry. A well-known liberal, Israel resigned in 1936 from the national executive board of the American League for Peace and Democracy and in 1940 from the Advisory Youth Congress, charging that both groups had fallen into communist hands. One of the first clergymen to use radio for the presentation of his lectures and sermons, Israel's words were frequently quoted by President Franklin D. Roosevelt.

At the beginning of the Nazi period, Israel joined Stephen S. Wise of New York in developing a plan to boycott firms selling German imports. He led a movement to demonstrate at the Port of Baltimore when the German battleship *Emden* docked there. Popular with all elements of the Jewish and the general community, Israel was president of the Synagogue Council of America at the time of his death. He considered his principal work to be creating unity of Jewish consciousness.

In 1919 Israel married Amelia Dryer of Cincinnati; they had two sons: Charles and Edward L. Israel, Jr. Edward Israel died in Cincinnati on October 19, 1941.

Writings (partial listing): *Aspects of Individual Relations* (Cincinnati, 1931), pp. 55–61; "The Occupations of Jews," Central Conference of American Rabbis *Yearbook* 36 (1926); *The Philosophy of Modern Mysticism* (Evansville, IN, 1922); "The Social Philosophy of Judaism," in *Aspects of Individual Relations* (Cincinnati, 1931); "The Synagog [*sic*] and the Forces of Antagonism," Central Conference of American Rabbis *Yearbook* 42 (1937): 276–308; "Zionism Reaffirmed," *Baltimore Evening News*, June 15, 1939.

References: *Baltimore Sun*, obituary, October 20, 1941; Edward Paul Cohn, "A Rabbi Named Israel: The Life and Works of Rabbi Edward L. Israel" (Rabbinic thesis), Hebrew Union College–Jewish Institute of Religion, Cincinnati, 1974); "Nearprint Biographies File," "Diaries, Box Nos. 1707–1709," American Jewish Archives; Albert Vorspan, *Giants of Justice* (New York, 1960), pp. 160–71; *Who Was Who in America* (Chicago, 1943), 1:621.

A.S.

ISSERMAN, FERDINAND M. (1898–1972). Rabbi. Ferdinand M. Isserman was born in Antwerp, Belgium, on March 4, 1898, the son of Alexander and Betty Brodheim Isserman. In 1906 his family migrated to the United States and settled in Newark, New Jersey, where he attended grade school and high school.

Isserman received his A.B. at the University of Cincinnati in 1919 (where he received a letter in basketball) and was ordained a rabbi at Hebrew Union College in Cincinnati in 1922. In 1924 he received an A.M. from the University of Pennsylvania. He also did graduate study at the University of Toronto (1926–1927) and at the University of Chicago (1928). In 1941 he received an honorary D.L. from Douglas University for his interracial work. Isserman received an honorary degree from Central College (Methodist) in Fayette, Missouri, in 1944 and an honorary D.H.L. from HUC-JIR, Cincinnati, in 1950.

On his ordination, Isserman became assistant rabbi of Rodeph Shalom Congregation in Philadelphia, remaining there until 1925, when he was called to be rabbi of Holy Blossom Temple in Toronto, where he remained until 1929. He then became rabbi of Temple Israel in St. Louis, Missouri, and remained until his retirement on March 4, 1963.

Isserman served in the U.S. Army during World War I, volunteering for the infantry even though he was exempt as a theological student. He served overseas during World War II with the American Red Cross, attached to the First Armored Division as volunteer field director in the Tunisian Campaign. He was a member of Headquarters Staff, A.R.C., in Algiers and founded Town Hall, an educational form of entertainment that flourished in the Mediterranean theater of operations until the close of the war. He received citations from the Treasury Department and from the Red Cross.

Isserman organized the first goodwill dinner among Catholics, Protestants and Jews in the history of the Dominion of Canada. He participated in the first pulpit exchange with Protestant clergy in the history of the British Empire and led a campaign to abolish corporal punishment in Toronto public schools. He arranged for the first interdenominational Armistice Day service in Toronto. An interfaith goodwill prize bearing his name was established at the University of Toronto.

Isserman was chairman of the CCAR Justice and Peace Commission for many years. His efforts on behalf of world Jewry began with his leadership in the World Union for Progressive Judaism, serving as chairman of its American board. His visits to Europe and Germany in 1933 and 1934 prompted him to raise the cry of the impending danger of Nazism to the Jewish and non-Jewish world.

Isserman displayed a broad range of leadership activities, especially in the ecumenical movement and the early civil rights movement and as a proponent of an interracial nursery. He acted to break down religious prejudices and make people acknowledge the problems involving society.

Isserman passionately preached and wrote about the evils of bigotry and injustice. These concerns were addressed during his weekly radio broadcasts from a leading St. Louis radio station for almost 25 years. He was contributing editor of the *Canadian Jewish Review* (1925–1929), editorial contributor to the *Modern View*, St. Louis, Missouri (1929–1941) and the author of numerous books. He served on the Board of Governors, Hebrew Union College (1930–1938). Isserman was president of the Jewish Student Foundation, University of Missouri (1933–1947), and inspired a movement to build a chapel for Jewish students at the University of Missouri. In 1958 a plaque in his honor was placed at the University of Missouri to commemorate his 16 years as president of its Jewish Student Foundation. He was also chairman of the Inter-Racial Commission, Synagogue Council of America; chairman, American Institute on Judaism and a Just and Enduring Peace; chairman, Institute on Judaism and Race Relations (1945); chairman and organizer of the Social Justice Commission of St. Louis (1930–1931); vice chairman and founder of the St. Louis Seminar of Jews and Christians (1929–1935); member of the board, St. Louis Community Chest (1946); vice president, Missouri Welfare Board; vice chairman, Child Labor Committee of Missouri; and member of the Board, Urban League of St. Louis.

Isserman developed close friendships with the Christian clergy and arranged and organized the St. Louis Armistice Day Peace Parade. He was a member of the board of the Bible College, University of Missouri, and served on the national executive committee of the National Conference of Christians and Jews. In 1967 the clergy of Missouri chose Isserman for the Regional Clergyman of the Year Award from Religious Heritage of America, a nonsectarian group, in recognition of his contribution in building bridges between religions.

Isserman served as president of the HUC-JIR Alumni Association in 1950, the first president after the merger of HUC and JIR. He also headed the Rabbinical Council in 1952, organized to support the Combined Campaign, a fund-raising arm of HUC-JIR and the UAHC. In 1952 Isserman joined Jacob Rader Marcus on a five-week exploration of the public and private archives and collections in several West Indies countries to collect over 5,000 pages of manuscript material for the American Jewish Archives.

On June 6, 1923, he married Ruth Frankenstein of Chicago; they had two children: Irma Gertz and Ferdinand M. Isserman, Jr. Ferdinand Isserman died on March 7, 1972.

Writings (partial listing): *The Jewish Jesus and the Christian Christ* (St. Louis, 1950); *A Rabbi with the American Red Cross* (New York, 1958); *Rebels and Saints: The Social Message of the Prophets of Israel* (St. Louis, 1933); *Sentenced to Death: The Jews of Nazi Germany* (St. Louis, 1933; rev., 1961); *This Is Judaism* (New York, 1944).

References: Robert A. Cohn, "His Brave Voice Sounded Warning of Nazi Holocaust," *Jewish News*, September 20, 1979, pp. 64–66; "Nearprint Biographies Box," American Jewish Archives; *Who Was Who in America* (Chicago, 1973), 5:365.

A.D.R.

J

JANOWSKI, MAX (1912–1991). Cantor, composer, conductor, pianist, organist. Born in Berlin to musical parents (his mother, Miriam, was an opera singer, and his father, Chayim, coached cantors and choirs), Max Janowski showed early musical ability at the piano. Having studied at the Schwarenka Conservatory in Berlin, he won a piano contest shortly after graduation. As a result, he was appointed professor of music and head of the piano department of the Mosashino Academy of Music in Tokyo in 1933. There, in addition to concerts, teaching and recording, he made arrangements of Japanese folk songs for piano.

After his arrival in the United States in 1937, Janowski devoted himself largely to composition for the synagogue. Except for service in U.S. Navy Intelligence from 1942 to 1946, he served K.A.M. Isaiah Israel Congregation, Chicago, as musical director from 1938 until his death. He also served as musical consultant to other local synagogues. Janowski gave concerts and lecture recitals nationwide.

Janowski published over 500 compositions for youth choirs, adult choruses, orchestras, cantatas and oratorios; recordings have been made of his works. He founded Friends of Jewish Music, which is primarily responsible for the publication of his music. Among his most well-known compositions are "Avinu Malkeinu" and "Sim Sholom." Janowski's music is rich in its use of traditional prayer chant and cantillation motifs in a contemporary idiom. Rhythmically vigorous, his works are frequently built on the variation of small melodic modules, producing an effective and often memorable thematic impression. Whether large- or small-scale, his works are accessible to both audience and congregant.

In 1984 the Hebrew Union College School of Sacred Music honored him. Janowski also received the K'vod Award from the Cantors Assembly and two Solomon Schecter Awards from the United Synagogue of American for outstanding contributions to Jewish music.

In 1945 he married Gretel Haas. Max Janowski died in Hyde Park, Illinois, on April 8, 1991.

Writings (partial listing): *And I Will Plant Them upon Their Land* (Chicago, 1970); *Avodath Hakodesh Shel Kehilath Anshe Maarav* (New York, 1947); *Kol B' Ramah Nishma* (Chicago, 1974); *Memorial Service for the High Holidays* (Chicago, 1966); *Ovinu Malkeinu* (Chicago, 1950); *Recording: The Music of Max Janowski* (Chicago, 1978); *Shem Kileynu* (Chicago, 1969); *Sim Sholom* (Chicago, 1950); *Un' taneh Tokef—Uv' shofar Gadol* (Chicago, 1974); *Yaaleh* (Chicago, 1966).

References: ''Nearprint Biography Box,'' American Jewish Archives.

G.C.G.

K

KAHN, ROBERT IRVING (1910–   ). Rabbi. The son of Morris L. and Sadie Finkelstein Kohn, Kahn was born on December 10, 1910, in Des Moines, Iowa. After attending Des Moines lower schools, Kahn simultaneously enrolled in the University of Cincinnati (B.A., 1932) and Hebrew Union College (ordination, 1935). After ordination, he accepted an appointment as assistant rabbi at Congregation Beth Israel in Houston, Texas. With some interruption, Kahn would continue to serve the Houston, and Texas, Jewish community for over 40 years.

Kahn held his position at Beth Israel until 1939, when he was appointed associate rabbi. He served in this capacity until 1943, although he was not actually present for the last years of his term. Kahn was on the other side of the world, serving as a chaplain in the U.S. Infantry (1942–1945) in New Guinea and the Philippines. In 1944, Kahn accepted the pulpit at Houston's Congregation Emanu El, a post he would hold until 1978, when he was appointed rabbi emeritus.

While serving his congregations in Houston, Kahn quickly assumed a role of leadership in the Jewish and secular community. Kahn traveled as a Jewish Chautauqua Lecturer all over Texas and Louisiana. He taught a course in Judaism at St. Thomas University and a course in contemporary Jewish life at St. Mary's Seminary and served as guest lecturer in Bible and in Jewish values at the University of Houston. After his retirement, Kahn returned to HUC-JIR in Cincinnati as alumnus professor-in-residence for 1979–80. Kahn chaired the Central Conference of American Rabbis Liturgy Committee during the development and publishing of *Gates of Prayer* (1975). He served as president of his local B'nai B'rith Lodge (1937), of Texas Rabbis (1939), of Southwest Region of the CCAR (1973–1975) and of the Houston Rotary Club (1968). In 1979, Kahn became District Governor of Rotary.

In 1940, Kahn married Rozelle Rosenthal of Dallas, Texas. They have three children: Alfred J., Edward B. and Sharon F.

Writings: *Lessons for Life* (Garden City, NY, 1963); *The Letter and the Spirit* (Waco, TX, 1972); *May the Words of My Mouth* (Houston, 1984); *Ten Commandments for Today* (New York, 1964).

References: *Who's Who in American Jewry* (Los Angeles, 1980), p. 240; *Who's Who in World Jewry* (New York, 1981), p. 389.

KAISER, ALOIS (1840–1908). Cantor. Kaiser was born on November 10, 1840, in Szobohst, Hungary, the son of David Loeb Kaiser. After an early synagogue education with Henry Zirndorf, he was educated at the Realschule and the Teacher's Seminary and Conservatory, both in Vienna. Kaiser also studied at the Conservatory of Music in Prague and Johns Hopkins University in Baltimore.

Kaiser sang in the choir of Solomon Sulzer at the age of ten. Before coming to the United States, he was assistant cantor at Fünfhaus in Vienna (1859–1862) and at the Neusynagogue in Prague (1861–1866). He came to New York City in 1866 and moved to Baltimore to serve Congregation Oheb Shalom, a position he held until his death. There he worked with Benjamin Szold toward the abolition of rituals he considered insignificant to the modern Jew. He also worked to establish decorum in worship.

Said to be the founder of the American cantorate, Kaiser was president of the Society of American Cantors and was made an honorary member of the Central Conference of American Rabbis in 1895. He was also president of the Hebrew Education Society in Baltimore.

Kaiser and William Sparger compiled the music for the first *Union Hymnal* (1897), and he contributed articles to the *Jewish Encyclopedia*.

Alois Kaiser died in Baltimore on January 5, 1908.

Writings: *Cantata for Simchath Torah*; with William Sparger, *Confirmation and Consolation Hymns; Psalms 1, 29, 112, 125; Requiem for the Day of Atonement; Zimrath Yah*, 4 vols. (1871–1885).

References: *American Jewish Yearbook* 5; Central Conference of American Rabbis *Yearbook* 18 (1908): 175–78; *Jewish Encyclopedia* (New York, 1942), 7:292; *Universal Jewish Encyclopedia* (New York, 1942), 7:292.

KAPLAN, KIVIE (1904–1975). Businessman, philanthropist. Kaplan was born on April 1, 1904, in Boston, the son of Benjamin Kaplan and Celia Solomont Kaplan. He attended English High School in Boston, Massachusetts. At his retirement, he was president and general manager of Colonial Trading Co., Inc., in Boston, Massachusetts.

Active in the cause for social justice and well-known for his distribution of "Keep Smiling" cards translated in various languages and distributed throughout the world, he became president of the National Association for the Advancement of Colored People in 1966, a position he held until his death. At the NAACP, he endowed the Kivie Kaplan Life Membership Award and was the architect of its life membership program. He retired from business and devoted his life to social causes, primarily the NAACP. He promoted and led many causes devoted to the establishment of civic and social equality for all citizens. His humanitarian efforts embraced the young, the sick and the community at large. He was also affiliated with Newton-Wellesley Hospital; American Arbitration Association; Newton Community Chest; director for life and honorary treasurer, the Jewish Memorial Hospital (Boston); treasurer, B'nai B'rith Career and Counseling Services National Commission; treasurer, Roxbury Cemetery Association; and president, 210 Associates, Inc.

Kaplan was active as vice chairman of the Union of American Hebrew Congregations (and honorary life chairman) and as a member of its Social Action Commission (elected in 1958), as well as a co-founder and life trustee of Temple Emanuel in Newton, Massachusetts, and Temple Israel in Boston, Massachusetts. He was also a member of the National Health Planning Committee Council of Jewish Federations and Welfare Boards, and the North American Board of the World Union for Progressive Judaism.

He also served on the boards of the Hebrew Free Loan Society, Lincoln University (Pennsylvania) and Tougaloo College (Mississippi); life trustee, Combined Jewish Philanthropies; treasurer, Combined Jewish Appeal; life member, Board of Fellows, Brandeis University Associates.

He received numerous honors, including the Man of Vision Award from Bonds for Israel; (hon.) D.H.L., Hebrew Union College–Jewish Institute of Religion; (hon.) D.H.L., Portia Law school; (hon.) D.L., Wilberforce University (Ohio); D.H., Lincoln University; (hon.) D.H.L., Central State University (Wilberforce, Ohio); Human Rights Award, NAACP, Pittsburgh, Pennsylvania; Modern Community Developer's First Annual Averell Harriman Equal Housing Opportunity Award; Temple Reyim Brotherhood Man of the Year Award; Brotherhood Award, Temple Israel, Boston, Massachusetts; Brotherhood Award, Temple Emanuel, Newton, Massachusetts; Human Rights Award, Temple Sha-arey Shalom, Springfield, New Jersey; William S. Stashenfeld Award, National B'nai B'rith Career and Counseling Services (1974); and T. Kenyon Holly Award for Outstanding Humanitarian Service in Civic, Cultural and Philanthropic Fields.

Due to his generosity, facilities throughout the world bear his family name, including the admissions office, Newton-Wellesley Hospital; building of the Jewish Memorial Hospital; Lincoln Hall at Brandeis University; wing of Jewish Memorial Hospital; reception hall, Boston Dispensary; Rehabilitation Institute (Boston); NAACP Boston branch building; Religious Action Center of Reform Judaism in Washington, D.C.; dormitory at UAHC Eisner Camp-Institute in Great Barrington, Massachusetts.

In 1925, Kaplan married Emily Rogers. They had three children: Sylvia Grossman, Jean Green and Edward. He died in May 1975.

References: Norman Feingold and William Silverman, eds., *Kivie Kaplan: A Legend in His Own Time* (New York, 1976); *Who Was Who in America* (Chicago, 1976), 6:219.

KATZ, ROBERT L. (1917–   ). Rabbi. Born on September 18, 1917, Robert Katz is a native of Fort Dodge, Iowa, and the son of Raphael and Rebecca Rebbe Katz. He graduated with honors from Lake Forest College (B.A., 1938) and was ordained from HUC-JIR (1943), where he also received an M.H.L.

From 1943 to 1944, Katz was rabbi of Temple Beth El in Steubenville, Ohio. He then served as a chaplain with the Eighty-fifth Division of the Fifth Army in Italy (1944–1946). After World War II, he returned to HUC-JIR as a graduate fellow (1946–1947). He was named Director of Field Activities in 1947. Katz became Director of Admissions and eventually Coordinator of Human Relations, teaching courses during his career at HUC-JIR. He earned his D.H.L. (1952), writing on the work of Micah Joseph Berdichewsky. Katz was promoted to full professor in 1957, when he founded the Department of Human Relations at HUC-JIR, Cincinnati. Katz received training in human relations in the Department of Psychiatry, University of Cincinnati, and at the Moreno Institute. He also participated in the Gallahue Seminar on Religion and Psychiatry at the Menninger Foundation in Topeka, Kansas. He received training in group dynamics at the National Training Laboratories in Group Development and is a graduate of the Intensive Post Graduate Training Program of the Gestalt Institute of Cleveland.

A pioneer in the field of rabbinical counseling, Katz is the Helen and Joseph Regenstein Professor Emeritus of Religion, Ethics, and Human Relations at the HUC-JIR. As professor and coordinator of HUC-JIR's department of human relations for almost 40 years, Katz made an entire generation of Reform rabbis aware of the role that empathic counseling plays within the Jewish religious tradition.

Katz has been a member of the National Institute of Mental Health's Task Force on the Family and a consultant to the U.S. Navy on the spiritual needs of young adults. He has taught in the Department of Sociology of the University of Cincinnati and Antioch College and is a member of the Reform movement's Task Force on Jewish Identity, sponsored by the UAHC, HUC-JIR and the CCAR. He is a member of its Task Force on Research.

Katz's first book, *Empathy: Its Nature and Uses*, is still considered a classic in its field. His *Pastoral Care and the Jewish Tradition* is used as a textbook in Christian and Jewish seminaries alike.

Katz retired from the HUC-JIR faculty in 1988 but continues to teach.

In 1948 he married Miriam Katz; they had three children: Jonathan, Amy and Michael (deceased).

Writings: "Empathy in Modern Psychotherapy and the Aggada," *Hebrew Union College Annual* 30 (1959): 191–215; *Empathy: Its Nature and Uses* (New York, 1963); "Martin Buber and Psychotherapy," *Hebrew Union College Annual* 46 (1975): 413–32; *Pastoral Care and the Jewish Tradition* (Philadelphia, 1985); "The Rabbi as Preacher/ Counselor: A Frame of Reference," *Central Conference of American Rabbis Journal* 5 (June 1958): 22–35.

References: "Nearprint Biography Box and File," American Jewish Archives.

J.R.K.

KIEV, ISAAC EDWARD (1905–1975). Rabbi, librarian. The son of Nathan and Anna Radin Kiev, I. Edward Kiev was born in New York City on February 28 (some sources record March 5), 1905. He was raised on the Lower East Side.

Kiev attended public schools until he entered the Jewish Institute of Religion in 1923. As a student, he earned money by working in the library, paging and shelving books. Because he did not complete the course of study that included writing a thesis in order to earn a bachelor's degree, he was not formally ordained with his class in 1927 but was given a *hatarat hora'ah*, a certificate recognized by the State of New York, which permitted him to function as a rabbi.

Kiev's first rabbinic position was as chaplain at a city-run hospital. Since the chaplaincy was a part-time position, he continued to work as assistant librarian in the library of the Jewish Institute of Religion. Eventually the library became his primary employment, although he continued to serve as hospital chaplain until his death. In 1930 Kiev was considered for the position of librarian. While members of the administration and faculty felt he had the knowledge to perform competently in the capacity, the overriding feeling was that his lack of a university degree made it impossible for him to function on the same level as his peers at New York Public Library, Jewish Theological Seminary and Hebrew Union College. In 1942, when the position next came open, Kiev's experience and abilities were recognized, and he was named librarian. He held the position until his death. It was also at that time that he was formally made a rabbi, for the institute's catalogue thereafter listed him as "rabbi extra ordinem." In 1956 HUC-JIR awarded him the D.D. degree.

After World War II, Rabbi Kiev was involved in the promotion of Jewish libraries and books. He served as secretary to the Jewish Cultural Reconstruction, the body responsible for the reporting and inventory of surviving Jewish artifacts. He was president of the Jewish Librarians Association from 1951 to 1959. He was also very active in the Jewish Book Council, serving as treasurer from 1954 to 1958, secretary from 1958 to 1966 and as associate editor of *Jewish Book Annual* from 1952 to 1975, where his bibliographical article "American Jewish Non-Fiction Books" appeared annually.

Kiev served on the board of directors of *Studies in Bibliography and Booklore* from 1953 to 1975. He also chaired the Book Selection Committee of the National Federation of Temple Brotherhoods' Jewish Chautauqua Society, which assists in putting books of Jewish interest in college and university libraries. An avid Hebraist, he was for many years the chairman of the Israel Matz Fund, a foundation that supports Hebrew writers in Israel and the Diaspora.

Gifted with a prodigious memory and the ability to recall countless bibliographic citations, Kiev was consulted frequently by scholars, researchers and writers. In 1971 his colleagues presented him with a festschrift on his sixty-fifth birthday, *Studies in Jewish Bibliography, History, and Literature in Honor of I. Edward Kiev*.

During the almost 50 years that Rabbi I. Edward Kiev worked in the library at 40 West 68th Street, the collection grew from less than 10,000 volumes to over 100,000. He was responsible for its growth and development. As long as the library was on West 68th Street, many people, especially the regular visitors to the library from outside the college-institute, routinely referred to it as "the Kiev library."

Kiev married Mary Nover on December 20, 1930; they had two children: Ari and Aviva. I. Edward Kiev died suddenly at work on November 3, 1975.

References: *American Jewish Yearbook* 77 (1977): 598; *Hadoar* 55, no. 2, pp. 21, 30; "Nearprint Biography Box," American Jewish Archives; *New York Times*, November 5, 1975; *Who Was Who in America* (Chicago, 1976), 6:226.

P.E.M.

KLAU, DAVID (1894–1961). Businessman. Born in New York City on October 2, 1894, Klau was the son of Nathan and Paula Klau. He graduated from the High School of Commerce in New York City and served in the army during World War I.

David Klau was president and treasurer of Weiss and Klau Co., president and treasurer of Airex Venetian Blind Co. and a member of the Board of Directors of Standard Coated Products, Inc. He was president and chairman of the David W. Klau Foundation and trustee and vice-president of Montefiore Hospital in the Bronx, New York, where he had contributed a 250-bed wing known as the Klau Pavilion. Klau was also a member of Columbia University Industry Advisory Committee on Hospital and Medical Care in New York State and served as fund-raising chairman of the Window Shade Industry for the Federation of Jewish Philanthropies (New York) and the United Jewish Appeal, as well as cochairman of the Housewares Division of the Greater New York Fund. He was also a trustee of Temple Emanu-El (New York).

During World War II, Klau served as a member of the Venetian Blind Industry Advisory Committee of the War Production Board. He was also named vice president of the Board of Governors of Hebrew Union College–Jewish Institute of Religion in 1960, which he had served as a member since 1955. Klau and his wife were the principal supporters of the archaeological expeditions in Israel's Negev under HUC-JIR's president Nelson Glueck.

On February 21, 1922, he married Sadie Klingenstein. They had four children: James, Felice Shea, Lucille Stern and Paula Oppenheimer. He died on March 12, 1961, in New York City.

References: *New York Times*, obituary, March 13, 1961.

KLAU, SADIE (1898–   ). Philanthropist. Sadie Klingenstein was born in New York City on July 19, 1898, the daughter of Jacob Klingenstein and Clara Buttenweiser Klingenstein. She attended Hunter College, where she received a B.A. in 1919. After graduation, she taught public school for one year. In 1974, she received the honorary D.H.L. from Hebrew Union College–Jewish Institute of Religion. In 1976, she received the President's Medal from Hunter College.

She was a trustee of the Board of Montefiore Hospital, as well as of its

Women's Auxiliary. Klau also serves as trustee of Hunter College and the UJA/ Federation of Jewish Philanthropies of Greater New York. She was also a trustee of the Mosholu Community Center and the Sunshine Nursery School and Day Care Centers. She is an honorary member of the Board of Governors of HUC-JIR, where, in tribute to the support of David and Sadie Klau, the libraries at the Cincinnati and New York schools bear the Klau name.

On February 21, 1922, she married David Klau. They had four children: James, Felice Shea, Lucille Stern and Paula Oppenheimer.

KLAUSNER, ABRAHAM (1915–). Rabbi. Born on May 18, 1915, in Memphis, Tennessee, Abraham Klausner is the son of Joseph and Tillie Binstock Klausner. As a child he moved to Denver, Colorado, where he attended lower schools. Klausner received a B.A. (1937) and an M.A. (1938) from the University of Denver. In 1942 he received an M.H.L. from Hebrew Union College, where he was ordained in 1943. In 1948 he became the youngest person to receive an honorary D.D. from Hebrew Union College.

After ordination, Klausner served Temple Mishkan Israel in New Haven, Connecticut (1943–1945). After serving as an army chaplain (1945–1948), Klausner was appointed provost at HUC-JIR (1948–1949). From 1949 to 1953, he served Temple Israel in Boston. In 1953 he was named rabbi at Temple Emanuel in Yonkers, New York, a position he retains.

While an army chaplain, Klausner worked intimately with those in D.P. camps in Germany, having been attached to the combat forces that liberated Dachau in 1945. There he helped to lay the foundation for the revival of Jewish life in Germany by organizing the Central Committee of Liberated Jews of Germany, of which he was honorary chairman. He worked closely with the Central Committee to organize hospitals, sanitoria, clinics, farms, schools, synagogues, newspapers and workshops. When he returned to the United States, Klausner devoted himself to the cause of the displaced Jews by campaigning for the United Jewish Appeal.

While in Boston, Klausner taught in Boston University's School of Theology. During the same period of time, when the CCAR decided to initiate the publication of its rabbinic journal, Klausner was appointed its first editor. He became well known as an advocate for and officiant at ecumenical wedding ceremonies.

In 1951 he married Judith Haskell; they had two children: Jeremiah and Amos. In 1966 he married Judith Steinberg Pressman.

Writings: *Bicentennial Haggadah* (Yonkers, 1974); *Child's Holyday Prayer Book* (Yonkers, 1974); *A Sabbath Bar Mitzvah Service* (Yonkers, 1977); *Sharit Ha-Platah* (Dachau, 1945); *Weddings* (Columbus, OH, 1986).

References: "Nearprint Biography Box," American Jewish Archives; *Who's Who in American Jewry* (Los Angeles, 1980), p. 262; *Who's Who in World Jewry* (New York, 1981), p. 418.

KOHLER, KAUFMANN (1843–1926). Rabbi, theologian, scholar. On May 10, 1843, Kaufmann Kohler was born in Fuerth, Bavaria, the son of Rabbi Moretz and Babett Lowenmayer Kohler. Initially filled with the spirit of Orthodoxy, he studied with Rabbi Jacob Ettlinger in Altona and the neo-Orthodox leader Rabbi Samson Raphael Hirsch in Frankfurt, whom Kohler recalled as being the greatest influence on him in his youth. This early traditionalism was shattered by university study. Kohler's doctoral thesis for the University of Erlangen (1867), *Der Segen Jacobs*, a radical treatment of Genesis 49, underscored the extent of his transformation. This work raised a storm of opposition, making it impossible for Kohler to obtain a rabbinical position in Germany. On the recommendation of Abraham Geiger, Kohler came to the United States in 1869. After serving as rabbi in Detroit and Chicago, Kohler succeeded his father-in-law, David Einhorn, as rabbi of New York's Beth El Congregation in 1879. In 1903 he left to assume both the presidency and the chair of Jewish theology at Hebrew Union College, positions he retained until 1921.

Kohler was a brilliant thinker and articulate speaker who devoted his life to the furtherance of Jewish life in America. He advanced his views from the pulpit and through hundreds of articles in the American Jewish press and scholarly journals. He wrote scientific articles as well as textbooks and guides for the young.

In 1885 Kohler gave a series of lectures defending Reform against the attacks of the more conservative rabbi Alexander Kohut, a debate that attracted wide attention. Crystallizing the Reform position, Kohler convened the Pittsburgh Conference. As the major architect of the resulting "Pittsburgh Platform" (1885), Kohler became the chief spokesman of classical Reform. This platform was the philosophical foundation for the movement and its rationalist view of Judaism, stressing the concepts of ethical monotheism and universal mission while denying Jewish nationhood and rejecting ceremonies foreign to modern sensibilities. Kohler's crowning achievement, *Jewish Theology, Systematically and Historically Considered* (1918), traced the development of Jewish religious thought from the viewpoint of nineteenth-century Reform. Although not an original contribution to Jewish thought, it became the standard exposition of classical Reform.

While Kohler strove to articulate a Judaism consistent with modern science and rational thought, he also worked to nurture spirituality in Reform. As president of Hebrew Union College, Kohler revamped the curriculum, introducing higher biblical criticism and reducing the time spent on Talmud study. Yet he also strove to instill a religious atmosphere through daily religious services and a reverent mode of instruction. Especially in his later years, he stressed the importance of ceremony and piety. Kohler's vehement opposition to political Zionism remained untempered. He sought to influence the college on this issue, a posture that contributed to the resignation of several faculty members with known Zionist leanings.

Kohler worked throughout his life with more traditional American Jewish religious leaders on many projects, including the American Jewish Historical Society. Kohler was instrumental in the success of the *Jewish Encyclopedia* (1901–1906). As head of the department of philosophy and theology and of the executive committee of the editorial board for the publication, Kohler wrote over 300 articles and edited countless more, leaving a strong imprint on the work as a whole. He was one of the editors responsible for the Jewish Publication Society's English translation of the Bible (1917), the society having previously published Kohler's own translation of the book of Psalms (1903).

Kohler was a crucial figure in the history of American Reform Judaism. He crystallized the classical Reform position of the late nineteenth century and helped root it in traditional rabbinic texts.

Kohler married Johanna Einhorn in 1870; they had four children: Max, Edgar, Rose and Lili. Kaufmann Kohler died in Cincinnati on January 28, 1926.

Writings (partial listing): *Hebrew Union College and Other Addresses* (Cincinnati, 1916); *Jewish Theology, Systematically and Historically Considered* (New York, 1918); *A Living Faith: Selected Sermons and Addresses from the Literary Remains of Dr. Kaufmann Kohler*, ed. Samuel S. Cohon (Cincinnati, 1948); *Studies, Addresses and Personal Papers* (New York, 1931). For a listing of Kohler's works, see Adolph S. Oko, "Bibliography of Rev. Kaufmann Kohler, Ph.D., 1867–1913," in *Studies in Jewish Literature Issued in Honor of Prof. Kaufmann Kohler Ph.D. on the Occasion of his Seventieth Birthday* (Berlin, 1913), pp. 299–301.

References: Samuel S. Cohon, "Kaufmann Kohler the Reformer," in *Mordecai M. Kaplan Jubilee Volume on the Occasion of His Seventieth Birthday* (New York, 1953), pp. 137–55; Clifford Day, "Reflections of Kaufmann Kohler: Changes and Dreams of American Reform, 1903–1918" (Term paper, Hebrew Union College–Jewish Institute of Religion, Cincinnati, 1973); H. G. Enelow, "Kaufmann Kohler," *American Jewish Year Book* 28 (1926): 234–60; "Kaufmann Kohler Manuscript Collection," American Jewish Archives; Robert J. Marx, "Kaufmann Kohler as Reformer" (Rabbinic thesis, Hebrew Union College–Jewish Institute of Religion, Cincinnati, 1951); Michael A. Meyer, *Response to Modernity: A History of the Reform Movement in Judaism* (New York, 1988); David Philipson, "Kaufmann Kohler," *Publications of the American Jewish Historical Society* 31 (1928): 268–71; idem, "Kaufmann Kohler," Central Conference of American Rabbis *Yearbook* 36 (1926): 170–77.

S.R.S.

KORN, BERTRAM WALLACE (1918–1979). Rabbi, historian. The son of Manuel and Blanche Bergman Korn, Bertram Korn was born in Philadelphia on October 6, 1918. After attending the University of Pennsylvania and Cornell, he completed his A.B. at the University of Cincinnati in 1939. He was ordained at Hebrew Union College in 1943 and earned his D.H.L. there in American Jewish History in 1949. He later received honorary doctorates from Delaware Valley College of Science and Agriculture (formerly the National Farm School), 1967; HUC-JIR, 1968; Temple University, 1975; Dropsie University, 1976; and Gratz College, 1979.

On ordination, Korn accepted a position at Congregation Shaarai Shomayim of Mobile, Alabama. Within the year he entered the U.S. Navy as a chaplain, giving distinguished service in China. When he returned, Korn began his doctoral studies at Cincinnati while serving the congregation in Mansfield, Ohio. In 1948 Korn received an invitation to become the senior rabbi of the congregation in which he was reared, Keneseth Israel of Philadelphia, where he remained for the rest of his life.

A powerful preacher and dedicated pastor, Korn gave himself unstintingly to his congregants while maintaining a heavy schedule of scholarship and communal activities. He served as visiting professor of American Jewish history at HUC-JIR in New York and at Dropsie University. He was an active board member of the Reconstructionist Rabbinical College. Each summer found him maintaining his obligations to the U.S. Naval Reserve, which earned him citations and ultimately a promotion to rear admiral, the first rabbi to achieve so high a rank in the armed forces.

His scholarship displayed itself in an outpouring of well-researched, seminal volumes in the field of American Jewish history, making him the outstanding disciple of his teacher, Jacob Marcus. His articles appeared in many journals. Korn pioneered in studying and publishing books and articles on the middle period of American Jewish history, 1840–1880. His expertise was widely recognized, and he was invited to join Marcus and Professor Moshe Davis in writing a history of America's Jews, a three-volume work that was translated into Hebrew for Israeli readers.

Korn was president of the American Jewish Historical Society and recipient of its Lee M. Friedman Gold Medal. For many years he edited the yearbooks of the Central Conference of American Rabbis and served as chairman of the Chaplaincy Committee as well as chairman of the Jewish Welfare Board's Chaplaincy Commission.

Korn married Rita Rosenfeld on June 28, 1951; they had two children: Judith and Bertram W., Jr. He subsequently married Rita Packman Dogole. Both marriages ended in divorce. Bertram Korn died in New Orleans on December 9, 1979.

Writings (partial listing): *American Jewry and the Civil War* (Philadelphia, 1951); *The Early Jews of New Orleans* (Waltham, MA, 1969); *The Middle Years of American Jewish History*, in Hebrew (Jerusalem, 1970).

References: *Encyclopaedia Judaica* (Jerusalem, 1971), 10:1205; Richard C. Hertz, "Memorial Tribute," in Central Conference of American Rabbis *Yearbook* 90 (1980): 231 ff.; "Nearprint Biography Box," American Jewish Archives; Marc Lee Raphael, "Necrology," *American Jewish History* 69, no. 4 (June 1980): 506 ff.; *Who's Who in American Jewry* (Los Angeles, 1980), p. 270; *Who Was Who in America* (Chicago, 1981), 7:328.

KRAUSKOPF, JOSEPH (1858–1923). Rabbi. Born in Ostrowo, Prussian Posen, on January 21, 1858, Joseph Krauskopf was the son of Hirsch Krauskopf, a lumber merchant. After the death of his father, Joseph, age 14, emigrated to

America to join an older half-brother in Trenton, New Jersey. Sadly, his brother had been robbed and killed the day before Joseph arrived. Joseph had the address of a married first-cousin in Fall River, Massachusetts, so he went there and soon became employed by a tea merchant. The Christian widow of a newspaper editor gave the young immigrant permission to borrow books from her late husband's library to improve his English. In 1875 she read of Isaac M. Wise's intention to open a seminary in Cincinnati for training American rabbis. She wrote to Wise recommending Krauskopf as an ideal student, "because he has all the Christian virtues."

Krauskopf enrolled in the first class of Hebrew Union College, sharing a rented room with Henry Berkowitz. The two students wrote a periodical for Jewish youth, *Sabbath Visitor*, as well as three textbooks for religious education. On ordination in 1883, Krauskopf chose the growing pioneering community at Kansas City, Missouri. There his sermons proved so popular that they were carried in the local press. In 1884 he instituted a nonsectarian Poor Man's Free Labor Bureau that served as a successful free employment agency for the indigent. Krauskopf's espousal of a rational Reform, then called radical, brought him national attention.

In 1885, motivated by the debate in the Jewish press between the New York rabbis Kaufmann Kohler of Beth El and Alexander Kohut of Ahawath Chesed (now Central Synagogue), Krauskopf wrote Kohler proposing a meeting of like-minded rabbis. The result was the Pittsburgh Platform. No one was stronger in applying its principles than Joseph Krauskopf. He became one of the first advocates of Sunday worship for Jews, which he instituted in Philadelphia's Congregation Keneseth Israel. He was called there in 1887 to succeed Samuel Hirsch, who was retiring.

Among Krauskopf's other innovations were a large mixed choir, departmentalized religious school classes and classes in Bible ethics for adults—taught in both English and German. For young adults he created the Society of Knowledge Seekers and inspired them to revitalize the defunct Jewish Publication Society with national backing. His new synagogue included a free lending library for the neighborhood, and he encouraged the women of the congregation to create a sewing circle to aid charitable causes.

Appalled at the unsanitary condition of Philadelphia's slums, Krauskopf sought to enlist community leaders to provide better housing with a profit motive. The result was an increase in public attention to the problem, leading to improved sanitation. Another of his idealistic schemes was the Personal Interest Society, an attempt to have successful Jews develop one-to-one relationships with poor Jews. This gained few adherents.

Concerned with the mass immigration of Jewish refugees from Tsarist Russia and the pogroms that caused the exodus, Krauskopf sought to go to Russia in 1894. He was denied a visa on the grounds that Jews could not travel freely in Russia. In a public address to Civil War veterans, Krauskopf opened the issue to widespread publicity when he insisted that under the Russian-American trade treaty, any American had the right to travel freely. A resolution was brought to Congress to abrogate the trade treaty, and Krauskopf secured his visa. Shown a model Jewish farm at Odessa, Krauskopf returned to Philadelphia and purchased a farm some miles away in Doylestown. There he began his most famous project, the National Farm School, designed to take immigrant lads from the urban ghettos of America and train them in agricultural pursuits.

Krauskopf brought together some of the clergy of Philadelphia to form the Liberal Ministers Conference, from which came the National Federation of Religious Liberals. In 1901 he revitalized the local Board of Jewish Ministers, which previously had excluded Reform rabbis.

In 1903 Krauskopf was elected the third president of the Central Conference of American Rabbis. The Alumni Association of Hebrew Union College asked him to serve as director of the Isaac Mayer Wise Memorial Fund to develop an endowment for this alma mater.

Krauskopf applauded the agricultural efforts in Palestine. He recognized Herzl's dream of a land of refuge but objected to its nationalism. Instead he urged fighting anti-Semitism with knowledge of the Jew. In 1916, after a family trip to Palestine, he restated his position. While believing in Judaism as a religion and not as a nation, he opposed those who said Palestine could not support a growing population of Jews and denounced those who were fearful of dual loyalty. Krauskopf had become a defender of Zionism against the anti-Zionists.

Krauskopf was married twice. Six months after his ordination he had a double wedding with his classmate Henry Berkowitz, when he married Berkowitz's sister, Rose. They had three surviving children: Harold, Eleanore and Manfred. After Rose's death in 1893, he married Sybil Feineman, the daughter of the president of Krauskopf's Kansas City congregation. They had one daughter: Madeline. Joseph Krauskopf died in Atlantic City on June 12, 1923.

Writings (partial listing): coauthor, *Bible Ethics* (Cincinnati, 1893); *Evolution and Judaism* (Kansas City, 1887); coauthor, *First Hebrew Reader* (Cincinnati, 1884); coauthor, *The Jews and Moors in Spain* (Kansas City, 1887); coauthor, *Second Hebrew Reader* (Cincinnati, 1884); *Service Manual* (Philadelphia, 1892); *Service Ritual* (Philadelphia, 1888).

References: Richard F. Address, "Rabbi Joseph Krauskopf: Selected Thoughts" (Term paper, Hebrew Union College–Jewish Institute of Religion, Cincinnati, 1969); Martin Beilfield, Jr., "Joseph Krauskopf: 1887–1903" (Rabbinic thesis, Hebrew Union College–Jewish Institute of Religion, Cincinnati, 1975); William W. Blood, *Apostle of Reason* (Philadelphia, 1973); Abraham J. Feldman, "Joseph Krauskopf," *American Jewish Yearbook* 26 (1924): 420–47; "Nearprint Biography File and Box," American Jewish Archives.

L

LANDMAN, ISAAC (1880–1946). Rabbi, interfaith activist. Landman was born in Sudilkev, Russia, on October 24, 1880, the son of Louis Hymanson and Ada Gedaliah Landman. He emigrated as a child to Cincinnati, Ohio, where he attended the University of Cincinnati (B.A., 1906). That same year he was ordained at Hebrew Union College, which he had been attending concurrently. Later he did graduate work at the University of Pennsylvania.

After ordination, Landman accepted the invitation to serve as assistant rabbi at Keneseth Israel in Philadelphia, where he remained from 1906 to 1910, serving under the tutelage of a great classical reformer, Joseph Krauskopf. Following in the footsteps of his newly found mentor, Landman was appointed executive secretary of the National Farm School (1906–1916) and in 1911 helped established a farm colony of Jews in Clarion, Utah.

In 1916 he served a year as a U.S. Army chaplain with General John J. Pershing's forces in Mexico. During World War I, Landman worked closely with the Jewish Welfare Board in organizing its first training school.

In 1917 Landman went to Temple Israel in Far Rockaway, New York, remaining until 1928. While in Far Rockaway, Landman became editor of the *American Hebrew*, a major English-language Jewish weekly. He left Temple Israel to devote more time to the *American Hebrew* and to the planning of the *Universal Jewish Encyclopedia*. Although Landman managed to attract considerable editorial and writing talent for his *Universal Jewish Encyclopedia*, the result proved inferior to the earlier *Jewish Encyclopaedia*.

Americanism constituted the organizing core of Landman's worldview. His fight against political Zionism and American anti-Semitism was balanced by his enthusiastic endorsement of the interfaith movement that was emerging in the United States during the 1920s.

As editor of the *American Hebrew*, Landman began promoting three areas that would provide a focus for his career: Americanism, the emerging interfaith movement and non-Zionism. An ambitious young man, he rose through the ranks of the CCAR, elected secretary in 1915 (serving till 1917). At the same time he pursued his lifelong interest in drama, publishing a modest biography of Moses Hyman Luzzato. He collaborated with his brother in writing several original plays. Primarily as a result of Landman's activity with the *American Hebrew*, his influence broadened. In 1922 he was called before the Foreign Affairs Committee of the House of Representatives to give his opinion on House Resolution 52, which expressed "satisfaction at the recreation of Palestine as the national home of the Jewish race." In his controversial testimony, Landman declared his opposition to political Zionism and maintained that the Arab-Jewish problem in Palestine would be solved through collaboration. Landman was equally outspoken in combating domestic anti-Semitism during the 1920s, especially that of the Ku Klux Klan and Henry Ford's *Dearborn Independent*, a stance that won him the nickname "Two-fisted Rabbi."

The *American Hebrew* paid special attention to cooperative efforts among America's various religious groups. After the 1927 Massena Incident, a short-lived affair involving talk of a blood-libel in the aftermath of a murder in a small upstate New York village, Landman organized the Permanent Commission on Better Understanding among Catholics, Protestants and Jews in America. That same year he traveled to Mexico to preside at a commission-sponsored conference, held at the palace of the Bishop of Tabasco, dealing with religious problems in Mexico. The commission ceased functioning shortly after the formation of the National Conference of Christians and Jews in 1929. The work of the Permanent Commission is exemplified by a collection of short essays by leading interfaith figures, edited by Landman and entitled *Christian and Jew: A Symposium on Better Understanding*.

The economic dislocations of the Great Depression forced him to return to the pulpit. He was appointed rabbi of Beth Elohim in Brooklyn, New York, in 1931, where he remained until his retirement in 1942. In Brooklyn he founded the Academy of Adult Education in 1931.

Active in many areas, Landman was secretary of the New York Executive Committee of the UAHC (1919–1930); representative for the CCAR-UAHC Joint Delegation to the Paris Peace Conference (1919); CCAR delegate to the founding of the World Union for Progressive Judaism (London, 1926); and president of the Synagogue Council of America, elected shortly before his death.

In 1913 Landman married Beatrice Eschner; they had three children: Ames, David and Louise. Isaac Landman died in New York on September 3, 1946.

Writings (partial listing): *Christian and Jew: A Symposium on Better Understanding* (New York, 1929); *Keneseth Israel Sunday Discourses* (Philadelphia, 1907–1914); *Moses Human Luzzato, First Hebrew Playwright* (Cincinnati, 1907); *Stories of the Prophets* (Cincinnati, 1912).

References: Central Conference of American Rabbis *Yearbook* 56 (1946): 264; "Near-print Biography Box," American Jewish Archives; *New York Times*, obituary, September 5, 1946; Lance J. Sussman, "Toward Better Understanding: The Rise of the Interfaith

Movement and the Role of Rabbi Isaac Landman," *American Jewish Archives* 24 (April 1982): 35–51; *Universal Jewish Encyclopedia* (New York, 1942), 6:527–29; *Who's Who in American Jewry* (1939), p. 585.

LAUTERBACH, JACOB Z. (1873–1942). Rabbinic scholar. The son of Israel and Taube Bandler Lauterbach, Jacob Lauterbach was born in Monasterzyska, Galicia, Austria, on January 6, 1873. He received his Ph.D. at the University of Goettingen and his ordination from the Hildesheimer Rabbinerseminar in Berlin. Emigrating to the United States in 1904, he became an editor of the *Jewish Encyclopedia*, to which he contributed 260 articles on Talmudic and rabbinic literature. After serving as a congregational rabbi in Illinois, New York and Alabama, he was appointed to the faculty of Hebrew Union College in 1911 as professor of Talmud. He held this position until his retirement in 1934.

Lauterbach's scholarship centered on the textual, historical and contextual aspects of rabbinic literature. His most enduring contribution was his edition and translation of the tannaic midrash *Mekilta de-Rabbi Ishmael*, accompanied by a critical apparatus, explanatory notes in English and an introduction that traced the development of the misrashic literature and described in detail Lauterbach's methodology in preparing the text. His 1916 study, "Midrash and Mishna," was a comprehensive statement of his view of the history of the early halakah. It was included, along with a number of articles on the Pharisees and Saducees, in *Rabbinic Essays*, a 1951 anthology edited by his colleagues and students.

Lauterbach's studies of Jewish customs were collected for a second anthology in 1970. In tracing the history of such ritual practices as the breaking of a glass at weddings, the naming of children and the *tashlik* ceremony, he described how such customs were ultimately adopted by and assimilated into halakic Judaism, often despite initial rabbinic opposition to their original folkloristic or pagan elements.

From 1923 to 1933, Lauterbach served as chairman of the Responsa Committee of the Central Conference of American Rabbis, in which capacity he directly influenced the development of the halakic process in Reform Judaism. Unlike those written by his predecessors, Lauterbach's responsa were suffused with the atmosphere of the rabbinic academy. Although he did not abandon his liberal stance, Lauterbach's basic frame of reference in these decisions was defined by the Talmudic and halakic sources; even the later rabbinic authorities were frequently cited. This affirmative approach to the halakic tradition was reflected in the many responsa authored by Lauterbach's student Solomon B. Freehof. Among Lauterbach's responsa, a number of which are reprinted in *American Reform Responsa*, were essays on the covering of the head during worship; autopsy; birth control; and the ordination of women as rabbis.

Jacob Lauterbach died on March 20, 1942.

Writings (partial listing): *Mekilta de-Rabbi Ishmael*, ed. and trans., 3 vols. (Philadelphia, 1933–1935); *Rabbinic Essays* (Cincinnati, 1951); *Studies in Jewish Law, Custom and Folklore* (New York, 1970).

References: Bernard J. Bamberger, "Jacob Z. Lauterbach: An Informal Memoir," *Central Conference of American Rabbis Journal* 11 (June 1963): 3–8; Lewis M. Barth, "Rabbinics," in *Hebrew Union College–Jewish Institute of Religion at One Hundred Years*, ed. Samuel E. Karff (Cincinnati, 1976), pp. 317–82; "Chronicle of Lauterbach Family," "Nearprint Biographies File," "Testimonials and Resolutions Honoring Lauterbach on his Retirement," American Jewish Archives; Solomon B. Freehof, "Introduction to Lauterbach," in *Rabbinic Essays*, by Jacob Lauterbach (Cincinnati, 1951); idem, "Jacob Z. Lauterbach and the Halakah," *Judaism* 1 (July 1952): 270–73.

M.E.W.

LAZARON, MORRIS (1888–1979). Rabbi, ecumenical leader, founder and leader of American Council for Judaism. The son of Samuel Louis and Alice de Castro Lazaron, Morris Lazaron was born in Savannah, Georgia, on April 16, 1888. Lazaron grew up and began his education in Savannah. He was ordained at the Hebrew Union College in 1914. After serving briefly at a congregation in Wheeling, West Virginia, Lazaron was invited to Baltimore Hebrew Congregation, where he served for over 31 years as rabbi and rabbi emeritus.

During his tenure at Baltimore Hebrew Congregation, Lazaron's association with the congregation was bittersweet. He ushered in a new era of youthfulness and energy focused on creative and innovative rituals, programs and forums. He initiated one of the first temple bulletins, which later served as a model for other congregations. He was committed to the youth and religious program, seeing both as vehicles for ensuring future generations of educated, committed Jews. Yet Lazaron's activity was later overshadowed by an adversarial relationship with his congregation. His congregation disagreed with his vocal anti-Zionist stance and disapproved of his participation in the American Council for Judaism. A breach caused Lazaron to sever his formal relationship with Baltimore Hebrew; he relinquished his title of rabbi emeritus in 1949.

Lazaron was a pioneer of the Interfaith Movement, which later developed into the National Conference of Christians and Jews. He toured the United States and other countries on behalf of the conference. In 1933, along with Father John Ross and Dr. Everett Clinchy, Lazaron traveled 9,000 miles to speak in 38 cities to over 60,000 people and 119 meetings. That year the three were awarded the Richard Gottheil Medal by Zeta Beta Tau Fraternity. His years of service to the causes of the NCCJ resulted in two books, *Common Ground: A Plea for Intelligent Americanism* and *Bridges Not Walls*. By 1946, mounting pressure from Zionists on the leaders of the NCCJ forced Lazaron's official involvement in conference activities to wane.

Lazaron's career as a pulpit rabbi and leader in the fight to promote better understanding between Christians and Jews was overshadowed by his fervent association with the anti-Zionist movement in America in the late 1930s and early 1940s and by his leadership in the American Council for Judaism (founded in 1942). Early in his career, Lazaron expressed some sentiment toward Zionism, but he quickly became disenchanted and embittered by what he felt was a corrupt Zionist Organization of America. He was opposed to political aspirations to rebuild a Jewish homeland, stressing instead the ethical principles of Judaism and the universalistic interpretation of Jewish history. Unlike many other anti-Zionists, Lazaron maintained his positions after the establishment of Israel. However, in a 1973 essay, "Looking Back," Lazaron conceded a role for the State of Israel in Jewish life.

In 1963, at the age of 75, Lazaron was recognized by the HUC-JIR with an honorary D.D. degree.

Lazaron married Pauline Horkheimer on May 1, 1916; they had three children; Morris, Jr., Harold and Clementine. After Pauline Lazaron's death, Lazaron married Hilda Rothschild Rosenblatt, with whom he shared 34 years. Morris Lazaron died on June 5, 1979.

Writings: *Address in Three Dimensions* (Philadelphia, 1954); *As I See Him* (Buckinghamshire, UK, 1978); with Albert K. Weinberg, *Ask the Rabbi* (New York, 1927); *Bridges Not Walls* (New York, 1959); *Common Ground: A Plea for Intelligent Americanism* (New York, 1938); *The Consolation of Our Father* (Baltimore, 1928); *Homeland or State: The Real Issue* (New York, 1940); *In the Shadow of the Catastrophe* (New York, 1956); *Is This the Way* (Baltimore, 1942); *Olive Trees in Storms* (New York, 1955); *Side Arms: Readings, Prayers and Meditations for Soldiers and Sailors* (Baltimore, 1918).

References: "Morris Lazaron Manuscript Collection," American Jewish Archives; Scott Shpeen, "A Man against the Wind: A Biographical Study of Rabbi Morris S. Lazaron" (Rabbinical thesis, Hebrew Union College–Jewish Institute of Religion, Cincinnati, 1984).

S.L.S.

LELYVELD, ARTHUR JOSEPH (1913–   ). Rabbi. The son of Edward Joseph and Dora Cohen Lelyveld, Arthur Lelyveld was born in New York City on February 6, 1913. After attending lower schools in New York City (he is featured in the Hall of Fame at George Washington High School in the Bronx), in 1929 Lelyveld enrolled at Columbia College, Columbia University, receiving an A.B. in 1933. He worked his way through college as a musician. He then attended Hebrew Union College in Cincinnati, receiving an M.H.L. and his ordination in 1939. In 1955 he was awarded an honorary D.D. from Hebrew Union College–Jewish Institute of Religion. He was also awarded an honorary Litt.D. from the Cleveland College of Jewish Studies (1986). After ordination, Lelyveld served Bene Israel, Hamilton, Ohio (1939–1941), while simultaneously studying at Hebrew Union College, Cincinnati, as the Edward L. Heinsheimer Fellow.

In 1939, while studying and serving a congregation, Rabbi Lelyveld was also director of youth activities for the Union of American Hebrew Congregations. There he was instrumental in initiating summer youth conclaves and was an organizer of the National Federation of Temple Youth. From 1944 to 1946, he was executive director of the Committee on Unity for Palestine. From 1946 to 1947, Lelyveld was assistant national director and then, from 1947 to 1956, national director of the B'nai B'rith Hillel Foundations. From 1956 to 1958, he served as executive vice-chair of the American-Israel Cultural Foundation. He is a member of the Board of Trustees of the Martin Luther King, Jr., Center for Social Change.

In 1958, he was named Senior Rabbi of Anshe Chesed Congregation (Fairmont Temple) of Cleveland, and in 1986 he became Senior Rabbi Emeritus. Since 1980, Lelyveld has been the Bernard Rich Hollander Lecturer in Jewish Thought at John Carroll University.

While working for the Zionist cause in the early forties, Lelyveld won the support of Harry Truman's former partner, Eddie Jacobson, for the idea of a Jewish homeland; and then in 1946, with Jacobson as the door-opener, Lelyveld was among the first to speak with Truman on behalf of the idea of a Jewish state.

Lelyveld went to Mississippi during the summer of 1964 as part of a team of Cleveland clergy to serve as minister-counselor to the Council of Churches Commission on Race and Religion. During this stay, he was severely beaten by segregationists.

In 1964, the Cleveland community honored Lelyveld's services to Zionism and to the Jewish National Fund by creating the Rabbi Arthur J. Lelyveld Forest in the State of Israel. In 1965 he received an award for "distinguished service to the NAACP and the cause of Freedom" and, in 1977, the Prime Minister's Medal from State of Israel Bonds. From 1967 to 1973, Lelyveld chaired the American-Israel Dialogues of the American Jewish Congress in Rehovot, Haifa and Jerusalem.

As a well-rounded scholar, Lelyveld has written numerous monographs in the area of Jewish thought, often writing in response to contemporary radical theology. He is also known to speak his conscience and act on it, especially in the area of Zionism and race relations.

Lelyveld was president of the Central Conference of American Rabbis (1975–1977) and the Synagogue Council of America (1979–1981) and honorary national president of the American Jewish Congress and the American Jewish League for Israel. He was a founder and first president of the Jewish Peace Fellowship, from 1941 to 1944.

In 1982, Lelyveld was honored by the American Civil Liberties Union of Ohio Foundation for distinguished service on behalf of civil rights and liberties. During John Carroll University's centennial observance in 1986, Lelyveld was honored as one of the recipients of the John Carroll University "Centennial Medal." In 1988, the Histradrut in Israel established a scholarship in Lelyveld's honor at the Afro-Asian Institute in Israel, and in 1989, Lelyveld held the Walter and Mary Tuohy Chair of Interreligious Studies at John Carroll University. That same year, he served as Alumni Scholar-in-Residence at HUC-JIR, New York.

Lelyveld contributed several articles in theology to the *Universal Jewish Encyclopedia* and is one of the authors represented in *Religion and the State University*, published in 1958 by the University of Michigan.

In 1933, Lelyveld married Toby Bookholtz. They had three children: Joseph,

David and Michael. In 1964, Lelyveld married Teela Stovsky. They had two children: Benjamin (d. 1987) and Robin.

Writings (partial listing): *Atheism Is Dead* (Lanham, MD, 1968); *For and Against Books*, series (Denver, CO, 1971, 1973); *The Social Relevance of the Eighth Century Prophet* (Cincinnati, 1973); *The Unity of the Contraries—Paradox as a Characteristic of Normative Jewish Thought* (Syracuse, 1984).

References: Zvi Ganin, *Truman, American Jewry, and Israel* (New York, 1979); Berney Green, ''Arthur Lelyveld: Celebrating 50 Years in the Rabbinate,'' *Jewish News*, May 26, 1988; *Who's Who in America* (Wilmette, IL, 1991), 2: 1957; *Who's Who in World Jewry* (New York, 1981), p. 463.

LEVITT, NORMA (1917–   ). Born Norma Uttal on March 11, 1917, in New York City, the daughter of Henry and Anna Probstein Uttal, Levitt received a B.A. (Phi Beta Kappa) from Wellesley College in 1937. She pursued graduate studies at the University of California at Berkeley and the University of Chicago. She has also participated in human relations and growth seminars with the National Training Laboratories.

Levitt has served the Reform movement in a wide variety of leadership capacities, including the Executive Committee, Board of Trustees, of the UAHC. She was the first woman to be elected an officer in that organization, serving as vice chairman in 1979. She was also cochairman of the UAHC Centennial Committee in 1973; member of the Social Action Committee, UAHC; and treasurer, Steering Committee, Association for Reform Zionists of America. Levitt blazed the trail for women in other organizations as well by becoming the first chairman of the Executive Committee of the World Union for Progressive Judaism and the first woman officer of the Synagogue Council of America, where she served as secretary in 1979 and chairman of its Task Force on Israel, the U.S. and the Third World.

Levitt was chairman of the Program Committee for its International Conference in 1974 and 1976. She served as president of the Jewish Braille Institute of America and the National Federation of Temple Sisterhoods; was vice president of the American Association for Jewish Education and the American Section of the World Jewish Congress; and a member of the Board of Governors of Hebrew Union College–Jewish Institute of Religion. She was a member of the Interreligious Affairs Commission of the American Jewish Committee.

Levitt has also been vice president of the Jewish Theatre for Children and Chairman of Leadership Conferences of National Jewish Women's Organizations as well as organizer and first chairman of its Subcommittee on Jewish Poverty and the Elderly Poor and chairman of its committee on the International Year of the Child. She was elected president of the World Conference on Religion and Peace in 1984.

Levitt was accredited to the U.S. mission to the United Nations as a nongovernmental representative in 1979, to UNICEF on behalf of the World Jewish

Congress, to the Office of Public Information for the World Union for Progressive Judaism and to many other important positions as organizational representative.

Norma Levitt has been honored by numerous organizations. In 1972 she received the Eleanor Roosevelt Award from the North Shore Division of the American Jewish Congress. In 1981, the UAHC and the Jewish National Fund organized the Norma U. Levitt Forest in Israel. In addition, she is an accomplished poet and writer.

In 1938 she married David M. Levitt, president of DCA Food Industries, Inc.; they have three children: Sally Steinberg, Nancy Hoffman and Andrew.

Writings (partial listing): *Confirmed in Righteousness* (New York, 1962); *The Days of Creation* (Great Neck, NY, 1956); *Here I Am, Hineni* (New York, 1965).

References: "Autobiography," "Nearprint Biography Box," American Jewish Archives; *Who's Who in World Jewry* (New York, 1980), p. 477.

LEVY, CLIFTON HARBY (1867–1962). Rabbi, writer. Levy was born on June 21, 1867, in New Orleans to Eugene H. and Almeria Moses Levy. His ancestors were prominent Jews who had settled in the South in 1740. He finished high school in Cincinnati, then went on to the University of Cincinnati (A.B., 1887) while simultaneously enrolled at Hebrew Union College. He was ordained by Hebrew Union College in Cincinnati in 1890. Later he pursued graduate study at Johns Hopkins University (1895–1896).

On ordination, Levy served Congregation Gates of Hope in New York City (1890–1891); Congregation Shaarai Shomayim in Lancaster, Pennsylvania (1892–1894); and Congregation Eden St. Temple in Baltimore, Maryland (1894–1896). In New York, Levy was superintendent of classes for immigrant children under the Baron de Hirsch Fund, believed to be one of the first formal attempts at Americanization. In Baltimore, he opened the first Jewish kindergarten in a religious school and launched the first United Hebrew Charities. He was also the editor of the *Jewish Comment* (1894–1896). Disenchanted with congregational life, Levy returned to New York City to pursue a writing career, having gained experience earlier by publishing a five-act Purim play.

While in New York, Levy wrote for various Jewish newspapers, publishing articles on the subject of biblical archaeology. He was also involved in founding and organizing Tremont Temple in the Bronx, where he served from 1906 to 1921. He organized the International Copyright Bureau in 1909 and briefly managed it.

In 1923 a group interested in Jewish Science approached him for leadership. Together they founded the Centre for Jewish Science, which functioned until Levy's death in 1962. The Centre sponsored religious services, classes in spiritual culture and a magazine, *Jewish Life*, written primarily by Levy. Under the auspices of the Centre, Levy published a Jewish Science handbook. Levy's goal was to provide exemplary programs that other Reform rabbis could adapt for their congregations rather than start a separate synagogue or movement.

Levy understood Jewish Science as an antidote to the absence of spirituality from the American Reform synagogue. He challenged his colleagues to attend the needs of individuals who hungered for emotional and spiritual content within the synagogue and who were turning to groups like Christian Science to meet their needs. Levy's greatest accomplishments were in making Jewish Science appear legitimate to the rabbis of the CCAR and in persuading other rabbis to start spiritual education circles in their congregations. He was also a founding member of the American Council for Judaism.

Late in life, Levy developed an interest in Jewish art. He published two volumes on the subject and served as art editor of the *Universal Jewish Encyclopedia*. He also served on the Board of Boy Scouts of America and the Society for the Prevention of Cruelty to Children. He was a member of B'nai B'rith and Masons, president of the New York Board of Rabbis and member of the New York Association of Reform Rabbis, which he helped found.

In 1891 he married Sarah Lang. After her death, he married Cora Bacharach in 1903. Clifton Levy died in New York in 1962.

Writings (partial listing): *The Bible in Art* (New York, 1936); *Haman and Mordecai* (Cincinnati, 1886); *The Helpful Manual* (New York, 1926); *The Jewish Life* (New York, 1925); *Principles of Reform Judaism* (New York, 1922).

References: John Appel, "Christian Science and the Jews," *Jewish Social Studies* 31 (April 1969): 100–121; "Autobiography," "Nearprint Biography Box," American Jewish Archives; *Universal Jewish Encyclopaedia* (New York, 1942), 7:9; *Who Was Who in America* (Chicago, 1973), 5:428.

R.T.A.

LEVY, LIPMAN (1836–1918). Lawyer. Born in Prussia on August 25, 1836, Lipman Levy was the son of Lewis and Kittie Levy. His family came to the United States in 1898 and settled in Cincinnati, Levy began his education in Prussia, continuing in England before completing it in Cincinnati. After a short time in business, he attended Cincinnati Law School, where he graduated in 1875. In 1876 he joined a law firm that became Moulton, Johnson and Levy (later Johnson and Levy).

Levy was among the 13 men who signed the original call in 1872 to form the organization that eventually became the UAHC. At its preliminary meeting in 1873, he was elected secretary of the UAHC, a post he held until 1917, when he left Cincinnati. Affiliated with the Mound Street Temple, he was a member of F. and A.M., the I.O.O.F. and B'nai B'rith. Levy also served as a delegate to the United Jewish Cemetery Association in 1909.

On August 30, 1860, Levy married Henrietta Feder; they had seven children: Selena, Belle Johnson, Rachel Seitner, Addie Spear, David M., Esther and Florence. Lipman Levy died on March 25, 1918.

Writings: ed., *Proceedings of the Union of American Hebrew Congregations*, 1873–1917.

References: *American Jewish Yearbook* (Philadelphia, 1905), 7: 80; *Centennial History of Cincinnati* (Chicago, 1904).

LICHTENSTEIN, MORRIS (1889–1938). Rabbi, founder of the Society for Jewish Science. The son of Eliezer and Hannah Surasky Lichtenstein, Morris Lichtenstein was born in Lithuania in 1889 and studied at *yeshivot* in Bialystok and Lomza. He emigrated to the United States in the early years of the twentieth century. He was one of the first Eastern European students to attend Hebrew Union College, enrolling in 1910 and receiving rabbinic ordination in 1916. Lichtenstein received a B.A. from the University of Cincinnati in 1916 and an M.A. from Columbia University in 1919.

From 1920 to 1922, Lichtenstein served a congregation in Athens, Georgia. It is likely that while serving in Georgia, he became aware of Jewish Science and of its chief proponent, Rabbi Alfred Geiger Moses of Congregation Shaarai Shomayim in Mobile, Alabama. In 1922 Lichtenstein returned to New York City to found the Society for Jewish Science. The Society held meetings two afternoons a week, ran Friday evening and Sunday morning services and had weekly instructional classes for Jewish Science practitioners who were trained in the art of healing. For some time, a Jewish Science reading room was open daily. The society also functioned as a congregation, developing a Ladies Auxiliary, a Sunday School program and a group for teenagers.

Jewish Science acted as a Jewish response to Christian Science and employed many Christian Science concepts and techniques, translated into a Jewish framework. Lichtenstein identified the God of Israel with the metaphysical Divine Mind. The Divine Mind was the source of good; the human mind created hatred, greed, fear and worry. The proponents of Jewish Science used the techniques of prayer, affirmation, visualization and relaxation to enable people to overcome their "wrong thinking" and properly approach the Divine Mind. The Psalms were the essential text through which these techniques were carried out.

Lichtenstein was a prolific writer. He published a monthly journal, *Jewish Science Interpreter*, and authored seven volumes over a 13-year period.

Lichtenstein married Tehilla Hirschenson in June 1919; they had two sons: Michael and Emmanuel. Lichtenstein died of cancer on November 11, 1938, in New York City. His wife succeeded him as leader of the Society for Jewish Science. Tehilla Lichtenstein died on February 23, 1973, in New York City. The Society for Jewish Science remains in existence.

Writings: *Cures for Minds in Distress* (New York, 1936); *How to Live* (New York, 1929); *Jewish Science and Health: The Textbook of Jewish Science* (New York, 1925); *Joy of Life* (New York, 1938); *Judaism* (New York, 1934); *Peace of Mind* (New York, 1927).

References: Abraham Holtzberg, "Memorial Address," Central Conference of American Rabbis *Yearbook* 49 (1939): 298–300; "Nearprint Biography File," American Jewish Archives; *Universal Jewish Encyclopedia* (New York, 1942), 7:48–49.

R.T.A.

LICHTENSTEIN, TEHILLA (1894–1973). Rabbinic leader. The daughter of Rabbi Hayim Hirschenson, Lichtenstein was born in Jerusalem on May 16, 1894. The Hirschenson family arrived in Hoboken, New Jersey, in 1904. Tehilla received a B.A. in classics from Hunter College in 1915 and subsequently earned an M.A. in English literature from Columbia University.

Lichtenstein interrupted her doctoral studies in English literature in June 1919 in order to marry Rabbi Morris Lichtenstein. The couple moved to Athens, Georgia, where Morris served as rabbi. The Lichtensteins returned to New York in 1922, where Morris founded the Society for Jewish Science. During her husband's lifetime, Lichtenstein served as principal of the Sunday School and editor of the movement's magazine, *Jewish Science Interpreter*.

In 1938, Morris Lichtenstein died. On December 4, 1938, Tehilla Lichtenstein assumed the role of Spiritual Director for the Society for Jewish Science. She served in that role until her death in 1973. She was the first woman in the United States ever to hold a rabbinic post. For 35 years she gave weekly sermons, taught classes in Jewish Science and in Bible, trained all the Jewish Science practitioners and counseled those who came to her for guidance. She did weekly Jewish Science radio broadcasts and wrote and edited the *Jewish Science Interpreter*.

Lichtenstein's main interest as leader of the Society for Jewish Science was in espousing a Judaism based on a deep connection to a personal God, and a profound sense of optimism about the human spirit. Jewish Science articulated a vision of happiness and health set within a context that was specifically Jewish. Lichtenstein maintained that Jewish Science was no more than applied Judaism— the application of Jewish teachings to everyday life. Her goal was to awaken Jews spiritually, to tell them not to follow Christian Science. Instead, all faith is in Judaism. Lichtenstein was also an ardent Zionist and an active member of the American Mother's Committee, an interfaith group. She was also committed to equality for women within Judaism and lived out that commitment in her life's work.

Lichtenstein had two sons: Emmanuel and Michael. She died in New York City on February 23, 1973.

Writings: ed., *Jewish Science Interpreter*, 1938–1972; "Jewish Science," *Universal Jewish Encyclopedia* (New York, 1942), 6:142.

References: *New York Post*, January 26, 1951; *New York Times*, December 5, 1938.

R.T.A.

LIEBMAN, JOSHUA LOTH (1907–1948). Rabbi, pioneer in applying modern psychology to religion. The son of Simon and Sabina Loth Liebman, Joshua Liebman was born in Hamilton, Ohio, on April 7, 1907. His parents were divorced when he was a small child, and he went to live with his paternal grandfather, Rabbi Lippman Liebman. He was a child prodigy, completing Walnut Hills High School at age 15. At 19 he received a B.A. from the University of Cincinnati. Liebman was descended from a line of Reform rabbis, and there-fore his family assumed that he was destined for the rabbinate, enrolling him at Hebrew Union College at age 13. While completing his rabbinic studies, Liebman served as the Taft Teaching Fellow in Philosophy at the University of Cincinnati, from 1926 to 1929. On his ordination in 1930, Liebman served as rabbi in

Lafayette, Indiana, on weekends, pursued his doctoral studies at HUC in Cincinnati and taught Bible and commentaries there.

Liebman received the Simon traveling fellowship, which enabled him to study at Hebrew University in Palestine (1929–1930). It was there that his deep-seated love of Zion awakened.

In 1934 Liebman succeeded Rabbi Solomon B. Freehof as the rabbi of Congregation Kehillath Anshe Maarav, the oldest Reform congregation in Chicago. He served as rabbi from 1934 to 1939. During those years, he completed his D.H.L. degree in Jewish philosophy.

While in Chicago, Liebman became absorbed in the study of psychology. He interwove his own liberal Jewish understanding of Judaism with his knowledge of psychology. The synthesis of his study, experience and teaching was articulated in his book *Peace of Mind*, published in 1946. It soon became an enormous best seller, his face familiar in the printed media and his name renowned. To a generation of Jews beleaguered by the traumatic events of World War II, this book brought comfort and solace. For the first time in a modern context, psychology and Jewish religion were brought together.

In 1939 he was called to Congregation Adath Israel of Boston, where he served until his death. He gained a reputation as a radio preacher and visiting professor at Boston University and the Andover-Newton Theological Seminary. At Temple Adath Israel, he was responsible for redirecting the life of this classical Reform congregation into the mainstream of American Judaism. He discontinued the Sunday morning service, reestablished Friday evening services, expanded the use of Hebrew, advocated the establishment of a Jewish homeland in Eretz Yisrael and introduced the bar mitzvah as early as 1939. Shortly before his death, he achieved his dream of appointing a social worker to the temple staff. He saw this as the integration of his Jewish worldview and the discipline of psychology.

Liebman married Fannie Loth on July 4, 1928; they adopted one child: Leila Bornstein. Joshua Liebman died on June 9, 1948.

Writings: *Hope for Man* (New York, 1966); *Peace of Mind* (New York, 1946); *Psychiatry and Religion* (Boston, 1948). His dissertation, "The Religious Philosophy of Aaron ben Elijah," and other essays and sermons are maintained in the Fannie and Joshua Loth Liebman Papers, Twentieth Century Archives, Boston University.

References: Rebecca Alpert, *Faith and Freedom* (London, 1987), pp. 177–91; William G. Braude, "Recollections of a Septuagenarian," *Rhode Island Jewish Historical Notes* 8, no. 3 (November 1981); Albert Goldman, introduction to *Psychiatry and Religion* (Boston, 1948); Arthur Mann, ed., *Growth and Achievement: Temple Israel, 1854–1954* (Cambridge, MA, 1954), pp. 100–114; "Nearprint Biography Box," American Jewish Archives; Sefton D. Temkin, "Liebman, Joshua Loth," in *Encyclopaedia Judaica* (New York, 1971), 11:224–25.

B.H.M.

LILIENTHAL, MAX (1815–1882). Rabbi. Born in Munich, Bavaria, on November 6, 1815, Lilienthal studied with Rabbi Moses Wittelbucher and attended the *yeshivah* of Wolf Hamburger in Fuerth. He was ordained by Hirsch Aub, then rabbi of Munich. Lilienthal studied at the University of Munich (Ph.D., 1857). He had been offered a government post but refused it when he learned that it required a conversion to Catholicism. He was unable to find work as a rabbi in Bavaria, so he turned his talents to contributing columns in *Allgemeine Zeitung des Judenthums* based on Hebrew manuscript work he was doing in the royal library of Munich. He received the attention of the editor, Ludwig Philipson, who eventually recommended him for a position with a new school opening in Riga. He became director of the Jewish School of Riga (1830), which opened the following year. He also became the community rabbi. Quickly he became known for his sermons (later published). As a result of his friendship with the Russian minister of education, Sergius Uvarov, he was invited to draw up a project for the establishment of state schools for Jews to provide them with a European-style education. His famous address to the Russian Jews—"Maggid Yeshua" ("A Tale of Salvation")—was issued during this period. While trying to persuade leaders in the Pale of Settlement, he encountered opposition and mistrust. Communities felt that his plan was a cover for the government attempt to convert the Jews. He utilized the authority of the government and began to issue threats to coerce people into cooperating. As a result, he encountered physical abuse. Eventually, as the government started to issue anti-Jewish laws, Lilienthal began to see the plan as had his coreligionists, and he secretly left the country, although he had been invited to serve the community of Odessa as its rabbi. There is some speculation that he was being asked to convert as well.

Lilienthal immigrated to the United States in 1845 and settled in New York City, quickly developing a love for America as a home of religious liberty. Shortly after his arrival (in 1846), he was invited to serve as rabbi of a short-lived union of three New York City German congregations (including Anshe Chesed, Shaare Shomayim and Rodeph Shalom). He withdrew from two of them and stayed a short time with Anshe Chesed. Already a moderate Reformer, he left and then devoted his time to a day school he had developed (Hebrew Union School) for boys from around the country. He directed it until 1855, when he was invited to serve K. K. Bene Israel in Cincinnati. Both in New York and in Cincinnati he led the congregations in the direction of moderate Reform. Throughout his career he wavered between traditional Judaism and Reform, yet he warned against inconsistency. He was critical of German Reform but looked to secure decorum in worship. In New York he preached in German, organized a choir and formed one of the earliest confirmation classes in a U.S. synagogue. He replaced the prayer for the monarchy with one representing a republican form of government. Lilienthal actively worked with Isaac Mayer Wise in promoting Reform Judaism throughout the Midwest and was associated with Wise's *American Israelite*. In Cincinnati, he led the congregation to abolish the sale of *aliyot* (Torah honors) and the reading of *piyyutim* (prayer poems) as well as other sections in the Sabbath service. Not everyone was particularly responsive to his reforms. When he refused to be present for a Tisha B'av service, a large contingency left to form its own congregation (She'arith Israel). He did not believe in a return to the land of Israel (or Palestine). Instead, the universalism of Judaism formed the basis of his preaching and teaching.

Believing strongly in interfaith work, Lilienthal joined Christian clergy in numerous civic causes. He was a leading exponent of excluding all religious instruction from public schools. During the Civil War period, he preached in favor of the Union and did relief work for the South after the end of the war.

Lilienthal was a member of the Cincinnati Board of Education (1860–1869), a trustee of the University of Cincinnati (1872–1882) and president of the Board of Trustees of its medical college (1867–1870). Lilienthal was also president of the National Saengerfest held in Cincinnati in 1870. He was founder of the Rabbinic Literary Association (1879) and published the *Sabbath (School) Visitor* from 1874 to 1896. He taught at Hebrew Union College from its opening in 1875 and served on its board of governors until his death. He was instrumental (with Wise) in the founding of the first association of rabbis in the United States, which they called a Beth Din (to which he was elected president). Lilienthal participated in the major rabbinical conference held in the United States during his lifetime. He also served as editor of the short-lived *Hebrew Review* and was a frequent contributor to *Die Deborah, Occident, Asmonean, Volksblatt* and *Volksfreund*.

Lilienthal married Josephine (Peppi) Nettre. They had four children: Jesse, Albert, Philip and Eliza Werner. Lilienthal died in Cincinnati on April 5, 1882.

Writings: *Freiheit, Frühling and Liebe* (Cincinnati, 1857); *Predigten in der Synagogue zu Riga* (Riga, 1841).

References: Central Conference of American Rabbis *Yearbook* 25 (1915): 191–220; *Der deutsche Pioneer* 14 (1882): 102–70, 211–16; *Encyclopaedia Judaica* (Jerusalem, 1971), 11:243–45; *Hebrew Review* 1 (1880): 184–90; *Hebrew Union College Annual* 18 (1943/1944): 32–52, and 12–13 (1937/1938): 825–39; *Jewish Encyclopedia* (New York, 1964), 8:86–87; David Philipson, ed. *Max Lilienthal, American Rabbi: Life and Writings* (New York, 1915); *Universal Jewish Encyclopedia* (New York, 1942), 7:62–63.

LITMAN, RAY (RACHEL) FRANK (1866[?]–1948). Journalist, teacher, orator. Born on April 10, 1866 (?), to Bernard Frank, a San Francisco Indian agent who claimed descent from the Gaon of Vilna, Ray Frank attended California public schools. Her college education at Berkeley was interrupted by her mother's death in 1888, whereupon Frank began teaching in Ruby Hill, Nevada, a poor mining town. There she earned a reputation for compassion, offering free classes to the parents of her students.

Litman's experience living and working among non-Jews caused her to devote her early journalism to combating anti-Semitism. Later she concentrated on short stories, but despite the encouragement of Ambrose Bierce, her fiction remained mediocre. She supported herself by writing feature stories for West Coast publications and teaching in the first Sabbath school in Oakland, California. Litman's class was so popular with children and adults that she received invitations to lecture in other cities, where she impressed audiences with her great oratorical skills and her contagious enthusiasm for Judaism.

An Orthodox Jew in her early years, Litman preached toleration and favored some modernization in religious practice. Her greatest talent was the ability to foster community cooperation, often between Russian and German or between Reform and traditional Jews. At a time when women rarely occupied Jewish pulpits, Litman preached regularly in synagogues throughout the West and Midwest, often receiving requests that she stay on as rabbi.

The most acclaimed of these incidents occurred in Spokane, Washington. On the road as a correspondent, Litman found that factional bickering had blocked the organization of High Holy Day services. She gathered the community, led services and delivered an eloquent sermon that convinced the Jews of Spokane to found their first synagogue. The West Coast press gave wide coverage to their reporter-turned-celebrity, incorrectly dubbing Litman the first woman rabbi.

Though Litman sat in on some Hebrew Union College classes, she never sought ordination and publicly opposed the ordination of women. Among the first Americans to supply domestic feminist arguments to Judaism, she insisted that women were capable of being rabbis but that they could better preserve Judaism by being mothers. In her 1893 address before the Jewish Women's Congress of the World Parliament of Religions at the Chicago World's Fair, Litman glorified motherhood, declaring the home sacred and stressing its influence in developing future commitment to Judaism. Rather than pushing to expand the role of women, she demanded recognition and status for women's traditional roles within Judaism, often publicizing long-ignored biblical heroines as role models. She also believed that when properly observed, Judaism provided women and men with complementary but equal roles. Litman saw little need for the women's rights movement and opposed women's suffrage, though once women had the vote, she encouraged them to use it wisely and organized a chapter of the League of Women Voters in Champaign, Illinois. Her positions were echoed in the National Council of Jewish Women, which she helped found at the 1893 Jewish Women's Congress. She also organized the Oakland, California, section of that organization.

From 1899 to 1901, Litman lived in London, associating especially with Rabbi Hermann Adler, Nettie Adler, Nina Davis and Lily Montague. There she also met and married an economics professor, Simon Litman. His career took them to Champaign, Illinois, where Litman frequently hosted Jewish students in her home. These activities evolved into the University of Illinois Hillel. In Champaign, she helped found that city's first Reform temple as well as a Hadassah chapter while continuing to lecture occasionally.

Ray Litman died on October 10, 1948, after a lengthy illness, in Peoria, Illinois.

Writings: "The Arch Enemy of the Jew," *American Jewess* (October 1895); Jewish Messenger (May 23, June 20, 1890); *Papers of the Jewish Women's Congress* (Philadelphia, 1894), pp. 52–65; "Ray Frank Litman Manuscript Collection," American Jewish Historical Society.

References: Anita Libman Lebeson, *Recall to Life* (New York, 1970), pp. 161, 178, 205–7; Simon Litman, *Ray Frank Litman: A Memoir* (New York, 1957); Nahida Remy, *The Jewish Woman*, trans. Louise Mannheimer (Cincinnati, 1895), pp. 221–26; Frances Willard and Mary Livermore, eds., *A Woman of the Century: Leading American Women* (Buffalo, 1893), pp. 299–300.

F.R.

LOTH, MORITZ (1832–1913). Businessman. Loth was born on December 29, 1832, in Milotitz, Moravia, Austria, the son of Bernard and Pauline Strassman Loth. The twelfth son of 22 children, he was educated at home and in the public schools of Moravia. Loth was apprenticed to a goldsmith before entering the German army. His entrepreneurial acumen won him free passage to America. Loth settled in Hartford, Connecticut, where he opened a dry goods store and speculated in local bank currency. He moved to Cincinnati as a wealthy man in 1858. In Cincinnati he opened a store and took an active part in the community as a lobbyist for tax concessions beneficial to Cincinnati traders.

Loth was president of Congregation Bene Jeshurun, where Isaac M. Wise served as rabbi. He was a founder of the Board of Trade, which developed the Cincinnati Southern Railroad. He was also general manager for the Central, Western and Southern departments of the United States Credit System Company of New York, the original credit insurance company. Loth was president of the convention that founded the Union of American Hebrew Congregations by calling together congregations in the South and West. While Isaac M. Wise had attempted to call together a congregational union in 1845 and almost succeeded in 1867, it was Loth who successfully did so, avoiding Wise completely. He served as president of the First Council of the UAHC and led it for 18 years. During this time, Hebrew Union College was established. Afterward he continued on the executive board of the UAHC as a member of its Board of Synagogue and School Extension.

Loth also founded the Ladies' Educational Aid Society to assist needy students of HUC. He also drafted the Free Port of Entry bill, making every interior city equal to a seaport, and through an active editorial-writing campaign, he succeeded in securing its passage through Congress. While a member of the Committee on Transportation of the Board of Trade, Loth was instrumental in abolishing the toll at the Portland Canal; as a member of the Committee on Public Improvements on the same Board of Trade, he inaugurated the Cincinnati Zoological Gardens. His work on the Board of Trade was recognized when a Cincinnati street was named in his honor.

A consummate fund-raiser, Loth was editor-in-chief of the *Fair Journal*. The publication was used to raise funds to rebuild the Cincinnati Union Bethel Building. He was a member-for-life of the Bethel Society.

Loth was a businessman with unusual astuteness and means (gaining and losing millions of dollars several times in his life) and an author of novels and short stories. He was editor and publisher of *Monitor Magazine* for children. A committed Reform Jew, he was conservative in regard to his ritual observances and highly suspicious of radical Reform.

He married Frederica Wilhartz; they had five children: Laura Loth Newburgh, Ida Jacobs, Paul Loth, Mrs. Leo Newburgh and Steven Loth. Moritz Loth died in Cincinnati in May 1913.

Writings: *The Forgiving Kiss* (New York, 1874); *On a Higher Plane* (Cincinnati, 1899); *Our Prospects* (Cincinnati, 1870); *Pearls from the Bible* (Cincinnati, 1894).

References: *American Jewish Year Book* (Philadelphia, 1906), 7:83; *Cincinnati Enquirer*, obituary, May 1913; "Nearprint Biographies Box," American Jewish Archives; *Universal Jewish Encyclopedia* (New York, 1943), 7:205.

M

MAGNES, JUDAH L. (1877–1948). Rabbi, academician, community organizer, Zionist leader. Born on July 5, 1877, in San Francisco, California, Judah Magnes was the son of David Magnes and Sophie Abrahamson Magnes. (Magnes was born with the name Julian but changed it to Judah early in his life.) He attended school in Oakland, California, and studied at local orthodox synagogues until San Francisco's leading Reform rabbi, Jacob Voorsanger, was attracted to him and became his teacher. He attended the University of Cincinnati (B.A. 1898), where he was editor of *The Cincinnatian*. He resigned as editor when the president of the university attempted to suppress the students' freedom to roast faculty members. In Cincinnati, he initiated the Zionist Club and its settlement house. He attended Hebrew Union College, where he was ordained in 1900.

After ordination, Magnes studied at the Universities of Berlin and Heidelberg (Ph.D. 1902), as well as at the Lehrenstadt für der Wissenschaft des Judenthums. There he started the National Association of Students, which eventually dissolved. After his return to the United States, he served as librarian and instructor in Bible at Hebrew Union College. He served Temple Israel in Brooklyn, New York (1904–1905), and as assistant rabbi at Congregation Emanu-El in New York City (1906–1910). His shift toward traditionalism (already seen by 1904 in his relationship with Solomon Schechter) led to a break with Emanu-El, from which he resigned in 1910. Among other things, he called for a return to traditional liturgy. He wanted Hebrew taught in the religious schools (he would later call Reform Judaism "all Reform and no Judaism"). While at Emanu-El, he vociferously defended those among the Hebrew Union College who were accused of Zionism. He served B'nai Jeshurun, a conservative synagogue (1910–1912), but left to dedicate his life to public service. Even B'nai Jeshurun was too liberal. He argued for the removal of its organ almost as soon as he arrived. In 1909 he organized Ahva (modeled after the Society of Lovers of Zion in

Odessa), but it lasted only until 1912. In 1922 he organized the Society for the Advancement of Judaism (which was later revived to embody the philosophy of Mordecai Kaplan). In 1908, Magnes founded the Kehillah and served as its president (until its demise in 1922). The Kehillah was designed to advance and coordinate Jewish life in New York City and dealt vigorously with such internal problems as religious life and Jewish education. Magnes was the driving force behind the development of its pioneering Bureau of Jewish Education (with Samson Benderly) and other departments.

He served as a liaison between uptown and downtown Jews, was active in labor arbitrations and helped to repress crime in the immigrant areas of the city. But Magnes's fiery leadership and conscience would eventually cause him to resign from most of his leadership positions. He can best be described as a maximalist Jew rather than a maximalist Zionist. He was able to inspire but unable to organize sufficiently to build a foundation for the organizations he led.

As an active Zionist, Magnes participated in the Zionist Congress in Basle in 1905 and served the American Federation of Zionists (secretary 1905–1908). He resigned from the Zionist Executive Committee over a conflict with Louis Brandeis regarding popular representation. He assisted Henrietta Szold in her Youth Aliyah work and was chair of the Emergency Council of Hadassah in Palestine. He was also chairman of the Middle East Advisory Council of the American Joint Distribution Committee (which he helped found during World War I). In 1939 he helped establish the Hebrew University–Hadassah Hospital.

Magnes was a disciple of Ahad Ha-am, whom he called "harmonious jew." Magnes would later call his own vision "synthetic Judaism," to harmonize Judaism with modern culture. He constantly sought an accord with Palestinian Arabs and wanted Israel established as a binational state.

In the community, Magnes led the largest Jewish demonstration against the pogroms in Kishinev in 1903 and established the Jewish Defense Association, which sought funds to smuggle arms to Russian Jews. After Kishinev, he helped establish the American Jewish Committee. In 1916 Magnes headed the first commission that went to Europe to arrange for the distribution of American Jewish relief funds, where he was criticized for his pacifism.

Magnes helped found the Yiddish *Der Tag* and sponsored the Intercollegiate Menorah Association. With Israel Friedlaender, he founded Young Judea.

Magnes left for Palestine in 1922. He served as chancellor of Hebrew University, which he helped to found (1925–1935), and later as president (1935–1945). The latter role was more honorific and carried with it no decision-making responsibilities. Before the opening of the university, he developed several institutes into which the university grew, including the Institute for Jewish Culture (1925). He saw the university (originally conceived by Herman Schapira at the First Zionist Congress in 1897) as the spiritual center of the entire Jewish people. He was a member of the international board of the Technion, where he fought for Hebrew as the language of instruction. He helped found local religious institutions in Israel as well as Jeshurun Synagogue.

Magnes was a pacifist who rallied against the entrance of the United States in World War I. In spite of his pacifism, he called for war against Germany (during World War II) and served as chairman of the Supply Board, Scientific Advisory Committee of the War. He assisted Jews in escaping to Turkey.

Hebrew University honored Magnes by publishing *Sefer Magnes* (*The Book of Magnes*) in 1938 and named its university press in his honor, as well as its chair of Bible. He was also granted its first honorary degree (along with Chaim Weizman).

In 1908, he married Beatrice Lowenstein. They had three children: David, Jonathan and Benedict (Baruch). Magnes died in New York City during a visit on October 27, 1948.

Writings (partial listing): *Addresses by the Chancellor of Hebrew University* (Jerusalem, 1940); *The Bond* (Jerusalem, 1939); *In the Perplexity of the Times* (Jerusalem, 1946); *Like All the Nations?* (Jerusalem, 1930); with Martin Buber and E. Simon, *Toward Union in Palestine* (Jerusalem, 1943); *War-time Addresses, 1917–1921* (New York, 1923).

References: *American Hebrew*, July 9, 1937, pp. 5, 20; Norman Bentwich, *For Zion's Sake: A Biography of Judah L. Magnes* (Philadelphia, 1954); David Bichel, *Judah L. Magnes: Pioneer and Prophet* (Berkeley, 1973); William M. Brinner and Moses Rischin, *Like All the Nations? The Life and Legacy of Judah L. Magnes* (Albany, 1987); *Encyclopaedia Judaica* (Jerusalem, 1971), 11:715–18; Nelson Glueck, *The Lion of Judah* (New York, 1958); Arthur Goren, *New York Jews and the Quest for Community: The Kehillah Experiment, 1908–1922* (New York, 1970); Marc Gruber, "Judah Leon Magnes: Zionist Pacifist and Democrat" (Rabbinic thesis, Hebrew Union College–Jewish Institute of Religion, Cincinnati, 1981); *Universal Jewish Encyclopedia* (New York, 1941), 7:276–77.

MAGNIN, EDGAR FOGEL (1890–1984). Rabbi, civic leader. The son of Samuel and Lillian Fogel Magnin, Edgar Magnin was born in San Francisco on July 1, 1890. He began his education in San Francisco and then attended the University of Cincinnati and Hebrew Union College, where he was ordained in 1914.

After ordination, Magnin briefly served his first rabbinical post in Stockton, California. In 1915 he moved to Los Angeles, which he called the "Athens of the Western World," to become rabbi of the B'nai B'rith Temple, today known as Wilshire Boulevard Temple. Magnin served in this position until his death. During his tenure at Wilshire Boulevard Temple, the congregation grew from 400 to 2,000 families, as the Los Angeles Jewish community exploded in size. Magnin's ability to adjust the mission of the Temple to accommodate this growth—increasing his public visibility in proportion to the expansion of his constituency—is directly related to the heightened stature of the Temple. His personal involvement extended to assisting in the drawing of blueprints for the landmark building that now houses the Wilshire Boulevard congregation.

Magnin became a widely known public figure, serving as Reform Judaism's de facto spokesperson for the western United States. He was interested particularly in Jewish-Christian dialogue and in disseminating the perspective of progressive Judaism in radio and television broadcasts and newspaper columns. He was a columnist for the *Los Angeles Herald-Examiner* and the Anglo-Jewish weekly *Heritage*.

Among Magnin's many civic activities, his work during World War II stands out. Throughout the war years, Magnin represented the Jewish Welfare Board, working with the USO and traveling to combat zones under the auspices of the National Conference of Christians and Jews.

Deeply interested in Jewish education, Magnin served as a lecturer at the University of Southern California from 1935 to 1955. In the mid-1940s, he became founding president of the College of Jewish Studies, which later became the Rhea Hirsch School of Education of Hebrew Union College–Jewish Institute of Religion, Los Angeles. He was later honored with the dedication of the Edgar F. Magnin School of Graduate Studies at the same campus. Magnin is best known to many for delivering the prayer at the 1969 inauguration of Richard Nixon. He was a founder of the National Council of Alcoholism and published a popular book, *How to Live a Richer and Fuller Life*. In 1980 the city of Los Angeles, Orange County and the State of California renamed the block of Wilshire Boulevard Temple the "Edgar F. Magnin Square."

In 1916 Magnin married Evelyn Rosenthal; they had two children: Henry and Mae. Edgar Magnin died in Los Angeles on July 17, 1984.

Writings: *How to Live a Richer and Fuller Life* (New York, 1951).

References: Samson Levey, "Magnin: People Cannot Remain Neutral towards This 20th Century Rabbinical Giant," *B'nai B'rith Messenger*, July 11, 1975; "Nearprint Biography File and Box," American Jewish Archives; oral history memoir of Magnin in Bancroft Library, University of California Library, Berkeley, California.

H.J.F.

MARCUS, AUDREY FRIEDMAN (1931–   ). Educator, publisher. The daughter of Julius and Anne Rosenberg Ritter, Audrey Marcus was born on June 6, 1931, in New York City. After attending lower schools in Westtown, Pennsylvania, she attended Smith College and Wesleyan University (Middletown, Connecticut) before graduating from the University of Denver in 1970. She received an M.A. in Jewish Education from HUC-JIR, Rhea Hirsch School of Education, Los Angeles, in 1976.

From 1969 to 1973, Marcus originated and codirected the Rocky Mountain Curriculum Planning Workshop, which published curicula written by college students during these retreat workshops. In 1972 she became director of education at Temple Micah in Denver, a post she would hold for two years. In 1974–1975 she served as Junior High School Coordinator at Temple Judea in Tarzana, California, She left this post to become a full-time free-lance consultant in Jewish education. Marcus's career has focused on writing, editing and publishing innovative materials for Jewish education. Marcus was editor and publisher of *Alternatives in Religious Education* from 1970 until it ceased publication in

1979. Since 1973, she has been vice president of Alternatives in Religious Education, an innovative and trendsetting publishing house of Jewish educational materials, resources and textbooks.

Formerly active in the organizations of her profession, Marcus was a board member of the National Association of Temple Educators (NATE); a member of the Joint Commission on Jewish Education of the Union of American Hebrew Congregations and the Central Conference of American Rabbis; and chair of Task Force #1 on Jewish Identity, UAHC-CCAR National Curriculum Project. In 1970–1971 she received NATE's Emanuel Gamoran Memorial Award. Marcus has been affiliated with many other organizations, including the National Federation of Temple Sisterhoods, serving on its Board of Directors (1969–1975), Member Commission of Projections for the Future, and Executive Committee (1971–1973). She is currently first vice president of the Hillel Council of Colorado. In 1980 she became a Fellow in Religious Education.

Very concerned with issues of women's equality, Marcus served as vice president of the National Organization for Women, Denver chapter, and as state coordinator of the Equal Rights Amendment Coalition (Colorado, 1972); she was a member of the Governor's Commission on the Status of Women. In 1973 she was honored by Denver NOW for advancing the quality of women. Marcus also focused her energies on illuminating women's stake in issues of specifically Jewish concern as chair of the Women's Plea for Soviet Jewry, as a steering committee member of the Denver Committee of Concern for Soviet Jewry and as a vice president of Denver's chapter of the National Council of Jewish Women.

Audrey Ritter married Don Friedman; they had three children: Jill Fixler, Dayle and Glen Friedman. In 1974 she married Fred Marcus, a retired Jewish educator. From this marriage she has two stepchildren: Vivian and David Marcus.

Writings (partial): coauthor, *Bioethics: A Jewish View* (Denver, 1984); coauthor, *Death, Burial and Mourning in the Jewish Tradition* (Denver, 1976); coauthor, *A Family Education Unit on Bar and Bat Mitzvah* (Denver, 1977); coauthor, *The Holocaust: A Study in Values* (Denver, 1976); coauthor, *The Jewish Principals Handbook* (Denver, 1983); coauthor, *Shabbat Can Be* (New York, 1979).

References: *Who's Who in American Jewry* (Los Angeles, 1980), pp. 324–25.

MARCUS, JACOB RADER (1896–   ). Rabbi, historian, professor, administrator. The son of Aaron Marcus and Jennie Rader, Jacob Marcus was born in Connellsville, Pennsylvania (actually in an unincorporated area called New Haven), on March 5, 1896. He was the second of four children: Isaac and twins Frank and Ethel.

At age four, Marcus moved to Homestead, Pennsylvania, where his father opened a clothing shop. In 1907 the family moved to Pittsburgh and less than two years later to Wheeling, West Virginia. Marcus had been attending both public school and heder since the age of nine or ten. In Wheeling, where the family would live until 1915, he went to the Reform Jewish Sunday School and to the Reform Eoff Street Temple. In 1909 he was confirmed in the Reform Sunday School but observed his bar mitzvah in the Orthodox synagogue.

In 1910, Rabbi Harry Levy of Eoff Street Temple told Marcus that he was going to prepare him for the Reform rabbinate. Despite the Orthodox aspects of Marcus's background and with a rebuff from the Jewish Theological Seminary, Jacob Rader Marcus, just 15 years of age, went to Cincinnati in the fall of 1911. He attended Hughes High School, the University of Cincinnati and Hebrew Union College. Apart from his studies, Marcus was active in the University of Cincinnati's Jewish Menorah Society, ultimately becoming its president. He edited the Hebrew Union College's student journal, *Hebrew Union College Monthly*, beginning in 1917. He was also in the Ridgeway Players, a drama group.

In 1917 Marcus volunteered for the U.S. Army. Stationed near Cincinnati, he was able to receive his A.B. in June of that year.

In June 1920, a year after his return from the army, Marcus was ordained a rabbi at Hebrew Union College in Cincinnati. After ordination, he was appointed to the Hebrew Union College faculty as an instructor in Bible and rabbinics, declining an offer by Rabbi Israel Mattuck to become associate rabbi in a London synagogue.

In 1922 he left for Germany to continue his studies, spending a semester at the University of Kiel and the remainder of his time at the University of Berlin (Ph.D., 1925, magna cum laude). His dissertation was a study of commercial relations between England and Germany during the years 1576 to 1585. After postgraduate studies in Paris (Ecole Rabbinique) and Jerusalem (Hebrew University, 1925 to 1926), he returned to Hebrew Union College, where he remained, moving up the ranks from assistant professor in 1926 to associate professor in 1929 and full professor in 1934. In 1946 Marcus was named Adolph S. Ochs Professor of American Jewish History; since 1965 he has been the Milton and Hattie Jutz Distinguished Service Professor of American Jewish History.

Between 1928 and 1947, Marcus published several important studies on Central European Jewry. He was profoundly affected by the Holocaust. Before 1945, Marcus theorized that a new center of world Jewish life was being formed in the United States on the threshold of a Golden Age. In 1947, as one part of an age was coming to an end, a new one was formed with Marcus's creation and direction of the American Jewish Archives.

Marcus can be credited with almost single-handedly establishing and developing American Jewish history as a legitimate academic discipline and making the American Jewish Archives one of the great archives of the world. He instituted the semiannual *American Jewish Archives* journal and remains its editor. In 1956 he founded the American Jewish Periodical Center. Since that time he has published numerous pioneering works on American Jewry. A prolific scholar, he is best known for his research in colonial Jewish history as well as for his publications of numerous collections of primary documents illustrating virtually every aspect of American Jewish life.

Marcus served as president (1949–1950) and was subsequently named honorary president of the Central Conference of American Rabbis; president of the

Jewish Community Relations Council of Cincinnati; and president of the American Jewish Historical Society (1956–1959). Marcus also served as trustee for the Jewish Academy of Arts and Sciences and as a member of the executive committee of the American Academy of Jewish Research. He is the recipient of honorary degrees from the University of Cincinnati (LL.D., 1950), Dropsie College (LL.D., 1959), Spertus College of Judaica (D.H.L., 1977), Gratz College (D.H.L., 1978), and Wayne State University (D.H.L.). He received the Frank L. Weil Award, National Jewish Welfare Board (1955); and the L. M. Freidman medal for distinguished service to history (1961).

In 1925 he married Antoinette Brody (d.); they had one daughter: Merle (d.).

Writings (partial listing from a bibliography that numbers over 250 items): *The American Jewish Woman, 1654–1980* (New York, 1981); *The American Jewish Woman: A Documentary History* (New York, 1981); *American Jewry: Documents, Eighteenth Century* (Cincinnati, 1958); *Colonial American Jew*, 3 vols. (Detroit, 1970); *Communal Sick-Care in the German Ghetto* (Cincinnati, 1947); *Early American Jewry*, 2 vols. (Philadelphia, 1951–1953, 1974); *The Jew in the Medieval World: A Source Book, 315–1791* (Cincinnati, 1938); *Memoirs of American Jews, 1775–1865*, 3 vols. (Philadelphia 1955, 1974); *The Rise and Destiny of the German Jew* (Cincinnati, 1934); *This I Believe* (Northvale, NJ, 1991); *To Count a People: American Jewish Population Data, 1585–1984* (Lanham, MD, 1990); *United States Jewry, 1776–1985*, 4 vols. (Detroit, 1990).

References: *American Jewish Biographies* (New York, 1982), pp. 223–24; *A Bicentennial Festschrift for Jacob Rader Marcus* (Waltham, MA, 1976); *Biz Hundert un Tzvantsik! A Tribute Volume for Dr. Jacob Rader Marcus on the Occasion of His 90th Birthday* (Cincinnati, 1986); *Essays in American Jewish History: To Commemorate the Tenth Anniversary of the Founding of the American Jewish Archives under the Direction of Jacob Rader Marcus* (Cincinnati, 1958); ''Jacob R. Marcus Manuscript Collection,'' American Jewish Archives; *Who's Who in America* (several editions); *Who's Who in American Jewry* (Los Angeles, 1980), p. 325.

A.J.P.

MARCUSON, ISAAC EDWARD (1872–1952). Rabbi. Born in Cincinnati, Ohio, on December 18, 1872, Isaac Marcuson was the son of Marcus and Adele Marx Marcuson. He attended Cincinnati public schools. In 1894 he received his B.L. from the University of Cincinnati and was ordained by Hebrew Union College, where he had been studying simultaneously. In 1939 he received an honorary D.D. from Hebrew Union College.

Immediately after ordination, Marcuson went to Temple Beth Israel, where he served for nine years. In 1903, due to health problems, he resigned his pulpit and returned to Cincinnati. There he studied chemistry and in 1905 accepted a position as a chemist in Sandusky, Ohio. In Sandusky, Marcuson organized a congregation and became its rabbi without compensation. In 1910, his health restored, he accepted a pulpit from Congregation Beth Elohim in Charleston, South Carolina, where he remained until 1915. From 1915 to 1918, he served United Hebrew Congregation in Terre Haute, Indiana. In 1918 he returned to Macon, Georgia, to serve Temple Beth Israel, a position he held until his death.

In 1915 Marcus became editor of all CCAR publications. In 1917, he began his 35-year tenure as secretary of the CCAR, becoming an authority on the organization's procedures, practices, historical declarations and policies. The CCAR honored him for his service several months before his death. The Southeast Region of the UAHC also honored him in 1946.

Marcuson was deeply influenced by Isaac M. Wise, and his career reflected that influence. He ministered to the poor and spoke out on their behalf.

In 1903, he married Rose Thorner. He died on September 2, 1952, in Macon, Georgia.

References: Central Conference of American Rabbis *Yearbook* 63 (1953): 225–26.

MARSHALL, LOUIS (1856–1929). Lawyer. Louis Marshall was born on December 14, 1856, in Syracuse, New York, the son of Jacob Marshall and Cilli Strauss Marshall, German-Jewish immigrants. After attending public school in Syracuse, he served as an apprentice for two years in a Syracuse law firm.

In 1877, he graduated from Columbia University Law School, having completed his two-year program in only one year, at which time he returned to Syracuse to join a law firm, where he remained until 1894. That year, he came to New York as a partner of Guggenheimer, Untermeyer and Marshall. Later, he received an (hon.) L.L.D. in 1913 from Syracuse University and an (hon.) L.H.D. in 1920 from Hebrew Union College.

As an attorney, Marshall was a specialist in constitutional and corporate law. While he was once considered for the Supreme Court, he never ran for public office. He did, however, argue numerous cases before the Supreme Court and was the first person in the United States to serve three times as a member of the New York State constitutional conventions (1870, 1893 and 1915). He also participated in local and national politics as a Republican. Such participation led him to help establish the New York State College of Forestry (serving as president for 20 years) while serving on the board of Syracuse University (where he bequeathed his law library). The State College of Forestry was named in his memory at Syracuse University in 1930, after the erection of a new building. He was also chairman of the committee on amendment of law of the Association of the Bar of New York.

Marshall eschewed the Gentile tendency of the time to refer to Jews as Hebrews or Israelites, while at the same time he argued that he was more than a Jew, he was also an American. Although Marshall was a Reform Jew, he condemned radical Reform, clinging closely to his roots. A manifestation of his sense of *Klal Yisrael* (an inclusive Jewish community) can be seen when he served as president of (Reform) Temple Emanu-El in New York, while at the same time he was chairman of the board of directors of (conservative) Jewish Theological Seminary of America. He oversaw the merger of Temple Emanu-El and Temple Beth El (in 1927). He was president of the American Jewish Joint Relief Committee in World War I and helped to organize and guide the American Jewish Joint Distribution Committee. As a nonpolitical Zionist who was not interested in Palestine as a political entity, Marshall worked with Chaim Weizman to establish a venue for non-Zionists who believed in Palestine as a center of settlement for Jews, to support its upbuilding and relieve its beleaguered inhabitants. These efforts, opposed by Stephen S. Wise and others, eventually led to the establishment of the Jewish Agency, which included Zionists and non-Zionists. Articulating his non-Zionist policy in an attempt to assuage both elements in the American Jewish Committee, Marshall said, "Zionism is a theory and anti-Zionism is a folly."

Best called the foremost spokesperson for the American Jewish elite, Marshall demonstrated his leadership on the national scene when he led the successful campaign against the United States–Russian Commercial Treaty Affair of 1832. Some years later, in 1912, Marshall was president of the American Jewish Committee, a post he held until 1929. Always playing the role of mediator, Marshall was involved in the bitter struggle over the establishment of the American Jewish Congress and was a member of the Jewish delegation to the Paris Peace Conference in 1919, helping to steer the way for Jewish minority rights in the new Eastern European nation-states.

An ardent opponent of anti-Semitism, Marshall fought Henry Ford and his distribution of *The Protocols of the Elder of Zion*, causing Ford to write a formal apology to the Jewish community in 1927. And in 1913, Marshall participated in the unsuccessful legal defense of the wrongfully accused Leo Frank in Atlanta, Georgia. Marshall was involved in the campaign to delay legislation aimed at restricting immigration and intervened in 1922 when Harvard University announced that it would put into place a quota system for Jewish students. Through his efforts, this plan was reversed. In 1929, Marshall joined others in opposing the Ku Klux Klan and publicly condemned the Massena ritual murder libel.

Marshall's work was not limited to the Jewish community. He championed minority rights as an active member of the National Association of Colored People and in 1920 defended the right of five socialist assemblymen who were refused their seats in the New York State Legislature.

In 1895, he married Florence Lowenstein. They had three sons: George, James and Robert. He died in Zurich, Switzerland, on September 11, 1929.

Writings: For selected papers and writings, see Charles Reznikoff, ed., *Louis Marshall: Champion of Liberty*, 2 vols. (Philadelphia, 1957).

References: Morton Rosenstock, *Louis Marshall: Defender of Jewish Rights* (Detroit, 1965); Simon E. Sobeloff, *Louis Marshall* (New York, 1956); Horace Stern, *Louis Marshall: An Appreciation* (N.p., 1930); Sol M. Stroock, *Louis Marshall, His Achievements as Factors in the Lives of the Jewish Community Today* (New York, 1936); *Universal Jewish Encyclopedia* (New York, 1943), 7:380–85; *Who's Who in American Jewry* (New York, 1928), p. 474.

MARTIN, BERNARD (1928–1982). Rabbi, teacher, academician. The son of Benjamin and Helen Hershkowitz Martin, Bernard Martin was born on March 13, 1928, in Soklence, Czechoslovakia. He came to America in 1934. Martin entered the University of Chicago, where he received a B.A. with honors in 1947. He studied law for a year at the University of Virginia. Afterward Martin entered Hebrew Union College, where he received a B.H.L. with honors in 1949, as well as an M.H.L. and ordination in 1951.

After ordination, Martin became rabbi of Sinai Temple in Champaign, Illinois. He served until 1957, except from 1953 to 1955, when he was a chaplain in Japan for the U.S. Army. Martin became associate rabbi of Chicago Sinai Congregation in 1957 and served until 1961, when he became senior rabbi at Mount Zion Hebrew Congregation in St. Paul, Minnesota. He retained that position until 1965. During most of his years in Champaign and Chicago, Martin was enrolled at the University of Illinois, where he received an M.A. (1957) and a Ph.D. (1961) in philosophy.

Martin left the pulpit in 1966 to become Abba Hillel Silver Associate Professor of Jewish Studies at Case Western Reserve University in Cleveland (named professor in 1968), a position he held until his death.

As a philosopher and theologian, Martin actively participated in learned societies such as the American Philosophical Association, American Academy for Jewish Research, Society of Biblical Literature, American Academy of Religion, National Association of Professors of Hebrew and the Association for Jewish Studies. He was also a member of the Central Conference of American Rabbis and edited its *Journal of Reform Judaism* (formerly *Journal of the Central Conference of Reform Rabbis*) from 1975 to 1982. He was invited to give papers and lectures at the meetings of these organizations as well as at colleges and universities throughout the world, including the University of Paris (Sorbonne), Oxford University, Keio University (Tokyo) and Hebrew University (Jerusalem). He was the recipient of research grants from the Memorial Foundation for Jewish Culture (Geneva), the Leonard, Faye and Albert Fatner Foundation (Cleveland) and the Pritzker Foundation (Chicago). His essays in philosophy formed substantial chapters in edited books. Martin wrote and edited multivolume works that "illuminated the complexities of modern theological and philosophical thought." His work "opened access to a wide range of important literature," according to the citation he received on being awarded an honorary D.D. from HUC-JIR in 1976.

In an effort to maintain his commitment to community, an interest that transcended his academic and scholarly pursuits, Bernard Martin was active in his university community. He served on many internal committees and as chairman of the Department of Religion. He was also active in the civic community as a member of the Board of Trustees of the Cleveland Jewish Community Federation, among others.

In 1955 Martin married Nancy Louise Platt; they had two children: Rachel and Joseph. Bernard Martin died in Cleveland on January 18, 1982.

Writings: *The Existentialist Theology of Paul Tillich* (New York, 1963); ed., *Great Twentieth Century Jewish Philosophers* (New York, 1970); trans. *History of Jewish Literature* (Cleveland and Cincinnati, 1972–1978); *A History of Judaism* (New York, 1974); *Prayer in Judaism* (New York, 1968).

References: "Biography Nearprint File," American Jewish Archives; *Who's Who in World Jewry* (New York, 1981), pp. 524–25; *Who Was Who in America* (Chicago, 1985), 8:262.

MERZBACHER, LEO (1809–1856). Rabbi. Leo Merzbacher was born on March 16, 1809, in Fuerth, Bavaria, the son of Salman and Rachel Merzbacher. His mother died when he was two, and his father married his mother's sister Dina. In Bavaria he studied under the Hatam Sofer R. Moses Schreiber of Pressburg. Although Merzbacher pursued graduate studies at the University of Erlangen (and perhaps Munich) and was known as "Doctor," it is unclear whether he completed his doctoral studies. Merzbacher emigrated to the United States in 1841, although he may have arrived as late as 1843, according to I. M. Wise (*American Israelite*, July 24, 1965).

Considered America's first Reform rabbi, Merzbacher's first position was as a teacher with Congregation Rodeph Sholom in New York, one he held for two years. In 1843 he became preacher and teacher at New York City's Anshe Chesed. He seems to have held these positions simultaneously. After a seminar in 1845, in which he argued against the practice of married women covering their hair, his appointment was not renewed. As a result, his supporters formed Congregation Emanuel, merging their efforts with those of the recently formed Cultus Verein, a group of young German Jews unaffiliated with any congregation. When the Verein became Temple Emanu-El, it invited Merzbacher to serve as its rabbi. He did so until his death in 1856.

In the early years at the new congregation, organized in 1845 as Temple Emanu-El, reforms were moderate. Merzbacher delivered a sermon (or *Vorksung*) each Shabbat, a radical departure from the prevailing tradition. In 1848 he introduced confirmation and in 1855 compiled an abbreviated prayer book for use at worship. As the rabbi of the first Reform congregation in New York City, he became a force in the organization and development of Reform Judaism in the United States.

While Merzbacher's deteriorating health (tuberculosis) limited his activities and impact on his congregation in New York, he did participate in the founding of the Independent Order of True Sisters. He was active in the Independent Order of B'nai B'rith and is credited with suggesting its name, as well as preparing its first ritual for burial.

Leo Merzbacher died in New York City on October 21, 1856.

Writings: *Seder Tefillah* (New York, 1855).

References: Bernard Cohn, "Leo Merzbacher," *American Jewish Archives* 6 (January 1954): 21–24; Hyman B. Grinstein, *The Rise of the Jewish Community of New York, 1654–1860* (Philadelphia, 1945); *Menorah Monthly*, 1887; "Necrology of Leo Merzbacher," *Die Deborah* 2 (1856): 81; Ronald Sobel, "A History of New York's Temple Emanu-El" (Ph.D. dissertation, New York University, 1980); *Universal Jewish Encyclopedia* (New York, 1942), 7:497.

MEYER, MICHAEL ALBERT (1937–   ). Historian. The son of Charles Matthaeus and Susanne Paula Frey Meyer, Michael Meyer was born in Berlin on November 15, 1937. He and his family emigrated to the United States in 1941. During his youth, Meyer served as president of the National Federation of Temple Youth. He attended the University of California at Los Angeles, receiving a B.A. with honors in history and philosophy in 1959. He enrolled in HUC-JIR, Los Angeles, and received a B.H.L. in 1960. Leaving the rabbinic program, Meyer transferred to the Cincinnati campus of HUC-JIR to complete his education, earning a Ph.D. in Jewish history in 1964.

Meyer returned to the Los Angeles campus of HUC-JIR to teach from 1964 to 1967, then joined the Cincinnati faculty, where he has remained since. A specialist in German-Jewish history and with a strong interest in Jewish historiography, Meyer is currently professor of Jewish history. He has been a visiting member of the faculties of UCLA, Antioch College, the University of Haifa, Ben Gurion University in Beersheba and Hebrew University in Jerusalem. He has lectured frequently at other colleges and universities in the United States and abroad.

A prolific author, his *Origins of the Modern Jew* won an award from the Jewish Book Council and the Milberry Prize. The first comprehensive history of the Reform movement in 80 years, *Response to Modernity* won the Gerrard and Ella Berman Award. From 1978 to 1980, Meyer was the first president of the Association for Jewish Studies, the leading professional society of Judaica scholars in North America. He currently chairs the American Section of the International Association of Historical Societies for the Study of Jewish History and serves as chair of the Publications Committee of the Hebrew Union College Press.

Meyer married Margaret Mayer, a Reform rabbi, in 1961; they have three children: Daniel, Jonathan and Rebecca.

Writings (partial, not including nearly 200 articles and reviews or editorial work): "Alienated Intellectuals in the Camp of the Religious Reform: The Frankfurt Reformfreunde, 1842–45," *Association of Jewish Studies Review* 6 (1981); "A Centennial History," in *Hebrew Union College–Jewish Institute of Religion at One Hundred Years*, ed. Samuel E. Karff (Cincinnati, 1976); *Ideas of Jewish History* (New York, 1974); "Judaism after Auschwitz," *Commentary*, June 1972; "Ob Schrift? Ob Geist?—Die Offenbarungsfrage im deutschen Judentum des neunzehnten Jahrhunderts," in *Offenbarung im jüdischen und christlichen Glaubensverstandnis* (Freiburg, 1981); *The Origins of the Modern Jew: Jewish Identity and European Culture in Germany, 1749–1824* (Detroit, 1967); *Response to Modernity: A History of the Reform Movement in Judaism* (New York, 1988).

References: "Nearprint Biography Box," American Jewish Archives; *Who's Who in American Jewry* (Los Angeles, 1980); *Who's Who in World Jewry* (New York, 1981), p. 539.

MIELZINER, MOSES (1828–1903). Talmudic scholar, rabbi. The son of Rabbi Benjamin and Rosa Caro Mielziner, Moses Mielziner was born on August 12, 1828, in Schubin, Posen, Germany. Mielziner pursued general studies in

Germany as well as rabbinic studies under Samuel Holdeim and Leopold Lowe. Faced with strong opposition from Orthodox authorities, the liberal Mielziner was forced to abandon his rabbinic position in Mecklenberg. He moved to Denmark, where he headed a Jewish school in Copenhagen while pursuing doctoral studies. He received his Ph.D. from the University of Giessen in 1859. His doctoral dissertation was on the institution of slavery in biblical and rabbinic law. Emigrating to the United States, Mielziner served as a pulpit rabbi and Jewish educator in New York City until 1879, when Isaac Mayer Wise appointed him professor of Talmud at the Hebrew Union College in Cincinnati. When Wise died in 1900, Mielziner, as senior faculty member, was chosen interim president of the college until a suitable successor could be found. He served in that position until his death three years later.

Remembered by his students as a respected and patient teacher, Mielziner devoted most of his scholarly attention to the task of guiding American students through the vast and complex rabbinic literature. His *Jewish Law of Marriage and Divorce* was a concise and useful summary of the halakic material and its relationship to modern concerns and sensibilities. He afforded a similar treatment to some aspects of rabbinic civil and criminal law in a work published in 1898. The crowning work of his career, however, was his *Introduction to the Talmud*, published in 1894 and reissued three times. While the work's historical and literary introduction is outdated, Mielziner's treatment of Talmudic methodology is a lasting achievement. "Like any other branch of science and literature," he noted, "the Talmud has its peculiar system of technical terms and phrases adapted to its peculiar methods of investigation and demonstration." More than any previous author, he presented a systematic description and discussion of these technical terms that form the skeletal structure of Talmudic debate and hermeneutics. Mielziner's *Introduction* remains a virtually indispensable tool in helping the beginning student follow the intricate process by which the Talmud analyzes concepts of halakah and Haggadah. The work includes the author's "Outlines of Talmudical Ethics," as well as his address to Talmud classes at the college, on the continuing relevance of Talmud study for modern Jews and for liberal rabbis. The most recent edition of the *Introduction*, published in 1968, contains an updated bibliography compiled by Alexander Guttmann.

A charter member of the Central Conference of American Rabbis, Mielziner was regarded as the consummate rabbinic teacher to his generation of the Reform rabbinate. His remarks and scholarly papers on subjects of practical import, which exercised an important influence in discussions of conference policy, were featured in the early volumes of the CCAR *Yearbook*.

Mielziner married Rosette Levald in 1861; they had seven children. Moses Mielziner died in Cincinnati on February 18, 1903.

Writings: *The Institution of Slavery among the Ancient Hebrews, According to the Bible and Talmud* (Cincinnati, 1894; translation of his doctoral thesis); *Introduction to the Talmud* (Cincinnati, 1894; fourth edition, with expanded bibliography, New York, 1968); *The Jewish Law of Marriage and Divorce in Ancient and Modern Times, and Its*

Relation to the Law of the State (Cincinnati, 1884); *Legal Maxims and Fundamental Laws of the Civil and Criminal Code of the Talmud* (Cincinnati, 1898).

References: Lewis M. Barth, "Rabbinics," in *Hebrew Union College–Jewish Institute of Religion at One Hundred Years*, ed. Samuel E. Karff (Cincinnati, 1976), pp. 317–82; *Encyclopaedia Judaica* (Jerusalem, 1971), 11:1526; Michael Meyer, "A Centennial History," in *Hebrew Union College*, ed. Karff, pp. 23–25; Ella Mielziner, *Moses Mielziner, 1828–1903* (New York, 1931); "Nearprint Biography Box," American Jewish Archives; William Rosenau, *A Tribute to Moses Mielziner* (Baltimore, 1929).

M.E.W.

MIHALY, EUGENE (1918–   ). Rabbi, professor, administrator. Born in Hungary on September 29, 1918, Eugene Mihaly is the son of Hillel and Ida Kahn Mihaly. After emigrating to the United States in 1930, Mihaly attended Yeshiva University (B.A., 1940), graduating magna cum laude, and was ordained a rabbi in its Rabbi Isaac Elchanan Theological Seminary in 1941. He then entered Hebrew Union College and was ordained again at Hebrew Union College in 1949. Mihaly received an M.A. from HUC-JIR and received the Simon Lazarus Prize, the highest scholastic award conferred by HUC, given annually to the senior who achieves the best academic standing of the graduating class during the entire period of study.

Mihaly began teaching at HUC-JIR in 1951, when he was granted a teaching fellowship, returning for graduate study and receiving his Ph.D. from HUC-JIR in 1952. Mihaly has remained at HUC-JIR throughout his career, being named assistant professor of Rabbinics in 1953; associate professor; professor of rabbinic literature and homiletics in 1951 (emeritus in 1989); academic coordinator in 1975; executive dean for academic affairs in 1976; academic vice president in 1985; and Deutsch Professor of Jewish Jurisprudence and Social Justice until his retirement in 1990.

A radical reformer, Mihaly advocates rabbinic officiation at mixed marriages and the offication of marriages on Shabbat. In 1974 Mihaly was chosen president of the newly formed but short-lived Association for a Progressive Reform Judaism, dedicated to "reforming Reform Judaism." He believed that the new association was created to defend the openness to change and development central to Reform Judaism, which he thought was being restricted by an attempt to appease the Orthodox and Conservative establishments rather than addressing the needs and concerns of the Reform constituency.

Mihaly is a contributor to the *Encyclopaedia Britannica* and the *Encyclopaedia Judaica*. He has also issued several major responsa.

On June 25, 1945, Mihaly married Cecile Louise Bramer Kahn; they have two sons: Eugene Bramer Mihaly and Marc Bramer Mihaly from her previous marriage.

Writings (partial listing): "The Breaking of the Tablets," in *Jews in a Free Society*, by Edward Goldman (Cincinnati, 1978), pp. 163–75; "Halakhah Is Absolute and Passe," *Judaism* 29, no. 1 (Winter, 1980): 68–75; "Isaac Abravanel on the Principles of Faith," *Hebrew Union College Annual* (1955), pp. 481–502; "Marriage on the Sabbath: A Responsum'' (Cincinnati, 1976); ''Responsum on Homosexuality'' (Cincinnati, n.d.); *A Song to Creation* (New York, 1975); ''Teshuvot on Jewish Marriage, with Special References to Reform Rabbis and Mixed Marriages'' (Cincinnati, 1985).

References: ''Nearprint Biography File,'' American Jewish Archives; *Who's Who in American Jewry* (Los Angeles, 1980), pp. 338–39.

MINDA, ALBERT (1895–1977). Rabbi. Albert Minda was born on July 30, 1895, in Holton, Kansas, to Hyman L. and Rachel Leah (Greenberg) Minda, both immigrants from Lithuania. After attending school in Kansas City, Missouri, Minda studied at the University of Cincinnati (A.B., 1918), having graduated from Hughes High School in the same city in 1914. Minda attended Hebrew Union College, where he was ordained in 1919. At HUC, he was business manager of the *HUC Monthly*, president of the HUC Literary Society and president of the HUC Student Body, and he delivered the valedictory address at graduation. Later, he did graduate work at Columbia University, the University of Minnesota and the University of Chicago. In 1947, he was awarded the (hon.) D.D. by HUC.

After ordination, he served Temple Beth El in South Bend, Indiana, from 1919 to 1922. In 1922, he became rabbi of Temple Israel in Minneapolis, Minnesota, a position he held until his retirement in 1963. In the year following his retirement, he served as Distinguished Alumni Lecturer in Homiletics at Hebrew Union College—Jewish Institute of Religion, Cincinnati. While in Minneapolis, he was Lecturer on Judaica at Hamline University in St. Paul.

Minda's entry into community affairs came early in his rabbinate; he pursued community interest, saying the duty of a religious leader was ''not to build walls but bridges.'' As a picturesque illustration of his interest, he bobbed for apples to publicize an antivandalism Halloween Committee he helped to organize. He served as a kind of chaplain to boxers and show-business people and was a familiar figure at Golden Gloves boxing tournaments in the 1930s and 1940s. He was also well known for representing Judaism at interfaith gatherings.

During his career, he participated in many communal and civic activities. He served the Central Conference of American Rabbis as president in 1961–1963 and as chairman of its Committees on Church and State and Religious Work in Universities. He was vice president of the World Union for Progressive Judaism. He was one of the organizers and the first president of the Minneapolis Federation for Jewish Service, organizer of the Minneapolis Urban League, chairman of the Citizen's Committee on Education, member of the Advisory Committee of Minnesota Poll, member of the Advisory Committee of Better Sports Committee, member of Board of Council of Social Agencies, member of Speakers Committee–Community Fund and member of Governor's Mental Health Committee. Minda was also a Mason and chaplain and scholarship commissioner of Phi Epsilon Phi and Pi Tau Pi (Hai Resh). He was also a member of American University Seminar to Palestine in 1931 and a member of Sherwood Eddy Seminar to Europe in 1938. In 1945, Minda received a citation from the Minneapolis

Urban League and in 1947, a citation from the Minneapolis Round Table of National Conference of Christians and Jews, which he had earlier helped to organize. In 1949, he was designated one of "The One Hundred Living Great of Minnesota" by the Minnesota Territorial Centennial Committee. The Jewish National Fund dedicated a forest in his honor.

In 1922, Minda married Frances G. Salinger. They had one son: Roland. Minda died in Minneapolis on January 15, 1977.

Writings (partial listing): *America, America* (Minneapolis, 1974); *The Fire on the Altar* (Minneapolis, 1948); *Over the Years: Papers and Addresses by Albert G. Minda* (New York, 1963); *Peace and Fellowship* (Cincinnati, 1937); *Sanctuary of the Home* (Minneapolis, 1944); *Speak to the Heart* (Minneapolis, 1956); *Temple Etiquette and Procedure* (Minneapolis, 1943); coauthor, *Ten Commandments for Modern Living* (Minneapolis, 1952); *Why I am a Jew* (Minneapolis, 1925).

References: *Minneapolis Tribune*, obituary, January 16, 1977; *Who's Who in American Jewry* (New York, 1938), p. 747; *Who Was Who in America* (Chicago, 1981), 7:406.

MORGENSTERN, JULIAN (1881–1976). Rabbi, Bible scholar, academician. The son of Hannah Ochs Morgenstern and Samuel Morgenstern, Julian Morgenstern was born in St. Francisville, Illinois, on March 18, 1881. He attended the University of Cincinnati (B.A. 1901) while simultaneously studying at Hebrew Union College, where he was ordained (1902). After ordination, he studied in Europe at the University of Berlin (1902–1903) and the University of Heidelberg (Ph.D., 1904). His dissertation, which was later published, was titled *Doctrine of Sin in the Babylonian Religion.* Later he received an honorary D.H.L. (1937) from Jewish Theological Seminary and a D.L. (1947) from the University of Cincinnati. In 1954, the University of Heidelberg renewed his degree, an unusual honor.

When he returned to the United States, he served Ahavath Achim (later Temple Israel) in Lafayette, Indiana (1904–1907), and then returned to Hebrew Union College to teach on its faculty as instructor in Bible and Semitic Languages, beginning in 1907 (promoted to assistant professor 1910, professor 1913). In 1921 he served as acting president of HUC and then was named president the following year (1922–1947), the first HUC alumnus to hold this office and the first American-born scholar to become a regular, permanent member of its faculty. He held this position until retirement, when he was named professor emeritus. After retirement, Morgenstern continued to teach at HUC in Cincinnati until 1960, when he moved to Macon, Georgia.

Under his presidency, Hebrew Union College grew dramatically. While it was originally included in the charter of the Union of American Hebrew Congregations, Morgenstern saw to it that HUC would be chartered separately. He established departments of education, social studies and music. He built new buildings and developed an endowment fund. Under his direction, the HUC School of Religious Education was instituted in New York City. Morgenstern also started the *Hebrew Union College Annual* in 1924, a major scholarly journal, especially in the area of the Bible. He wrote in the publication extensively. To promote interfaith relations, Morgenstern was among the first to develop exchange lectureships with American Christian seminaries.

As a Bible scholar, he was originally a follower of Wellhausen. But he became increasingly independent in his thinking and relied chiefly on differences in economic, social and political backgrounds rather than on the vocabulary and style of biblical authors and editors. Even his attempt to date festivals reflected what he perceived as changes in the life of the people of Israel. He saw a strong trend toward proselytism in the post-Exhilic period that ended catastrophically with the destruction of the Second Temple. In the area of the history of religion, Morgenstern argued that the Israelites retained many ceremonies whose origins can be traced to solar worship. Morgenstern wrote very little in his early years and only later began to publish with an ever increasing tempo. His theories were often insightful and unpopular, but he stated them boldly. Perhaps his most notable accomplishment in this regard was the so-called Kenite hypothesis, in which he argued that Moses learned about monotheism from his father-in-law Jethro, a Kenite. Morgenstern also served as the Bible specialist on the board of editors for the *Universal Jewish Encyclopedia*, where his method and outlook in Bible are clearly evidenced.

Morgenstern believed that universalism and particularism complemented one another. Preferring the term *American Judaism* over *Reform Judaism*, he saw American Judaism as more pragmatic and less dogmatic than early Reform. He contended that Reform and Conservative Judaism would ultimately merge. Morgenstern was originally an anti-Zionist, but he later modified his position.

Morgenstern is also noted for the rescue of scholars from Germany during World War II. He invited them to teach at HUC and, in doing so, saved their lives and helped to bring their high standards of scholarship to the Reform rabbinical seminary.

As a result of his Hebrew Union College presidency and his scholarly interest, Morgenstern was active in many organizations. Among others, he was a member of American Academy for Jewish Research, B'nai B'rith, Theta Phi, Central Conference of American Rabbis (secretary, 1907–1913), American Oriental Society (president, Western branch, 1913–1920; president, general society, 1927–1928), Society of Biblical Literature and Exegesis (president, Midwest branch, 1938–1939; president, general society, 1940–1941), Alumni Association of Hebrew Union College (president, 1916–1918), World Union of Progressive Judaism (American vice president), executive of Jewish Agency and Society for Oriental Research (honorary fellow).

Morgenstern married Helen Thorner on April 18, 1906. They had one daughter: Jean Greenebaum. Morgenstern died in Macon, Georgia, on December 4, 1976.

Writings (partial listing): *Amos Studies* (Cincinnati, 1941); *As a Mighty Stream* (Philadelphia, 1949); *The Book of Genesis* (New York, 1965); *Doctrine of Sin in the Babylonian Religion* (Berlin, n.d.); *The Fire on the Altar* (Chicago, 1963); *Judaism and the Modern World* (San Francisco, 1929); *The Message of Deutero-Isaiah* (Cincinnati,

1961); *Rites of Birth, Marriage, Death, and Kindred Occasions among the Semites* (Cincinnati, 1966).

References (partial listing): Bernard Bamberger, ''The Impact of Julian Morgenstern on American Jewish Life,'' *Central Conference of American Rabbis Journal* 4 (April 1957): 1–4; *Encyclopaedia Judaica* (Jerusalem, 1971), 12:317–19; Louis Finkelstein, *Thirteen Americans: Their Spiritual Autobiographies* (New York, 1948), pp. 253–372; ''Julian Morgenstern Manuscript Collection,'' American Jewish Archives; M. Liebman, *Hebrew Union College Annual* 32 (1961): 1–8.

N

NEUMARK, DAVID (1866–1924). Rabbi, scholar, philosophy professor, Reform Jewish thinker. Born in Lemberg Galicia on August 3, 1866, the son of Solomon and Schifrah Schuetz Neumark, David Neumark entered heder. Precociously he began his studies of Hebrew at age two and *gemara* at age six. In 1892 he graduated from the II K.K. Obergymnasium in Lemberg. After pursuing a variety of studies, he received his doctorate from the University of Berlin in 1896. In 1897 he was ordained as rabbi at the Hochschule Fuer die Wissenschaft des Judenthums in Berlin, where he was awarded the Mendelssohn Prize (1894).

From 1897 to 1904, Neumark served as rabbi in Rakonitz (Rakovnik), Bohemia. He was invited to become Rabbino Maggiore of Rome and accept the presidency of the Collegio Rabbinico, but he withdrew his candidacy. From 1904 to 1907, he lived in Berlin and was editor-in-chief of the division of Jewish philosophy and halakah for the proposed Hebrew encyclopedia *Otzar Ha-Yahadut*, whose specimen volume on the essence and philosophy of Judaism he edited in 1906. In 1906, he was considered for the pulpit of the Central Jewish Congregation of Berlin. In 1907 he served briefly as professor of Jewish philosophy at the Veitel-Heine-Ephraimschen Lehranstalt in Berlin. Then, at the invitation of Kaufmann Kohler, he went to Hebrew Union College in Cincinnati, where he served as professor of philosophy from 1907 to 1924, to the consternation of the faculty at the Hochschule who had tried to persuade him to return to Berlin and teach there. In 1919 Neumark founded the *Journal of Jewish Lore and Philosophy*, which was renamed the *Hebrew Union College Annual* in 1921.

Neumark was unmistakably progressive in his thinking. According to him, Judaism was a constantly evolving, changing religion. Its enduring and life-giving core was ethical monotheism. Jewish philosophy had the task of understanding, clarifying and defending this ethical monotheism. Scripture, specifically the Torah, was written by human beings, fallible men. Accordingly, Scripture was a source of fallible knowledge—one could disagree with its teachings, since they were not binding.

Neumark's philosophy enabled him to connect Zionism with Reform Judaism. In an age when most Reform Jewish leaders opposed Zionism, Neumark was a forceful and vocal exception within the Reform movement. Zionism for him was an essentially Jewish movement and, far from being secular, ethnic or at most ethical, was grounded in historically evolving Jewish religion. Neumark opposed the secular nationalism of Ahad Ha-Am.

In his scholarly writings, Neumark sought to demonstrate that throughout their history, Jews remained committed to their religion and survived as a separate religious group because the Jewish concept of God (ultimate reality) and the ethics of Judaism were superior to those of other religions.

His major scholarly work was a history of Jewish philosophy, in German (*Geschichte der juedischen Philsophie des Mittelalters* [1907–1910]) and Hebrew (*Toledot Hafilosofiah beYisrael* [1922, 1929]) but not in English.

David Neumark married Dora Turnheim on June 7, 1898; they had two children: Sulamith Brainin and Immanuel Kant. Neumark died in Cincinnati, Ohio, on December 15, 1924.

Writings: *Essays in Jewish Philosophy* (Austria, 1929); *History of Dogmas of Judaism* (Odessa, 1919); *Judah Halevi's Philosophy* (Cincinnati, 1908); *The Philosophy of the Bible* (Cincinnati, 1918); *The Principles of Judaism in the Historical Outline* (Cincinnati, 1919); *Toledot Hafilosofiah beYisrael* (New York, 1921).

References: Reuben Brainin, "David Neumark," in *Collected Works of Reuben Brainin* (New York, 1938) [Hebrew]; Central Conference of American Rabbis *Yearbook* 35 (1925): 240–42; *Encyclopaedia Judaica* (Jerusalem, 1971), 12:1014; *Hebrew Union College Monthly*, January 1924; *HUCA* 2 (1925); "Nearprint Biography File and Box," "Biographies File," American Jewish Archives; Meyer Waxman, "David Neumark," in *A History of Jewish Literature* (New York, 1960), 4: 927–33.

                                                                          A.D.H.

NEWFIELD, MORRIS (1869–1940). Rabbi, social worker. Mor Newfield (as he was known in Hungary) was born in Homanna, Hungary, on January 31, 1869, the son of Seymon Shabsi Newfield and Lena Klein Newfield, his father's second wife. Poverty-stricken, Newfield was forced to leave home as a teen. He went to the Jewish Theological Seminary in Budapest to study in 1884, earning a B.D. in 1889. He also matriculated at the Royal Catholic Grand Gymnasium in Budapest, graduating in 1889. Newfield enrolled at the Medical College at the University of Budapest. In 1891 he left medical school, fulfilling a deathbed promise made to his father, and sailed to the United States to attend Hebrew Union College. Attending the University of Cincinnati concurrently, Newfield received his B.A. from there in 1895, the same year he was ordained at HUC. While at HUC, he taught a course in Talmud and was superintendent of the John Street Temple Sunday School.

On ordination, Newfield went to Temple Emanu-El in Birmingham, Alabama, a position he would retain until his death, having gained life tenure in 1924. In Birmingham he taught Hebrew and Semitics at Howard College and quickly established himself as a leader of civil liberalism, fighting the conservative majority over issues of prohibition and Sunday blue laws. He offered religious and social leadership to both Christians and Jews, reconciling and accommodating both groups. He sometimes found himself at odds with Christian clergy, especially over Sunday blue laws. A classical reformer, Newfield believed in the mission of the Jews to develop a "Kingdom of God" on earth and worked toward that end.

Newfield was also involved with social-welfare concerns, hoping to integrate his Social Gospel theology into societal efforts. He was instrumental in establishing the city's first free kindergarten and in 1909 helped established the Associated Charities. Newfield was involved in the CCAR's formal opposition to child labor. Having joined the Alabama Child Labor Committee, he helped establish institutions like the Juvenile Court in Birmingham in 1911 and the Department of Child Welfare in 1919. Active in the fight against tuberculosis, Newfield was among the founders of the Anti-Tubercular Society in 1910 and of the Alabama Anti-Tubercular League in 1914, serving as president from 1919 to 1921. Newfield was also active in the local Red Cross, reflecting an extensive activity in community concern for social welfare. A charter member of the Civilian Relief Committee in 1917 (Jefferson County Chapter), serving as chairman of its Home Service Committee from 1917 to 1939, Newfield actively assisted returning veterans. In 1917 Newfield was president of the Alabama Sociological Congress, helping to develop the Alabama Children's Aid Society, supporting local child-welfare work. In 1928 Newfield was elected chairman of the Red Cross Advisory Case Committee, responsible for assisting caseworkers in solving the most difficult case-relief problems. That same year he and several Christian colleagues founded the Birmingham chapter of the National Conference of Christians and Jews. He often lectured as part of a Catholic-Jewish-Protestant interfaith team and was well known for his work in interfaith relations.

As extensive as were his efforts in the wider community, Newfield was also a founder of the local Federation of Jewish Charities, later known as the United Jewish Fund. He was instrumental in organizing the Alabama Jewish Religious School Teachers Association, which he served as president for two years.

Although an advocate of peace, Newfield served as a part-time chaplain at Camp McClellan in nearby Anniston, Alabama, during World War I. He wanted to show his Christian neighbors that Jews were patriotic.

Newfield served as CCAR president from 1931 to 1933, having served as secretary for the preceding five years. It was while he held that office that his position on non-Zionism became manifest. Yet by 1938, Newfield had become a Zionist in response to the rise of Nazism.

In 1901 Newfield married Leah Ullman; they had six children: Seymon, Emma, Mayer, Lena, Lincoln and John.

Morris Newfield died on March 7, 1940, in Birmingham, Alabama.

Writings: "A History of the Birmingham Jewish Community," *Reform Advocate*, November 4, 1911, pp. 6–33.

References: Mark Cowett, *Birmingham's Rabbi: Morris Newfield and Alabama, 1895–1940* (University, AL, 1986); Sylvia Blascoer Kohn, *By Reason of Strength: The Story of Temple Emanu-El's Seventy Years, 1882–1952* (Birmingham, 1952); ''Morris Newfield Collection,'' Alabama State Department of Archives and History, Montgomery; ''Morris Newfield papers,'' American Jewish Archives.

O

OKO, ADOLPH SIGMUND (1883–1944). Librarian, Spinoza scholar, philanthropist. The son of Tebel and Mariam Deborah Popolyek Oko, Adolph Oko was born in Kharkov, Russia, on January 5, 1883. Educated in Germany, Oko came to the United States in 1902. After working at the Astor Library in New York City, he was appointed in 1906 librarian of Hebrew Union College in Cincinnati, Ohio. He enlarged the library's holdings greatly, acquiring some 18,000 volumes, including the Edward Birnbaum music collection, and bringing to the library a comprehensive Spinoza collection, the Chinese-Jewish manuscripts of Kai-Feng-Fu and an outstanding collection of incunabula. Under his leadership, the library outgrew its quarters in 1913 and again in 1931, in which year HUC awarded him an honorary D.H.L. degree. Oko also aided in the founding of the Hebrew Union College (now Skirball) Museum.

After his second marriage in 1933, Oko left HUC and moved to England, where he completed his *Spinoza Bibliography*. In 1938 the Okos returned to the United States, where Oko joined the staff of the American Jewish Committee. In 1943 Oko became associate editor of the American Jewish Committee magazine, *Contemporary Jewish Record*, in which capacity he served until his death the following year.

Oko wrote numerous essays and bibliographies. Many of his articles were printed in the *Menorah Journal*, of which he was an associate editor. He was a lifelong admirer of Baruch Spinoza, so much so that he signed many of his articles with the pseudonym "S. Baruch." He was a founder and the U.S. secretary of Societas Spinozana and a trustee of Domus Spinoza in the Hague.

Though not a wealthy man, Oko was active in philanthropic work, making use of his reputation as a librarian and scholar and persuading friends to provide necessary funds. He made tremendous efforts to rescue colleagues, friends and their families and friends from Europe before World War II and was expert in providing funds for impoverished colleagues in a manner that would not injure their pride.

Oko's first wife, Etta Weisinger, died in 1924; they had two sons: Adolph S. and Benjmain. His second marriage was to Dorothy Kuhn in 1933. Adolph Oko died in New York on October 3, 1944.

Writings (partial listing): *A History of the Hebrew Union College Library and Museum* (Cincinnati, 1944); *Jewish Book Collections in the United States* (reprinted in the *American Jewish Yearbook*, vol. 45, 1943); *Selected List of the Writings of Gotthard Deutsch* (Cincinnati, 1916); *The Spinoza Bibliography* (Boston, 1964).

References: "Adolph S. Oko Papers," American Jewish Archives; *B'nai B'rith Magazine*, April 1977; *Cincinnati Post*, January 15, 1939; *Contemporary Jewish Record*, October 1944, pp. 451–52; *New York Times*, obituary, October 4, 1944; Fred Wenger, "The Life, Activity and Personality of Adolph Sigmund Oko" (Term paper, Hebrew Union College–Jewish Institute of Religion, Cincinnati, 1967).

F.L.W.

OLAN, LEVI ARTHUR (1903–1984). Rabbi, theologian, civic leader. The son of Max and Bessie Olan, Levi Olan was born on March 22, 1903, in Cherkassy, Russia (near Kiev). His family settled in Rochester, New York, in 1906. He was educated in public school, attended the University of Rochester from 1921 to 1923, received his B.A. from the University of Cincinnati in 1925 and was ordained by the Hebrew Union College in 1929. Olan was awarded an honorary D.D. by HUC-JIR in 1955, an honorary D.H.L. by Austin College in 1967 and an honorary doctorate from Southern Methodist University in 1968.

Olan's rabbinic career began in Worcester, Massachusetts, where he served for 20 years, and continued for 21 years in Dallas, Texas, where he became rabbi emeritus in 1970.

A lifelong student of philosophy, theology and general literature, Olan was a daily student of the Torah. He had a logical mind, a clear style and an incisive wit and brought all these to bear on his writing and lecturing. Olan delivered papers frequently at the annual convention of the Central Conference of American Rabbis, stimulated the formation of a Special Interest Group in Jewish Theology, which he chaired, and became president of the CCAR in 1968. He was also a visiting lecturer on a regular basis at both the Perkins School of Theology at Southern Methodist University and the Department of Religion at Texas Christian University.

Olan described himself as a religious liberal, a rationalist who stressed the role of reason and experience in the search for truth. He was keenly aware of the conflict between the religious and secular points of view, and he sought to narrow the gap. This was especially important to a movement that removed itself from what it perceived as the yoke of tradition and to a world that was redeeming itself in the face of an enlightened modern world order to have its dreams shattered by the realities and vagaries of history.

Olan had been exposed to socialist ideals in his youth and was inspired during his seminary years by Dr. Moses Buttenweisser's courses about the Hebrew prophets. In Worcester, he not only became president of the United Jewish Charities and a board member of the Red Cross and Community Chest but also helped organize the People's Forum, presenting such speakers as Norman Thomas and Clarence Darrow.

In Dallas, following a path hewn out by his predecessor, Dr. David Lefkowitz, Olan continued a weekly radio, and later television, program on the religious issues of life. Thousands of requests came in through the years for copies of his messages. He goaded Dallas into facing up to the problems of racial segregation, becoming so well known that in the 1960s a writer for Fortune Magazine described him as "the conscience of Dallas." He was also appointed chairman of the Housing Authority, board member of the Human Relations Commission, twice a member of the Goals for Dallas civic group and regent of the University of Texas.

After his retirement in 1970, Olan continued his scholarly work and was invited to lecture at the University of Texas, Emory University in Atlanta, the University of Texas at Arlington, the Institute of Religion in Houston and the Leo Baeck College in London, England.

Olan married Sarita Messer of Cincinnati on June 9, 1931; they had three children: Elizabeth, Francis and David. Levi Olan died on October 17, 1984, in Dallas, Texas.

Writings: *Judaism and Immortality* (New York, 1971); *Maturity in an Immature World* (New York, 1984); *A Prophetic Faith and the Secular Age* (New York, 1982).

References: *D: The Magazine of Dallas*, November 1975; *Dallas Morning News*, February 16, 1981; *Dallas Times Herald*, October 11, 1970, and October 10, 1981; Benjamin J. Leinow, "Glimpses into the Life of a Cultured American Jew" (Term paper, Hebrew Union College–Jewish Institute of Religion, Cincinnati, 1964); "Nearprint Biography Box and File," "Correspondence File," American Jewish Archives; *Who Was Who in America* (Chicago, 1985), 8:306.

R.I.K.

P

PETUCHOWSKI, JAKOB JOSEF (1925–1991). Rabbi, scholar. Jakob Petuchowski was born in Berlin on July 30, 1925, the son of Siegmund and Lucie Loewenthal Petuchowski. In 1939 he left Germany and lived in London until 1947, when he left to come to the United States. Petuchowski attended Adath Israel (elementary school) in Berlin before his emigration. He received his high school education at the University Tutorial College in London, from which he graduated in 1944. Petuchowski had received his early Jewish education at Kibbutz Hachsharah in Wittingehame, Scotland, as well as at the Glasgow Yeshivah (Rabbinical College). He had private instruction in Berlin with Alexander Altmann and in London with Benno Jacob, Isaac Markon, Leo Baeck and A. Loewenstamm.

While in England, Petuchowski was education director of the Youth Association of Synagogues in Great Britain. He also was a social worker in the D.P. Reception Camp at Windermere, as well as a Hebrew and religion teacher at the West London Synagogue. In addition, Petuchowski was chaplain to the D.P. Tuberculosis Sanatorium in England. In addition, he was an executive member of the University of London Jewish Union Society; member of the panel of speakers, Association of Jewish Youth, England; and a member of a study group of Youth Association of Synagogues in Great Britain. He attended the University of London, where he received a B.A., with honors, in 1947. He continued his studies in semitics at the University of London for another year. Petuchowski received his B.H.L. (1949), M.A.H.L. (1952) and Ph.D. (1958) from HUC-JIR. Petuchowski was ordained at HUC-JIR in 1952. From 1952 to 1955, he was a Heinsheimer Memorial fellow at HUC-JIR.

Petuchowski served as rabbi at Temple Emanuel in Welch, West Virginia (1949 to 1955), and Beth Israel Synagogue in Washington, Pennsylvania (1955 to 1956), and was the High Holy Day rabbi of Temple B'nai Israel in Laredo, Texas, since 1956. In 1956 he joined the faculty of HUC-JIR as instructor in

Jewish Theology. He was later named the Sol and Arlene Bronstein Professor of Judaeo-Christian Studies and Research Professor of Jewish Theology and Liturgy. He was the first rabbi and director of Jewish Studies at HUC-JIR, Jerusalem, and a visiting professor of Jewish Philosophy at Tel Aviv University, Divinity School of Harvard University, Oxford University, Antioch College and Theologische Fakultät Luzern in Switzerland. Petuchowski appeared often at universities and on lecture circuits in Germany, the United States and Switzerland.

As a result of its rather traditional theological perspective, Petuchowski's writings have helped to serve as a bridge between Reform Judaism and the rest of the Jewish world. In his *Ever Since Sinai*, he articulated a belief in the authority of revelation and halakha, while interpreting both in an evolutionary system, of which Reform is simply another stage in the process. He was also an outspoken critic of secular Zionism, positing that Israel should be a legitimate continuation of Jewish history.

Petuchowski was a Fellow of the American Academy for Jewish Research. He authored over 35 books or pamphlets and was a contributor to various encyclopedias in the United States and Israel. His articles were frequently published in English, German and Hebrew periodicals.

In 1979 Petuchowski received an honorary Ph.D. from the University of Cologne in recognition of his contributions to the study of Jewish liturgy and Jewish thought, his encouragement of better German-Jewish relations and his interest in the progress of Judaic studies at the University of Cologne. That same year, he received an honorary D.L. degree from Brown University. He held an honorary Fellow of Humane Letters degree from Maimonides College in Winnipeg, Canada. Petuchowski has received the Order of Merit First Class of the Federal Republic of Germany.

In 1980 Petuchowski received the Ecumenical Award of Xavier University in Cincinnati. In 1985, a German volume, with 22 Catholic and Protestant theologians as contributors, was published in honor of Petuchowski. The title in translation, was "Judaism Is Alive—I Have Encountered It: Experiences by Christians."

In 1946 he married Elizabeth Mayer; they had three children: Samuel, Aaron and Jonathan. Petuchowski died in Cincinnati, Ohio, on November 12, 1991.

Writings (partial listing): *Ever Since Sinai* (New York, 1961, 1979); *Heirs of the Pharisees* (New York, 1970); coeditor, *Lexikon der juedisch-christlichen Begegnung* (*Encyclopedia of the Jewish-Christian Encounter*) (Munich, 1989); *Prayerbook Reform in Europe* (New York, 1968); *The Theology of Haham David Nieto* (New York, 1954, 1970).

References: "Autobiography," Nearprint Biography File," American Jewish Archives; *Who's Who in American Jewry* (Los Angeles, 1980), p. 371.

PHILIPSON, DAVID (1862–1949). Rabbi, historian. David Philipson, later called "The Dean of American (Reform) Rabbis," was born in Wabash, Indiana, on August 9, 1862, to Louisa and Joseph Philipson. He began his rabbinic career as a member of the first graduating class of Hebrew Union College in 1883. He also received a B.A. from McMicken University (the University of Cincinnati) in 1883 and a D.D. from HUC in 1886. As one of the college's first graduates, Philipson was close to Isaac Mayer Wise and Max Lilienthal and saw himself as their successor.

Shortly after his ordination, Philipson accepted the pulpit of Har Sinai Congregation in Baltimore, which he served until 1888. In Baltimore, Philipson received valuable experience, including an invitation to participate in the Pittsburgh Conference (1885). In 1888 Philipson returned to Cincinnati to lead the Bene Israel Congregation until his death. In Cincinnati, which was then a leading center of the Reform Movement and the home to its institutions, Philipson became a leader in the community and among his fellow rabbis. He became a standard bearer for Classical Reform Judaism. Philipson especially defended the Reform belief in Jewish universalism and the Jewish mission concept.

The corollary to Jewish universalism, antinationalism, was primary among Philipson's principles. He was fiercely opposed to Zionism, mostly out of a devotion to universalism, Americanism and the belief that no person could espouse two nationalities. As an acculturated, native-born American and a religious Jew, he could not accept claims of Jewish national allegiance. Thus, he consistently opposed Zionism from the pulpit and with his pen. In 1918 Philipson attempted to form a national anti-Zionist organization, primarily to oppose the Balfour Declaration. It failed when Jacob Schiff, a non-Zionist, refused to lend Philipson his support.

Philipson was active in the Union of American Hebrew Congregations, the Hebrew Union College and the Central Conference of American Rabbis, which he helped Wise found in 1889. For the UAHC, Philipson chaired the joint UAHC-CCAR Commission on Jewish Education (1903 to 1942), which published hundreds of textbooks and other educational resources. At the college, Philipson taught homiletics, Bible and the history of Reform Judaism, as well as serving on the Board of Governors for years. Although he aspired to the HUC presidency, he never succeeded in winning that post, although for many years he was as powerful as (or more so than) the president. Philipson served a term as CCAR president (1907 to 1909) and sat on the Conference Executive Committee for decades. The CCAR committees he chaired from time to time included Church and State, Prayer Book Revision and Arbitration. Philipson was elected Honorary President of the CCAR in 1929.

Deeply committed to interfaith work, Philipson was a speaker at the 1892 Chicago World's Fair Parliament of Religions. He was an early advocate of the National Conference of Jews and Christians.

As a writer, Philipson was a prolific, though not outstanding, scholar. He wrote or edited ten books and numerous articles, as well as hundreds of sermons and addresses. His particular interest was the history of Reform Judaism, and his most significant work was *The Reform Movement in Judaism* (1907). He also wrote biographical studies of his mentors, Wise and Lilienthal. Although not a trained historian, Philipson was careful in collecting and arranging facts. He was a founder and vice president of the American Jewish Historical Society. He also served on the Jewish Publication Society's Publication Committee and chaired several of its subcommittees. Most important, Philipson is credited with helping to forge the cooperative union of the CCAR and the JPS that produced the 1917 English-language Jewish translation of the Bible.

Philipson married Ella Hollander in 1885. David Philipson died in Boston, Massachusetts, on June 29, 1949, while attending a CCAR convention in New Hampshire.

Writings: *Centenary Papers and Others* (Cincinnati, 1919); *The Jew in English Fiction* (Cincinnati, 1889; 5th ed., rev., New York, 1927); *Letters of Rebecca Gratz* (Philadelphia, 1929); *Max Lilienthal: American Rabbi* (New York, 1915); *My Life as an American Jew* (Cincinnati, 1941); *The Oldest Jewish Congregation in the West—Bene Israel, Cincinnati* (Cincinnati, 1894); *Old European Jewries* (Philadelphia, 1894); *The Reform Movement in Judaism* (New York, 1907; rev., 1931; rev., 1967); ed., *Isaac M. Wise: Reminiscences* (Cincinnati, 1901; rev., 1945); ed., with Louis Grossman, *Selected Writings of Isaac Mayer Wise* (Cincinnati, 1900).

References: "Addresses and Testimonials . . . on the Occasion of . . . David Philipson's Fortieth Anniversary with Congregation Bene Israel" (Cincinnati, 1928); *American Jewish Archives* 3 (1951): 28–31; *Central Committee of American Rabbis Journal* 15, no. 1 (1968): 4–8; Stanley F. Chyet, "Isaac Mayer Wise: Portraits by David Philipson," in *A Bicentennial Festschrift for Jacob Rader Marcus* (New York, 1976), pp. 77–92; Solomon B. Freehof, "Introduction," in Philipson, *The Reform Movement in Judaism* (New York, 1967), pp. ix–xxi; Douglas J. Kohn, "The Dean of American Rabbis: A Critical Study of . . . David Philipson" (Rabbinical thesis, Hebrew Union College–Jewish Institute of Religion, Cincinnati, 1987); *Services at the Installation of Rev. Dr. David Philipson* (Cincinnati, 1888).

                                                                                                     D.J.K.

PLAUT, W. GUNTHER (1912–   ). Rabbi, author. Gunther Plaut was born to Jonas and Selma Gumprich Plaut on November 1, 1912, in the German city of Münster. He studied law at the Universities of Heidelberg and Berlin and in 1934 obtained his degree of Doctor Juris from the latter, one of the last Jews in Germany to do so. When Nazi measures ended his legal career, Plaut turned to Jewish studies and was tutored by Abraham Joshua Heschel. He attended the Hochschule (later, Lehranstalt) for die Wissenschaft des Judentums, whose president was Rabbi Leo Baeck. In 1935, Plaut and four other students accepted an invitation to study at Hebrew Union College in Cincinnati, Ohio, where he was ordained in 1939.

In addition to serving American and Canadian congregations, Plaut has occupied many posts of national and international leadership. His first congregation was B'nai Abraham Zion in Chicago. In 1943 Plaut enlisted in the U.S. Army, served as a chaplain in the infantry at the European front and was present at the liberation of the Dora-Nordhausen concentration camp in April 1945. His service earned him the Bronze Medal.

Plaut returned to Chicago, then in 1948 accepted a call to Mt. Zion Temple in St. Paul, Minnesota. In 1961 he went to Holy Blossom Temple in Toronto, Canada, where he served as Senior Rabbi until 1977 and thereafter as Senior Scholar. Various schools accorded him honorary degrees: Hebrew Union College (D.D., 1964), University of Toronto (LL.D., 1977), Cleveland College of Jewish Studies (D.H. L., 1978) and York University (Toronto, 1987).

In Chicago he became a founder of the camp movement for Jewish students. In St. Paul he served as president of the Minnesota Rabbinical Association and chaired the Twin Cities committee for the defense and support of Israel; he was appointed a member of the Minnesota Human Relations Committee (1949), headed the Governor's Commission on Ethics in Government (1958 to 1961) and was elected president of the St. Paul Gallery and School Arts (1953 to 1959). After he moved to Canada he held many Jewish and general posts: president, World Federalists of Canada (1966 to 1968); founding member and (1975 to 1977) cochairman, the Canada-Israel Committee; chairman, United Jewish Appeal of Metropolitan Toronto (1970); president, Canadian Jewish Congress (1977 to 1980); president, Central Conference of American Rabbis (1983 to 1985); and vice chairman, Ontario Human Rights Commission (1979 to 1985), for which he published a quarterly, *Affirmation*. In 1987 Plaut was appointed by the Ontario Human Rights Commission to discharge judicial functions in cases of human-rights violations. From 1984 to 1985, he served the Canadian government by conducting a one-person study of refugee legislation.

Plaut's wide range of interests made him a popular lecturer throughout the world. He appeared at universities and in congregations in North America, Europe, Israel, South Africa and Australia. He holds a visiting lectureship at the University of Haifa and is a Fellow at York University. For many years he made weekly radio and television broadcasts. Plaut was honored by many organizations, among them the Canadian Council of Christians and Jews, the Urban Alliance on Race Relations and the Jewish National Fund. In 1978 he was made an officer of the Order of Canada.

Early in his career, Plaut wrote many scholarly and general articles; his first books were histories of his congregation in St. Paul and of Judaism in Minnesota. In his theological writings, as well as his communal endeavors, Plaut is a religious liberal significantly influenced by Jewish tradition. His theological writings include *Judaism and the Scientific Spirit*, which argued for the compatibility of liberalism and traditionalism, and *The Case for the Chosen People*, which supported the continuing validity of the concept of selection. By far his most influential work is as editor and principal author of *The Torah—A Modern Commentary*. Robert Alter has called this "the finest commentary [on the Torah] in English or, for that matter, in any language." Plaut has also written fiction and the libretto for an opera.

Plaut married Elizabeth Strauss in Cincinnati on November 10, 1938; they have two children: Jonathan and Judith. They live in Toronto.

Writings: *The Case for the Chosen People* (Garden City, NY, 1965); libretto for Lothar Klein opera, *A Father and His Son* (prod. Banff, 1988); *The Growth of Reform*

Judaism (New York, 1965); *Hanging Threads* (Toronto, Ontario, 1978); *Judaism and the Scientific Spirit* (New York, 1962); *The Rise of Reform Judaism* (New York, 1963); *The Torah—A Modern Commentary* (New York, 1981); contributing ed., *Universal Jewish Encyclopedia*, (New York, 1943). A *Festschrift* in honor of Plaut, produced on his seventieth birthday, includes a complete bibliography of his writings up to 1982, encompassing some one thousand items: Jonathan V. Plaut, ed., *Through the Sound of Many Voices* (Toronto, Ontario, 1982).

References: Robert Alter, "Reform Judaism and the Bible," *Commentary* 73 (February 1982): 31–35; *The Canadian Encyclopedia* (Edmonton, 1985), 3:1693; *Encyclopaedia Judaica* (Jerusalem, 1971), 13:631; "Nearprint Biography File," "Genealogies File," American Jewish Archives.

J.V.P.

POLISH, DAVID (1910–   ). Rabbi. David Polish was born in Cleveland, Ohio, on January 16, 1910, the son of Morris and Mollie Feinberg Polish. After attending (Case) Western Reserve University, he studied at the University of Cincinnati (B.A., 1931). In 1934 he was ordained at Hebrew Union College, where he received a D.H.L. in 1942 and an honorary D.D. in 1959. In 1959, Polish studied at Hebrew University in Jerusalem. After ordination, he served in Cedar Rapids, Iowa (1934–1939); Hillel Foundation at Cornell University (1939–1942); Waterbury, Connecticut (1942–1947); and Temple Mizpah in Chicago, Illinois (1947–1950). In 1950 he became the founding rabbi of Beth Emet—The Free Synagogue of Evanston, a position he held until his retirement in 1980.

An ardent Zionist, Polish organized a statewide Zionist movement while in Cedar Rapids. In Chicago he introduced *selihot* services to his congregation, a renewed practice that was also adopted by other Reform congregations. In 1957 he published *Guide for Reform Jews*, which also emphasized traditional practices.

Polish served as founding president of the Chicago Board of Rabbis (1958–1960) and of the Chicago Board of Reform Rabbis. He was visiting professor at Garrett Biblical Institute in 1959. Polish served as national chairman of the Committee on Unity for Palestine. He was a member of the administrative committee of the Chicago Zionist Federation (president, 1975–1976). He served as vice president of ARZA. Polish was also a member of the Committee on Liturgy and Projects for Israel for the Central Conference of American Rabbis (president, 1971–1973). He was a member of the Commission on Education of the UAHC and a member of the editorial board of *The Reconstructionist*. In 1980 Polish served as alumnus-in-residence at HUC-JIR, Los Angeles, and has been a member of the Board of Governors of HUC-JIR. Polish also taught courses at Northwestern University.

Polish is the author of numerous books. His *Higher Freedom* won the Frank and Ethel S. Cohen Award by the Jewish Book Council of America in 1966 as an outstanding work in the field of Jewish thought.

In 1938 he married Aviva Friedland; they have two children: Daniel, a Reform rabbi, and Judith Shenker.

Writings: *Are Zionism and Reform Judaism Incompatible?* (N.p., 1973); *The Eternal Dissent* (published in Hebrew as *Ha-Maavak Ha-Nitzchi*; New York, 1961); coauthor, *Give Us a King* (Hoboken, NJ, 1989); *Guide for Reform Jews* (New York, 1957); *Higher Freedom* (Chicago, 1965); *Israel: Nation and People* (New York, 1975); *Renew Our Days: The Zionist Issue in Reform Judaism* (Jerusalem, 1976).

References: *Encyclopaedia Judaica* (Jerusalem, 1971), 13:797; "Nearprint Biograhy File," American Jewish Archives; *Who's Who in American Jewry* (Los Angeles, 1980), p. 376.

POZNANSKI, GUSTAVUS (1805?–1870). Hazzan, religious leader, reformer. The son of Joseph and Sarah Poznanski, Gustavus Poznanski was born in Storchnest, Prussia. He received a traditional Jewish education and acquired an impressive familiarity with Talmudic and Hebraic literature. Poznanski briefly settled in Hamburg, where he may have been exposed to the Hamburg Temple and the early stirrings of the Reform movement in Europe.

The precise year of Poznanski's emigration to the United States is unknown. The minutes of New York Congregation Shearith Israel indicate that he was appointed ritual slaughterer (*shochet*) in 1832. In addition to these duties, he was also the assistant hazzan and shofar blower for the High Holy Days. When the position of hazzan became available at Beth Elohim of Charleston, South Carolina, the congregation invited him to assume the position for a probationary period of two years.

Arriving in Charleston in January 1837, Poznanski's ministrations met with such success that he was elected minister for life even before the expiration of his term. This widespread communal approbation ended, however, in 1840 when Poznanski openly sided with a liberal faction of the congregation. The liberals wanted an organ installed in the new building, then under construction to replace their previous one, which had been destroyed by fire. Traditionalist opponents to the organ resented Poznanski for endorsing this reform. They were incensed two years later when, on Passover 1843, he suggested in a sermon that second-day observances of the Holidays be abandoned. For the next three years, the two factions battled in court over installing the organ in the synagogue.

Although the South Carolina courts ultimately sided with the liberal faction, Poznanski apparently felt it was not a real victory because the congregation had been divided. In 1847 he resigned and expressed his hope that a new religious leader might reunify the community. The board rejected his resignation, but Poznanski was adamant. Although he remained an active member of Beth Elohim for the next 15 years, he never again assumed the official mantle of religious leadership. After the Civil War ended, Poznanski resided part of the year in New York, where he had family, and part of the year in Charleston, where he had both friends and property.

The factors underlying Poznanski's intellectual development seem to have been intensely personal. He showed no interest in controversy and largely ignored opponents when they attacked his beliefs in the press. Poznanski remained staunchly nonpartisan; he contributed money for the construction of a building for the breakaway congregation established by his traditionalist opponents in Charleston. Years later, when he returned to New York City, he rejoined traditional Congregation Shearith Israel while retaining his membership in Beth Elohim of Charleston.

Poznanski married Esther G. (Hetty) Barrett on December 5, 1838; they had four children: Isaac, Joseph, Gustavus, Jr., and Sarah. Gustavus Poznanski died in New York on January 7, 1879.

Writings: Unfortunately, the only writings of Poznanski's known to have survived are a few excerpts of his speeches, which were periodically quoted in the Charleston press and the *Minute Books of the Congregation Beth Elohim*, 1838–43, 1846–52.

References: "Biographies File," American Jewish Archives; Solomon Breibart, *The Reverend Dr. Gustavus Poznanski: First American Jewish Reform Minister* (Charleston, SC, 1979); Barnett A. Elzas, "Gustavus Poznanski," *Dictionary of American Biography* (1935); idem, *The Jews of South Carolina* (Philadelphia, 1905); Carol Hess Long, "Gustavus Poznanski" (unpublished essay in the Klau Library, Hebrew Union College–Jewish Institute of Religion, Cincinnati, 1977); Michael A. Meyer, *Response to Modernity* (New York, 1988); Allan Tarshish, "The Charleston Organ Case," *American Jewish Historical Quarterly* 54, no. 4 (June 1965): 411–49. See also Lewis Levin, *The Congregation Beth Elohim, 1870–1883* (Charleston, SC, 1883); David Philipson, *The Reform Movement in Judaism* (New York, 1931); Charles Reznikoff and Uriah Z. Engelman, *The Jews of Charleston* (Philadelphia, 1950); Isaac Mayer Wise, *Reminiscences* (Cincinnati, 1901).

G.P.Z.

PRIESAND, SALLY J. (1946–   ). Rabbi. The daughter of Irving T. and Rose E. Welch Priesand, Sally Priesand was born on June 27, 1946, in Cleveland, Ohio. After attending lower schools in Cleveland, Priesand entered the University of Cincinnati, where she received a B.A. in English in 1968. After graduation, she entered HUC-JIR, where she received a B.H.L. (1971) and an M.A.H.L. (1972). In 1972 Priesand was the first woman to be ordained a rabbi.

On ordination, Priesand assumed the position of assistant rabbi at Stephen S. Wise Free Synagogue in New York City, where she served until 1979, having been named associate rabbi two years earlier. When the senior rabbi retired, the synagogue was still not ready to name a woman as his replacement. Priesand next became chaplain at Lenox Hill Hospital in New York City, serving simultaneously as rabbi of Temple Beth El in Elizabeth, New Jersey. After a two-year tenure in these positions, Priesand became rabbi of Monmouth Reform Temple in Tinton Falls, New Jersey, where she has served since 1981.

Priesand's commitment to the cause of justice and peace, to equal opportunity for women, to the needs of the hungry and the homeless and to the survival of Israel is reflected in her many organizational affiliations. She is a member of B'nai B'rith Women, Hadassah, the American Jewish Committee and the American Jewish Congress. She has served on the Executive Board of the Central Conference of American Rabbis (1977–1979) and was a founding member of the Association of Reform Zionists of America (ARZA).

Priesand belongs to the National Organization for Women and is a strong supporter of the Equal Rights Amendment. She is a member of the Advisory Board of the Brookdale Center for Holocaust Studies and is a member of the boards of trustees of the following organizations: Jewish Federation of Greater Monmouth County, Planned Parenthood of Monmouth County, Monmouth Campaign for Nuclear Disarmament and Interfaith Neighbors.She chairs the Religious Affairs Committee of Planned Parenthood and currently serves as vice president of Interfaith Neighbors, an organization whose primary purpose is to provide rental assistance and support services for the homeless.

In 1972 Priesand was chosen Ohio's Outstanding Young Woman of the Year and named one of the Ten Outstanding Young Women in America. She has been honored by numerous organizations, including B'nai B'rith Women (1971) and Hadassah. She is a recipient of the World Gratitude Day Award. In 1973 she was awarded on honorary D.H.L. from Florida International University. In 1978 she was honored on a medallion struck by the Judaic Heritage Society, and later that year she was named one of 50 Extraordinary Women of Achievement by the National Conference of Christians and Jews in New York City.

In 1980 Priesand received the Eleanor Roosevelt Humanities Award given each year by the State of Israel to a woman who has distinguished herself through service to others. In 1982 she was honored by the Wings Club as a Woman of Accomplishment for her contribution to the field of religion. In 1988 Priesand was named a Woman of Achievement by the Monmouth County Advisory Commission on the Status of Women in recognition of her contributions to the community.

Writings: "From Promise to Reality," *Keeping Posted* 17 (April 1972: 17–19); *Judaism and the New Woman* (New York, 1975).

References: Sherry Levy, "Meet the World's First Woman Rabbi," *Ladies Home Journal*, June 1972; Jacob R. Marcus, *The American Jewish Woman: A Documentary History* (New York, 1981); Norman Mirsky, *Unorthodox Judaism* (Columbus, 1978); "Nearprint Biographies File," American Jewish Archives; Priscilla Proctor and William Proctor, *Women in the Pulpit* (New York, 1976); *Who's Who in America* (Wilmette, IL, 1990–1991), p. 2649.

R

REGNER, SIDNEY L. (1903–   ). Rabbi, administrator. Born to Hungarian immigrant parents, Martin and Kate Lichtman Regner, in New York City on September 25, 1903, Sidney Regner attended high school in Rochester, New York. He attended the University of Cincinnati, where he majored in philosophy (B.A., 1924, Phi Beta Kappa). In 1927 he was ordained at Hebrew Union College, where he received his B.H.L. in 1923 and the I. Fleischer Prize and the Simon Lazarus Prize. He received an honorary D.D. from HUC-JIR in 1954.

After ordination, Regner became rabbi of Temple Oheb Shalom in Reading, Pennsylvania (1927–1954). In Reading, he was active in many community organizations, including its Council of Social Agencies (president, 1942–1943), Reading Congregation B'nai B'rith (1935–1936) and United Jewish Campaign Budget and Scope Committee (chairman, 1936–1948). He was a member of the board of the Jewish Welfare League, the Visiting Nurse Association, the Planned Parenthood center, the Guidance Institute and Fellowship House. He was a member of the executive committee of the Jewish Community Council and the Reading Round Table of Christians and Jews. Regner was also a member of the Community Chest Board (1933–1934, 1937–1947) and the executive committee of Central Atlantic States Region of Council of Jewish Federations and Welfare Funds (1943–1947). During World War II, he served as chief of the emergency welfare service of the Berks County Defense Council and as a member of the Regional War Labor Board.

When the CCAR established its central office in New York in 1954, Regner became its first executive vice president and remained in that position until his retirement in 1971. Under Regner's guidance, the CCAR developed into a recognized professional association with annual regional *kallot* (study retreats) in addition to the annual convention. Regner had been financial secretary of the CCAR (1939–1952), chairman of its publication committee (1952–1954) and secretary of the HUC Alumni Association (1936–1939).

During his tenure at the CCAR, Regner served as a member of the Governing Body of the World Union for Progressive Judaism (1957–1971) and the Executive Committee of the Synagogue Council of America (1955–1971). He also edited the CCAR *Yearbook* from 1954 until 1971. After his retirement, Regner has served as the vice president of the Jewish Peace Fellowship (since 1980), reflecting his career-long interest in social justice with a special emphasis on peace. In 1957 Regner was honored by the New York Federation of Jewish Philanthropies in recognition of his service to the community.

In 1931 Regner married Dorothy Marcus (d., 1971); they had three children: Norman (d., 1960), Babette Melmed and James.

Writings: "The Earliest Jews in Berks County," *Historical Review of Berks County*, January 1942.

References: "Nearprint Biography File," American Jewish Archives; *Who's Who in American Jewry* (Los Angeles, 1980), p. 390.

REINES, ALVIN JAY (1926–   ). Rabbi, philosopher. Born September 12, 1926, in Paterson, New Jersey, the son of Louis and Celia Rubin Reines, Alvin Reines attended the Rabbi Joseph Jacob School and the Talmudical Academy before entering Yeshiva University (B.A., 1947). After graduation, he attended law school at New York University before entering Hebrew Union College, where he was ordained with an M.A.H.L. in 1952. After ordination, he was awarded the Mrs. Henry Morgenthau Fellowship by HUC-JIR for study at Harvard University (Ph.D., 1958). In 1958 he was appointed to the faculty of HUC-JIR, Cincinnati, and later promoted to Professor of Jewish Philosophy, a position he still holds.

While Reines specialized in medieval philosophy and the work of Moses Maimonides in particular, he is more widely known for his conception of "polydox" religion and its application to Reform Judaism. Polydoxy is a radical interpretation of Judaism that begins with the premise that, philosophically speaking, there is a multiplicity of truths on which Judaism can be based. It holds that Jewish religious activity should be pluralistic and highly responsive to cultural change. For instance, Reines rejects the idea of a seventh-day Sabbath and instead defines Shabbat as a "state of being." In 1971 he founded the Institute of Creative Judaism and served as chair of its board of trustees. The institute is a nonprofit research organization dedicated to producing philosophical, educational and liturgical materials for the understanding and practice of what Reines suggests is a free Judaism in the concrete religious life of the community.

In 1962 Reines married Hera Ginsberg; they have three children: Jennifer, Kip and Adam.

Writings (partial listing): coauthor, *Elements in the Philosophy of Reform Judaism* (Cincinnati, 1976); "Freud's Concept of Reality and God: A Text Study," *Hebrew Union College Annual* 61 (1990): 219–70; *Haggadah: A Passover Service for the Family* (Cincinnati, 1956); *Maimonides and Abrabanel on Prophecy* (Cincinnati, 1976); *The Patriarchal Family* (Cincinnati, 1975); *Polydoxy; Explorations in a Philosophy of Liberal*

Religion (Buffalo, 1987); *Reform Judaism as a Polydoxy*, 4 vols. (Cincinnati, 1970–1973).

References: "Nearprint Biographies File," American Jewish Archives.

RIVKIN, ELLIS (1918–   ). Historian. The son of Moses I. and Beatrice Leibowitz Rivkin, Ellis Rivkin was born on September 7, 1918, in Baltimore and raised as an Orthodox Jew. Rivkin entered Johns Hopkins University, receiving his B.A. (1941) and Ph.D. in history (1946). During his early years at Johns Hopkins, he was concurrently enrolled at Baltimore Hebrew College (now University) and was awarded the B.H.L. degree in 1943. After receiving his doctorate, Rivkin served as the Cyrus Adler Post-Doctoral Research Fellow at Gratz College in Philadelphia (1946–1948), remaining at Gratz to teach history until 1949.

In 1949 Rivkin was appointed assistant professor of Jewish history at HUC-JIR, Cincinnati (appointed professor in 1953; named Adolph S. Ochs Professor in 1965). He remained at HUC-JIR until his retirement in 1988. A popular teacher, he is well known as a keen and insightful analyst of the relationship between Jewish culture and its surrounding milieu. Rivkin advocates the idea that the "unity principle" monotheism is the salient element in Jewish history. He is also known for applying his "trans-historic" methodology to the problems of Jewish history.

Throughout his career, Rivkin has served as a visiting faculty member at various institutions, including Antioch, Dropsie University, University of Utah, Southern Methodist University and the University of San Francisco. In 1962 he was awarded a Simon Guggenheim fellowship to do archival research in Vienna on the role of Jews in the early development of capitalism. He is a member of many learned societies, to which he has presented numerous papers, including the American Historical Association, the Economic History Association, the Medieval Academy of America, the Society of Biblical Literature, the American Academy of Political and Social Science and the American Academy of Religion.

In recognition of his work, the American Association for the Advancement of Science elected Rivkin a Fellow (1966), and Baltimore Hebrew College granted him an honorary D.H.L. in 1975. In 1977 Rivkin established the Globalist Research Foundation, which focuses on the field of international affairs with emphasis on Israel and the Middle East. He is the author of more than 100 articles and has published five books covering the whole range of Jewish history, with emphases on the "Pharisaic revolution," the Marranos, messianism and the intertestamental period.

Rivkin married Zelda Zafren in 1941; they have two daughters: Roslyn and Sharon.

Writings (partial listing, books only): *The Dynamics of Jewish History* (Sarasota, 1970); *A Hidden Revolution: The Pharisee's Search for the Kingdom Within* (New York, 1971); *Leon da Modena and the Kok Sahkol* (Cincinnati, 1952); *The Shaping of Jewish*

History: A Radical New Interpretation (New York, 1971); *What Crucified Jesus* (Nashville, 1984).

References: *American Jewish Biographies* (New York, 1982), pp. 355–56; *Encyclopaedia Judaica* (Jerusalem, 1971), 14:198; "Nearprint Biographies File and Box," American Jewish Archives; *Who's Who in America* (Wilmette, IL, 1990–1991), p. 2753; *Who's Who in American Jewry* (Los Angeles, 1980), p. 396; *Who's Who in World Jewry* (New York, 1981), pp. 632–33.

ROSENAU, WILLIAM (1865–1943). Rabbi, professor. Born in Wollstein, the Prussian province of Posen, on May 30, 1865, William Rosenau was the son of Rabbi Nathan and Johanna Braun Rosenau. He was educated in the public schools and gymnasium of Hirshberg, Silesia, before immigrating to the United States in 1876. After arriving in Boston, his father was called to Philadelphia, where William attended public schools. Later he attended high school in Cincinnati, Ohio. Rosenau received a B.A. from the University of Cincinnati (1888) and was ordained at Hebrew Union College the following year (1889), where he was studying concurrently. He received an honorary D.H.L. from Hebrew Union College in 1933.

After ordination, he served Temple Israel in Omaha, Nebraska (1889–1892). He left to lead Congregation Oheb Shalom in Baltimore, Maryland, where he served until 1939, when he was named rabbi emeritus. While in Baltimore, Rosenau studied semitics at Johns Hopkins University (Ph.D., 1900) and served on its faculty (1898–1932).

While steeped in a broad knowledge of rabbinics, Rosenau was radical in regard to ritual. In Nebraska he refused either to wear tallit or to cover his head and rewrote both Friday evening and Saturday morning services. While at Oheb Shalom, he changed the language of prayers and sermons from German to English. The compulsory requirement to wear a head covering was abolished. Late Friday evening worship was introduced. He was a non-Zionist and member of the American Council for Judaism.

When Kaufmann Kohler retired as president of Hebrew Union College, Rosenau was nearly elected his successor. As a matter of fact, the *American Israelite* even predicted his election with a header, "Dr. Rosenau will probably be elected President of Hebrew Union College." But he lost the vote to Julian Morgenstern. Rosenau had been invited to serve several large congregations but generally declined and remained in Baltimore.

Rosenau was an active member of the Baltimore Board of Education (1900–1919). He served various offices of the Central Conference of American Rabbis (second vice president, 1896–1897; corresponding secretary, 1902; president, 1915–1917). Rosenau was also active in the Mt. Pleasant Sanitorium, Associated Jewish Charities, Maryland Society for the Study and Prevention of Tuberculosis, Maryland Prisoner's Aid Society, (Maryland) Governor's Commission on State College and (Maryland) Governor's Commission on Higher Education of Negroes. He was a member of the Hebrew Union College Board of Governors

(1917–1943). Rosenau was among the founders of the Jewish Welfare Board, the Jewish Chautauqua Society (where he served as chancellor) and the World Union for Progressive Judaism. He also was a member of the Commission on Jewish Education for the Reform movement, as well as the American Oriental Society and the Society for Biblical Literature.

Rosenau edited the *Jewish Comment* for four years and was a contributor to the *Jewish Encyclopedia*. He was also an editor of the revised *Union Prayer Book* and *Union Haggadah*.

Rosenau married Mabel Hellman in 1893. They had two children: Marguerite Keifer and William. After Mabel's death, he married Myra Kraus in 1925. He died on December 9, 1943, in Baltimore.

Writings (partial listing): *The Book of Esther* (New York, 1917); *Consolations* (Baltimore, 1914); *Hebraisms in the Authorized Version of the Bible* (Baltimore, 1902); *Jewish Biblical Commentators* (Baltimore, 1906); *Jewish Ceremonial Institutions and Customs* (Baltimore, 1902); *The Rabbi in Action* (New York, 1937); *Seder Hagadah* (Baltimore, 1906); *Semitic Studies in American Colleges* (Baltimore, 1896).

References: *American Jewish Year Book* 5 (1904): 90–91; *Jewish Encyclopedia* (New York, 1906), 10:473; William F. Rosenblum, *The Life and Work of Rev. Dr. William Rosenau* (Cincinnati, 1946); "William Rosenau Manuscript Collection," American Jewish Archives.

ROSENWALD, LESSING JULIUS (1891–1979). Merchant. Born on February 10, 1891, in Chicago, Illinois, Lessing Rosenwald was the son of Julius and Augusta Nusbaum Rosenwald. After graduating from the University of Chicago's elementary and high schools (1909), he studied at Cornell University but left in 1911.

That same year, Rosenwald entered his father's company, Sears, Roebuck and Company, as a shipping clerk, working his way up in the company. After his naval service in World War I, Rosenwald managed the Sears plant near Philadelphia. He remained in the Philadelphia area the rest of his life. On the elder Rosenwald's death in 1932, Lessing Rosenwald became chairman of the board of Sears, a position he held until 1939.

In 1934 Rosenwald became a representative of industry on the Regional Labor Board of Philadelphia. Active in Philadelphia cultural life, he was also a member of Congregation Keneseth Israel. He was chairman of the National United Jewish Appeal from 1942 to 1963. He also served on the Regional Labor Board and the Philadelphia Labor Mediation Tribunal (1935). Rosenwald was on the board of the University of Chicago and the Princeton Institute for Advanced Study. Rosenwald was also director of the American Research and Development Company. A vigorous anti-Zionist who campaigned before the United Nations against the establishment of a Jewish state in Palestine, Rosenwald helped to found the American Council for Judaism in 1943 and was its first president (until 1955; cochairman of the board, 1956 to 1966; honorary chairman, 1966 to 1968). Rosenwald saw his anti-Zionism as an outgrowth of classical Reform Judaism.

Briefly, in 1940, Rosenwald joined the National Committee of America First. Later he served as a member of the local Board of Appeal of the Selective Service System (1939 to 1941). In 1941 he headed the Offices of Production Management's silk commodity section. For the reorganization of the defense system, in September 1941 Rosenwald was named Chief of the Bureau of Industrial Conservation and later served as director (when it was raised to the level of a division) until 1943.

Rosenwald was a noted rare-book collector who financially supported the National Gallery of Art and the Library of Congress, to whom he bequeathed his books. He was a leader of the Community Fund and president of the Federation of Jewish Philanthropies (1930 to 1934), as well as director on the Board of Jefferson Medical College and secretary of Dropsie College. In 1937 he became trustees chairman of the Rosenwald Family Foundation, which was endowed to support his father's philanthropic interests—to further interracial understanding.

Rosenwald received honorary doctorates from the University of Pennsylvania (1947), Lincoln University (1954), Jefferson Medical College (1954), LaSalle College (1965), Colby College (1966) and Williams College (1969). He also received the following awards: Philadelphia Award, Artists Equity Association; Distinguished Achievement Award, the Philadelphia Art Alliance; the Philadelphia Award; Donald F. Hyde Award, Princeton University; Sir William Osler Award, Johns Hopkins University; and the title of Knight First Class, Royal order of Vasa, Sweden.

In 1913 he married Edith Goodkind (whose mother had married Rosenwald's widowed father 17 years earlier); they had five children: Julius II, Janet Becker, Helen Snellenbus, Robert and Joan Scott. Lessing Rosenwald died on June 26, 1979, at his home, "Alverthorpe" (deeded to Abington Township), in Jenkintown, Pennsylvania.

Writings: *The Death of Dance* (Paris, 1945); *The Early Illustrated Book* (Washington, DC, 1982); *Five Centuries of Print-Making* (Philadelphia, 1931).

References: *American Jewish Yearbook* (Philadelphia, 1981); *Current Biograhy* (New York, 1947); "Nearprint Biography File," "Scrapbooks," American Jewish Archives; *New York Times*, January 26, 1988; *Universal Jewish Encyclopedia* (New York, 1943), 9:255; M. R. Werner, *Julius Rosenwald* (New York, 1939); *Who's Who in American Jewry* (New York, 1939), p. 891; *Who Was Who in America* (Chicago, 1981), 7:492.

ROTHSCHILD, JACOB (1911–1973). Rabbi. Jacob Rothschild was born on August 4, 1911, in Pittsburgh, Pennsylvania, the son of Meyer and Lillian Abrams Rothschild. He attended public school in Pittsburgh and one year at the University of Pittsburgh (at the age of 15). He entered the University of Cincinnati, where he received an A.B. degree in 1932, and was ordained by Hebrew Union College in 1936. In 1960 he received an honorary D.D. from HUC-JIR.

After his ordination, Rothschild first served Temple Emanuel in Davenport, Iowa (1936–1937), then served, as assistant rabbi, Rodef Shalom Congregation in Pittsburgh, Pennsylvania (1937–1946), the congregation in which he had been raised. He took a leave from his congregation to serve in the U.S. Army from 1942 to 1945, seeing combat in Guadalcanal from 1942 to 1943. Rothschild served temporary duty in the Office of Chief of Chaplains (1944) and special duty in the Information and Education Branch (1943–1944). In 1946 he was named rabbi of the Temple, Hebrew Benevolent Congregation, in Atlanta, Georgia, a position he held until his death.

One of Rothschild's first acts in Atlanta was to establish an Institute for the Christian Clergy. He was active in the pursuit of interfaith relations and civil rights, and he gained national attention in 1958 when a bomb exploded, partially destroying the Temple. Although Rothschild received intimidating phone calls and threats of violence to himself and his family, nothing deterred him from his positive racial stand. A few years later, he asserted his leadership in seeing that Atlanta pay honor to Martin Luther King, Jr., on the occasion of King's receiving the Nobel Peace Prize in 1964.

In Atlanta, Rothschild was president of Gate City Lodge, B'nai B'rith (1950); cochairman, UJA (1949–1950); member, National Conference of Christians and Jews; and member, the Kiwanis Club. He was president of the Atlanta Federation of Jewish Social Services (1954–1957) and served on the executive committee of the Anti-Defamation League's Southeast Regional Advisory Board and the Greater Atlanta Council on Human Relations. He served as chairman of the Commission on Social Action and as a member of the Advisory Committee for the Religious Action Center of Reform Judaism. Rothschild was also president of the Atlanta Rabbinical Association. In 1962 he joined the Board of Governors of HUC-JIR. Rothschild was a founding member of the Atlanta Community Relations Commission. His work in the commission represented his often articulated belief in religious and racial tolerance.

Rothschild was honored twice by the Anti-Defamation League; he received its Citation of Merit in 1954 and then the Abe Goldstein Human Relations Award in 1968.

In 1946 Rothschild married Janice Oettinger Blumberg; they had two children: Marcia and William, a Reform rabbi and attorney. Jacob Rothschild died on December 31, 1973.

References: Jacob M. Rothschild Manuscripts, Special Collection, Robert W. Woodruff Library, Emory University, Atlanta, Georgia; "Nearprint Biographies Box," American Jewish Archives; Janice Rothschild, *As But a Day* (Atlanta, 1966, 1987); idem, *One Voice* (Atlanta, 1988).

S

SANDMEL, SAMUEL (1911–1979). Rabbi, professor. Born in Dayton, Ohio, on September 23, 1911, Samuel Sandmel was the son of Morris and Rebecca Lenderman Sandmel. He attended public schools in St. Louis, graduated with an A.B. from the University of Missouri in 1932 and was ordained in 1937 after studying at Hebrew Union College. Sandmel served as a naval chaplain during World War I. He was director of the Hillel Foundation at Yale University (1946–1949) while studying there toward his Ph.D., which he received in 1949.

Sandmel taught Jewish literature and thought at Vanderbilt University from 1949 to 1952, when he joined the faculty of Hebrew Union College. He was appointed provost (1957–1966), Distinguished Service Professor of Bible (1966) and director of the graduate program. He retired in 1979 to accept a position as Helen A. Regenstein Professor of Religion at the University of Chicago Divinity School. Sandmel had taught previously at the University of Chicago, including in 1976 when he was Nuveen Visiting Professor of Religion. He had also been director of the Weil Institute for Studies in Religion and the Humanities as well as editor of the *Hebrew Union College Annual* (1970–1973). In 1968 and 1969 he was the Honorary Visiting Principal of Leo Baeck College in London.

The author of 17 scholarly volumes and one novel, Sandmel served as head of a group of 29 specialists who produced the Oxford Study Edition of the *New English Bible with Apocrypha*. He was a specialist in the intertestamental period, especially focusing on Judaism in the early age of Christianity. By writing his first book, *A Jewish Understanding of the New Testament*, he became the first American Jewish scholar to publish a study of the New Testament from a Jewish point of view. In 1961 Sandmel served as president of the Society for Biblical Literature.

Widely acclaimed as a leader in interfaith relations, Sandmel spent a lifetime building bridges between Christians and Jews, with his interpretive scholarship, widespread lectures to clergy, students and laypersons and many publications.

Several of his books received awards, including the Jewish Book Award in 1973 for *Two Living Traditions*.

Sandmel was the recipient of numerous awards and citations: Distinguished Alumni Citation from the University of Missouri (1966), honorary D.H.L. from the University of Vermont, Nicholas and Hedy Munk Brotherhood Award of the Canadian Council of Christians and Jews (posthumously, 1979), National Brotherhood Media Award of the National Conference of Christians and Jews, honorary D.H.L. from Xavier University and honorary D.L. from Rosary College.

In 1977 scholars at seminaries and universities in Ohio established an annual Mid-American Scholars Dialogue to honor Sandmel.

In 1940 Sandmel married Frances Langsdorf Fox; they had three children: Charles E. F., Benjamin F. and David F. Samuel Sandmel died in Cincinnati on November 4, 1979.

Writings (partial listing): *Alone atop the Mountain* (New York, 1973); *The Genius of Paul* (New York, 1958); *A Jewish Understanding of the New Testament* (Providence, 1974); *Judaism and Christian Beginnings* (Oxford, 1978); *A Little Book on Religion* (Chambersburg, PA, 1975); *When a Jew and Christian Marry* (Knoxville, 1977).

References: Michael J. Cook, *The Legacy of Samuel Sandmel* (Cincinnati, 1979); Frederick E. Greenspahn et al., *Nourished with Peace: Studies in Hellenistic Judaism in Memory of Samuel Sandmel* (Chicago, 1984); "Nearprint Biography File and Box," American Jewish Archives; *New York Times*, obituary, November 7, 1979; *Who Was Who in America* (Chicago, 1981), 7:500.

SCHEUER, SIMON HAAS (1891–1979). Businessman, philanthropist. Born in New York on October 7, 1891, Simon Scheuer was the son of Jonas Scheuer and Olga Haas Scheuer.

Scheuer attended Columbia College, where he received his B.A. in 1913. He also attended Columbia Law School during his last year at college. In 1967, Hebrew Union College–Jewish Institute of Religion awarded him the (hon.) D.H.L.

Scheuer liquidated his stock holdings before the crash of 1929. This enabled him to acquire control of a number of commercial and residential real estate companies in the New York area. He also became the principal stockholder in two Houston-based companies: Southdown, Inc., and CLC of America, Inc. Likewise, Scheuer was involved in the Rouse Co., Eastern Gas and Fuel Associates, and as a director of the Florida East Coast Railway.

Active in many areas of philanthropy, Scheuer maintained an interest in subsidized housing for the elderly, most notably in the Scheuer House at Coney Island. He was also interested in the development of Brandeis University, City College, Columbia University and Hebrew Union College.

He served on the board of Hillside Hospital. In 1972 he received the Distinguished Communal Service Award from the Federation of Jewish Philanthropies (New York).

In 1916, he married Helen Rose. They had five children: Richard, James, Walter, Steven and Amy Cohen. He died on October 22, 1979, in New York City.

References: *American Jewish Year Book* 82 (1981): 375; *New York Times*, obituary, October 25, 1979.

SCHINDLER, ALEXANDER MOSHE (1925–   ). Rabbi, UAHC president. The son of Sali Hoyda Schindler and Eliezer Schindler, Alexander Schindler was born in Munich, Germany, on October 4, 1925. He emigrated to the United States with his parents on July 30, 1938. The remainder of Schindler's formative years were spent in New York, where he attended the College of the City of New York (B.S., 1950), graduating cum laude with honors in history. He also attended Hebrew Union College for Teachers in New York. After graduation, he attended HUC-JIR, Cincinnati, where he received an M.H.L. and was ordained a rabbi in 1953. He was awarded the Mother Hirsch Memorial Prize for the highest scholastic level in the competition for the B.H.L. degree. While in Cincinnati, he served two years as Director of the B'nai B'rith Hillel at the University of Cincinnati and three years as Jewish Chaplain at Longview State Hospital for the Mentally Ill. Schindler served in the U.S. Army Ski Troops during World War II, seeing service in Europe, and was awarded a Purple Heart and Bronze Star.

After ordination, Schindler was assistant rabbi of Temple Emanuel in Worcester, Massachusetts (1953–1955), and associate director (1955–1959) then director of the UAHC New England Region (1959–1963). While in Worcester, he also served as director of the Hillel Foundation of Clark University and Worcester Polytechnic Institute. From there he returned to New York to direct the UAHC Department of Education (1963–1967). He remained in that position until named vice president in 1967. In 1973, after the death of Maurice Eisendrath, Schindler was named president of the UAHC, a position he still holds.

Throughout his career, Schindler has been associated with numerous organizations, serving as chairman, Conference of Presidents of Major American Jewish Organizations (1976–1978); vice president, World Jewish Congress and Memorial Foundation for Jewish Culture; member, Governing Body, Jewish Agency for Israel; member, Board of Trustees, United Jewish Appeal; member, Board of Governors, HUC-JIR; member, Board of Directors, American Joint Distribution Committee; member, Board of Governors, United Nations Association of the USA.

An outspoken proponent for Reform Judaism's innovative programs, Schindler has been the driving force behind the UAHC Torah commentary, the first liberal commentary. He endorsed the UAHC outreach programs, encouraged converts to Judaism and welcomed non-Jews (married to Jews) into the synagogue. He was the force behind the official adoption of patrilineal descent by the CCAR.

Schindler has served as literary editor of the *CCAR Journal* and was the founding editor of *Dimensions*.

He received an honorary D.D. from HUC-JIR and honorary degrees from the University of Southern California (1987) and Lafayette College (1988). He has also received the Bublick Prize of Hebrew University (1978). A JNF forest was planted in his honor.

On September 29, 1956, Schindler married Rhea Rosenblum; they have five children: Elisa, Debra Trautmann, Joshua, Judith and Jonathan.

Writings: *Consultation on Conscience* (Washington, DC, 1985); *Contradictory Vatican Statements about Jews and Judaism* (New York, 1987); *East-West Relations* (New York, 1985); *From Discrimination to Extermination* (Cincinnati, 1949); *Jewish Community Service in Support of People with AIDS* (Los Angeles, 1989).

References: ''Nearprint Biographies Box,'' ''Biographies File,'' American Jewish Archives; *Who's Who in American Jewry* (Los Angeles, 1984), p. 432; *Who's Who in World Jewry* (New York, 1981), p. 683.

SCHINDLER, SOLOMON (1842–1915). Rabbi. Schindler was born on April 24, 1842, in Neisse, Silesia, Germany, the son of an Orthodox rabbi, Julius Schindler, and Bertha Algan Schindler. At age 13, he went to Breslau to study for the rabbinate. Two years later, objecting to Orthodoxy, he left his rabbinical studies, graduating from the Breslau gymnasium and later receiving the requisite training for qualifying as a teacher. In 1870 he graduated from the Royal Teachers' Seminary in Buren, Germany.

In 1868 Schindler led a small congregation in Westphalia, but it was not prepared for his already pronounced liberal position. This conflict came to a head when he was forced to leave Germany as a result of a speech he gave attacking Bismarck's conduct in the Franco-Prussian War on the very day the victorious Prussian armies returned to Berlin. Immigrating to the United States in 1871, he first tried to make a living as a shoelace peddler. However, poverty forced him, shortly after his arrival, to secure a position as rabbi of a small Orthodox congregation, Adath Emono Congregation in Hoboken, New Jersey. He held this position until 1874, when he was elected to the pulpit of Congregation Adath Israel (later Temple Israel) in Boston, where he remained until 1894. Schindler steered the congregation of the traditional synagogue toward Reform Judaism by introducing the organ, family pews, prayers in the vernacular and, in 1885, Sunday services. While Temple Israel was ready for moderate Reform Judaism, it was not ready for Schindler's religious radicalism. He left his pulpit to follow the ''religion of social reform'' as articulated by Edward Bellamy, whose work he translated, offering an English sequel to *Looking Backward*.

A strong preacher who was influenced by Darwinism and the emerging school of biblical criticism, Schindler attracted large audiences and a great deal of attention through his sermons and lectures. He was closely associated with Minot Savage (who later founded the Community Church of New York), the first American clergyperson to reconcile Christianity and Darwinism. He was closely aligned with other non-Jews strongly attracted to the Free Religionists. He was also active with the American Psychical Society and was a colleague of Hamlin Garland's.

Schindler was a radical thinker, considered assimilationist by some (from which he eventually returned to a more moderate position). His liberalism took him too far, and he left Temple Israel and the congregational rabbinate in 1894. He had moved too fast in adopting Sunday services and had also outraged his congregation in the early 1890s by advocating intermarriage between liberal Jews and Christians.

Schindler was active in charitable work. He became superintendent of the Federation of Jewish Charities and then the Leopold Morse Home for Infirm Hebrews and Orphanage at Mattawan, Massachusetts, in 1899. From 1888 to 1894, he also served as a member of the Boston School Board, chosen by popular election.

A litterateur, Schindler prepared the *Illustrated Hebrew Almanac for the Year 5641* (1881). He frequently offered representative Jewish opinion on general Boston community issues. He was a frequent contributor to leading journals, especially in the area of education, immigration and race relations.

Working toward a theology modeled after unitarianism, Schindler came to terms with the study of comparative religions, biblical criticism and the evolutionary hypothesis. He worked toward dissolving misconceptions that Jews had about Christianity, as well as those that Christians had about Judaism, minimizing the differences between both groups. He rejected the beliefs in a personal God and the divine origin of the Bible and the notion of a Messiah.

In 1866 Schindler married Henrietta Schultz; they had three sons: Otto, Paul and William. Solomon Schindler died in 1915.

Writings: *Dissolving Views in the History of Judaism* (Boston, 1888); *Messianic Expectations and Modern Judaism* (Boston, 1886); *Young West* (Boston, 1894).

References: *American Jewish Year Book* (Philadelphia, 1905), 7:99–100; *Encyclopaedia Judaica* (Jerusalem, 1972), 14:967; Arthur Mann, *Growth and Achievement of Temple Israel, 1854–1954* (Boston, 1954), pp. 45–62; *History of the Jews of Boston* (Boston, 1892); *Massachusetts of Today* (Boston, 1890); *One of a Thousand* (Boston, 1890); idem, *Yankee Reformers in an Urban Age* (Cambridge, Massachusetts, 1954), pp. 42–72; "Nearprint Biography Boxes," "Personal Scrapbooks," American Jewish Archives; *Who Was Who in America* (Chicago, 1943), 1:1087.

SCHOEN, MYRON E. (1920–   ). Administrator. Myron Schoen was born in the Bronx on January 9, 1920, the son of Murray S. and Anna Stein Schoen. While his father and grandparents on both sides were from Hungary, his mother was born in the United States. Growing up in New York, Schoen received his B.B.A. from the Baruch School of Business Administration, CUNY, in 1948, doing graduate work at Brooklyn College (1949–1950) and again at the Baruch School (1951–1952). Before entering college, Schoen served as an Information and Education Specialist in the U.S. Army from 1943 to 1946. He became a Fellow of Temple Administration in 1964.

In 1952 Schoen was appointed assistant to the national director, B'nai B'rith Hillel Foundations, where he remained for two years. In 1954 he entered the world of synagogue administration when he became executive secretary of the Stephen S. Wise Free Synagogue in New York City. He relinquished this post in 1957 to become the director, UAHC-CCAR Commission on Synagogue Administration (now Management), serving until his retirement in 1987. In this capacity he applied the modern business skills of management to the American synagogue. In doing so, he helped build the profession of synagogue adminis- tration and trained lay and rabbinic leaders in the management, finance and administration of the modern synagogue.

Throughout his career, Schoen has served the Reform movement in various capacities: Director of Placement, National Association of Temple Administra- tors (1967–1987); consultant to NATA Placement Service (from 1981); member, NATA Executive Board (from 1957); secretary, Board of Certification for Tem- ple Administrators of the Union of American Hebrew Congregations, NATA and CCAR; Professional Advisory Committee, School of Jewish Communal Service, HUC-JIR; Honorary Life Member, CCAR (1987); Board of Governors, Commission on Synagogue Relations of Federation of Jewish Philanthropies of New York City; chairman, Sterling Committee, Interfaith Commission on Family Financial Planning, American Council on Life Insurance; Secretary, Lemberg Scholarship Loan Fund.

In addition, Schoen has lectured on synagogue management at various insti- tutions, including the Lown School at Brandeis University and Center for Church Management at American University. He served as a columnist for "On the Synagogue Scene" for the *National Jewish Post and Opinion* (1962–1981) and the *Jewish Week* in New York (1981–1984).

Schoen married Charlotte Klepper in 1944; they have two children: Deborah Nan Stern and Marc Aaron.

Writings: coed., *The American Synagogue: A Progress Report* (New York, 1958); coauthor, *Successful Synagogue Administration* (New York, 1964); coed., *The Temple Management Manual* (New York, 1984).

References: *National Association of Temple Administrators Journal* (Fall/Winter, 1987), p. 6; "The Story of NATA" (videotape, New York, 1987); "UAHC—Mid- Atlantic Council News" (Nisan, 1987), p. 3.

SCHULMAN, SAMUEL (1864–1955). Rabbi, scholar, theologian, orator, communal leader. The son of Tanhum and Rachel Alterman Schulman, born in Kalvaria, Russia, on February 14, 1864, Samuel Schulman came to the United States at age four. On entering public school, he had an extensive knowledge of Hebrew, and by age 13, he had mastered several tractates of Talmud. Schulman received his B.A. at the College of the City of New York in 1885 and continued his studies at the University of Berlin (1885–1889) and at the Hochschule für die Wissenschaft des Judentums, where he received rabbinic ordination. In 1904, he received a D.D. at the Jewish Theological Seminary, and in 1925, Schulman was awarded the honorary D.H.L. by Hebrew Union College.

Schulman's distinguished rabbinic career included service as rabbi of Congregations Shalom, New York City (1889–1890); Emanu-El, Helena, Montana (1890–1893); B'nai Jehudah, Kansas City, Missouri, (1893–1899); Beth-El, New York City (1899–1927), which merged with Emanu-El, New York City (1927–1934; emeritus, 1934–1955). Schulman served as president of the CCAR (1911–1913), president of the Association of Reform Rabbis of Greater New York and Vicinity (1921–1926) and member of the Union of American Hebrew Congregations Commission on Jewish Education (1927–1940). Schulman was chairman of the UAHC Youth Education Committee, which led to the establishment of the National Federation of Temple Youth in 1939. He served as a founder and organizer of the Hebrew Union College School for Teachers, New York, and of the World Union for Progressive Judaism in 1926.

Other noteworthy accomplishments include founding president of the Synagogue Council of America (1934–1935) and director, vice president, and education committee chairman of the Young Mens Hebrew Association of New York. Schulman was one of the editors of the Jewish Publication Society Bible Translation (1909–1916) and a member of the board of editors of its *Jewish Classics* series. While his writings are numerous, they are mostly tracts, magazine and journal articles, as well as an extensive number of published sermons. He also served as an officer of the Jewish Publication Society.

Schulman's theology is characterized by a theistic, God-centered orientation to Judaism. He therefore vigorously opposed humanism, ethical culture, atheism and other secular philosophies. He viewed Law as an essential element of Judaism, teaching divine revelation but identifying such revelation only with the Prophets and their moral imperatives. Unlike other classical Reformers, he held a positive view of ritual and ceremony, which he believed served to discipline a person for the rigors of moral law. Schulman called for a greater inclusion of ritual in the Reform movement and was a moderating influence. His theology was imbued with an indomitable hope, inspired by a deep commitment to the principle of Israel's divine election. A full presentation of Schulman's theology was presented for consideration for the 1937 Columbus Platform of the CCAR. Although not adopted by the convention, it was nevertheless published in that year's CCAR *Yearbook*. He was also an outspoken opponent of mixed marriage.

Like other Reform leaders of the day, he rejected nationalistic conceptions of Israel as a contradiction of the mission of Israel. Despite his untiring opposition to political Zionism, however, he was an early proponent of Palestinian development and Jewish immigration and became a non-Zionist member of the Jewish Agency in 1929. Schulman held a fervent love for America as the ideal representation of democracy and the best opportunity for the realization of Judaism's potential. Schulman claimed to have coined the term *melting pot* before its use by Israel Zangwill and others to refer to the symbol of America.

In 1949, Congregation Emanu-El established the Reverend Dr. Samuel Schulman Lectureship on Judaism in Its Relations to Philosophy, Science and Ethics at HUC-JIR, Cincinnati. In 1952 the Samuel Schulman Publication Fund for Biblical Studies was established by the Jewish Publication Society as a tribute to the veteran religious leader who was a key translator of the Hebrew Bible in 1917. It was the society to which Schulman devoted most of his time outside of the pulpit.

In 1890 Schulman married Emma Weinberg; they had three children: Aubrey, Walter and Dorothy Masback. Samuel Schulman died in New York on November 2, 1955.

Writings (partial listing): *America and Palestine in the Light of My Recent Travels* (New York, 1955); "Israel," Central Conference of American Rabbis *Yearbook* 45 (1935): 260–311; *Jewish Ethics* (Cincinnati, n.d.); *Judaism and the Destiny of the Individual* (London, 1939); *A Set of Holiday Sermons* (New York, 1909).

References: Lewis H. Kamrass, "The Life and Works of Rabbi Samuel Schulman as Reflected in His Writings: A Critical Historical Study of One of Reform's Most Significant Leaders" (Rabbinical thesis, Hebrew Union College–Jewish Institute of Religion, Cincinnati, 1985); Samuel Schulman Manuscript Collection, American Jewish Archives; *Who Was Who in America* (Chicago, 1960), 3:765

L.H.K.

SCHWARTZMAN, SYLVAN DAVID (1913–   ). Rabbi, academician. The son of Jacob and Rose Padve Schwartzman, Sylvan Schwartzman was born on December 13, 1913, in Baltimore. After attending schools in Baltimore, Schwartzman enrolled in the University of Cincinnati, where he was awarded an A.B. in 1936. Simultaneously matriculating at Hebrew Union College, he received a B.H.L. (1936) and was ordained in 1941, when he received an M.H.L. Schwartzman received a Ph.D. from Vanderbilt University (1952) and an M.B.A. from the University of Cincinnati (1970). He also received an honorary D.D. from HUC-JIR in 1981.

After ordination, Schwartzman served as rabbi at the Augusta, Georgia, Congregation Children of Israel (1941–1947). He left to become Director of Field Activities for the U.A.H.C. (1947–1948). After this short tenure in field service, he assumed the pulpit at the Temple in Nashville, Tennessee (1948–1950). He then was named professor of Jewish Religious Education at HUC-JIR, Cincinnati, where he remained until his retirement in 1981 (having served shortly as dean in 1975). Immediately on retirement, he relocated to Albuquerque, New Mexico, and has taught at the University of New Mexico, New Mexico Highlands University, the College of Santa Fe and Chapman College.

Much of Schwartzman's career focused on the work of the rabbi as educator and congregational administrator. He also expressed concern for the financial well-being of the individual rabbi and the Reform rabbinate in general. This career focus is evidenced in his many memberships and activities in the National Association of Temple Educators, Religious Education Association, American Association of University Professors, Joint Commission on Jewish Education

(1951–1981) and Central Conference of American Rabbis (financial secretary, chairman of Budget and Finance Committee, executive board member, 1981–1983).

In recognition of his accomplishments in education, Schwartzman was given Honorary Life Membership by the National Association of Temple Educators in 1950. He was awarded the Emanuel Gamoran Curriculum Award in 1963 by the same organization for *Our Religion and Our Neighbors*.

Schwartzman married Sylvia Cohen on September 22, 1940; they have two children: Judith Paley and Joel.

Writings (partial listing): coauthor, *Elements of Financial Analysis* (New York, 1989); coauthor, *Our Religion and Our Neighbors* (New York, 1959; rev., 1963; rev., 1971); *Reform Judaism in the Making* (New York, 1955); *Rocket to Mars* (Cincinnati, 1953; rev., 1969); *The Story of Reform Judaism* (New York, 1949; rev., 1958).

References: "Nearprint Biographies File," American Jewish Archives; *Who's Who in American Jewry* (Los Angeles, 1980), p. 440; *Who's Who in Religion* (Chicago, 1975), p. 508.

SCHWARZ, JACOB D. (1883–1962). Rabbi, administrator. Born in Cincinnati, Ohio, on December 6, 1883, Jacob Schwarz was the son of David and Dora Mendel Schwarz. After attending schools in Cincinnati, he studied at the University of Cincinnati (B.A., Phi Beta Kappa, 1906). Concurrently he attended Hebrew Union College, where he received rabbinic ordination in 1906. In 1952 he received an honorary D.D. from HUC-JIR. After ordination he went to Pensacola, Florida, to serve Temple Beth El. After six years, he left to join the UAHC as assistant director of Synagogue and School Extension, serving until 1919, when he was appointed assistant secretary of the UAHC. Schwarz left that position when he was named national director of Synagogue Activities in 1932, a position he held until his retirement in 1952.

As national director of Synagogue Activities, Schwarz counseled the UAHC's affiliated congregations in the areas of administration, architecture, attendance, worship and other related matters. He edited the monthly house publication, *Synagogue Service Bulletin*. In 1945 Schwarz organized and directed the first two conferences on synagogue architecture for the purpose of modernizing and raising the standard of synagogue design and facilities. These conferences set the pattern for the contemporary and functional type of synagogue architecture used for many years in North America.

Schwarz played a major role in the movement within Reform Judaism for wider use of ceremonies and ritual. He also conducted the first nationwide survey of the organizational structure and activities of American Reform congregations. On the basis of his survey, the UAHC planned the information service that it provided for many years to its affiliates in the United States and abroad.

Under the pseudonym Montgomery Prunejuice, a mythical trustee, Schwarz wrote a series of letters, published in 1957, entitled *The Life and Letters of Montgomery Prunejuice*, a satire of Reform Judaism.

Jacob Schwarz died on December 8, 1962.

Writings (partial listing): *Adventures in Synagogue Administration* (Cincinnati, 1936); *Ceremonies in Modern Jewish Life* (Cincinnati, 1937); *Financial Security for the Synagogue* (Cincinnati, 1935); *In the Land of Kings and Prophets* (Cincinnati, 1928); *Into the Promised Land* (Cincinnati, 1927); *New Trustees in a New Age* (Cincinnati, 1938).

References: "Nearprint Biography File," American Jewish Archives; *Who's Who in American Jewry* (New York, 1939), p. 954.

SEASONGOOD, MURRAY (1878–1983). Lawyer, civic leader. The son of Alfred and Emily Fechheimer Seasongood, Murray Seasongood was born in Cincinnati, Ohio, on October 27, 1878. He attended Harvard University, where he earned his A.B. in 1900, A.M. in 1901 and LL.B. in 1903. Seasongood was the recipient of honorary degrees from numerous institutions, including HUC-JIR. Admitted to the Ohio bar in 1903, he practiced law in Cincinnati, where he was a partner of the firm Paxton and Seasongood.

Seasongood was a leader of the 1924 political reform movement that destroyed the power of the Boss Cox political machine in Cincinnati. It led to the adoption of a city charter and the creation of the city-manager form of municipal government. He was one of six founders of the Charter Committee as well a drafter of Cincinnati's charter. Seasongood served as mayor of Cincinnati for two terms (1926–1930). During that time, he was chairman of the City Planning Commission (1926–1930).

Seasongood founded the Hamilton County Good Government League and served as its president (1934–1945). He was elected a County Charter Commissioner to draft a home-rule charter and was a member of the Republican Executive Committee.

At the state level, Seasongood served on the Ohio Commission for the Blind (chairman, 1915–1925), the Ohio Commission of Code Revision (1945–1949), the Advisory Committee of the Ohio Civil Service Council (chairman) and the Citizens' Library Committee of Ohio (vice chairman).

Seasongood was president of the National Municipal League and the National Association of Legal Aid Organizations. The U.S. Supreme Court appointed him to membership on the Advisory Board on Rules of Criminal Procedure (1941–1944). He was also a member of the U.S. Civil Service Commission's Loyalty Review Board (1947–1953), the Advisory Council of the Proportional Representation League, the National Civil Service League (vice president) and the President's Housing Conference (1932). Seasongood served the U.S. Atomic Energy Commission's Personnel Clearance Security Board as counsel (1954–1959) and was a trustee of the Julius Rosenwald Fund for the Well-being of Mankind (1930–1934).

As professor in the College of Law of the University of Cincinnati (1925–1959), Seasongood taught a course on municipal corporations. In 1932 he delivered the Godkin Lecture at Harvard Law School, where he later was a Visiting Professor of Law (June and July in both 1947 and 1948).

While Seasongood's major interests lay in the civic community, he also assumed leadership within the Jewish community. He was a member of the Board of Governors of Hebrew Union College (1913–1942) and served on the Council and Board of Directors of the American Jewish Joint Distribution Committee and on the Executive Committee of the American Jewish Committee. A classical Reform Jew, he was a member of the Board of Rockdale Temple in Cincinnati.

Seasongood spoke about Cincinnati and local government, law and educational subjects throughout the nation and was a lecturer for Phi Beta Kappa Associates. He contributed to numerous law reviews and other publications. Seasongood was also a member of the board of many civic and cultural institutions in Cincinnati.

Seasongood married Agnes Senior on November 28, 1912; they had one daughter. Murray Seasongood died in Cincinnati, Ohio, on February 21, 1983.

Writings: *Cases on Municipal Corporations* (Chicago, 1934); "Cincinnati and Home Rule," *Ohio State Law Journal*, 2958; description of contents in "The Murray Seasongood Papers," William A. Baughin (Cincinnati, December 7, 1965); "The Future of Local Self-Government, *American Scholar* 5, no. 2 (1936): 164–71; "How Political Gangs Work," *Harvard Graduates' Magazine*, March 1930; *Local Government in the United States: A Challenge and an Opportunity* (Cambridge, MA, 1933); "The Municipal Prospect," *Ohio Reporter*, November 15, 1937; Papers, 1848–1978, MSS 578, Cincinnati Historical Society; "Papers, Addresses, Reviews, and Other Writings of Murray Seasongood, Compiled and Presented to the Cincinnati Public Library, Cincinnati," 13 vols. (1955); "Political Service by Lawyers in Local Government," *Syracuse Law Review*, Spring 1951, pp. 210–27; "References to Murray Seasongood, Cincinnati, 1947–1960, preserved by the family and law office and presented to the Public Library of Cincinnati and Hamilton County"; *Selections from Speeches (1900–1959) of Murray Seasongood*, comp. Agnes Seasongood (New York, 1960); "The Triumph of Good Government in Cincinnati," in *Annuals of the American Academy of Political and Social Science* (Philadelphia, 1938).

References: *American Israelite*, February 24, 1983; William A. Baughin, "Murray Seasongood and Civil Service," *University of Cincinnati Law Review*, 44, no. 4 (1975): 663–64; idem, "Murray Seasongood: Twentieth-Century Urban Reformer" (Ph.D. dissertation, University of Cincinnati, 1972); idem, "Murray Seasongood—Urban Reformer and Champion of Merit Employment: A Tribute," *Good Government*, 902 (1973): 1–7; *Cincinnati Enquirer*, February 23, 1983; *Cincinnati Post*, February 22, 1983; Iola O. Hessler, *The Citizen and County Charter Movement in Hamilton County, Ohio, 1926–1935* (Cincinnati, 1958); "Nearprint Biography File and Box," American Jewish Archives; *New York Times*, February 23, 1983.

J.A.B.

SHARLIN, WILLIAM (1920–   ). Cantor, educator. Born on January 7, 1920, in New York City, William Sharlin is the son of Isaac and Ida Halaban Sharlin. At an early age he attended Yeshiva D'Harlem, transferring to Yeshiva D'Bronx after his family moved to the Bronx. Raised in a traditionally observant family, he continued his studies at the Talmudical Academy at Yeshiva University in New York City for two years after bar mitzvah. Later he attended the Bet Midrash

L'Morim (Teachers Seminary) at the same institution. In 1935 the Sharlin Family moved to Palestine (where his parents had been born), settling in Jerusalem. After his mother's death in 1936, Sharlin took refuge in his music, entering the Jerusalem Conservatory of Music while simultaneously studying at the Bet Midrash L'morim Mizrachi (Teachers Seminary), also in Jerusalem. In 1939 his father moved the family back to the United States, where Sharlin attended high school at night to finish the requirements for his diploma. After high school graduation, he reentered the Bet Midrash L'Morim at Yeshiva University. He remained only a year, leaving to enroll in the Manhattan School of Music, where he remained (except for army service, 1942–1945), receiving both his B.A. and M.A. (1949).

Entering the School of Sacred Music at HUC-JIR in 1949 as a special student, he later transferred into its cantorial program, graduating in 1951. After investiture, Sharlin went to HUC-JIR in Cincinnati as a Fellow and Music Director (1951–1954) to pursue further graduate studies. He also studied at the Cincinnati Conservatory of Music.

In 1954 Sharlin became part-time cantor at the newly formed Leo Baeck Temple in Los Angeles, California, where he remained until his retirement in 1988. While in Los Angeles, he also taught as adjunct professor at HUC-JIR and later was named chairman of the Department of Sacred Music, a position he continues to hold. There he established a local program for cantorial certification and a course of study for Temple organists.

In 1989 Sharlin served as a guest instructor at HUC-JIR, Jerusalem, and was the musical scholar-in-residence at the School of Sacred Music, HUC-JIR, New York. On numerous occasions Sharlin has been cantorial scholar-in-residence at congregations throughout the country. An active composer and arranger, he has produced numerous pieces, from short simple ditties to major choral and orchestral works. In 1988 the American Conference of Cantors paid tribute to him, and its West Coast chapter is sponsoring the publication of a collection of his work.

In 1958 Sharlin married Jacqueline Drucker; they have two daughters: Ilana and Lisa.

Writings: A full catalogue of Sharlin's writings and compositions is included in Janece Erman Cohen, ''The Life and Music of Cantor William Sharlin'' (Master's thesis, Hebrew Union College–Jewish Institute of Religion, New York, 1990).

SILVER, ABBA (ABRAHAM) HILLEL (1893–1963). Rabbi, Zionist leader. Born in Neustadt-Schirwindt, Lithuania, on January 28, 1893, Silver was the son of Rabbi Moses Silver and Dianna Seaman Silver. He immigrated to the United States in 1902. While a student at the Yeshiva Etz Chaim (later, the Rabbi Isaac Elhanan Theological Seminary) in New York City, he established, with his brother Maxwell (and Israel Chipkin) the first Zionist youth organization in the United States, called the Dr. Herzl Zion Club. (This eventually grew into Young Judea.) There he edited the *Hebrew Herald* and its Hebrew counterpart

Ha B'Surah. Silver attended Townsend Harris Hall (High School) and then the University of Cincinnati (B.A., 1915). He simultaneously attended Hebrew Union College, where he was ordained the same year. While a student at Hebrew Union College, he encountered opposition to his vocal Zionism. While at HUC, he founded the *Hebrew Union College Monthly*. And at the University of Cincinnati, he founded and edited the *Scribe*, a monthly literary magazine. Later, in 1925, he earned the D.D. from Hebrew Union College.

After ordination, he became rabbi of Congregation Leshem Shomayim in Wheeling, West Virginia. In 1917 he became rabbi of The Temple—Tifereth Israel in Cleveland, Ohio—where he remained until his death. On arriving in Cleveland, he immediately placed a *Sefer Torah* in the ark, where there had been none, and instituted Saturday morning services (Sunday morning services had been the norm of the congregation).

Silver's contributions were in the following four areas. First, he was devoted to prophetic Judaism, which was to permeate all of Jewish living. For Silver, the Hebrew prophets were men of action who spoke out against evil and corruption in the world, constantly trying to improve social conditions while speaking in the name of God. It was this role model that Silver tried to emulate. Second, he saw himself as a defender of the people of Israel, especially to a non-Jewish world. Third, he sought the maintenance of basic Jewish tradition. As a result he was often critical of what he saw as the weaknesses of Reform Judaism. Silver challenged its leadership to respond to the needs of *Klal Yisrael*. While critical of the Pittsburgh Platform, Silver was instrumental in shaping the spirit of the 1937 Columbus Platform. Last, he articulated a program of Zionism. However, he did not see Zionism as a total expression of Judaism. At the core of his commitment he saw the mission of Israel to be a moral and spiritual force in the world.

Silver spoke out against segregation, assailed class domination, supported the right of labor to organize and battled for its right to bargain collectively. In the 1930s, against the advice of leaders of the Cleveland Jewish community who thought him extreme, Silver organized a boycott of German goods by establishing (with Samuel Untermayer) the Non-sectarian Anti-Nazi League to Champion Human Rights. He resigned from the Cleveland Chamber of Commerce over its anti-union policies. He opposed "open shops" and fought against the proposed "right to work" constitutional amendment in Ohio in 1958. Earlier, as a member of a special state labor commission, he drafted Ohio's first unemployment insurance law.

With Stephen S. Wise, Silver formed the American Zionist Emergency Council, which brought the question of Israel's statehood before the U.S. Congress. In 1944 the council split over the leadership of Wise and Silver, who often clashed. Silver resigned but was later recalled to the chairmanship. It was Silver who announced to the United Nations that Israel had declared itself an independent state. It has been speculated that had Claim Weizmann not become the first president of Israel, Silver might have been selected for that position.

Active in over 30 organizations, Silver established the Cleveland Bureau of Jewish Education and served as its president (1924–1932). He was also president of the Cleveland Jewish Federation (1935–1941) and national chairman of the board of governors of the State of Israel Bonds. Silver was president of the Central Conference of American Rabbis (1945–1947), national chairman of the United Palestine Appeal, national cochairman of the United Jewish Appeal, chairman of the Hebrew Union College board of alumni overseers (1952) and president of its alumni association (1936–1937), member of the board of governors of Hebrew University, chairman of the American section of the Jewish Agency (1946–1949) and president and honorary chairman (1957–1958) of the Zionist Organization of America (1945–1946).

Silver was the recipient of many awards and honors, beginning in his college days. Silver offered the prayer at the inauguration of Dwight D. Eisenhower. He received an honorary L.D. from (Case) Western Reserve University, an honorary D.H.L. from Hebrew Union College (1941), Cardozo Memorial Award of Tau Epsilon Rho law fraternity (1941), national service award of Phi Epsilon Pi (1948), distinguished service award of the New England region of the Zionist Organization of America (1950), honorary D. H. from the University of Tampa (1951), medal of merit from the Jewish War Veterans (1951), the National Human Relations Award of the National Conference of Christians and Jews (1959) and Louis Brandeis Award of the American Zionist Council. A village in Israel is named to honor his memory, and in 1950 a poll conducted by the *National Jewish Post* named him the leading American Jew.

Silver married Virginia Horkheimer in 1923; they had two sons: Rabbi Daniel Jeremy and Raphael. Silver died on November 28, 1963, in Cleveland, Ohio.

Writings (partial listing): *The Democratic Impulse in Jewish History* (New York, 1928); *A History of Messianic Speculation in Israel* (New York, 1927); *Moses and the Original Torah* (New York, 1961); *Religion in a Changing World* (New York, 1930); *Vision and Victory* (New York, 1949); *Where Judaism Differed* (New York, 1956).

References (partial listing): *Encyclopaedia Judaica* (Jerusalem, 1972), 14:1543–44; *Herald Tribune*, November 29, 1963; *The Plain Dealer*, November 29, 1963, pp. 1, 10; Marc Lee Raphael, *Abba Hillel Silver: A Profile in American Judaism* (New York, 1989); Daniel Silver, *In the Time of Harvest* (New York, 1963); *Universal Jewish Encyclopedia* (New York, 1943), 9:536–37.

SILVER, DANIEL JEREMY (1928–1989). Rabbi. Daniel Silver was born on March 26, 1928, in Cleveland, Ohio, the son of Abba Hillel and Virginia Horkheimer Silver. After attending schools in Cleveland, he studied at Harvard University, graduating with honors (A.B., 1948). He was ordained in 1952 after attending HUC-JIR in Cincinnati. In 1977 he received an honorary D.D. from HUC-JIR. After his ordination, Silver served as a chaplain in the U.S. Navy during the Korean War (1952–1954). After naval service he studied at the University of Chicago (Ph.D., 1962) while also serving as rabbi of Chicago's Beth Torah Congregation. In 1956 Silver became associate rabbi at The Temple,

Tifereth Israel, in Cleveland. He was named senior rabbi in 1963, succeeding his father. He served as senior rabbi until his death, although his last two years were fraught with illness.

Over the years Silver commented in sermons and interviews on many public and political issues. He opposed teaching religion in public schools, advocated civil rights for blacks and other minorities and proposed in 1958 that the United States recognize China. In 1966 Silver was a member of a Jewish delegation that met with Arthur Goldberg, then U.S. ambassador to the United Nations, to advocate support of Israel. Silver also promoted reforms to help the poor and hungry in the Cleveland community.

Deeply interested in scholarship, Silver wrote several books and many journal articles. He was also adjunct professor of religion at Case Western Reserve University from 1968 to 1986. He taught at Cleveland State University from 1973 to 1986 and edited the *Central Conference of American Rabbis Journal* from 1964 to 1972.

In 1973 Silver was Dorfler Memorial Lecturer at Leo Baeck College in London and was a senior fellow at the Oxford Post Graduate Center for Hebrew Studies in England in 1979.

Silver has served as president of the National Foundation for Jewish Culture; chairman, Israel Task Force, Cleveland Jewish Federation; vice president, Cleveland Museum of Art; and member of the executive boards of the Jewish Community Federation, United Appeal (Cleveland), America-Israel Public Affairs Committee and the Synagogue Council of America. He was also a member of the boards of the Cleveland Red Cross, Family Service Association, Boy Scouts of America, UNICEF and the Cleveland Society of the Mentally Retarded.

In 1956 Silver married Adela Zeidman; they had three children: Sarah, Jonathan and Michael. Daniel Silver died in Cleveland on December 20, 1989.

Writings (partial listing): coauthor, *A History of Judaism* (New York, 1974); *Images of Moses* (New York, 1982); *In the Time of Harvest* (New York, 1963); *Judaism and Ethics* (New York, 1970); *Maimonidean Criticism and the Maimonidean Controversy, 1180–1240* (Leiden, 1965); *The Story of Scripture* (New York, 1990).

References: "Nearprint Biography File and Box," American Jewish Archives; *Who's Who in American Jewry* (Los Angeles, 1980), p. 461; *Who's Who in World Jewry* (New York, 1981), p. 731.

SILVERMAN, JOSEPH (1860–1930). Rabbi. Born in Cincinnati, Ohio, on August 25, 1860, Joseph Silverman was the son of Michael Silverman and Ulrika Piorkowsky Silverman. He attended the University of Cincinnati, receiving his A.B. in 1883, and studied at Hebrew Union College, where he was ordained (as valedictorian) in 1884. Later, he received a D.D. from HUC in 1887.

Between the years 1884 and 1888, Silverman was kind of circuit preacher in the South and West, which led to the establishment of synagogues in those areas. After ordination, he served Temple Emanu-El in Dallas, Texas (1884–1885); Temple B'nai Israel in Galveston, Texas (1885–1888); and Temple Emanu-El in New York City from 1888 to 1922, when he was named rabbi emeritus. In New York he served as assistant until 1897, when he was elected sole rabbi. While at Temple Emanu-El, Silverman was founder and president of Emanu-El Brotherhood and a trustee of its Sisterhood and introduced the *Union Prayer Book* for congregational use. He was also extended the title of honorary rabbi of Temple Emanu-El in Brooklyn, New York, in 1925.

An advocate of an American Synod, he favored a precise statement of the principles of Judaism and proposed a definition of Judaism and a uniform catechism for use in Reform religious schools.

Silverman served as a consulting editor of the *Jewish Encyclopedia* and was a member of the Committee for Religious Congress of the Chicago World's Fair in 1893. He served as president of the Central Conference of American Rabbis (1900–1903), which he took an active part in founding, and was honorary president of the New York Board of Jewish Ministers as well as founder and first president (later honorary president) of the Association of Reform Rabbis of New York City and Vicinity. Silverman was honorary vice president of the Palestine Foundation Fund and was a Four-minute Man during World War I. He was also a member of the executive committee, Masonic Palestine Fund; member, American Committee of Palestine Jewish Exploration Society; member, American Jewish Committee; member, B'nai B'rith; member, Zionist Organization of America; member, Palestine Research Society; member, Ohio Society; and member, New York Federation of Jewish Philanthropic Societies.

On returning from a visit to Palestine in 1923, under the auspices of the Palestine Foundation Fund, he penned a series of articles for the *New York Tribune*, as well as "Pen Pictures of Palestine." Following this trip, he lectured extensively throughout the country, encouraging the rehabilitation of Palestine. It was in his retirement that he became an active Zionist, but he cautioned against political Zionism during the CCAR convention in 1897 and in his CCAR presidential address in 1901. Silverman was also a secretary of the Emanu-El Seminary Association; member, Council World's Fair Religious Parliament; and member, National Council of Actors Church Alliance.

A frequent contributor to leading Anglo-Jewish periodicals such as *American Israelite*, *Jewish American* and *Menorah Journal*, he also contributed to *North American Review* and the *Standard Encyclopedia*. Silverman was also instrumental in the adoption of the *Union Hymnal* by the CCAR.

In 1886, Silverman married Henrietta Bloch. He died on July 26, 1930.

Writings: *Catechism on Judaism* (Galveston, 1885); *The Renaissance of Judaism* (New York, 1918).

References: *American Jewish Year Book* 5 (1904): 99–100; Central Conference of American Rabbis *Yearbook* 41 (1931): 230–38; *Jewish Encyclopedia* (New York, 1964), 11:744; *New York Times*, obituary, July 27, 1930; *Universal Jewish Encyclopedia* (New York, 1943), 9:538.

SIMON, ABRAM (1872–1938). Rabbi. Abram Simon was born in Nashville, Tennessee, on July 14, 1872, the son of David and Rachel Lederhandler Simon. In 1894 he received the degree of B.L. from the University of Cincinnati. He was ordained at Hebrew Union College that same year. In 1917 he received a Ph.D. from George Washington University. Simon wrote his dissertation on "The Constructive Character and Function of Religious Progress As Illustrated by the Religion of Israel." In 1925 he received an honorary D.H.L. from Hebrew Union College.

After his ordination, Simon served B'nai Israel in Sacramento, California (1894–1899); Temple Israel in Omaha, Nebraska (1899–1904); Washington Hebrew Congregation in Washington, D.C. (1904 until his death in 1938). In Washington he was among the first to hold separate worship services for college students.

As a volunteer during World War I, Simon served overseas with the Red Cross. While in Washington, he served as a member of the Board of Education for seven years, including service as its president (1920–1923). He was also a trustee of Columbia Hospital for Women (president, 1921–1927), the Public Library (president, 1929–1933) and the Jewish Chautauqua Society. He was a president of the CCAR (1923–1925), where he had served previously as treasurer and vice president and as chairman of the committee on the Harmonization of Jewish and Civil Laws of Marriage and Divorce. He was chairman of the Synagogue Council of America (1928), which he had helped to found. Simon was also an organizer of the Washington Chapter of the National Conference of Christians and Jews. As such, he was instrumental in bringing together an interfaith assembly of clergy for the study of religious life in the nation's capital. In 1929 he was appointed as a non-Zionist member of the Jewish Agency.

Simon was a member of the faculty of the short-lived Correspondence School of the Jewish Chautauqua Society for the Training of Teachers. He was one of the founding members of the Reform movement's Committee on Jewish Education. Simon was not a radical Reformer. Instead, he chose a more receptive approach to tradition and appreciated the points of view of other interpretations.

In 1949 the Washington (D.C.) Board of Education named an elementary school in his memory.

In 1896 Simon married Carrie Obendorfer; they had two children: Leo and David. Abram Simon died in Washington on December 24, 1938.

Writings: *A Child's Ritual* (Washington, DC, 1909); coauthor, *History of Jewish Education* (Washington, DC, 1916); *The Principle of Jewish Education in the Past* (Washington, DC, 1909).

References: "Abram and Carrie Simon Manuscript Collection," American Jewish Archives; *American Hebrew*, January 25, 1929, p. 407; Central Conference of American Rabbis *Yearbook* 49 (1939): 303–8; *Universal Jewish Encyclopedia* (New York, 1943), 9:545; *Who's Who in American Jewry* (New York, 1926), p. 573.

SIMON, CARRIE OBENDORFER (1872–1961). Communal leader. The daughter of Leo William and Mary Wise Obendorfer, Carrie Simon was born in Uniontown, Alabama, on March 5, 1872. Raised in Cincinnati, her first involvement in Jewish communal life was as secretary of a local chapter of the

National Council of Jewish Women founded by her mother in 1895. On August 5, 1896, she married Rabbi Abram Simon. After moving briefly to Sacramento, California, and Omaha, Nebraska, they moved to Washington, D.C., in 1904, where Abram Simon held a pulpit until his death in 1938.

Throughout her marriage, Carrie Simon retained a keen interest in Jewish communal affairs. She was particularly interested in working with other women to help revitalize the religious life of American Jewry. Convinced that such efforts needed to be coordinated on a national level, she founded the National Federation of Temple Sisterhoods in 1913. Established with the support of the Union of American Hebrew Congregations in Cincinnati, the federation brought together local women's auxiliaries and sisterhoods to aid in "the preservation of Jewish life and the development and expression of that life in varied forms of activity." Its earliest committees, conceived and organized by Simon as president, included a National Committee on Religion, which organized religious schools, devised new methods to increase synagogue attendance and issued annual Jewish art calendars; a museum committee, to collect Jewish ceremonial objects and hold art exhibitions (whose efforts led to the establishment of the Hebrew Union College Art Museum); and a Committee on Hebrew Union College Scholarships, which established scholarships for young men interested in entering HUC's rabbinical program and raised funds for lay religious educational work by the UAHC. A later committee, of which Simon became chair and to which she contributed significantly, was a committee established to raise funds to erect a student dormitory at HUC, subsequently erected in 1925.

Starting with an initial membership of 49 local sisterhoods, the federation quickly grew in size and by 1915 boasted 101 chapters and represented 15,000 women. Though Simon's tenure as president ended in 1919, she remained active in the federation as honorary president. She also became chair of the Conference Committee of National Jewish Women's Organizations, speaking in numerous pulpits throughout the United States on behalf of Jewish women.

Carrie and Abram Simon had two children: Leo and David. Carrie Simon died in Washington, D.C., on March 3, 1961.

Writings: Carrie Simon's presidential speeches at the NFTS biennial conventions are included in published *Proceedings*.

References: "Abram and Carrie Simon Manuscript Collection," American Jewish Archives; *American Jewish Year Book* 63 (Philadelphia, 1962): 562; *Universal Jewish Encyclopedia* (New York, 1943), 9:545; *Who's Who in American Jewry* (New York, 1926), p. 573.

                                                                                     E.M.U.

SKIRBALL, JACK (1896–1985). Rabbi, movie producer, real estate developer, philanthropist. Born in Homestead, Pennsylvania, on June 23, 1896, the son of Abraham and Sarah (Sally Davis) Skirball, Jack Skirball followed diverse pursuits throughout his life.

His academic education was fairly conventional: a B.A. from Case Western

Reserve University, a rabbinic degree from Hebrew Union College and post-graduate work in philosophy and sociology at the University of Chicago. After ordination at HUC in 1921, Skirball served as assistant rabbi in Cleveland, Ohio (1924–1926), and spent seven years as rabbi in Evansville, Indiana (1926–1933). From the beginning, Skirball distinguished himself in activities beyond the pulpit, including his work as a founder of the Big Brothers Association in Cleveland, president of the Southern Indiana Red Cross Society and chairman of the Anti-Tuberculosis Society in Indiana.

In 1933 Skirball's career underwent an unusual change when he took a leave of absence from the Evansville congregation, a leave that would last the rest of his life. He became manager of the Educational Films Corporation, briefly in New York and then in Los Angeles, pioneering in the field of audiovisual material for schools. During this time he produced *Birth of a Baby*, the motion picture of which he would always be proudest. This was the first time the actual birth of a child was brought to theater screens. It proved to be a controversial landmark in cinema, earning nine pages of coverage in *Life* magazine and the opposition of the Catholic church, which stopped the film's sale in several cities.

He went on to become president of Skirball Productions, responsible for such films as *The Howards of Virginia*, with Cary Grant (1940); *Saboteur* (1942) and *Shadow of a Doubt* (1943), both directed by Alfred Hitchcock; and *Payment on Demand*, starring Bette Davis (1951).

Beginning in the 1950s, Skirball turned his considerable energies to real estate development, establishing a number of bowling alleys as president-director of Bowlero Corporation. He also created innovative Vacation Village in San Diego, which would be a model for resort hotels across America.

Skirball's involvement with public-service projects, increasing in later life, included Hope for Hearing, at the University of California at Los Angeles, and the American Jewish Committee. Although Skirball never returned to the pulpit rabbinate, he remained active in the Reform movement, assisted in the establishment of new congregations, served as regional president for the Union of American Hebrew Congregations and financially supported HUC-JIR. He spearheaded the development of HUC-JIR's Los Angeles campus and established the Skirball Museum at HUC-JIR, Los Angeles, the Skirball Gallery at the Cincinnati school and the Skirball Museum and Archeological Building on the Jerusalem campus. During the last year of his life, he founded the Skirball Institute on American Values of the American Jewish Committee for Interreligious and Interethnic Research into Core American Values.

Skirball married Audrey A. Marx Tobias on April 7, 1949; they had two daughters: Sally and Agnes. Jack Skirball died in Los Angeles on December 8, 1985.

References: *Los Angeles Times*, November 10, 1985, and December 10, 1985; "Near-print Biographies Box," American Jewish Archives; *San Diego Tribune*, August 29, 1985.

                                                                             A.C.W.

SLONIMSKY, HENRY (1884–1970). Scholar, teacher. Born in Minsk, Russia, on October 9, 1884, Henry Slonimsky was the son of Moses and Sarah Epstein Slonimsky. He emigrated to the United States in 1890 and attended Philadelphia schools, Haverford College (1902) and the University of Pennsylvania (1902–1904). He did graduate work at the University of Berlin (1905–1907) and the University of Marburg (Germany), where he studied with Hermann Cohen and received his Ph.D. in 1912.

On returning to America, Slonimsky served as an instructor at Columbia University (1914–1915), then assistant professor of philosophy at Johns Hopkins University (1915–1921). In 1921 he joined the faculty of Hebrew Union College in Cincinnati as Professor of Ethics and the Philosophy of Religion, until he was invited to join the faculty of the Jewish Institute of Religion as Professor of Midrash and Philosophy in 1924 (JIR merged with HUC in 1950). Slonimsky was named dean of JIR in 1935 and retired in 1952 but taught occasional courses until his death. He was instrumental in shaping the academic structure of JIR throughout his tenure, particularly as dean, defining JIR as "a free school, free from dogmas, free from orthodoxy, free from reform, where teachers are free to teach what they think best and where students are not bound by any obligation to conform."

Slonimsky was a master of language, but it was in philosophy that he made his greatest contribution. His *Mythos of the Growing God* blended humanist ideas with the God concept. Slonimsky saw man as the creation of God through whom God's spirit flows in such a fashion that man and God build and grow together. In light of the suffering and injustice that prevail on earth, Slonimsky tempered his view of an absolute God. Yet he rejected the humanist view that the human species is absolute. Without the other, each is impotent.

In 1927 Slonimsky married Minnie Tennenbaum. He died on March 12, 1970, in New York City.

Writings: *Essays* (Cincinnati, 1967); *Heraklit und Parmenides* (Giessen, 1912); *Judaism and the Religion of the Future* (New York, 1955).

References: Richard Aldington, *Life for Life's Sake*; "Nearprint Biography Box and File," American Jewish Archives; *Who's Who in American Jewry* (New York, 1939), pp. 1006–7.

SOLOMON, HANNAH GREENEBAUM (1858–1942). Communal worker. Born on January 14, 1858, in Chicago, Illinois, Hannah Solomon was the daughter of Michael and Sarah Spiegel Greenebaum. While Solomon became an accomplished musician and linguist, she devoted her life to nurturing the interests of all Jewish women. She was the first woman in America to shape Jewish women into a movement, working toward a new level of consciousness and activity. She and her sister were the first Jewish women invited to join the Chicago women's club; Solomon was a member of its board during the Chicago World's Fair. In 1890 Solomon was appointed a member of the Women's Committee for the World's Parliament of Religions, held during the World's Fair.

In 1893 she prepared the first paper on religion ever presented before the Chicago Women's Club: "A Review of Spinoza's Theologico-Politicism."

In 1891 Solomon organized the Jewish Women's Congress in Chicago, with the approval of the Parliament Women's Committee. This organization, which stressed religious, educational and philanthropic activities, subsequently evolved into the National Council of Jewish Women—the first organized women's group that constituted a cross-section of Jewish women. Solomon served as the organization's president from 1893 to 1908, when she was named honorary president.

Active in other women's activities as well, Solomon organized the first conference of Chicago Women's Organizations in 1884. In 1895 she founded the Illinois Federation of Women's Clubs, which she served as vice president. She founded in 1897 the Bureau of Personal Service for aiding immigrants, an organization that she led as president from 1897 to 1910, when it was incorporated into the Associated Jewish Charities. Under her direction, the bureau made a survey of the Jewish population of Chicago, one of the first surveys of this nature undertaken in the United States. She then participated in the founding of the Juvenile Court, served on the board of the Civic Federation and worked toward the establishment of the Associated Charities of Chicago. Representing the National Council of Jewish Women, Solomon was treasurer of the Council of Women of the United States in 1899. With Susan B. Anthony in 1904, she was sent by the council as a delegate to the convention of the International Council of Women in Berlin. There she was made chairman of the nominating committee.

In 1907 Solomon was elected president of the Illinois Industrial School for Girls, where the rehabilitation of the school stands as testimony to her achievements on behalf of ill and neglected children. The school evolved into the Park Ridge School for Girls, whose entrance building is called the Solomon Cottage in her honor.

During World War I, Solomon was chairman of city wards of the Women's Division of the State Council of Defense, where she organized the city wards for service. Wherever she worked, she was interested in the welfare of children and was, therefore, involved with the censorship of movies. Later, Chicago Sinai honored her by establishing the Hannah Solomon Peace Fund used to award the author of an essay on peace from among its religious school students. An ardent defender of Reform Judaism, Solomon encountered some opposition from traditional elements within the Council of Jewish Women. In one instance, when she was attacked for not being a traditional Sabbath observer, she replied, "I consecrate every day."

In 1910 Solomon established the Chicago Women's City Club, which she served as vice president. She led Chicago's women in a movement against city government, forcing it to find a better method of handling garbage and cleaning up water supplies. She was also active in the Chicago Round Table of Christians and Jews.

In 1938 Sigma Delta Tau awarded her its first award to a Jewish woman. Alpha Epsilon Phi sorority made her an honorary member in 1931.

In 1879 she married Henry Solomon; they had three children: Frank, Helen Levy and Herbert. Hannah Solomon died in Chicago on December 7, 1942.

Writings: *Fabric of My Life* (New York, 1940); *A Sheaf of Leaves* (Chicago, 1911), which contains a collection of articles, mostly on women, women's organizations and Judaism, including "The Religious Mission of Women," "Our Debt to Judaism," and "The Practical Results of Women's Clubs."

References: Philip Breystone, *Chicago and Its Jews* (Chicago, 1933), pp. 42–43; 66–67; *The First Fifty Years: A History of the National Council of Jewish Women, 1893–1943* (N.p., 1943), pp. 9–12, 21–22.

SONNESCHEIN, ROSA FASSEL (1847–1932). Publisher, editor, Zionist, feminist. Rosa Sonneschein was born in Hungary on March 12, 1847, the youngest of nine children. Her father, Dr. Hirsch Baer Fassel, was a prominent rabbi known for his scientific publications. On October 30, 1864, at her father's insistence, she married Rabbi Solomon Hirsch Sonneschein. In 1868 they went to New York and in 1869 moved to St. Louis, Missouri, where Solomon became rabbi of the Reform congregation Shaare Emeth.

Rosa Sonneschein soon gained recognition as a leading figure in St. Louis literary circles and as an active charity worker. Headstrong and independent, she endured what by all accounts was a disastrous marriage until 1891 when, with three of her four children grown, she left her husband. To support herself, she began a literary career. Serving as St. Louis correspondent to newspapers in New York and Chicago, she also wrote stories for the local St. Louis press. In 1895 she founded and became publisher and editor of the *American Jewess*, the first independent American Jewish journal published by a woman for other women.

Through the *American Jewess*, Sonneschein sought to report on world events of interest to Jews, especially Jewish women. At the same time she hoped to delineate areas of mutual concern to all American women interested in national, social and religious issues. Favorably reviewed by the Jewish and secular press, *American Jewess* enjoyed a brief but popular run, boasting a circulation of 29,000 subscribers. Most of its articles were written by women and included reports on women's organizations, biographical sketches of American women, short stories and reviews of contemporary music and art. Sonneschein herself was a regular contributor, critically reporting on the activities of the CCAR, the Union of American Hebrew Congregations and the National Council of Jewish Women, which she hoped would become "the representative body of Jewish womanhood in America."

As a feminist and a liberal Jew, Sonneschein frequently wrote articles defending women's struggle for equality in Jewish religious life. A fervent Zionist, she attended the first Zionist Congress in Basel in 1897 and, though critical of the congress for its disenfranchisement of women, devoted much space in subsequent issues of her journal to the writings and thought of major Zionist leaders. This exposure brought them to the attention of Americans for the first time.

Financial difficulties forced the *American Jewess* to cease publication in 1899.

Though Sonneschein's literary career came to an end, she retained a lively interest in world affairs.

Sonneschein had four children: Ben, Fanny, Leontine and Monroe. Little more is heard about Rosa Sonneschein until her death in St. Louis on March 5, 1932.

Writings: The best source of her written work remains the *American Jewess* (1895–1899); see too *The Pioneers: An Historical Essay* (St. Louis, 1880).

References: Jack Nusan Porter, *American Jewish Archives*, November 1980, pp. 124–31, and *American Jewish History* 68 (September 1978): 57–63.

E.M.U.

SPIRO, JACK DANIEL (1933–   ). Rabbi, educator. The son of Rebecca and Jack Spiro, Spiro was born on March 4, 1933, in New Orleans. He lived in Louisiana through his graduation from Tulane University in 1953. Spiro then enrolled at Hebrew Union College in Cincinnati, from which he received a B.H.L. (1955), an M.A.H.L. (1958), his ordination (1958) and a D.H.L. (1962).

From 1958 until 1961, Spiro served as a chaplain in the U.S. Air Force, responsible for Jewish personnel in Great Britain and Scandinavia. After his return to the United States in 1961, he was appointed rabbi of Temple Anshe Emeth in New Brunswick, New Jersey, a post he held for six years. In 1967 he was appointed National Director of Education of the Union of American Hebrew Congregations. He held this post until 1973, during which period he also served as visiting professor of education at HUC-JIR, New York. In 1973 Spiro left the UAHC to assume the pulpit of Congregation Beth Ahabah in Richmond, Virginia.

Although he is still at Congregation Beth Ahabah, since 1979 Spiro has also devoted himself to another career: Director of Judaic Studies at Virginia Commonwealth University. Spiro has been a prolific author and editor, producing over 50 articles and more than 40 edited books. He has hosted and produced a weekly radio program, "Jewish Dimensions," for eight years. He has contributed to several magazines as an editor (*Compass*, which he founded, *Pedagogic Reporter*, *Reform Judaism*, *Menorah Review* and *Religious Education*) and produced numerous teaching guides, filmstrips and educational aids.

Spiro has been very active as a religious and civic leader in Richmond. Among the posts he has held are president of Virginia League for Planned Parenthood and the Association of Virginia Planned Parenthood Affiliates; member of Red Cross Executive Committee and chair of International Committee; president and member of Executive Committee of Richmond Area Clergy Association; and member of the executive committee of United Way of America. For his work as an educator and community leader, Spiro has been recognized by various organizations. He is a recipient of a Citation for Outstanding Service by the National Association of Temple Education, a Citation from the Union of Liberal and Progressive Synagogues of Great Britain for outstanding service and the Brotherhood Award of the Richmond chapter of the National Conference of Christians and Jews.

In 1956 Spiro married Marilyn Loevy; they have three children: Hillary Hawkins, David and Ellen.

Writings (partial listing): "Biblical Criticism and Archaeology," in *Currents and Trends in Contemporary Jewish Thought*, ed. Benjamin Efron (New York, 1965); with John S. Spring, *Dialogue: In Search of Jewish/Christian Understanding* (New York, 1975); with Sylvan D. Schwartzman, *The Living Bible* (New York, 1963); "Rabbi in the South: A Personal View," in *Turn to the South: Essays on Southern Jewry* (Charlottesville, VA, 1979); *A Time to Mourn* (New York, 1967).

References: "Nearprint Biography File," American Jewish Archives.

STEINBERG, BEN (1930–   ). Musician, composer. Ben Steinberg was born in Winnipeg, Manitoba, Canada, on January 22, 1930. His father, Alexander Steinberg, a cantor, had emigrated to Canada from Zhitomir, Russia, in 1912 and his mother from Odessa in 1927. Steinberg was raised in Toronto, where he attended school and studied with the faculties of music at the University of Toronto (graduating in 1961). He also attended Toronto's Royal Conservatory of Music.

For many years Steinberg taught music in Toronto's public schools. He has been involved with synagogue music nearly his entire life, singing as a child soloist at age eight and conducting his first synagogue choir at 12. Steinberg was head of the music department of the Forest Hill Collegiate (1963–1986) and served as director of music at Holy Blossom Temple (1960–1969). Since 1970 he has been director of music at Temple Sinai in Toronto.

Active in various musical organizations, Steinberg has been chairman of the Music Committee, Canadian Jewish Congress (Central Region) since 1967; president of the Jewish Music Society of Toronto; member of the executive board of the National Music Council of the JWB; and a member of the Canadian League of Composers. He is also an associate composer of the Canadian Music Centre.

Steinberg's career has revolved around his teaching of the history of Jewish music as well as the composition of Jewish music, especially for the synagogue. His commissioned works include three Sabbath services, five cantatas for chorus and orchestra, numerous choral settings, instrumental chamber works and solo songs. His book on synagogue youth choirs won numerous awards. Steinberg has received the Gabriel Award in 1979 for his cantata "Echoes of Children," commemorating the children who perished in the Holocaust. He was honored by the CBC in 1979, which devoted an entire broadcast to his music. The Cantors' Assembly awarded Steinberg its Kavod Award in 1983, and the American Harp Society presented him with a composer's award in 1983. In 1978 and 1980 he served as artist-in-residence for the city of Jerusalem.

In 1951 Steinberg married Mildred Tameanko; they have two children: David and Ruth.

Writings: "Ashrei" (Toronto, 1986); "Ata Echad" (New York, 1984); "L'cha Anu Shira" (New York, 1969); "Pirchay Shir Kodesh" (New York, 1963); *Together Do They Sing* (New York, 1961).

References: "Ben Steinberg Manuscript Collection," American Jewish Archives."

S.H.A.

STEINBERG, PAUL (1926–). Rabbi, psychologist, academician. Born in New York City on January 29, 1926, Paul Steinberg is the son of Abraham and Lena Schimelman Steinberg. After attending lower schools in New York City, Steinberg attended the College of the City of New York, where he received a B.S. with honors in 1946, was a fellow in its Department of Education (1946–1948) and received an M.S. degree in 1948. Steinberg also attended the Jewish Institute of Religion, where he received an M.H.L. and rabbinic ordination (1949). Later he attended Teachers College, Columbia University, receiving an Ed.D. in 1961. In 1985 he was awarded an honorary D.H.L. from Baltimore Hebrew University.

Receiving a Guggenheim Fellowship for research and travel in Israel after ordination, Steinberg served as lecturer in the Department of Education and in the School of Social Welfare, Hebrew University (1949–1950). After returning to the United States, he was appointed director of the Hillel Foundation at the University of California at Berkeley (1950–1952). In 1952 he was named rabbi of Temple Israel in Croton-on-Hudson, New York, where he remained until 1958. During most of this time Steinberg was also chaplain at Franklin Delano Roosevelt VA Hospital in Montrose, New York (1952–1957), and taught at New York University's School of Education (1956). Before leaving Temple Israel, Steinberg began an association with HUC-JIR which he has maintained throughout his career: instructor in human relations and education (1955–1957); assistant professor (1957–1959); associate professor (1959–1961); professor of human relations and dean (1961–1985); Eleanor Sinsheimer Distinguished Service Professor of Jewish Education (1970); and vice president and dean of faculty (since 1985). From 1963 until 1970, Steinberg was executive dean of the Hebrew Union College Biblical and Archaeological School, Jerusalem, and continues to serve as the director of the American Office of the HUC-JIR Jerusalem School and director of the Summer Programs in Israel, conducting an extensive program in archaeological excavations. In 1967 he was named a New York State Department of Education Research Fellow in Israel.

Steinberg served as consultant to industry and management (Richardson, Bellows, and Henry, 1958 to 1960) and as expert examiner for municipal and state civil service commissions. He has lectured at executive-development programs conducted by the U.S. Department of Defense and the American Management Associations. He has been a professional associate with B.F.S. Psychological Associates of New York since 1961.

Steinberg is a certified psychologist in the State of New York and a Fellow of the American Association for the Advancement of Science. Among the professional organizations with which he is affiliated are the CCAR, the American Psychological Association, the American Personnel and Guidance Association, the American Association of University Professors and Phi Delta Kappa, the national professional honor society in education. Steinberg has been a member of the Board of Directors of the Council of Higher Educational Institutions of the City of New York (1957–1973), the Religious Education Association and

Interfaith Council for Family Financial Planning. He is a member of the Board of the Albright Institute of Archaeology of the American Schools of Oriental Research in Jerusalem. He is also a member of the Board of Trustees of the Jewish Braille Institute.

In 1947 he married Trude Strudler; they have two children: Alana Wittenberg and Alan.

References: "Nearprint Biography File," American Jewish Archives; *Who's Who in American Jewry* (Los Angeles, 1980), p. 482; *Who's Who in World Jewry* (New York, 1981), p. 757.

STERN, CHAIM (1930–   ). Rabbi. A direct descendant of Rashi, Stern was born in Brooklyn, New York, on August 8, 1930, the son of Pinkas and Leah Frankel-Teomim. After graduation from Boys' High School (Brooklyn) in 1948, he attended CCNY, where he received a B.A. in 1952. Stern attended Harvard Law School the following year but resigned to enter Hebrew Union College–Jewish Institute of Religion, where he was ordained in 1958, having received an M.H.L. with honors. Later, in 1983, he was awarded an (hon.) D.D. from HUC-JIR.

After ordination, he assumed the pulpit of Temple Sholom in River Edge, New Jersey, as its first full-time rabbi; formerly he had held that position as a student rabbi. While in River Edge, he was an instructor at the HUC-JIR School of Sacred Music. He left that position in 1962 to become associate minister (then acting senior rabbi) of the Liberal Jewish synagogue in London, England, a position he held for three years, when he left to serve Congregation Emanu-El B'ne Jeshurun in Milwaukee, Wisconsin. He left Milwaukee in 1967 to assume the pulpit at Westminster synagogue. In 1968, he left England to serve Temple Beth El of Northern Westchester in Chappaqua, New York, a position he still holds. While in London, Stern was an instructor in liturgy at the Leo Baeck College.

In 1971, Stern was appointed by the Central Conference of American Rabbis to edit the new liturgy of the Reform movement. As such, he is responsible for the "Gates" series of prayer books. He also served as coeditor for the new prayer books of the liberal movement in Great Britain.

Stern served as president of the Northern Westchester and Putnam Valley (New York) Rabbinic Council and the Chappaqua Interfaith Council and was a member of the regional board of the Anti-Defamation League of B'nai B'rith.

In 1951, he married Susan Bank. They had three children: David, Philip and Michael. In 1986, he married Carol Morgan.

Writings (partial listing): ed., *Gates of Forgiveness* (New York, 1980); ed., *Gates of Freedom* (Bedford, NY, 1982); ed., *Gates of Heaven* (New York, 1979); ed., *Gates of Prayer* (New York, 1975); ed., *Gates of Repentance* (New York, 1968); ed., *Gates of the House* (New York, 1977).

References: "Biography File," American Jewish Archives; *Who's Who in World Jewry* (New York, 1987), p. 540.

STERN, HARRY J. (1897–1984). Rabbi. Born in Lithuania on April 24, 1897, Harry Stern was the son of Morris and Hinda Markson Stern. After immigrating to the United States at age six, Stern was educated in Steubenville, Ohio, public schools. He received his B.A. from the University of Cincinnati in 1920 and his B.H.L. in 1919 from Hebrew Union College, where he was ordained a rabbi in 1922. He also did graduate work at the University of Chicago. In 1938 he received an honorary L.L.D. from McGill University, in 1947 an honorary D.D. from Hebrew Union College, and in 1970 an honorary D.L. from the College of Steubenville.

After his ordination, Stern served Temple Israel in Uniontown, Pennsylvania (1922–1927). He then went to Temple Emanu-El in Montreal, serving from 1927 until his retirement in 1972.

Stern was active in Montreal in the furtherance of goodwill and amity between various religious, racial and national groups. He was a pioneer in interfaith dialogue in Canada, using Temple Emanu-El as a forum for major figures in religion, politics and the city. Stern was often a controversial figure, particularly because of his liberal attitude toward mixed marriage.

Within Temple Emanu-El, Stern founded the Institute on Judaism for Christian Clergy and Education, the annual Fellowship Dinners for Catholics, Protestants and Jews, the College of Jewish Studies, the Book Lover's Forum and the Aron Museum.

Stern was a member of Kiwanis; Masons; B'nai B'rith; Pi Lambda Pi; American Academy of Political and Social Science; honorary life member, Central Conference of American Rabbis; Biblical Society of Canada; Dominion Executive Canadian Jewish lifelong member, Zionist Revisionist Organization; vice president, Royal Empire Society; the Canadian Club; first chairperson of the Canadian Conference of Reform Rabbis; president and cofounder, Board of Jewish Ministers of Greater Montreal; and cofounder of the Synagogue Council of Greater Montreal.

Stern received the B'nai B'rith Humanitarian Award, the Legion of Honor of Kiwanas International, and life membership in the Jewish Chautauqua Society of America. In 1937 he was decorated with the Coronation Medal by King George VI. At the First World Jewish Congress held in Geneva in 1936, he was elected secretary. In 1978 Stern was honored as the Great Montrealer in Religion, and in 1980, former Israeli Prime Minister Menachem Begin presented Stern with the Jabotinsky Centennial Award.

The author of several publications, Stern was contributing editor of the *Canadian Jewish Chronicle*. He was also heard on radio broadcasts for many years.

In 1937 Stern married Sylvia Goldstein (d. 1979); they had two children: Justine Bloomfield and Stephanie Glaymon. Harry Stern died on September 2, 1984, in Atlantic City.

Writings: *Jews and Christians* (New York, 1927); *Judaism and the War of Ideas* (New York, 1937); *Martyrdom and Miracle* (New York, 1951); *One World or No World* (New York, 1973); *Pilgrimage to Israel* (Montreal, 1951); *The Spirit Triumphant* (New York, 1943).

References: Kenneth Cleator and Harry J. Stern, *A Rabbi's Journey* (New York, 1981); "Nearprint Biography File," American Jewish Archives; *Who's Who in American Jewry* (Los Angeles, 1980), p. 454.

STERN, MALCOLM HENRY (1915–   ). Rabbi, historian, genealogist. The son of Henrietta Berkowitz Stern and Arthur Kaufman Stern, Malcolm Stern was born on January 29, 1915, in Philadelphia, Pennsylvania. He attended lower schools in Philadelphia and the Ecole La Villa in Lausanne, Switzerland (1925–1926). Graduating from the University of Pennsylvania in 1935 with a B.A. in Semitics, winning the Hilda Nietzsche Prize, he entered Hebrew Union College, where he was ordained a rabbi with an M.A.H.L. (1941) and received a D.H.L. in American Jewish History (1957) and an honorary D.D. (1966).

After ordination, Stern served as assistant rabbi at Reform Congregation Keneseth Israel in Philadelphia (1941–1943, 1946–1947). From 1943 to 1946, Stern served as a chaplain in the U.S. Army Corps, narrowly escaping death in a plane crash at Casablanca en route to India. In 1947 he became rabbi of Congregation Ohef Sholom in Norfolk, Virginia, where he remained until 1964, when he became the first director of the Rabbinical Placement Commission of Reform Judaism, a position he held until his retirement in 1980. Since then, Stern has worked as a fieldwork supervisor and lecturer on Jewish history at HUC-JIR, New York.

Stern's interest in Jewish genealogy and Jewish music led him beyond a well-established, pastoral-centered, congregational rabbinate. He helped to create a professional placement system for Reform rabbis and congregations. As the staff genealogist (since 1950) of the American Jewish Archives, he created a genealogical resource base for further study and research. Stern served as the president of the Jewish Genealogical Society and is the only Jewish Fellow of American Society of Genealogists (since 1966, as well as its past president). Stern has also been president of the Jewish Historical Society of New York and an officer of the American Jewish Historical Society, along with other historical and genealogical societies. Stern has written widely in the field of genealogy. His first volume, *Americans of Jewish Descent*, was the most important volume of its kind. It was used as a source for Stephen Birmingham's *The Grandees*. For many years Stern contributed the weekly column "Some of My Best Jews" in *Jewish Week*.

Stern has been honored widely. He was named B'nai B'rith Man of the Year in Norfolk (1964), was named one of New York's "Living Treasures" by an organization promoting the Statue of Liberty Anniversary known as View from the Bridge '86 and was presented the George Williams Award for distinguished service in genealogy by the Federation of Genealogical Societies and the Lee Max Friedman Award by the American Jewish Historical Society (1979).

In 1941 Stern married Louise Bergman.

Writings (partial listing): coauthor, *American Airlines Guide to Jewish History in the Caribbean* (New York, n.d.); *Americans of Jewish Descent* (Cincinnati, 1960; rev.

as *First Families*, 1978); coauthor, *Life Begins at 40* (New York, 1980); ed., *Shaarei Shirah* (New York, 1987).

References: *Encyclopaedia Judaica* (Jerusalem, 1971), 15:389–90; "Nearprint Biography File and Box," American Jewish Archives; "Uncles, Goats, and Family Trees," *Reform Judaism* 11 (Fall 1982): 18; *Who's Who in American Jewry* (Los Angeles, 1980), pp. 484–85; *Who's Who in World Jewry* (New York, 1981), p 761.

STOLZ, JOSEPH (1861–1941). Rabbi. Born in Syracuse, New York, on November 3, 1861, Joseph Stolz was the son of David and Regina Strauss Stolz. He attended public schools in Syracuse. He received his B.L. in 1883 from the University of Cincinnati and was ordained from Hebrew Union College the following year, where he had been studying concurrently as a member of its second class. In 1890 he received a D.D. from HUC and was awarded the honorary D.H.L. in 1931. After ordination, Stolz served B'nai Israel Temple in Little Rock, Arkansas (1884–1887), and Zion Temple in Chicago, Illinois, where he assisted Bernard Felsenthal (1887–1895). In 1895, as Jews were moving to the South Side of Chicago, Stolz was elected to the pulpit of Isaiah Temple in Chicago (which later merged to form Isaiah-Israel) and served until his retirement in 1929. He then was named rabbi emeritus.

Concerned that Reform Judaism was closing its doors to the working middle class and seeking to encourage its affiliation, Stolz introduced a Sunday service as early as 1887. He passionately believed that the synagogue, as the cornerstone in the Jewish community, should be a democratic institution.

Active in community and civic concerns, Stolz was a member of the Chicago Board of Education (1899–1905) and the Chicago Criminal Commission beginning in 1910. He was secretary of the Jewish Training School and Home for Aged Jews. He was a member of the Union of American Hebrew Congregations executive committee and of the Central Conference of American Rabbis (president, 1905–1907), where he was responsible for changes in liturgy and ceremonial observances. Stolz was also active in the Chicago Rabbinical Association (president, 1920–1925) and the Chicago Federation of Synagogues.

In 1890 Stolz married Blanche Rauh; they had three children: Edna Brody, Leon and Regina Greenebaum. Joseph Stolz died in Chicago on February 7, 1941.

Writings: "Funeral Agenda for Jews," Central Conference of American Rabbis *Yearbook* 7 (1897): 27–47; "History of Chicago Jewry," *Chicago Sentinel* 91, no. 12 (1933): 6, 27, 31, and no. 13 (1933): 6, 26.

References: *Advocate*, February 14, 1941; *American Jewish Year Book* (Philadelphia, 1942), 43:441–46; Tobias Schanfarber, "Joseph Stolz," Felix Levy, "Joseph Stolz," Central Conference of American Rabbis *Yearbook* 51 (1941): 249–53; Felix Levy and Joseph Stolz, *A Victorious Life and Words of Appreciation* (Chicago, 1936); "Nearprint Biography File," American Jewish Archives; *Universal Jewish Encyclopedia* (New York, 1943), 10:69.

SZOLD, BENJAMIN (1829–1902). Rabbi. Benjamin Szold, the son of Boruch and Chaile Szold, was born on November 15, 1829, in Nemiskert, Neutra Komitat, Hungary, where his family were the only Jews. Since there were no schools, he studied with an itinerant rabbi. He received ordination at the age of 14 from Judah Oszad and Simon Sidon, after studying at the Pressburg Yeshiva. He went to Vienna to pursue further study but was expelled from the city for his activities following the revolution of 1848. Between 1849 and 1855, he was a private tutor in Pressburg. Szold studied at the University of Breslau and the Breslau Rabbinical Seminary, where he came under the influence of Zacharias Frankel and Heinrich Graetz.

In 1857 he officiated for the High Holy Days in Brieg, Silesia, and in 1858, in Stockholm, Sweden. In both places, he was offered the position of rabbi but declined. He might have taken the position in Stockholm had Ludwig Lewisohn not suggested a pulpit exchange with Oheb Shalom Congregation in Baltimore, Maryland. In 1859, Szold accepted the position of rabbi at Oheb Shalom and held it until 1892, when he was named rabbi emeritus. He opposed radical Reform at Oheb Shalom and was widely known as an advocate of moderate Reform. His *siddur Avodat Yisrael* (a modified Orthodox prayer book) was adopted by numerous congregations throughout the United States.

Active in various liberal and humanitarian causes, Szold participated in the founding of numerous charitable organizations that aided the Russian Jewish refugees who came to the United States in the wave of immigration of the 1880s. He wrote extensively in Hebrew. As a Hebraist and Zionist, Szold, with his daughter Henrietta, organized study groups for immigrants. He also provided the initial impetus for the Hebrew Hospital and Asylum Association and the Hebrew Orphans' Asylum in Baltimore. In recognition of his efforts, the Independent Order of B'rith Abraham named its local group the Benjamin Szold Lodge.

In 1859 he married Sophia Schaar. They had eight daughters; only four survived him: Henrietta, Rachel Jastrow, Bertha Levin and Adele Seltzer. Benjamin Szold died on July 31, 1902, in Berkeley Springs, West Virginia.

Writings (partial listing): *Advocat Yisrael* (Baltimore, 1867); *Book of Job* (Baltimore, 1886); *Hegyon Libi* (Baltimore, 1867); *Moses Mendlesohn* (Baltimore, 1879); *Outline of the System of Judaism* (Wilmington, NC, n.d.); *Proverbs of Judaism* (Baltimore, 1874); *Sefer Hachayim* (Baltimore, 1887); *Urim Vethumim* (Baltimore, 1867).

References: Central Conference of American Rabbis *Yearbook* 13 (1903): 357–63; *In Honor of the Seventieth Birthday of Rev. Benjamin Szold* (Baltimore, 1899); A. L. Levin, *Szolds of Lombard Street: A Baltimore Family* (Philadelphia, 1960); "Nearprint Biography File," American Jewish Archives; William Rosenau, *Benjamin Szold* (Baltimore, 1929).

V

VOGELSTEIN, LUDWIG (1871–1934). Businessman. Vogelstein was born in Pilsen, Bohemia, Czechoslovakia, on February 3, 1871, the son of Rev. Dr. Heinemann Vogelstein and Rosa Kobrak Vogelstein. He attended Jewish parochial schools and a gymnasium in Stettin, Germany. After graduation, he entered the metal firm of Aron Hirsch and Sohn in Halberstadt, Germany, where he remained until 1896. He immigrated to the United States in 1897, as a representative of this firm. Later, he founded his own firm under the name Ludwig Vogelstein and Co., which he merged with the American Metal Co., Ltd., in 1920. Vogelstein went on to serve this new company first as vice president (1920) and then as chairman of the board (1924). Active in the metals industry, he founded and developed several mining and metal companies in the United States and Canada and wrote technical articles for the Daily Metal Reporter. He also gathered a valuable collection of books on metals and minings.

Although Vogelstein was a philanthropist and favored the raising of funds for the relief of German Jewry, he was an outspoken opponent of anti-Hitler demonstrations in the United States. An ardent Reformer, believing that Reform Judaism was the only form of Judaism that would survive modernity, he predicted the ultimate unity of all Jews in a Reform synagogue. He was also an anti-Zionist.

He served as chairman, Union of American Hebrew Congregations (1925–1934); vice president, Federation for the Support of Jewish Philanthropic Societies of New York; vice president, World Union for Progressive Judaism; member, board of governors, Hebrew Union College; member, board of directors, Jewish Publication Society; president, Temple Beth El (New York City) and trustee and chairman of the finance committee (after its merger with Congregation Emanu-El). He was also active in the National Council for Jewish Education.

In recognition of his services to Reform Judaism, the UAHC presented him with a gold cup in 1931.

Vogelstein died in New York City on September 23, 1934.

References: *American Hebrew and Jewish Tribune*, September 28, 1934, pp. 371, 373; *Who's Who in American Jewry* (New York, 1928), p. 724.

VOORSANGER, JACOB (1852–1908). Rabbi, publicist, classicist. The son of Wolf and Alicia Voorsanger, Jacob Voorsanger was born in Amsterdam, Holland, on November 13, 1852. After graduating from the Amsterdam Jewish Theological Seminary, Voorsanger immigrated to America in 1872 and within a few years received his doctorate from the new Hebrew Union College. After holding pulpits in the East and South, he became assistant rabbi of San Francisco's Congregation Emanu-El in 1886 and senior rabbi three years later, after the death of his mentor and predecessor Elkan Cohn.

For almost two decades as the spiritual leader of the most prestigious synagogue in the American West, Voorsanger tirelessly advocated the principles of Classical Reform Judaism set forth in the Pittsburgh Platform of 1885. He fought bitterly against Orthodox East European "rabbinism" and "legalism," as he put it, and also staunchly opposed Zionism. But although he performed services bareheaded, married Jew to non-Jew and introduced the radical *Union Prayer Book*, he maintained some traditions, such as his opposition to Sunday observance of the Sabbath.

In 1895 Voorsanger founded the *Emanu-El*, a publication he edited for the next thirteen years. It became the most influential Jewish journal on the West Coast. A 20-page weekly, it included fiction, philosophy, scholarship and reports on Jewish communities throughout the world, as well as on local institutions.

Voorsanger, who mastered 13 languages, many of them ancient, was an accomplished biblical scholar who founded and taught in the Department of Semitics (today's Department of Near Eastern Studies) at the University of California, Berkeley. He also tutored, as teenagers, such future rabbis as Judah L. Magnes, Martin A. Meyer (his successor at Emanu-El) and his own son Elkan.

While involved in many philanthropic efforts to aid the East European Jews who arrived in California in large numbers after the turn of the century, Voorsanger also exhibited a mistrust and prejudice toward East European Jewry. He was an advocate of lowering immigration quotas for East European Jews, and supported limits on their numbers on the West Coast and, especially, in San Francisco.

Voorsanger was very active in civic affairs. He was a major figure in rebuilding Jewish communal institutions (including Emanu-El's magnificent Sutter Street Temple) as well as San Francisco in general after the great earthquake and fire of 1906.

Voorsanger married Eva Korper; they had eight children: Alice, William,

Miriam, Leon Morais, Julian (Julius Henry), Ray, Emmanuel and Elkan. Jacob Voorsanger died in San Francisco on April 27, 1908.

Writings: *The Chronicles of Emanu-el* (San Francisco, 1990); *Sermons and Addresses* (New York, 1913).

References: "Nearprint Biography File," American Jewish Archives; Marc Lee Raphael, "Rabbi Jacob Voorsanger on Jews and Judaism: The Implications of the Pittsburgh Platform," *American Jewish Historical Quarterly* 63 (December 1973): 185–203; Fred Rosenbaum, *Architects of Reform* (Berkeley, 1980).

F.Ro.

VORSPAN, ALBERT (1924–   ). Social-action activist, administrator. The son of Fanny Swidelsky and Benjamin Vorspan, Albert Vorspan was born on February 12, 1924, in St. Paul, Minnesota. He attended the University of Minnesota, then New York University, where he received a B.A. (1946). He also attended the New School for Social Research in New York City. During World War II, he served as a gunnery officer on a destroyer escort in the Pacific (1943–1946).

In 1948 Vorspan was named assistant to the national coordinator of the National Community Relations Advisory Council. In 1953 he was appointed executive secretary of the (UAHC) Commission on Social Action and concurrently assistant director of the (UAHC) Department of Synagogue Activities. Currently, he is a senior vice president and director, Commission on Social Action at UAHC.

During his career with the Union of American Hebrew Congregations, Vorspan has been a leading participant in the civil rights struggle, the nuclear peace movement and interfaith activities. In acknowledging this work, he was honored by the Stephen S. Wise Free Synagogue in New York City and Temple Emanuel in Denver. He received the Allard Lowenstein Memorial Award, given by the American Jewish Congress (1984), and the Maurice N. Eisendrath Bearer of Light Award by the UAHC (1987). For his long years of service to the Reform movement, he received an honorary D.H.L. from HUC-JIR (1988).

In 1946 Vorspan married Shirley Nitchum; they have four children: Charles, Roberta, Kenneth and Deborah.

Writings (partial listing): *Giants of Justice* (New York, 1960); *Great Jewish Debates and Dilemmas* (New York, 1980); *Jewish Values and Social Crisis* (New York, 1968); *Justice and Judaism* (New York, 1956); *My Rabbi Doesn't Make House Calls* (New York, 1969); "Soul-searching," *New York Times Magazine*, May 8, 1988.

References: *Who's Who in American Jewry* (New York, 1981), p. 506.

W

WATTERS, GERTRUDE WILE (NATHAN) (1887–). Communal leader and businesswoman. Born on February 22, 1887, in Buffalo, New York, Gertrude Watters is the daughter of Isaac and Fannie Stettenheim Wile. She received her education in Buffalo preparatory schools.

After her first husband, Henry Nathan (president and cofounder of A. Victor and Co.), was killed in an accident while visiting France, she took over A. Victor and Co. Thereafter she served as director of A. Victor and Co., furniture merchants, and the Belgert Reality Co.

Watters was president of the National Federation of Temple Sisterhoods (1934–1941) and a member of the board of managers of the Department of Synagogue and School Extension of the Union of American Hebrew Congregations. Watter's other involvements included member of the board, women's division, Federation for Support of Jewish Philanthropic Societies of New York City; member, board of governors, Jewish Federation for Social Service, Buffalo; member, National Committee for Youth Aliyah; life member, board of directors, Women's Temple Society of Buffalo; director, Jewish Fresh Air Camp, Buffalo; director, women's board, Millard Filmore Hospital, Buffalo; director, Buffalo Symphony Society.

Watters was the first woman elected to the Board of Governors of Hebrew Union College. She was also on the executive board of the UAHC. She and Mrs. A. L. Warner were the first two women selected to sit on the board of Temple Beth Zion (Buffalo). Later, she was a director of the New York section of the National Council for Jewish Women and, as a member of Temple Emanu-El (New York City), was a director of its Women's Auxiliary Board. Active in the promotion of interfaith cooperation and goodwill, she served on the executive committee of the National Conference of Christians and Jews. When World War II erupted in Europe, Gertrude Watters added to her array of activities by participation in the British War Relief and the United Jewish Appeal.

In 1907, she married Henry Nathan (d. 1931); they had two children: Robert and Frances. In 1936 she married Leon Watters and moved to New York City; they had one child: Ichel.

References: Selias Adler and Thomas Connally, *From Ararat to Suburbia* (Philadelphia, 1961; *American Hebrew*, January 8, 1937, p. 747, and January 15, 1937, p. 777; *Universal Jewish Encyclopedia* (New York, 1941), 10: 476–77; *Who's Who in American Jewry* (New York, 1938), pp. 1106–7.

WECHSLER, JUDAH (1832–1907). Rabbi. Born on March 24, 1832, in Bavaria, the son of Hirsch Wechsler, Judah Wechsler studied at the talmudical academy of Wuerzburg. He was ordained as an Orthodox rabbi by Seligman Baer Bamberger, a leader of German Orthodoxy known as the Wuerzburger Rav, but after coming to America, he called himself Reverend, then Reverend Doctor, abandoning all traces of his Orthodox training and ordination.

On arriving in this country in 1857, he briefly served a congregation in Portsmouth, Ohio, having originally been hired as hazzan and schohet. He next served in Indianapolis, Indiana, from 1861 to 1864 (apparently leaving because of congregational financial difficulties); Richmond, Virginia (1864–1867); then back to Indianapolis Hebrew Congregation (1867–1869); Columbus, Ohio (1869–1872); New Haven, Connecticut (1872–1882); Temple Mt. Zion, St. Paul, Minnesota (1882–1892); and Meridian, Mississippi (1892–1897). In retirement, he returned to Indianapolis, where he remained until his death.

During his initial tenure in Indianapolis, he was the first Jew to preach in the George Street Methodist Church. While in New Haven, he attracted attention for his interfaith services.

In St. Paul, unable to abide traditional Judaism, Wechsler worked hard to place the Temple squarely within the mainstream of the Reform movement. The UAHC had been founded before his arrival, but the congregation had not accepted an invitation to join the new national body. There, Wechsler worked hard to apply the philosophy of Reform Judaism to traditional ritual. For Wechsler, religion knew no inertia. It was either progress or retrogression.

While in St. Paul, Wechsler began his association in 1892 with a colony near Painted Woods, North Dakota, a potential settlement for the large number of immigrants leaving czarist Russia and, after arriving in New York, sent westward. As the patron of the enterprise, gaining financial support from congregation members, Wechsler wanted to channel as many immigrants as possible into Painted Woods and similar colonies. At its height, over 230 persons settled there, but the colony ultimately failed, and its settlers moved away. It is possible that Wechsler's resignation from Mt. Zion was a result of his disappointment over the failure of Painted Woods.

Not avoiding controversy, while in Meridian, Mississippi, he took a courageous stand in advocating and working toward improving the education and status of blacks. The senior high school that he insisted be built for black children when a bond issue was floated for constructing new city schools (for whites) bears his name. This is a marked change from his antiabolitionist views for which he was cautioned when he went to Indianapolis Hebrew Congregation the second time.

Wechsler was a regular contributor to the *American Israelite*. His articles on refugees and their settlement also appeared in the *Jewish Messenger* and were often translated into Hebrew for distribution in the European press. He was a member of the Central Conference of American Rabbis from its founding in 1889.

Wechsler died in Indianapolis on August 8, 1907.

Writings: "Portland Jewry as Seen by a Minnesota Rabbi in 1884," *Western States Jewish Historical Quarterly* 15 (October 1982): 22–23; "A Minnesota Rabbi's Impression of San Francisco in 1884," *Western States Jewish Historical Quarterly* 16 (January 1984): 134–38.

References: *American Israelite*, obituary, August 15, 1907, p. 6; Judith E. Endelman, *One Jewish Community of Indianapolis* (Bloomington, IN, 1984); W. Gunther Plaut, *The Jews in Minnesota* (New York, 1959); idem, *Mt. Zion, 1856–1956: The First Hundred Years* (St. Paul, MN, 1956).

WEIL, FRANK LEOPOLD (1894–1957). Lawyer, communal and lay religious leader. The son of Leopold and Rebecca Weil, Frank Weil was born in New York City on March 6, 1894. He earned a B.S. from Columbia College in 1915 and an LL.B. from Columbia University Law School in 1917. He received an honorary D.H.L. from the HUC-JIR in 1945. He was admitted to the bar in 1917 and ultimately became a partner in the New York law firm of Weil, Gotshal and Manges.

Governor Herbert A. Lehman appointed Weil one of three employer representatives on the New York State Unemployment Insurance State Advisory Council (1935–1949). Weil also served as a member of the New York Commission Against Discrimination (1944) and was appointed to the National Advisory Panel to Study Juvenile Delinquency (1946).

Weil was involved in many social, religious and cultural activities, including serving as president of the National Jewish Welfare Board from 1940 until 1947. During Weil's presidency, the wartime United Service Organizations was created; he served as its director from 1940 until 1950. As president of the Jewish Welfare Board during World War II, Weil mobilized United States Jewry in support for the American military on a scale unprecedented in the history of American Jewish life.

In 1946 President Harry Truman awarded Weil the Medal of Merit, the nation's highest civilian award, in recognition of his "selfless, courageous and wholly objective contribution to the war effort and a lasting contribution to the welfare of the nation." Weil was a member of the United States National Commission on UNESCO (1946–1948). In 1948 President Truman named him chairman of the President's Committee on Religion and Welfare in the Armed Forces.

Weil was president of the 92nd Street Young Men's Hebrew Association in

New York (1932–1940) and founder and president of the World Federation of Young Men's Hebrew Associations and Jewish Community Centers (1947–1957). He served as a director of the Joint Distribution Committee and on the Advisory Council of the American Jewish Committee.

Vice president and a member of the National Executive Board (1940 –1957) of the Boy Scouts of America, chairman and director of personnel (1940–1954), Weil served as chairman of the Jewish Committee on Scouting. From 1943 until 1948, Weil was vice president of the Association of Youth Serving Organizations. A member of the National Executive Committee of the National Social Welfare Assembly (1946–1949), he served as its president (1949–1951).

A member of the Board of Governors of HUC-JIR (vice chairman, 1948–1957), Weil became the first chairman of the Board of Governors who was not a Cincinnati resident (1957). In his memory, HUC-JIR established the Frank L. Weil Institute of Advanced Studies in Religion and the Humanities. He also served on the Board of Trustees of Brandeis University and as chairman of its University Fellows.

A lifelong member of Congregation Emanu-El in New York, Weil served as trustee (1934–1957), chairman of the religious school committee and vice president of the congregation (1949–1957). In 1955 he was Reform Judaism's "Man of the Year." In that same year, Weil and his wife were selected "Mr. and Mrs. New York." Weil was a director of the Lincoln Center for Performing Arts.

Weil made a vital contribution to the promotion of unity in the Jewish community, especially during the stressful postwar years. While working for unity, he recognized that ideological diversity was a healthy part of the Jewish community.

Weil married Henrietta Amelia Simons, the granddaughter of Governor Moses Alexander of Idaho (the first Jewish governor in the United States), on July 7, 1924; they had three sons: John, Thomas and Peter. Frank Weil died in New York City on November 10, 1957.

Writings: Address, National Jewish Welfare Board (Atlanta, 1944); "Community Morale in the Emergency," Harry L. Gluckson Memorial Lectures (1941); "A Great Past—A Greater Future," Founders' Day Address, Hebrew Union College–Jewish Institute of Religion (New York, 1957); *Scouting and the Jewish Boy*, foreword (New York, 1943); "United or Divided," Founders' Day Address, Dropsie College (Philadelphia, 1945).

References: *American Israelite*, November 14, 1957; "Frank L. Weil Papers, 1898–1958," American Jewish Archives; *Frank L. Weil: In Memoriam*, tributes of Nelson Glueck, Julius Mark, Theodore Tannenwald, Jr., and Sylvan Gotshal (Cincinnati, 1958); *New York Times*, November 11, 1957; Weil Necrology by S. D. Gershovitz, *American Jewish Historical Quarterly* 47 (1958): 230–33.

J.A.B.

WEINER, LAZAR (1897–1982). Composer, conductor, pianist. Lazar Weiner was born in Cherkass, near Kiev in Russia, on October 24, 1897, the son of Samuel and Gussie Kahan Weiner. He began his studies at the State Conservatory in Kiev (1910–1914) but left at the age of 17 to emigrate to the United States. Since his family was not very observant, his early (*cheder*) religious education ended at the age of seven.

Weiner's first job in New York was as an accompanist to a Carnegie Hall vocal teacher. He also served as librarian and later conductor of the Little Symphony Amateur Orchestra. He gave recitals of his own compositions at New York City's Aeolian Hall (1923) and Town Hall (1930). Weiner also served as accompanist for Nina Tarasova from 1920 until 1930. He organized and conducted the Freiheit Singing Society (1923–1928), the Kultur Gezelshaft Chorus (1930–1934), the Workmen's Circle Chorus (1930–1950), the Central Synagogue Choir (1930–1974), the Message of Israel "chorus" (1935–1974) and the International Ladies Garment Workers Union Chorus (from 1934). From 1937 to 1939, he was an active member of the Mailamm Society, advancing Jewish music in the United States and Palestine. In 1939 Weiner helped to found a Jewish Music Forum. In 1944 he was involved in the formation of the Jewish Music Council of the Jewish Welfare Board. In 1963 he helped to found the Jewish Liturgical Music Society of America (which evolved into the American Society for Jewish Music in 1974).

During Weiner's experience with the Amateur Orchestra, he developed a friendship with Nahum Baruch Minkoff, violinist and Yiddish poet. Through Minkoff, his circle of friends widened to include Yehoash, David Pinski and Peretz Hirschbein. In fact, many of Weiner's works are settings of Yiddish poetry or translations of poems into the Yiddish language. He wrote larger works, including *To Thee America* (1942), based on a text by A. Leyeleas, and *Legend of Toil* (1934), based on a poem by I. Goichberg.

Weiner taught at the School of Sacred Music of HUC-JIR from 1952 until his death. He was self-taught in *nusach hatefillah* (prayer modes) and cantillations. It was the modal musical tradition that provided him with a foundation for much of his well-known later music, especially the art songs. Weiner's inspiration came from his former countrymen and coreligionists. The Jewish flavor emanated from the selection of poetry for the lyric as much as from the music itself.

In 1956, Weiner won the Jacob Weinberg Synagogue Composition Prize, awarded by the Hebrew Union College School of Sacred Music, for his *Ashre Haish, Psalm I*. His synagogue music demonstrates a strong feeling for the Eastern European traditional melodic style combined with a complex harmonic background. His complete Friday Eve and Sabbath Morning services, including a *Chassidic Service*, are used frequently in North American synagogues. He was also recognized in 1949 by the American Society of Composer, Authors, and Publishers (ASCAP); in 1958 by the Jewish Congress for Yiddish Culture; in 1961, 1965 and 1969 by various branches of the Women's Circle; in 1962 by the Cantor's Assembly; in 1968 by the City University of New York; and in 1978 by Herzliah and Touro College (honorary D.J.L.).

In 1921 Weiner married Naomi Shumiatcher; they had two children: David and Yehudi (who later changed his surname to Wyner). Lazar Weiner died in New York on January 10, 1982.

Writings: *Anim Z'miros* (New York, 1964); *Ashre Haish, Psalm I* (New York, 1956); *The Golem* (New York, 1950, 1956); *Likras Shabos* (New York, 1954); "Nigun," "Dos Gold fun Deine Olgen," "Stile Light" (New York, 1968); *Shir L'Shabat* (New York, 1963).

References: *American Jewish Year Book* (Philadelphia, 1984), p. 341; Marsha Bryan Edelman, "In Memoriam: Lazar Weiner (1897–1982)," *Musica Judaica* 14, no. 1 (1981–1982): 99–105; "Lazar Weiner: A Tribute," *Congress Bi-Weekly*, 34, no. 16 (November 20, 1967): 16; "Nearprint Biography File," American Jewish Archives; *New York Times*, obituary, January 11, 1982.

S.H.A.

WERNER, ERIC (1901–1988). Musicologist, educator. A native of Vienna, the son of Julius and Helen Donath Werner, Eric Werner was born on August 1, 1901. Well grounded in music theory and practice, he became an avid student of philosophy, Semitics, literature and, above all, music, between 1919 and 1928, at the Universities of Graz, Prague, Vienna, Berlin and Goettingen. Werner earned his doctorate in musicology at the University of Strasbourg in 1928. He briefly taught in the gymnasium of Holzminden, Brunswick, which led to posts at the gymnasium and conservatory at Saarbruecken.

With the advent of Nazism, Werner was forced to leave his position and found employment in Breslau, lecturing at the Rabbinical Seminary and teaching Latin and music at the local Jewish high school. In 1938 he was brought by Julian Morgenstern to the faculty of Hebrew Union College in Cincinnati to become professor of Jewish music (then sacred music). In addition to becoming professor of liturgical music, he was organist and choir director.

In 1948 Werner founded the School for Sacred Music. With the merger of Hebrew Union College and the Jewish Institute of Religion, the school of Sacred Music moved to New York. Werner became the official director of the school, first advising it, then teaching one semester in Cincinnati and one in New York and eventually moving to New York. Under his direction, the school became the first formal training school for American cantors.

In 1957 Werner was awarded a Guggenheim Fellowship to study liturgy. In 1967 HUC-JIR awarded him an honorary D.H.L. He has taught at the Universities of Rochester, Cincinnati and Columbia and at European universities in Cologne, Heidelberg and Vienna.

Werner convened the first International Congress of Jewish Music in Paris in 1959. The same year saw the publication of his monumental book *The Sacred Bridge: The Interdependence of Liturgy and Music in Synagogue and Church during the First Millenium*. This highly original, ecumenical study earned him citations from the Vatican. Werner was invited by the CCAR's Committee on Synagogue Music to serve as musical editor of the *Union Songstar: Songs and Prayers for Jewish Youth*. Often frustrated, he resigned from the project again and again. He did, however, complete the project in 1960. Werner's musical biography of Felix Mendelssohn is considered definitive. It was published in German in 1963 and subsequently translated into English, Hebrew and Italian.

Werner is the author of over 200 articles and ten books, each carefully researched and annotated. Typical of his work is *A Voice Still Heard: The Sacred Songs of the Ashkenazic Jews*. It remains a standard textbook on the subject.

Although Werner composed a few musical works, including a *Rosh Hashanah Service*, his compositions went largely unnoticed. He also participated in the biblical film series titled *The New Media Bible*. He was a fellow of the American Musicological Society, a fellow of the American Academy of Jewish Research and president of the American sector of the International Society of Jewish Music.

In 1966 Werner was invited to develop a Department of Musicology at Tel Aviv University. From 1966 to 1971, he served as its head, having retired from HUC-JIR. In 1982 he received the Great Golden Sign of Merit, first class, from the Republic of Austria, which he declined to accept if it came with the signature of Prime Minister Kurt Waldheim. The Minister of Culture signed it instead. The National Jewish Welfare Board named him the first winner of the National Jewish Music Awards from the Jewish Board's Jewish Music Council.

In 1932, Werner married Elizabeth Mendelssohn. Eric Werner died in New York in 1988.

Writings (partial listing): *The Choir Loft* (New York, 1957); *Mendelssohn* (New York, 1962); *The Sacred Bridge* (New York, 1959); *A Voice Still Heard* (Philadelphia, 1976).

References: ''Nearprint Biography Box and File,'' ''Correspondence File,'' American Jewish Archives.

WIENER, MAX (1882–1950). Rabbi, theologian. The son of Isidor and Amalie Marcus Wiener, Max Wiener was born in Oppeln, Upper Silesia, Germany (now Opole, Poland), on April 22, 1882. Max Wiener was born into an Orthodox family. Wiener studied at the University of Berlin and the University of Breslau (Ph.D., 1906) and at the Jüdisch-theologische Seminar in Breslau and at the Lehranstalt für die Wissenschaft des Judentums in Berlin, from which he received ordination in 1908.

From 1909 until 1912, Weiner served as assistant rabbi in Dusseldorf under Leo Baeck. He accepted a call as senior rabbi to Stettin (now Szczecin, Poland) in 1912. During 1917 and 1918 he officiated as army chaplain in France. In 1926 Weiner became one of the communal rabbis for the liberal Jewish community in Berlin. For several years he directed an adult-education program in that community (Jüdische Volkschochschule). He also served as student pastor at the University of Berlin until 1933. He was chair in Jewish philosophy and theology at the Lehranstalt from 1934 to 1939. Concurrently, Wiener was a member of the national board of directors of the Judischer Kulturbund, an organization that directed such activities as theater performances, concerts and lectures for the Jewish community during the Nazi period.

In 1939 he was invited to lecture at Hebrew Union College in Cincinnati, where he taught Talmud, liturgy and Jewish philosophy until 1941 while also serving as rabbi in Fairmont, West Virginia. After his tenure there, he moved to New York, where he served as part-time assistant rabbi at Congregation Habonim, did some free-lance writing and served on the board of editors of the *Reconstructionist*.

Throughout his congregational career, Wiener was deeply concerned with the religious education of young and old. He sought to make Jewish tradition relevant to physicians and lawyers by offering special courses comparing Jewish law and medical wisdom of the past with that of his day.

Wiener's first book was *Die Anschauungen der Propheten von der Sittlichkeit* (*The Prophetic View of Ethics*) (1909). Inspired by the philosophy of Hermann Cohen, Wiener departed from pure rationalism and stressed revelation, which he saw as underlying the force and enthusiasm of the prophetic message. In his later writings the stress on the uniqueness of the religious experience through revelation is given increased emphasis. Wiener's major work *Juedische Religion im Zeitalter der Emanzipation* (1933)—Hebrew translation, *Ha-Dat Ha-Yehudit Bi-Tekufat Ha-Emantsipatsyah*, Jerusalem, Mosad Bialik (1974)—analyzed the enormous changes in Jewish thought brought about by the Emancipation, particularly in Germany.

In addition to his larger studies, Wiener wrote many articles in various Jewish periodicals. He also served as editor of the religion department of the *Jüdisches Lexikon* (1927–1930). Many of these articles were adapted for the *Universal Jewish Encyclopedia* (1939–1943). He likewise participated in the incomplete German *Encyclopaedia Judaica* (1928–1934). After coming to the United States, he also wrote articles in English, many appearing in the *Reconstructionist*.

Wiener married Toni Hamburger on November 11, 1913; they had two sons: Theodore and Emanuel. Max Wiener died in New York on June 30, 1950.

Writings: comp., *Abraham Geiger and Liberal Judaism: The Challenge of the Nineteenth Century* (Philadelphia, 1962; reprint, Cincinnati, 1981); *Die Anschauungen der Propheten von der Sittlichkeit* (Berlin, 1909); *Ha-Dat Ha-Yehudit Bi-Tekufat Ha-Emantsipatsyah* (translation of *Juedische Religion im Zeitalter der Emanzipation*) (Jerusalem, 1974); *J. G. Fischtes Lehre vom Wesen und Inhalt der Geschichte* (Berlin, 1906); For a bibliography of his writings, see Guido Kisch, ed., *Das Breslauer Seminar (The Breslau Seminary)* (Tubingen, 1963), pp. 439–40.

References: *Hebrew Union College Annual* 56 (1985): 29–46; "Miscellaneous File," American Jewish Archives; *New York Times*, July 2, 1950, p. 24; *Treue zur Thora, Beitragen zur Mitte des christlich-judischen Gesprachs, Festschrift fur Gunther Harder zum 75. Geburstag*, hrsg. von Peter von der Osten-Sacken (Berlin, Institut Kirche and Judentum, 1977), pp. 101–7; World Congress of Jewish Studies, *Proceedings* (1982), Division C, Hebrew section, pp. 111–16.

                                                                                              T.W.

WINE, SHERWIN T. (1928–   ). Born on January 25, 1928, in Detroit, Michigan, the son of William and Tillie Israel Wine, Sherwin Wine received both an A.B. (1950) and A.M. (1951) in philosophy from the University of Michigan. He entered HUC-JIR, Cincinnati, where he received his M.A.H.L. and was ordained in 1956. In 1981 he was awarded an honorary D.D. from HUC-JIR.

On his ordination, Wine served as a chaplain with the U.S. Army in Korea from 1956 to 1958. Wine served as assistant rabbi at Temple Beth El in Detroit from 1958 to 1960. He then moved to Temple Beth El in Windsor, Ontario, Canada, serving from 1960 to 1963.

While in Windsor, he began to formulate what he eventually called Humanistic Judaism, a movement founded in response to what Wine considered the "conservatisation" of Reform Judaism. In 1963 he returned to Detroit to found the Birmingham Temple, the first of several organizations he nurtured to support a humanistic philosophy in Judaism. In 1969 Wine cofounded the Society for Humanistic Judaism. He was also instrumental in establishing the Institute for Secular Humanistic Judaism in Jerusalem.

Wine defines Humanistic Judaism as "the philosophy of those who affirm their Jewish identity, their independence of supernatural authority, and the right to determine the purpose and course of their own lives." With a strong commitment to human reason, Wine espouses that emphasis must be placed on creating a Judaism that acknowledges and is responsive to the needs of the individual in a modern, scientific and ever-changing society.

Wine contends that traditional liturgy does not reflect the values or beliefs embraced by many contemporary Jews. This liturgy, which is prayer-centered according to Wine, defines a world in which God has the power to contravene natural law, to issue commands and to respond to the petitions of those who seek his intervention. Wine argues that it is hypocritical to continue using such liturgy for those who no longer find prayer efficacious. He further argues that reinterpreting traditional prayers in an attempt to make them conform to a scientific worldview is a futile act. Wine says honesty demands that a new liturgy be created, one that affirms the beliefs of the contemporary Jew. As a response, he believes that humanistic liturgy celebrates the ongoing evolution of the Jewish people while articulating the values of human dignity, integrity and autonomy.

Wine has written liturgical materials for the Shabbat and holidays, as well as two books that explain the nature of Humanistic Judaism. He has traveled extensively discussing Humanistic Judaism and aiding in the formation of groups dedicated to its growth.

While Wine's major focus continues to be as a humanistic rabbi, he is involved in supporting ethical and social positions that uphold human freedoms and the separation of church and state. Wine also is involved in educational projects that promote and articulate humanistic philosophy in general. In 1979 he founded the Center for New Thinking and has been director of the Michigan Foundation for the Arts.

Writings: *High Holidays for Humanists* (Detroit, 1979); *The Humanist Haggadah* (Detroit, 1979); *Humanistic Judaism* (Buffalo, 1978); *Judaism Beyond God* (Detroit, 1985); *Meditation Services for Humanistic Judaism* (Detroit, 1976).

References (partial listing): Atheist Rabbi Doesn't Let 'Non-beliefs' Get in His Way," *Southern Israelite*, January 20, 1978; Lev Bearfield, "Saturday the Rabbi Had Nothing to Worship," *Jerusalem Post International Edition*, July 27, 1985, p. 11; Nor-

man B. Mirsky, *Unorthodox Judaism* (Columbus, 1978), pp. 112–25; "Nearprint Bi-
ography File and Box," American Jewish Archives; "One Detroit-area Synagogue Has
an Atheistic Rabbi, and Half of Its Congregants are Atheists," (Buffalo) *Jewish Review*,
December 23, 1977; Irving Spiegel, "Jewish 'Ignostic' Stirs Convention," *New York
Times*, June 20, 1965; Hiley H. Ward, "Godless Rabbi Raps Revered Jewish Hero,"
Detroit Free Press, December 7, 1964.

R.B.B./T.F.B.

WISE, ISAAC MAYER (1819–1900). Rabbi, principal organizer of Reform
Judaism in North America. Wise was born in Steingrub, Bohemia, and received
a traditional Talmudic education at various *yeshivot*. He was certified as a *Re-
ligionsweiser* (religious officiant) and served the small Jewish community of
Radnitz, Bohemia, for three years before emigrating to the United States in 1846.
The exact circumstances of his departure from Europe are unknown, but it is
possible that either his liberal political views or his unauthorized officiation at
weddings was brought to the attention of Hapsburg officials.

Less than a month after arriving in New York, Wise introduced himself to
Max Lilienthal, the chief rabbi of New York's three traditional German synagogues. Lilienthal, who subsequently embraced Reform Judaism, engaged the
articulate and energetic newcomer as his personal emissary. A speaking trip to
Albany, New York, resulted in a rabbinic position for Wise at the local synagogue, Beth El. Empowered by his new situation and liberated by the democratic
traditions of his adopted country, Wise began to fashion a uniquely American
Judaism with the hope of organizing the chaotic U.S. Jewish community under
its banner.

Controversy erupted at Beth El because of Wise's introduction of select religious reforms, his increasingly heterodox beliefs and, primarily, his unwill-
ingness to be controlled by his lay leadership. In 1850, following a widely
reported melee in the synagogue on Rosh Hashanah, Wise's supporters organized
a new congregation, Anshe Emeth, and named him its rabbi. The new synagogue
was the first in the United States to allow mixed seating. The congregation had
bought a church and decided to use its family pews. Apparently, the idea of
men and women sitting together at Anshe Emeth was not debated.

In 1854 Wise moved to Cincinnati to serve as rabbi of Congregation Bene
Jeshurun (recently renamed the Wise Center) and remained there for the rest of
his life. Shortly after relocating in the "Queen City," he began publishing an
English-language paper, the *Israelite* (subsequently renamed the *American Israelite*) and a German supplement called *Die Deborah*. Both papers enjoyed a
national circulation. The following year, Wise organized his first successful
rabbinic conference. Meeting in Cleveland, a small group of moderate Reformers, including the leading spokesman for traditional Judaism in America, Isaac
Leeser, endorsed a number of Wise's ideas. Leeser would later distance himself
from the positions and programs adopted at the conference. The harshest criticism
of the Cleveland meetings, however, came from radical Reformers, especially
David Einhorn, who claimed that Wise had conceded too much to the Orthodox

camp. Undeterred, Wise issued his own prayer book, *Minhag America*, in 1856. He continued to call for a union of congregations as well as a college to train rabbis in the United States.

During the Civil War, Wise articulated what is widely held to have been the political position of the majority of American Jews of the period. A Copperhead Democrat, he was prepared to tolerate slavery to preserve the Union. Wise even flirted with the idea of running for public office in Ohio until his congregation forced him to drop the idea. During the war years, Bene Jeshurun built in downtown Cincinnati a monumental brick sanctuary that combined Moorish and Gothic themes. Now a national historic landmark, the Plum Street Temple helped to popularize the "cathedral synagogue" concept in the United States.

After the war, Wise and Einhorn resumed their fierce ideological struggle. Wise attended a rabbinic conference organized by Einhorn in Philadelphia in 1869 but determined that its radical decisions were inconsistent with his vision of a united American Jewry. The German radicals, on the other hand, boycotted meetings called by Wise in Cleveland, Cincinnati and New York. Frustrated by the sharp divisions in the American rabbinate, laymen, largely associated with Wise's congregation, took matters into their own hands and organized the Union of American Hebrew Congregations in 1873. One of the union's principal goals was to establish a rabbinic school, and in 1875 the Hebrew Union College was organized. Wise was named president and successfully built the Cincinnati-based institution into an important center of modern Jewish scholarship. Largely estranged from the radicals who prepared the Pittsburgh Platform in 1885, Wise gathered his rabbinical allies and graduates from Hebrew Union College and organized the Central Conference of American Rabbis in 1889 as a regional organization. The conference quickly developed a national following and emerged as the third and final of the parent bodies that continue to shape the development of American Reform Judaism.

Although he was remarkably prolific and addressed nearly all the major issues of philosophy, religion and science of the nineteenth century, Wise was not a systematic thinker. Scholars continue to debate the content of his personal religious beliefs. Influenced by Mendelssohnian ideas while still in Europe, he also felt challenged by the rational religion of Unitarianism in the United States. He rejected biblical criticism and, late in life, vociferously opposed political Zionism. Wise's intellectual flexibility and personal dynamism greatly contributed to his effectiveness as a religious leader in the United States during the nineteenth century. He never abandoned his vision of a singular American Judaism but, in effect, established the basic pattern of denominational Judaism in North America. The current institutional strength of the American Reform movement is testimony to his foresightedness and tenacity.

Wise married Therese Block in 1844; they had ten children. Therese died in 1874. Two years later, Wise married Selma Bondi; they had four children, including Rabbi Jonah B. Wise. Isaac Wise died on March 24, 1900, in Cincinnati.

Writings: *History of the Israelitish Nation*, vol. 1 (Albany, 1854); *Minhag America* (for Day of Atonement) (Cincinnati, 1856); *Minhag America* (Cincinnati, 1866); *Reminiscences*, ed. and trans. David Philipson (Cincinnati, 1901, 1945); *Selected Writings of Isaac M. Wise, with a Biography*, ed. David Philipson and Louis Grossman (Cincinnati, 1900; rev. 1969); *The World of My Books* (Cincinnati, n.d.).

References: James G. Heller, *Isaac M. Wise: His Life, Work and Thought* (New York, 1965); "Isaac M. Wise Manuscript Collection," American Jewish Archives; Benny Kraut, "Judaism Triumphant: Isaac Mayer Wise on Unitarianism and Liberal Christianity," *AJS Review* 7–8 (1982–1983): 179–230; Michael A. Meyer, *Response to Modernity: A History of the Reform Movement in Judaism* (New York, 1988); Sefton D. Temkin, "Isaac Mayer Wise and the Civil War," *American Jewish Archives* 15 (November 1963): 120–42.

WISE, JONAH BONDI (1881–1959). Rabbi. Born in Cincinnati on February 21, 1881, Jonah Wise was the twin son of Isaac Mayer Wise and his second wife, Selma Bondi. Wise grew up in Cincinnati and was the only one of his father's children to enter the rabbinate. Wise graduated simultaneously from the University of Cincinnati and Hebrew Union College in 1903. After ordination, he studied at the Lehrenstält für Wissenschaft des Judentums and the University of Berlin, as well as at the University of Berne. Wise was granted honorary degrees from New York University, Hebrew Union College (1935) and the Jewish Theological Seminary of America (1949). On returning to the United States, he served Temple Mizpah in Chattanooga, Tennessee (1904–1906). He then served Temple Beth Israel in Portland, Oregon (1906–1925), where he was active also in civic and state affairs. While in Portland, he established a weekly Jewish newspaper, the *Scribek*. In 1925 he came to Central Synagogue, New York City, where he served until his death.

Early in his career, Wise emerged as a valiant and indefatigable battler for social welfare, civic service, interfaith activities and peace. In Portland, he was particularly active on behalf of Jewish immigrants from Eastern Europe. Wise was an outspoken pacifist from the outbreak of war in 1914 until the United States entered the war three years later. Wise was active in Jewish War Relief and, beginning in 1915, spearheaded the West Coast drive. This involvement gave him the national exposure that would eventually lead to his selection as rabbi at Central Synagogue and as chairman of the Joint Distribution Committee.

Wise again attracted national attention in 1934 when, while in his early days at Central Synagogue, he launched the first nationwide Jewish inspirational broadcast, "The Message of Israel." He coordinated the production entirely from the sanctuary of his synagogue.

Wise's strength lay in public leadership. Deeply devoted to American ideals and the validity of a liberal approach to Judaism, he was passionately dedicated to the welfare of world Jewry. Wise avoided the sensational, subordinating his personality to the causes he served. He was a realist who was concerned with the practical task of salvaging the survivors of Nazi persecution rather than the grandiloquent oratory of Zionists of his era.

Beginning in 1931, Wise became a leader of the Joint Distribution Committee and the United Jewish Appeal. He was named national chairman in 1939, working to raise million of needed dollars and reorganizing programs of financial support in order for these organizations to carry on their work of rescue and resettlement. As a result of his work, President Roosevelt chose Wise as a delegate to the International Refugees Conference held at Evion-les-Bains in France.

In 1935, Wise became treasurer and representative of the Workers Aim Association, which dealt with the Farm Resettlement Administration. He continued in this role until 1940, when government participation in the farmsteads ceased and members of the cooperative became full-fledged individual homeowners.

Shortly after Chaim Weizmann's inauguration as the first president of Israel, he cited Wise for outstanding contributions toward the establishment of the state of Israel. Wise accepted the honor, but he never set aside his reservations about political Zionism. He argued against the pro-Zionist resolution contained in the Columbus Platform in 1937 and was angered by the CCAR support of the Jewish legion in 1942 (apparently contrary to a compromise among members of the CCAR that no public stand regarding Zionism would be taken until seven years after the Columbus Platform was accepted). Wise joined others in a strong protest against the legion, penning a position paper that was released to the press over his objections. Eventually, he joined in creating the American Council for Judaism but resigned after only seven weeks. Wise was a non-Zionist, not an anti-Zionist. Thus, as a non-Zionist and an active supporter of Israel, Wise was indeed a contradictory figure.

Wise also served as a member of the Book Selection Committee and Religious Books Round Table of the American Library Association. He briefly served as editor of the *American Israelite*.

Although Wise never formally retired, he withdrew from public life after his wife's death. In the last years of his life, Wise became discontented with himself and had his then assistant, David Seligson, elevated to take over most of his rabbinical duties at Central Synagogue.

Wise married Helen Rosenfeld in 1909 (d. 1950); they had three children: David, Elsa Hertzberg and Joan Kaufman. Jonah Wise died on February 1, 1959, in New York City.

References: Sam Cauman, *Jonah Bondi Wise* (New York, n.d.); "Nearprint Biography File and Box," American Jewish Archives; Julius J. Nodel, *The Ties Between* (Portland, 1959); *Who Was Who in America*, (Chicago, 1960), 3:931.

WISE, STEPHEN SAMUEL (1874–1949). Rabbi, Zionist leader, social reformer, academician. Born on March 12, 1874, in Budapest, Hungary, Stephen S. Wise was the son of Sabina de Fischer Farkashazy Wise and Rabbi Aaron Wise (Weist). He immigrated to the United States in 1875. His father had come 15 months earlier, working first as a bricklayer, then as rabbi of Congregation Beth Elohim in Brooklyn and finally at Congregation Rodeph Shalom in Manhattan. Stephen Wise studied at the College of the City of New York (1887–1891) and then Columbia College (B.A., 1892) before going on to Columbia

University (Ph.D., 1901). He studied toward a private ordination with Gustav Gottheil, Alexander Kohut, Henry Gersoni, Max Margolis and Adolf Neubauer (of Oxford).

Wise had enrolled in absentia at Hebrew Union College in Cincinnati. With Isaac Mayer Wise's permission, Stephen S. Wise was to go to Cincinnati for examination, but he never did so. Instead he went to Vienna in the summer of 1893 to study with its chief rabbi, Adolf Jelinek, and then returned to assist Henry Jacobs at Congregation B'nai Jeshurun in New York City. Wise was elected its rabbi the following year when Jacobs became ill. While at B'nai Jeshurun, he had organized the Sisterhood for Personal Service, which provided for needy families on the Lower East Side and established a religious school there. This foreshadowed the Social Service Division he later created (with Sidney Goldstein) at the Free Synagogue.

Already disheartened by traditional Judaism, he accepted a call to Congregation Beth Israel in Portland, Oregon, in 1900—not even having sought the position. He knew that he would return to New York but wanted to establish a reputation elsewhere. He hoped to bring Zionism to the West but quickly realized that it was freedom of the pulpit that he wanted to exercise. There he exchanged pulpits with Christian ministers, introduced voluntary contributions for dues, established worship services for children and published his sermons, all progressive activities for the rabbinate of his era. From the beginning of his tenure in Portland, he preached social reform. His Judaism was a religion that combined the social-justice teachings of the Hebrew prophets with Jewish nationalism. There he served as the first vice president of the Oregon State Conference of Charities and Corrections (1902). He was invited to serve in the cabinet of Mayor Henry Lane, whom he helped get elected, but declined. Although he eschewed political appointments, he did accept an appointment as Commissioner of Child Labor in Oregon (1903). He spoke out against assimilation, although he realized it would not put an end to anti-Semitism.

In 1906 he was invited to Congregation Emanu-El in New York City to preach a trial sermon, a practice he denounced. He was never elected to the pulpit because he refused to relinquish, on principle or in practice, the right of a rabbi to freedom of speech in the pulpit (without censure by a synagogue's board of trustees). Wise also recognized that to develop a great career, he had to do so outside of synagogue activity. He felt that the constraints of Emanu-El would not allow him to do so. Nevertheless, he resigned in Oregon to return to New York to found (in 1907) the Free Synagogue, whose platform also included free unassigned pews. By this time Wise had abandoned most Jewish ritual practices in exchange for what he considered a kinship with the Jewish people. He believed that Judaism had a universal world message to offer. Wise was an eloquent preacher who appealed to Jews and non-Jews in the Sunday services he led, first at the Hudson Theater and Clinton Hall and eventually at Carnegie Hall (before the building of his own synagogue). He attacked the injustices of the steel industry, championed a shorter work week for women in the canning industry, denounced evils in the needle trades and led the City Affairs Committee of New York in its attack on the administration of Mayor James Walker.

Wise was at the heart of the Zionist movement in America. However, he did not entertain the notion of living in Palestine himself. He believed that Zionism was a means of uniting the entire Jewish people as much as it was an attempt to resettle refugee Jews in Palestine. He attended the Second Zionist Congress (Basle 1898), serving as a delegate and translator for the English section. That year he went on to cofound the Zionist Organization of America, which he served as president (1912, 1937–1938). He was chairman of the United Palestine Appeal and represented the Zionist interest at the Versailles Peace Conference. While a member of the International Zionist Executive Committee, he frequently resigned and returned over differences with Chaim Weizmann. In the 1940s, Wise served as chairman of the American Emergency Committee for Zionist Affairs. He also led a militant self-defense against Hitlerism.

In 1922 Wise established the Jewish Institute of Religion in New York City. He believed in the need for a rabbinic training institution that would protect the sectarian interest of Jews and would provide liberal rabbinic leadership in New York. Although the Jewish Institute of Religion eventually merged with Hebrew Union College in 1950, he contended that Hebrew Union College did not provide for the needs of American Jewry. Wise technically retired from the Jewish Institute of Religion in 1948, and became president emeritus, but he stayed in the Free Synagogue pulpit until his death. Nelson Glueck, then president of Hebrew Union College, was president of both institutions until plans for the formal merger took place, when Glueck became president of the merged institution.

Wise's activities led him to prominence in various organizations. He actively supported the National Association for the Advancement of Colored People and the American Union Against Militarism. He established the American Jewish Congress as a democratic body representing a cross-section of American Jewry in distinction to what he saw as elitism in the American Jewish Committee. Wise served as president from its founding in 1924 until his death (excluding 1929–1934, when the presidency was held by Bernard Deutsch). Later he organized the World Jewish Congress and chaired its executive committee (in 1936).

As he did with other organizations, Wise repeatedly resigned and returned as a member of the Central Conference of American Rabbis when he saw its leadership turn toward traditionalism. As a result, he never served as an officer.

Wise was honored by numerous institutions and organizations. He received the Chevalier of the Legion d'Honneur (France 1919), the award of merit of the Decalogue Society of Lawyers in Chicago for his "courageous leadership in defense of civil rights and the human dignity of every man in the land" (1948), a citation from the 92nd Street YMHA in New York (1949) and the Zeta Beta Tau Richard Gottheil medal for the most distinguished service in the cause of Jewry during 1925. Wise received honorary degrees from Temple University, Syracuse University, Bates College, Roanoke College, Rollins College and Hebrew Union College. The American Jewish Congress established (in 1949) four annual awards in his honor in recognition of outstanding service or creative contributions in major areas in Jewish activity.

In 1900 Wise married Louise Waterman. They had two children: Justine Wise Polier and James Waterman Wise. He died on April 19, 1949, in New York City.

Writings (partial listing): *Beth Israel Pulpit*, 2 vols. (Portland, 1905–1906); *Challenging Years* (New York, 1949); *Child Versus Parent* (New York, 1922); *The Free Synagogue Pulpit*, 10 vols. (New York, 1908–1950); *The Great Betrayal* (New York, 1930); *How to Face Life* (New York, 1917); "What I Owe My Father," in Sidney Strong, *What I Owe My Father* (New York, 1931); trans., *The Improvement of the Moral Qualities*, by Solomon ibn Gabirol (New York, 1902).

References (partial listing): *Current Biography* 2 (1941): 81–83; *Jewish Encyclopedia* (New York, 1964), 12–543; Justine Wise Polier and James Waterman Wise, eds., *The Personal Letters of Stephen Wise* (Boston, 1956); Robert Shapiro, *The Reform Rabbi in the Progressive Era* (New York, 1988); "Stephen S. Wise Manuscript Collection," American Jewish Historical Society; *Universal Jewish Encyclopedia* (New York, 1943), 10:543–44; Melvin I. Urofsky, *A Voice That Spoke for Justice: The Life and Times of Stephen S. Wise* (Albany, 1982); Carl Hermann Voss, *Stephen S. Wise: Servant of the People: Selected Letters* (Philadelphia, 1969); Moses Weiler, *Stephen S. Wise: People's Champion* (New York, 1972).

WOLF, ALFRED (1915–   ). Rabbi and communal organizer. Born in Eberbach, Germany, to Hermann and Regina Levy Wolf, he entered the United States after high school graduation in 1935, earned a B.A. at the University of Cincinnati in 1937, was ordained at Hebrew Union College, Cincinnati, in 1941, and completed a Ph.D. in Religion at the University of Southern California in 1961. Wolf held pulpits in Toronto, Ontario, and Dothan, Alabama (1941–1946), and served simultaneously as Union of American Hebrew Congregations Southeast Council Regional Director (1944–1946) and Western Regional Director (1946–1949) before his election in 1949 to the rabbinical staff at Wilshire Boulevard Temple in Los Angeles, where he was active for a generation alongside Edgar F. Magnin and Maxwell Dubin. Retiring as Senior Rabbi of the Temple in 1985, he remained in Los Angeles to assume the directorship of the American Jewish Committee's Skirball Institute on American Values.

Wolf, as UAHC regional director and as rabbi at Wilshire Boulevard Temple, has been a notable builder of Reform Judaism in Southern California. He has devoted himself to West Coast intergroup relations, helped found the first Los Angeles Human Relations Conference and the Interreligious Council of Southern California and was also instrumental in developing his temple's Camp Hess Kramer and Gindling Hilltop Camp in Malibu. Wolf has had an impact on many other organizations, to name a few among them: the Southern California Board of Rabbis, the Pacific Association of Reform Rabbis (an affiliate of the Central Conference of American Rabbis), the Hebrew Union College-Jewish Institute of Religion Board of Governors, the National Commission on Interfaith Relations co-sponsored by the UAHC and the CCAR, the American Jewish Committee's Executive Board in Los Angeles, the Los Angeles Jewish Federation Council, United Way of Los Angeles, and the American Academy of Religion. In addition, he has lectured at Loyola Marymount University, the University of Southern California, and the California State University at Los Angeles, as well as the College of Jewish Studies in Los Angeles.

In 1940, Wolf married Miriam Office, of Dayton, Ohio. They had two sons, David and Dan, a daughter, Judith, who died in 1988, and four grandchildren.

Writings: "Ecology—New Word, Old Ideal," *Loyala* 5:5 (Feb. 1971): 18–21; co-editor with Joseph Gaer, *Our Jewish Heritage* (New York, 1957); co-author with Royale Vadakin, *A Journey of Discovery: A Resource Manual for Jewish-Catholic Dialogue* (Valencia, CA, 1989); and with Dan Wolf, *Wilshire Boulevard Temple Camps 1949–1974* (Los Angeles, 1975).

References: *Who's Who in America* II (1982–1983), p. 3615; *Who's Who in American Jewry* (Los Angeles, 1980), p. 528.

S.H.L.

WOLF, ARNOLD JACOB (1924–   ). Rabbi, teacher. The son of Nettie Schanfarber and Max A. Wolf, Arnold Wolf was born on March 19, 1924, in Chicago, Illinois. After attending the University of Chicago (A.A., 1942), Wolf entered the University of Cincinnati (B.A., Philosophy, 1945). Subsequently, he entered and was ordained at Hebrew Union College in 1948. Some years later, he attended the Oriental Institute at the University of Chicago (1955–1957). Serving in the U.S. Navy during the years 1951 to 1953, Wolf received a Korean Service Ribbon and the U.N. Medal for his work as the only Jewish naval chaplain in the Far East.

After ordination, Wolf served as assistant rabbi at Emanuel Congregation in Chicago (1948–1955); rabbi at B'nai Jehoshua in Chicago (1955–1957); founding rabbi of Congregation Solel in Highland Park (1957–1972); Jewish chaplain at Yale University (1972–1980); and rabbi of K.A.M.-Isaiah Israel in Chicago (since 1980).

Outspoken on various social issues, Wolf is a founding contributing editor of *Sh'ma*. He has lectured widely and taught at HUC-JIR, the University of Chicago Divinity School, the (Chicago) College of Jewish Studies and Yale University.

Wolf was the first official Jewish representative to the World Council of Churches Assembly. He has conducted his own radio and television programs over Midwest CBS and ABC affiliates. He was honored with the National Conference of Christians and Jews Brotherhood Award in 1962. He was chairperson of Breira, a project on shared responsibility between Israel and Diaspora Jewry (1973–1975), as well as a founding director of Camp Institutes for the National (now North American) Federation of Temple Youth. He is also a board member of the Jewish Peace Fellowship, the Jewish Council on Urban Affairs and other human-rights organizations. For three years, he was a commissioner of the Board of Ethics of the City of New Haven. He served on the Commission of Ethics and the Human Services Task Force for the Mayor of Chicago.

Wolf married Lois Blumberg in 1963 (div.); they had three children: Jonathan, Benjamin and Sarah Berger. In 1987 he married Grace Wolf. She has three children: Justine, Sara-Anne and Dara Henning.

Writings (partial listing): *Challenge to Confirmands: An Introduction to Jewish Thinking* (New York, 1963); "The Last Lecture," *Religion and Intellectual Life* 5, no. 2 (Winter 1988): 101–8; "Makers of a Modern American-Jewish Theology," in *Handbook of American-Jewish Literature* (Westport, CT, 1988), pp. 239–60; "Post-Liberal Judaism," *Reconstructionist* 56, no. 4 (Summer, 1991): 5–6; *Rediscovering Judaism* (Chicago, 1965); *What is Man?* (Washington, DC, 1968).

References: "Nearprint Biography File," American Jewish Archives; *Who's Who in American Jewry* (Los Angeles, 1980), p. 528.

Z

ZEPIN, GEORGE (1878–1963). Rabbi, administrator. Born in Kiev, Russia, on June 8, 1878, George Zepin was the son of Otto and Hannah Matzov Zepin. He immigrated to the United States with his parents in 1882. After attending secondary school in Cincinnati, Zepin entered the University of Cincinnati (B.A., 1900) and Hebrew Union College concurrently, where he was ordained in 1900. In 1942, Hebrew Union College conferred on him the honorary D.D. degree.

After his ordination, Zepin served B'nai Israel Congregation in Kalamazoo, Michigan, from 1900 to 1903. In 1904 he began his first association with the Union of American Hebrew Congregations as director of the Union of American Hebrew Congregations Department of Synagogue and School Extension (1904–1906), a position to which he would later return. He served as director of the United Social Agencies of Chicago from 1907 to 1908. He returned to the pulpit to serve Congregation Beth El in Fort Worth, Texas, from 1909 to 1910. While in Ft. Worth, Zepin was appointed commissioner of charities of that city. In 1910 he returned to the UAHC, again to direct the Department of Synagogue and School Extension, a position he held until 1917, when he was named UAHC Executive Secretary. In 1941 he retired from that position and was named honorary secretary of the UAHC and honorary vice chairman and secretary of the Rabbinical Pension Board.

During Zepin's three decades of service to the UAHC, he was responsible for the UAHC's expansive publication program of educational materials (while he himself wrote little more than a few articles for the *Universal Jewish Encyclopedia*), as well as the establishment of the first systematic programming for synagogues.

Zepin also had a major role in the organization and early development of the National Federations of Temple Sisterhoods, Temple Brotherhoods, and Temple Youth—as well as the Rabbinical Pension Board.

In 1914 Zepin married Laura Lehman. George Zepin died in Cincinnati on April 9, 1963.

Writings: *The Falashas* (Cincinnati, 1912).

References: "Nearprint Biography File and Box," American Jewish Archives; *Universal Jewish Encyclopedia* (New York, 1941), 10:640; *Who's Who in American Jewry* (New York, 1938), p. 1170.

ZWERIN, RAYMOND A. (1936–   ). Rabbi, educator, author, publisher. Born in Cincinnati, Ohio, on November 28, 1936, to Irwin and Mary Sadacca Zwerin, Raymond A. Zwerin attended school in Culver City, California. He received his A.B. in psychology from UCLA in 1958, moving on to HUC-JIR in Cincinnati, where he received a B.H.L. (1960) and an M.A.H.L. (1964) and rabbinic ordination (1964). During the years 1960 and 1961, Zwerin went to Hebrew University in Jerusalem for graduate studies, having been awarded the Louis A. and Rose Chase Fellowship. While in Israel, he covered the trial of Adolph Eichman for the Copley Press, writing a series of feature articles. In 1989, HUC-JIR awarded him an honorary D.D. in recognition of his 25 years in the rabbinate. After ordination, he became assistant rabbi at Temple Emanuel in Denver, Colorado (1964–1967). He then founded Temple Sinai in Denver, where he remains serving as its rabbi.

While most of Zwerin's career has focused on education, he has been active in other local and national projects and organizations, including serving as founder of Babi Yar Park Memorial to the Holocaust and to the cause of Soviet Jewry and as founder of the Theodor Herzl Jewish Day School of Denver. He served as a board member of the ADL of B'nai B'rith, Arapahoe Mental Health Center, Colorado State Commission for Health Planning, Denver Technological Center Ministries, Rose Medical Center, the William Petschek National Jewish Family Center of the American Jewish Committee (for research and programming on the Jewish family) and other organizations. Zwerin also serves as an adjunct professor of Old Testament and Judaism at the Colorado Women's College in Denver.

Zwerin's impact on Jewish education is most evident in his work as cofounder, with Audrey Friedman Marcus, and president of Alternatives in Religious Education, Inc., a major producer of creative Jewish educational materials for children and adults. His articles have been published in journals and magazines, and a selection of his sermons has been published in *American Rabbi* magazine. He is the author of numerous books and minicourses.

Zwerin married Rifka (Rikki) Finci in 1961; they had three children: Ron, Robyn (d.) and Dina.

Writings (partial listing): *For One Another: How Jewish Organizations Help* (New York, 1975); *High Holy Day Dictionary* (New York, 1983); *Our Synagogue* (New York, 1974); *A Purim Album* (New York, 1982); co-ed., *Jewish Principal's Handbook* (Denver, 1984).

References: "Nearprint Biography File," American Jewish Archives.

UNION OF AMERICAN HEBREW CONGREGATIONS

PRELUDE AND BIRTH[1]

From almost the moment of his arrival in America in 1846, Isaac Mayer Wise dreamed of strengthening American Judaism by ventures that would unite American Jewry. Within a year he had joined a *beth din* of New York rabbis with a view to creating texts for Jewish education and worship, but only Wise fulfilled the commitment by creating a prayer book. His vision of a congregational union attracted the enthusiastic endorsement of Rev. Isaac Leeser of Philadelphia, the most influential Jewish religious leader of his day. Leeser espoused the idea in a series of articles in the the *Occident*. In the December 1848 issue, Wise issued an invitation to rabbis and lay leaders for the formation of a religious union. Earlier that year, Wise had proposed his idea from Rabbi Max Lilienthal's pulpit in New York. Despite a number of favorable responses in print from both rabbis and laymen, the meeting set for New York in 1849 had to be cancelled. The New York congregations remained divided by rivalries, and only one offered to send a delegate. Subsequent rabbinic conferences widened the gap between Wise and his eastern colleagues. For radicals like David Einhorn, he was too much of a traditionalist; for Leeser and the Orthodox, he was too Reform.[2]

The Civil War and its Americanizing influences on the German Jews, combined with a growing and prospering Jewish population, encouraged Wise's plans for a school to train American rabbis. The failure of his prewar Zion College had demonstrated the need of lay support for such an institution. Before 1870, Wise's most successful contribution to the unity of American Jews was his prayer book, *Minhag America*. Ostensibly to revise it for postwar needs, Wise called several rabbinical gatherings of those colleagues who were using it—in Cleveland (summer 1870), New York (fall 1870), and Cincinnati (June 1871). The first two meetings were fraught with bickering among the few rabbis who attended. With

27 rabbis present, the Cincinnati conference issued a call for a congregational union, but the newspaper report of one rabbi's disbelief in a personal God again condemned Wise in the eyes of the Eastern "establishment." Wise's own congregation, Bene Jeshurun, endorsed his ideas. Its president, Moritz Loth, addressed an invitation to southern and midwestern congregations to form a union to establish a rabbinical seminary, but reaction was dilatory. In the fall of 1872, Loth put together a committee of 12 members of Bene Jeshurun to again issue a call, but it was not until the following March, when Loth brought together representatives of the five Cincinnati congregations, that a formal invitation was forthcoming for a meeting to be held in Cincinnati that summer. Delegates from 34 congregations in 28 southern and midwestern cities assembled at Melodeon Hall on July 8, 1873, and promptly voted to create a Union of American Hebrew Congregations (UAHC), whose main purpose would be to establish a "Hebrew Theological College." The Union was to meet annually (changed in 1881 to biennially). At the Cleveland meeting in 1874, 21 more congregations were enrolled, and others soon followed.[3]

Although creating the Hebrew Union College and raising funds for its support remained the major function of the UAHC, it soon turned its attention to serving the needs of congregations and to American Jewish life.

SOCIAL ACTION

Despite Wise's opposition to the idea, the 1877 convention of the UAHC in Philadelphia voted to absorb the Board of Delegates of American Israelites. In 1880 the Board published a census of Jews in the United States. Beginning in 1876, it prevailed on the UAHC to raise funds for agricultural settlements of immigrant Jews, but this effort failed to elicit sufficient support and was abandoned by 1886. The Board sought State Department intervention for the rights of oppressed Jews in such foreign lands as Romania, Morocco and tsarist Russia. In 1882 the UAHC secured committees in congregations to aid the growing group of immigrants from Russia and subsequently chartered the Hebrew Sheltering and Immigrant Aid Society (forebear of the Hebrew Immigrant Aid Society, known as HIAS). The opening decades of the twentieth century saw the birth of other organizations that assumed the civil-rights and social-action roles, so the Board of Delegates on Civil and Religious Rights (as it was then known) faded into oblivion in 1925.[4]

After participating with Christian leaders at the organizational meeting of the United Nations in San Francisco in 1945, Maurice Eisendrath urged the UAHC Executive Board to create a joint CCAR-UAHC commission in the area of social action. By 1951 the UAHC had appointed its delegation and selected Rabbi Eugene J. Lipman, the Director of Synagogue Activities, to also direct this joint commission. Two years later he was joined by the creative mind of Albert Vorspan, who succeeded Lipman as director in 1961. In 1963 the Kivie Kaplan Center was opened in Washington, D.C. Ten years later Rabbi David Saperstein became Vorspan's associate and dynamic director of the Kaplan Center, where not only the UAHC but also Jewish defense agencies are housed. They function as a strong lobby for causes espoused by the UAHC and raise consciousness for these causes through committees on social action established in individual congregations.[5]

By 1879 the UAHC was urging rabbis in the field to ride circuit to assist isolated Jews and small congregations. This program grew for a number of years until the Hebrew Union College began sending students as weekend rabbis.[6]

PUBLICATIONS AND EDUCATION

Wise had expressed the hope of using the UAHC to create a publication society and dreamed of publishing an inexpensive edition of the Bible, but the limited funds of the UAHC went elsewhere. Wise himself published a catechism for religious schools. In 1877 the UAHC offered a prize for a hymnal for Sabbath schools, but there is no record of an award. One of the submissions was *Z'mirot Yisrael: Jewish Hymns for Sabbath-Schools and Families*, with hymns in English and German, published by Rev. Simon Hecht of Evansville, Indiana. The UAHC did not become involved with music publishing until 1976, when it was presented with Transcontinental Music Publications by Mari Freudenthal, the widow of its founder. Under the direction of Judith Tischler, this arm of the UAHC has become the leading publisher and distributor of music for the synagogue.[7]

In 1886 the Hebrew Sabbath School Union was established with the aim of expanding religious schools, developing a uniform curriculum and training teachers. It began publishing educational works, primarily in the form of pamphlets, but included books on Bible, biblical history and pedagogy. In 1905 the UAHC combined the Sabbath School Union with its own circuit endeavors in religious education and created the Department of Synagogue and School Extension. Efforts were made to encourage congregations to conduct weekday afternoon classes as well as weekend classes, but under pressures from merchant congregants, for whom Saturday was the busiest day of the week, most congregations moved their Sabbath schools to Sunday morning, with a few holding special classes during the week. Attempts were also made to establish educational facilities for isolated groups, immigrant groups and others as part of a larger welfare program, but lack of funds limited and ended this effort.[8]

Continuing dissatisfaction with the results of Jewish education in the Reform movement led the Central Conference of American Rabbis to form, with the UAHC, the Joint Commission on Jewish Education, at first a division of the Department of Synagogue and School Extension. By 1941 it had become a separate entity. The engagement, in 1923, of Emanuel Gamoran as its first professional director brought the Commission and the UAHC to the forefront in American Jewish education. Attractive textbooks and workbooks were published for all age groups, from preschool to adults. Formal curricula for each age group were produced and circulated. Other movements in American Jewish life began purchasing and imitating the UAHC output. The attractiveness of the UAHC's shelf list was greatly enhanced with the employment of Max Singer, an expert book designer. As a result, the UAHC received a number of awards for books that not only were superior for Jewish education but also were works of beauty. Until the establishment of Hebrew Union College's School of Education, the UAHC conducted sporadic teacher-training programs and institutes. Under Gamoran's editorship it published a quarterly, *Jewish Teacher*, aimed at enhancing pedagogical methods and substance. From 1922 to 1940, a children's magazine, *Young Israel*, was issued, to be replaced after World War II by *Keeping Posted*, aimed at junior- and senior-high youth. Edited first by Edith Samuel and until recently by Aron Hirt-Mannheimer, *Keeping Posted* was published both in a reader's edition and with a teacher's guide.

In May 1943 the UAHC began publishing an illustrated periodical for the members of affiliated congregations, *Liberal Judaism*, subsequently retitled *American Judaism* and now called *Reform Judaism*. Under a variety of editors, its scope has grown from purely in-house for Reform congregations to wider issues that affect Jews everywhere. After Gamoran's retirement in 1958, a variety of successors enlarged on the foundations he had established. One of the most significant publishing ventures of the UAHC was its issuance in 1981 of *The Torah: A Modern Commentary*, edited by Rabbi W. Gunther Plaut. It provides full Hebrew text with English translation and critical commentary for the Torah and all haftarah portions. Despite the advent of many competing publishers in the field of Judaica, the UAHC continues to exert an influence.[9]

GROWTH AND LEADERSHIP

The UAHC grew with the Reform movement, maintaining its headquarters in Cincinnati through the administrations of Lipman Levy, who served as secretary from 1873 to 1917, and Rabbi George Zepin, who assumed the title of executive vice-president, retiring in 1941. During their tenure, the UAHC's main functions continued to be raising funds for the support of Hebrew Union College and developing service to congregations. Until 1941, dues paid by congregations were only one dollar per member. The Great Depression severely reduced congregational growth. At the 1941 biennial convention in Detroit, Rabbi Louis Mann delivered a lecture—"The Failures of the Union and Where Do We Go from Here?"—that galvanized the Board of Trustees to retire Zepin and elect Rabbi Edward Israel, who unfortunately died during his first board meeting. He was succeeded briefly by Professor Nelson Glueck, whose call to serve the U.S. government in the Middle East led to the temporary appointment of Rabbi Maurice Eisendrath of Toronto. As Glueck's term of service with the Office of Strategic Services was lengthened by the war, Eisendrath insisted that, in fairness to his congregation, he be either released by the UAHC or retained with the title of director. In September 1943 he was elected director. On the death of Adolph Rosenberg, the last lay president, in 1946, the Executive Board of the UAHC approved the election of a lay chairman of the board, and Eisendrath was given the title of president.[10]

From the outset, Eisendrath offered a larger vision of the role of the UAHC. He considered the UAHC and Hebrew Union College separate entities with differing missions. To expand the Reform movement, he created regional offices of the UAHC, at first using part-time congregational rabbis to help the founding, growth and servicing of congregations. With the movement of large Jewish populations to the suburbs after World War II, full-time regional rabbis were engaged and offices established in regions throughout the United States and Canada, now totaling 13.[11]

For many years the UAHC occupied offices in the Merchants Building, at 34 West Sixth Street in downtown Cincinnati. With the expansion of its activities came the need for larger quarters. In 1944 funds were appropriated to erect a building on the campus of Hebrew Union College, but war shortages made this unfeasible. At the 1947 biennial, Eisendrath reiterated an oft-spoken recommendation of earlier UAHC leaders to move the base of operations to New York, and a temporary office shared the facilities of the New York Federation of Reform Synagogues, adjacent to Temple Emanu-El at 3 East 65th Street. Meanwhile, the Cincinnati headquarters were maintained. Eisendrath's larger dream was realized in October 1951 when, thanks to the generosity of Dr. Albert Berg, the basic funds were provided for the UAHC to erect and dedicate a seven-story structure (later expanded to ten), named the Berg Memorial–House of Living Judaism, at Fifth Avenue and 65th Street in New York City. From this conspicuous site, Eisendrath developed the UAHC's significance in the larger Jewish community.[12]

On Eisendrath's death in 1973, Rabbi Alexander Schindler became president of the body. Under his leadership, UAHC membership is rapidly approaching 850 congregations in the United States and Canada. He has continued to add staff and substance to the UAHC program and has earned ever greater recognition for the UAHC's positions and stature in world Jewry.[13]

DEVELOPMENT OF AFFILIATES

With the growth of the number of congregations came the birth of affiliated bodies. Most Reform congregations increasingly relied on the women of the community for many chores within the temples. One of the earliest principles enunciated by the Reform movement was the equality of women. The 1891 UAHC convention accepted its first woman delegate—from Congregation Berith [sic] Kodesh of Rochester, New York. By the end of the nineteenth century, every congregation had its Ladies' Auxiliary, later called Sisterhood. At the 1913 Council of the UAHC, Carrie Obendorfer Simon of Washington, D.C., organized the Sisterhood representatives into the National Federation of Temple Sisterhoods (NFTS). This affiliate grew rapidly and holds biennial conventions of its own concurrently with those of the UAHC. From the beginning, NFTS has successfully shared program ideas among sisterhoods and has strengthened and supported religious schools and youth programs. NFTS has also raised funds, primarily through the sale of Uniongrams (greetings for life-cycle occasions), to provide scholarships for students of the Hebrew Union College and to build the first dormitory on that institution's Cincinnati campus, dedicated in 1925. NFTS also made an important financial contribution to the UAHC's New York headquarters. Within individual congregations, sisterhood presidents came to be welcomed on temple boards of trustees and, as they went out of office, moved to elected positions on the board. In 1956 Helen Dalsheimer, of Baltimore Hebrew Congregation, pioneered as the first woman president of a congregation, a situation now common.[14]

From 1933 to 1976, NFTS enjoyed the strong directorship of Dr. Jane Evans, whose outspoken advocacy of many social-action causes preceded and paralleled that of Maurice Eisendrath. In 1941, hers was one of the first voices to denounce the government's internment of Japanese-Americans on the West Coast. Her interest in the Jewish Braille Institute led NFTS to sponsor the distribution of large-print and braille Judaica to the sight-impaired. Projects for Israel, Soviet Jewry and the aging are ongoing concerns of NFTS, as are scholarships for rabbinic students at Hebrew Union College–Jewish Institute of Religion. On Evans's retirement, she was succeeded by Eleanor Schwartz, who had the difficult role of continuing the effectiveness of NFTS in an era when women were moving both into the workplace and into positions of leadership in the movement. The Executive Board of the UAHC accorded *ex officio* status to NFTS presidents, but it was the 1960s before women were elected to that body.

The National Federation of Temple Brotherhoods (NFTB) was formed in 1923 as a service agency to brotherhoods but found its major mission when it took over the operation of the Jewish Chautauqua Society in 1939, providing rabbis as lecturers on Judaism at college campuses, developing Judaica libraries on the campuses and creating interfaith understanding through the production of radio and television programs. The varied activities of local brotherhoods, together with articles of special interest, appear in the periodic NFTB publication originally called *Jewish Layman*, now called *Brotherhood*. Many of these projects were developed by NFTB's longtime executive director, Sylvan Lebow, and his associate Avram Bondarin.[15]

The National (now North American) Federation of Temple Youth (NFTY) was instituted at the 1939 Council of the UAHC at the instigation of Rabbi Samuel Shulman, who had long been urging the movement to meet the needs of young people between the ages of confirmation and marriage. Richard Bluestein of Cincinnati was elected the first of a number of national presidents who were to take their place in the leadership of the Reform movement. Rabbi Selwyn D. Ruslander was engaged as the first full-time director. He succeeded in bringing many of the congregational youth groups into NFTY and led the movement into interfaith programming. He enlisted the enthusiastic support of Rabbis Eugene Sack and Samuel Cook in directing the first of NFTY's highly successful summer-camp programs at a rented camp in eastern Pennsylvania. When World War II summoned Ruslander into the U.S. Navy, NFTY's directorship went to Miss Helen Goldstrom until Samuel Cook returned from the chaplaincy to take her place. Under Cook's inspired leadership, youth leaders were trained in special seminars, and the UAHC embarked on purchasing its own camp institutes, now nine in number, in all parts of the country, catering to all age groups. NFTY conducts innumerable programs for youth in the United States and Canada and in Israel, where the UAHC sponsors two kibbutzim.[16]

The UAHC has been interested in the World Union for Progressive Judaism (WUPJ) since it was founded in England in 1926 to coordinate liberal Jewish congregations outside the United States and Canada. With the devastation of Europe's Jews and European Jewry's financial resources at the end of World War II, the leadership of WUPJ turned to the UAHC for help. Financial solic- itations on behalf of WUPJ accompanied bills to UAHC congregations. In 1951 WUPJ asked for office space in the House of Living Judaism, which was even- tually granted. Thanks to Eisendrath's stimulus, an American Board of World Union was established to develop funds primarily to support a Reform movement in Israel. Eventually, the UAHC underwrote WUPJ's payment of salaries to Israel's liberal rabbis. The Leo Baeck College in London, sponsored by WUPJ, was established in 1956 to train non-Orthodox rabbis, most of whom serve congregations outside the United States and Canada. A number of rabbis serving WUPJ congregations have also been trained at the Hebrew Union College–Jewish Institute of Religion. Rabbis from abroad, aided by NFTS scholarships, have been obligated to give a minimum of three years of service to WUPJ congre- gations. WUPJ holds biennial conventions, with delegates and speakers from all parts of the liberal Jewish world. Long headquartered with the UAHC in New York, WUPJ's main office is now on the Jerusalem campus of HUC-JIR, with Rabbi Richard Hirsch as executive director. Under his leadership, the Reform movement has gained reluctant but increasing recognition in Israel, with a grow- ing number of congregations there and with major cultural centers in Jerusalem and Tel Aviv. The UAHC still houses the Office of the American Board of WUPJ to service liberal congregations in Latin America and the Caribbean.[17]

The 1920s and 1930s saw the development of large congregations in major cities, producing the need for professional business managers, originally known as temple secretaries. By 1941 there were enough of them to band together and form the National Association of Temple Secretaries (NATS). Its original purpose was to prepare and disseminate administrative information and procedures to member congregations of the UAHC. As congregations grew and more people joined the group, its title was changed to National Association of Temple Ad- ministrators (NATA), and it acquired its own Office of Synagogue Administration at the House of Living Judaism, ably headed for many years by Myron Schoen. To encourage professionalization, NATA has devised a curriculum leading to the granting of the title of Fellow in Temple Administration. NATA also provides placement service to congregations seeking professionals in this field.[18]

By 1955 so many congregations were retaining full-time religious educators that the National Association of Temple Educators (NATE) was born. Aimed first at giving the religious educators representation in the deliberations of the UAHC, it has expanded its efforts to encourage people to enter the professional field of Jewish education and to stimulate interest in Jewish education in local communities. With the assistance of NATE, the UAHC's periodical *Compass* replaced *Jewish Teacher* as the UAHC's educational publication.[19]

Before World War II, cantors were the exception rather than the rule in Reform congregations. The emergence of a growing group of cantors trained at Hebrew Union College's School of Sacred Music led to their increased acceptance in the movement and the formation of the American Conference of Cantors (ACC) in 1953. Eligibility for membership is based on professional cantorial training. The ACC works with the UAHC to foster the use of trained cantors in congregations and encourages the composition of new music for the synagogue, as well as the publication of music that is out of print. The ACC also maintains a placement service. The ACC takes an active role in the UAHC-promoted Joint Commission on Synagogue Music, headed by Rabbi Daniel Freelander. The Commission now assumes responsibility for all musical portions of each biennial.[20]

HOW THE UAHC FUNCTIONS

The UAHC operates on the principle that its individual member congregations are autonomous and that the UAHC has no right to interfere in their forms of worship, programs of education or internal organization. Each congregation pays dues to the UAHC, currently forming about one-eighth of its budget. In addition, individuals are encouraged to contribute to the Fund for Reform Judaism. A share of the UAHC's collected funds goes to the support of Hebrew Union College–Jewish Institute of Religion.

The UAHC's biennial conventions, usually held in major cities, attract an ever larger gathering of delegates, alternates and local laity to hear lectures, attend educational and inspirational workshops, debate resolutions on current issues and worship together. Each member congregation is entitled to two delegates for the first 100 members and one delegate per 100 members or part thereof over the first 100. The high level of education and the quality of professionalism among the participants engenders informed, serious discussions, and, often, heated debates. The emphasis on liberal agenda seems to spark an excitement that has many attendees returning to convention after convention. Similar activities take place in alternate years at regional conventions of the UAHC.[21]

A large Board of Trustees—consisting of officers, an Executive Committee (originally labeled Administrative Committee) and members-at-large—is entrusted with carrying out the decisions of the conventions and the ongoing business of the UAHC. In preparation for conventions, and to advise and be informed by the various departments of the UAHC, numerous committees and joint commissions (the latter involving other bodies, most notably the Central Conference of American Rabbis) are appointed by the Chairman of the Board for the central body, whereas the elected regional chairpersons appoint committees for their regions.[22]

ZIONISM

Of all the issues debated in the conventions of the UAHC, none has been more significant than the Reform movement's changing attitudes toward Zionism. The first Zionist conference in Basel in 1897 and the subsequent formation of the Federation of American Zionists, headed by the son of Temple Emanu-El's rabbi, Professor Richard Gottheil of Columbia University, provoked the 1898 biennial convention of the UAHC to pass a resolution expressing its sympathy for oppressed Jews in foreign lands but also its unalterable opposition to political Zionism:

The Jews are not a nation, but a religious community. . . . America is our Zion. . . . The mission of Judaism is spiritual, not political. Its aim is not to establish a State, but to spread the truths of religion and humanity throughout the world.[23]

Despite the pro-Zionist activities of a number of Reform rabbis, notably Stephen S. Wise and Abba Hillel Silver, as well as some lay leaders, the anti-Zionist stance remained dominant in the entire Reform movement until 1937, when it had become obvious that Palestine could well serve as a place of refuge for central Europe's beleaguered Jews. At its biennial in New Orleans, the UAHC passed the following resolution:

The UAHC, in Council assembled, expresses its satisfaction at the progress made by the Jewish Agency in the upbuilding of Palestine. We see the hand of Providence in the opening of the gates of Palestine for the Jewish people at a time when a large portion of Jewry is so desperately in need of a friendly shelter and a home where a spiritual, cultural center may be developed in accordance with Jewish ideals. The time has now come for Jews, irrespective of ideological differences, to unite in the activities leading to the establishment of a Jewish homeland in Palestine, and we urge our constituency to give financial and moral support to the work of rebuilding Palestine.[24]

In the summer of 1942 a group of rabbis, angered by the Central Conference's passage of a resolution favoring a Jewish brigade in the British Army of North Africa, met at the call of Rabbi Louis Wolsey and formed the American Council for Judaism. With subsequent strong lay support, this group became the representative for anti-Zionism.

In early 1943, as word of Hitler's "Final Solution" for the Jewish people reached America, the UAHC joined other national Jewish organizations in attempting to create a representative body, the American Jewish Conference. The 38th Council of the UAHC, held in New York on April 2–3, 1943, authorized the appointment of a lay-rabbinic committee, from which a subcommittee, representative of both Zionist and anti-Zionist views, drafted a "Declaration of

Principles on Post-War European Jewry and Palestine,'' urging the new American Jewish Conference to push for complete civic equality and rehabilitation for Europe's Jews, with world support. Reiterating the 1937 resolution, the Declaration urged the postwar ''concert of nations'' to provide for large-scale immigration to a Palestine administered by this concert of nations, enabling the establishment of a democratic government in which church and state would be separated while preserving the inviolability of all holy places of various faiths.

The American Jewish Conference, meeting in New York on August 31– September 2, 1943, proved to be dominated by Zionist voices that voted a strong platform urging Jewish control of immigration to Palestine and the establishment of a Jewish commonwealth there. This led the UAHC to convoke a series of meetings. One gathering of rabbis, conducted by Rabbi Solomon Freehof, considered neutral on the issue, reiterated the UAHC's more moderate proposal, urging its acceptance by the American Jewish Conference, and expressed the hope that the UAHC would remain affiliated with the Conference. The UAHC Executive Board was split almost evenly on the Conference's Palestine Resolution and resolved to put the matter before the next biennial. The delay did not suit proponents of both views, and the UAHC, rather than the Conference, became the battleground. Resolution after resolution was discussed, with the outcome that the Executive Board proposed that the UAHC, in the interest of world Jewry, remain in the American Jewish Conference but take no action on the Palestine Resolution, leaving it to individuals to determine their own views. The Executive Board ended with a plea for loyalty to the UAHC. At that point the UAHC still had a lay president, Adolph Rosenberg. He had been invited to serve as cochairman of the American Jewish Conference's Interim Committee and sought the counsel of the Executive Board. They approved him but left it up to him to decide whether to serve. He seems not to have accepted cochairmanship but was on the committee as the UAHC's representative, along with Eisendrath. Both fought the Conference's becoming a permanent agency to represent American Jewry, though they did support its efforts for Jewish rescue and rehabilitation. Eisendrath was among those sent by the American Jewish Conference to San Francisco to be a consultant for the formation of the United Nations. In the ensuing publicity, it was clear that the UAHC was among those Jewish organizations that had taken no position on the question of the Jewish Commonwealth.

At the 1946 biennial council, Rosenberg defended the UAHC's participation in the Conference. Eisendrath pointed out that Isaac M. Wise had disassociated the UAHC from the Pittsburgh Platform. He underscored the fact that neither Zionism nor anti-Zionism was a tenet of Reform Judaism; therefore, the UAHC would be hospitable to all views. After much strong debate, the plenum voted that the UAHC would remain a member of the American Jewish Conference but would stay neutral on the Palestine Resolution. Despite agitation to have the UAHC withdraw from the Conference, Eisendrath secured the approval of his Executive Board for him to accept the chairmanship of the Committee on Future

Organization of the American Jewish Conference. The dream of creating a permanent American Jewish Assembly, however, came to naught. Only the political upheavals that were leading to the formation of the State of Israel kept the Conference alive until the end of 1948. In March 1948 the UAHC Executive Board voted by a narrow margin to support Eisendrath's plea that the UAHC join other national Jewish bodies in pressuring the United Nations and the U.S. government to act on the Palestine question. But the vote was so close that the Board felt constrained to maintain the previous biennial's insistence on neutrality. At the following biennial in November 1948, Eisendrath's presidential message chastised the gathering for what he called their "archaic neutrality" and called on them to lend their support to the moral issues of Jewish survival in the new state. This evoked the following resolution:

That this 40th General Assembly of the Union of American Hebrew Congregations enthusiastically hails the creation of the State of Israel and prays that peace may soon come to that now troubled land and its people. This Assembly respectfully petitions that the United Nations' decision of November 29, 1947, be fully and swiftly implemented by the United Nations.[25]

The resolution was adopted, but pockets of anti-Zionist opposition, largely fomented by the American Council for Judaism and its members, were to remain until Israel's victory in the Six-Day War of 1967. The excitement generated by the birth and growth of the State of Israel was reflected in congregational growth and programming and consequently in the enlarged programs of the UAHC.

Over the years of his administration, Eisendrath taught his constituency how the UAHC could make its presence felt in the American scene. The move to its own headquarters building in New York, the establishment of the Commission on Social Action and its Washington, D.C., base and the passage and dissemination of biennial resolutions on many issues far beyond the former in-house concerns of the UAHC membership all attest to the membership's acceptance of the direction of the UAHC.

At Eisendrath's instigation, the UAHC in 1955 began a program of financial support for the World Union for Progressive Judaism, which led to the creation of the Leo Baeck High School in Haifa and the underwriting of liberal congregations and rabbis in Israel, as well as to the headquartering of WUPJ in New York until its move to Israel. Subsequent years saw the establishment of exchanges of Israeli and American Youth and the growth of the liberal youth movement in Israel.[26]

The decade following the Six-Day War saw efforts to enlarge the recognition of Reform Judaism in Israel, culminating in the 1977 establishment of the Association of Reform Zionists of America (ARZA). To avoid the problem of residual isolationists, ARZA is an organization of individuals in the Reform movement devoted to achieving Jewish pluralism in Israel and to strengthening the Israeli Reform movement. So rapid was the growth of ARZA that for the

1987 quinquennial meeting of the World Zionist Congress, it won 33 of the highly contested seats in that body, the largest single contingent in the American delegation. It has become a significant element in the conduct of the Jewish Agency and in world Zionism.[27]

OTHER ISSUES

The birth and development of the State of Israel influenced the American Reform movement internally. As the UAHC approached its first centennial, a committee of rabbis and lay leaders was appointed, under the chairmanship of Rabbi Dudley Weinberg, to prepare a platform for the new century. Rabbi Weinberg's illness and subsequent death delayed the effort. When Professor Eugene Borowitz assumed the chairmanship, it was evident that the Reform movement was no longer the monolith of the earlier Pittsburgh Platform, nor even the dichotomy of the Columbus Platform of 1937, when Zionism was effectively challenging the movement. As a result, the committee decided to define the state of this very dynamic movement in 1973 rather than dictate the directions it might go. The result was "Centenary Perspective," which recognized the wide diversity in Jewish practice and in attitudes toward God and Israel, underscoring the autonomy of both individuals and congregations in matters of belief and ritual.[28]

Since its beginnings, Reform Judaism has recognized the reality of intermarriage, especially in America. While officially deploring the inroads into Jewish loyalty, the movement has capitalized on the opportunities intermarriage offers for new converts to Judaism. In larger cities, and at the UAHC headquarters in New York, formal classes in Judaism have for many years been instructing both non-Jews and their intended Jewish spouses. With the increase in the intermarriage rate, the UAHC has embarked on a highly successful program to help integrate non-Jewish mates and Jews by choice into Reform congregations. These outreach programs, administered from the House of Living Judaism by the staff of the Joint Commission on Outreach, afford such individuals the opportunity of venting their feelings, sharing their common problems and learning to be comfortable in the Jewish scene.[29]

CONCLUSION

The history of Judaism has been one of factionalism. Isaac M. Wise's dream of a union for all American Jewry could never be realized, as he himself discovered. But what he created in the spirit of liberalism has become a very diverse, constantly growing and, in many ways, effective union that challenges and often inspires its constituency. Each UAHC biennial convention is larger than the last, not only because of the growth in the number of member congregations but also because so many of those who experience the excitement of one convention return to other conventions for the inspiration they derive. As one attendee described it, "The biennials give us the opportunity of seeing so many Reform Jews excited about their Judaism."[30] The success of the UAHC can also be measured by the fact that so many of its institutions have been imitated by the other denominations of American Judaism.[31]

NOTES

1. Details of the Union of American Hebrew Congregations (UAHC) can be found in the *Proceedings of the Union of American Hebrew Congregations* issued in *Annual Reports* (hereafter cited as *AR*). These reports include résumés of proceedings of the biennial councils, popularly referred to as biennials. Also included are résumés of proceedings of the Executive Committee. After 1940, the Executive Committee met less frequently, and an Administrative Committee of its members functioned between meetings; its minutes were published as well. Until 1950, the Board of Governors of Hebrew Union College reported as a UAHC affiliate. In the interest of efficiency and economy, several years' activities might be bound together, with the final date on the cover of the volume. Unless otherwise noted, the information in this article is derived from these *AR* or from the personal knowledge of the authors.

2. David Philipson, *Reminiscences by Isaac M. Wise* (Cincinnati, 1901), ch. 3; "First Movement for a Union," in *Selected Writings of Isaac Mayer Wise*, edited by David Philipson and Louis Grossman (Cincinnati, 1900), ch. 4.

3. James G. Heller, *Isaac Mayer Wise: His Life, Work and Thought* (New York, 1965), chs. 17, 26–27.

4. Jacob R. Marcus, *United States Jewry, 1776–1985* (Detroit, 1991), pp. 312ff; Heller, *Isaac Mayer Wise*, pp. 438ff.

5. *AR*, October 1947, pp. 94, 145, 272, December 1955, p. 262; *Who's Who in American Jewry* (Los Angeles, 1980).

6. *Proceedings of the UAHC* 2 (1879–1885): 8 and (1898): 10.

7. The preface to the second edition of Hecht's hymnal (Evansville, IN, 1877) is our source for information on the UAHC prize. This work, with the many hymn texts and tunes by non-Jews, is characteristic of the hymnals produced by the Reform movement until the 1930s. Hecht's own "We Meet Again in Gladness" was reprinted in a number of later hymnals. Malcolm H. Stern, "A Century of Jewish Music," *Reform Judaism* (Fall 1988), pp. 14–15.

8. *American Jewish Year Book (AJYB)* 5660 (1899–1900): 55; Kehillah of New York City, *The Jewish Communal Register of New York City, 1917–1918* (New York, 1918), p. 1194.

9. *Universal Jewish Encyclopedia*; *AR*, passim, reports of the Commission on Jewish Education.

10. *AR*, passim. Mann's sermon was retitled by Eisendrath as "While the Union Slept," and it is remembered that way. He was elected president by the Executive Board. *AR*, October 1947, p. 151.

11. *AR*, 1943 and after; also Eisendrath's reports to each Executive Board and his presidential reports, "The State of Our Union," delivered to each biennial. These were printed in *AR* through 1955, then published separately until his final one in 1973.

12. *AR*, October 1947, pp. 34, 52, December 1955, pp. 3, 51, 81, 90ff.

13. In a move to add spirituality to his biennial messages, Schindler has made them

the Shabbat morning sermon of each biennial. These too have been published as individual pamphlets. The UAHC's actions and views on Jewish issues are reflected annually in *AJYB*.

14. *United Jewish Encyclopedia* 8:121. The German rabbinical conferences of 1843–1845 had recommended equality for women. In 1845, Berlin's Reform congregation abolished the women's gallery and permitted women in the choir but preserved their separation on the main floor of the sanctuary. Isaac M. Wise introduced family pews in Albany in 1851. By the time of the UAHC's establishment in 1873, family pews were the norm in Reform temples in the United States. See "Women" in the index to David Philipson, *The Reform Movement in Judaism* (New York, 1931). Rose Greenberg, *The Chronicle of Baltimore Hebrew Congregation, 1830–1975* (Baltimore, 1976), p. 68.

15. *AR*, May 1940, pp. 76ff., and other reports of NFTB in each issue of *AR*. See also issues of the periodicals.

16. Periodic reports of NFTY in *AR*.

17. *AR*, December 1955, pp. 43, 131, 389; Eisendrath's "State of Our Union" messages, passim; *Reports* and *Bulletins of WUPJ*.

18. See NATA reports in *AR*, passim; "Directory of National Jewish Organizations," *AJYB*, passim.

19. Ibid and the periodicals mentioned.

20. *AJYB*, UAHC biennial programs.

21. Biennial and regional programs.

22. *AR*, passim; centerfold in *1991 Directory of Member Congregations, UAHC*.

23. *Proceedings of the UAHC*, (1898): p. 4002.

24. *Proceedings of the UAHC*, (1937): p. 158.

25. *Proceedings of the UAHC*, (1950): p. 287.

26. It is interesting to follow the movement of the UAHC from a strong anti-Zionist stance to one almost totally pro-Israel. The facts presented here are nearly all derived from *AR*.

27. *ARZA Newsletter*; *AJYB*, passim; "Directory of National Jewish Organizations." ARZA's success at the 1987 World Zionist Congress is reported in *AJYB*, 1989, p. 218.

28. "Centenary Perspective"; Charles A. Kroloff, "Unity within Diversity," *Tanu Rabbanan: Our Rabbis Taught; Essays in Commemoration of the Centennial of the CCAR* (New York, 1989), pp. 89ff.

29. Publications of the Joint Commission on Outreach.

30. Oral reports and personal observations.

31. "A Union of Conservative Congregations: The United Synagogue of America," *Encyclopedia of Conservative Judaism* (forthcoming), cites the formation of the National Women's League of the United Synagogue and the National Federation of Jewish Men's Clubs, both modeled on Reform predecessors. The United Synagogue cantors, administrators, and educators organized after World War II, as did its Joint Social Action Commission, all following Reform precedent. *AJYB*, 1989, p. 469, shows the Union of Orthodox Jewish Congregations of America, founded in 1898, with a National Conference of Synagogue Youth (1954) and Women's Branch (1923).

HEBREW UNION COLLEGE– JEWISH INSTITUTE OF RELIGION

THE DREAM

Even as a newcomer to America in 1846, Isaac Mayer Wise dreamed of creating a union of congregations that would produce an institution of higher learning for Jews where rabbis could be trained to serve the growing American community.

Shortly after his arrival in Cincinnati in 1855, he began publishing a weekly newspaper, *Israelite*, and in one of its first editorials he urged the creation of a college. He evoked enough favorable response to announce the formation of the Zion Collegiate Association to serve as a fund-raising body for his Zion College. New Yorkers assumed that the college would be located in the largest Jewish community, but Wise, without consulting them, proceeded to open the school in Cincinnati in November 1855 with 14 students, two of them Christian, and with five professors. Wise defended his action to the New Yorkers by stating that Cincinnati was more central and had the second-largest Jewish population. The New York group, however, withdrew all support. The school lasted only one year. The immigrant German Jews were neither affluent enough nor sufficiently Americanized in the 1850s to see the value of sending their sons to an institution of higher learning or to grasp the need for English-speaking rabbis.[1]

THE REALITY

The Civil War deferred further action, but in the postwar era the failure of the Rabbinical Conference of 1869 to bear any fruits led Wise to campaign for the fulfillment of his dreams. In June 1871, Wise had brought to Cincinnati a group of southern and midwestern colleagues who were using his prayer book, *Minhag America*. He used the occasion to resubmit the idea of a rabbinical seminary and publicized the idea in his *Israelite*. He found surprising support from the editor of the *New York Herald*, who wrote as follows on June 11, 1871:

A GREAT NEED

[There is] the great need of an English ministry for our Jewish congregations . . . if the rising generations of Hebrews are to be kept within the fold of Judaism and obedient to the faith of their fathers. There is not a single such rabbi in this city and very few such in the country. They are all of foreign importation.

One of Wise's New York opponents, Rev. Samuel M. Isaacs of Congregation Shaarey Tefila, took the *Herald* to task in his newspaper, the *Jewish Messenger*, for overestimating the importance of the Cincinnati conference. Isaacs assured the *Herald* that the Orthodox were aware of the need for English-speaking rabbis and for a seminary in which to train them. He advised the *Herald* to "leave Jewish law to the Rabbis and the Jews." The *Herald*'s editor, undaunted, pursued the argument in a lengthy editorial published on July 22, 1872, in which he reiterated the need for English-speaking rabbis and preachers: "to maintain Judaism in America something more than a mere recitation of prayers in Hebrew and German is necessary." Give Jewish youth "religious as well as secular education in their vernacular, and there will not be much cause to complain of empty pews and neglected synagogues." This struck such a responsive chord in Isaacs's heart that he republished the entire editorial in the *Jewish Messenger*.[2] But the many factions in New York could not get together to create a seminary at that time.

The determination of Moritz Loth, the president of Wise's Congregation Bene Jeshurun, produced the 1873 gathering that founded the Union of American Hebrew Congregations (UAHC), whose aim was the creation of a "Hebrew Theological College." The Panic of 1873, whose reverberations were to keep the country depressed for at least five years, augured poorly for the establishment of Wise's Hebrew Union College (HUC), but at the first council of the UAHC in July 1874, delegates from 55 congregations voted unanimously for the college to be located in Cincinnati, with Isaac M. Wise as president. A number of factors contributed to the timing. The Civil War had unleashed much public anti-Semitism, largely leveled against German-Jewish immigrants. The war had a strong Americanizing influence on these immigrants and, even more, on their sons who had been in uniform. From 1869 to 1873, Cincinnati had been the locus of a series of well-publicized court cases fighting to have Bible reading eliminated from the public schools, exposing the Jews to uncomfortable limelight. So the Jewish community was very ready for the education of American spokesmen. When the University of Cincinnati opened in 1873, it made possible Wise's plan that his ordinees would be university graduates. Furthermore, in 1870 Henry Adler of Lawrenceburg, Indiana, offered Wise $10,000 to open the school, and in 1873 he threatened to withdraw the gift if plans were not forthcoming.[3]

The formal opening of HUC took place on October 3, 1875, at Wise's Plum

Street Temple. Addresses were given by Bernhard Bettmann, who had been elected president of the newly appointed board of governors and was to serve in that office until 1910, and by Wise's colleagues Solomon Sonnenschein of St. Louis and Max Lilienthal of Cincinnati. Wise limited his own remarks to saying that his joy in seeing his 25-year dream achieved left him without words to do justice to his feelings.[4]

THE PRESIDENTS AND THE FACULTIES

Each of the presidents has been treated in individual biographies elsewhere in this volume. The first president was Isaac Mayer Wise, 1875–1900. After Wise's death, Professor Moses Mielziner was acting president until his own death in February 1903, when Professor Gotthard Deutsch completed the semester. Kaufmann Kohler served from 1903 to 1921, succeeded by the first alumnus to be elected to the office, Julian Morgenstern, 1921–1947. Stephen Wise created his Jewish Institute of Religion (JIR) and served as its president from 1922 to 1948, when Nelson Glueck, Morgenstern's successor at HUC, became president of JIR as well. After the two institutions combined in 1950, Glueck served as president of HUC-JIR until his death in 1971. Since that date, Alfred Gottschalk has led the ever-growing HUC-JIR. Details of their administrations and of the faculties who served under them for the school's first century can be found in *Hebrew Union College–Jewish Institute of Religion at One Hundred Years*, edited by Samuel E. Karff (Cincinnati, 1976).

THE CAMPUSES

Cincinnati

The first class met the day after the dedication, in the basement vestry rooms of Lilienthal's Mound Street Temple. By 1877, with the need for three classrooms, the school was moved to the more commodious basement of Wise's Plum Street Temple. A new class was added each year, and in January 1880, in anticipation of the fifth council of the UAHC, Wise notified Loth, the UAHC president, that with six classes anticipated for the following year, a building had become a necessity. Wise described his ideal: a building of three stories, 50 by 60 feet, that would cost about $27,500; with a "Home" (dormitory), the cost might be $60,000. The UAHC council authorized the donation or purchase of land for the erection of a building. A committee was appointed and by 1881 had secured a bargain, paying $25,250 for the former Slevin Homestead at 484 West Sixth Street in a fashionable neighborhood. The three-story building was easily converted to provide a president's office and library on the ground floor, classrooms on the second and, eventually, a chapel on the third.[5]

By the first decade of the twentieth century, the majority of Cincinnati's established Jews had fled to the suburban hills, taking boarding students with them, and the University of Cincinnati had moved to the Clifton area. In 1910 the Hughes High School, attended by many entering students of HUC, was given a new building across from the university. The HUC library was pushing out its walls. All these factors demanded a new campus. As early as 1903 the UAHC had appointed a committee to explore a move. Eventually an 18-acre plot was purchased for $31,000. By then the UAHC's primary concern was dealing with the desperate needs of the growing East European refugee community; raising funds for a new HUC was secondary. The Eastern Jewish establishment was contributing its resources to the Jewish Theological Seminary, considering it a way of helping Americanize the Russian Jews. Fortunately, a gift of $50,000 from the Chicago philanthropist Julius Rosenwald and $25,000 from New York's tireless donor to Jewish causes, Jacob Schiff, paid for the two-story classroom administration building, while Isaac W. Bernheim, a successful Louisville distiller, contributed the full cost of a library building. Both were erected in the crenellated Tudor-style brick that was the fashion for school architecture in America just before World War I. The formal dedication of the new buildings took place on January 21–23, 1913, during a biennial of the UAHC. A historic address was delivered by Solomon Schechter, president of the Jewish Theological Seminary.[6]

In 1916 the Cincinnati physician Hiram B. Weiss began urging the board of governors to be more concerned with student health. World War I precluded more than the formation of a committee to investigate the quality of the homes where students were boarding, but by the early 1920s plans were afoot to create a dormitory. The National Federation of Temple Sisterhoods raised the necessary quarter of a million dollars, and the building was in use by the fall of 1924, despite the fact that the architect had failed to put closets in each room, which had to be added. Mrs. J. Walter Freiberg, widow of a former UAHC president, was inspired to have a separate gymnasium built, complete with swimming pool. It was opened soon after the dormitory. The Bernheim Library, whose collections had been organized and greatly expanded by the energetic librarian Adolph S. Oko, was outgrown. Oko prevailed on the board of the UAHC to permit him to raise the funds needed for a new library building, built to Oko's design and dedicated in 1931.

The post–World War II expansion of Reform Judaism in America led the College's board of governors to develop in 1957 a master plan for the next 20 years. In anticipation of a growing student body and faculty and the need for enlarged and renovated facilities, the board in 1959 authorized the construction of a new high-rise library and administrative building on the Cincinnati campus. Attached to it was a wing for housing the rare-book and manuscript collections. The Sisterhood dormitory was totally renovated, its dining room enlarged and a separate apartment made for the resident matron as well as several bedrooms and a basement suite for official guests. Two ground-floor rooms were altered for meeting or classroom use.

Although funds for these expansions had to be furnished through bank loans,

President Nelson Glueck decided to build an additional dormitory in a valley behind the older dormitory. His initial thought was to provide housing for the increasing number of married students, but they rejected the thought of communal living. He then announced that the new building would be for graduate rabbinical students, leaving the older dormitory for undergraduates. In the end, the new dormitory became a residence for occasional visiting groups and an overflow storage for the American Jewish Archives and the library.

Subsequently, the original administration building was altered to provide more classroom space. The chapel was redecorated with the surviving ark from a Polish synagogue, the choir loft removed and the *bima* platform lowered and expanded. The former reading room of the Oko Library building was converted into a museum to house the college's growing collection of ceremonial objects and Glueck's archaeological artifacts. When much of this material was moved to the Los Angeles campus, the space was converted to a gallery for changing exhibits.

In 1988 the former Odd Fellows Hall adjacent to the campus was put up for sale and, largely through the generosity of Manuel D. Mayerson of the board of governors, was acquired as a conference center and museum exhibit space.[7]

New York

For Stephen Samuel Wise, Hebrew Union College was too mired in the German-Jewish traditions of universalism, anti-Zionism and assimilation. By 1922 he and his Free Synagogue had achieved stellar recognition on the New York scene as champions of liberalism, free speech and social activism. Wise had already provided study programs for would-be rabbis and had given private *s'michah* to Louis I. Newman. The prospective erection of the Free Synagogue's own building at 40 West 68th Street provided a locus for a rabbinical school, although during the first year, classes had to be held at Temple Israel. Attempts to secure UAHC sponsorship failed. Nor was Wise able to find a competent leader to succeed him as president. Wise ended up raising funds, presiding over the school, recruiting the students and selecting the faculty for the rest of his life. The Jewish Institute of Religion from 1922 to 1949 was in every way his baby. For most of that period, the four-story Tudor-style building proved adequate for both JIR and the Free Synagogue. A number of attempts to merge HUC and JIR ended in failure until mid-1948, when economic pressures on JIR, Wise's advancing years and the succession of Nelson Glueck to the presidency of HUC made the time ripe for a merger, not totally completed until 1950, by which time Wise had died. The combined school came to be known as Hebrew Union College–Jewish Institute of Religion (HUC-JIR).[8] One of the first acts of Glueck's building program was to add a fifth floor to the New York campus to provide space for the growing library.[9]

In 1976 Dr. Jules Backman, Research Professor of Economics at New York University, became chairman of the HUC-JIR board of governors. He and Dean

Paul Steinberg determined to follow the example set by HUC in California and by the Jewish Theological Seminary and to move the New York campus close to a major university. Once again the chief motivations were a growing student body, an aging facility and an ever-expanding library. A large parking lot adjacent to the NYU campus at the corner of Fourth Street and Broadway was purchased. With major financial assistance from the Brookdale Foundation, a six-story building, designed by the leading architectural firm of Harrison & Abramowitz, was built and dedicated on October 29, 1979. Its ground floor contains a handsome chapel with ark and windows designed by the Israeli artist Yaakov Agam. A museum gallery affords changing displays of contemporary Jewish artists. A study center provides opportunities to consult microfilms of the materials at Cincinnati's American Jewish Archives. On the floor below is a dividable conference center and student lunchroom, as well as practice rooms for cantorial students and a well-equipped educational resource center. The upper floors contain a spacious library and stacks, administrative offices and classrooms. The roof can be used for seasonal celebrations.

Los Angeles

The growth of the Los Angeles area after World War II made it home to the largest Jewish community outside New York. To meet the needs of that community, HUC in 1947 established a part-time College of Jewish Studies aimed at teacher training and adult education. The Conservative movement's similar institution, called the University of Judaism, was promoted as the West Coast branch of the Jewish Theological Seminary. Motivated by the alumnus Jack Skirball, who had left the pulpit rabbinate for a very successful career producing motion pictures and acquiring real estate, the board of governors and President Nelson Glueck were persuaded to open a prerabbinic program at Wilshire Boulevard Temple in 1954. Two years later, a former home for asthmatic Jewish girls at 8745 Appian Way, high in the Hollywood Hills, was purchased to provide the first two years of rabbinic studies. The student body and the library expanded rapidly, and the difficulty of access to the site made evident the need for a move. By 1970, land adjacent to the University of Southern California had been acquired, and a handsome, functional building was erected at 3077 University Avenue, primarily with funds raised locally. It was formally dedicated on November 5, 1971. In addition to classrooms and chapel, the building houses the nationally recognized Skirball Museum of Jewish Art, whose rapid growth helped precipitate the creation of the Hebrew Union College Cultural Center for American Jewish Life on a 15-acre site adjacent to the San Diego Freeway, between West Los Angeles and the San Fernando Valley. In addition to an enlarged museum of art and artifacts of American Jewish life, the Center has an auditorium and conference center.[10]

Jerusalem

Nelson Glueck's heart was in the land of Israel, so as soon as the State of Israel became a reality he began efforts to achieve an HUC presence in Jerusalem. His stature as an archaeologist earned him generous concessions from the government of the new state. In 1954 they offered him a two-acre site at 13 King David Street on payment of one Israeli pound per year, provided a building was erected within five years. Vehement opposition from the Orthodox rabbinate and problems with a building contractor delayed completion of the first building. It was dedicated in festive ceremonies March 27–31, 1963, with most of Israel's dignitaries participating. Academic programs were introduced the following July at a summer dedication attended by 150 members of the Central Conference of American Rabbis. The building, designated the Center for Biblical Archaeology, houses classrooms, offices and a synagogue in whose design Glueck took special pride. Its windows are narrow open slits, and the building was sited to catch the prevailing winds, thereby providing natural air conditioning.[11]

After the Six-Day War in 1967, American interest in Israel reached its zenith, and increasing groups of Reform Jews visited the land and the College. The Progressive movement (as Reform in Israel is called) expanded, and so did programs at the Jerusalem school of HUC-JIR. By 1983, two additional acres had been secured, and designs for more buildings on the Jerusalem campus had been prepared by the prize-winning architect Moshe Safdie. The week of November 3–10, 1986, marked the dedication of the first of several new buildings: the Skirball Center for Biblical and Archaeological Research, housing classrooms, a laboratory and a museum; and the Academic Center, with space for rabbinic and cantorial classes. On March 10, 1988, the large Abramov Library was formally opened. The campus includes Beit Shmuel Youth Center, a hostel sponsored by the World Union for Progressive Judaism.[12]

THE STUDENTS

When Isaac M. Wise began his first class there were about ten students, most of them children from his religious school. Seven others joined the group during the first year, including an 11-year-old girl. Wise remembered the group as "fourteen noisy boys [of whom] four wanted to study, and ten solely to create a disturbance." The four serious students were characteristic of those whom Wise was to attract to his school. They remained for eight years, attending classes first at high school and then at the University of Cincinnati. Their HUC classes came after school. These four lads were to become his first graduates. They ranged in age from David Philipson, 13, to Henry Berkowitz, 18. All came from modest circumstances and from different communities. Israel Aaron was from Lancaster, Pennsylvania, the son of the deceased cantor of that community; Joseph Krauskopf, the only foreign-born member of the class, was an orphan from Fall River, Massachusetts; Philipson came from Columbus, Ohio; and Berkowitz was from Pittsburgh.[13]

To secure students, Wise took advantage of every speaking engagement to promote his college. New York remained diffident toward the inland school, although Rabbi Gustav Gottheil of Temple Emanu-El in 1879 opened a pre-rabbinic program partially financed by the UAHC. He ran it for two years before it petered out.[14]

In the school's fourth year, the board of governors, in an attempt to stimulate academic excellence, offered an award to the two best students in the oldest class. In what seems to have been the first in a long history of student challenges of administrative decisions, the five students indicated their wish not to be subjected to discrimination from their classmates. In later years endowed prizes became part of the annual graduation exercises, but after many years of being announced at the time of ordination, they are now awarded by the faculty after the close of the academic year.[15]

The size of the rabbinic school's student body has fluctuated widely over the years due to economic and recruitment patterns. The threat of wartime drafts enlarged the student body; depressions and recessions depleted it. Twice during Isaac M. Wise's administration and twice during Kohler's, only one student was ordained. Resistance to the Vietnam War produced classes that reached an all-time high of 56 ordinees in 1974. The size of graduating classes is a source of tension between the Union of American Hebrew Congregations, which wants rabbis available for any congregation that can afford one, and the Central Conference of American Rabbis, which is concerned that flooding the market leaves rabbis unemployed and decreases the opportunities for upward mobility.[16]

HUC has always been open to women students. Isaac M. Wise, in reports to the board of governors, made frequent and proud allusions to the two women—Emily Bloch, his niece, and Jenny Mannheimer, the daughter of Professor Sigmund Mannheimer—to whom he granted degrees that gave them teaching careers. The former received a B.H. and B.A., the latter a B.H. and B.L. It remained for the daughter of another faculty member, Martha Neumark, to challenge the administration on the right of women to be ordained. This evolved from the national furor over women's right to vote. The HUC debate opened in the spring of 1921 with Martha's request to be considered for a holiday pulpit should one be available. A joint committee drawn from the faculty and board of governors produced an equivocal report on whether to ordain women, and the faculty issued its own somewhat negative acceptance of the idea. The CCAR was consulted at its 1922 convention and voted overwhelmingly in favor, but the board of governors determined to maintain the status quo. This evoked the following protest from one of Wise's first students and an honorary member of the board of governors, Rabbi Henry Berkowitz, then living in retirement in Atlantic City:

Dear Colleagues:

It was with deep regret that I learned from the report of the proceedings at a recent meeting of the Board that action was taken adversely to the proposal that the full freedom of the Hebrew Union College be officially granted to a woman and the possibility of her attaining to the degree of ''Rabbi'' was denied.

When the Board submitted this question to the Central Conference of American Rabbis it created the presumption that in such a matter the action of the Conference was sought because this was a question to be left to rabbinic decision. That decision overwhelmingly declared that there could be no just reason for barring any duly qualified woman who might claim it from achieving the title of ''Rabbi.'' The Board by its action seems to me to have deliberately repudiated the authority to which it submitted the question.

As the Conference embodies the entire body of our graduates the Board has evidently set aside the wishes of its own Alumni. From its inception the founder of the College welcomed girls as students. This fact justifies the presumption that he believed the time had passed when sex was to be held to be an insuperable barrier to a woman's claims to share in the service of the ministry.

For all these reasons I ask that a record be made of my demurrer against the decision of the Board in this matter and of my request that the decision be reconsidered.

The board remained firm in its decision, a signal that lay domination over the rabbinate still prevailed. Over the next half century women, including the convert Regina O'Hara, were admitted to classes, but ordination was denied until 1972, by which time women had achieved full recognition in all other positions in the Reform movement. In that year Sally Priesand, with much fanfare, was heralded as the pioneer woman rabbi, to be followed by others: enrollment of women at HUC-JIR is now rapidly approaching 50 percent of the student body. Acceptance of women as rabbis is now taken for granted in Reform congregations. The Conservative movement, reluctantly persuaded to follow the Reform example, remains divided on the issue.[17]

During the 1980s, similar debates confronted all branches of the Reform movement over the admission and ordination of homosexuals. For many years, all applicants to HUC-JIR were subjected to psychological screening aimed at rejecting, among others, those predisposed to homosexuality. When most members of the psychological community announced that homosexuality was innate rather than a condition of choice, the College, over the vehement objections of some members of the faculty, began admitting any applicant suitable to the rabbinical calling regardless of sexual orientation.[18]

In the early years of the Cincinnati school, only junior and senior students were permitted to serve in congregations, and then only on the holidays. They were expected to preach from memory using the published sermons of ordained rabbis. By the time of Morgenstern's presidency, the number of congregations had grown to the point where students were needed on a more frequent basis, especially in congregations too small to afford a rabbi. An ever-growing program of weekly, biweekly and monthly positions developed, providing these congregations with part-time rabbinic ministations and offering the students hands-on training. In recent years, all campuses have offered students opportunities to render service in hospitals, social-service agencies, the organizations of Reform Judaism and youth work and as interns attached to larger congregations.

HUC-JIR is rapidly approaching its 125th anniversary and the ordination of its 2000th rabbinic graduate. Not every graduate has desired or proved suitable to the congregational rabbinate, nor has the growth of the number of congregations in the UAHC kept pace with the number of rabbis available. As a consequence, HUC-JIR graduates can be found in numerous occupations in all parts of the world. As Professor Jacob Rader Marcus loves to boast, "The sun never sets on a graduate of the Hebrew Union College!" Outside the United States and Canada, alumni can be found in Australia, Brazil, Chile, the United Kingdom, Germany, Israel, New Zealand, South Africa and the Virgin Islands. Some are serving congregations affiliated with other movements or unaffiliated; others staff national bodies of Reform Judaism and other agencies. Still others are chaplains in the armed forces or institutions. Hillel Foundations and other college service or academic posts account for another group. Some are educators outside congregations, while a large group has left the rabbinate for a variety of secular enterprises.[19]

SCHOOLS AND PROGRAMS

Education

Among Isaac M. Wise's many dreams was that his college would serve as a university of service to the larger Jewish community. The first successful effort to reach out toward the training of other than rabbis occurred in 1923, when Morgenstern, at the instigation of the New York Association of Reform Rabbis, agreed to sponsor the HUC School for Teachers, headed by Abraham Franzblau, later to teach at the Cincinnati campus. Classes were held at Temple Emanu-El, and an ever-growing group of would-be teachers took courses or completed the program until the Depression ended it, despite attempts by New Yorkers and the UAHC to keep it alive. In January 1947, under Franzblau's direction, the School of Education was revived in New York, eventually offering degrees in education. After an initial spurt of activity, this school declined in enrollment but remains a part of the academic curriculum of the New York campus of HUC-JIR, providing training for teachers and principals in Reform Jewish education and offering an M.A. in the field. In addition, extension programs, under the direction of Rabbi Kerry Olitzky, are conducted by the School of Education in various parts of the New York metropolitan area. In 1967, before its move from Appian Way, the California campus, at the instigation of Professor William Cutter, opened the Rhea Hirsch School of Education, which now, directed by Professor Sara S. Lee, offers Ph.D. and M.A. programs in Jewish Education;

conducts joint degree programs with the University of Southern California; trains teachers, librarians, and early educators; and conducts summer institutes.[20]

School of Sacred Music

For most Reform temples before World War II, music was provided by non-Jewish organists, choir directors, choirs and/or soloists. Only the larger congregations in the Northeast and a few elsewhere had cantors, and many of these lacked training in the tradition, relying totally on composers—including non-Jews—to supply their musical agenda. The growing demand for Jewish authenticity that accompanied and followed the birth of the State of Israel produced the HUC School of Sacred Music, opened at the New York campus in 1948, at first under the direction of Professor Abraham Franzblau and later influenced by the musicologist and polymath professor Eric Werner, who had first advocated the school. The original five-year program not only prepared cantors in all aspects of music and the Jewish tradition but also provided them with substantive courses in Hebrew language, literature, Jewish education, history and philosophy. In 1983 the School of Sacred Music became postgraduate, requiring all applicants for admission to have completed a bachelor's degree. The course was reduced to four years, and the School was authorized to grant a degree of Master of Sacred Music to those who completed the program and were invested as cantors. Beginning in 1986, all entering classes, like those in the rabbinical school, spend their first year at the Jerusalem campus, thereby enhancing their grasp of the Hebrew language. In New York the cantorial students frequently perform in concerts for the public, both as soloists and as a chorus, at the campus and in various concert halls. More than 250 cantors have been invested by the school, whose program has become a model for other movements in Judaism.[21]

Communal Service

California has been the source of many innovations in the Reform movement. During his tenure as dean of the California campus, Alfred Gottschalk responded to the growing demand of Jewish philanthropic and social-service agencies for professionals who would be schooled in advanced Judaica by proposing that HUC create a School of Jewish Communal Service. This came into existence in 1968, with Gerald Bubis as its first director. The school has grown rapidly, providing individuals already in the field and those preparing for it with opportunities for certification or master's degrees, not only in communal service, but also—in cooperation with other graduate schools—in education, social work, public administration and gerontology.[22]

Graduate Studies

From its very beginning, HUC has welcomed the attendance of Christian clergy. This attitude became institutionalized in 1947 when a School of Graduate

Studies for both Jewish and Christian clergy was created on the Cincinnati campus, offering doctoral studies and degrees. Interfaith fellowships were established for Christians, many of whom have become academics in seminaries and universities and help spread their knowledge of Jews and Judaism.

For rabbis in the field, HUC-JIR has from its inception offered programs leading to doctoral degrees. Originally the degree earned was Doctor of Divinity (D.D.). In more recent years, that degree has been granted *honoris causa* to alumni who have rendered good service to the movement after 25 years in the field. Currently, candidates can earn a Doctor of Hebrew Letters (D.H.L.) with minimal residence requirements or a Doctor of Ministry (D.Min.) degree in pastoral care. A Ph.D. may be pursued only in residence.[23]

Biblical Archaeology

From its inception under Nelson Glueck's direction, the Jerusalem campus has set a high priority on the study of Bible and on exploration in biblical archaeology. With occasional cooperation from other institutions of higher learning, it has conducted ongoing digs and has achieved some remarkable finds, notably at Tel Dan. Volunteers spend varying amounts of time under the guidance of Professor Avraham Biran, learning both science and lore in the process.[24]

Archives and Libraries

The American Jewish Archives, founded in 1947 by Professor Jacob Marcus, took over the facilities of the original Bernheim Library on the Cincinnati campus. The building, subsequently remodeled, provides a state-of-the-art archive for the study and preservation of the Western Hemisphere Jewish experience through research, publications, collection of important source materials and a vigorous public-outreach program. The large collection of data on microfilm at the American Jewish Archives is available at each of the HUC campuses. The Archives offers fellowships to researchers, publishes books and periodicals and cosponsors the American Jewish Periodical Center, which preserves on microfilm all available Jewish periodicals published in America before 1925 and selected items since. Professor Marcus was responsible for building the Archives collections and directing its operations. Abraham Peck is the current administrative director.

The College's original library, according to Isaac M. Wise, consisted of a few donated prayer books that were stored in a wooden trunk "to keep out the mice." By the time the College had acquired its first building in 1881, the library had begun to acquire the tools of the trade, necessitating the appointment of librarians, usually professors. In 1906 the Cincinnati campus secured from the cataloguing department of the New York Public Library the college's first professional librarian, Adolph S. Oko. A year later Oko succeeded Professor Schloessinger as librarian and began to exert a profound influence on the entire campus with his strong personality and opinions to match. In the aftermath of World

War I, Oko went to Europe and acquired many of the library's unique incunabula and rare manuscripts. His own interests in Spinoza and in Jewish music led to separate rooms for the large collections of each in the library built to his specifications in 1931. He was succeeded by an alumnus, Walter Rothman, a pale personality by comparison with Oko, whose mantle fell on his longtime cataloguer Moses Marx. Marx's training in the Prussian army made him a feared martinet, but his knowledge of Judaica and Hebraica was encyclopedic. Another alumnus, Irving Levey, followed Rothman, but the library became the institution that it is today under the direction of Herbert Zafren, an able professional who became librarian in 1966. The New York campus, from the days of Stephen Wise, rejoiced in its librarian, I. Edward Kiev, a genial alumnus. He accumulated many outstanding collections of both classic and modern Jewish works while the two institutions were independent. Kiev was succeeded by the scholarly Dr. Philip I. Miller, a professional librarian. Los Angeles and Jerusalem have also developed remarkable collections under their librarians, to the point where the combined resources are rapidly approaching 650,000 volumes. The Abramov Library in Jerusalem, dedicated in 1900, houses, among other collections, that of the late Dr. Fritz Bamberger, who for many years served as special assistant to Presidents Nelson Glueck and Alfred Gottschalk. Bamberger's great interest in Spinoza provides Jerusalem with valuable material that complements the Cincinnati collection of the works of this seminal thinker. The Abramov Library has also acquired the archaeological library of the late Yigael Yadin. With the destruction of Europe's centers, the HUC-JIR libraries now compose one of the world's largest collections of Hebraica and Judaica from the tenth century to the present.[25]

Museums

For many years the Cincinnati campus accumulated artifacts from a variety of donors, a collection that received sporadic display in its buildings. Some of the Nelson Glueck's archaeological findings needed appropriate display space, so the 1931 library building was remodeled for the purpose. With the building of the California campus, space was provided for the rapidly growing Skirball Museum, and many of Cincinnati's objects were sent there. A small gallery for traveling exhibits remains in the Cincinnati building. The New York campus also provides gallery space, which has been the site of changing exhibits devoted primarily to the works of little-known Jewish artists working in varied media. The Jerusalem campus also has a display area, primarily for the school's archaeological discoveries.[26]

Outreach

This quadri-based university has been recognized as a significant center of Jewish scholarship. Each of the campuses annually hosts scholars, alumni-in-residence and speakers of note. Each campus conducts scholarly seminars on a variety of spiritual topics, involving not only distinguished members of the faculty but also other scholars of eminence in the disciplines addressed. The ideas and influence emanating from Hebrew Union College–Jewish Institute of Religion cannot be measured. They reach all parts of the globe in more than 1,000 liberal congregations, in major Jewish organizations and institutions, in the academic world of research and scholarship and in the cultural life of many communities. The dreams of Isaac Mayer Wise and of Stephen Samuel Wise have far exceeded their imaginations in fulfillment.

NOTES

1. James G. Heller, *Isaac Mayer Wise: His Life, Work and Thought* (New York, 1965), ch. 17; Michael A. Meyer, "A Centennial History," in *Hebrew Union College–Jewish Institute of Religion at One Hundred Years*, ed. Samuel E. Karff (Cincinnati, 1976), p. 15. Heller, p. 275, mistakenly dates the opening of Zion College to 1856.

2. Heller, *Wise*, pp. 396ff.; Morris U. Schappes, "On Rabbinical Education," *A Documentary History of the Jews in the United States, 1654–1875* (New York, 1950), pp. 554–57, 733, n. 7.

3. "Panic of 1873," *Encyclopedia of American History*, ed. Richard B. Morris (New York, 1965), pp. 251, 539; Max B. May, *Isaac Mayer Wise, the Founder of American Judaism: A Biography* (New York, 1916), pp. 294ff.; Morris Schappes, "Separating Religion from Public Schools," *A Documentary History*, pp. 520–37; Meyer, "Centennial History," p. 17.

4. May, *Wise*, pp. 298ff.

5. Ibid.; *Proceedings of the Union of American Hebrew Congregations* 2:794, 924ff.; Meyer, "Centennial History," p. 19.

6. Meyer, "Centennial History," pp. 70ff.; the dedication date is derived from *American Jewish Year Book* 15 (1913): 253; Schechter's address is excerpted in "The College and the Seminary, 1901–1913," *American Jewish Archives* 26 (November 1974): 153ff.

7. Meyer, "Centennial History," passim. In building the new dormitory, Glueck revealed some thoughts to me. Still smarting from his failure to diminish the New York school (Meyer, pp. 187ff.), he stated, "I've spent four million dollars to anchor this school to Cincinnati!" Mayerson Hall acquisition and dedication are reported in *HUC-JIR Annual Report* for 1988, 1989.

8. Meyer, "Centennial History," pp. 137ff.

9. Ibid., pp. 205ff.

10. Ibid., pp. 190ff.; *HUC-JIR Annual Reports*, 1988–1991.

11. Meyer, "Centennial History," pp. 208ff.

12. *HUC-JIR Annual Reports*, 1988–1991.

13. Jacob R. Marcus describes the first class in "Hebrew Union College–Jewish Institute of Religion—A Centennial Documentary," *American Jewish Archives* 26 (November 1974): 104. Wise's reminiscence originally appeared in his German-language periodical *Die Deborah*, quoted by Heller, *Wise*, p. 416; data on Israel Aaron can be found in David A. Brener, *The Jews of Lancaster, Pennsylvania* (Lancaster, 1979), p. 51.

14. Gottheil reported starting his second year with 35 students and ending with 29. Among those he graduated were Bernard Drachman, who adhered to Orthodoxy, finished

his rabbinical education at Breslau and later became one of the founding professors of the Jewish Theological Seminary. Gottheil's son Richard became a noted professor at Columbia University. *Proceedings*, 1879–1885, 2:880.

15. Ibid.

16. *The Graduates of Hebrew Union College–Jewish Institute of Religion: A Centennial Register* (1975); minutes of the Joint Commission on Rabbinical Placement, passim.

17. Meyer, "Centennial History," pp. 98ff.; letter from Berkowitz to the board of governors dated June 9, 1923 (copy in the American Jewish Archives).

18. "Report of the Ad Hoc Committee on Homosexuality and the Rabbinate," CCAR *Yearbook* 99 (1989): 133ff.

19. Reports of the Director of Placement, CCAR *Yearbooks*, passim; *HUC-JIR Rabbinic Alumni Roster*, 1988, p. 69.

20. Meyer, "Centennial History," passim; *American Jewish Year Book* 89 (1989): 460.

21. *HUC-JIR Annual Reports*, 1977–1991.

22. Meyer, "Centennial History," p. 198; *American Jewish Year Book* 89 (1989): 460; *HUC-JIR Annual Reports*, 1977–1991.

23. *HUC-JIR Annual Reports*, 1977–1991.

24. Ibid.

25. Meyer, "Centennial History," passim; *HUC-JIR Annual Reports*, 1977–1991.

26. Ibid.

CENTRAL CONFERENCE OF AMERICAN RABBIS

PRELUDES

Among Isaac M. Wise's many plans for American Jewry was the creation of an ongoing rabbinic body to synthesize the best ideas for the promotion of Judaism. Before coming to this country, Wise had attended the conference of Reform rabbis in Frankfurt-am Main in 1844. Although his participation has not been fully documented, the conference probably motivated his efforts to train leaders for America's Jews.[1]

It was Wise, the recently arrived immigrant, who in 1848 first proposed a lay-rabbinic conference, which never materialized. Rabbis did come together in Cleveland in 1855 and in Philadelphia in 1869 in what Wise and other attendees hoped would become annual meetings. Later, in his first presidential message in 1890 to the Central Conference of American Rabbis (CCAR), Wise specified why these previous meetings had failed. He cited, as the primary cause, divisions of opinion as to the amount and nature of reform. Five years earlier Wise had recognized that the Pittsburgh Conference over which he reluctantly presided had produced a platform that enunciated an extreme view of Reform Judaism. At the very session that approved the Pittsburgh Platform, Wise said, "Gentlemen, what are we going to do with this Declaration of Independence?" Experience had taught him that such a statement could only prove divisive, and indeed it did, pushing the more traditional Easterners into opening the Jewish Theological Seminary as a rival to Wise's Hebrew Union College. The 18 rabbis at Pittsburgh planned to convene the following May in Cincinnati. As with all the previous conferences, there was no immediate sequel.[2]

BIRTH OF THE CCAR

On March 29, 1889, Wise turned 70, an occasion marked by his congregation on April 6 with an outpouring of testimonials from all parts of the city and the country. Disciples and representatives of many organizations added their tributes. Cantor Moritz Goldstein of Congregation K.K. Bene Israel (now Rockdale Temple) composed and performed a cantata. This occasion was followed by a celebration at Hebrew Union College (HUC). The euphoria of these celebrations undoubtedly induced Wise to further his dream of an enduring rabbinical conference. Despite the furor engendered by the Pittsburgh Platform, a number rabbis had endorsed it. By the summer of 1889, Wise had ordained 20 of his students. These rabbis provided him with a putative power base, predominantly in the Midwest and South. Wise arranged with David Philipson, by then rabbi of Cincinnati's Bene Israel, to prepare and circulate a proposal to rabbis who might be attending the July 9–10 council of the Union of American Hebrew Congregations (UAHC) for the formation of a "Central Conference of American Rabbis."[3]

On July 9, 1889, Philipson's resolution was passed and a committee of five was appointed to plan the organization. The following day the committee presented a resolution that pointed to the failure of prior conferences but proposed to go ahead with an executive of five officers. The work of prior conferences in Germany and America would serve as guides "in an endeavor to maintain in unbroken historic succession the formulated expression of Jewish thought and life of each era." Any rabbi who was serving a Hebrew congregation or who had held such office could be admitted if he applied before the following Passover. Thereafter, membership would be open to a wide gamut of categories that included not only Ph.D.s with ordination but also autodidactic preachers, teachers of religion, authors of eminent books on Jewish theology or literature or anyone who rendered practical service to the cause of Judaism, all subject to majority vote of the body in order to be admitted. Annual dues were set at five dollars, with paid-up members entitled to a free copy of the association's publications. Members were expected to attend all meetings or provide a letter excusing their absence.

Rabbi Samuel Adler, the only surviving attendee of all post-1840 conferences, was named honorary president. Wise had wanted Adler to be president of the CCAR, but Adler refused, so Wise was elected unanimously and continued in office for the rest of his life. Elected with him were Samuel Sale of St. Louis, vice-president; Henry Berkowitz of Kansas City, recording secretary; David Philipson of Cincinnati, corresponding secretary; Aaron Hahn of Cleveland, treasurer; and as Executive Committee: Lippmann Mayer of Pittsburgh, Professor Moses Mielziner of Cincinnati, Max Samfield of Memphis, Solomon H. Sonneschein of St. Louis, Joseph Stolz of Chicago, Maximilian Heller of New Orleans and Adolph Moses of Louisville.[4]

The preliminary meeting resolution also anticipated that the CCAR would meet annually in conjunction with the councils of the UAHC, but provision was made for the rabbis to set their own meeting schedule at other times. Business was to be completed at each session unless referred to a committee. Proceedings were to appear in an annual yearbook, which might also include appropriate essays and communications approved by the body. Copies of the yearbook would be distributed gratis to members, to the press and to interested parties, with additional copies available for sale. The outcome of the preliminary meeting would be sent to every Jewish paper in the land, inviting all rabbis to submit their names and payment of dues before the following Passover. The initial yearbook would include transcriptions in English of all prior conferences. One half of the five-dollar annual dues would be set aside as the "Relief Fund of the Conference" to prevent colleagues and their families from becoming objects of charity.

The resolution passed unanimously, and the CCAR was born.[5]

GROWTH AND DEVELOPMENT

By the first convention in Cleveland, July 13–15, 1890, Wise could boast in his President's Message that 90 rabbis had affiliated. From that auspicious beginning, the CCAR has grown beyond 1500 members in 1991 and increases by 40 to 50 annually. The patterns established at its beginnings have been maintained, testimony to Isaac M. Wise's ability to organize. Each session opens with a challenging presidential message, which is then referred to a committee with the responsibility of recommending appropriate actions to the plenum. The constitution and bylaws ratified by the first convention have been enlarged and amended occasionally, but the basics have survived. The originally broad admission requirements have necessarily narrowed to maintain high professional standards. Each convention contains its measure of worship, scholarship, resolutions on timely topics, many of which are ardently debated, and proposals of projects of service to the Reform movement. Lectures are presented by knowledgeable members or outside experts. For many years, tyros in the CCAR were "seen but not heard." In recent years, active participation of all age groups has been encouraged. By 1892, the convention had become separated from the councils of the UAHC and extended over five days, from Wednesday through Sunday. The earliest conventions were held in July to conform to the rabbis' vacation time, but as the CCAR grew in stature in the eyes of the movement, it was found feasible to hold conventions in June. This summer tradition was broken in 1889 when the CCAR paid tribute to its founder's 70th birthday by meeting in Cincinnati in March. March was not chosen again until 1970, when the CCAR held its first convention in Jerusalem. Although June remains the preferred month, the Executive Board has occasionally opted for spring meetings. Until 1968, the conventions ran over the Sabbath, with Friday evening devoted to the Conference Lecture and Saturday morning to the Conference Sermon. So many rabbis found it necessary to return to their congregations for weekend responsibilities that the conventions are almost invariably held from Sunday through Thursday.

YEARBOOK

More than 100 annual yearbooks have now been published. Each contains the record of that year's activities and includes the President's Message, reports of officers, full reports of committees and commissions, all major addresses, memorial tributes, resolutions and responsa (answers to queries, usually ritual) and the roster of membership. In 1892, the convention voted to engage a professional stenographer to record the proceedings. Until 1952, every debate was included in full, but since that date, only debates on major issues have been recorded; for others, only the outcome has been stated. The appendices now include a page of tribute to Isaac M. Wise, a list of charter members, a necrology, locations of past conventions, past presidents and honorary presidents, constitution and bylaws, actions of the convention and of the Executive Board, the year's audited balance sheet, the convention program and rosters of officers, committee personnel, honorary members and members listed both alphabetically and geographically. The volumes of the yearbook have been indexed individually and cumulatively. The yearbooks remain an invaluable source of data on the changing thought in the Reform movement and on the rabbinic participation in those changes.[6]

LEADERSHIP

The death of Isaac Mayer Wise in 1900 after 11 years as founding president brought to the post of president Joseph Silverman, of New York's Temple Emanu-El, who was recognized for having done more than anyone else to bond the recalcitrant eastern Reform rabbis to the Central Conference. He served for three years, to be followed by colleagues, most of whom served for two one-year terms. In CCAR elections, the most-sought office has been that of vice president, since this is tantamount to president-elect. Over the years this has led to considerable electioneering and pressures on the annual Committee on Nominations, which was appointed at the beginning of each convention and met in a series of late-night sessions in order to report its slate before the close of the convention. In 1975 the assemblage voted to move the nominating process away from conventions, and this has dignified the process.

Editing the yearbook was the responsibility of the elected recording secretary. In 1915 Isaac Marcuson was chosen for that office. As rabbi in Terre Haute, Indiana, and subsequently Macon, Georgia, he devoted more and more of his time to serving the CCAR, diligently editing all works produced by the organization until his death in 1952. He became in effect the CCAR's administrative secretary, not only editing the yearbook but also handling the sales of all CCAR publications. His post-office box in Macon became the CCAR's mailing address. His footlocker filled with books and files would arrive at each convention to serve as his CCAR office equipment. For many years his able assistant at conventions was the stenographer Rosie Mark from Cleveland. Both prided themselves on knowing the membership by name and face. Marcuson's death caused President Joseph Fink to designate Recording Secretary Sidney Lefkowitz to handle the paper work, Bertram Korn to edit the *Yearbook* and Sidney Regner to deal with publications.

Marcuson's demise brought the CCAR to the realization of its need for a permanent office in New York City with a full-time administrator. In November 1953, a special subcommittee met and defined the role of Executive Vice President. HUC-JIR had offered space on its campus. Rabbi Sidney L. Regner was unanimously elected and installed at the 1954 convention as Executive Vice President, and he served until his retirement in 1971. Regner demonstrated a splendid capacity for handling the myriad of administrative details and was vigilant in controlling the expenditures. As the CCAR's representative at many of the national bodies and meetings of various organizations, he was a bold defender of the CCAR's prerogatives and an advocate of Reform Judaism's positions. Past attempts to create regional associations of rabbis had been met by the CCAR with the fear that regional groups might fragment the body and dissipate its effectiveness. In 1946 the rabbis in the far West felt themselves to be so remote from headquarters that they organized a Western Association of Reform Rabbis. By 1955 the CCAR had come to recognize the value of regional groups and approved their formation with guidelines so that the central body would retain the right to be spokesperson. Regner began attending as many of the regional meetings as he could fit into his schedule, finding that they gave him both a platform and a sounding board. The subsequent members of the CCAR executive staff have followed this pattern of attendance. Many of the elected presidents also try to attend regional sessions.

Regner's announced retirement in 1971 brought Rabbi Joseph Glaser from a position as UAHC Regional Director for Northern California and the Pacific Northwest to the office of Executive Vice President. Glaser, who had acquired a degree in law before entering HUC-JIR, had already proved himself in the realms of social action and in government lobbying. An ardent and outspoken Zionist, he not only encouraged the CCAR to meet in Israel every seven years but also became actively involved with many of Israel's leaders. To the CCAR he brought a vision of its potential as a significant participant in all phases of Jewish and American life. He soon enlarged its committee structure and the scope of its activities.

In 1963 the CCAR had approved the employment of an administrative assistant to Sidney Regner. Norman Mirsky, a newly ordained rabbi, served for one year before finding a more congenial position on the HUC-JIR faculty. In the summer of 1974, Joseph Glaser secured the assistance of a rabbinical student from HUC-JIR, Elliot L. Stevens. On his ordination in 1975, the CCAR hired Stevens as Glaser's full-time administrative assistant, a position he has continued to hold, with the title Administrative Secretary of the CCAR. Among his many responsibilities are designing, producing and selling publications, editing the yearbooks, organizing conventions, serving as parliamentarian and compiling and producing statistics and compendia of CCAR resolutions, responsa and guidelines.

PLACEMENT

Until the late 1940s, when HUC and JIR merged into one institution, the placement of graduates of both HUC and JIR was usually negotiated by the president of each seminary. The presidents also assisted rabbis desirous of moving, although much of the mobility was determined by congregational committees that selected from rabbis of their acquaintance or recommended by persons they knew. Over the years, the CCAR conventions raised the issue of regulating placement, but no actions were taken. In 1947, 147 rabbis emerged from the World War II chaplaincy. Many sought new posts. In the ensuing scramble, three young, comparatively inexperienced rabbis secured three of the largest positions available, and the CCAR pressed for a placement system that would place higher priorities on experience. In 1951 a Provisional Placement Committee was established, with Rabbi Sidney Regner for the CCAR, Rabbi Louis Egelson for the UAHC and Richard Bluestein for HUC-JIR. The Provisional Committee was created as a service to rabbis and congregations, and both groups were encouraged but not obligated to use it. In the course of a decade, both the rabbis and the committee felt that a better system was needed. The rabbis approved the idea of taxing themselves to engage a full-time placement director, while a joint CCAR-UAHC committee hammered out the specifics of a placement plan. In 1963, CCAR President Leon Feuer chose Rabbi Malcolm Stern as director, subject to the eventual approval of the movement's three constituent bodies. Installed in 1964, Stern initiated a newsletter announcing all openings and the development of categories of eligibility based on years from ordination vis-à-vis the size of the congregation. Individual rabbis were pledged to seek positions only through the placement office and to act in accordance with its guidelines. To handle breakdowns of rabbi-congregation relationships, the late Theodore Broido of the UAHC staff developed a Joint Commission on Rabbinical-Congregation Relationship. Staffed by a part-time UAHC director with cochairpersons from the UAHC and CCAR, this commission can be summoned either by a rabbi or by congregational leadership to conciliate or arbitrate a dispute.

Malcolm Stern served as placement director from 1964 to 1980, when A. Stanley Dreyfus became his successor. Dreyfus's extensive knowledge of Jewish liturgy contributed immeasurably to the CCAR's output in this field. He began placement service in 1979 and retired in 1991, to be succeeded by Arnold Sher, a rabbi-lawyer, who remains in that position.

HEADQUARTERS

In the early 1960s, it became evident to both the CCAR and HUC-JIR that the expanded activities of the Conference demanded larger office space than

HUC-JIR could provide. In 1964 a suite in a new office building at 790 Madison Avenue was obtained. By 1980, major publishing operations forced the CCAR to find larger quarters, and an entire floor was rented at 21 East 40th Street until 1985, when inflationary rents forced it to move to a less expensive location at 192 Lexington Avenue, where the CCAR was joined by the Rabbinical Pension Board.

LITURGICAL PUBLICATION

The CCAR's first mandate from Issac Mayer Wise was to create a set of prayer books to help unify America's Reform movement, since the earlier liturgies of David Einhorn, Isaac Mayer Wise and Benjamin Szold had factionalized America's liberal Jews. At the 1890 meeting, a heavily debated process began that eventually chose Isaac Moses's English adaptation of David Einhorn's German *Olath Tamid*, the most radical of the prototypes. Volume 1 for Sabbaths, festivals and weekdays appeared in 1892, with the holy day volume 2 published two years later. An attempt to add Isaac M. Wise's hymnal (volume 4 of his *Minhag America*) was defeated, and the Cantors' Association of America, headed by Alois Kaiser, was given the task of producing a new hymnal, published in 1897.[7]

Despite their adoption by a large majority of Reform congregations, dissatisfaction with the contents of these prayer books was soon evident. The stilted Victorian English, much influenced by Germanic style, lost appeal for an American-born generation. The contents of the new Bible translation eventually published in 1917 by the Jewish Publication Society required changing many liturgical passages, and a revised volume 1 was published. The end of World War I, the "war to end all wars," brought a euphoric belief in the human potential that demanded a theological change in the prayers, so volume 2 was even more revised and appeared in 1922. In these revisions it was recognized that most congregants were ignorant of Hebrew, and only basic rubrics—mostly to be sung by the choir—appeared in the sacred tongue. The Great Depression and the beginnings of Hitler's persecution made these editions obsolete in tone, and by 1940 a "Newly Revised" volume 1 offered five varied services for Sabbath eve. Under the influence of the "Guiding Principles of Reform Judaism" promulgated at its Columbus, Ohio, convention in 1937, the new liturgy included more Hebrew texts, and the fifth service offered a much-disputed prayer for Zion. The news of Hitler's "Final Solution" had a profound effect on the "Newly Revised" volume 2 that appeared in 1944, but the old German tradition of omitting the Hebrew text of *Kol Nidre* was preserved.[8] The birth of the State of Israel and Reform's embrace of a pro-Israel stance, especially after the Six-Day War of 1967, made the older prayer books obsolete for most rabbis, and the holy day volume *Gates of Repentence* was published in 1973 to be followed two years later by the more complex *Gates of Prayer*. Both volumes dropped the archaic "thee" and "thou." *Gates of Prayer*, in recognition of the multiplicity of theological and ritual viewpoints then prevalent, provided ten Sabbath eve services and six for Sabbath morning ranging in content from the more traditional prayer book to a humanistic service in which God is not mentioned. Another innovation was to recognize in print those rabbis who had created the volumes, thereby annulling the CCAR tradition of liturgical anonymity. The evolution of feminism and the ordination of increasing numbers of women rabbis have produced a demand for liturgy with gender-neutral prayer language. Experimental versions are being issued by the CCAR.

Over its century of existence, the CCAR has also produced varied versions of a *Union Haggadah*, the latest being illustrated by the noted artist Leonard Baskin. The CCAR has also published volumes of prayer for private devotion, rabbis' manuals, responsa and recently a whole series of *Gates: of Understanding* (commentaries on the prayer books); *of Mitzvah* (life-cycle ceremonies); *of the House* (home rituals); *of Shabbat* (shabbat observance); *of the Seasons* (festival observance); *of Forgiveness* (Selichot: late-Saturday-night penitential service before the New Year); *of Healing* (for those who are ill). Children's liturgical volumes and home prayers are also part of the output. In a vain effort to make the festivals more meaningful spiritually and intellectually, the CCAR produced *The Five Scrolls*, but few congregations seemed interested. Like the prayer books, the *Union Hymnals* have reflected the changing views in the Reform movement.[9]

OTHER PUBLICATIONS

In 1896 the CCAR brought out a volume of *Sermons by American Rabbis*. From 1906 to 1947, an annual set of holy day sermons was issued. Apparently more useful to the contemporary rabbinate has been the quarterly periodical begun in 1953 as *CCAR Journal*, now called *CCAR Journal: A Reform Jewish Quarterly*. It contains scholarly discussions, literary expressions, how-to pieces and other exchanges of ideas. In 1961, after the death in office of President Israel Bettan, longtime Professor of Homiletics at the Cincinnati campus of HUC-JIR, an *Israel Bettan Memorial Volume* was produced with articles and data about preaching. For the CCAR's 75th anniversary, it published a volume of essays, *Retrospect and Prospect*, on its history and its changing views on theology, liturgy, social justice, church and state, the Jew in the modern world, Jewish education, the organized American Jewish community and the role of the rabbi. For its 1989 centennial observance, the CCAR issued *Tanu Rabbanan: Our Rabbis Taught*, updating the CCAR's history and views.

MAJOR ISSUES

The first issue of concern to the CCAR at its initial convention was the question of whether adult male proselytes needed to be circumcised. Henry Berkowitz was given the task of surveying the rabbinate, and many responded. The CCAR was not yet strong enough to adopt a decisive view in the face of so many opinions, so it published all the responses.[10] This seems to have established the CCAR's unwritten pattern that the majority of its decisions are not binding on the individual member.

The question of lay participation in making decisions more authoritative was hotly debated from 1903 to 1906, but no consensus could be reached. The same era saw debates on the then popular Sunday services and whether they replaced the Sabbath ones. This was resolved by a decision that the historical Sabbath be preserved and that Sunday worship be categorized as weekday, necessitating the publication of weekday services. Sunday services in some congregations lasted through World War II. Since then, a number of congregations have introduced daily services.

Intermarriage and the rabbi have been frequently discussed. In 1909 the CCAR adopted the following negative resolution: "Mixed marriages are contrary to the tradition of the Jewish religion and should therefore be discouraged by the American rabbinate." Several attempts to strengthen this resolution were defeated. In 1971 the opponents of rabbis officiating at intermarriages raised the issue again. An *ad hoc* committee brought a new resolution to the 1973 convention that again was strongly debated and much amended until the following text was adopted:

The Central Conference of American Rabbis, recalling its stand adopted in 1909 . . . now declares its opposition to participation by its members in any ceremony which solemnizes a mixed marriage.

[It] recognizes that historically its members have held and continue to hold divergent interpretations of Jewish tradition.

In order to keep open every channel to Judaism and *K'lal Yisrael* for those who've already entered into mixed marriage, the CCAR calls upon its members:

1. to assist fully in educating children of such mixed marriages as Jews;
2. to provide the opportunity for conversion of the non-Jewish spouse; and
3. to encourage a creative and consistent cultivation of involvement in the Jewish community and the synagogue.[11]

Attempts to enunciate a Reform theology proved equally difficult. Although the assimilative Pittsburgh Platform was never officially adopted by any of the movement's organizations, its sentiments prevailed in the movement until the 1930s. By then, an increasing number of East European, pro-Zionist and pro-ritual rabbis felt that Pittsburgh Platform Judaism could not serve the faith. A statement of "Guiding Principles for Reform Judaism" was subjected to considerable debate but eventually adopted at the 1937 convention in Columbus, Ohio. It is remembered as Reform's first formal statement in support of the upbuilding of Zion and, more vaguely, as an expression of Jewish peoplehood.

The issue of Zionism had divided the CCAR since the early Zionist conventions in Basel. As the price for permitting the passage of the 1937 pro-Zionist statement and in a vain effort at making peace between factions, the Zionists accepted a gentlemen's agreement not to bring Zionist issues to the floor of the CCAR convention. In 1942 a resolution in support of a Jewish brigade in the British army in North Africa was deemed a violation of the agreement. A group of anti-Zionists led by Louis Wolsey met after the convention and organized the American Council for Judaism. It proved to be the last organized gasp of the anti-Zionists. With the birth of Israel in 1948, most of the rabbis, including Wolsey, resigned from the Council. The Six-Day War of 1967 effectively buried the Council and brought the entire Reform movement into active support of the new state. The resultant blossoming of the movement, with its many divergent viewpoints on theology, ritual and social action, made it impossible for the joint commission of the UAHC and CCAR to draft a new platform. Instead of proposing new directions for the movement, the commission produced in 1976 "A Centenary Perspective," which defined the movement as it existed in the early 1970s, pointing to an affirmation of God's existence and role in the lives of humanity. It also stressed the peoplehood of Jewry, the ongoing revelation of Torah and obligations to the performance of ritual and to the State of Israel as well as to survival and to serving humanity. Maintaining that "Jewish survival is warrant for human hope," the "Perspective" ends by stating that "we remain God's witness that history is not meaningless," so we continue to work and wait for the Messianic era.

In his presidential address at the 1979 UAHC Biennial, Rabbi Alexander Schindler called on the CCAR to redefine "Who Is a Jew?" to include patrilinear as well as matrilinear descent, provided that the parents announce that they are rearing their child Jewishly or that the child receives formal Jewish education. For many Reform rabbis, this had been accepted practice and was specifically stated in the 1961 revision of the *Rabbi's Manual*. Despite strong objections from Maram (the embattled Israeli Reform rabbinate) and a number of other CCAR members who sympathized with it, the North American members of the CCAR endorsed the report of the Committee on Patrilineality.[12]

Now in its second century, the CCAR has enunciated and disseminated resolutions on every human concern evoked by each generation. Through a proliferation of committees and commissions, it acts, resolves and labors for human benefit.

THE RABBI AND THE RABBI'S FAMILY

The CCAR has always demonstrated deep concern for assuring and maintaining high standards of performance, intellectuality and spirituality among its membership. The programs of each national and regional convention contain sessions, and the CCAR supports separate workshops and seminars, devoted to these goals. Manuals, guidelines and source books have been published. Increasing time at each convention has been devoted to Torah study sessions. In addition to daily worship, conventions offer regular programs for soul-searching and spiritual growth.

Over the years, support mechanisms have been developed in an effort to ease the pressures on rabbis and their families. A pension program begun in 1943 has grown more sophisticated and is well monitored and staffed by the Rabbinical Pension Board, a joint UAHC-CCAR commission. A Task Force on Women in the Rabbinate has assured the movement's almost total acceptance of women rabbis and makes ongoing recommendations to meet any special problems or needs. A highly organized Spouse Support Group offers programs on mutual concerns at each convention and provides a network of helpfulness in every region. In 1982 Paul Gorin organized the expanding group of retired rabbis into the National Association of Retired Reform Rabbis and since 1984 has been meeting at annual conventions, alternating between the East and West Coasts. For rabbinic families experiencing difficulties, Jason Edelstein, a qualified counselor, maintains the CCAR's Rabbinic Hotline. In addition, committees have been established to study and make recommendations on all aspects of rabbinic work and family life.

THE INFLUENCE OF THE CCAR

It would be impossible to measure the scope of influence of the CCAR. Its individual members serve not only as congregational rabbis in all parts of the world but also as military and institutional chaplains. They direct and staff communal organizations and serve in academia, and a sizable group can be found in a variety of secular occupations. As part of their work, rabbis lead and serve local and national organizations in many fields and exert influence on Jewish communal and secular governmental policies.

In 1926 the CCAR reached out to the UAHC and to the Conservative and Orthodox rabbinic bodies and their lay constituencies to create the Synagogue Council of America as the representative religious body of American Jewry. The Conference of Presidents of Major Jewish organizations has its CCAR member. Resolutions approved by each CCAR convention are forwarded to appropriate agencies of government in the United States, Canada, Israel and elsewhere and have influenced legislation.[13]

The late Bertram Korn summed up the major significance of the CCAR when he wrote:

Though the Reform movement—led by its rabbinical leaders who are the members of the Conference—has made many mistakes and has failed many times, its major virtue has been the strength of its determination to be honest, forthright, vigorous and direct.

It is perhaps in this area that its contribution has been greatest, whatever its affirmative leadership in the movement and nation has been: namely, the strength which it has given to its own members. . . . The Conference has helped its members to retain their sense of proportion and guides them again and again to that true humility without which no religious leader can fulfill his [or her] responsibilities.

If one aspect of the life of the Conference ought to be mentioned . . . it is the warmth, the gaiety, the great comradeship of its members. The lot of the rabbi is and needs to be a very lonely one. . . . In the bosom of the Conference its members can share everything.[14]

NOTES

1. James G. Heller, *Isaac Mayer Wise: His Life, Work and Thought* (New York, 1965), pp. 83–85.

2. "First Movement for a Union," in *Selected Writings of Isaac M. Wise*, edited by David Philipson and Louis Grossman (Cincinnati, 1900), ch. 4; Central Conference of American Rabbis *Yearbook* (hereafter cited as *CCARY*) 1 (1890): 13–15; "Authentic report of the proceedings of the rabbinical conference held at Pittsburg [sic], Nov. 16, 17, 18, 1885," in *The Changing World of Reform Judaism: The Pittsburgh Platform in Retrospect*, ed. Walter Jacob (Pittsburgh, 1985), pp. 109, 123.

3. Heller, *Wise*, p. 477; *The Graduates of Hebrew Union College–Jewish Institute of Religion: A Centennial Register* (Cincinnati, 1975); David Philipson, *My Life as an American Jew: An Autobiography*, (Cincinnati, 1941), pp. 69–70. The term "Central" was chosen to distinguish the new organization from the short-lived Jewish Ministers Association formed by the easterners and from the Conference of Southern Rabbis, both created in 1885. Bertram W. Korn, ed., *Retrospect and Prospect: Essays in Commemoration of the 75th Anniversary of the Founding of the Central Conference of American Rabbis, 1889–1964* (New York, 1965), pp. 2ff. The southerners were invited and joined the CCAR.

4. Berkowitz, Philipson, Stolz and Heller had been ordained by Wise at HUC. Conspicuous by his absence from the CCAR's founding and early years was Joseph Krauskopf, who had been the featured speaker at the April 1889 celebration of Wise's birthday. Krauskopf had just moved from Kansas City to Philadelphia and was undoubtedly active in the eastern Jewish Ministers Association. Members of the Jewish Ministers Association seem to have refused to participate in the third convention of the CCAR when it met in New York in July 1892, since formal thanks are specifically "expressed to the individual Rabbis of New York and Brooklyn, to whose untiring efforts the success of the present meeting has been largely due." (*CCARY* 3, p. 51). Although Krauskopf appears on the "List of Members" from 1895 on, he did not attend until 1898, when the CCAR met in Atlantic City (*CCARY* 8, p. 17). Despite this, he was elected the organization's third president in 1903.

5. *CCARY* 1, pp. 1–5.

6. *CCARY*, passim. Unless otherwise indicated, the *Yearbooks* and the authors' personal knowledge are the sources for what follows.

7. The details of the gestation of these first *Union Prayer Books* are analyzed by Lou H. Silberman in Korn, *Retrospect*, ch. 3, pp. 46–61.

8. The debate on whether to include *Kol Nidre* was intense. A printing with the Hebrew text was withdrawn and replaced with an English paraphrase followed by:

Kol Nidre (in Hebrew)
(The Kol Nidre Chant) (in English) (p. 130)

9. For a history of Reform hymnology, see Malcolm H. Stern, "A Century of Jewish Music," *Reform Judaism*, Fall 1988, pp. 14–15.

10. *CCARY* 2, pp. 66–128.

11. *Tanu Rabbanan: Our Rabbis Taught; Essays on Commemoration of the Centennial of the Central Conference of American Rabbis* (New York, 1990), p. 47.

12. *Rabbi's Manual*, rev. ed. (New York, 1961), p. 112; *CCARY* 93, pp. 44–160. The issues of women in the rabbinate and of homosexuality in the rabbinate are discussed in the chapter on HUC-JIR.

13. Further details on many aspects of the CCAR can be found in *Tanu Rabbanan: Our Rabbis Taught; Essays in Commemoration of the Centennial of the Central Conference of American Rabbis* (New York, 1990), issued as *CCARY*, 1989, volume II.

14. Korn, *Retrospect*, pp. xiv–xvi.

APPENDICES

1. UNION OF AMERICAN HEBREW CONGREGATIONS
(Founded 1873)

UAHC CHAIRMEN OF THE BOARD

1873–1889	Moritz Loth
1889–1903	Julius Freiberg
1903–1907	Samuel Woolner
1907–1911	Louis J. Goldman
1911–1921	J. Walter Freiberg
1921–1925	Charles Shohl
1925–1934	Ludwig Vogelstein
1934–1937	Jacob W. Mack
1937–1943	Robert P. Goldman
1943–1946	Adolph Rosenberg
1946–1951	Jacob Aronson
1951–1954	Samuel S. Hollender
1955–1959	Solomon Elsner
1959–1963	Emil N. Baar
1963–1967	Irvin Fane
1967–1971	Earl Morse
1971–1972	Sidney I. Cole
1972–1974	Harry K. Gutman
1974–1979	Matthew H. Ross
1979–1983	Donald S. Day
1983–1987	Charles J. Rothschild, Jr.

1987–1991   Allan B. Goldman
1991–   Melvin Merians

EXECUTIVE OFFICERS

1890–1907   Lipman Levy[1]
1907–1941   George Zepin, executive secretary
1941–1942   Nelson Glueck[2]
1943–1973   Maurice Eisendrath, director, then president
1973–   Alexander Schindler, president

[1]The organzation was led entirely by lay leaders between 1873 and 1900, in consultation, sometimes strained, with Isaac M. Wise. After Wise's death, Levy supervised a modest office.

[2]Edward Israel was selected for this appointment in 1941 but died at his first board meeting. Glueck held the office for a year but never really served. While he remained in Palestine, Eisendrath was appointed interim director.

2. HEBREW UNION COLLEGE–JEWISH INSTITUTE OF RELIGION (Founded 1875)

PRESIDENTS OF HEBREW UNION COLLEGE
(Founded 1875)

1875–1900   Isaac Mayer Wise

1900–1903   Moses Mielziner (acting)

1903   Gotthard Deutsch (acting, February–June)

1903–1921   Kaufmann Kohler

1921–1947   Julian Morgenstern

PRESIDENT OF THE JEWISH INSTITUTE OF RELIGION
(Founded 1922)

1922–1948   Stephen S. Wise

PRESIDENTS OF HEBREW UNION COLLEGE–JEWISH INSTITUTE OF RELIGION

1947–1971   Nelson Glueck[1]

1971–   Alfred Gottschalk

[1]Note: HUC and JIR merged in 1950; Glueck served as president of JIR from 1948 until the formal merger took place.

CHAIRMEN OF THE BOARD OF GOVERNORS

Hebrew Union College

1875–1910   Bernhard Bettmann
1910–1917   Edward L. Heinsheimer
1917–1937   Alfred M. Cohen
1937–1943   Ralph W. Mack
1943–1947   Hiram E. Weiss

Hebrew Union College–Jewish Institute of Religion

1947–1953   Lester A. Jaffe[2]
1953–1956   Herbert R. Bloch
1957   Frank L. Weil
1958–1962   Robert P. Goldman
1962–1966   Sidney Meyers
1966–1972   S. L. Kopald, Jr.
1972–1976   Theodore Tannenwald, Jr.
1976–1982   Jules Backman
1982–1991   Richard Scheuer
1991–   Stanley Gold

Jewish Institute of Religion

1923–1928   Lee K. Frankel
1928–1950   Julian W. Mack

---

[2]Jaffe was chair during the merger between Hebrew Union College and the Jewish Institute of Religion.

3. CENTRAL CONFERENCE OF AMERICAN RABBIS
(Founded 1889)

PRESIDENTS OF THE CENTRAL CONFERENCE OF AMERICAN RABBIS

1889–1900	Isaac M. Wise
1900–1903	Joseph Silverman
1903–1905	Joseph Krauskopf
1905–1907	Joseph Stolz
1907–1909	David Philipson
1909–1911	Maximilian Heller
1911–1913	Samuel Schulman
1913–1915	Moses J. Gries
1915–1917	William Rosenau
1917–1919	Louis Grossman
1919–1921	Leo M. Franklin
1921–1923	Edward N. Calisch
1923–1925	Abram Simon
1925–1927	Louis Wolsey
1927–1929	Hyman G. Enelow
1929–1931	David Lefkowitz
1931–1933	Morris Newfield
1933–1935	Samuel H. Goldenson
1935–1937	Felix A. Levy
1937–1939	Max. C. Currick
1939–1941	Emil W. Leipziger

1941–1943	James G. Heller
1943–1945	Solomon B. Freehof
1945–1947	Abba Hillel Silver
1947–1949	Abraham J. Feldman
1949–1950	Jacob R. Marcus
1950–1952	Philip S. Bernstein
1952–1954	Joseph L. Fink
1954–1956	Barnett R. Brickner
1956–1957	Israel Bettan
1957–1959	Jacob Philip Rudin
1959–1961	Bernard J. Bamberger
1961–1963	Albert G. Minda
1963–1965	Leon I. Feuer
1965–1967	Jacob J. Weinstein
1967–1969	Levi A. Olan
1969–1971	Roland B. Gittelsohn
1971–1973	David Polish
1973–1975	Robert I. Kahn
1975–1977	Arthur J. Lelyveld
1977–1979	Ely E. Pilchik
1979–1981	Jerome R. Malino
1981–1983	Herman E. Schaalman
1983–1985	W. Gunther Plaut
1985–1987	Jack Stern, Jr.
1987–1989	Eugene J. Lipman
1989–1991	Samuel Karff
1991–	Walter Jacob

EXECUTIVE VICE–PRESIDENTS OF THE CENTRAL CONFERENCE OF AMERICAN RABBIS

1954–1971	Sidney L. Regner
1971–	Joseph B. Glaser

4. AMERICAN CONFERENCE OF CANTORS (Founded 1953)

PRESIDENTS OF AMERICAN CONFERENCE OF CANTORS

1953–1955	Walter A. Davidson
1955–1957	Benjamin Grobani
1957–1959	Gunther Hirschberg
1959–1961	Robert Miller
1961–1963	Arthur Wolfson
1963–1965	Marshall M. Glatzer
1965–1967	George Weinflash
1967–1969	Norman Summers
1969–1971	Alex Zimmer
1971–1973	Norman Belink
1973–1975	Ephraim Steinhauer
1975–1977	Harold Orbach
1977–1979	Ramon Gilbert
1979–1981	Murray E. Simon
1981–1983	Howard Stahl
1983–1985	Richard Botton
1985–1987	Jay I. Frailich
1987–1989	Paul Silbersher
1989–1991	Ed Fogel
1991–	Vicki Axe

5. NATIONAL ASSOCIATION OF TEMPLE ADMINISTRATORS
(Founded 1941)

PRESIDENTS OF NATA

1941–1948	Irving I. Katz
1948–1955	Max Feder
1955–1957	Bernard I. Pincus
1957–1958	Louis J. Freehof
1958–1961	Nathan Emanuel
1961–1963	Henry S. Jacobs
1963–1965	Frank J. Adler
1965–1967	Henry Fruhauf
1967–1969	Julian Feldman
1969–1971	Bernard Lepoff
1971–1973	David I. Mitchell
1973–1975	Frank L. Simons
1975–1977	Melvin S. Harris
1977–1979	Walter C. Baron
1979–1982	Henry Ziegler
1982–1985	Shirley M. Chernela
1985–1987	Harold Press
1987–1989	Ilene H. Herst
1989–	William Ferstenfeld

6. NATIONAL ASSOCIATION OF TEMPLE EDUCATORS
(Founded 1955)

PRESIDENTS OF NATE

1956	Toby K. Kurzband
1957–1958	Norman Drachler
1959	Herbert Zuckerman
1960	James J. Levbarg
1961	Heinz Warschauer
1962	Samuel Nemzoff
1963–1964	Alan D. Bennett
1965–1966	Max Frankel
1967–1968	Ceil Singer
1969–1970	Marvin Walts
1971–1972	Louis Lister
1973–1974	Phillip Chapman
1975–1976	Rolf Schickler
1977–1978	Raymond Israel
1979–1980	Fred W. Marcus
1981–1982	Richard M. Morin
1983–1984	Joel I. Wittstein
1985–1986	Kenneth A. Midlo
1987–1988	Robert E. Tornberg
1989–1990	Zena W. Sulkes
1991–	Robin Eisenberg

EXECUTIVE VICE–PRESIDENTS OF NATE

1956–1961   James J. Levbarg

EXECUTIVE SECRETARIES OF NATE

1962–1964   James J. Levbarg
1965–1976   Alan D. Bennett
1984–   Richard M. Morin

7. NATIONAL FEDERATION OF TEMPLE SISTERHOODS
(Founded 1913)

PRESIDENTS OF NFTS

1913–1919	Carrie Simon
1919–1923	Hattie Wiesenfeld
1923–1929	Stella Freiberg
1929–1934	Martha Steinfeld
1935–1941	Gertrude Watters
1941–1946	Reina Hartmann
1946–1953	Frieda Rosett
1953–1957	Helen Dalsheimer
1957–1961	Daisy Monsky
1961–1965	Beatrice Hollobow
1965–1967	Marjorie Rukeyser
1967–1973	Norma Levitt
1973–1977	Betty Benjamin
1977–1981	Lillian Maltzer
1981–1985	Constance Kreshtool
1985–1989	Dolores Wilkenfeld
1989–	Judith Hertz

8. NATIONAL FEDERATION OF TEMPLE BROTHERHOODS
(Founded 1923)

PRESIDENTS OF NFTB

1923–1931	Roger W. Straus
1932–1933	Charles P. Kramer
1933–1939	Samuel B. Finkel
1939–1941	Albert F. Mechlenberger
1941–1943	Charles P. Kramer
1943–1948	Jesse Cohen
1948–1951	S. Herbert Kaufman
1951–1955	Harold W. Dubinsky
1955–1957	Leo Wertgame
1957–1960	J. Robert Arkush
1960–1962	Edward Lee
1962–1964	J. Jacques Stone
1964–1966	Seymour M. Liebowitz
1966–1968	Philip A. Lehman
1968–1970	Milton E. Harris
1970–1972	Herbert Portes
1972–1974	Morton L. Kemper
1974–1976	Bernard Hirsh
1976–1978	Robert E. Katz
1978–1980	Lawrence M. Halperin
1980–1982	David N. Krem

1982–1984	Herbert Panoff
1984–1986	Marshall Blair
1986–1988	Carl Burkons
1988–1990	Richard D. Karfunkle
1990–	Alvin R. Corwin

9. WORLD UNION FOR PROGRESSIVE JUDAISM
(Founded 1926)

PRESIDENTS OF WUPJ

1926–1938	Claude G. Montefiore
1938–1953	Leo Baeck
1954–1959	Lily H. Montagu
1959–1964	Solomon B. Freehof
1964–1970	Jacob K. Shankman
1970–1972	Bernard J. Bamberger
1972–1973	Maurice N. Eisendrath
1973–1980	David H. Wice
1980–1988	Gerard Daniel
1988–	Donald Day

EXECUTIVE DIRECTORS OF WUPJ

1959–1962	Hugo Gryn
1962–1972	William A. Rosenthall
1972–	Richard G. Hirsch

NORTH AMERICAN DIRECTORS OF WUPJ

1972–1979	Ira Youdovin
1979–1982	Paul Kushner
1982–1985	Benjamin Kamin
1985–	Martin Strelzer

10. ASSOCIATION OF REFORM ZIONISTS OF AMERICA
(Founded 1977)

PRESIDENTS OF ARZA

1977–1984	Roland B. Gittelsohn
1984–1989	Charles A. Kroloff
1989–	Norman D. Schwartz

EXECUTIVE DIRECTORS OF ARZA

1977–1983	Ira Youdovin
1983–1992	Eric H. Yoffie
.1992–	Ammiel Hirsch

11. KADIMA (Founded 1977)

PRESIDENTS OF KADIMA

1977–1986	Michael S. Stroh
1986–	Dow Marmur

EXECUTIVE DIRECTORS OF KADIMA

1977–1986	Arthur Grant
1988–	Daniel Komito Gottlieb

BIBLIOGRAPHY

ANNUAL REPORTS, PROCEEDINGS, ORGANIZATION MAGAZINES AND JOURNALS

American Conference of Cantors. *Proceedings* (of the annual conventions). New York: 1953–).

American Jewish Archives. Cincinnati: 1948– .

Association of Reform Zionists of America. *Newsletter*. New York: 1977– .

Central Conference of American Rabbis. *Central Conference of American Rabbis Journal*. New York: April 1953–Winter 1978.

———. CCAR *Journal: A Reform Jewish Quarterly*. New York: Fall 1991– .

———. *Journal of Reform Judaism*. New York: Spring 1978–Summer 1991.

———. *Newsletter*. New York: 1970– .

———. *Yearbook*. Cincinnati: 1889– .

Griffel, Suzanne, and Polokoff, Eric. *The Guide: A Directory to Programs, Services and Resources of the UAH Congregations and the Reform Movement*. New York: 1987–1988.

Hebrew Union College. *Annual*. Cincinnati: 1904, 1924– .

———. *Bulletin*. Cincinnati: March 1942–1948.

———. *Catalogue of the Hebrew Union College–Jewish Institute of Religion*. Cincinnati: 1984– .

———. *Hebrew Union College Monthly*. Cincinnati: 1914–1949.

———. *H.U.C. Journal*. Cincinnati: October 1896–1903.

———. *HUC'r*. Cincinnati: 1936–1940.

Hebrew Union College–Jewish Institute of Religion. *Annual Report*. New York: 1977– .

———. *Bulletin*. New York: 1948–1954.

———. *Chronicle*. New York: February 1977– .

———. *Vessels*. Cincinnati: Spring 1987– .

Jewish Institute of Religion. *Quarterly*. New York: 1924–1929.

Journal of Jewish Lore and Philosophy. Cincinnati: January 1919–October 1919.

Kadima Newsletter. Ontario, Canada.

National Association of Temple Administrators. *NATA Journal*. Chicago: 1978–   .
———. *NATA Quarterly*. New York: 1941–   .
National Federation of Temple Brotherhoods. *Brotherhood*. New York: September–October 1967–   .
———. *Temple Brother Monthly*. Cincinnati, 1935–1951.
National Federation of Temple Sisterhoods. *Index of Resolutions Adopted by NFTS, 1913–1983*. New York: 1985.
———. *Topics & Trends*. Cincinnati: 1935–1951.
National Federation of Temple Youth. *Ani V'atah*. New York: December 1981–   .
———. *The Messenger*. Cincinnati: 1945–1954.
Religious Action Center. *Rac-up*. Washington, DC: 1976–1977.
Resolutions of the Central Conference of American Rabbis Passed by the Central Conference of American Rabbis, 1889–1974. Rev. ed. New York: 1975.
Studies in Bibliography and Booklore. Cincinnati: 1953–   .
The Synagogue, Its Relation to Modern Thought and Life: Papers Delivered at the 32nd Council, Union of American Hebrew Congregations. Philadelphia: 1931.
Union of American Hebrew Congregations. *Aging Concerns*. New York: 1985–   .
———. *American Judaism*. New York: 1951–1964.
———. *Annual Report*. Cincinnati: 1891–   .
———. Board of Trustees. *Minutes*. New York: 1979–   .
———. Bureau of Synagogue Activities. *Synagogue Service Bureau*. Cincinnati: September, 1933–1961.
———. *Compass*. New York: 1955–   .
———. Department of Synagogue and School Extension. *Jewish Teacher*. Cincinnati: 1932–1966.
———. *Dimensions*. New York: 1966–1971.
———. *Family Concerns*. New York: 1986–   .
———. *Jewish Connection*. New York: March 1981–   .
———. *Just for You*. New York: April 1986–   .
———. *Keeping Posted*. New York: October 1954–1991.
———. *Liberal Judaism*. Cincinnati: 1933–1951.
———. *Monthly Report*. Cincinnati: 1932–1935.
———. *Proceedings*. Cincinnati: 1885–   .
———. *Reform Judaism*. New York: 1971–   .
———. *Union Bulletin*. Cincinnati: 1911–1923.
———. *Union Home Study Magazine*. Cincinnati: 1909–1922.
———. *Union Tidings*. Cincinnati: 1919–1930.
———. *Visions*. New York: Fall 1978–Winter 1980–1981.
———. *What's Happening?!* New York: 1975–1984.
———. *Young Israel*. Detroit: 1907–1911; Cincinnati: 1912–1917, 1922–1940.
———. *Youth Leader*. Cincinnati: 1932–1938.
Where We Stand: Social Action Resolutions Adopted by the Union of American Hebrew Congregations. Rev. ed. New York: 1980.
World Union for Progressive Judaism. *American Annual Manual*. N.p.: 1955.

SELECTED WORKS BY KEY LEADERS

Adler, Felix. *Creed and Deed*. New York: 1877.
Adler, Liebman. *His Life through Letters*. Ed. Joan Weil Saltzstein. N.p.: 1975.

Bamberger, Bernard J. "The American Rabbi in the Changing Role." *Judaism* 3 (1954): 488–97.

———. *The Story of Judaism*. New York: 1964.

Bemporad, Jack, ed. *A Rational Faith*. New York: 1977.

Berger, Elmer. *The Jewish Dilemma*. New York: 1945.

———. *Judaism or Jewish Nationalism*. New York: 1957.

———. *Memories of an Anti-Zionist Jew*. Beirut: 1978.

———. *A Partisan History of Judaism*. New York: 1951.

Berkowitz, Henry. *Intimate Glimpses of the Rabbi's Career*. Cincinnati: 1921.

———. *Judaism on the Social Question*. New York: 1888.

Bial, Morrison David. *Liberal Judaism at Home: The Practices of Modern Reform Judaism*. Summit, NJ: 1967.

———. *Your Jewish Child*. New York: 1978.

Blank, Sheldon H. *Prophetic Faith in Isaiah*. New York: 1958.

———. *Prophetic Thought*. Cincinnati: 1977.

———. *Understanding the Prophets*. New York: 1969.

Borowitz, Eugene B. *Choosing a Sex Ethic*. New York: 1969.

———. "Liberal Jewish Theology in a Time of Uncertainty." Central Conference of American Rabbis *Yearbook* 87 (1977): 124–70.

———. *Liberal Judaism*. New York: 1984.

———. *The Mask Jews Wear: The Self-Deception of American Jewry*. New York: 1974.

———. *Modern Varieties of Jewish Thought: A Presentation and Interpretation*. New York: 1981.

———. *A New Theology in the Making*. Philadelphia: 1968.

———. "On Being a Reform Jew Today." *Central Conference of American Rabbis Journal* 20 (Summer 1973): 55–61.

———. *Reform Judaism Today*. New York: 1977.

———. "Reform's Interest in Halacha." *Reconstructionist* 21 (February 10, 1956): 9–13.

Borowitz, Eugene B., and Patz, Naomi. *Explaining Reform Judaism*. New York: 1985.

Central Conference of American Rabbis. *Retrospect and Prospect*. Ed. Bertram W. Korn. New York: 1965.

Cohen, Henry. *Justice, Justice: A Jewish View of the Negro Revolt*. New York: 1968.

———. *Talmudic Sayings*. Cincinnati: 1894.

Cohen, Henry. *Why Judaism?* New York: 1973.

Cohon, Samuel S. *Judaism—A Way of Life*. Cincinnati: 1948.

———. "Reform Judaism in America." *Judaism* 3 (1954): 333–53.

———. "The Theology of the UPB." Central Conference of American Rabbis *Yearbook* 38 (1928): 246–94.

———. *What We Jews Believe*. Cincinnati: 1931.

Cutter, William. "The Future of Reform Judaism." Central Conference of American Rabbis *Yearbook* 79 (1969): 256–58.

———. "Reading for Ethic." *Journal of Reform Judaism* 30 (Spring 1984): 50–64.

Deutsch, Gotthard. "The Jewish Reform Movement Historically Considered." *Hebrew Union College Monthly* 6 (March/April 1920): 131–41.

Doppelt, Frederic. *A Dialogue with God*. Philadelphia: 1943.

Eichhorn, David Max. *Conversion to Judaism: A History and Analysis*. New York: 1965.

———. *Jewish Intermarriages: Fact and Fiction*. Satellite Beach, FL: 1974.

Eisendrath, Maurice N. *Can Faith Survive: The Thoughts and Afterthoughts of an America Rabbi*. New York: 1964.

———. "The Present Task." In *Aspects of Progressive Jewish Thought*, ed. Israel I. Mattuck, pp. 70–84. New York: 1955.

Feldman, Abraham J. *Reform Judaism: A Guide for Reform Jews*. New York: 1956.

Feuer, Leon. *Prophetic Religion in an Age of Revolution*. Cincinnati: 1962.

———. "Some Reflections on the State of Reform Judaism." *Journal of Reform Judaism* 27 (Summer 1980): 22–31.

———. *Why a Jewish State?* New York: 1942.

Fields, Harvey J. *Bechol Levavcha*. New York: 1975.

———. "We Must Fashion Keva and Kevannah." *Central Conference of American Rabbis Journal* 20 (Spring 1973): 78–81.

Franklin, Leo M. *The Rabbi, the Man and his Message*. New York: 1938.

Freed, Isador. *Harmonizing the Jewish Modes*. New York: 1958.

Freehof, Solomon B. *Current Reform Responsa*. Cincinnati: 1969.

———. *Modern Jewish Preaching*. New York: 1941.

———. *Modern Jewish Responsa*. Cincinnati: 1971.

———. *Reform Jewish Practice*. 2 vols. Cincinnati: 1952.

———. "Reform Judaism in America." *Jewish Quarterly Review* 5 (April 1955): 350–62.

———. *Reform Responsa*. Cincinnati: 1960.

———. *The Responsa Literature*. Philadelphia: 1955.

———, ed. *A Treasury of Responsa*. Philadelphia: 1963.

Gittelsohn, Roland B. *Love, Sex and Marriage*. New York: 1980.

Glueck, Nelson. *Addresses, 1947–1954*. New York: 1955.

———. *Deities and Dolphins: The Story of the Nabataeans*. New York: 1965.

———. *Letters of the American Schools Oriental Research*. Jerusalem: 1943.

———. "What Is Reform Judaism." *American Jewish Archives* 26 (1974): 214–16.

Gottschalk, Alfred. "Israel and Reform Judaism: A Zionist Perspective." *Forum* 36 (1979): 143–60.

———. "A Strategy for Non-Orthodox Judaism in Israel." *Judaism* 31 (Fall 1982): 421–24.

———. *Your Future as a Rabbi*. New York: 1967.

Gries, Moses J. *The Union: Its Past and Its Future*. Atlanta: 1907.

Grollman, Earl A., ed. *Concerning Death: A Practical Guide for the Living*. Boston: 1974.

———, ed. *Explaining Death to Children*. Boston: 1967.

Grossman, Louis. *Judaism and the Science of Religion*. New York: 1889.

Guttman, Alexander. *Rabbinic Judaism in the Making*. Detroit: 1970.

———. *The Struggle over Reform in Rabbinic Literature*. Jerusalem: 1977.

Harris, Maurice Henry. *Selected Addresses*. New York: 1895.

Heller, James G. *Reform Judaism and Zionism*. Cincinnati: 1944.

Herscher, Uri D., and Chyet, Stanley. *On Jews, America and Immigration*. Cincinnati: 1980.

Hirsch, Emil G. *My Religion*. New York: 1925.

———. *Reform Judaism and Unitarianism*. N.p.: 1905.

———. *Reformed Judaism*. Chicago: 1883.

———. *Twenty Discourses*. New York: 1906.

Hirsch, Richard G. "Jewish Peoplehood: Implications for Reform." *Central Conference of American Rabbis Yearbook* 89 (1979): 164–73.
———. *Reform Judaism and Israel*. New York: 1972.
———. "A Response to Tabory." *Judaism* 31 (1982): 425–30.
———. *Thy Most Precious Gift: Peace in Jewish Tradition*. New York: 1974.
———. *The Way of the Upright: A Jewish View of Economic Justice*. New York: 1973.
Hirsch, Samuel. *Book of Essays*. London: 1905.
———. *The Reform in Judaism and Its Calling in the Contemporary World*. Leipzig: 1844.
Hoffman, Lawrence. *The Art of Public Prayer: Not for Clergy Only*. Washington: 1989.
———. *Beyond the Text: A Holistic Approach to Liturgy*. Bloomington, IN: 1987.
———. *The Canonization of the Synagogue Service*. Notre Dame: 1979.
———. *Gates of Understanding, Vol. I*. New York: 1977.
———. *Gates of Understanding, Vol. II*. New York: 1984.
———. "The Language of Survival in American Reform Liturgy." *Central Conference of American Rabbis Journal* 24 (Summer 1977): 87–106.
———, ed. *Land of Israel: Jewish Perspectives*. South Bend, IN: 1986.
Holdheim, Samuel. "Rabbi Jochanan ben Sakai, ein Retter und Reformator des Judenthums." In *Predigten uber die judische Religion* 3 (Berlin, 1855): 289–310.
———. *Sein Leben und seine Werke*. Berlin: 1865.
Idelsohn, Abraham Z. *Jewish Music in Its Historical Development*. New York: 1929.
———, ed. *Thesaurus of Hebrew Oriental Melodies*. 10 Vols. Berlin and Leipzig: 1925–1932.
Jacob, Walter, ed. *American Reform Responsa*. New York: 1983.
———. *Contemporary American Reform Responsa*. New York: 1987.
———. "The Source of Reform Halachic Authority." Central Conference of American Rabbis *Yearbook* 90 (1980): 31–36.
Jacob, Walter, and Staitman, Mark. "A Responsa to Law and Freedom in Reform Judaism." *Journal of Reform Judaism* 30 (Winter 1983): 98–104.
Kahn, Robert I. "Shall We Frame a Reform Halacha?" *Central Conference of American Rabbis Journal* 11 (April 1963): 62–66.
Karff, Samuel E., ed. *Hebrew Union College–Jewish Institute of Religion at One Hundred Years*. Cincinnati: 1976.
Katz, Robert L. *Changing Self-Concepts of Reform Rabbis*. Cincinnati: 1975.
———. *Pastoral Care and the Jewish Tradition*. Philadelphia: 1985.
———. "The Rabbi as Preacher/Counselor: A Frame of Reference." *Central Conference of American Rabbis Journal* 5 (June 1958): 22–35.
Kiev, Edward I., and Tepfer, John L. "Jewish Institute of Religion." *American Jewish Year Book* 49 (1947): 91–102.
Kohler, Kaufmann. *Backwards or Forwards?* New York: 1885.
———. *Hebrew Union College and Other Addresses*. Cincinnati: 1916.
———. *Jewish Theology, Systematically and Historically Considered*. New York: 1918.
———. *A Living Faith*. Ed. Samuel S. Cohon. Cincinnati: 1948.
———. *Studies, Addresses and Personal Papers*. New York: 1931.
Kohut, Alexander. *The Ethics of the Fathers*. New York: 1885.
Korn, Bertram W. *Eventful Years and Experiences*. Ed. Jacob R. Marcus. Cincinnati: 1954.

————. "Isaac Mayer Wise on The Civil War." *Hebrew Union College Annual* 20 (1947): 635–58.

————, ed. *Retrospect and Prospect*. New York: 1965.

Kushner, Lawrence. *Honey from the Rock*. Woodstock VT: 1977.

————. *The River of Light*. Woodstock, VT: 1981.

Langer, Michael, ed. *A Reform Zionist Perspective: Judaism and Community in the Modern Age*. New York: 1977.

Lauterbach, Jacob Z. "The Ethics of the Halakhah." Central Conference of American Rabbis *Yearbook* 23 (1913): 249–87.

————. *Rabbinic Essays*. Cincinnati: 1951.

————. *Studies in Jewish Law, Custom and Folklore*. New York: 1970.

Lazaron, Morris S. *Bridges Not Walls*. New York: 1959.

Lelyveld, Arthur J. *Atheism Is Dead*. Cleveland: 1968.

Levy, Beryl Harold. *Reform Judaism in America*. New York: 1933.

Liebman, Joshua Loth. *Peace of Mind*. New York: 1946.

Lipman, Eugene. "Women's Liberation and Jewish Tradition." *Jewish Heritage* 13 (Winter 1971/1972): 21–23.

Lipman, Eugene, and Vorspan, Albert, eds. *A Tale of Ten Cities: The Triple Ghetto of American Religious Life*. New York: 1962.

Magnes, Judah L. *War-time Addresses, 1917–1921*. New York: 1923.

Mann, Jacob. *The Collected Articles of Jacob Mann*. Israel: 1971.

Marcus, Jacob R. "Isaac M. Wise—Fighter for Women's Rights." *Jewish Digest* 19 (June 1974): 73–75.

Margolis, Max Leopold. "The Theological Aspect of Reform Judaism." Central Conference of American Rabbis *Yearbook* 13 (1903): 185–308.

Margolis, Max Leopold, with Alexander Marx. *A History of the Jewish People*. Philadelphia: 1927.

Martin, Bernard. "The Americanization of Reform Judaism." *Journal of Reform Judaism* 27 (Winter 1980): 33–58.

————. *Prayer in Judaism*. New York: 1968.

————, ed. *Contemporary Reform Jewish Thought*. Chicago: 1968.

————, ed. *Great Twentieth Century Jewish Philosophers*. New York: 1970.

Meyer, Michael. "Abraham Geiger's Historical Judaism." In *New Perspectives on Abraham Geiger: An HUC-JIR Symposium*. Cincinnati: 1975.

————. "Jewish Religious Reform and Wissenschaft de Judentums." *Leo Baeck Institute Yearbook* 16 (1971): 19–44.

————. *Response to Modernity: A History of the Reform Movement in Judaism*. New York: 1988.

Mielziner, Moses. *Introduction to the Talmud*. Cincinnati: 1894.

————. *The Jewish Law of Marriage and Divorce in Ancient and Modern Times, and Its Relation to the Law of the State*. Cincinnati: 1884.

Mihaly, Eugene. "Religious Discipline and Liberal Judaism." Central Conference of American Rabbis *Yearbook* 85 (1975): 174–83.

Mirsky, Norman B. *Unorthodox Judaism*. Columbus: 1978.

Morgenstern, Julian. *As a Mighty Stream: The Progress of Judaism through History*. Philadelphia: 1949.

Newman, Louis I. *A New Reform Judaism and the New Union Prayer Book: A Personal Statement*. N.p.: 1943.

Olan, Levi. *Judaism and Immortality*. New York: 1971.
————. "The Limits of Liberal Judaism." *Judaism* 14 (Spring 1965): 146–58.
————. "Plural Modes within Halacha." *Judaism* 19 (Winter 1970): 77–89.
————. *Prayerbook Reform in Europe: The Liturgy of European Liberal and Reform Judaism*. New York: 1968.
————. "Problems of Reform Halakhah." In *Contemporary Reform Jewish Thought*, ed. Bernard Martin. Chicago: 1968.
————. *A Prophetic Faith and the Secular Age*. New York: 1982.
————. "Reform Benedictions for Rabbinic Ordinations." *Hebrew Union College Annual* 37 (1966): 177–78.
————. "Speaking to and about God." *Jewish Spectator* 48 (Winter 1983): 29–36.
Philipson, David. *The Reform Movement in Judaism*. New York: 1907. Revised, New York: 1931. Reissue, New York: 1967.
Philipson, David, and Grossman, Louis, eds. *Selected Writings of Isaac Mayer Wise*. Cincinnati: 1900.
Pilchik, Ely E. *Judaism outside the Holy Land*. New York: 1964.
————. "Stumbling Blocks to Prayer." *Central Conference of American Rabbis Journal* 14 (January 1967): 65–67.
Plaut, W. Gunther. *Book of Proverbs*. New York: 1961.
————. "Can We Speak of Reform Halacha?" Central Conference of American Rabbis *Yearbook* 90, part 2 (1980): 63–65.
————. *The Case for the Chosen People*. Garden City, NY: 1965.
————. *The Growth of Reform Judaism: American and European Sources until 1948*. New York: 1965.
————. "Is Reform Ambiguous." *Reform Judaism* 3 (October 1974): 1.
————. "Reform Judaism: Past, Present and Future." *Journal of Reform Judaism* 27 (Summer 1980): 1–11.
————. *The Rise of Reform Judaism: A Sourcebook of Its European Origins*. New York: 1963.
————. *Time to Think and Other Columns from the Globe and Mail*. Toronto: 1977.
————. *The Torah—A Modern Commentary*. New York: 1981.
Polish, David. "The Changing and the Constant in the Reform Rabbinate." *American Jewish Archives* 35 (1983): 286–98.
————. *The Higher Freedom*. Chicago: 1965.
————. *Israel, Nation and People*. New York: 1975.
————. "The New Reform and Authority." *Judaism* 23 (Winter 1974): 8–22.
————. "Opportunities for Reform Judaism." *Central Conference of American Rabbis Journal* no. 19 (October 1957): 13–18.
————. "An Outline for Theological Discourse in Reform." *Journal of Reform Judaism* 29 (Winter 1982): 1–13.
————. *Renew Our Days: The Zionist Issue in Reform Judaism*. Jerusalem: 1976.
Polish, David, and Doppelt, Frederic A. *A Guide for Reform Jews*. New York: 1957.
Priesand, Sally. "From Promise to Reality." *Keeping Posted* 17 (April 1972): 17–19.
————. *Judaism and the New Woman*. New York: 1975.
————. "They Did Build the House of Israel." *Dimensions* 5 (Winter 1971): 27–29.
Reform Judaism: Essays by Hebrew Union College Alumni. Cincinnati: 1949.
Reines, Alvin. "Authority in Reform Today." *Central Conference of American Rabbis Journal* 8 (April 1960): 17–20.

Rivkin, Ellis. *The Shaping of Jewish History: A Radical New Interpretation*. New York: 1971.

Rosenau, William. *Jewish Ceremonial Institutions and Customs*. Baltimore: 1903.

Schindler, Solomon. *Messianic Expectations and Modern Judaism*. Boston: 1886.

Schoen, Myron E., Feldman, Julian, and Fruhauf, Henry, eds. *The Temple Management Manual*. New York: 1984.

Schwartzman, Sylvan. *Reform Judaism in the Making*. New York: 1955.

———. *Reform Judaism—Then and Now*. New York: 1971.

———. *The Story of Reform Judaism*. New York: 1949; rev., 1958.

———. "Who Wants Reform All-Day Schools?" *Central Conference of American Rabbis Journal* (April 1964): Vol. 12:3–10.

Seltzer, Robert M. *Jewish People, Jewish Thought: The Jewish Experience in History*. New York: 1980.

Silberman, Lou M. "Concerning Jewish Theology in North America: Some Notes on a Decade." *American Jewish Year Book* 70 (1969): 41–45.

Silver, Abba Hillel. *A History of Messianic Speculation in Israel*. New York: 1927.

———. *Moses and the Original Torah*. New York: 1961.

———. *Religion in a Changing World*. New York: 1930.

———. *Vision and Victory*. New York: 1949.

———. *Where Judaism Differed*. New York: 1956.

———. *A Word in Its Season*. Vol. 2. New York: 1972.

Silver, Daniel Jeremy, ed. *Judaism and Ethics*. New York: 1970.

Silver, Samuel. *How to Enjoy This Moment*. New York: 1967.

———, ed. *The Quotable American Rabbis*. Anderson, SC: 1967.

———, ed. *To My Knowledge*. New York: 1961.

Skirball, Henry F., and Rayner, John D., ed. *The Jewish Youth Group*. London: 1958.

Slonimsky, Henry. Essays. Cincinnati: 1967.

Spiro, Jack D. *A Time to Mourn: Judaism and the Psychology of Bereavement*. New York: 1967.

Stern, Harry Joshua. *Judaism in the War of Ideas*. New York: 1937.

———. *One World or No World*. New York: 1973.

———. "Our Obligations: Religious Practice." *Central Conference of American Rabbis Journal* 24 (Spring 1977): 59–64.

Stern, Jack. "President's Message." Central Conference of American Rabbis *Yearbook* 96 (1986): 1–10.

Stern, Malcolm. "Reforming of Reform Judaism—Past, Present and Future." *American Jewish Historical Quarterly* 63 (1973): 111–18.

Sturzenberger, Doris C., ed. *A Guide to the Writings of Isaac Mayer Wise*. Cincinnati: 1981.

Syme, Daniel. *The Jewish Home: A Guide for Jewish Living*. New York: 1988.

Syme, Daniel, and Sonsino, Rifat. *Finding God: Ten Jewish Responses*. New York: 1986.

Voorsanger, Jacob. *The Chronicles of Emanu-El*. San Francisco: 1900.

Vorspan, Albert. *To Do Justly*. New York: 1971.

Weinstein, Jacob J. *The Rabbi as Pastor, Community Worker, Preacher*. Cincinnati: 1950.

Wine, Sherwin T. *Humanistic Judaism*. Buffalo: 1978.

Wise, Isaac M. *The Cosmic God*. Cincinnati: 1876.

————. *History of the Israelitish Nation*. Vol. 1. Albany: 1854.

Wise, Stephen S. *The Personal Letters of Stephen Wise*. Ed. Justine Wise Polier and James Waterman Wise. Boston: 1956.

Wolf, Arnold Jacob. *Challenge to Confirmands*. New York: 1963.

————, ed. *Rediscovering Judaism: Reflections on a New Theology*. Chicago: 1965.

MEMOIRS, AUTOBIOGRAPHIES, BIOGRAPHIES AND SERMONS

Adler, Felix. *Life and Destiny: or, Thoughts from the Ethical Lectures of Felix Adler*. New York: 1905.

————. *The Religion of Duty*. New York: 1905.

Bamberger, Bernard. "Jacob Z. Lauterbach: An Informal Memoir." *Central Conference of American Rabbis Journal* 11 (June 1963): 3–8.

————. *Sermons*. New York: 1955.

Berkowitz, Henry. *The Kol Nidre Comes to Life*. Portland, OR: 1940.

Berkowitz, Max E. *The Beloved Rabbi: The Life of Henry Berkowitz*. New York: 1932.

Blumberg, Janice Rothschild. *One Voice: Rabbi Jacob M. Rothschild and the Troubled South*. Atlanta: 1985.

Braude, William. *It Is Good to Know That All of Us Are Sinners*. Providence, RI: 1948.

Brav, S. R., ed. *Telling Tales Out of School: Seminary Memories*. Cincinnati: 1965.

Breibart, Solomon. *The Reverend Dr. Gustavus Poznanski: First American Jewish Reform Minister*. Charleston, SC: 1979.

Calisch, Edith. *Three Score and Twenty*. Richmond, VA: 1945.

Central Conference of American Rabbis, ed. *Sermons by American Rabbis*. Chicago: 1896.

————. *A Set of Holiday Sermons, 1959–60*. New York: 1959.

Chyet, Stanley F. *Jacob Rader Marcus: A Biographical Sketch*. Cincinnati: 1958.

Clar, Reva, and Kramer, William M. "The Girl Rabbi of the Golden West: The Adventurous Life of Ray Frank in Nevada, California and the Northwest." *Western States Jewish History* 18 (1986): 99–111, 223–36, 336–51.

Cohn, Bernard N. "David Einhorn: Some Aspects of His Thinking." In *Essays in American Jewish History to Commemorate the Founding of the American Jewish Archives*, pp. 315–24. Cincinnati: 1958.

Cohon, Samuel S. "Kaufmann Kohler the Reformer." In *Mordecai M. Kaplan Jubilee Volume*, pp. 137–55. New York: 1953.

————. *A Living Faith*. Cincinnati: 1948.

————, ed. *Lives and Voices*. Philadelphia: 1972.

Congregation Emanu-El of New York City. New York: 1945.

Dreyfus, Stanley, ed. *Henry Cohen: Messenger of the Lord*. New York: 1963.

Einhorn, David. *David Einhorn Memorial Volume*. Ed. Kaufmann Kohler. New York: 1911.

————. *Inaugural Sermon and Personal Recollections*. Baltimore: 1855.

Eisendrath, Maurice N. *The Never Failing Stream*. Toronto: 1939.

Enelow, Hyman. *Reform Judaism*. New York: 1913.

————. *Selected Works of Hyman G. Enelow*. 4 vols. Kingsport, TN: 1935.

————. *The Synagogue in Modern Life*. New York: 1916.

Feldman, Abraham J. *The Faith of a Liberal Jew*. Hartford, CT: 1931.
———. *God's Fool*. Philadelphia: 1923–1924.
———. *Hills to Climb*. Hartford, CT: 1931.
———. "Joseph Krauskopf: A Biographical Sketch." *American Jewish Yearbook* 26 (1924): 420–47.
———. *Kiddush Hashem*. Hartford, CT: 1929.
———. *Religious Action*. Philadelphia: 1923.
Feldstein, Janice J., ed. *Rabbi Jacob J. Weinstein: Advocate of the People*. New York: 1980.
Felsenthal, Bernhard. *The Beginnings of Chicago Sinai Congregation*. Chicago: 1898.
Feuer, Leon I. "Abba Hillel Silver: A Personal Memoir." *American Jewish Archives* 19 (1967): 107–26.
Freehof, Solomon B. *Bible Sermons for Today*. New York: 1973.
———. *Cheap Phrases of a Vulgar Age*. Pittsburgh: 1947.
———. *The Italian Ex-Rabbi—and Others Who Deserted Intermarried Converts—and Others Who Join Us*. Pittsburgh: 1945.
———. *K.A.M. Pulpit*. Chicago: 1924–1934.
———. *Preaching the Bible: Sermons for Sabbath and High Holy Days*. New York: 1974.
———. *Rodef Shalom Pulpit, New Series*. Pittsburgh: 1963.
———. *The Sermon Continues*. Pittsburgh: 1982.
———. *Spoken and Heard*. Pittsburgh: 1972.
Friedlander, Albert H. *Leo Baeck: Teacher of Theresienstadt*. New York: 1968.
Gittelsohn, Roland B. *Here I Am—Harnessed to Hope*. New York: 1988.
———. *Man's Best Hope*. New York: 1961.
Glueck, Nelson. *Dateline Jerusalem: A Diary by Nelson Glueck*. Cincinnati: 1968.
Goldenson, Samuel H. *World Problems and Personal Religion*. Pittsburgh, 1975.
Gordis, Robert, ed. *Max Leopold Margolis: Scholar and Teacher*. Philadelphia: 1957.
Gottheil, Richard. *Memoir of a Priest in Israel*. Williamsport, PA: 1936. (On Gustav Gottheil.)
Grand, Samuel, and Gamoran, Mamie, eds. *Emanuel Gamoran: His Life and His Work*. New York: 1979.
Greenberg, Gershon. "Mendelssohn in America: David Einhorn's Radical Reform Judaism." *Leo Baeck Institute Yearbook* 27 (1982): 281–94.
———. "The Messianic Foundations of American Jewish Thought: David Einhorn and Samuel Hirsch." *Proceedings of the Sixth World Congress of Jewish Studies* 2 (1975): 215–26.
———. "The Reformers' First Attack Upon Hess' Rome and Jerusalem: An Unpublished Manuscript of Samuel Hirsch." *Jewish Social Studies* 35 (1974): 179–97.
———. "The Significance of America in David Einhorn's Conception of History." *American Jewish Historical Quarterly* 63 (1973): 160–84.
Greenspoon, Leonard. *Max Leopold Margolis: A Scholar's Scholar*. Atlanta: 1987.
Gumbiner, Joseph Henry. *Isaac Mayer Wise: Pioneer of American Judaism*. New York: 1959.
———. "Last Leader of a Winning Cause: The Founder of American Reform Judaism Reconsidered." *Judaism* 1 (1912): 171.
Heller, James G. *Isaac M. Wise: His Life, Work and Thought*. New York: 1965.

Heller, Maximilian. *Remembrance Atonement: Sermons Delivered on the Eves of Rosh Hashanah and Yom Kippur, 5648*. New Orleans: 1887.

Hirsch, David Einhorn. *Rabbi Emil G. Hirsch: The Reform Advocate*. Chicago: 1968.

Hirsch, Emil G. *Discourses*. Chicago: n.d.

Hirsch, Samuel. *Dr. Jastrow und sein Gebaren in Philadelphia*. Philadelphia: 1888.

———. *My Religion and the Crucifixion Viewed from a Jewish Standpoint*. New York: 1973.

Hirt-Manheimer, Aron. "Jane Evans: A Builder of Reform Judaism." *Reform Judaism* 12 (Fall 1983): 30.

Samuel Holdheim Collection, Central Archives for the History of the Jewish People, Jerusalem.

Hubsch, Julia, ed. *Rev. Dr. Adolph Hubsch: Late Rabbi of the Ahawath Chesed Congregation, New York*. New York: 1885.

Idelsohn, A. Z. "My Life: A Sketch." *Jewish Music Journal* 2 (1935): 8–11.

In Honor of Dr. Joseph L. Fink. Buffalo: 1949.

Isserman, Ferdinand. *A Rabbi with the Red Cross*. New York: 1958.

Jacob, Walter. *A Selection of Sermons*. Pittsburgh: 1969.

———. *Thus We Begin*. Pittsburgh: 1967.

Kahn, Robert. *Judaism and the Space Age and Other Sermons*. Houston: 1962.

———. *Lessons for Life*. Garden City, NY: 1963.

———. *May the Words of My Mouth*. Houston: 1984.

Katz, Jacob. "The Historical Origins of God and Man: Samuel Hirsch's Luxembourg Writings." *Leo Baeck Institute Yearbook* 20 (1974): 192–48.

———. "Samuel Hirsch—Rabbi, Philosopher, and Freemason." *Revue des études juives* 192 (1970): 205–15.

Kohler, Kaufmann. "David Einhorn: The Uncompromising Champion of Reform Judaism." *Central Conference of American Rabbis Yearbook* 19 (1909): 215–70.

———, ed. *Dr. David Einhorn's Ausgewahlte Predigten und Reden*. New York: 1881.

Kohler, Max J. "Isaac Harby: Jewish Religious Leader and Man of Letters." *Publications of the American Jewish Historical Society* 23 (1931): 35–53.

Kohut, Rebeka. *His Father's House: The Story of George Alexander Kohut*. New Haven: 1938.

Krauskopf, Joseph. *Evolution and Judaism*. Kansas City: 1887.

———. *Glint-Lights on the Ten Commandments*. Philadelphia: 1892.

———. *Sunday Lectures before Congregation Keneseth Israel*. Philadelphia: 1887–1923.

Kraut, Benny. *From Reform Judaism to Ethical Culture: The Religious Evolution of Felix Adler*. Cincinnati: 1979.

———. "Judaism Triumphant: Isaac Mayer Wise on Unitarianism and Liberal Christianity." *Association of Jewish Studies Review* 7–8 (1982–1983): 179–230.

———. "A Unitarian Rabbi? The Case of Solomon H. Sonnenschein." In *Jewish Apostasy in the Modern World*, ed. Todd M. Endelman. New York: 1987.

Lazaron, Morris. *Seed of Abraham . . . Ten Jews of the Ages*. New York: 1930.

Lefkowitz, David. *Medicine for a Sick World*. Dallas: 1952.

Lelyveld, Arthur J., Rudavsky, Benjamin, and Braude, Samuel. *Narrowing the Gap*. Cleveland: 1962.

Levy, Clifton Harby. *The Jewish Life*. New York: 1925.

Levy, Jacob C. "The Reformed Israelites." *Southern Quarterly Review* 5 (1844): 3–8.

Levy, Sherry. "Meet the World's First Woman Rabbi." *Ladies Home Journal* (June 1972).

Lichenstein, Morris. *How to Live*. New York: 1929.

Liebeschitz, Hans. "Max Wiener's Reinterpretation of Liberal Judaism." *Leo Baeck Institute Yearbook* 5 (1960): 35–57.

Lipman, Eugene J. *Yamin Noraim*. Washington, DC: 1987.

Litman, Simon. *Ray Frank Litman: A Memoir*. New York: 1957.

Luz, Ehud. "Max Wiener as a Historian of Jewish Religion in the Emancipation Period." *Hebrew Union College Annual* 56 (1985): Hebrew section, 29–46.

Magnin, Edgar F. *How to Live a Richer and Fuller Life*. New York: 1951.

Mann, Arthur. *Growth and Achievement: Temple Israel, 1854–1954*. Cambridge, MA: 1954.

———. "Solomon Schindler, Boston Radical." *New England Quarterly* 23 (1950): 453–76.

Mann, Louis L. *In Quest of the Bluebird*. Chicago: 1938.

Marcus, Jacob Rader. "Israel Jacobson." Central Conference of American Rabbis *Yearbook* 38 (1928): 386–498.

———. *Israel Jacobson: The Founder of the Reform Movement in Judaism*. Cincinnati: 1972.

Martin, Bernard. "The Religious Philosophy of Emil G. Hirsch." *American Jewish Archives* 4 (1952): 66–82.

———. "The Social Philosophy of Emil G. Hirsch." *American Jewish Archives* 6 (1954): 151–65.

May, Max B. *Isaac Mayer Wise, the Founder of American Judaism: A Biography*. New York: 1916.

Meyer, Michael A. "Aron Bernstein—The Enigma of a Radical Religious Reformer." *Proceedings of the Ninth World Congress of Jewish Studies* 3 (1986): 9–16.

———. "Caesar Seligmann and the Development of Liberal Judaism in Germany at the Beginning of the Twentieth Century." *Hebrew Union College Annual* 40–41 (1969–1970): 529–54.

———. "Samuel S. Cohon: Reformer of Reform Judaism." *Judaism* 15 (1966): 319–28.

Mielziner, Ella McKenna Friend. *Moses Mielziner*. New York: 1931.

Minda, Albert G. *The Fire on the Altar*. Minneapolis: 1948.

———. *Over the Years*. New York: 1963.

Moise, Harold. *The Moise Family of South Carolina and Their Descendants*. Columbia, SC: 1961.

Moise, L. C. *Biography of Isaac Harby, with an Account of the Reformed Society of Israelites of Charleston, S.C., 1824–1833*. Macon, GA: 1931.

Nathan, Anne, and Cohen, Harry I. *The Man Who Stayed in Texas*. New York: 1941. (On Henry Cohen.)

Oko, Adolph S. "Kaufmann Kohler." *Menorah Journal* 12 (1926): 513–21.

Olan, Levi. *Maturity in an Immature World*. New York: 1984.

Petuchowski, Jakob J. "Abraham Geiger and Samuel Holdheim: Their Differences on Germany and Repercussions in America: *Leo Baeck Institute Yearbook* 22 (1977): 139–59.

———, ed. *New Perspectives on Abraham Geiger*. Cincinnati: 1975.

Philipson, David, ed. *Centenary Papers and Others*. Cincinnati: 1919. (On Isaac M. Wise, Lilienthal.)

———. *Max Lilienthal: His Life and Writings*. New York: 1915.

———. *My Life as an American Jew: An Autobiography*. Cincinnati: 1941.

Pilchik, Ely E. *Bachya ibn Pakuda's "Duties of the Heart."* Newark, NJ: 1953.

———. *Jerusalem Sermons*. New York: 1957.

———. *A Preface to Judaism and Science*. Newark, NJ: 1958.

———. *A Touch of Torah*. Newark, NJ: 1953.

Pinckney, Henry L., and Moise, Abraham, eds. *A Selection from the Miscellaneous Writings of the Late Isaac Harby*. Charleston, SC: 1829.

Plaut, W. Gunther. *The Hard Way of Reform Judaism*. Toronto: 1961.

———. *Unfinished Business: An Autobiography*. Toronto: 1981.

Polier, Justine Wise, and Wise, James Waterman. *The Personal Letters of Stephen J. Wise*. Boston: 1956.

Polish, David. *Sermons by David Polish*. Evanston, IL: 1961.

———. *Sermons for the Yamim Noraim, 1962*. Evanston, IL: 1962.

Raisin, Max. *Great Jews I Have Known: A Gallery of Portraits*. New York: 1952.

Raphael, Marc Lee. "Rabbi Jacob Voorsanger on Jews and Judaism: The Implications of the Pittsburgh Platform." *American Jewish Historical Quarterly* 63 (1973): 185–203.

Reform Judaism in Large Cities: A Survey. Cincinnati: 1931.

Ritter, Immanuel H. "Samuel Holdheim: The Jewish Reformer." *Jewish Quarterly Review* 1 (1889): 202–15.

Rosenau, William. *The Child as Bread-Winner*. Baltimore: 1912.

Rosenbaum, Fred. *Architects of Reform: Congregational and Community Leadership, Emanu-El of San Francisco, 1849–1980*. Berkeley: 1980.

———. *Feeling and Thought in Religion*. Baltimore: 1895.

———. *Irreparable Losses*. Baltimore: 1895.

———. *The Place of Authority in Life*. Michigan: 1916.

———. *Sounding God's Praise*. Baltimore: 1898.

———. *A Tribute to Moses Mielziner*. Baltimore: 1929.

Rubenstein, Aryeh. "Isaac Mayer Wise: *A New Appraisal*." *Jewish Social Studies* 39 (1977): 53–74.

Rudin, Jacob. *Very Truly Yours*. New York: 1971.

Sabbath Sermons. Cincinnati: 1937.

Schulman, Samuel. *Sermons Delivered at the Beth-El Temple, New York City*. New York: 1919–1926.

Sermons by American Rabbis. Chicago: 1896.

Shusterman, Abraham. *The Legacy of a Liberal*. Baltimore: 1967. (On David Einhorn.)

Silver, Abba Hillel. *Sermons Delivered at the Temple*. Cleveland: 1919–1925.

———. *Therefore Choose Life*. Ed. Herbert Weiner. Cleveland: 1967.

———. *The World Crisis and Jewish Survival*. New York: 1941.

Silver, Samuel. *Portrait of a Rabbi*. Cleveland: 1959. (On Barnett Brickner.)

———, ed. *A Treasury of Jewish Thought*. New York: 1964.

Silverman, Joseph. *The Renaissance of Judaism*. New York: 1918.

Spicehandler, Ezra, and Wiener, Theodore. "Bernard Felsenthal's Letters to Osias Schorr." In *Essays in American Jewish History*, pp. 394–96. Cincinnati: 1958.

Stern, Harry J. *Entrusted with Spiritual Leadership*. New York: 1961.

————. *Jew and Christian*. Montreal: 1937.

————. *The Jewish Spirit Triumphant*. New York: 1943.

————. *Judaism in the War of Ideas*. New York: 1937.

————. *Martyrdom and Miracle*. New York: 1950.

————. *One World or No World*. New York: 1973.

Stern, Malcolm. "National Leaders of Their Time: Philadelphia's Reform Rabbis." In *Jewish Life in Philadelphia, 1830–1940*, ed. Murray Friedman. Philadelphia: 1983.

Stern, Myer. *The Rise and Progress of Reform Judaism . . . Temple Emanu-El of New York*. New York: 1895.

Stern, Richard M. "Arnold B. Erlich: A Personal Recollection." *American Jewish Archives* 23 (1971): 73–85.

Studies in Jewish Literature Issued in Honor of Professor Kaufmann Kohler, ed. David Philipson, David Neumark, and Julian Morgenstern. Berlin: 1913.

Temkin, Sefton D. "Isaac Mayer Wise and the Civil War." *American Jewish Archives* 15 (1963): 120–42.

————. "Rabbi Max Lilienthal Views American Jewry in 1847." In *A Bicentennial Festscrift for Jacob Rader Marcus*, ed. Bertram Wallace Korn, pp. 589–608. Waltham, MA: 1976.

Teplitz, Saul I., ed. *Best Jewish Sermons*. 2 vols. New York: 1952.

————, ed. *The Rabbis Speak*. New York: 1986.

Urofsky, Melvin I. *A Voice That Spoke for Justice: The Life and Times of Stephen S. Wise*. Albany: 1982.

Voorsanger, Jacob. *Sermons and Addresses*. New York: 1913.

Vorspan, Albert. *Giants of Justice*. New York: 1960. (On Edward Israel.)

Weiner, Herbert, ed. *Therefore Choose Life: Selected Sermons, Addresses, and Writings of Abba Hillel Silver*. Cleveland: 1967.

Weinstein, Jacob J. *Doctrine Distilled as the Dew*. Chicago: 1954–1955.

————. *My Pen Is a Ready Tongue*. Chicago: 1961.

————. *The Place of Understanding: Comments on the Portions of the Week and Holiday Cycle*. New York: 1959.

Wise, Isaac Mayer. *Reminiscences*. Ed. and trans. David Philipson. Cincinnati: 1901.

————. *Selected Writings of Isaac M. Wise, with a Biography*. Ed. David Philipson and Louis Grossman. Cincinnati: 1900.

————. *The World of My Books*. Cincinnati: n.d.

Wise, James Waterman. *Legend of Louise: The Life Story of Mrs. Stephen S. Wise*. New York: 1949.

Wise, Stephen S. *As I See It*. New York: 1944.

————. *Challenging Years: The Autobiography of Stephen S. Wise*. Ed. James Waterman Wise. New York: 1949.

————. *Free Synagogue Pulpit Sermons and Addresses*, vol. 1. New York: 1908.

————. *Stephen S. Wise, Servant of the People: Selected Letters*. Ed. Carl Hermann Voss. Philadelphia: 1969.

Wolsey, Louis. *Sermons and Addresses*. Philadelphia: 1950.

Zlotowitz, Bernard. *Radio Sermons*. Freeport, NY: 1962.

————. *Sermonettes by Bernard Zlotowitz*. Freeport, NY: 1962.

Zola, Gary P. "Reform Judaism's Pioneer Zionist: Maximilian Heller." *American Jewish History* 73 (June 1984): 375–97.

SYNAGOGUE HISTORIES*

Abington, Pennsylvania. *Dedication*. 1951. (On Old York Road Temple.)

Akron, Ohio. *Yesterday, Today and Tomorrow*. 1953 (On Temple Israel.)

Albany, New York. *Beth Emeth Congregation*. 1910, 1911, 1914, 1914–1922.

———. *Congregation Beth Emeth—130th Anniversary*. 1968.

———. "A History of the Congregation." In *Centenary Celebration*. 1938 (On Beth Emeth Congregation.)

Albuquerque, New Mexico. *Congregation Albert, 1897–1972. Albuquerque, New Mexico*. By Gunther Rosenberg. 1972.

Alexandria, Louisiana. *Seventh-fifth Anniversary Service*. 1936. (On Congregation Gemiluth Chassodim.)

Alexandria, Virginia. *Beth El Hebrew Congregation, 1859–1984*. 1984. (On Temple Beth El.)

———. "Beth El History and the Jews of Northern Virginia." By Leonard S. Bendheim. *Record* 6 (December 1971): 27–32.

———. *Temple Beth El: A Centennial History of Beth El Hebrew Congregation Serving Northern Virginia since 1959*. By Max Rosenberg and Arthur Marmor. [1962].

Altoona, Pennsylvania. *100 Years of Praise to God—100th Anniversary, 1874–1974*. 1974. (On Temple Beth Israel.)

———. *75th Anniversary, 1874–1949*. 1949. (On Beth Israel Congregation.)

Amsterdam, New York. *75th Anniversary, 1873–1948*. 1948. (On Congregation Temple of Israel.)

Anchorage, Alaska. *History of Congregation Beth Shalom*, Anchorage, Alaska. By Bernice Bloomfield. 1968.

Ann Arbor, Michigan. *Temple Beth Emeth: The First Fifteen Years, 1966–1981*. Ed. Linda Vanek and Rose Vainstein. 1982.

Ardmore, Oklahoma. *A Short History of the Congregation Temple Emeth, Ardmore, Oklahoma, 1898–1948*. By Norman Kahanowitz. 1948.

Asheville, North Carolina. *Dedication Program—New Temple*. 1949. (On Congregation Beth HaTephila.)

———. *The Golden Book of Memoirs*. 1941. (On Congregation Beth HaTephila.)

———. *75th Anniversary, Beth HaTephila, 1891–1966*. 1966.

Astoria, New York. *Third Anniversary*. 1929. (On Astoria Center of Israel.)

Atlanta, Georgia. *As But a Day: The First Hundred Years, 1868–1967*. By Janice O. Rothschild. 1967 (On Hebrew Benevolent Congregation.)

———. "The Bomb That Healed: A Personal Memoir of the Bombing of the Temple in Atlanta, 1958." By Janice Blumberg. *American Jewish History* 73 (September 1983): 20–38. (On Hebrew Benevolent Congregation.)

———. *A History of the Hebrew Benevolent Congregation [the Temple] of Atlanta . . . Fiftieth Anniversary*. By David Marx. 1917.

*Primary Sources: Alexandra Korros and Jonathan Sarna, *American Synagogue History* (New York, 1988), and Malcolm H. Stern, comp., "American Reform Judaism: A Bibliography," *American Jewish Historical Quarterly* 63 (December 1973): 120–137.

Augusta, Georgia. *Congregation Children of Israel: Into a Second Century, 1845–1945*. 1945.

——. *United for Worship and Charity: A History of Congregation Children of Israel*. By Jack Steinberg. 1983.

Austin, Texas. *Congregation Beth Israel Diamond Jubilee Anniversary, 1876–1951*. 1951.

Bainbridge, Georgia. *Historical Sketch of Temple Beth El*. 1956.

Bakersfield, California. *25th Anniversary, 1947–1972*. 1972. (On Temple Beth-El.)

Baltimore, Maryland. "Address Containing the History of Har Sinai Congregation of Baltimore City." By William Harper. In *Har Sinai Souvenir: Jubilee Year, 1842–1892*. 1892.

——. *A Brief History of Congregation Oheb Shalom, Baltimore, Maryland*. By William Rosenau. 1903.

——. *A Brief History of Congregation Oheb Shalom, Baltimore, Maryland, 1853–1928*. By William Rosenau. 1928.

——. *A Brief History of Congregation Oheb Shalom, Baltimore Maryland, 1853–1938*. By William Rosenau. 1938.

——. *The Chronicle of Baltimore Hebrew Congregation, 1830–1975*. By Rose Greenberg. 1976.

——. *Har Sinai Souvenir: Jubilee Year, 1842–1892*. 1892.

——. *History*. N.d. (On Har Sinai Congregation.)

——. *History of Har Sinai Congregation of the City of Baltimore*. By Charles Aaron Rubenstein. 1918.

——. *The History of Oheb Shalom, 1855–1953*. By Louis F. Cahn. 1953.

——. *A History of the Baltimore Hebrew Congregation [Nidhe Yisrael], 1830–1905*. By Adolph Guttmacher. 1905.

——. *The Legacy of a Liberal*. By Abraham Shusterman. 1967. (On Har Sinai Congregation.)

——. *The 1942 Yearbook of the Har Sinai Congregation, Founded 1842 at Baltimore, Maryland*. 1942.

——. *The One Hundredth Anniversary of the Baltimore Hebrew Congregation*. 1930.

Beaumont, Texas. *Temple Emanuel . . . Golden Jubilee*. 1950.

Beckley, West Virginia. *History of the Beckley Jewish Community (Beckley, West Virginia) and of Congregation Beth El (the Beckley Hebrew Association) (including Raleigh and Fayette Counties, West Virginia), (1855–1955)*. By Abraham I. Shinedling and Manuel Pickus. 1955.

Belmont, Massachusetts. *Welcome Friends and Neighbors to Beth El Temple Center*. N.d.

Benton Harbor, Michigan. *Dedication Program*. 1949. (On Temple Beth El.)

Birmingham, Alabama. *Temple Emanu-El: A Century of Reverence, 1882–1982*. 1983.

Bluefield, West Virginia. *History of Congregation Ahavath Shalom, 1904–1957*. 1957.

Blytheville, Arkansas. *Temple Israel, Silver Anniversary, 1947–1972*. 1972.

Boston, Massachusetts. *Eightieth Anniversary, 1854–1934*. 1935. (On Congregation Adath Israel [Temple Israel].)

——. *Growth and Achievement: Temple Israel, 1854–1954*. Ed. Arthur Mann. 1954.

——. *The Social History of the Changes within Temple Adath Israel, 1854–1911*. By Susan R. Abramson. 1973.

——. *The Story of Adath Israel: Issued on the Occasion of the Tenth Anniversary of*

    the Dedication of the Present House of Worship of the Congregation. By Stella
    D. Obst. 1917.

Bradford, Pennsylvania. *75th Anniversary, 1880–1955.* 1955. (On Temple Beth Zion.)

Bridgeport, Connecticut. *Dedication.* 1958. (On Congregation B'nai Israel.)

Brockton, Massachusetts. *Yearbook.* 1927. (On Congregation Israel.)

Bronx, New York. *History, 1884–1961.* 1961. (On Sinai Congregation of the Bronx.)

Brookline, Massachusetts. *At Sinai, 1939–1959.* 1959. (On Temple Sinai.)

————. *At Sinai, 1939–1964.* By David A. Lurensky. 1964. (On Temple Shalom.)

————. *Brotherhood Temple Ohabei Shalom.* 1922.

————. *The By-Laws of Temple Ohabei Shalom, Boston, Massachusetts, Prefaced with
    an Historical Sketch.* By M. Stone. 1907.

————. *Congregation Ohabei Shalom, Pioneers of the Boston Jewish Community: An
    Historical Perspective of the First One Hundred and Forty Years, 5603–5743,
    1842–1982.* By Jeanette S. and Abraham E. Nizel. 1982.

————. "The Dedication of Massachusetts' First Synagogue." By Lee M. Friedman.
    In *Jewish Pioneers and Patriots*, pp. 116–29. 1942. (On Temple Ohabei Shalom.)

————. *Dedication Program.* 1944. (On Temple Sinai.)

————. *History . . . 1843 to . . . 1893.* 1893. (On Temple Ohabei Shalom.)

————. *The History of Temple Ohabei Shalom, Boston: Principal Events from Its Or-
    ganization in 1842 to the Fiftieth Anniversary Celebration, 1893.* By Simon
    Simmons. 1893.

————. "Memoirs of Temple Ohabei Shalom, 1843 to 1918." By Abraham G. Daniels.
    In *Commemoration of the Temple's Seventh-Fifth Anniversary.* 1918.

————. *Temple Ohabei Shalom, 110th Anniversary Celebration.* 1953.

Brooklyn, New York. *A Brief History of the Congregation Beth Elohim.* 1936.

————. *Congregation Beth Elohim . . . Temple House Dedication, Brooklyn.* 1926.

————. *History, 1861–1936.* 1936. (On Congregation Beth Elohim.)

————. *History, 1911–1961.* 1961. (On Temple Beth Emeth of Flatbush.)

————. *Temple Ahavath Sholom 50th Anniversary, 1912–1962.* 1962.

————. *Twentieth Anniversary . . . 1912–1932 [with a Brief Chronicle of Congregation
    Ahavath Sholom].* 1932.

————. *Twenty-fifth Anniversary.* 1937. (On Temple Ahavath Sholom.)

————. *Union Temple of Brooklyn: One Hundred Twentieth Anniversary Souvenir, 1969.*
    1969.

Brownsville, Tennessee. *History of the Temple* [1867–1967]. 1967. (On Temple Adas
    Israel.)

Brunswick, Georgia. *Seventh-fifth Anniversary, 1886–1961.* 1961. (On Temple Beth
    Tefilloh.)

Buffalo, New York. *Celebration: 50th Anniversary of Dedication First Temple Beth Zion
    . . . Including a History of the Congregation, 1864–1915.* 1915.

————. *[Dedication], 1967.* (On Temple Beth Zion.)

Canton, Ohio. *Temple Israel Dedication.* 1954.

Chappaqua, New York. *Temple Beth El of Northern Westchester.* By Alice Wolff. 1974.

Charleston, South Carolina. *American Impact: Judaism in the Early Nineteenth Century.*
    By Lou H. Silberman. 1964.

————. "America's First Reform Jewish Congregation." By Lee M. Friedman. In
    Pilgrims in a New Land, pp. 151–60. 1948. (On the Reformed Society of Isra-
    elites.)

———. *A Bi-Centennial Anniversary in Charleston: The Story of Congregation Beth Elohim*. By Allan Tarshish. 1950.

———. *Biography of Isaac Harby with an Account of the Reformed Society of Israelites, South Carolina, 1824–1833*. By I. C. Moise. 1931.

———. *Centennial Booklet Commemorating the Introduction of Reform Judaism at Kahal Kadosh Beth Elohim*. Comp. Jacob S. Raisin. 1925.

———. "The Charleston Organ Case." By Allan Tarshish. In *Publications of the American Jewish Historical Society* 54 (June 1965): 411–99. (On Kahal Kadosh Beth Elohim.)

———. *The Congregation Beth Elohim, 1870–1883*. By Lewis Levin. 1883.

———. "Harby's Discourse on the Jewish Synagogue." By Isaac Harby. In *Publications of the American Jewish Historical Society* 32 (1931): 49–51. (On Kahal Kadosh Beth Elohim and the Reform Society of Israelites.)

———. *History of Congregation Beth Elohim of Charleston, South Carolina, 1800–1810: Compiled from Recently Discovered Records*. By Barnett A. Elzas. 1902.

———. *History of the Congregation Beth Elohim, Charleston, South Carolina*. N.d.

———. "Jewish Education in Charleston, South Carolina, during the Eighteenth and Nineteenth Centuries." By Uriah Engelman. In *Publications of the American Jewish Historical Society* 42 (September 1952): 43–70. (On Kahal Kadosh Beth Elohim.)

———. *The Reformed Society of Israelites*. By Barnett A. Elzas. 1916.

———. *Since 1750—The Story of the Kahal Kadosh Beth Elohim, American Judaism through Two Centuries*. 1950.

———. *The Story of Kahal Kadosh Beth Elohim of Charleston, South Carolina: The Oldest Synagogue in Continuous Use in the United States of America—since 1749*. 1977.

———. "The Synagogue of Kahal Kadosh Beth Elohim, Charleston." By Solomon Breibart. In *South Carolina Historical Magazine* 80 (July 1979): 215–35.

Charleston, West Virginia. *History, 1873–1948*. 1948. (On Congregation B'nai Israel.)

———. *History of the Congregation, Charleston, West Virginia, B'nai Israel Congregation (The Virginia Street Temple)*. By Samuel Volkman. N.d.

———. *Virginia Street Temple—A Little Chronicle of Origins and Events*. 1948. (On Congregation B'nai Israel.)

Chattanooga, Tennessee. *A Century of Reform Judaism, 1866–1966*. 1966. (On Mizpah Congregation.)

———. *Diamond Jubilee, 1888–1963*. 1964. (On Congregation B'nai Zion.)

———. *The Golden Book of B'nai Zion Congregation, Chattanooga, Tennessee, 1888–1938*. 1938.

———. *History of the Mizpah Congregation, Chattanooga, Tennessee, 1866–1946*. By Abraham Feinstein. N.d.

Cherry Hill, New Jersey. *Our First Thirty Years*. 1980. (On Temple Emanuel.)

Chicago, Illinois. *The Beginnings of the Chicago Sinai Congregation: A Contribution to the Inner History of American Judaism*. By Bernhard Felsenthal. 1898.

———. *Centennial Anniversary, 1861–1961*. 1961. (On Chicago Sinai Congregation.)

———. *Centennial, 1871–1971*. 1971. (On Temple Beth-El of Chicago.)

———. *Dedication*. 1950. (On Chicago Sinai Congregation.)

———. *Dedication Services*. 1924. (On Isaiah Temple.)

———. *Dedication Services, Chicago Sinai Congregation*. 1912.

————. *Fortieth Anniversary, 1864–1904*. 1904. (On Zion Congregation of West Chicago.)

————. *A History*. 1951. (On Kehilath Anshe Maariv.)

————. *History of Kehilath Anshe Maarib (Congregation of the Men of the West): Issued under the Auspices of the Congregation on the Occasion of Its Semi-Centennial Celebration, November 4, 1897*. By Bernhard Felsenthal and H. Eliassof. 1897.

————. *A History of Kehilath Anshe Mayriv Congregation of the Men of the West, Founded 1847*. 1959.

————. *History of Sinai Congregation*. By I. Hirsch. 1949.

————. *History of Temple Isaiah Israel, Chicago, Illinois (United Congregation B'nai Shalom, Temple Israel and Isaiah Temple), 1852–1952*. By Morton M. Berman. 1952.

————. *Isaiah Temple, 1896–1921*. 1921.

————. "The New Temple of Congregation B'nai Sholom Temple Israel." In *Reform Advocate* 45, no. 14 (May 31, 1913): 496.

————. *100th Anniversary, 1867–1967*. 1967. (On Temple Sholom.)

————. *120 Years: A History of K.A.M. Temple, 1847–1967*. 1967.

————. *Our First Century*. 1952. (On Temple Isaiah Israel.)

————. *70th Anniversary and Testimonial to Rabbi Louis Binstock*. 1938. (On Temple Sholom.)

————. *Seventy-fifth Birthday Celebration*. 1936. (On Chicago Sinai Congregation.)

————. *Special Number Commemorating the Fiftieth Anniversary of the Founding of Chicago Sinai Congregation*. 1911.

————. *Yearbook 1926*. 1926. (On Temple Sholom.)

Chicago Heights, Illinois. *Highlights from the History of Temple Anshe Shalom*. 1964.

Cincinnati, Ohio. *As Yesterday When It is Past: A History of the Isaac M. Wise Temple, Kehillat Kodesh Bene Yeshurun, of Cincinnati . . . 1842–1942*. By James Butheim Heller. 1942.

————. *The History of the Kehillat Kodesh Bene Yeshurun of Cincinnati, Ohio, from the Date of Its Organization . . . in Commemoration of the Fiftieth Anniversary*. 1892.

————. *The Oldest Jewish Congregation in the West: Bene Israel, Cincinnati [One Hundredth Anniversary, 1824–1924, Rockdale Avenue Temple]*. By David Philipson. 1924.

————. *The Oldest Jewish Congregation in the West [Bene Israel, Cincinnati]: Souvenir of Seventieth Anniversary, 1824–1894*. By David Philipson. 1894.

————. *One Hundred Twenty-Fifth Anniversary . . . 1949*. 1949. (On Bene Israel.)

————. *Program of Ceremonies at the Dedication of the Temple Kehillat Kodesh Bene Yeshurun of Cincinnati*. 1866.

————. *Tell Us the Wise Temple Story*. 1972. (On Isaac M. Wise Temple.)

————. *Temple Sholom, 1954–1964: 10th Anniversary Souvenir, A Personal Memoir*. By Stanley Brav. 1964.

————. *Temple Sholom, 1954–1974*. 1974.

————. *Yearbook*. 1926–1927, 1927–1928, 1928–1929, 1930–1981. (On Congregation Bene Yeshurun.)

Clarksdale, Mississippi. *Beth Israel Anniversary Issue, 1939*. 1939.

Cleveland, Ohio. *Centennial Anniversary: 1846–1946 [the Hundred Years of Religious Progress by S. M. Silver]*. 1946. (On Euclid Avenue Temple.)

————. *[Fairmont Temple] Centennial Anniversary, 1846–1946*. 1946.
————. *History of the Euclid Avenue Temple, Cleveland, Ohio, 1846–1936*. [1936].
————. *The Temple, 1850–1950*. 1950.
————. *The Temple: Fiftieth Anniversary Services*. 1900.
————. *This Tempting Freedom: The Early Years of Cleveland Judaism and Anshe Chesed Congregation*. By Allan Peskin. 1973.
Columbia, South Carolina. *The Tree of Life: Fifty Years of Congregational Life at the Tree of Life Synagogue, Columbia, South Carolina*. By Helen (Kohn) Hennig. 1945.
————. *The Tree of Life Temple, 1896–1971*. By Susan Eleanor Fischer. 1971.
Columbus, Ohio. *125th Anniversary*. 1971. (On Temple Israel.)
————. *Temple Israel: One Hundredth Anniversary Celebration, 1846–1946*. 1946.
Concord, New Hampshire. *Temple Beth Jacob [Golden Anniversary], 1917–1967*. 1967.
Corpus Christi, Texas. *History of the Jewish Community . . . Corpus Christi, Texas*. 1957. (On Temple Beth El.)
Cumberland, Maryland. *Congregation B'er Chayim: The Anniversary Story, 1853–1955*. N.d.
————. *Diamond Jubilee, [1853–1928]*. 1928. *(On Congregation B'er Chayim.)*
Dallas, Texas. *1872–1947: 75th Anniversary*. 1947. (On Temple Emanu-El.)
————. *Temple Emanu-El: 90th Anniversary, 1872–1962*. 1962.
Davenport, Iowa. *100th Anniversary, 1861–1961*. 1961 (On Temple Emanuel.)
Dayton, Ohio. *Centennial Program*. 1950. (On Congregation Israel [Temple Israel]).
————. *History*. 1863. (On Congregation Israel [Temple Israel]).
————. *History of the Congregation Israel, Dayton, Ohio, 1850–1944*. [1944]. (On Temple Israel.)
Decatur, Illinois. *Dedication [of the New Temple]*. 1958. (On Temple B'nai Abraham.)
Deerfield, Illinois. *Congregation Beth Or, 1960–1970*. 1970.
Denver, Colorado. *75th Anniversary*. 1949. (On Congregation Emanuel.)
————. *Temple Emanuel of Denver: A Centennial History*. By Marjorie Hornbein. 1974. (On Congregation Emanuel.)
Des Moines, Iowa. *75th Anniversary, 1873–1948*. 1948. (On Temple B'nai Jeshurun.)
Detroit, Michigan. *The Beth El Story with a History of the Jews in Michigan before 1850*. By Irving I. Katz. 1955.
————. *Congregation Beth El: A History . . . 1850–1900*. 1900.
————. *[Congregation Beth El]: An Outline History . . . from Its Founding 1850, to . . . Ninetieth Anniversary, 1940*. Edited by Leo M. Franklin. 1940.
————. "The Early Sites and Beginnings of Congregation Beth El." By Irving I. Edgar. In *Michigan Jewish History* 10, no. 2, and 11, no. 1 (June 1970).
————. "The Early Sites and Beginnings of Congregation Beth El of Detroit, Michigan." By Irving I. Edgar. In *Michigan Jewish History* 20 (January 1980).
————. *1861–1951: Commemorating Its 90th Anniversary*. N.d. (On Congregation Shaarey Zedek.)
————. "The First Synagogue of Congregation Beth El: The Room above the Store of Silberman and Hirsch, 1852–1859." In *Michigan Jewish History* 10 (November 1970): 5–11.
————. *Highlights of the History of Temple Beth El, Detroit, 1850–1950*. 1950.
————. *A History of Congregation Beth El, Detroit, Michigan, Compiled and Edited under the Auspices of the Historical Committee*. 1900–1910.

————. *A History of Temple Beth-El, Detroit, 1840–1945*. Comp. Irving I. Katz. [1945].

————. "Jewish Education at Temple Beth-El, 1850–1871." By Irving I. Katz. In *Michigan Jewish History* 8 (June 1968): 24–31.

————. *110 Years of Temple Beth-El, Detroit, 1850–1960: Highlights of Its History*. By Irving I. Katz. [1960].

Dothan, Alabama. *Temple Emanu-el: Silver Anniversary Year Book, 1929–1955*. 1955.

Duluth, Minnesota. *Temple Emanuel Story*. By Ida B. Davis. 1967.

Easton, Pennsylvania. *Ninety-fifth Anniversary Celebration, 1842–1937*. 1937. (On Temple Covenant of Peace.)

————. *100th Anniversary Program*. 1942. (On Temple Covenant of Peace.)

Elmira, New York. *Centennial Celebration, 1862–1962*. 1962. (On Temple B'nai Israel.)

El Paso, Texas. *1898–1928 Temple Mt. Sinai Year Book: Issued in Honor of the Thirtieth Year of Its Charter*. 1928.

————. *75th Anniversary, Temple Mt. Sinai, 1898–1973*. 1973.

Erie, Pennsylvania. *The Temple*. 1930. (On Congregation Anshe Hesed.)

Evansville, Indiana. *100th Anniversary, Washington Avenue Temple, 1857–1957: Congregation B'nai Israel, Evansville, Indiana*. 1957.

Fargo, North Dakota. *Temple Beth El: History*. 1951.

Flint, Michigan. *Dedication Book*. 1950. (On Temple Beth El.)

Florence, South Carolina. *Temple Beth Israel: Dedication*. 1970.

Flushing, New York. *The Free Synagogue of Flushing: History*. By Samuel Jaros. 1921.

Fort Lauderdale, Florida. *Temple Emanu-El: History, 1925–1941*. By S. H. Baron. 1941.

Fort Wayne, Indiana. *Congregation Achduth Ve Sholom, 1848–1948*. 1948.

————. "Passover Edition: Commemorating the One Hundredth Anniversary . . . [of] Congregation Achduth Ve Sholom." In *Indiana Jewish Chronicle* 27 (1948).

Forth Worth, Texas. *50th Anniversary*. 1972. (On Beth-El Congregation.)

Gadsden, Alabama. *A Brief History of the Congregation Beth Israel*. 1948.

————. *History, 1908–1933*. 1933. (On Congregation Beth Israel.)

Galveston, Texas. *The First Hundred Years*. 1968. (On Congregation B'nai Israel.)

Garden City, New York. *25th Anniversary of the Garden City Jewish Center*. 1978.

Gary, Indiana. *Anniversary Album of Temple Beth-El, 1908–1938*. 1938.

————. *The Story of Temple Israel*. 1959.

Glencoe, Illinois. *The First Fifty Years*. N.d. (On North Shore Congregation Israel.)

Grand Rapids, Michigan. *History of Temple Emanuel: Published on the Occasion of the Dedication of the New Temple in the 97th Consecutive Year of Its Existence, 1857–1954*. 1954.

————. *Seventieth Anniversary*. 1941. (On Temple Emanuel.)

Greensboro, North Carolina. *To Honor the 75th Anniversary, 1907–1982*. (On Temple Emanuel.)

Greenville, Mississippi. *Hebrew Union Congregation: Early History, 1850–1855*. By Herman W. Solomon. 1972.

Hagerstown, Maryland. *80 Years: Congregation B'nai Abraham, 1892–1972*. 1972.

Hamden, Connecticut. *Dedication*. 1960. (On Congregation Mishkan Israel.)

Harrisburg, Pennsylvania. *75th Anniversary*. 1926. (On Temple Ohav Shalom.)

————. *Temple Ohav Shalom Dedication Book, 1853–1953*. 1953.

Harrisonburg, Virginia. *History*. 1954. (On Hebrew Friendship Congregation.)

Hartford, Connecticut. *Binding the Generations Each to Each*. 1968. (On Congregation Beth Israel.)

————. *Our Message to the Future . . . Temple Beth Israel*. By Abraham Jehiel Feldman. 1933.

————. *Remember the Days of Old: An Outline History of the Congregation Beth Israel, 1843–1943, One Hundredth Anniversary*. By Abraham J. Feldman. 1943.

Hazleton, Pennsylvania. "History of the Congregation." By Allan Tarshish. In *Congregation Beth Israel, Hazleton, Pennsylvania, 30th Anniversary*. 1937.

————. "History of the Congregation." By Allan Tarshish. In *Congregation Beth Israel, Hazleton, Pennsylvania, 40th Anniversary*. 1946.

Henderson, Kentucky. *History, 1879–1942*. 1942. (On Adas Israel Congregation.)

Highland Park, Illinois. *Some Facts about Lakeside Congregation for Reform Judaism*. 1961.

Hoboken, New Jersey. *Seventieth Anniversary Celebration, 1871–1941*. 1941. (On Congregation Adas Emuno.)

————. *Souvenir Journal, 75th Anniversary*. 1946. (On Congregation Adas Emuno.)

Hoffman Estates, Illinois. *Beth Tikvah Congregation from Hope to Fulfillment: The First 25 Years*. 1982.

Hollywood, California. *The History of Temple Israel of Hollywood, 1926–1931*. By Louis M. Barth. 1959.

Honesdale, Pennsylvania. *Centennial Year, 1849–1949*. 1949. (On Temple Beth Israel.)

————. *Congregation Beth Israel History Compiled for the Congregation's 125th Anniversary*. By Marie R. Freund. N.d.

Honolulu, Hawaii. *Dedication*. 1960. (On Temple Emanuel.)

Hot Springs, Arkansas. *Bibilog: In Commemoration of Seventy-Five Years' Service to God and Man*. 1950. (On Temple Beth Israel.)

Houston, Texas. *The Centenary History: Congregation Beth Israel of Houston, Texas, 1854–1954*. By Anne Nathan Cohen. 1954.

Indianapolis, Indiana. *80th Birthday Celebration: [History of] the Indianapolis Hebrew Congregation, 1856–1936*. 1936.

————. *History, 1856–1956*. 1956. (On Indianapolis Hebrew Congregation.)

————. "125 Years of Judaism." By Lloyd B. Walter. In *Indianapolis Sunday Star Magazine*, n.d., pp. 6–15. (On Indianapolis Hebrew Congregation.)

————. *To 120 Years! A Social History of the Indianapolis Hebrew Congregation, 1856–1976*. By Ethel and David Rosenberg. 1979.

Jackson, Michigan. *85th Anniversary Celebration of the Founding of Temple Beth Israel and 70th Anniversary Celebration of the Founding of Hebrew Union College*. 1945.

————. *History, 1862–1949*. By Irving I. Katz. 1949. (On Temple Beth Israel.)

Jackson, Mississippi. *Congregation Beth Israel, Jackson, Mississippi: History of the Congregation, 1860–1961*. By Perry Nussbaum. 1961.

————. *History of Congregation (Beth Israel), 1859–1935*. By Charles Heuman. N.d.

Jacksonville, Florida. *Dedication: The Temple and Educational Recreational Buildings*. 1950. (On Ahavath Chesed Congregation.)

————. *The Temple Ahavath Chesed 75th Anniversary Congregation History, 1882–1957*. 1957.

————. *That Ye May Remember: Congregation Ahavath Chesed, 1882–1982*. By Natalie Glickstein. 1982.

Jasper, Alabama. *Our Fiftieth Year, 1922–1972*. 1972. (On Temple Emanuel.)

Johnstown, Pennsylvania. *Dedication of the New Beth Zion Temple*. 1951.

Jonesboro, Arkansas. *Fiftieth Anniversary*. 1948. (On Temple Israel.)
————. *History*. By Sam Leavitt. 1965. (On Temple Israel.)
Kansas City, Missouri. *The Kansas City Experiment with Reform Judaism: The First 80 Years*. By Harry G. Mayer. 1953. (On Congregation B'nai Jehudah.)
————. *Roots in a Moving Stream: The Centennial History of Congregation B'nai Jehudah of Kansas City, 1870–1970*. By Frank J. Adler. 1972.
Kenosha, Wisconsin. *Temple Beth Hillel*. 1939.
————. *Twenty-fifth Anniversary . . . History and Program*. 1949. (On Temple Beth Hillel.)
Kingston, New York. *One Hundredth Anniversary*. N.d. (On Temple Emanuel.)
————. *Reflections: A Jewish Bicentennial Edition*. 1975. (On Temple Emanuel.)
Knoxville, Tennessee. *Centennial History, Temple Beth El, Knoxville, Tennessee*. By Matthew I. Darby. 1974.
————. *Earliest History of Temple Beth El, Knoxville, Tennessee*. By Matthew I. Darby. 1974.
————. *A Short History of Temple Beth El, Knoxville, Hebrew Congregation Beth El*. By Matthew I. Darby. N.d.
————. *Temple Beth El, 80th Anniversary*. 1947.
Kokomo, Indiana. *Dedication, Temple B'nai Israel*. 1942.
Lafayette, Indiana. *One Hundred Year History, 1849–1949*. 1949. (On Temple Israel.)
Lancaster, Pennsylvania. *Congregation Shaarei Shomayim . . . Ninetieth Anniversary*. 1946.
————. *Lancaster's Gates of Heaven, Portals to the Past: The 19th Century Jewish Community of Lancaster, Pennsylvania, and Congregation Shaarai Shomayim, 1856–1976*. By David A. Brener. 1976.
————. *100th Anniversary, 5617–5717*. 1957. (On Congregation Shaarai Shomayim.)
La Porte, Indiana. *Notes on the History of the Jewish Congregation and Cemetery B'nai Zion of La Porte, Indiana*. N.d.
Lawrence, Massachusetts. *Dedication*. 1957. (On Temple Emanuel.)
————. *50th Anniversary Year, 1920–1970*. 1970. (On Temple Emanuel.)
Lawrence, New York. *Celebrating the Thirtieth Anniversary of the Founding of the Temple and the Tenth Anniversary of W. B. Schwartz's Ministry*. 1938. (On Temple Israel.)
Lexington, Kentucky. *Kehillat Kodesh Adath Israel [Ashland Avenue Temple] History*. 1926.
Little Rock, Arkansas. *The Centennial History of Congregation B'nai Israel*. By Ira E. Sanders and Elijah E. Palnick. 1966.
Los Angeles, California. *Congregation B'nai B'rith [Wilshire Boulevard Temple] History, 1860–1947*. By Marco Newmark. 1947.
————. *Congregation B'nai B'rith [Wilshire Boulevard Temple], [Seventh-fifth Anniversary, 1862–1937]*. 1937.
————. *Fifteenth Annual of the Congregation B'nai B'rith, Los Angeles, California*. 1915.
————. "The First Synagogue in Los Angeles." By Tom Owen. In *Western States Historical Quarterly* 1 (October 1968): 9–13.
————. "Wilshire Boulevard Temple: Congregation B'nai B'rith, 1862–1947." By Marco R. Newmark. In *Historical Society of Southern California* 38 (June 1956): 167–184.

Louisville, Kentucky. *Dedication Service*. 1951. (On B'rith Sholom Congregation.)

————. *History of the Congregation Adath Israel, Louisville, Kentucky, and the Addresses Delivered at the Dedication of Its New Temple, September 6, 7, and 9, 1906*. 1906.

Lynbrook, New York. *50th Anniversary*. 1920. (On Temple Emanu-El.)

Lynchburg, Virginia. *Agudath Sholom, 5658–5718, 1897–1951: A Dedication to the Future*. 1957.

Macon, Georgia. *Centennial Celebration, 1859–1959*. 1959. (On Temple Beth Israel.)

————. *A History of Temple Beth-Israel of Macon, Georgia*. By Newton J. Friedman. 1955.

Manchester, New Hampshire. *Dedication*. 1959. (On Temple Adath Yeshurun.)

————. *Silver Anniversary, 1912–1937*. 1937. (On Temple Adath Yeshurun.)

Marblehead, Massachusetts. *Twenty-fifth Anniversary, 1954–1979*. 1979. (On Temple Emanu-El.)

Martinsburg, West Virginia. *History: 50th Anniversary, 1913–1963*. 1963. (On Congregation Beth Jacob.)

Memphis, Tennessee. *Temple Israel: Our First Century, 1854–1954*. Ed. Ernest Lee. 1954.

Miami, Florida. *Dedication Book*. 1955. (On Temple Israel.)

————. *History of Temple Israel, Miami, Florida*. By Herbert Feibelman. 1955.

————. *Synagogue in the Central City: Temple Israel of Greater Miami, 1922–1972*. By Charlton W. Tebeau. 1972.

Michigan City, Indiana. *The History of Sinai Temple*. 1953.

Middletown, Ohio. *Dedication Book*. 1956. (On Temple Beth Shalom.)

Milwaukee, Wisconsin. *Congregation Emanu-El, Ten Years*. By S[igmund] Hecht. 1898.

————. *1869–1919: Golden Anniversary*. 1919. (On Congregation Emanu-El.)

————. *Recollections of the Old Temple Emanuel in Milwaukee*. By Henry C. Friend. 1972.

Minneapolis, Minnesota. *The Story of Temple Israel, Minneapolis, Minnesota: A Personal Account*. By Albert G. Minda. 1971.

Mobile, Alabama. *Congregation Shaarai Shamayim, 1844–1944*. 1944.

————. *One Hundred Twenty-fifth Anniversary, Springhill Avenue Temple, 1844–1969*. N.d. (On Congregation Sha'arai Shomayim, also known as Springhill Avenue Temple.)

Monessen, Pennsylvania. *Dedication*. 1954. (On Knesseth Israel Synagogue.)

Monroe, Louisiana. *Congregation B'nai Israel, 1868–1915*. 1915.

Montgomery, Alabama. *Diamond Jubilee, 1852–1927*. 1927. (On Kahl Montgomery.)

————. *The First 100 Years of Kahl Montgomery, Published on the Occasion of Its 100th Anniversary*. 1952.

Mount Vernon, New York. *Treasure Hunt Journal*. 1945. (On Sinai Temple.)

Nashville, Tennessee. *The Temple of Congregation Ohabai Sholom: Dedication*. 1955.

Natchez, Mississippi. *Story of Temple B'nai Israel, Natchez, Mississippi*. By Julius Kerman. 1955.

Newark, New Jersey. *The Ninetieth Anniversary Celebration . . . 1938*. 1938. (On Congregation B'nai Jeshurun.)

————. *The Seventh-Fifth Anniversary Celebration*. 1923. (On Congregation B'nai Jeshurun.)

Newark, Ohio. *History of Ohav Israel Congregation, 1907–1957*. [1957].

Newburgh, New York. *The Anniversary Story, 1854–1954*. 1954. (On Congregation Beth Jacob.)

New Castle, Pennsylvania. *Temple Israel: 25th Anniversary, 1926–1951*. 1951.

New Haven, Connecticut. *Centennial Volume . . . 1840–1940*. 1940. (On Congregation Mishkan Israel.)

———. *History of the Congregation Temple Mishkan Israel, 1840–1940*. N.d.

———. "Innovation and Consolidation: Phases in the History of Temple Mishkan Israel." By Jonathan D. Sarna. In *Jews in New Haven*, Ed. Barry E. Herman and Werner E. Hirsch, pp. 101–9. 1981.

New Iberia, Louisiana. *Congregation Gates of Prayer: History*. By Louis Newhart Ackerman. N.d.

New Orleans, Louisiana. *A History*. [1968]. (On Touro Synagogue.)

———. *A History of Touro Synagogue, New Orleans*. By Leo A. Bergman. 1968.

———. *Jubilee Souvenir of Temple Sinai, 1872–1922*. By Max Heller. 1922.

———. *One Hundredth Anniversary, 1850–1950, Congregation Gates of Prayer, New Orleans, Louisiana*. 1950.

———. *Our First One Hundred Years*. 1970. (On Temple Sinai.)

New Rochelle, New York. *The History of Temple Israel of New Rochelle, New York*. By Jacob K. Shankman. 1977.

———. *Temple Israel: The First Fifty Years, 1908–1958*. 1958.

———. *30th Anniversary Celebration: 1908–1938*. 1938. (On Temple Israel.)

New York, New York. *Celebration of the Ninetieth Anniversary of the Founding of Congregation Shaaray Tefila, West End Synagogue*. 1935.

———. *Centenary Celebration [1845–1945] of Congregation Emanu-El of the City of New York*. 1945.

———. *Central Synagogue Centennial, 1846–1946: Commemorating a Century of Service to God and America*. 1946.

———. *Central Synagogue, 140 Years [1839–1979]*. Ed. Stella J. Fuld, Mildred Ross and Janet Stone. N.d.

———. "Central Synagogue Portfolio: Centennial for Central Synagogue." *National Jewish Monthly* 85 (December 1970): 39.

———. *Congregation Rodeph Shalom: Its Past*. 1948.

———. *Congregation Rodeph Shalom: 10th Anniversary, 1842–1942*. 1942.

———. *Dedication of Temple Beth El, September 18, 1891*. 1891. (On Congregation Beth El.)

———. *40th Anniversary . . . 1907–1947*. 1947. (On Free Synagogue.)

———. *Golden Jubilee*. 1924. (On Temple Beth-El.)

———. "Historical Review of Congregation Shaaray Tefila [West End Synagogue]." By Nathan Stern. In *Celebration of the Ninetieth Anniversary of the Founding of Congregation Shaaray Tefila, West End Synagogue*. 1935.

———. "A History of New York's Temple Emanu-El: The Second Half Century." By Ronald B. Sobel. Ph.D. dissertation, New York University, 1980.

———. "History of the Beth-El Congregation (NY)." By Max Kohler. *American Hebrew* 40 (September 1891): 158–61. (On Temple Beth-El.)

———. *The History of the Congregation . . . from the Date of Its Organization, 1842*. [1892]. (On Congregation Rodeph Shalom.)

———. *Isaac Mayer Wise and Emanu-El*. By Isadore Levi. 1930.

————. *Journal of the Ninetieth Anniversary Celebration*. 1932. (On Congregation Rodeph Shalom.)

———— "The Minute Book of Lilienthal's Union of German Synagogues." By Hyman B. Grinstein. *Hebrew Union College Annual* 28 (1944): 324–52.

————. *140 Years: A Proud Tradition . . . A Vital Future*. [1979]. (On Central Synagogue.)

————. "One Hundred Years of Congregation Emanu-El." By Nathan A. Perilman. In *Moral and Spiritual Foundations for the World of Tomorrow: The Centenary Series . . . Prepared for the Hundredth Anniversary of Congregation Emanu-El of the City of New York*. 1945.

————. "Reforms at Temple Emanuel of New York: 1860–1890." By Hyman B. Grinstein. *Historia Judaica* 6 (1944): 163–74.

————. *The Rise and Progress of Reform Judaism, Embracing a History Made from the Official Records of Temple Emanu-El of New York, with a Description of Salem Field Cemetery*. By Myer Stern. 1895.

————. *Seventh-fifth Anniversary Celebration of Congregation Emanu-El of New York City*. 1920.

————. *75th Anniversary (1870–1945)*. 1945. (On Temple Israel.)

————. *Shaaray Tefila: A History of Its Hundred Years, 1845–1945*. By Simon Cohen. 1945.

————. *The Synagogue and Social Welfare: A Unique Experiment (1907–1953)*. By Sidney Emanuel Goldstein. 1955.

————. *Temple Emanu-El, 1880–1900*. By Rita Rubinstein Heller. 1961.

————. *Your Temple*. 1958. (Reprinted 1960). (On Central Synagogue.)

Norfolk, Virginia. *One Hundred and Twenty-fifth Anniversary: Ohef Sholom Temple, 1844–1969*. By Elise Levy Margolius. 1970.

————. "Some Notes on the History of the Organized Jewish Community of Norfolk." By Malcolm H. Stern. In *Journal of the Southern Jewish Historical Society* 1 (November 1963): 12–336. (On Ohef Sholom Temple.)

Oakland, California. *First Hebrew Congregation: Seventy-fifth Anniversary of Temple Sinai*. 1950.

————. "The History of the First Hebrew Congregation of Oakland, 1875–1975." By Fred Rosenbaum. In *1875–1975: Temple Sinai, Oakland, California*, pp. 8–27. 1975.

Oak Park, Illinois. *History, 1864–1958*. 1958. (On Oak Park Temple B'nai Abraham Zion.)

Oklahoma City, Oklahoma. *50th Anniversary, 1903–1953*. 1953. (On B'nai Israel Congregation.)

————. *Year of Dedication, 1955*. 1955. (On B'nai Israel Congregation.)

Olympia Fields, Illinois. *Dedication*. 1964. (On Temple Anshe Sholom.)

————. *Temple Anshe Sholom: A Beth Torah of Olympia Fields*. By Leo and Gerry Slov. 1977.

Omaha, Nebraska. *Consider the Years 1871–1971: Congregation of Temple Israel, Omaha, Nebraska*. By Suzanne Richards Somberg and Silvia Greene Roffman. 1971.

Parkersburg, West Virginia. *Centennial Service*. 1956. (On Temple B'nai Israel.)

Peoria, Illinois. *Yearbook, 1959–1960*. 1960. (On Temple Anshai Emeth.)

Petoskey, Michigan. "Congregation B'nai Israel of Petoskey." By Zalman B. Fryman. In *Michigan Jewish History* 11 (1971): 20–23.
———. *75th Anniversary Celebration.* 1971. (On Congregation B'nai Israel.)
Philadelphia, Pennsylvania. *From . . . the Pulpit.* 1964. (On Congregation Rodeph Shalom.)
———. "Hebrew German Society Rodeph Shalom in the City and County of Philadelphia (1800–1950)." By Jeanette W. Rosenbaum. In *Publications of the American Jewish Historical Society* 41 (September 1951): 83–93.
———. *History, 1943–1964.* 1964. (On Beth David Reform Congregation.)
———. *The History of Rodeph Shalom Congregation, Philadelphia, 1802–1926.* By Edward Davis. 1926.
———. *90th Anniversary Record.* 1937. (On Reform Congregation Knesseth Israel.)
———. "Notes on the History of the Earliest German Jewish Congregation in America." By Harry Berkowitz. In *Publications of the American Jewish Historical Society* 9 (1901): 123–37. (On Congregation Rodeph Shalom.)
———. *Proceedings of the Laying of the Corner Stone for the Synagogue of the Congregation Rodeph Shalom, July 20, 1869.* 1869.
———. *Reform Congregation Keneseth Israel, 1847–1972.* 1972.
———. *Reform Congregation Keneseth Israel: Its First 100 Years, 1847–1947.* 1950.
———. "Rodeph Shalom, Philadelphia, 1800–1850." By Jeanette W. Rosenbaum. *Liberal Judaism* 18 (September 1950): 41–46.
———. *Rodeph Shalom: Tradition and Innovation, 1927–1987.* By Ellen Norman Stern. 1987.
———. *Temple Judea: Silver Anniversary, 1930–1955.* 1955.
———. *Temple Judea: Thirty-fifth Anniversary, 1930–1965.* 1965.
———. *Three Aspects of the Development of the Rodeph Shalom Congregation of Philadelphia, 1810–1940.* By Joseph Levine. 1956.
Phoenix, Arizona. *Dedication Souvenir.* 1950. (On Temple Beth Israel.)
———. *Yovel, Temple Beth Israel, 1920–1970.* 1970.
Pine Bluff, Arkansas. *History and Activities of Congregation Anshe Emeth.* By Raphael Goldstein. 1917.
Pittsburgh, Pennsylvania. *Centennial and Dedication Festival Recollections, 1856–1956.* 1956. (On Rodef Shalom Congregation.)
———. *One Hundred Twenty Years, Rodef Shalom Congregation, Pittsburgh, Pennsylvania.* By Marcus L. Aaron. 1976.
———. "Pittsburgh and the Synagogue Tradition." By Walter Jacob. In *Carnegie Magazine* 56 (May/June 1983).
Pittsfield, Massachusetts. *The History of Congregation Anshe Amonim.* By Robert G. Newman. 1961.
Plattsburg, New York. *Beth Israel Congregation, 75th Anniversary, 1861–1936.* 1936.
———. *The Jewish Congregations of Plattsburg.* By Henry K. Freedman. 1975.
Pontiac, Michigan. *Dedication Volume.* 1955. (On Temple Beth Jacob.)
———. *50th Anniversary, 1923–1973.* 1973. (On Temple Beth Jacob.)
Portland, Oregon. "Beth Israel Anniversary Supplement." In *The Jewish Tribune*, June 26, 1914. (On Temple Beth Israel.)
———. *A Brief History of the Congregation Beth Israel, Portland, Oregon, 1858–1888.* N.d.
———. *Congregation Beth Israel, 1858–1933.* 1933.

———. *1858–1933: Seventy-Fifth Anniversary Program and Historical Review.* 1933. (On Congregation Beth Israel.)

———. *The Ties Between: A Century of Judaism in America's Last Frontier.* By Julius J. Nodel and Alfred Apsler. 1959. (On Temple Beth Israel.)

Portsmouth, Ohio. *Congregation Beneh Abraham: 100th Anniversary, 1858–1958.* 1958.

Providence, Rhode Island. *Congregation of the Sons of Israel and David: One Hundred Twenty Fifth Anniversary, A Pictorial Memoir.* 1980. (On Temple Beth El.)

———. "Congregation of the Sons of Israel and David (Temple Beth El), the Early Years." By David C. Adelman. In *Rhode Island Jewish Historical Notes* 3 (May 1962): 195–261.

———. *Dedication of Temple Beth El Congregation of Sons of Israel and David.* 1954.

———. *Journal of the Ninetieth Anniversary, 1844–1934.* 1934. (On Temple Beth El/ Congregation Sons of Israel and David.)

———. "We Look Back." By William G. Braude. In *Rhode Island Jewish Historical Notes* 5 (May 1967): 120–26. (On Temple Beth El.)

Pueblo, Colorado. *History of Temple Emanuel, 1900–1956.* 1956.

———. *Temple Emanuel: History of the Founding of the Temple.* By Simon F. Elliot. 1956.

Raleigh, North Carolina. *Golden Anniversary.* 1936. (On Congregation Beth Or.)

———. *A New Beth Or: "Light for Tomorrow."* 1976.

Reading, Pennsylvania. *100th Anniversary, 1864–1964.* 1964. (On Oheb Shalom.)

———. *Seventh-Fifth Anniversary of Reform Congregation Oheb Shalom, 1864–1939.* 1939.

Richmond, Virginia. *A Commemorative History of Congregation Beth Ahabah, 1841–1966.* Edited by Saul Viener. 1966.

———. *A History of Congregation "Beth Ahabah," Richmond, Virginia, from Its Organization to Its Sixtieth Anniversary, 1841–1901.* 1901.

———. *The Light Burns On, 1841, 1891, 1941: Centennial Anniversary, Congregation Beth Ahabah, Golden Jubilee.* 1941.

———. *125th Anniversary Celebration . . . Valentine Museum Exhibit.* 1966. (On Beth Ahabah Congregation.)

———. *Richmond, City of Churches: A Short History of Richmond's Denominations and Faith.* [1957]. (On Congregation Beth Ahabah.)

Ridgefield, Connecticut. *History, 1966–1969.* 1969. (On Temple Shearith Israel.)

Rochester, New York. *Temple Brith Kodesh, 1848–1948.* [1948].

Sacramento, California. "The Old Jewish Synagogue on 15th Street." By Martha Wire. 1961. (On Congregation B'nai Israel.)

St. Louis, Missouri. *Dedication.* 1963. (On Temple Emanuel.)

———. *The First Twenty Years . . . Temple Emanuel, 1956–1978.* By Estelle Shamski. 1976.

———. *Golden Jubilee History of Temple Israel, 1886–1936.* 1937.

———. *The Oldest Jewish Congregation West of the Mississippi River: The United Hebrew Congregation, St. Louis, Missouri.* By Jane Driwer. 1963.

———. *One Hundredth Anniversary, United Hebrew Congregation, 1838–1938.* 1938.

———. *Origin and Early History of the United Hebrew Congregation of St. Louis, 1841–1959, the First Jewish Congregation in St. Louis.* By Donald I. Makovsky. 1958.

St. Paul, Minnesota. *Mount Zion, 1856–1956: The First Hundred Years.* By W. Gunther Plaut. 1956.

————. *95th Anniversary [of Mount Zion Hebrew Congregation]*. 1952.

————. *75th Anniversary of the Founding of Mount Zion Hebrew Congregation*. 1932.

St. Petersburg, Florida. *St. Petersburg, Florida, Temple Beth-El: History of the Temple, 1926–1951*. By Eva Radzinsky. 1951.

Salt Lake City, Utah. "Congregation Kol Ami: Religious Merger in Salt Lake City." By Hynda Rudd. In *Western States Jewish Historical Quarterly* 10 (July 1978): 311–26.

San Antonio, Texas. *Diamond Jubilee, 1874–1949*. 1949. (On Temple Beth-El.)

San Diego, California. *The Anniversary Story: Souvenir History and Program Commemorating the 75th Anniversary of Congregation Beth Israel, San Diego, California, 5637–5712*. 1952.

————. "The First Temple Beth Israel: San Diego." In *Western States Jewish Historical Quarterly* 11 (January 1979): 153–61.

Sandusky, Ohio. *Dedication Program*. 1956. (On Congregation Oheb Shalom.)

San Francisco, California. *Architects of Reform: Congregational and Community Leadership, Emanu-El of San Francisco, 1849–1980*. By Fred Rosenbaum. 1980.

————. "The Cantorate at Sherith Israel, 1893–1957." By Kenneth C. Zerwin. In *Western States Jewish Historical Quarterly* 17 (January 1985): 114–50.

————. *Divre Yeme Emanuel: The Chronicles of Emanu-El, Being an Account of the Rise and Progress of Congregation Emanu-El which was founded in July, 1850, and Will Celebrate Its Fiftieth Anniversary December 23, 1900*. By Jacob Voorsanger. 1900.

————. "A Merger of Synagogues in San Francisco." By Carolyn L. Winer. In *Jewish Journal of Sociology* 14 (December 1972): 167–96.

————. *100th Anniversary . . . 1850–1950*. 1950. (On Congregation Sherith Israel.)

————. "An Orthodox Rabbi and a Reforming Congregation in Nineteenth Century San Francisco." In *Western States Jewish Historical Quarterly* 15 (April 1983): 275–81. (On Congregation Sherith Israel.)

————. *Program: 90th Anniversary, 1850–1940*. 1940. (On Congregation Sherith Israel.)

————. *The Sage of Congregation Emanu-El, San Francisco, California, 1850–1950*. 1950.

————. "The Sage of the First Fifty Years of Congregation Emanu-El, San Francisco." By Edgar M. Kahn. In *Western States Jewish Historical Quarterly* 3 (April 1971): 129–47.

————. "A San Francisco Synagogue Scandal in 1893." By Norton B. Stern. In *Western States Jewish Historical Society* 6 (April 1974): 196–203.

————. "Temple Emanu-El of San Francisco: A Glory to the West." By Allan Temko. In *Commentary* 26 (August 1958): 107–118.

San Jose, California. *Centennial Anniversary, 1861–1961*. 1961. (On Temple Emanu-El.)

Sarasota, Florida. *Souvenir Dedicatory Program*. 1962. (On Temple Emanu-el.)

Savannah, Georgia. *Congregation Mickve Israel, Savannah, Georgia, 1840–1860*. By Walter Blumenthal. 1957.

————. *Culture, Practices and Ideals of Congregation Mickve Israel, Savannah, Georgia*. By Morris M. Hershman. 1956.

————. *A Short History of Congregation Mickve Israel*. 1957.

————. *Third to None: The Sage of Savannah Jewry, 1933–1983*. By Saul Jacob Rubin. 1983. (On Congregation Mickve Israel.)

Schenectady, New York. "History of Our Congregation." By Nathan Sahr. In *100th Anniversary of the Temple Gates of Heaven, 1854–1954*. 1954.

Schulenberg, Texas. *Temple Israel of Schulenberg, Texas, and Its Affiliated Cities and Institutions*. By Abraham I. Shinedling. 1960.

Scranton, Pennsylvania. *Congregation Anshe Chesed . . . Seventy-fifth Anniversary*. 1937.

————. *The Madison Avenue Temple, Congregation Anshe Chesed, 1860–1960*. 1960.

Seattle, Washington. *Dedication of the New Sanctuary*. 1960. (On Temple De Hirsch.)

Sharon, Pennsylvania. *Dedication . . . 1950*. 1950. (On Temple Beth Israel.)

Sherman, Texas. *History of the Community, 1846–1916*. N.d. (On Temple Beth Emeth.)

Sioux City, Iowa. *Dedication*. 1856. (On Mount Sinai Temple.)

South Bend, Indiana. *The First 75 Years, 1905–1980*. [1980]. (On Temple Beth-El.)

Springfield, Illinois. *History: Compiled in Commemoration of the Seventieth Anniversary*. 1935. (On Temple B'rith Sholom.)

————. *History of Temple B'rith Sholom, Springfield, Illinois*. By Seymour R. Mendelson. 1974.

Springfield, Ohio. *100th Anniversary, 1866*. 1966. (On Temple Sholom.)

Staunton, Virginia. *History*. 1968. (On Reform Congregation of Israel.)

Steubenville, Ohio. *Silver Anniversary, 1924–1949*. 1949. (On Temple Beth El.)

Sumter, South Carolina. *Temple Sinai: Brief Congregational History*. By Marian Moise. 1973.

Syracuse, New York. "The Days of the Years." By Benjamin Friedman. In *One Hundredth Anniversary, 1839–1939*. [1939]. (On Temple Society of Concord.)

————. *History, 1839–1964*. (On Temple Society of Concord.)

Tallahassee, Florida. *Service of Dedication*. 1973. (On Temple Israel.)

Tampa, Florida. *Golden Anniversary, 1894–1944*. 1944. (On Congregation Shaarai Zedek.)

————. *75 Years: Congregation Shaarai Zedek, Tampa, Florida, 1894–1969*. 1969.

Toledo, Ohio. *Dedication Program*. 1952. (On Congregation Shomer Emunim.)

————. *75th Anniversary, 1875–1950*. 1950. (On Congregation Shomer Emunim.)

Topeka, Kansas. *Topeka, Kansas, Temple Beth Shalom, Parliamentary Digest*. By Elbert L. Sapinsley. 1964.

Trinidad, Colorado. "A Synagogue for Trinidad, Colorado—1889." In *Western States Jewish Historical Quarterly* 11 (October 1978): 18–19.

————. *Temple Aaron in Commemoration of 3 Anniversaries*. 1949.

Troy, New York. *A Century of Temple Berith Sholom, 1866–1966*. By Samuel Rezneck. 1966.

Tucson, Arizona. *Commemorative Book in Recognition of the Sixtieth Anniversary of the . . . Founding as First Synagogue in the Territory of Arizona, March 10, 1910*. 1970. (On Temple Emanu-El.)

————. *Temple Emanu-El: Thirtieth Anniversary, 1910–1940*. 1941.

Tulsa, Oklahoma. *Memorial Volume, 1913–1943*. 1943. (On Temple Israel.)

Utica, New York. *Temple Emanu-El, History: Dedication and Tenth Anniversary*. N.d.

Waco, Texas. *Souvenir Fair Book*. 1899. (On Congregation Rodef Sholem.)

Washington, D.C. *Golden Jubilee (Exercises and Addresses Pronounced at the Fiftieth Anniversary of the Washington Hebrew Congregation, December 19, 1905)*. 1906.

————. "A History of the Washington Hebrew Congregation." By Bernard I. Nordlinger. In *Record* 4 (November 1969): 1–82.

————. *Washington, Hebrew Congregation: A History of the Congregation in Commemoration of Its Jubilee.* By Abram Stern. 1905.

Westfield, New Jersey. *A Historic Narrative: The Story of Temple Emanu-El [1950–1980].* By Evelyn Averick. 1981.

West Hempstead, New York. *25th Anniversary Journal.* 1970. (On Nassau Community Temple.)

Wheeling, West Virginia. *A Brief History of Congregation Leshem Shomayim, Wheeling, West Virginia.* By Harry Levi. 1899. (On Temple Shalom.)

Wilkes-Barre, Pennsylvania. *A Century with Wilkes-Barre: Congregation B'nai Brith of Wilkes-Barre, Pennsylvania, Announces the Completion of 100 Years of Service [1845–1945].* 1945.

————. *History of the Temple.* 1924. (On Congregation B'nai Brith.)

Williamson, West Virginia. *The Everlasting Light.* 1918. (On Temple B'nai Israel.)

Williamsport, Pennsylvania. *A Century of Illustrious Service.* 1965. (On Beth ha-Shalom Congregation.)

————. *Eightieth Anniversary Celebration, 1866–1946.* 1946. (On Beth ha-Shalom Congregation.)

————. *Four Score and Ten Years, 1866–1956.* 1956. (On Beth ha-Shalom Congregation.)

Wilmington, Delaware. *A Brief History Commemorating the Twentieth Anniversary of the Dedication and Use of the Temple of Truth, Congregation Beth Emeth.* 1928.

————. *Congregation Beth Emeth, 20th Anniversary Ball.* By Louis Mischkind. 1928.

————. *Reflections on the Past: A Few of the Memorable Highlights of Congregation Beth Emeth and Its Sisterhood.* 1983.

Wilmington, North Carolina. *Bibliography, Temple of Israel: Oldest Jewish Congregation in North Carolina.* 1976.

————. "Brief History of Temple of Israel, Wilmington, North Carolina." By Karl Rosenthal. In *Seventy-Fifth Anniversary, Temple of Israel, Wilmington, North Carolina.* 1951.

Worcester, Massachusetts. *Silver Anniversary Celebration.* 1946. (On Temple Emanuel.)

Yonkers, New York. *In Commemoration of the Consecration and Dedication of the New Temple Sanctuary and Religious School.* 1960. (On Temple Emanu-El.)

————. *Kodesh: The History, Art and Artifacts of Temple Emanu-El, Yonkers, New York.* By Abraham J. Klausner. 1976.

————. *Tercentary Journal.* 1955. (On Temple Emanu-El.)

York, Pennsylvania. *Dedication Exercises.* 1962. (On Temple Beth Israel.)

Youngstown, Ohio. *Congregation Rodef Shalom, 1867–1967.* 1967.

PRAYER BOOKS AND MANUALS

Brav, Stanley R. *A Guide for Religious Practice.* Cincinnati: 1962.

Bronstein, Herbert, ed. *A Passover Haggadah.* New York: 1974.

Calisch, Edward N. *A Book of Prayer for Jewish Worship.* Richmond: 1893.

Central Conference of American Rabbis. *Blessings and Praise.* Cincinnati: 1923.

————. *Gates of Forgiveness.* New York: 1980.

————. *The Isaac Harby Prayerbook.* Charleston: 1979.

————. *Revised Rabbi's Manual.* New York: 1946.

————. *A Ritual for Jewish Soldiers.* Cincinnati: 1916.

————. *Service for Confirmation Shavvos*. New York: 1962.

————. A Shabbat Manual. New York: 1972.

————. *Union for Jewish Worship*. Cincinnati: 1914.

————. *Union Haggadah*. [Cincinnati]: 1923.

————. *Union Hymnal: Musical Services for Sabbath and Festivals According to Newly Revised Union Prayer Book*. Cincinnati: 1942.

————. *Union Prayer Book, Part I: The Sabbath, the Three Festivals and the Daily Prayers*. Chicago: 1892.

————. *Union Prayer Book, Part II. New Year's Day, Day of Atonement*. Cincinnati: 1894.

Cohn, Edward L. *Evening Service for Israel Independence Day*. New York: 1920.

Day Book of Service at the Altar. Los Angeles: 1978.

Dreyfus, A. Stanley, ed. *Book of Prayers*. Cincinnati: 1948.

Einhorn, David. *Olat Tamid*. [Chicago]: 1896.

Feldman, Abraham J. *Reform Judaism: A Guide for Reform Jews*. New York: 1956.

————, ed. *Confirmation*. New York: 1948.

Folkman, Jerome D. *Design for Jewish Living: A Guide for the Bride and Groom*. New York: 1955.

Friedland, Eric L. *"Olath Tamid* by David Einhorn," *Hebrew Union College Annual*, 45 (1974): 313–18.

Harby, Isaac. *The Sabbath Service and Miscellaneous Prayers of the Reformed Society of Israelites*. Reprint. Columbia, SC: 1974.

Hirsch, Emil G., trans. *Dr. David Einhorn's Book of Prayers for Jewish Congregations*. Chicago: 1896.

Knobel, Peter, ed. *Gates of Seasons*. New York: 1983.

Krauskopf, Joseph. *The Mourner's Service*. Philadelphia: 1895.

————. *The Service-Ritual*. Philadelphia: 1888.

————, ed. *Service Manual*. Philadelphia: 1892.

————, ed. *Service Ritual/Service Hymnal*. Philadelphia: 1888.

Lazaron, Morris. *Religious Service for Jewish Youth*. Baltimore: 1927.

Levy, J. Leonard. *A Book of Prayer*. 2d ed. Pittsburgh: 1902.

Margolies, Israel Raphael, ed. *Temple Emanu-El Prayerbook for Sabbath and Festivals*. Englewood, NJ: 1950.

Maslin, Simeon J., ed. *Gates of Mitzvah*. New York: 1979.

Maslin, Simeon J., and Max Janowski. *The Sabbath Eve Seder*. Chicago: 1971.

Ner Tamid: Die Lehre des Judenthums, dargestellt fur Schule und Hans. Philadelphia: 1866.

Olat Tamid: Gebetbuch fur Israelitishce Reform—Gemeinde. Baltimore: 1858.

Olitzky, Kerry M. "Rituals for the Sunday Sabbath." *Journal of Reform Judaism*, Summer 1984, pp. 66–71.

Petuchowski, Jakob J. "Manuals and Catechisms of the Jewish Religion in the Early Period of Emancipation." In *Studies in Nineteenth Century Jewish Intellectual History*, ed. Alexander Altmann. Cambridge, MA: 1964.

Reform Congregation Beth-El of Sudbury River Valley. *V'Taher Libenu*. Sudbury, MA: 1981.

Renaissance Liturgical Service: Plum Street Temple, April 2, 1982. Cincinnati: 1982.

The Sabbath Service and Miscellaneous Prayers, Adopted by the Reformed Society of

Israelites. Charleston: 1830. Reprint, with an introduction by Barnett A. Elzas. New York: 1916.

Schusterman, Abraham. *A Prayerbook for Jewish Children*. Baltimore: 1966.

Seder ha-avodat: Gebetbuch fur die offentliche und hausliche Andacht, nach dem Gebrauche des Neuen Israelitischen Tempels in Hamburg. Hamburg: 1841.

Seder Tefilah: Gebetafur den offentlichen Gottesdienst der Tempelgemeinde Ahawath Chesed. 2 vols. New York: 1872.

Service for Erev Shabat at the Plum Street Temple. Cincinnati: 1982.

Shirim U-Zemirot—Songs and Hymns: A Musical Supplement to Gates of Prayer. New York: 1977.

Siskin, Edgar E. *Family Worship Services*. Glencoe, IL: N.d.

Stern, Chaim. *Gates of Joy*. New York: 1979.

———, ed. *Days of Awe*. New York: 1971.

———, ed. *Gates of Freedom: A Passover Haggadah*. Bedford, NY: 1981.

———, ed. *Gates of the House*. New York: 1977.

———, ed. *Gates of Prayer: The New Union Prayerbook*. New York: 1975.

———, ed. *Gates of Repentance*. New York: 1978.

Union Hymnal. Cincinnati: 1932.

The Union Prayer-Book for Jewish Worship: Morning Services. New York: 1907.

Werner, Eric, ed. *Union Songster: Songs and Prayers for Jewish Youth*. New York: 1960.

Wise, Aaron, ed. *The Temple Service for the Sabbath and Festivals*. New York: 1897.

Wise, Isaac M. *Minhag America* (for Day of Atonement). Cincinnati: 1866.

———. *Minhag America*. Cincinnati: 1892.

Zion, Joel. *Sabbath Prayerbook for Young People*. Denver: 1953.

SECONDARY SOURCES

Arfa, Cyrus. *Reforming Reform Judaism: Zionism and the Reform Rabbinate, 1885–1948*. Tel Aviv: 1985.

Bernfeld, Simon. *Toledot ha-reformatsyon ha-datit be-yisrael*. Cracow: 1900.

Blau, Joseph Leon, ed. *Reform Judaism: A Historical Perspective*. New York: 1973.

Borowitz, Eugene B. *Liberal Judaism*. New York: 1984.

———. *Reform Judaism Today*. New York: 1977.

Cohn-Sherbok, Dan. "Law and Freedom in Reform Judaism." *Journal of Reform Judaism*, Winter 1983, pp. 88–97.

Cohon, Samuel S. "Reform Judaism in America." *Judaism* 3 (Fall 1954): 333–53.

"A Commentary on 'Reform Judaism, a Centenary Perspective.' " *Central Conference of American Rabbis Journal* 24 (Spring 1977): entire issue.

Eisen, Arnold M. *The Chosen People in America: A Study of Jewish Religious Ideology*. Bloomington, IN: 1983.

Fein, Leonard J., et al. *Reform Is a Verb: Notes on Reform and Reforming Jews*. New York: 1972.

Feldman, Abraham J. *The American Reform Rabbi: A Profile of a Profession*. New York: 1965.

Fox, Steven A. "On the Road to Unity: The UAHC and American Jewry, 1873–1903." *American Jewish Archives* 32 (1980): 145–93.

Furman, Freda Kerner. *Beyond Yiddishkeit: The Struggle for Jewish Identity in a Reform Synagogue*. Albany: 1987.

Gamoran, Emanuel. *A Curriculum for the Jewish Religious School*. Cincinnati: 1937.

———. *A Survey of 125 Religious Schools Affiliated with the Union of American Hebrew Congregations*. Cincinnati: 1925.

Gertman, Stuart A. *"And You Shall Teach Them Diligently: A Study of the Current State of Religious Education in the Reform Movement*. New York: 1977.

——— "The Language of Survival: Curriculum and Textbook." *Central Conference of American Rabbis Journal* 24 (Summer 1977): 37–47.

Glasner, Samuel, and Rosenstock, Elliot D. "The Case for/against a Reform Jewish Day School." *Dimensions in American Judaism*, Summer 1969, pp. 36–39.

Greenstein, Howard R. *Turning Point: Zionism and Reform Judaism*. Chico, CA: 1981.

Gutmann, Joseph. "How Traditional Are Our Traditions?" *Central Conference of American Rabbis Journal* 15 (April 1968): 59.

Guttman, Alexander. *The Struggle over Reform in Rabbinic Literature during the Last Century and a Half*. New York: 1977.

Hertz, Richard C. *The Education of the Jewish Child: A Study of 200 Reform Jewish Religious Schools*. New York: 1953.

Hertzberg, Arthur. "The Changing American Rabbinate." *Midstream*, January 1966, pp. 16–29.

Jacob, Walter, ed. *The Changing World of Reform Judaism: The Pittsburgh Platform in Retrospect*. Pittsburgh: 1985.

Karff, Samuel, E., ed. *Hebrew Union College—Jewish Institute of Religion at One Hundred Years*. Cincinnati: 1976.

Kaufmann, Manahem. *Lo-tsiyonim be-amerikah be-ma'avak al ha-medinah*. Jerusalem: 1984.

Knee, Stuart E. "From Controversy to Conversion: Liberal Judaism in America and the Zionist Movement, 1917–1941." *YIVO Annual* 17 (1978): 260–89.

Korn, Bertram W., ed. *Retrospect and Project: Essays in Commemoration of the Seventy-fifth Anniversary of the Founding of the Central Conference of American Rabbis, 1889–1964*. New York: 1965.

Kraut, Benny. "The Ambivalent Relations of American Reform Judaism with Unitarianism in the Last Third of the Nineteenth Century." *Journal of Ecumenical Studies* 23 (1986): 58–68.

Kukoff, Lydia. *Choosing Judaism*. New York: 1981.

Lenn, Theodore. *Rabbi and Synagogue in Reform Judaism*. New York: 1972.

Levy, Beryl Harold. *Reform Judaism in America: A Study in Religious Adaptation*. New York: 1933.

Lewis, Irving. "Reform Jews and Zionism, 1919–1921." *American Jewish Archives* 14 (1962): 3–19.

Liberales, Robert. "Conflict over Reforms: The Case of Congregation Beth Elohim, Charleston, South Carolina." In *The American Synagogue: A Sanctuary Transformed*, ed. Jack Wertheimer. Cambridge, England: 1987.

———. "The Rabbinical Conferences of the 1850s and the Quest for Liturgical Unity." *Modern Judaism* 3 (1983): 309–17.

Lieberman, Morris. "The Role and Functions of the Modern Rabbi." *Central Conference of American Rabbis Yearbook* 79 (1969): 211–24.

Liebman, Charles. "Changing Social Characteristics of Orthodox, Conservative, and Reform Jews." *Sociological Analysis* 27 (1966): 210–22.

Maller, Allen S., and Raphael, Marc Lee. "The Cost of Mixed Marriages." *Central Conference of American Rabbis Journal* 18 (April 1971): 83–85.

Marcus, Jacob R., and Peck, Abraham J., eds. *The American Rabbinate: A Century of Continuity and Change, 1883–1983*. Hoboken, NJ: 1985.

Martin, Bernard, ed. *Contemporary Reform Jewish Thought*. New York: 1968.

Mervis, Leonard J. "The Social Justice Movement and the American Reform Rabbi." *American Jewish Archives* 7 (1955): 171–230.

Messer, Ellen. "Franz Boas and Kaufmann Kohler: Anthropology and Reform Judaism." *Jewish Social Studies* 48 (1986): 127–40.

Meyer, Michael A. "American Reform Judaism and Zionism: Early Efforts at Ideological Rapproachement." *Studies in Zionism* 7 (Spring 1983): 49–64. Hebrew version in *Ha-Tsiyonut* 9 (1984): 95–110.

———. "Beyond Particularism." *Commentary*, March 1971, pp. 71–76.

———. "The Establishment of the Hamburg Temple." [Hebrew]. In *Studies in the History of Jewish Society in the Middle Ages and the Modern Period Presented to Professor Jacob Katz*. Jerusalem: 1980.

———. *Response to Modernity: A History of the Reform Movement in Judaism*. New York: 1988.

Neusner, Jack, ed. *Sectors of American Judaism*. New York: 1975.

Olitzky, Kerry M. "Rituals for the Sunday Sabbath." *Journal of Reform Judaism*, Summer 1984, pp. 66–71.

——— "The Sunday-Sabbath Movement in American Reform Judaism." *American Jewish Archives* 34 (April 1982): 75–88.

Philipson, David. "The Pittsburgh Rabbinical Conference." Central Conference of American Rabbis *Yearbook* 45 (1935): 193–96.

———. *The Reform Movement in Judaism*. New York: 1931, 1967.

Plaut, W. Gunther. *The Growth of Reform Judaism*. New York: 1965.

———. *The Rise of Reform Judaism*. New York: 1963.

Poppel, Stephen M. "The Politics of Religious Leadership: The Rabbinate in Nineteenth Century Hamburg." *Leo Baeck Institute Yearbook* 28 (1983): 439–70.

Raphael, Marc Lee. *Profiles in American Judaism: The Reform, Conservative, Orthodox and Reconstructionist Traditions in Historical Perspectives*. San Francisco: 1984.

Regner, Sidney L. "The Rise and Decline of the Sunday Service." *Journal of Reform Judaism*, Fall 1980, pp. 32–38.

Reinhart, Arthur L. *The Voice of the Jewish Laity: A Survey of the Jewish Layman's Religious Attitudes and Practices*. Cincinnati: 1928.

Ritter, Immanuel Heinrich. *Geschichte der judischen Reformation*. 4 vols. Berlin: 1858–1902.

Rockaway, Robert A. "The Progress of Reform Judaism in Late 19th and Early 20th Century Detroit." *Michigan Jewish History*, January 1974.

Rosenberg, Adolph, et al. *Statement of the Union of American Hebrew Congregations on the American Jewish Conference*. N.p.: 1945.

Rosenthal, Gilbert S. *Contemporary Judaism: Patterns of Survival*. New York: 1986.

———. *The Many Faces of Judaism: Orthodoxy, Conservative, Reconstructionist, Reform*. New York: 1978.

Sarna, Jonathan D. "New Light on the Pittsburgh Platform of 1885." *American Jewish History* 76 (1986–1987): 358–688.

Schein, Jeffrey. "Changes in the Reform Curriculum." *Journal of Reform Judaism,* Spring 1982, pp. 58–68.

Schoolman, Leonard A. *Welcome to Reform Judaism.* New York: 1981.

Schreiber, Emanuel. *Reformed Judaism and Its Pioneers: A Contribution to Its History.* Spokane, WA: 1892.

Schwartzman, Sylvan David. *Reform Judaism in the Making.* New York: 1955.

———. *Reform Judaism Then and Now.* New York: 1971.

Schwarz, Jacob D. *Ceremonies in Modern Jewish Life.* Cincinnati: 1973.

Seligmann, Caesar. *Geschichte der judischen Reformbewegung.* Frankfurt a/m: 1922.

Showstack, Gerald L. *Suburban Communities: The Jewishness of American Reform Jews.* Atlanta: 1988.

Silberman, Lou H. *American Impact: Judaism in the United States in the Early Nineteenth Century.* Syracuse: 1964.

Silver, Daniel Jeremy, ed. *In the Time of Harvest: Essays in Honor of Abba Hillel Silver on the Occasion of His 70th Birthday.* New York: 1963.

Statistics of the Jews of the United States, compiled under the authority of the Board of Delegates of American Israelites and the Union of American Hebrew Congregations. Philadelphia: 1880.

Stern, Malcolm. "America's First Reform Jews." *American Jewish Historical Quarterly* 63 (1973): 118–29.

———. "Reforming of Reform Judaism: Past, Present and Future." *American Jewish Historical Quarterly* 63 (1973): 111–37.

Sussman, Lance J. "The Suburbanization of American Judaism as Reflected in Synagogue Building and Architecture, 1945–1975." *American Jewish History* 75 (1985/1986): 31–47.

Syme, Daniel B. "Reform Judaism and Day Schools: The Great Historical Dilemma." *Religious Education* 78 (1983): 153–81.

Tarshish, Allan. "The Board of Delegates of American Israelites (1859–1878)." *Publications of the American Jewish Historical Society* 49 (1959/1960); 16–32.

Temkin, Sefton D. *The New World of Reform.* Bridgeport: 1974.

———. "The Pittsburgh Platform: A Centenary Assessment." *Journal of Reform Judaism,* Fall 1985, p. 172.

Umansky, Ellen. "Women in Judaism: From the Reform Movement to Contemporary Jewish Religious Feminism." In *Women of Spirit: Female Leadership in the Jewish and Christian Traditions,* Rosemary Ruether and Eleanor McLaughlin, eds. New York: 1979.

Union of American Hebrew Congregations. *Jewish Students: A Survey Dealing with the Religious, Educational, Social and Fraternal Activities among Jewish Students at Universities and Colleges.* Cincinnati: 1915.

Weiner, Herbert. "Conversion: Is Reform Judaism So Right?" *Dimensions in American Judaism,* Winter 1971, pp. 4–7.

Winer, Mark L. "Jewish Demography and the Challenges to Reform Jewry." *Journal of Reform Judaism* 31 (Winter 1984): 1–27.

———. *Leaders of Reform Judaism: A Study of Jewish Identity, Religion, Practices, Belief and Marriage Patterns.* New York: 1987.

Zehavi, Y. Zvi. *Tenuat ha-hitbolelut be-yisrael.* Tel Aviv: 1943.

Zeitlin, Joseph. *Disciples of the Wise: The Religious and Social Opinions of American Rabbis*. New York: 1945.

UNPUBLISHED WORKS

Address, Richard F. "Rabbi Joseph Krauskopf: Selected Thoughts." Term paper, Hebrew Union College—Jewish Institute of Religion, Cincinnati, 1969.

Akselrad, Sidney. "Studies in the Development of Conservative and Reform Judaism in the United States." Rabbinical thesis, Hebrew Union College, Cincinnati, 1947.

Alpert, Rebecca Trachtenberg. "From Jewish Science to Rabbinical Counseling: The Evaluation of the Relationship between Religion and Health by the American Reform Rabbinate, 1916–1954." Ph.D. dissertation, Temple University, 1978.

Annes, Charles A. "The Life and Works of Joseph Krauskopf." Rabbinical thesis, Hebrew Union College–Jewish Institute of Religion, Cincinnati, 1954.

Arian, Avram. "Reform Rabbis and the Movement for Official Authority: The Abrogation of Modernity." Thesis, Brown University, Providence, RI, 1971.

Arnold, Stephen A. "Ideas of Immortality in American Reform Ritual." Rabbinical thesis, Hebrew Union College–Jewish Institute of Religion, Cincinnati, 1960.

Bleiberg, James S. "The Debate over Day School Education in Reform Judaism: A Historical Study." Rabbinical thesis, Hebrew Union College–Jewish Institute of Religion, Cincinnati, 1982.

Bornstein, Lewis Richard. "Halachic Problems of Reform Judaism: Twenty Questions and Answers." Rabbinical thesis, Hebrew Union College–Jewish Institute of Religion, Cincinnati, 1972.

Borowitz, Eugene B. "The Jewish Religion According to the Liberal Reform Tradition." Ed.D. dissertation, Columbia University, 1958.

Boxman, Bradd H. "The Significance of Brit Milah in Reform Judaism." Rabbinical thesis, Hebrew Union College–Jewish Institute of Religion, Cincinnati, 1986.

Caminker, Harold Floyd. "Reform Judaism in the United States and Its Relationship to Zionism as Reflected Primarily in Sources Heretofore Not Researched, 1889–1948." Rabbinical thesis, Hebrew Union College–Jewish Institute of Religion, Cincinnati, 1978.

Cogdell, Gaston D. "American Reform Judaism as Reflected in the *Proceedings of the UAHC*, 1898–1903." Unpublished paper, Hebrew Union College–Jewish Institute of Religion, Cincinnati, 1962.

Cohen-Gavarian, Jody Ruth. "The Omer Celebration of Matitayahu Shelem: An Instance of Creative Jewish Ritual and Its Relevance to Reform Communities Today." Rabbinical thesis, Hebrew Union College–Jewish Institute of Religion, New York, 1984.

Cohn, Edward P. "Reform Judaism as Reflected in the Conference Messages of the Presidents of the CCAR from 1920–1945." Unpublished paper, Hebrew Union College–Jewish Institute of Religion, Cincinnati, 1971.

———. "Reform Judaism in the Nineteen-Sixties." Unpublished paper, Hebrew Union College–Jewish Institute of Religion, Cincinnati, 1973.

Datz, Michael. "Poor Cousin or Parent Body? The World Union for Progressive Judaism during its First Fifty Years, 1926–1976." Rabbinical thesis, Hebrew Union College–Jewish Institute of Religion, Cincinnati, 1987.

Downing, Thomas A. "Bernard Felsenthal: His Identities and Work." Unpublished paper, Hebrew Union College–Jewish Institute of Religion, Cincinnati, 1974.

Eichhorn, Jonathan. "Attempts at Creedal Formulations in American Reform Judaism." Rabbinical thesis, Hebrew Union College–Jewish Institute of Religion, Cincinnati, 1962.

Engel, Steven W. "A Critical Psychobiography of Kivie Kaplan against the Backdrop of Black-Jewish Relations." Rabbinical thesis, Hebrew Union College–Jewish Institute of Religion, Cincinnati, 1988.

Falk, Gustave F. "The Doctrine of Revelation in Reform Judaism with Special Emphasis on Geiger, Holdheim, Einhorn, Wise and Kohler." Rabbinical thesis, Hebrew Union College–Jewish Institute of Religion, Cincinnati, 1928.

Foster, Steven E. "The Development of the Social Action Program of Reform Judaism, 1878–1969." Rabbinical thesis, Hebrew Union College–Jewish Institute of Religion, Cincinnati, 1970.

Frank, David M. "Tisha B'Av: A Reform Perspective." Rabbinical thesis, Hebrew Union College–Jewish Institute of Religion, New York, 1983.

Frank, Emmet A. "The Attitude toward Music and Ritual in the Evolution from Orthodoxy to Reform in the American Synagogue as Reflected in Congregational Histories." Rabbinical thesis, Hebrew Union College–Jewish Institute of Religion, Cincinnati, 1952.

Freehling, Allen I. "Reform Judaism: An Anvil for Social Justice." Ph.D. dissertation, Kensington University, Glendale, CA, 1977.

Friedland, Eric Lewis. "The Historical and Theological Development of the Non-Orthodox Prayerbooks in the United States." Ph.D. dissertation, Brandeis University, 1967.

Gershon, Phillip S. "A History of Reform Judaism, 1885–1900." Rabbinical thesis, Hebrew Union College–Jewish Institute of Religion, Cincinnati, 1955.

Gitlin, Seymour. "American Jewish Reform as Reflected in the *Proceedings of the UAHC*, 1891–1897." Unpublished paper, Hebrew Union College–Jewish Institute of Religion, Cincinnati, 1961.

Glassman, Linda L. "Wise and Cincinnati: The Heart and Heartbeat of Reform Judaism." M.A. thesis, University of Cincinnati, 1965.

Gold, Stephen D. "Trends in Reform Judaism as Reflected in the *Journal of Reform Judaism*." Term paper, Hebrew Union College–Jewish Institute of Religion, Cincinnati, 1984.

Goldberg, Robert E. "Hyman G. Enelow: Rabbi, Scholar and Preacher." Rabbinical thesis, Hebrew Union College–Jewish Institute of Religion, Cincinnati, 1945.

Goldman, Joseph. "An Inquiry into the Significance of the High Holy Days for Reform Jews." Rabbinical thesis, Hebrew Union College–Jewish Institute of Religion, Cincinnati, 1959.

Goldstein, Jerrold. "Reform Rabbis and the Progressive Movement." M.A. thesis, University of Minnesota, 1967.

Goldstein, Ronald M. "Trends in American Reform as Reflected in the CCAR Yearbooks for 1960–1964." Unpublished paper, Hebrew Union College–Jewish Institute of Religion, Cincinnati, 1965.

Gordon, Theodore H. "The Liturgy of the Reform Movement in America to the Union Prayer Book." Rabbinical thesis, Hebrew Union College–Jewish Institute of Religion, Cincinnati, 1933.

Grand-Golomb, Deborah. "Women and Reform Jewish Education." M.A. thesis, He-
    brew Union College–Jewish Institute of Religion, New York, 1975.
Grollman, Jerome W. "The Emergence of Reform Judaism in the United States." Rab-
    binical thesis, Hebrew Union College–Jewish Institute of Religion, Cincinnati,
    1948.
Grumbacher, Peter Henry. "The Sabbath Concept in Reform Judaism." Rabbinical thesis,
    Hebrew Union College–Jewish Institute of Religion, Cincinnati, 1972.
Halpern, Audrey. "The American Experience: Influences on the Music of Reform and
    Conservative Judaism." M.A. thesis, Hebrew Union College–Jewish Institute of
    Religion, New York, 1987.
Hart, Stephen A. "An Historical Overview of the Function of Music in the American
    Reform Synagogue." Rabbinical thesis, Hebrew Union College–Jewish Institute
    of Religion, Cincinnati, 1986.
Heilbrunn, Bernice Ann. "Emil G. Hirsch: Reform Advocate." Paper submitted in partial
    fulfillment of requirements for B.A., Radcliffe College, Cambridge, MA, 1970.
Henry, Sharyn H. "An Analysis of the Changing Attitudes toward Ritual Mitzvot in the
    American Reform Movement, 1885–1987." Rabbinical thesis, Hebrew Union
    College–Jewish Institute of Religion, Cincinnati, 1988.
Herman, Floyd F. "Some Aspects of the Life of Stephen S. Wise to 1925." Rabbinical
    thesis, Hebrew Union College–Jewish Institute of Religion, Cincinnati, 1964.
Hermann, Bennett. "Trends in American Reform as Reflected in the Proceedings of the
    Union of American Hebrew Congregations, 1945–1955." Unpublished paper,
    Hebrew Union College–Jewish Institute of Religion, Cincinnati, 1965.
Herscher, Uri David. "Stephen S. Wise: His Character and Values Manifested in
    Speech." Rabbinical thesis, Hebrew Union College–Jewish Institute of Religion,
    Cincinnati, 1970.
Hoffman, Sydney L. "An Historical Analysis of Some Changing Concepts in the Reform
    Rabbinate between the Two World Wars on the Basis of the CCAR *Yearbook*,
    1918–1942." Rabbinical thesis, Hebrew Union College–Jewish Institute of Re-
    ligion, Cincinnati, 1956.
Horowitz, David M. "The Use of the Halacha Dealing with Marriage in the Reform
    Movement as Seen through the Reform Responsa on Marriage." Rabbinical thesis,
    Hebrew Union College–Jewish Institute of Religion, Cincinnati, 1969.
Huber, Gary A. "A Comparative Study of the Prayerbooks of Krauskopf, Landsberg,
    Szold, Union Prayerbook, Minhag Amerika and Einhorn's Olat Tamid: The The-
    ological Significance of the Difference." Term paper, Hebrew Union College–
    Jewish Institute of Religion, Cincinnati, 1977.
Jessel, David. "American Jewish Reform as Reflected in the *Proceedings of the UAHC*,
    1886–1890." Unpublished paper, Hebrew Union College–Jewish Institute of Re-
    ligion, Cincinnati, 1961.
Jick, Leon A. "The Efforts of Isaac Mayer Wise to Establish a Jewish College in the
    United States." Hebrew Union College–Jewish Institute of Religion, Cincinnati,
    N.d.
Kamrass, Lewis H. "The Life and Works of Rabbi Samuel Schulman as Reflected in
    His Writings: A Critical Historical Study of One of Reform's Most Significant
    Leaders." Rabbinical thesis, Hebrew Union College–Jewish Institute of Religion,
    Cincinnati, 1985.
Kanter, Morton M. "Conceptions of Jewishness among the Laity in American Reform

Congregations.'' Rabbinical thesis, Hebrew Union College–Jewish Institute of Religion, Cincinnati, 1956.

Karol, Lawrence P. ''Rabbinic Leadership in the Reform Movement as Reflected iin the Life and Writings of Rabbi Abraham Jehiel Feldman (1893–1977).'' Rabbinical thesis, Hebrew Union College–Jewish Institute of Religion, Cincinnati, 1981.

Karol, Stephen A. ''Reform Jewish Life in the U.S., 1897–1910, as Reflected in the Yearbooks of the CCAR.'' Unpublished paper, Hebrew Union College–Jewish Institute of Religion, Cincinnati, 1976.

————. ''Reform Judaism during the Depression, 1929–1941: A Period of 'Retrenchment.' '' Unpublished paper, Hebrew Union College–Jewish Institute of Religion, Cincinnati, 1975.

Kasdan, Peter. ''Some Aspects of Nihum Avelim in the Tradition and in Reform Jewish Practice Today.'' Rabbinical thesis, Hebrew Union College–Jewish Institute of Religion, Cincinnati, 1966.

Katzman, Aviva. ''The Development of Music in the 20th Century American Reform Synagogue.'' M.A. thesis, Hebrew Union College–Jewish Institute of Religion, New York, 1987.

Kaufman, Jay H. ''Antecedents and Beginnings of the Reform Movement in American Judaism.'' Rabbinical thesis, Hebrew Union College–Jewish Institute of Religion, Cincinnati, 1946.

Kohn, Douglas J. ''The Dean of American Rabbis: A Critical Study of . . . David Philipson.'' Rabbinical thesis, Hebrew Union College–Jewish Institute of Religion, Cincinnati, 1987.

Kolsky, Thomas A. ''Jews against Zionism: The American Council for Judaism, 1942–1948.'' Ph.D. dissertation, George Washington University, 1986.

Levitan, Kalman L. ''The Problem of Ritual and Practice in Reform Judaism.'' Rabbinical thesis, Hebrew Union College–Jewish Institute of Religion, New York, 1948.

Levy, David C. ''The Transition from Classical to Neo-Reform in the Period following World War II.'' Term paper, Hebrew Union College–Jewish Institute of Religion, Cincinnati, 1985.

Librach, Clifford E. ''Judaism beyond Autonomy: A Philosophy of Halaka for Liberal Jews.'' Rabbinical thesis, Hebrew Union College–Jewish Institute of Religion, Cincinnati, 1986.

Loeb, Garry A. ''The Changing Religious Role of the Reform Jewish Woman.'' Rabbinical thesis, Hebrew Union College–Jewish Institute of Religion, Cincinnati, 1981.

Ludlow, Victor. ''Bernhard Felsenthal: Quest for Zion.'' Ph.D. dissertation, Brandeis University, 1984.

Ludwig, Stephen. ''Trends, Changes and Goals in American Reform as Reflected in the *Proceedings of the UAHC*, 1873–1900.'' Unpublished paper, Hebrew Union College–Jewish Institute of Religion, Cincinnati, 1972.

Martin, Bernard. ''The Message of Emil G. Hirsch's Sermons.'' Rabbinical thesis, Hebrew Union College–Jewish Institute of Religion, Cincinnati, 1951.

Marx, Robert J. ''Kaufman Kohler as Reformer.'' Rabbinical thesis, Hebrew Union College–Jewish Institute of Religion, Cincinnati, 1951.

Matzi, Milton. ''Theological Developments in American Reform Judaism as Reflected by the Proceedings of the CCAR during the Years 1890–1937.'' Rabbinical thesis, Hebrew Union College–Jewish Institute of Religion, Cincinnati, 1952.

Mecklenburger, Ralph D. "The Theologies of Isaac Mayer Wise and Kaufmann Kohler."
    Rabbinical thesis, Hebrew Union College–Jewish Institute of Religion, Cincinnati,
    1972.
Meisels, Stanley Darrell. "Reform and Conservative Judaism in the Mirror of Orthodoxy:
    An Historical Survey, 1939 to 1968." Rabbinical thesis, Hebrew Union College–
    Jewish Institute of Religion, Cincinnati, 1970.
Mendel, Norman T. "Glimpses into the Life of a Famous Rabbi and Zionist: Max Heller."
    Unpublished paper, Hebrew Union College–Jewish Institute of Religion, Cincin-
    nati, 1965.
———. "The Rise and Growith of Reform Judaism in Los Angeles." Rabbinical thesis,
    Hebrew Union College–Jewish Institute of Religion, Cincinnati, 1968.
Mervis, Leonard J. "The Social Justice Movement of the American Reform Rabbis,
    1890–1940." Ph.D. dissertation, University of Pittsburgh, 1951.
Mevorah, Barouh. "The Messiah Question in the Disputes over Emancipation and Re-
    form, 1781–1819" [Hebrew]. Ph.D. dissertation, Hebrew University, 1966.
Meyer, David J. "Elements of the Return to Tradition in American Reform Judaism from
    1885–1976." Rabbinical thesis, Hebrew Union College–Jewish Institute of Re-
    ligion, Cincinnati, 1987.
Milgrom, Shira. "Systematizations of Halaka and Implications for Liberal Judaism."
    Rabbinical thesis, Hebrew Union College–Jewish Institute of Religion, New York,
    1986.
Miller, Bennett F. "A Time to Sing: Reform Synagogue Music Today." Rabbinical
    thesis, Hebrew Union College–Jewish Institute of Religion, Cincinnati, 1974.
Newman, Max. "Basic Principles of American Reform Judaism and Their Reflection in
    the Movement's Program of Religious Education from 1848 to the Present."
    Ph.D. dissertation, Hebrew Union College–Jewish Institute of Religion, Cincin-
    nati, 1963.
Olitzky, Kerry M. "A History of Reform Jewish Education during Emanuel Gamoran's
    Tenure as Educational Director of the Commission on Jewish Education of the
    Union of American Hebrew Congregations, 1923–1958." D.H.L. dissertation,
    Hebrew Union College–Jewish Institute of Religion, Cincinnati, 1984.
———. "The Sunday Sabbath Movement in Reform Judaism." Rabbinical thesis, He-
    brew Union College—Jewish Institute of Religion, Cincinnati, 1981.
Pomerantz, Frederic S. "The Birth and Initial Expansion of the UAHC (1873–1903).
    Unpublished paper, Hebrew Union College–Jewish Institute of Religion, Cincin-
    nati, 1966.
Richman, Milton. "Studies of Three American Reform Temples between Two World
    Wars." Rabbinical thesis, Hebrew Union College–Jewish Institute of Religion,
    Cincinnati, 1952.
Robinson, Michael A. "The God Idea in American Reform Judaism." Rabbinical thesis,
    Hebrew Union College–Jewish Institute of Religion, Cincinnati, 1952.
Rosen, David Bennett. "A Critical Study of Reforms in Hilkhot Kashrut Based on the
    Responsa of the Rabbinical Assembly (Conservative) vis-à-vis Orthodox and Re-
    form Responsa." Rabbinical thesis, Hebrew Union College–Jewish Institute of
    Religion, Cincinnati, 1980.
Rosoff, Donald. "Toledat ha-reformatsyon ha-daht beyisrael." Rabbinical thesis, Hebrew
    Union College–Jewish Institute of Religion, Cincinnati, 1981.
Rubenstein, Aryeh. "Reshitah shel tenuat ha-reformah be-yahadut artzot ha-berit ve-ha-

pulmus sevivah ba-shanim, 1840–1969.'' Ph.D. dissertation, Hebrew University, 1973.

Ryback, Martin B. ''The East-West Conflict in American Reform as Reflected in the *Israelite*, 1854–1879.'' Rabbinical thesis, Hebrew Union College–Jewish Institute of Religion, Cincinnati, 1949.

Sajowitz, William N. ''History of Reform Judaism in San Antonio, Texas, 1874–1945.'' Rabbinical thesis, Hebrew Union College–Jewish Institute of Religion, Cincinnati, 1945.

Saltzman, Murray. ''The Development of Reform Judaism in New York City, 1885–1900.'' Rabbinical thesis, Hebrew Union College–Jewish Institute of Religion, Cincinnati, 1956.

Sapinsley, Elbert Lee. ''The Split between the Reform and Conservative Jewish Movements in America.'' Rabbinical thesis, Hebrew Union College–Jewish Institute of Religion, Cincinnati, 1954.

Satlow, Lewis A. ''The Evolution of the Reform Prayer Book.'' Rabbinical thesis, Hebrew Union College–Jewish Institute of Religion, Cincinnati, 1942.

Schulman, Avi M. ''Visionary and Activist: A Biography of Maurice N. Eisendrath.'' Rabbinical thesis, Hebrew Union College–Jewish Institute of Religion, Cincinnati, 1984.

Schwartzman, Allan H. ''William Rosenau: His Life and Work as Rabbi and Communal Leader.'' Rabbinical thesis, Hebrew Union College–Jewish Institute of Religion, Cincinnati, 1955.

Scott, Robert M. ''The Transition from Classical Reform to New Reform Judaism as Reflected in Synagogue and Other Publications.'' Rabbinical thesis, Hebrew Union College–Jewish Institute of Religion, Cincinnati, 1966.

Serotta, Isaac. ''Reform Judaism and Ritual Divorce.'' Rabbinical thesis, Hebrew Union College–Jewish Institute of Religion, New York, 1988.

Shapiro, Mark S. ''Reform Judaism in the Heyday of Classicity, 1905–1914.'' Unpublished paper, Hebrew Union College–Jewish Institute of Religion, Cincinnati, 1960.

Shapiro, Max A. ''An Historical Analysis and Evaluation of Jewish Religious School Textbooks Published in the United States, 1817–1903.'' Ed.D. dissertation, University of Cincinnati, 1960.

Shpeen, Scott L. ''A Man against the Wind: A Biographical Study of Rabbi Morris S. Lazaron.'' Rabbinical thesis, Hebrew Union College–Jewish Institute of Religion, Cincinnati, 1984.

Siegel, Lawrence M. ''The Neo-Reform Growth of American Reform Judaism as Reflected in the CCAR *Yearbook*, 1942–1959.'' Rabbinical thesis, Hebrew Union College–Jewish Institute of Religion, Cincinnati, 1961.

Smigel, Howard S. ''American Reform Judaism as Reflected in the *Proceedings of the UAHC*, 1873–1879.'' Unpublished paper, Hebrew Union College–Jewish Institute of Religion, Cincinnati, 1962.

Sniderman, Stephen Ludwig. ''Trends, Changes and Goals in American Reform as Reflected in the *Proceedings of the UAHC*, 1925–1955.'' Unpublished paper, Hebrew Union College–Jewish Institute of Religion, Cincinnati, 1973.

Spiro, John. ''Dissertation on Roland Gittelsohn. In progress.

Stahl, Samuel M. ''The 'About-Face' of American Reform Judaism since 1945.'' D.H.L.

dissertation, Hebrew Union College–Jewish Institute of Religion, Cincinnati, 1974.

Stern, Elizabeth Weiss. "Approaching God: Some Contemporary Reform Perspectives." Rabbinical thesis, Hebrew Union College–Jewish Institute of Religion, Cincinnati, 1984.

Stern, Jack. "The Doctrine of Immortality in Reform Judaism." Rabbinical thesis, Hebrew Union College–Jewish Institute of Religion, Cincinnati, 1952.

Stever, Ulrick B. "The Adaptation of the Synagogue to American Culture, with Particular Consideration of the American Reform Synagogue." M.A. thesis, University of Illinois, 1946.

Stillpass, Leo J. "The Attitude of Reform Judaism toward Intermarriage." Rabbinical thesis, Hebrew Union College–Jewish Institute of Religion, Cincinnati, 1944.

Syme, Daniel B. "The Growth of the Hebrew Union College–Jewish Institute of Religion in the United States and Abroad." Rabbinical thesis, Hebrew Union College–Jewish Institute of Religion, Cincinnati, 1972.

Temkin, Sefton D. "Isaac Mayer Wise, 1819–1875." Ph.D. dissertation, Hebrew Union College–Jewish Institute of Religion, Cincinnati, 1963.

Treister, Edward. "Robert P. Goldman: A Leader in Reform Judaism, 1943–1963." Term paper, Hebrew Union College–Jewish Institute of Religion, Cincinnati, 1969.

Wechman, Robert J. "Emanuel Gamoran: Pioneer in Jewish Religious Education." Ph.D. dissertation, Syracuse University, 1970.

Weiss, Gretel D. "Searching for Roots: Modernization and Demodernization in Reform Judaism." Thesis, Rutgers University, 1978.

Weiss, Kenneth. "Solomon B. Freehof–Reforging the Links: An Approach to the Authenticity of the Reform Rabbi in the Modern World." D.H.L. dissertation, Hebrew Union College–Jewish Institute of Religion, Cincinnati, 1980.

Winter, Nathan B. "The Emergence of Reform Judaism in Chicago, 1841–1861." M.A. dissertation, Northwestern University, Evanston, IL, 1949.

Wolf, Sylvin Lawrence. "Reform Judaism as a Process: A Study of the CCAR, 1960–1975." Ph.D. dissertation, St. Louis University, 1978.

Yedwab, Paul Michael. "Na'aseh V'nishma: Faith Development in a Liberal Jewish Context." Rabbinical thesis, Hebrew Union College–Jewish Institute of Religion, New York, 1986.

Zionts, Richard. "Reform Jewish Attitudes Regarding Intermarriage in the Light of Halakic and Historic Antecedents." Rabbinical thesis, Hebrew Union College–Jewish Institute of Religion, Cincinnati, 1965.

INDEX

CONTRIBUTORS

A.C.W.   Alfred C. Wolf, Rabbi, Director, Skirball Institute on American Values, American Jewish Committee, Los Angeles, CA.

A.D.H.   Anthony D. Holz, Rabbi, Kahal Kodesh Beth Elohim, Charleston, SC.

A.D.R.   Alvan D. Rubin, Rabbi Emeritus, Temple Israel, St. Louis, MO.

A.G.F.   Arnold Fink, Senior Rabbi, Beth El Hebrew Congregation, Alexandria, VA.

A.H.   Ammiel Hirsch, Executive Director, Association of Reform Zionists of America, New York City.

A.J.P.   Abraham J. Peck, Administrative Director, American Jewish Archives, Cincinnati, OH.

A.M.S.   Alan M. Sokobin, Rabbi, Temple Congregation Shomer Emunim, Sylvania, OH.

A.S.   Abraham Shusterman, Rabbi Emeritus, Har Sinai Congregation, Baltimore, MD.

Av.M.S.   Avi M. Schulman, Rabbi, Director, B'nai B'rith Hillel Foundation, University of Colorado, Boulder; Executive Director, Hillel Council of Colorado.

B.H.M.   Bernard H. Mehlman, Rabbi, Temple Israel, Boston, MA.

D.J.K.   Douglas J. Kohn, Associate Rabbi, Temple Oheb Shalom, Baltimore, MD.

E.A.G.   Edward A. Goldman, Rabbi, Professor of Rabbinic Literature, HUC-JIR, Cincinnati, OH.

E.M.U.	Ellen M. Umansky, Associate Professor of Religion, Emory University, Atlanta, GA.
F.L.W.	Faedra Lazar Weiss, Rabbi, Research Assistant, Girls Inc., National Resource Center, Indianapolis, IN.
F.R.	Faith Rogow, State University of New York, Binghampton.
F.Ro.	Fred Rosenbaum, Founder/Director, Lehrhaus Judaica, B'nai B'rith Hillel Foundation, University of California, Berkeley.
F.S.F.	Floyd S. Fierman, Rabbi Emeritus, Temple Mt. Sinai, El Paso, TX (deceased).
G.C.G.	Geoffrey C. Goldberg, Rabbi, Ph.D. candidate, School of Sacred Music, Jewish Theological Seminary of America; Music Librarian, HUC-JIR, NY.
G.G.	Gershon Greenberg, Professor of Judaic Studies, American University, Washington, DC.
G.P.Z.	Gary P. Zola, Rabbi, National Dean of Admissions, HUC-JIR, Cincinnati, OH.
H.C.C.	Henry C. Cohen, Rabbi, Beth David Reform Congregation, Gladwyne, PA.
H.J.F.	Harvey J. Fields, Rabbi, Wilshire Blvd. Temple, Los Angeles, CA.
I.A.G.	Israel A. Goldstein, Cantor, Director, School of Sacred Music, HUC-JIR, NY.
J.A.B.	Judith A. Bluestein, Rabbi, Congregation B'nai Israel, Hattiesburg, MS.
J.C.	Joseph Churman, Instructor, William Patterson College, Wayne, NJ; Leader, Ethical Culture Society of Bergen County, NJ.
J.R.K.	Jonathan R. Katz, Rabbi, Congregation Ner Shalom, Woodbridge, VA.
J.V.P.	Jonathan V. Plaut, Rabbi, Temple Emanual, San Jose, CA.
K.J.W.	Kenneth J. Weiss, Rabbi, Temple Mt. Sinai, El Paso, TX.
L.H.K.	Lewis H. Kamrass, Rabbi, Isaac M. Wise Temple, Cincinnati, OH.
L.P.K.	Lawrence P. Karol, Rabbi, Temple Beth Sholom, Topeka, KS.
L.Y.G.	Leslie Yale Gutterman, Rabbi, Temple Beth El, Providence, RI.
M.E.W.	Mark E. Washofsky, Rabbi, Assistant Professor of Rabbinics, HUC-JIR, Cincinnati, OH.
P.E.M.	Phillip E. Miller, Librarian, HUC-JIR, NY.
R.B.B.	Robert B. Baar, Rabbi, Beth Adam, Cincinnati Congregation for Humanistic Judaism.

R.C.H.	Richard C. Hertz, Rabbi Emeritus, Temple Beth El, Birmingham, MI.
R.I.K.	Robert I. Kahn, Rabbi Emeritus, Congregation Emanu-El, Houston, TX.
R.T.A.	Rebecca T. Alpert, Associate Director, Adult Education Program, Temple University, Philadelphia, PA.
S.F.C.	Stanley F. Chyet, Rabbi, Professor of American Jewish History and Director, Edgar F. Magnin School of Graduate Studies, HUC-JIR, Los Angeles, CA.
S.H.A.	Samuel H. Adler, Professor of Composition, Eastman School of Music, University of Rochester.
S.H.L.	Samson H. Levey, Professor Emeritus/Founding Director, Magnin School of Graduate Studies, Hebrew Union College–Jewish Institute of Religion, Los Angeles, CA.
S.L.S.	Scott L. Shpeen, Rabbi, Temple Beth Emeth, Albany, NY.
S.M.G.	Stuart M. Geller, Rabbi, Temple Emanu-El, Lynbrook, NY.
S.R.B.	Stanley R. Brav, Founding Rabbi, Temple Shalom, Cincinnati, OH.
S.R.S.	Shuly Rubin Schwartz, Assistant to the Dean, Albert A. List College of Jewish Studies, Jewish Theological Seminary of America, New York City.
T.F.B.	Terri Feldman Baar, Ph.D. candidate, University of Cincinnati.
T.P.L.	Thomas P. Liebschutz, Rabbi, Temple Emanuel, Winston-Salem, NC.
T.W.	Theodore Wiener, Rabbi, Judaic Cataloguer, Library of Congress, Washington, DC.
W.G.P.	W. Gunther Plaut, Rabbi, Senior Scholar, Holy Blossom Temple, Toronto, Ontario.
W.J.	Walter Jacob, Rabbi, Rodef Shalom Congregation, Pittsburgh, PA.

About the Editors

KERRY M. OLITZKY is Director of the School of Education at Hebrew Union College—Jewish Institute of Religion, where he also directs the Doctor of Ministry program. He is the author or editor of numerous books and journal articles, and he has written extensively on the Sunday Sabbath movement and the history of Reform Jewish education.

LANCE J. SUSSMAN is rabbi of Temple Concord in Binghamton, New York. He is also Adjunct Professor of History at SUNY Binghamton. An authority on the history of Judaism, he has written numerous scholarly articles and monographs.

MALCOLM H. STERN is Staff Genealogist of the American Jewish Archives and a lecturer in Jewish History at Hebrew Union College—Jewish Institute of Religion, where he also serves as Field Work Counselor. The author of many books and articles, his pioneer work, *Americans of Jewish Descent*, has become a classic in its field.